The American Christian Review

(Vol. 1, 1856)

Edited by
Elder Benjamin Franklin

Charleston, AR:
Cobb Publishing
2020

The American Christian Review, Vol. 1, 1856, is republished by Cobb Publishing, 2020.

Cobb Publishing
704 E. Main St.
Charleston, AR 72933
CobbPublishing@gmail.com
www.CobbPublishing.com
(479) 747-8372

ISBN: 978-1-947622-55-5

Publisher's Note:

Many hours of work have gone into the production of the volume you now hold in your hands. Many people have been a part of this project, and each one did it as a labor of love in order to bring this often forgotten part of Restoration Movement history to light once more. All students of the movement are at least aware of Campbell's two periodicals, *The Christian Baptist* and *The Millennial Harbinger*. Some have heard of Walter Scott's *The Evangelist* and Barton Stone's *Christian Messenger*. Most know about *The Gospel Advocate*, but may not be aware of its pedigree and history. But ask most members of the church of Christ, the Christian Church, or the Disciples of Christ (those who trace their history back to the Restoration Movement, though some distance themselves from the principles their spiritual forefathers fought for) about the *American Christian Review*, and you'll most likely end up with blank stares.

Elder Benjamin Franklin was a fierce conservative voice, standing for Jesus Christ and His church against any attacks. He was related to the famous American Patriot, Benjamin Franklin, though there has been some disagreement as to the exact relationship (grandson or nephew). Either way, he was named for this famous relative; and while the Patriot Franklin is better known, the Preacher Franklin did more and better work that matters eternally.

As much as is possible, we have tried to keep the original setup from the 1856 edition of the *American Christian Review*. This has been done so that any writers who have, or who will in the future, quote from or reference the *ACR* will not have readers scratching their heads if they look for the quote in this volume or in the original.

The text has been cleaned up visually, but no changes have been made to the text itself, except for a few very rare cases where there was an obvious typo (like "teh" instead of "the").

We hope you enjoy this piece of Restoration Movement history.

-The Publisher

THE

AMERICAN CHRISTIAN REVIEW.

A MONTHLY PERIODICAL,

DEVOTED TO

THE DEFENSE AND MAINTENANCE OF THE CHRISTIAN RELIGION,

CONTAINING

*Sermons, Essays, Reviews, Queries and Answers, Progress
of the Gospel, and important Items of News.*

EDITED BY

BENJAMIN FRANKLIN.

"Prove all things; hold fast that which is good."

CINCINNATI:

PUBLISHED BY BENJAMIN FRANKLIN

No. 60, WEST FOURTH STREET,
1856.

CONTENTS OF VOL. I.

	PAGE
Introductory Address	1
Labors in the Gospel	6
Our Position as a Religious Community	8
Review of Dr. Shaffer on Baptism	10
A Sermon	13
Organization—Ordaining Preachers	22
Mr. Quimby—the "*Star*"	24
Mr. Curry	26
Resurrection of the Dead	26
Revision of the English Scriptures	27
Second Epistle of Peter	27
The Duty of Rendering God's Word Plain to all	28
General Rule in Translating	29
Special Instruction	29
The Bible	29
Catechism for Calvinists	30
Editor's Table	31
The Mission of Infidels	33
Where is the Safe Ground?	35
Our Position as a Religious Community	39
Labors in the Gospel	41
Review of Dr. Shaffer on Baptism	44
A Sermon, by Elder M. B. Hopkins	46
The Temptation after Baptism	53
Evangelizing	55
Letter from B. K. Smith	57
Mr. Quimby—the "*Star*" once more	58
Queries Answered	58
The Christian	60
New Version—First Epistle of John	61
Editor's Table	64
Extract From Elder Challen's Book	65
Our Position as a Religious Community	70
Review of Dr. Shaffer on Baptism	72
The Christian Ministry	75
Mission of Infidelity	77
Organization	79
Reply	81
Letter from Elder Rogers	82
Letter, from Elder Raines	83
Trine Immersion	83
Letter from Elder W. M. Irvin	85
Remarks upon the Same	86
Creeds, Disciplines, etc.	87
Affairs about Indianapolis	89
Circles	91
Objects of the Bible Union	92
Bible Union a Scriptural Society	92
The great Heresy of the Age	83
The Bible Union in Germany	83
Protestantism the Hope of Humanity	93
New Version—Second Epistle of John	94
Editor's Table	95
A Sermon, by Elder *A.* Raines	97
Revision Meeting in Louisville	104
Our Position as a Religious Community	107
Evangelizing	109
Review of Dr. Shaffer on Baptism	111
Clerical Organization	114
A Serious Difficulty	117
The Ministerial Calling—Its Support	119
Wars and Rumors of Wars	121
Letter from Bro. J. T. Johnson	122
Is Man capable of Self-Government?	123
"Human" Creeds *v.* "Divine" Creeds	124
Little Heart's Ease	126
Bible Revision—Third Epistle of John	126
Gems of Thought	126
Editor's Table	127
Sermon, by Elder Wm. C. Rogers	129
Beecher's Conflict of Ages	135
Our Position as a Religious Community	139
Mission of Infidels	142
Kentucky Christian Union	144
Remarks Upon Same	146
Tour to Michigan	148
Evangelizing	151
Catching and Scattering the Sheep	154
Review of Dr. Shaffer	156
Letter from Elder J. F. Johnson	158
Editor's Table	159

	PAGE
Infidelity	167
Baptismal Repentance	169
Conclusion of the Noblesville Matter	172
Our Position as a Religious Community	173
Review of Dr. Shaffer on Baptism	176
The Contrast fairly Stated	178
Letter from Elder B. F. Hall	187
A Word to the Brotherhood	188
Letter From Texas	189
Editor's Table	191
Sermon, by Elder B. K. Smith	193
Letter of Elder J. T. Johnson	198
Our position as a Religious Community	199
The Contrast Fairly Stated	201
Preliminary Address on Infant Baptism	210
Five Arguments Against Union	212
Letter from Bro. Wharton	213
Correspondence	215
Where is the Safe Ground?	216
Letter from Wales	219
Repentance after Baptism	219
Gleanings from a Sacred Field	221
Editor's Table	223
The Beginning Corner	225
Our Position as a Religious Community	236
Noblesville Matter again	239
Review of Dr. Shaffer on Baptism	241
Politics and Religion	244
Independency and Co-Operation	247
Queries Answered	249
Bible Union—Father Maclay's Pamphlet	250
Letter from "Onesimus"	252
The Christian Profession, as compared with that of the Patriarch and Jew	369
"Sweet are the Uses of Adversity"	371
Industry in the Ministry—Its Support	372
The Political Campaign—The Cause	374
Letter from J. T. Johnson	376
Sunday School Address	377
Letter from Bro. Christy Sine	378
Conclusion of the Volume	380
Alexander Campbell	381
Editor's Table	382

THE AMERICAN CHRISTIAN REVIEW.

Vol. 1.]   CINCINNATI, JANUARY, 1856.   [No. 1.

INTRODUCTORY ADDRESS.

DEAR READER: In the good providence of our most gracious and merciful Heavenly Father, we are again before you in the capacity of an editor; and desire to introduce to your acquaintance "*The American Christian Review.*" How this enterprise shall operate, what its success shall be, and how long its course, is only fully known to Him who sees the end from the beginning; but we enter the work not for a year, nor five years; nor yet as a stepping stone to some other position; but as a legitimate mode of operations, and proper field of labor, with the intention that while the Lord shall afford us life and strength, and the work shall prosper, under His divine aid and protection, it shall undeviatingly continue. In looking over our history for the last six years, the reader may conclude we are addicted to *change,* and that our operations are not as reliable as could be wished. At least an apparent ground has been given for such a conclusion, in the several different arrangements we have passed through. But such is not the fact; and these changes have been caused by means beyond our control, and that cannot be fully explained nor understood till all the works of the children of men shall be fully spread out, in the last judgment.

This work is fully under our own control, and if it does not proceed with regularity, firmness and stability, the responsibility is *ours*. We are labor-

VOL. I., NO. 1.—1

ing under no disaffection from any of our former arrangements, have no ill or unkind feeling toward any with whom we have been associated, nor any in the whole kingdom of God; nor would we, for any consideration, lay a stumbling-block in the way of any one. We love all who love the Lord Jesus Christ, and desire the friendship, fellowship and fraternal cooperation of all engaged in the same great cause of humanity and redemption. Nor is this work the rival of any work now in the field, or an "opposition line" to any benevolent enterprise in which brethren are engaged; but it is intended as a co-operant in all that is pure, peaceable and lovely. The world is large enough for us all, and if we will work for the Lord, we shall find plenty of work for us all to do, and shall all meet our proper reward. Not only so, but we shall all find our proper level among men, and in the church of God. Let us not, then, look to the past, but look forward to the Author of the Christian profession, who, for the joy that was set before him, endured the cross, despised the shame, and is set down at the right hand of the throne of the Majesty in the Heavens. Let us work while it is called to-day, knowing that the night of death soon cometh, when no man can work; and let us remember that divine rule of discipleship laid down by the Lord himself: "By this shall all men know that you are my disciples, *if you have love one to another.*"

Nothing is a more certain evidence that a man is wrong, that he is not in the favor of God, nor engaged in the Lord's work, than the manifestation of vicious, malignant and revengeful feelings and actions. Even where we have been treated badly, this is not admissible; much less when difficulties, into which we fall from unwise arrangements and improper combinations, fall in our path. In all these things we must make great allowance for the imperfections of poor fallen and perverted human nature; nor must we think that this weakness and imperfection is wholly on the part of others, and that the allowance is wholly to be made for them. We must live under a continual sense of *our own* personal weakness, imperfection and liability to err, and the constant and imperious necessity of watchfulness, rigorous scrutiny and examination in regard to our own deportment, that we give no occasion of offense to Jew, Gentile, or the church of God.

We trust we are now in a safe, reliable and permanent business, and that our way will be clear for an extended system of operation, and, by the Divine blessing, we hope to achieve great good. We have passed through some transmutations, and much of the perplexities incident to an imperfect state, but we have found the cause of Christ the same, and our attachment to it only becomes more ardent as we become older and see more of the world, and realize more of the necessity of such a gracious system for the children of men. Mutation, change and uncertainty stand inscribed upon everything but the religion of Jesus Christ. It is founded upon a rock. "We have received a kingdom that cannot be moved." When the earth shall fail; when the powers of heaven shall be shaken; when the Lord shall fulfill the words: "Yet once more, I shake not the earth only, but also heaven," the things that cannot be shaken, or the things that remain, the kingdom of Christ shall abide. The hope of the Christian is sure and steadfast. How important it is that we constantly feel the value of this hope, reaching to that within the vail, as an anchor of the soul.

The more we see of the sectarian world, the more we become acquainted with the Bible, and reflect upon our position as a religious body, and the great principles developed by Christians since Barton W. Stone first began to rend the shackles of human traditions and call for a return to the original standard of the faith and practice of the children of God, the more we are confirmed in the importance of our mission as a religious community. We have not been called out from among all the jarring and warring elements of these times; from among all the different parties in Christendom, and united upon the word of the living God, upon the foundation of apostles and prophets, Jesus Christ being the chief cornerstone, to be scattered and come to naught in a day, a year, nor an age; nor has this great work been without the Divine purpose in it. His hand has been with every man who has attempted to maintain the purity of his cause, keep it separate and distinct from all that is corrupting, deteriorating, and merely human. He will continue to be with such to the end of time, and crown them with eternal honors at the end. We are as certain that God is in this great work, as that the Bible contains a revelation from him; and all who fight against it will be found fighting against him. Those who become cowards and forsake this cause, as those who have done so before, will ruin themselves, and bring, down shame upon their heads, that shall not only follow them to the end of their career in this world, but abash them in the eternal state.

No people on this earth occupy such a position as we. Our rule of faith and practice is the one given by the Lord himself, the whole of it, and nothing else; the truth of God, the whole truth, and nothing but the truth; the New Covenant, confirmed by the oath of God, the whole of it, and nothing else. This is "the perfect law of liberty;" the law to which all the disciples of Jesus have sworn an eternal allegiance; to which they are bound by the highest and most solemn obligations that can rest upon a human being. We cannot depart from it without a breach of the most solemn integrity and veracity. In our conversion, we did not merely subscribe to a class of *views of men,* but we became identified with the Redeemer of the world; placed ourselves

INTRODUCTORY ADDRESS.

under him, and, by all the honor there was in us—by all the integrity and veracity we possessed, we pledged ourselves to him, to follow him, serve him, honor him and love him forever. We professed to receive nothing but him and his law—to bind ourselves to no leader but him, and, to the extent of our ability, to adhere 'to him forever. In taking this position, we have left no room for any departure from our position, without a departure from him, a departure from his holy, perfect and infallible law. Our profession is, therefore, infallibly right, holy, just and true. If there is any failure, it must be in *us*, who have made the profession, and not in the profession itself. We can never fail, unless we have made the profession falsely, hypocritically, and pretendedly, or are false, unfaithful and untrue in the practice of it. The profession itself being infallibly right, if we were sincere When we made it, and practice it sincerely, we cannot fail to be right in the end. But if we fly from the true profession, desert it and shrink from it, after having taken it upon us, God will as certainly forsake us as he did king Saul after he had disobeyed the commands of the Lord.

The Bible contains the true religion, or there is none. There is light in the Bible to save the world, or the world is lost. Our only choice is between the Bible and nothing. Judaism is abolished. Mohammedanism has no claims in internal merit or external evidence. The fruits of all Paganism show that it is evil, and only evil, continually. Infidelity has nothing for the world. While it would take Christianity from us, it has nothing to propose. It is no system—no doctrine—teaches nothing and defends nothing. Its only province is to stand and deny. It finds fault with everything, starts doubts, destroys confidence, fills the world with fears, and spreads an eternal gloom over the prospects and hopes of all nations. Reason and the light of nature have been tried longer and more effectually than any system in the world. At least four thousand years have the pagan nations been trying what they could do for our race without a revelation from God. In all the experiments yet made, with no guide but reason and the light of nature, the tendency has been downward. Deterioration has been the universal result, without the light of the Bible. We then, cling to the Bible, and the religion it reveals, as the only hope of the world. If it fails, all must fail, and all must be lost. But it is folly of the most stupid order to speak of the Bible failing. Its Author is emphatically *the friend of man*. Its holy lessons are all for our good. All who have been led by it, are thankful that they ever knew it. It has never deceived one or misled one. No one has ever lamented being led by it. The more solemn and affecting the circumstances around us, and the greater the trials in which we are placed, the more comforting and precious are its holy consolations to the soul. It encourages all that is good, and discourages and condemns all that is evil; it is our guide and comfort through our journey of life; nor does it fail when we are sinking in death. No one who believed it before, in a dying hour denies and repudiates the Bible. But many determined infidels have recanted and repudiated their infidelity when sinking into the eternal state. That which they talked in health, that which dwelt upon their tongues in their mad career through life, they themselves condemned, in the most awful and solemn moments of life, and with their dying lips repudiated. How shameful and preposterous, that a man should live such a life of folly and inconsistency as to be compelled in his dying moments to condemn all his past life, with all the sentiments he had cherished and inculcated, and warn all men against them!

Some have expressed discouragement in this great cause, and have been disposed to hanker after the flesh-pots of Egypt, and look back to the tents of sectarianism. But this is all human weakness and folly. This cause will live, whether we stand or fall; whether we are true to it or not. But whether we live or not, depends upon our integrity, our faithfulness and devotion to the cause, and the Author of it. It is the cause of God, and if any man proves recreant to it, he will be destroyed; for he is untrue and recreant to the Author of his existence. Whoever falls upon this rock shall be broken; but upon whomsoever this rock shall fall, it shall grind him to powder.

Better were it for a man that he had never been born, than that he should trifle with this mightiest and greatest of all causes. Men may leave one human establishment and go to another, without affecting them much; but men who leave this cause, leave Christianity, the church of God, and the Head of the church: and all such men are ruined. They are fallen stars, for whom nothing remains but the blackness of darkness forever. Several have tried the fearful experiment, and everyone has found it his ruin. Men once enlightened cannot depart from the holy commandment without working their destruction.

We have seen the workings of this cause during the last twenty years, and have carefully considered its history since the first effort in the United States, to call the attention of the people to original Christianity, as well as the rise of Christianity in Jerusalem at the beginning. We have also carefully considered the means employed to oppose it, and impede its progress, and we are well prepared to **say** that it is the cause of God, and that it can be successfully maintained, defended, and extended, in defiance of all opposition. There is no cause on earth that can stand before it. We have no need to fear any opponents beneath the skies. No power this side of the throne of the Almighty can stay its progress. Its friends need not fear, hesitate nor falter, for it can never fail. No mere human party **can** stand before it. It contains the benevolence of God to a fallen race; its expansive philanthropy was contained in the precious promise to Abraham:"In thee, and in thy seed *all nations* shall be blessed." The same extended compassion is seen in the announcement of the heavenly host at the birth of our Redeemer: "We bring you good news of great joy, which shall be to *all people.* "The same wide and expanded gracious system, is set forth in the first Gospel sermon: "The promise is unto you, and your children, and *all them, that are afar off.* "The same is expressed in our Lord's commission "Go ye, therefore, and teach *all nations*"—"Go into all the world, and preach the Gospel to *every creature.* "In these passages is expressed the benevolence of God, extending to the human race; to all mankind. It does not include merely one nation or order, one country or one age, but all nations, all orders, all countries, and in all ages, from the birth of our Lord, down to the end of time.

Such is the ample system of grace, of benevolence and mercy provided for man by the Author of his being. Such too, must be the extended benevolence it must impress upon the hearts of all under its hallowed and gracious influence; they are not filled with a little love, feeling, and kindness for a little party; but they are filled with love, compassion and solicitude for all mankind. They love those whom God loved; labor to save those whom Christ came to save, and strive to live in union and fellowship with all who have washed their robes and made them white in the blood of the Lamb. They are not limited down to some little partisan scheme, with one, two or three ideas in it; but their system is the one revealed from heaven, the whole of it, and nothing else. Their faith is the whole of God's revelation to man; they are not their own; nor is the work. in which they are engaged, their own work: they belong to the Lord; he bought them with a price—his own precious blood—and the work in which they are engaged, is his work. It is, therefore, their duty to enlarge their hearts, widen their sphere of operations, and extend their horizon beyond all mere partisan human movements and above them, to the great, exalted, and extended work of the Almighty Father of heaven and earth.

This is our legitimate sphere, dear brethren, as a great religious community, raised up by the providence of God. We have a mission from God; not to any one nation, but to all nations; not to any one party, but to all parties; not to any one people, but to all people—to all mankind; not to convert them to *our views,* to our way, our faith, or our church, but to the one Lord, who, in his own time, will show who is the only potentate, the King of kings, and Lord of lords. To Him the world must pay homage; to Him the universe shall one day be subjected. Our mission is to call the world to Him—to His way and work. What

INTRODUCTORY ADDRESS.

he has said must be maintained, what he has commanded must be done, what he has promised will all be fulfilled. We have Him in our view; His authority we reverence, his works, we admire; in Him and his cause, we have all confidence. Twenty years ago, we identified our all with Him, for time and eternity. The farther we progress, the stronger is our confidence in the entire cause, and the more determined we are to persevere and maintain it to the end.

In this cause is the hope of our present and eternal happiness; in it is our only hope for our children, and the world. If the world is ever to be converted, this cause is to do it. Sectarianism has frittered off into powerless factions, and shown its utter imbecility in converting and saving man. Everything that has ever been tried, has failed and shown itself wholly inadequate, but the Bible. It has stood the wreck of ages, and those who have stood upon it have never *failed,* and never will to the day of eternity. To maintain this great cause, shall be the object of this work; we have nothing else in our mind, nor do we intend to devote our energies to anything else. We trust we have in years past and gone, given evidence of devotion to this work, satisfactory to all who know us. We have, to the best of our ability, been true to the trust committed to our hands so far, and hope and pray that we may continue true to the Lord and his people, in whatever position we may occupy. It is also our intention to make this magazine, to the extent of our ability, instrumental in the work of righteousness. Our continued prayer and anxiety is to attain the highest degree of usefulness, and we now have the assurance that the Lord has more fully opened our way than ever before. We are cut loose from worldly cares, so that we can give our entire time and energies to reading, writing, preaching and conversation upon the things that pertain to the kingdom of God, and the name of Jesus Christ. Our health is good, and we look upon labor as the highest pleasure, and purest happiness of this life. We can devote as many hours to reading, writing, and make as many pulpit efforts, in any given time, as any man we know. In one word, it is our meat and drink to be engaged in the work.

We have confidence too, in the great Christian brotherhood, as an honorable band of disciples of our Lord and Savior, Jesus Christ, and are thankful to the Lord for a place among them. We have confidence in the Christian ministry, and regard it, not only as a high, but a divine honor, to stand side by side with such men, and engage with them in the great struggle to rescue our country from the manacles of sin and death. We acknowledge that we owe eternal gratitude to God for raising us from obscenity and sin, to stand in such a noble rank, and participate in the greatest and most God-like work on this earth. It is the highest and most noble honor to which we expect to attain, to be enrolled with such a brotherhood, such a ministry, and permitted to labor for such a cause. May we be enabled to do the cause such a service, as its greatness and goodness demand, as shall be satisfactory to its friends, and well pleasing to the Father of us all.

In entering the editorial field again, we wish the friendship, the fellowship and cooperation of all those great and good brethren of the same calling. We enter the list, not as a competitor or rival, of any one of them, but a cooperator with them in the same great work, and we wish them all possible success. There is not the least danger of our circulating too many publications, any more than of our sending out too many preachers: the more preachers and papers, the better, if they are the *right kind.* Our magazine then, enters the list as the advocate of the Bible, of Christianity, of righteousness, peace and good will among men. Whatever is of good report, gentle, easy to be entreated, lovely and for the glory of God, in our estimation, we intend to maintain and defend in all meekness and kindness, with as much wisdom, discretion, and prudence as possible; to our brethren, we look for the balance. What support, dear brethren, will you give us? We already have assurance from many that we shall have a long list, and we entertain no doubt but that we shall be well sustained: to the Lord and to his people we look. If we can have the approbation of Heaven and the concurrence of the people of God, we fear no evil. May God be with us, and bless our effort, with all the efforts of his true Israel, who are striving to do his will; may we be kept in love and harmony, and possess the zeal and perseverance required by the greatest and best of all causes; may we follow peace and holiness, without which no man shall see the Lord, and to God our blessed, most merciful and gracious Father, through Jesus, the Christ, our glorious Redeemer and Saviour, be glory and dominion, majesty and power, now and forevermore. Amen.

BENJ. FRANKLIN.

-----o-----

Labors in the Gospel.

A BRIEF outline of a portion of the labors set forth in the following narrative, appeared some few weeks ago, in the *Christian Age,* edited by the beloved Eaton, of our city; but we could not then extend our observations to many things as we desired. We shall, therefore, give a fuller account, thus affording an opportunity for various comments upon matters in general, which cannot be introduced and spoken of so profitably in any other way. We had been for some months engaged wholly in the church on Clinton street, in this city, and the church in Covington, Kentucky, and had not during the present year gone scarcely beyond the smoke of our cities. In looking over the papers, we saw much said about "the decline of churches," "our cause a failure," "signs of the times," "cure for our downward tendency," etc., etc., and, as a matter of course, desired to look out through the country and see the shape of things. We proposed to the brethren on Clinton street to release us from our obligation to labor for them one-half of the time, and after mutual and Christian consultation, they released us for three months, that we might enjoy the privilege to go abroad.

Our first visit was to Smelser's Mills, Rush county, Indiana. At thirty minutes past six o'clock in the morning, on Monday after the second Lord's day in August, we took cars, and passing Hamilton, Ohio, Richmond and Cambridge City, Ind., we were set off at Ogden, Indiana, one hundred miles distant, at nine o'clock and thirty minutes. Here we met with Mr. Peter Smelser, who had met us with his carriage, to convey us to the place of meeting, some eleven miles distant. We became acquainted with this very pleasant and agreeable gentleman some six years ago, enjoyed his hospitality and friendship at his elegant residence, and entertained strong hopes that he was not far from the kingdom of God. But though he has advanced in goods and in years, and seems to object to nothing in Christianity, we could not with any certainty say that he had made any nearer approaches to the only name under heaven and among men, whereby he could be saved. How one so intelligent, so moral, so kind, and with such just conceptions of the Bible, the condition of the world and matters in general, surrounded by so many friends so deeply solicitous for his salvation, can refuse submission to the only Potentate, the King of kings and Lord of lords, is to us wholly inexplicable. May he yet secure an interest in the Saviour of the world!

About twelve o'clock we reached the large assembly upon the spacious seats spread out under the shady bower, with no shelter except the vast heavens spread above us by the Almighty and incomprehensible hand of the Infinite One, and the green foliage of the natural growth of the forest. The meeting had been commenced on the Friday preceding, and continued over Lord's day, by our youngest brother, David Franklin, who had just closed an address, and the solemn audience was listening to an affectionate and impressive exhortation from Bro. Daniel Van Buskirk, now gone to Bethany college to perfect his education, and more fully qualify himself for the Christian ministry. None had yet been added. In a few minutes we were dismissed for an hour and a half, when we met one of the most cheerful and hearty greetings in our life. In a few minutes, the kind and provident sisters spread out in rich profusion all that a hungry person could desire, of which all present were indiscriminately invited to partake. After all were fully satisfied, many baskets of fragments were carried away.

Here, in company with Bro. David, we also met our dear mother, some sixty-three years of age, whom we had not seen for some twelve months, but who has been striving to serve God for about forty years. Among the earliest incidents we can recollect, and what we still regard as of the greatest moment of all the incidents of this life, was that when she revealed to us the idea of the Deity—God, who made the universe, the Saviour of the world, and the lost and ruined condition of man, without his mediation; and we trust we shall never forget her many prayers and tears from our childhood to manhood; nor do we desire ever to become unmindful that we owe her a larger debt of gratitude for our first religious impressions, than any human being. Her joy now, and crown of rejoicing is, that her five sons, her only surviving children, are all in the ancient faith, and three of them in the Christian ministry. May Heaven comfort and sustain her in her declining years!

There is no church in this neighborhood, though there are some five or six in a few miles round. Here we met brethren with whom we labored and associated ten years ago, many of whom we had introduced into the kingdom of God. In the course of the meeting, elders Peter Wiles and Jacob Daubenspeck were some portion of the time present. These are old preachers and true, who contended for the faith long and hard, without any earthly remuneration, when the brethren were few and poor. The blessing of Heaven has attended them. The cause they maintained has, in their section of country, gained the victory, and now has more influence than all sectarian parties combined. They are both abundantly supplied with the good things of this life, and for years past have given liberally to the support of those wholly devoted to the ministry of the Word. The churches never should forget their indebtedness to such men, nor should young members become too proud to hear and encourage them. We make not this observation for these men alone, but for many more who stand in a similar attitude, only not so well provided for temporally. Old men are neglected. That wise adage, "Old men for counsel, but young men for war," has gone out of date. It is too far behind the times for "Young America," for "this age of progression and improvement." Aged men, such as God, under all dispensations, has required his people to honor and respect, are now sneered at, as, "common," "old fashioned," "fogies," that may do to speak "in the country," but not in towns and cities! Young and vain men are flattered and inflated with conceit, if not real foppery and dandyism encouraged. But in all such cases, the ruin of the cause, and frequently both the ruin of the old preacher and the young is wrought. Several cases within our horizon furnish sad comments, demonstrative of all this.

Our aged preachers must receive the respect, esteem, and consideration due them. They, must be treated with deference, and their counsels must be regarded and have their due weight. It is contrary both to reason and revelation for the younger to rule the elder. Young men, however, must be encouraged, their way opened for usefulness and improvement, and proper consideration given their efforts. All possible care should be taken to improve young brethren who are making efforts to preach, to make an open door for them, and make them useful; but there is both a rational and a scriptural place for both the elder and younger, that both be encouraged, sustained, and duly honored, and the cause saved from scandal.

Bro. Jacob Vail, one of the valuable county evangelists, whose whole time is devoted to preaching the Word, was with us all the time. Bro. Daniel Franklin, who is also employed by the Rush County Cooperation as an evangelist, was with us one day. We continued to address the large assemblies who resorted here to hear the Word, twice each day for one week. Some fifteen became obedient to the ancient faith, and were advised to unite with the most convenient congregation to them, till such time as it might be proper to form another church.

On Tuesday morning, by the kindness of Bro. Mock, we were conveyed in his carriage to Ogden, where we took cars and reached home in three hours, and found all well, under the same gracious Providence which has long been and is now our whole trust for time and eternity.

We now determined to ask the brethren in Covington, Kentucky, where one-half of our time was engaged for the present year, to release us for two months, that we might have our whole time to go abroad for a short time. On the fourth Lord's day we spoke to a respectable congregation in Covington, in the morning, and at night addressed a large and intelligent audience again in the same house, on the causes of opposition to the revision of the English Scriptures. At the close, the brethren heard and kindly granted our request to release us from our obligation to them for two months. By the request of one of the elders, the brethren sang a parting hymn, during which the members, with much Christian affection, extended to us the parting hand, expressive of their kind regard for us, and anxiety for our success in turning men to God. We owe our brethren in Covington, and many other brethren, a large debt of gratitude, not only for their usual kindness and liberality, but for their gratuitous free-will offering in our behalf, during forty days while our family was kept in awe and affliction, with that loathsome disease called *small pox*. In the place of stopping our support when we could no longer fill our post, as has been the case when preaching brethren have failed through affliction to fill engagements, in some instances, these brethren continued our regular support, and added an extra contribution of some forty dollars. We mention this to their praise, and as an inducement to lead other congregations, when the servant *Of God*, and their servant in the gospel, may be in affliction, to similar evidences of affection and liberality.

We had Bro. E. C. Payne, of New Orleans, with us during the day, and formed a short and happy acquaintance with him. He has passed through many severe trials within the last few years, but remains firm and unshaken in the Christian hope. We do hope and pray that peace may be restored in the little band of brethren in his great city, and that the love of God may again abound there.

B. F.

Our Position as a Religious Community. No. I.

THE position we have assumed, as a religious community, before the world, has been under most rigid and searching investigation for the last thirty years. It has been repeatedly tried in public oral discussions, in the most able and searching written investigations, and in the unfair and one-sided pulpit attacks of its enemies, where its friends had no liberty to reply; but it has stood the test, and is still standing it, in defiance of all assault. It has never had a fair contest where it did not gain a victory. It has grown with a regular and rapid growth, extended its borders, and planted itself down in vast regions of this country, and now presents a most invulnerable front, before the numerous hosts who stand opposed to it. In large districts, where we have traveled in this country, it has wider influence, greater command, and more power, than all the opposing systems combined. Indeed, there is no place where this cause has been fairly presented, and not betrayed nor deserted by its professed friends, where it has not permanently planted itself, gained an honorable position, and erected the ancient worship of the Living and True God.

Though some men have fought this cause through the main vigor of a lifetime, many died in the heat of war against it, and hosts of new champions have appeared, willing to distinguish themselves in doing battle against it, while it not only stands, but makes its regular onward march, regardless of all opposition; still the virulence of sectarian strife and party leaders appear no nearer abating than they did twenty years ago. Nor do we expect sectarian partisans ever to be conciliated to it, or a haughty clergy ever to look with complacency upon it. Such a thing is a natural impossibility. It ignores all clerical assumptions, haughty and pompous titles, and acknowledges no man master. It looks upon all that distinguished class of men called "the clergy," as mere *men*—nothing but *men*—two-legged mortals, as other men, and sets at naught the pages of Scripture—the only gospel of the grace of God. It also ignores all human names, as religious designations, human creeds, and human authorities of every description, as rivals to the Divinely authorized designations of the people of God, with the only unerring and infallible law for the government of the church and comfort of saints—the Divine Scriptures. It openly impeaches their neglect and perversions of the most solemn ordinances, with all their departures from the simplicity of the ancient faith, and uncompromisingly maintains that nothing will please God, or gain the approbation of the great Head of the church, short of a full and unreserved return to the faith and practice of the primitive church.

To such a position as this, men of sense never expect a proud and haughty clergy to become reconciled, nor the sectarian parties they guide. Parties that intend, at all hazards, to maintain their human names, their human creeds, with all their present customs and peculiarities, whether scriptural or not, that never intend to review their position, to see how far they may have departed from the Lord's name, the ancient faith, and ancient practice, but intend to go blindly on, as they are, no man of sense need expect ever to become reconciled to such a position as we occupy. They will hate it, and oppose it, as long as they are parties, because the elements of which they are composed are naturally and inherently in eternal hostility to each other. That we are right, in maintaining the law of God, as laid down in the Scriptures, as the only law, the only authority, the only creed, and that everything else, as a law, or rule of faith, is not only a redundancy, but treasonable, and subversive of the law and government of God, we can never doubt while we have our senses. That the man who believes the gospel of the grace of God, as set forth in the New Testament, receives it into a good and honest heart, conforms his life piously and devotedly to the law of God, as laid down in the Bible, has the approbation of his God now, and will be saved in the world to come, is not doubted by any man who believes the Bible contains a revelation from God; and if such a one is not safe, there is no safe road to travel in this world of tears and sorrows. But of the safety of such a position, we who have so long occupied it, can have no more doubt than we have of the existence of the Deity, of which we are as certain as that we exist. This position we can never yield, and until we do yield it, we can never become partisans—we can never countenance any law but the law of God.

Here is an issue—an issue which it is no use to try to disguise. We maintain that the law of Christ is the only law that man can enforce upon the church, without losing the approbation of heaven. Our opposers maintain that they can, not only innocently, but profitably, name, enforce, and govern the church, by another law. They appear determined not to give up this other law; and we are equally determined not to regard it. This is a palpable issue, such as cannot be slurred over—cannot be compromised, or ever settled, unless one or the other of the parties yields. Either we must yield our position, that the church of the Living God should be governed by the law of God alone, that it is subversive of the law of God to introduce any other law to govern his church, that it is treasonable, and a bold attempt to set aside and defy the authority of the Almighty, to acknowledge any other law than his—or those who maintain the authority of human creeds, their utility and necessity, must relinquish them, and disavow all allegiance to them. That we shall never yield our position on this point, that we *cannot* yield, without openly disrespecting the law of the Great King, despising his authority, and defying the majesty of God, no one can fail to see, who with half discernment, will look over the ground. And that the sectarian parties of these times will hold on to their creeds, defend and maintain them in one form or other, that they will hear to no reason against them, admit none of their pernicious tendencies, but continue to bind them upon as many as can be found weak enough to bow the neck to the yoke, we see no reason to doubt. The issue, then, between human creeds and the law of God, will continue, and the controversy must go

on all their authority to teach and enforce anything save the pure and holy doctrine of the Lord Jesus, as unfolded upon The friends of the Bible, the friends of the law of God, those who wish God to govern, those who desire the Lord to reign, those who would see the Lord's authority exalted above all authority, those who would be his subjects, who would serve him and honor him as the only rightful Lawgiver, the only Potentate, the King of kings and Lord of lords, as the Supreme Governor in the universe, the Head over all to the church, blessed forever and ever, may then gird on the armor, prepare themselves for the conflict, and rush on to the issue. It is nothing short of a plain and most palpable conflict between light and darkness, the law of God and the law of man, the authority of God and the authority of man, whether Jesus shall rule or man, whether Christ or man shall give laws to the people of God, whether God or man shall have the throne. Shall the Almighty Maker of heaven and earth rule? Shall his law set aside everything else? Those who are in favor of the Lord's ruling, of Jehovah maintaining the throne and reigning, and his law prevailing throughout the whole kingdom of God, may prepare themselves for the conflict, and hasten to the issue. If the contest must continue, let us continue it with energy. Let us make out and file our plea for the law of the Lord. Let us not be silent by day nor by night, but urge, with all possible earnestness; the superiority of the claims of the law of the Lord, its exalted character and supreme authority, and the simple reason why all men should submit implicitly to it.

We know we are in the right. We cannot be wrong here. If it is wiser to obey God than man, if an infallible law is better than a fallible, if a perfect law is better than an imperfect one, if a divine law is better than a human, if the authority of God is better than the authority of man, if the word of the Living God is better than a human creed, if the infallible teachings of inspiration are better than uninspired human creeds, if the teachings of the Holy Spirit of God are a safer guide to heaven than the teachings of erring men, if God should govern in preference to man, we are right, and our opposers wrong, on this transcendent point, and it is our duty to God and our fellow-creatures, that we maintain with manly zeal and fortitude that which is so manifestly and self-evidently the will of God. We never can falter. We have no ground to doubt or fear; but if we shrink or hesitate, it must be manifest indifference. While we hope, then, for the blessing of God upon us, and call upon God for his mercy, let us remember our fealty to him, and maintain our integrity to the day of his coming.　　　　　　　　　　　　　B. F.

-----o-----

Review of Dr. Shaffer on Baptism
No. 1.

Dr. H. M. SHAFFER is a Methodist Presiding Elder. His book, entitled *"A Treatise on Baptism, in two Parts—Part I., Infant Baptism.; Part II., the Mode of Baptism,"* made its appearance in its present' form, about three years since; though the introduction to it appears to have been written some ten years ago. We discussed the main points in it with the author, some eighteen months since, in Darke county, Ohio, in an oral debate of some four days, in the presence of several hundred people; and, as we have been repeatedly assured, gave the hearers very general satisfaction, not only of the incorrectness of the Doctor's position, but of the miserable sophistry of his attempt at argument, and the imposture of many of his bold, persistent and unwarrantable statements. At the close of the discussion, a gentleman arose and spoke of asking the audience to request the parties to write out their speeches and publish them for the people, in a book. To this, the Doctor and several of his ministering brethren warmly objected. After some remarks from several gentlemen on each side, every friend of the Doctor most pertinaciously opposed giving the audience the opportunity to make the request. It was seen that owing to the opposition of the Doctor and his friends, the motion could not be put, and the mover declined persisting, though satisfied that a large majority desired the audience to make the request. But many have insisted that for the good

of those not present, but especially those who have been annoyed with the Doctor's course for many years, who have had no satisfactory means of meeting him, we should review his book. This we promised to do, but up to this time have had no opportunity. But now we have the *time* and *room,* and intend to proceed with the work. By the way, reviewing this book will review a half-dozen more such books upon our shelf, and we pretend not to say how many more, circulating through the land. This one, however, suits our taste better for an example than any we have seen. It was printed for the author by the Methodist Book Concern, and, if our memory is not at fault, received a favorable notice from the *Western Christian Advocate.*

We think it more compatible to review his second part first, or what he calls the "mode," and see if we can determine what *that is,* before we inquire whether infants are entitled to it. On page 129, he says: "Our Baptist brethren say, 'Immersion is essential to baptism, and without baptism (immersion) you do not belong to the church of Christ.' Mr. Campbell and his disciples not only contend for the above position, but go farther, and say: ' Without immersion there is no remission of sins or salvation.'" This, the Doctor lays down as the ground upon which he takes issue with Baptists, with Mr. Campbell, and with his disciples. We shall not be at any trouble about either of the parties here assailed, but shall take issue with this book, and see what can be done for it. In order to do this, we shall define our position, and the exact issue we make with Dr. Shaffer. Our position is not that "immersion is essential to baptism," for this would be precisely equivalent to saying that immersion is essential to immersion, or baptism is essential to baptism. The literal definition of a word means precisely the same thing as the word itself, and not something else essential to that thing. Immersion *is baptism*—the identical thing itself—not a mode of the thing meant, something like it, a way of it, or something essential to it, but the precise thing meant—the whole of it—no more, no less. Hence in *his own* definitions, professedly quoted from lexicons, he has no less than nine that give *immerse,* not as "essential to baptism," but *baptize itself,* in English. *Immerse,* in English, means precisely the same thing, or expresses the same action as *baptizo* in Greek. *Baptizo* in Greek, is *immerse* in English. There is no ordinance of the New Testament, or of any other kind, in the Greek *baptizo* or the English *immerse,* as is clear to any unsophisticated mind, from the fact that the original word, *baptizo,* was used thousands of times and hundreds of years before the initiatory ordinance of the New Testament existed. It is used in the Septuagint version of the Old Testament, 2 Kings 5: 14, and in the New, Mat. 7:3; verse 8; Heb. 6: 2; 9: 10, where it has no reference to the ordinance, which could not be the case if the word meant an ordinance. If the Hydropathic physician baptizes a patient in his medical treatment, he does not administer any ordinance of the New Testament, though he performs precisely the same action, and it is expressed by the same word, as when a preacher of Christ baptizes a man in the name of the Lord; and though the action is precisely the same in both cases, the object and effect are as different as heaven and earth. In one case, the appointment is only of man, for a physical remedy to the body, and will serve the same purpose to an infidel as to a believer. In the other case, the appointment is of the Lord, and relates not to the physical relief of the body, but to the soul, and is of no value without faith in him who requires it. But we proceed with Dr. Shaffer.

1. His first argument is built upon baptizing *"with water"* He says: "The difference between the practice of the apostles and the Baptist churches, is this: the former baptized *with* water, and the latter baptize *in* water." Again, the Doctor says, "We believe the mode of baptism, as taught in the Scriptures, and practiced by the Apostles, was by *aspersion* or *affusion,* that is, they applied the water to the candidate; therefore, they baptized *with* water." [Page 124.] Still farther, he says the preposition *en,* which is generally in connection, and which is translated *with,* is a correct translation. Now, from all we know of the learning, the understanding the

Doctor has of the subject he attempts to criticize, and his candor, we are not prepared to say positively that *he knew* his argument upon this point was worth nothing. But we are prepared to say that we know that it is not only worth nothing, but that we can show it to be such to any unsophisticated person of common intelligence. The very first place where baptism is mentioned in the New Testament, it is said to be *in* (Greek, *en*) Jordan. How is this, Doctor? Should this read, baptized *with* Jordan? Come, my dear sir, tell us—did John baptize *with* Jordan? or, in the Baptist way of it, *in* Jordan? Did he apply the people to the river, or the river to the people? Did he baptize the river *upon* the people, or only baptize the people *in* the river? Come, my worthy old friend, let us look at the subject in a sociable and friendly manner. This Greek preposition *en*, you say, commonly in connection with *baptize,* is correctly translated *with*. **Now** I will not torture you by tracing this word all through the New Testament. We will look at it as it stands connected with baptize. I perceive, Mark i. 4, it is said, "John did baptize *in* (Greek *en*) the wilderness." Does this mean *with* the wilderness? John, iii. 23, John is said to be "baptizing *in* Enon." Would you translate it *"with* Enon?" I see a mention of "baptizing *in (en)* the cloud and *in (en)* the sea." 1 Cor. x. 2. Should this be "baptized *with* the cloud and *with* the sea?" We should be edified to see the Doctor administer a few baptisms *with* Jordan—*with* the wilderness—*with* Enon— *with* the cloud, and *with* the sea. It would be **a** mighty performance for a man, even such as Dr. Shaffer, to sprinkle the river Jordan upon people; sprinkle Enon upon them; sprinkle the cloud and the sea upon them; to say nothing of sprinkling the wilderness upon them! When we shall see some mighty man come sprinkling *with* a river, *with* a cloud, *with* the sea, and *with* the wilderness, we, as a matter of course, shall be silenced about Greek prepositions. The Doctor believes that the mode of baptism was *aspersion* or *affusion*—that is, in his style, baptized by *aspersion* or *affusion*. **In** the instances cited above, he would have it aspersion or affusion *with* Jordan, *with* Enon, *with* a cloud, *with* the sea, *with* the wilderness!

Now, if the Doctor had not decided that *with* is the correct translation' of the Greek preposition *en,* where it is connected with baptism, we should have continued to read these passages as the translators of the common version, all sprinklers, gave them to us, *in* Jordan, *in* Enon, *in* the cloud, *in* the sea, *in* the wilderness; but, to keep out of the water, he would baptize *with* Jordan, Enon, a cloud, sea, or wilderness. But even King James' translators forsake him here. It was too manifestly ridiculous for even their sense of faithfulness, to translate *en*, *with*, in these instances. Still, they show a great want of faithfulness. They commence Matt. i. 18, and before reaching chapter iii. 11, in nineteen occurrences of *en*, give us *among* once, *within* once, and *in* seventeen times, but not one *with!* Among these instances, we find: *in* those days, conceived *in* her, *in* the East, *in* Bethlehem, *in* all the coasts, *in* Rama, *in* Egypt, *in* the wilderness, and *in* Jordan. So far, they proceeded straight forward. But here they change, with no reason only the one the Doctor has in his eye, viz: *To keep out of the water.* They could not translate *en hudor, in* water, giving manifest evidence of immersion. But they were too late, in this instance, to dodge. After giving us "*in* Jordan," (Matt. iii. 6,) it was too late to give us "*with* water," only five verses afterwards, especially when the passage where they give us "*with* water" refers to the identical same baptizing which they had before told us was "*in* Jordan." This opens the way for me to open the Doctor's eyes a little, on what he calls the "difference between the practice of the Apostles and the Baptist churches."

His difference is, that the practice of the Apostles was to baptize *with* water, but that of the Baptists to baptize *in* water. Now, keep cool, sir, and hear me. I not only deny that the Apostles ever baptized *with* water, or that the New Testament in any place says that they baptized *with* water, but I deny that the common version, in a single place, says that the Apostles baptized *with* water. I deny that the words "*with* water," in a single instance, in the common version, are applied to the Apostolic practice. Let him refute me who can. I have examined every place where *baptize* is found, in any form, in the common version, and there is not one place where the Apostles, or any one of them, are ever said to baptize *"with* water." The only baptism which the common version makes *"with* water" is the baptism of John, and that, the same version tells us was *in* Jordan, *in* Enon, and because there was much water there. The words *"with* water," are a translation of the words of John the Baptist, *en hudor.* Mark i. 5, the common version has, "baptized of him *in* the river of Jordan." In this passage, *patamos* is translated *river.* But the same word is translated *water, 2* Cor. xi. 26, and *flood,* Matt. vii. 25-27; Rev. xii. 15-16. Here, then; John baptized *in,* as we have it in the common version, not *with,* but *in* the *river, waters,* or *floods* of Jordan. How then, Doctor, was this baptizing *"with* water" performed? It was *in* Jordan, *in* the river, waters or floods of Jordan.

The words baptized "with water," "with the Holy Ghost," and "with fire," as we have them in the common version, are the words of John the Baptist, and used no place in the New Testament, except when referring to him. These words never relate to the practice of the Apostles. Hence, the reference of the Doctor to them, for Apostolic practice, only shows how deficient his acquaintance is, even with the common version of the New Testament, and how totally unfit he is to criticize upon such grave matters.

-----o-----

A SERMON,
On the Eternal Purpose of God.
[BY THE EDITOR.]

TEXT.—"Be not thou, therefore, ashamed of the testimony of our Lord, nor of me, his prisoner; but be thou a partaker of the afflictions of the Gospel, according to the power of God; who hath saved us, and called us with a holy calling, not according to our works, but according to his own purpose and Grace, which was given us in Christ Jesus, before the world began." _2 Tim. i: 9,11.

BELOVED BRETHREN AND FRIENDS: By your permission, I invite your attention to the investigation of the Purpose of God. In the universe there is one eye that looks down through the long cycles of all the ages, and sees the end from the beginning. There is but one Being who can say "I am God, and there is none else; I am God, and there is none like me, declaring the end from the beginning, and from ancient times the things that are not yet done; saying, My counsel shall stand, and I will do all my pleasure." Isa. xlvi; 9,10. He who uttered this, and He alone, "worketh all things after the council of his own will." Eph. i: 2. He had a purpose, as mentioned in our text, before the world began, and it is according to this purpose we are saved and called with a holy calling. Hence, at the close of that beautiful expression, Eph. iii: 1, 10, where the apostle sets forth the object of the apostolic mission, and of the Church, he says, it is "According to the eternal purpose which he purposed in Christ Jesus, our Lord." Also, speaking of the inheritance which the apostles and prophets had obtained, and to which they were predestinated, he affirms, that it was "according to the purpose of Him who worketh all things after the council of his own will." Many speculations have obtained touching this, the highest, holiest, and most benevolent of all the purposes revealed to mortals in the flesh, which we shall not mention in this discourse; but the following conclusions are inevitable:

1st. This purpose was before all things. Hence, it is said to have been "before the world began," and called "the eternal purpose." The Infinite One had a purpose before he created man—created him for that purpose; had a purpose when he sent the Lord into the world—sent him for that purpose; had a purpose when he gave the Christian revelation, and gave it for that purpose. This great purpose of the Infinite Mind, runs through the whole revelation of God to man; and indeed, the dealings of the Almighty with his intelligent creatures, as set forth in the Volume of God, are but a series of developments of this purpose, which was before all things; but this we shall see more fully as we proceed.

2d. This purpose is connected with Christ: Both the purpose and grace, the apostle says, were given us "in Christ," or by him, and he says that the eternal purpose was "purposed *in Christ*

Jesus, our Lord." The eternal purpose looks down from before the creation of man, four thousand years this side of his creation, to the revelation of Christ, to the period when it should be fully developed through him. No one need, therefore, look for this purpose outside of, or separate from Him.

3d. Man is included in this purpose. It does not relate to angels nor any other beings, but to man; this will appear fully as we proceed.

4th. It has in view the saving of man and calling him with a holy calling.

We therefore, proceed to enquire into the object of man's creation. There is more importance in the first question of the Shorter Catechism., than some would at first think. That question is this: "What is the chief end of man?" Nor is the answer less to the point; it is as follows: "Man's chief end is to glorify God, and enjoy him forever." To the same effect, how beautifully the sweet Psalmist of Israel sang, as follows: "Out of the mouths of babes and sucklings hast thou ordained strength, because of thine enemies, that thou mightst still the enemy and the avenger. When I consider thy heavens, the work of thy fingers; the moon and the stars, which thou hast ordained: what is man that thou art mindful of him? and the son of man, that thou visitest him? for thou hast made him a little lower than the angels, and hast crowned him with glory and honor; thou madest him to have dominion over the works of thy hands; thou hast put all things under his feet." Ps. viii: 2, 6. The apostle Paul, however, more fully and clearly sets forth the object of man's creation, in his address in the Athenian court, immediately after introducing to that benighted people, God who made the world, in the following words: "And hath made of one blood all nations of men to dwell on all the face of the earth, and hath determined the times before appointed, and the bounds of their habitation; that they should seek the Lord, if haply they might feel after him and find him, though he be not far from every one of us." Acts xvii: 26, 27.

Now, as men's salvation is according to God's eternal purpose and grace, or what he purposed in Christ before the world began, and as the Lord made man, that he might seek the Lord and find Him, the Almighty must have anticipated the fall, or man's apostasy. Hence, the purpose contained the Savior, man, salvation, and the idea of man's returning and seeking his God. We do not know of any other solution of these passages, and do not believe there is any. If any inquire why he created, knowing that man would sin, and fall, we respond, because it was better to create than not to create. If it is inquired how we know this, we answer, that the fact that the Lord did create, is an infallible evidence that it was the best that could be done. What the Infinite One does, is the best that can be done in all cases. It is a fact that man was created; the Creator does the best that can be done: it was, therefore, the best that could be done to create. Not only so, but his design in creating man—"that he might have dominion"—"that he might seek God, and find him "be crowned with glory and honor," and "glorify and enjoy God forever," is the most merciful and benevolent object that ever prompted or instigated any purpose or resolve, in the universe. We therefore look upon the purpose of God, as his will, or his resolve, sent forth from his infinite goodness, guided by his infinite wisdom, executed by his infinite power, and developed to man by his Son, the express image of the invisible God, in whom dwells all the fullness of the God-head, bodily.

Now we must inquire what Christ came into the world for. In a single verse, the Lord tells us what he did not come into the world for, and what he did come for. We will hear first, what he did not come for. He says, "For God sent not his Son into the world to condemn the world;" John iii: 17. The word translated *condemn* is *krino,* which in some eighty-five instances, is translated *judge,* and evidently should have been so translated here. The Lord affirms in this passage, that he came not into the world to *judge* the world, the same as he affirms, John xii: 4, 7. In this passage he says: "If any man hear my words and believe not, I judge him not; for I came not to judge the world, but to save the world. He that rejecteth

A SERMON—BY THE EDITOR.

me, and receiveth not my words, hath one that judgeth him; the word that I have spoken, the same shall judge him in the last day." But our object is to inquire especially, what he did come into the world for. He says: "That the *world through him might be saved.* "This clearly implies, that without God sending his Son into the world, the world could not have been saved. Salvation was not possible to man, or it was not in the power of man to be saved, without the mission of Christ into the world. Hence, he came that man "might be saved," or to give man power or ability to be saved. This is a beautiful expression, and clearly expresses the purpose of God, in the mission of Christ, viz: To make it possible for man to return to God, or as Paul expresses it, to seek God and find Him.

This leads us legitimately to inquire into another point. What did the Lord give us the holy testimonies of Matthew, Mark, Luke and John for? For this John has furnished a direct and most pointed answer, in the following words: "Many other signs truly did Jesus, in the presence of his disciples, which are not written in this book; but these are written, that ye might believe that Jesus is the Christ, the Son of God;" John xx: 30, 31. This is a full and clear statement of the divine purpose in publishing these sacred testimonies. That gracious purpose was, that man *might believe,* or, in other words, to give him ability to believe.

We have now briefly hinted at, and shown the purpose of God in three points: 1st. In man's creation. 2d. In the mission of Christ. 3d. In the Divine testimonies. We have shown that his purpose in the first point was that man *might seek God and find him;* in the second, that he *might be saved,* and in the third, that he *might believe.* Now do these modern developments correspond with more ancient intimations, in reference to this same great purpose of the Almighty Father? The first clear and explicit development, in reference to the eternal purpose, found in the ancient records, is the promise to Abraham; it is contained in the following words: "In thy seed shall all nations of the earth be blessed; because thou hast obeyed my voice;" Gen. xxii: 18. Some-one, however, will say, how do you know that this is the same as the purpose of God? To this we respond, that we know that it is a development of the purpose of God, because it contains the same as we have found in the purpose. We have found that the purpose of God contained Christ, salvation, and man, and that those saved through Christ, according to the Gospel, were saved according to the purpose of God. What did this promise to Abraham contain? Paul says: "And the Scripture foreseeing that God would justify the heathen through faith, preached before the Gospel unto Abraham, saying: In thee shall all nations be blessed;" Gal. iii: 8. Now the Scripture foreseeing that God would justify the heathen through faith, is nothing more than the Scripture, before setting forth the purpose of God, to justify the heathen through faith, and preaching the Gospel to Abraham, was done, in simply communicating to him the purpose of God, to justify the heathen through faith in a promise in him to bless all nations. The blessing contained in this promise, was the Gospel, Christianity, or the salvation it presents to all nations. Abraham is presented with the original purpose of God, which is a blessing for all nations, while Paul comments upon the promise, and declares it to be the Gospel. The whole of Christianity is now simply, a full development of the eternal purpose of God, or of the promise to Abraham.

Let us then proceed to take one look at the benevolence of the eternal purpose of God. The promise to Abraham, shows that it reaches to all the nations of the earth. In perfect harmony with the development contained in the promise, is the following expression of the prophet: "The Lord hath made bare his holy arm, in the eyes of all nations; and all the ends of the earth shall see the salvation of our God;" Isa. lii: 10. To the same amount this prophet deposes again: "Look unto me, and be ye saved, all ye ends of the earth; for I am God, and there is none else;" Isa. xlv: 22. These are very clear exponents of the divine purpose, setting forth its expanded benevolence, as wide as the human race. Another development is made by Joel, to the same amount, as follows: "And it shall come to pass afterward, that I will pour out of my spirit upon all flesh;" Joel, ii: 28. Now that these expressions are developments of the benevolent purpose of God, and that they extend to the whole race of man, we think no one can doubt. But notwithstanding developments so clear to us, the matters contained in them were all hid in God—mysteries—secrets not known to the sons of men, for 'ages. During this dark and gloomy period, man had not the ability to come to God, and God did not hold him strictly accountable. This will appear more evident, as we proceed.

When the Apostle says of John the Baptist: "The same came for a witness, to bear witness of the light, that all men through him might believe" (John i: 6—9), he implies that the means of believing did not exist to the same extent before the light came, as since; and that, though lack of ability did exist, since the light had come it had been removed, and now all men, through him, *might* believe. This shows that the divine purpose in sending light into the world, was to remove inability, or to give ability to believe—and now, all men have the ability and may believe. The same sentiment is clearly inculcated in another expression, as follows: "If I had not come and spoken to them, they had not had sin; but now they have no cloak for their sins;" John xv: 22. If the Lord had not come and spoken to them, and, as expressed subsequently, "done among them the works which none other man did," they had not been placed under the same responsibility, from the fact that they would not have had the same ability. But the ability now afforded, by the coming of the Lord, his works, speaking to them, thus extending power to believe, they are left without excuse, or have no cloak for their sins.

Is not the same principle recognized by the Apostle in the following? "But when we were yet without strength, in due time Christ died for the ungodly;" Rom. v: 6. Now "without Strength," is without ability, power or means to come to God. They were all under sin, apostatized from God, and fallen, and consequently without strength to return. While the world was in this condition, all included in unbelief and under sin, God had mercy upon all. It should be carefully noticed, too, that he had mercy upon precisely the same *all* that were in unbelief, or under sin. The mercy he has had upon all, is to enable them to believe, repent and be saved from their personal transgressions, in their own actual and personal submission to Jesus Christ, and gives them an assurance of a full and complete deliverance from the consequences of the Adamic transgression, in the resurrection from the dead. When it is said, that "when we were without strength, in due time Christ died for the ungodly," it is clearly implied that he died to give us strength. When it is said that "he came into the world that the world through him might be saved," it is clearly implied that, without his coming, the world had not ability to be saved; but his coming gave ability. When John the Baptist "bore witness to the light, that all men through him might believe," it is clearly implied that without this testimony, all men had not the ability to believe, but with this testimony, all men *might* believe. In the same way, when John says, "these things were written that you might believe," he implies that before these testimonies were written or published, man had not the ability to believe, and that his writing was that he might believe, or to enable him to believe. When the Lord says that he had come "and spoken, and done works such as none had ever done before; therefore, you have no cloak for your sins," he shows that his coming, speaking and doing mighty works, has given ability, and stripped them of excuse.

All this corresponds with that expression in our Lord's intercessory prayer, "I pray for those who shall believe on me *through* their word;" also that expression of Paul: "Faith comes by hearing, and hearing by the word of God;" or the statement of Peter, that "God made choice among us, that the Gentiles, by my mouth, should hear the word of the gospel and believe." What is here called "their words," "the word of God" and "the word of the gospel," is manifestly all the same, and corresponds precisely to what John the Baptist calls "witness of the light," and what John the apostle means by "these things are written that you might believe." All this, and much more that might be collected, to the same amount, means the divine testimonies which God has given, to enable man, or give him ability to believe, that he may be left without excuse.

But what is it that is to be believed? What is it that the divine testimony is designed to prove? It is not a set of metaphysical speculations, men's views, reasonings and opinions about Trinity and Unity, Calvinism and Armenianism, nor any other learned system of doctrines and commandments of modern date, for the following reasons:

1. "They who seek shall find," said the Lord, in referring to what he placed before men to believe. Thousands have sought the Lord through the above-mentioned speculations, and sought him honestly, but never could find him; therefore they are not what we are required to believe.

2. The gospel of Christ is designed for the people at large. The people at large cannot understand enough about the above-mentioned speculations to be able to say whether they believe them or not. They cannot, therefore, be what the Lord required man to believe.

3. It is admitted by all intelligent men, that a man can be a Christian and not believe the above speculations. A man cannot be a Christian and not believe that which God requires man to believe. Therefore, these speculations are not what man is required to believe.

4. It is declared by the Lord, that he that believeth not that which he requires man to believe, shall be damned. It is admitted that man may not believe the theories in question, and not be damned. These speculations or theories, then, are not what the Lord requires man to believe.

5. Thousands heard, believed and received what the Lord required men to believe, on hearing a single discourse. Thousands could not understand, or know enough about the above-named speculations, on hearing only a single discourse, to be able to say whether they believed or not. Therefore, these speculations are not what man is required to believe.

What then is it that man is required to believe? There are three things about this matter, that never should be forgotten. 1. That faith is required of all—of the masses of the people. 2. It is required upon pain of damnation. 3. It is a fact, as before stated, that immense numbers—that thousands of the people, believed that which God requires man to believe, upon hearing a single discourse. It must have been something of the simplest and clearest nature. It must have been something of the most tangible kind. It must have been exceedingly short; otherwise so many, of every grade of intelligence, upon the hearing of a *single discourse,* could not have become believers. They had no time to hear, much less to digest, examine and decide upon the merits of lengthy and intricate systems, so as to say whether they believed or not. But they had something presented and were required to believe it on pain of condemnation. Whatever that was, they believed it; and the power of their faith was so great, that it changed the whole course of their after lives. What was it, then, that they believed? They believed that great fundamental proposition declared by the Almighty Father of heaven and earth, at the baptism of our Lord: "This is my Son, the beloved, in whom I am well pleased." Hence the Apostle Peter, when the Saviour asked him the question, "Who do you say that I am," responded, "Thou art the Christ, the Son of the living God." In view of this great confession, the Lord pronounced a blessing upon him, adding, "Flesh and blood hath not revealed it unto thee, but my Father who is in heaven: Math, xvi: 16, 17. In view of this same great oracle, the same Apostle, when advanced in years, and about to put off his tabernacle, said, "We have not followed cunningly devised fables, when we made known unto you the power and coming of our Lord Jesus Christ, but were eye witnesses of his majesty. For he received from God the Father, honor and glory, when there came such a voice to him from the excellent glory, 'This is my beloved Son, in whom I am well pleased.'"

2 Pet i: 16, 17.

In declaring Christ to be his Son, the beloved, the Father gave him "honor and glory." To the same amount, Paul mentions "that which God had promised before by his prophets, in the holy scripture, concerning his Son, Jesus Christ, our Lord, who was made of the seed of David, according to the flesh, and declared the Son of God with power, according to the Spirit of Holiness, by the resurrection from the dead." Rom. 1: 2, 4. No one, we think, can fail to see that these expressions contain the great Christian proposition, in which the whole system centers, or upon which all depends. But someone will inquire— How do you know that this was what God required man to believe? Because John says "these things are written that you might believe that Jesus is the Christ, the Son of God." This passage not only shows what the divine testimonies were written for, but precisely what it is that is to be believed—that *Jesus is the Christ, the Son of God.* But if any one doubts what it is, that is to be believed, we will hear Paul inquire about it and give the answer: "What saith it? The word is nigh thee, even in thy mouth, and in thy heart; that is, the word of faith, which we preach; that if thou shalt confess with thy mouth, the Lord Jesus, and shalt believe in thy heart that God hath raised him from the dead, thou shalt be saved." Rom. x: 8, 9. What is it that he requires man to believe in his heart and confess with the mouth? He is to believe that God raised our Savior from the dead, and confess him with the mouth.

This is a capital point; one in which the souls of all men are concerned, and we must make sure work here. There must be no mistake. We must know precisely what it is that must be believed. What did the Lord command the apostles to preach? "Go into all the world," said he, "and preach the *gospel* to every creature." The gospel, then, is what is to be preached. He then adds, "He that believeth and is baptized shall be saved." "He that believeth" what? As a matter of course, he that believeth what is preached—*the gospel.* The gospel, then, is what was preached, and what was believed. What, then, is the gospel? Paul defines it to be "that Christ died for our sins, according to the scriptures; that he was buried, and that he rose again the third day, according to the scriptures." 1 Cor. xv: 8. His gospel then, is that which he says must be believed in the heart, and confessed with the mouth—that Christ died, and that God raised him from the dead—or, which amounts to the same, confess Christ, that he is God's Son, and then honor him as God has done. But we must know that we are right here. What did the Apostles preach? Let us hear Peter: "Ye men of Israel, hear these words: Jesus of Nazareth, a man approved of God among you, - by miracles, and wonders and signs, which God did by him in the midst of you, as ye yourselves also know: Him being delivered by the determinate counsel and fore-knowledge of God, ye have taken, and by wicked hands have crucified and slain, whom God hath raised up, having loosed the pains of death; because it was not possible that he should be holden of it." Acts ii: 22, 24. Here he embraces the same great proposition concerning Christ, and, at verse 33, affirms that "this Jesus, God had raised up," and that they were all witnesses of the fact. This is the same that was announced to Saul to believe: "I am Jesus of Nazareth, whom thou persecutest," said the Lord to him. He believed this announcement, and immediately commenced preaching it to others. See Acts xxii: 8,9. The same was demanded of the Philippian Jailor. "Believe on the Lord Jesus Christ," said the preacher, "and thou shalt be saved." Acts xvi: 13. Philip, the evangelist, preached Christ to the eunuch. After hearing him preach Christ, he inquires, "What doth hinder me to be baptized?" The man of God answered: "If thou believest with all thy heart, thou mayest. He answered, I believe that Jesus Christ is the Son of God." Acts viii: 36, 38.

This is as extended a development as we can at present make of what was preached, what was believed and confessed, to save man. This, you perceive, is a single proposition, embracing the Messiahship of Jesus, and consequently his divine authority. This great fact, that he is the Messiah—the Saviour of the world—is the one contained in the eternal purpose of God, in his promise to Abraham, alluded to by so many of the prophets, and evinced to John the Baptist, at his baptism, by the voice from Heaven, when God conferred upon him glory and honor. If God had not given us this foundation fact of all piety, benevolence and humanity, we never could have had any Christian faith. But having given the fact—the great proposition to be believed, and the divine testimonies that confirm it, he has thus enabled the world to believe. The light now being come, that all men might believe—these things now being written, that you might believe—the world is left without excuse, and has no cloak for its sins. God has given ability to all to believe, and the responsibility is theirs if they do not believe.

But the inquiry arises, What advantage is there in faith? The Lord responds, "And that believing ye might have life through his name;" John, xxi: 31. Faith brings the believer in reach of life, or where he may obtain life, or gives him power to obtain it. "As many as received him, to them *gave he power* to become the sons of God, even to them that believe on His name;" John, i: 12. The simple circumstance of believing does not make a son of God, but it gives the believer power to become a son. The question therefore is, how the believer, who has power to become a son, proceeds, or what he does to become a son? We must look back to the purpose of God in establishing the apostolic mission, and see what it was designed for. We have seen that the purpose contained Christ, the divine testimonies to enable us to believe in him, and that this belief gives us power to become sons. Is there anything more in the divine purpose? Let us hear Paul: In the same passage before quoted to show that Jesus was declared the Son of God, the Apostle says: "By whom we have received grace and apostleship, for obedience to the faith among all nations, for his name;" Rom. i: 5. At the close of the same letter we find the following: "Now to him who is of power to establish you according to my gospel, and the preaching of Jesus Christ, according to the revelation of the mystery, which was kept secret since the world began, but now is made manifest, and by the scriptures of the prophets; according to the commandment of the everlasting God, made known to all nations for the obedience of faith;" Rom. xvi: 25-6. The revelation of the mystery, or making it manifest, as mentioned here, is the same as unfolding or developing the purpose of God; but it reaches beyond the mere idea of making believers, and introduces another element, viz: the *obedience of faith*. In revealing the eternal purpose, we find no *faith alone* system; but faith that gives power to become sons of God—faith that requires obedience. Having this same element of obedience before his mind, the apostle says of our Lord, that "Being made perfect, he became the author of eternal salvation unto all them that obey him;" Heb. v: 9. In the same spirit, he again says: "But God be thanked, that though ye were servants of sin, you have obeyed from the heart that form of doctrine which was delivered you. Being then made free from sin, ye became the servants of righteousness; Rom. vi: 17, 18. This passage brings us to another item, viz: "being made free from sin," or pardoned, and shows that it is connected with this obedience found in the eternal purpose of God, and means the same as *saved* and called according to his purpose and his grace.

We might rationally expect to find something to do to become sons, when we hear him say that, to as many as received him, to them gave he power to become sons. The fact that he gives those who believe power to become sons, strongly implies that they have something to do; otherwise, there would be no use in power. But does not the Scripture say, "Stand still, and see the salvation of the Lord?" It does, but where would you suppose that passage may be found? Surely not connected with the conversion of any sinner. "But does it not show that the sinner is wholly dead in sins, and that he cannot do anything?" By no means; for no sensible being would command one so dead that he could not do anything, to "stand still;" for, surely, one so dead that he could not do anything could not even *stand still*. It requires some ability to obey the command to stand still, as well as some intelligence to understand it. They are not only commanded to stand Still, which required some ability, but to "see the salvation of the Lord." Never let a man who contends that the sinner has no ability to understand a command, see salvation, or obey the voice of God, quote this passage; for the fact that God gave them the command to stand still, shows that they could understand a command—the fact they obeyed showed that they had ability to obey, the fact that he commanded them to see the salvation of the Lord, and that they did as commanded, shows that they could see salvation—shows that they were by no means in such a state of inability as we have mentioned. The passage is found in Ex. xiv: 19. It is the Lord's account of the deliverance of the Israelites from Egyptian bondage. The hosts of Israel had reached the Red Sea. On the right hand and on the left were impassable mountains. The Egyptian army was in the rear. Fear and dismay spread through the whole ranks of Israel. A cry is raised to heaven, what is to be done? Moses cried aloud to the people, "Fear ye not; stand still and see the salvation of the Lord." They stood still, and saw the sea parted before them—saw the salvation of the Lord. But they *only saw it,* but did not *get it,* standing still. Presently the Lord spoke unto Moses, and said: "Speak unto the children of Israel, that they go forward." Yes, go forward, and obtain the salvation which you only saw while you were standing still. Indeed, this is not all; but you must go forward *in baptism,* if you obtain this salvation, which you only saw while you were standing still. In obedience to the command of the Lord, they went forward, and "were all baptized into Moses, in the cloud and in the sea." The next thing we hear of them is a song of triumph.

As they went forward and were baptized into Moses, in the cloud and in the sea, so the first act of the penitent believer, in obedience to his Lord and Master, is to go forward and be baptized into his name, that he too may unite in songs of redemption—not from Egyptian bondage, but from the bondage of sin. Here, in the name of the Redeemer, by the blood of the covenant, by the spirit of our God, by the life of Christ, through faith, he is justified, and his soul is delivered from all past sins, according to the benevolent purpose of God. Here is the object of the apostolic mission. Hear an expression from Paul upon it: "I was made a minister according to the gift of the grace of God given unto me by the effectual working of his power: unto me, who am less than the least of all saints, is this grace given, that I should preach among the Gentiles the unsearchable riches of Christ; and to make all men see what is the fellowship of the mystery which from the beginning of the world hath been hid in God; who created all things, by Jesus Christ; to the intent that now unto the principalities and powers in heavenly places might be known by the church the manifold wisdom of God, according to the eternal purpose which he purposed in Christ Jesus, our Lord." Eph. iii: 7-11.

Here lies the fearful ground of condemnation for the impenitent. They find themselves included in the benevolent purpose of God, in the promise made to Abraham, in the salvation spoken of by the prophets, that should be to the ends of the earth, for all people, and the love of God to man. They find that the light of the world was for them, that Christ came into the world that they might be saved, that he died for them, shed his blood for them, and opened the way for them to the father, as much as any human beings. They find that he sent the gospel to them, with all its divine testimonies, as much as he did to any saint that ever entered heaven—that it is put completely in their power to come to God. They remember, too, that the Lord says he is not willing that any should perish, but rather that all should come to repentance—that he wills that all men be saved—that all the day long he stretches forth his hand to a gain-saying and disobedient people, saying, Whoever will, let him come to the fountain's of living water. They further reflect, too, that he cries, Harden not your hearts, as in the bitter provocation, but hear his voice, for now is the acceptable time, the day of merciful visitation—that he who comes, he will in no wise cast out—that those who seek shall find—that his yoke is easy and his burden light. He can say to the sinful man, in the day of judgment, I included you in my eternal purpose—that you, as much as any of the human family, were the object of my benevolent promise to my servant Abraham. That very salvation which I said should be to the ends of the earth, was as free for you as for any who have lived upon the earth. My love embraced you as much as any of the whole world. The very object of the mission of my son to your world was, that you might be saved. The very object I had in revealing my son to you was that you might have confidence in him, and lean your soul upon him and be saved. I authorized his holy witnesses to write and publish their divine testimonies for the special purpose that you might Believe. I sent the true light, that is for every man who comes into the world, to you, that you might believe. My son spoke to you, and did such works as no man ever did, that you might have no cloak for your sins. I have set before you the wages of sin, which is death, and the gift of God, eternal life. My holy prophets have wept over you. My apostles have preached to you, wept over you, prayed for you, and suffered martyrdom for your sakes. My Son taught in his own person, prayed over men, wept over them, did miracles among them, was condemned by Jews and Romans, nailed to the cross, crowned with thorns, buffeted, spit upon, his side pierced with a spear, his soul made an offering for sin—poured out his soul unto death. The cry has come from heaven to you, "Why will you die?" Preachers of the gospel have plead with you, exhorted you, and prayed over you with tears. Many pious fathers have plead, and wept, and grieved. Mothers have mourned, as none but mothers can mourn, over wayward children, followed them, begging of them to turn to God. Wives have struggled with inexpressible anxiety and anguish for husbands, and husbands for wives. Children have, with streaming tears, upon their knees, begged of their parents to hear the voice of warning, and turn to God.

But, in some cases, all this is resisted, and the sinner hardens his heart, and in wild infatuation rushes on till he falls into ruin. He is brought to a stand. He looks round!! The work is done I In thunder tones, the words, "He who is filthy, let him be filthy still," thrill his polluted soul. He cries aloud, Who has done all this? He answers, Not the Almighty, for he included all alike in his benevolent purpose, as well as in his merciful promise, and gave his son for all. Not our Lord Jesus Christ, for he died for all and commanded salvation to be sent to all. Not the holy apostles, for they were faithful to preach the gospel to all, and invite all to receive it. The kind friends we have alluded to are not to blame for this sad affair. Where, then lies the blame? Upon his own soul. What an eternal sting upon the souls of the lost, to have to upbraid and reproach themselves for having resisted the wisdom, goodness, mercy, and love of God; for having rejected the high and holy counsels of heaven against their own souls; for having rejected and opposed all that was tender, kind, lovely, endearing, and good; for having used the very lips which God made to praise him, in cursing; for having used the very strength given him to serve God, in barring the way, so that he never could get to Heaven! What an eternal pain to the soul, the consciousness of having wrought his own ruin, of having pulled down eternal ruin upon his own head!

Suppose he does reflect that the Lord was good! So much worse the condemnation for rejecting him! He remembers that the Lord is merciful; but this only adds to his misery, to think he could have had the hardness of heart to have rejected and despised such mercy! He may remember that the Lord is wise; but this only deepens the pangs of hell, to think that he was so perverse as to reject such wisdom. He may think of the New Jerusalem, of the pure and holy there, of all ages—of the holy martyrs, apostles, prophets, the ancient worthies, the angels of God, Jesus, the mediator of the new institution, and the Almighty Father of all—that he hears the united chorus rise up, in a shout of blessing, and glory, and honor, and power, and dominion, to him who sits upon the throne, and the Lamb forever and ever—he may imagine that he hears the innumerable throng, making the heavenly arches ring with "Hallelujah, salvation, and glory, and honor, and power, unto the Lord our God:" but this, too, would only augment the blame that lay upon his soul, for his unaccountable obstinacy and hardness of heart, in disinheriting himself forever, and plunging himself into ruin.

My hearers, the door of mercy is still open. The invitations are still tendered to poor, fallen man. These invitations are to each of you personally, full of the goodness and mercy of our God. Let me entreat of you that you act wisely upon this great question, in seeking the salvation of your souls. What shall it profit a man if he shall gain the whole world, and lose his own soul? or what shall a man give in exchange for his soul?

May God bless you! may you come to the Lord, and find redemption through the blood of Christ, to whom be praises and honor, forever and ever. Amen.

-----o-----

Organization, Ordaining Preachers, etc.

We have long discovered that even among good men—the best of men—there is a wonderful proneness to wander from the simplicity of the way of the Lord, to real innovations, endangering the peace, harmony, and union of the whole family of God on earth. It is a difficult task to induce men to fix their minds upon the wisdom of God, admire it, and show by their practice their full confidence in it. It is true, almost any man will admit the wisdom of God abstractly, extol it and show how infinitely above all human wisdom it is. But the wisdom of God is so unlike the wisdom of this world, that many of its brightest displays are not noticed by the mere worldly man, whether in the Church, or out of it; in the form, and under the name of a preacher, or not. The wisdom of this world never would have conceived the idea of giving the Redeemer of the world his birth-place in a stable, cradled in a manger, clad in swaddling bands; nor would it ever have entered into the heart of those under the influence of the wisdom of this world, for their Lord and Master to have been a homeless pilgrim, not having where to lay his head. In their estimation, this would have been an eternal disgrace. Nor could they see, either the wisdom, or the goodness of our Lord's continual attention to the poor, the halt, the maimed, deaf and blind, and his sharp and cutting rebukes of the rich and affluent. Much less could they have seen any wisdom in admitting a Judas—a traitor—to all his private counsels; and placing twelve illiterate, uninfluential and penniless fishermen of Galilee before the lords, nobles, princes and potentates of the earth, as the first preachers and defenders of the faith. But, to one spiritually minded, the wisdom of God is seen, the Divine mission of Jesus proved and the truth of Christianity established through this procedure, as it never could have been by an opposite course.

In the same way, the first preachers of the Gospel, by their close adherence to the example of Christ, in humility, devotion, and complete consecration to God, with a total disregard of worldly treasures, honors, and powers, gave great evidence of their confidence in the doctrine they preached, their Master, and their hope of a resurrection from the dead, and eternal glory in the world to come. They lived and acted under the motto, "We have no continuing city here;" or in different words; "The things that are seen, are temporal, but the things which are not seen, are eternal." They received their great impulse from the eternal, and not from the temporal. But a worldly ministry receive their main impulse from the temporal, and not from the eternal. They are governed continually, by worldly influences, appliances, and policies. They are constantly speaking and meditating upon what the world will say, or think of us, and not how they will please God. Indeed, this class do not read and meditate upon the word and works of God enough, to bring their minds and souls under the influence of what God has said and done, much less what he says he will do in time to come. Preachers of this mold, and there are many of them, we are sorry to be compelled to admit, in our time, are not addicted to grave and deliberate researches into antiquity, or profound biblical criticism, much as they are wont to make allusions to *learning* and *literature*. The main literature with them, is that which is current at the present time; they notice what comes under their own eye, with the movements and bearings of things around them. They see that, in some organizations, a mere boy—a perfect novice—one who has not been in the Church three months, is made class-leader, and moves all under him, at his bidding, with the weight of his authority. It is seen too, that he is clothed with this distinction and consideration, by a single touch of appointing power. The observer notices again, and sees a young man scarcely escaped from his teens, in the form of a circuit-rider, put in charge of a circuit of Churches, to whom the class-leader is a "subordinate officer." It is seen too, that when this Rev. functionary makes his appearance, both the subordinate officers and private members dwindle into insignificance, eclipsed by the glory that excelleth. This station of authority, it is perceived, is obtained with but very little preparation, or moral worth. Indeed, it is all conferred at a single dash, by the greater glory of an appointing power. This is an easy road to preferment, authority and power.

Again, the observer looks, and there comes the presiding elder, before whom mere circuit preachers and class-leaders dwindle into insignificance. He has charge of a whole conference of circuits, while all the circuit-preachers, class-leaders and private members are under him. Such a position as he occupies, is very tempting to a worldly preacher. Look at his preferment, authority and power among his subordinates! But we look once more, and behold a bishop, with authority over all his Churches in a sixth part of the United States, with all the presiding-elders, circuit-preachers, and class-leaders, *subordinate officers.* What honor! what authority! what power! what temptation to worldly ambition, and vain glory! The eye of the observer turns again, and looks upon a grave Synod, Assembly, Conference or Council of dignitaries—reverends— men in authority, with great deference paid them by the Church and the world. "Ah," says the preacher, "we have nothing like this, no distinctions and preferments. Ah! me, what a mistake the Christian Baptist made, in its unmitigated war upon all these great things!" He looks again, and behold an Episcopal bishop in robes! and above him an Arch-bishop! He sees the people bowing before him, hears the titles of Rev., Rt. Rev., and Rt. Rev. Doctor! The worldly preacher commences reasoning upon it, "Look," says he, "at that stately edifice! what a display of art, mechanism, taste and elegance, all combined with convenience and comfort! Listen to the solemn tones of that great organ, and elegant performance of that refined choir. Observe too, the elegance of the audience, with the Rt. Rev. Doctor, in his clerical gown. Nothing is seen here but elegance, taste and refinement. Look at the graceful, easy and lovely gestures of the preacher! Observe the softness of his voice, the clearness of his articulation, and elegance of pronunciation. Nor is there anything objectionable in the doctrine. Here is something elevated. Here is Christianity carried out to perfection.— How different all this from our uncomely, unadorned and common places of worship! How different this too, from our plain, and frequently home-spun and uneducated ministry! Look too, at our unqualified and nominal eldership! It is a disgrace to the age."

Such are the reflections of many, surrounded by these wretched temptations. The idea of men having no preferment, promotion, authority and power, except what is naturally acquired before the Church and the world, by a man's own labors, perseverance, and usefulness in the cause; his known and established integrity to God and the cause; his faithfulness, patience, devotion—his ardent love, earnestness and sacrifice—his continued care and anxiety for the good of man, his intelligence and ability, is intolerable with some men. This way to preferment is too straight, the ascent too gradual, the labor and perseverance of obtaining the height, too great; it is intolerable. By having the right kind of an organization, an aspirant may, at a single leap, especially if he has the right kind of friends in authority, bound into distinction, such as he would not have reached in a lifetime, upon his *own* merit. Not only so, but if we had good order, a young man with a little show of learning, though he had never given the least evidence of devotion to the cause, or concern for the good of man, by an ordination ceremony, and the appointment of some authoritative body, or tribunal, might be brought into distinction, and notice, such as he could not earn by his intelligence, moral worth and usefulness, in ten years, and, in many instances, in a life-time. Not only so, but ignorant, illiterate men, and all classes, such as some who think themselves learned and wise, are ashamed of; such as they think a disgrace to the cause; men who "work for nothing, and find themselves;" and who have done a large share of the hard labor in building up the Churches all over the land, would be shut out of the ministry, and prevented from standing in the way of an elevated, learned, and talented ministry.

Many considerations like these, demand a different kind of an organization from that which we now have; that authorized in the New Testament; that where a man has the place that his *own standing,* his moral worth, his labors and devotion to the cause, his sacrifices for Christ's sake, his intelligence, natural ability and acquirements, have won for him, in the religious communities, and the world, where his life is well known. But after all, if his moral character, his love to God and man, his devotion to the cause, his intelligence, talents and learning—his exhibition of his usefulness before the people at large, will not command attention, and carry him through, without some ecclesiastical machinery unknown to the New Testament, it is evident that it is because he is not adapted to the station of a public preacher of Christ, and it would be an imposition for any body of men to impose him upon the people as such. He is to preach to the masses—to the people at large; his labors are for them, and if his ability to do good, if his usefulness does not appear among them, and to them, it is because *he has none.*

The disciples at large, taken all together, under all circumstances, and in all cases, are **a** safer tribunal, and when a fair opportunity is offered, will give a more correct decision, where the character of a man is at stake, or in regard to his usefulness as a preacher in their midst, than any other tribunal on this earth, and they are less liable to abuse their authority than any other. It is true, communities will not decide as soon, in such grave matters, as some who think they should have a divine right to *decide for them,* may think they should, but they will decide—at the proper time, the decision will come, and, right or wrong, when it does come, it will be *final,* so far as this world is concerned. It will, however be more frequently right than any other that ever can be had on this earth. Not only so, but as it takes all the men in the community to make up the *whole* community, and if any man, or any number of men desire to express their opinion in any case, they have **a** right to do so, and that opinion should have its own natural force upon the mind of community, who know those who gave it; but allow it to possess no decisive authority like that of a magistrate or judge. In the same light, all Church decisions must be regarded, till God, the righteous Judge, shall pass the final sentence upon all men and angels.

B. F.

-----o-----

Mr. Quinby—The "Star."

FOR want of space, time and disposition for *small matters,* we must attend to them in **a** short way, or omit them. The *Star in the West,* poor thing, in some four different Nos., occupies much space in pouring upon our devoted head, freely and lengthily, its native billingsgate. He becomes so infuriated as to feel some need of a hell in which for us to be punished. In order, however, to be consistent, he informs us that he believes in a retribution in *this life.* Forgetting the scripture, as usual with him, and the power of God, he assumes *his* judgment seat in this world, and proceeds to inflict upon us the punishment of *his* Universalian hell, in the shape of the putrid masses of accumulated matter emitted from his pen. But this poisonous matter, naturally flowing from its native bitter fountain, professedly for our punishment, we only look at, without tasting or being infected by it; the scorpions with which he lashes, we handle without harm; the fires of *his* hell, we can extinguish—or, if endless, we can, in argument, tie, hand-cuff and imprison our highly incensed tormentor. He, poor thing! talk about retribution upon us! He is more powerless than Sampson, shorn by Delilah. His scribblings constantly remind men of sense, of a whipt gander, chuckling to his comrades after rising from his back in a quagmire, whence he had been sent by the force of a kick from an ox. He, the embodiment of conscious weakness, the last particle of his courage having oozed from the point of his pen, as helpless as a sucking infant, so far as maintaining his cause in argument is concerned, talk about retribution! What a retribution!

But what has kindled his wrath, and put him in the notion of wresting vengeance out of the hands of God? Poor man! he could not keep it to himself. The thing has gone from him. Accidentally, the truth escaped from his pen. He says *he knows us.* Yes, here lies the trouble with him—*he knows us.* Gentle reader, we will tell you how he got to *know us.* Some three years ago he ventured into a written discussion, to be published in the *Christian Age* and *Star in the West,* on the doctrine of a judgment after death, which we affirmed. He wrote his replies some three times as long as our affirmative articles. We continued our articles about the same length as commenced, and inserted about the same amount, each time, of his response, in regular order. In a short time, he commenced complaining that we did not each time insert the whole of his lengthy articles, insisting that it required more space to reply than we occupied, and in a short time refused to proceed. In this, he got to *know us,* so that he did not call upon us for any more light for some time. He would occasionally, when trying to aid in the downfall of Mr. J. B. Furgeson, give vent to enough of his malignant feelings to show that he had not forgotten us.

Some twelve months ago, Mr. Peters, another Universalian preacher of this city, challenged Bro. J. A. Dearborn to debate the question of the final holiness and happiness of all mankind. Bro. Dearborn, not desiring to gain any notoriety in that way, and not thinking Rev. Peters competent to conduct such a discussion, proposed through the *Daily Times,* the medium through which the challenge came, that the Universalists of this city select a man to whom they would confide their cause, and the Disciples, in like manner, select a man to meet him. About this time, if our memory is correct, we published a notice of the debate between Mr. Bacon and Mr. Smith, in Harrison, Ohio. Mr. Quinby made some comments upon this notice, in reply to which we addressed him a letter, which he honorably published, and in which we approved the proposal of Bro. Dearborn. Mr. Quinby told his readers that I had proposed myself in the place of Bro. Dearborn—a statement in which there was not one word of truth; and told his readers, as he has done repeatedly since, that we had made great professions of saintship—about which we had not said one word, as he and all knew who had read all we had said. He also proceeded to tell his readers that we could not be accepted as an opponent, for the reason that we were destitute of *moral honesty in debate.* As yet, we had not been proposed as the man to debate with them, nor mentioned, nor hinted at, by either Bro. Dearborn or myself.

After all this slang, Mr. Quinby entered a horrible complaint about the proposition of Mr. Peters, attributing it to myself, insisting that endless punishment should be discussed in connection with universal salvation, and assuring his readers that I would not discuss that subject. I wrote him immediately, assuring him that he was mistaken—that I had never refused to debate that question with the former, and that I would debate it with him, or any man he would endorse, through the *Star.* Here he got to *know us* again. Here "he "caved in!" His courage failed him. He declined, with the ignominious assertion that, if there was an endless punishment, we were sure of it. How infinitely little! Where was his prediction?' Where was his judgment? All shrivelled up. Our champion crawled back into his shell—a very small and thin shell, at that.

A few weeks ago, we had an appointment in Keene, Jessamine county, Kentucky. When we arrived, we were informed that Mr. Quinby had been there a short time before, and had preached on the rich man and Lazarus, and that the

Universalians desired us to preach on the same subject. We inquired if he read the sermon, and told the friends that we knew what was in his old sermon, and agreed to give them a discourse on the same subject. We announced the time when we would speak upon it, and when the time came, we devoted about two hours and a half to the subject. If there was but one opinion in the community about it, viz: that it was a *satisfactory confutation of Universalism, especially Mr. Quinby's sermon,* we did not hear it. In a short time, here came some three long articles, full of the most ignorant and stupid blunders, from some-one who claimed to have heard us, through the *Star,* accompanied by comments from the Editor, blaming us for saying that his sermon was *written,* but admitting that it was written; blaming us for saying that it was an *old sermon,* but admitting that it was an old sermon; blaming us horribly for saying that he read it, but admitting that he did read it; murmuring sorely because we said he had preached it as he passed round the country, but admitting that he had preached it in several places West, and clearly implying that he had preached it in the East, before he came West, some four years ago. In his fury he blames us, and, in the lowest and roughest manner, accuses us of lying, for stating in Covington, that considerable space had lately been occupied in the *Star,* touching our effort at Keene, while three numbers stare him in the face and evince all we said.

Here is the way he came to *know us.* That he now has a right to say he knows us, is clear. He knows more than some think; he not only knows the shallowness, emptiness and ridiculous character of the claims of Universalism— the shameful contradictions, sophistries, evasions and twistings employed in its defense, but he knows that we know them, and can show them up, to the discomfiture of any man he can produce. Here lies the trouble. Here lies the pain. Then, to hide his shame, he tells his readers that he cannot wrestle with a chimney sweep! He knows us, and that if we falls into our hands, his craft will be in danger—that his *Star* would twinkle more dimly than ever; and that a defeat, such as we can escort him through, in the presence of a popular assembly in our city, would be disastrous to his gull-trap, with which he attempts to catch dimes. Here lies the trouble, and he *knows it.* B. F.

-----o-----

Mr. Curry.

Some Universalian friend, while we were at Fincastle, Indiana, some months since, sent us a note, inviting us to an oral discussion with Mr. Curry, a Universalian preacher. We agreed to debate with him, if the *Star in the West* would endorse him as a competent man to defend the Universalian cause. As yet, we have seen no such endorsement. A short time since, we received a letter from a brother, stating that our Universalian friends say, that we may come on— that he will be thus endorsed. We are not willing to start till we *see the endorsement.* We cannot debate with every young man who may desire to distinguish himself, unless the interests of his party are sufficiently identified with him, to make his position worth taking. We cannot debate with young men merely to learn them how to debate. Let them call out Mr. Quinby, Gurley, or some man endorsed by them, and we will satisfy him and them. B. F.

-----o-----

Resurrection of the Dead.

Why may not God raise the dead? He has raised us into life, as we now are. "It is natural to derive existence from parents, and come up into the world, as we now are, in the ordinary way." Indeed, *natural!* But pray, who made nature, and endowed it with the wonderful and incomprehensible power to raise up, fill with life, endow with mind, and clothe with strength, the innumerable throngs that constantly people this earth? He who made nature, and gave it this great power, did not endow it with a greater power than he possessed. He, then, who gave nature the power to bring us into existence, certainly has power, when we fall into the grave, to bring us up again.

Revision of the English Scriptures.

We are aware that there is an intense desire to get possession of the Revised English Scriptures. No question has been so frequently presented to us as the question: "When will the Revised Version be out?" This question we are unable to answer; but intending to "post up" our readers as far as possible, and gratify their laudable anxiety about the greatest work of the age, we give them below the Second Epistle of Peter entire, as now published by the Bible Union. It will probably undergo some change yet. When our readers have examined this, compared it with the common version, and fully digested it, if they desire more, we will furnish them with other specimens. We give it in paragraphs, just as we received it.

THE SECOND EPISTLE OF PETER.

I. SIMEON PETER, a servant and an apostle of Jesus Christ, to those who have obtained like precious faith with us in the righteousness of our God and Saviour Jesus Christ: Grace unto you, and peace he multiplied in the knowledge of God, and of Jesus our Lord.

Forasmuch as his divine power hath given unto us all things that *pertain* unto life and godliness, through the knowledge of him who called us by glory and might: whereby he hath given unto us the exceeding great and precious promises, that by these ye might become partakers of the divine nature, having escaped from the corruption that is in the world through lust: but for this very reason also do ye, contributing all diligence, furnish in your faith fortitude; and in fortitude, knowledge; and in knowledge, self-control; and in self-control, patience; and in patience, godliness; and in godliness, brotherly kindness; and in brotherly kindness, love. For these things being yours, and increasing, render *you* not idle nor unfruitful as to the knowledge of our Lord Jesus Christ. For he that lacketh these things is blind, being nearsighted, having forgotten the cleansing away of his old sins. Wherefore the rather, brethren, be diligent to make your calling and election sure; for, doing these things, ye shall never fall: for so there shall be richly furnished unto you the entrance into the everlasting kingdom of our Lord and Saviour Jesus Christ.

Wherefore I will be not negligent to remind you always of these things, though ye know *them,* and are established in the present truth: but I think it right, so long as I am in this tabernacle, to stir you up by way of remembrance; knowing that the laying aside of my tabernacle is speedy, as also our Lord Jesus Christ showed me; but I will endeavor that ye may even at all times be able, after my departure, to call these things to mind.

For we had not followed cunningly devised fables, when we made known unto you the power and coming of our Lord Jesus Christ, but had been eye-witnesses of his majesty. For he received from God the Father honor and glory, a voice being borne to him such as this from the excellent glory: This is my beloved Son, in whom I am well pleased; and this voice we, being with him on the holy mount, heard borne from heaven. And we have more sure the prophetic word, whereunto ye do well that ye take heed, as unto a lamp shining in a dark place, until day dawn, and the daystar arise in your hearts; knowing this first, that no prophecy of Scripture cometh from one's own interpretation: for not by man's will was prophecy brought at any time, but holy men of God spake, being moved by the Holy Spirit.

II. But there were also false prophets among the people, as also among you there shall be false teachers, who privily shall bring in destructive sects, even denying the Master who bought them, bringing upon themselves speedy destruction. And many shall follow their lascivious ways, by reason of whom the way of the truth shall be evil spoken of; and in covetousness shall they with feigned words make merchandize of you; for whom the judgment from of old lingereth not, and their destruction slumbereth not. For if God spared not angels when they sinned, but, having cast *them* to hell, delivered *them* unto chains of darkness, being reserved for judgment; and spared not the old world, but kept Noah, a preacher of righteousness, with seven others, when he brought the flood upon the world of the ungodly; and, reducing to ashes the cities of Sodom and Gomorrah, condemned *them* to an overthrow, having made *them* an example of those that should afterward be ungodly; and delivered righteous Lot, worn down with the filthy behavior of the lawless: (for in seeing and hearing did the righteous man dwelling among them, day after day torment *his* righteous soul with *their* unlawful deeds:) the Lord knoweth how to deliver the godly out of temptation, but the unrighteous to reserve under punishment unto the day of judgment; but chiefly those who walk after the flesh in the lust of uncleanness, and despise government. Daring men, self-willed, they tremble not while railing at dignities; whereas angels, who are greater in strength and power, bring not against them before the Lord a railing judgment. But these, as natural brute beasts born for capture and destruction, railing in things that they understand not, shall utterly perish in their own corruption, and so receive the wages of unrighteousness. Accounting *it* pleasure *to* revel in the daytime; spots and blemishes; revelling in their own deceits, while feasting with you; having eyes full of an adulteress and ceasing not from sin; alluring unstable souls; having a heart exercised in covetousness; children of a curse; having forsaken the right way, they went astray, having followed the way of Balaam the *son* of Bosor, who loved the wages of unrighteousness, but had a reproof of his transgression; a dumb ass, having spoken with man's voice, restrained the madness of the prophet. These are wells without water, and mists driven by a tempest; for whom the blackness of darkness for ever hath been reserved. For, speaking great swelling *words* of vanity, they allure in the lusts of the flesh, by lascivious ways, those who were scarcely escaped from those who live in error; promising them liberty, while they themselves are slaves of corruption; for by what any one hath been overcome, by that hath he also been enslaved. For if, having escaped from the pollutions of the world through the knowledge of the Lord and Saviour Jesus Christ, they are yet entangled again therein, and overcome, the last state is become worse with them than the first. For it were better for them not to have known the way of righteousness, than, having known *it,* to turn back from the holy commandment delivered unto them. But there hath happened unto them that of the true proverb: A dog that turned back to his own vomit; and: A sow that was washed, into the wallowing-place of mire.

II. This second epistle, beloved, I now write unto you, in *both* which I stir up your pure mind by way of remembrance, that ye may be mindful of the words spoken before by the holy prophets, and of the commandment of us the apostles, of the Lord and Saviour: knowing this first, that there shall come at the end of the days mockers in mockery, walking according to their own lusts, and saying: Where is the promise of his coming? for, since the fathers fell asleep, all things continue thus from the beginning of the creation. For of this they are willingly ignorant, that, by the word of God, heavens were from of old, and earth out of water and by water consisting; whereby the world that then was, being flooded with water, perished: but the heavens which are now, and the earth, have by his word been laid up in store, being reserved for fire unto the day of judgment and destruction of the ungodly men.

But of this one thing be ye, beloved, not ignorant, that one day *is* with the Lord as a thousand years, and a thousand years as one day. The Lord is not tardy concerning his promise, as some account tardiness; but is long-suffering towards us, not willing that any should perish, but that all should come to repentance. But the day of the Lord will come as a thief in the night; in which the heavens shall pass away with a rushing noise, but the elements shall be dissolved with fervent heat, and the earth and the works therein shall be burned up.

Since, then, all these things are dissolving, what manner *of persons* ought ye to be in *all* holy behavior and godliness, looking for and hastening the coming of the day of God, in consequence of which the heavens being on fire shall be dissolved, and the elements melt with fervent heat. But, according to his promise, we look for new heavens and a new earth, wherein righteousness dwelleth.

Wherefore, beloved, looking for these things, be diligent that spotless and blameless ye may be found by him in peace; and the long-suffering of our Lord account salvation; even as also our beloved brother Paul, according to the wisdom given unto him, wrote unto you, as also in all the epistles, speaking in them of these things; among which are some things hard to be understood, which the unlearned and unstable wrest, as also the other scriptures, unto their own destruction. Do ye, therefore, beloved, knowing *these things* before, beware lest, carried away with the error of the lawless, ye fall from your own steadfastness. But grow in the grace and knowledge of our Lord and Saviour Jesus Christ. To him the glory, both now and unto the day of eternity. Amen.

-----o-----

The Duty of Rendering God's Word Plain to all.

DEUTERONOMY 4: 2.—Ye shall not add to the word that I command you, neither shall ye diminish *aught* from it.

DEUT. 27: 8.—And thou shalt write upon the stones all the words of this law very plainly.

PSALM 12: 6.—The words of the Lord are pure words: as silver tried in a furnace of earth, purified seven times.

PSALM 119: 140.—Thy word is very pure; therefore thy servant loveth it.

JEREMIAH 23 : 28.—He that hath my word, let him speak my word faithfully.

HABAKKUK 2: 2.—Write the vision, and make it plain upon tables, that he may run that readeth it.

MATTHEW 4: 4.—Man shall not live by bread alone, but by every word that proceedeth out of the mouth of God.

ACTS 20 : 27.—I have not shunned to declare unto you the whole counsel of God.

2 TIMOTHY 3: 16.—All Scripture is given by inspiration of God, and is profitable for doctrine, for reproof, for correction, for instruction in righteousness.

REVELATION 22: 18, 19.—For I testify unto every man that heareth the words of the prophecy of this book: If any man shall add unto these things, God shall add unto him the plagues that are written in this book. And, if any man shall take away from the words of the book of this prophecy, God shall take away his part out of the book of life, and out of the holy city, and from the things which are written in this book.

Every fault of translation, either takes from or adds to the Word of God. When such fault is unknown and unintended, after proper diligence has been exercised to discover it, guilt does not attach, but when the fault is known and permitted, or when ignorance results from negligence, culpability is unavoidable.

"The great principle for which we contend, is THAT ALL MEN OUGHT TO HAVE THE WORD OF GOD, UNMUTILATED AND UNDISGUISED."—*Rev. S. H. Cone, D. D.*

"Need Protestants be told that there can be but *one* standard of authority in religious matters—the Bible *as it came from God*. Just so far and no farther, as a version is a faithful mirror of this, reflecting all its divine features with fullness and distinctness, is it to be regarded as having claims upon our reverence and obedience. Unhappily our version was made under circumstances that did not allow of this strict fidelity to the original."—*Prof. G. W. Eaton, D. D.*

"God will bless *the Bible translated without addition, diminution or concealment.*"—*Rev. A. Maclay, D. D.*

General Rules
FOR THE DIRECTION OF TRANSLATORS AND REVISERS EMPLOYED BY THE AMERICAN BIBLE UNION.

" 1. The exact meaning of the inspired text, as that text expressed it to those who understood the original scriptures at the time they were first written, must be translated by corresponding words and phrases, so far as they can be found, in the vernacular tongue of those for whom the version is designed, with the least possible obscurity or indefiniteness.

"2. Wherever there is a version in common use, it shall be made the basis of revision, and all unnecessary interference with the established phraseology shall be avoided; and only such alterations shall be made, as the exact meaning of the inspired text and the existing state of the language may require.

" 3. Translations or revisions of the New Testament shall be made from the received Greek text, critically edited, with known errors corrected."

-----o-----

Special Instructions
TO THE REVISERS OF THE ENGLISH NEW TESTAMENT.

" The common English version must be the basis of the revision: the Greek Text, Bagster and Sons' octavo edition of 1851.

" 2. Whenever an alteration from that version is made on any authority additional to that of the reviser, such authority must be cited in the manuscript, either on the same page, or in an appendix.

" 2. Every Greek word or phrase, in the translation of which the phraseology of the common version is changed, must be carefully examined in every other place in which it occurs in the New Testament, and the views of the reviser be given as to its proper translation in each place.

" 4. As soon as the revision of any one book of the New Testament is finished, it shall be sent to the Secretary of the Bible Union, or such other person as shall be designated by the Committee on Versions, in order that copies may be taken and furnished to the revisers of the other books, to be returned with their suggestions to the reviser or revisers of that book. After being revised with the aid of these suggestions, a carefully prepared copy shall be forwarded to the Secretary."

-----o-----

From the Gospel Advocate.
The Bible.—No. II.

Brethren Fanning and Lipscomb:—Having, in my number first, shown that all nature, internal and external, all nations, ancient and modern, and all religions, true and false, are monumental proofs of the divine inspiration of the Bible, I wish, in this, to say something of

THE NATURE OF INSPIRATION.

Naturalists, Spiritualists, and Christians, all use the word *inspiration*. Do they use it in the same sense? No. Three words will show the difference. They are *Natural, Spiritual, Divine*. Naturalists teach that inspiration is *natural* to man, and that all nature is inspired. Spiritualists contend that there is a *ghost* inspiration in addition to natural or *intuitive* inspiration. But Christians believe that God is *Spirit,* and that he inspired Moses and the Prophets, and Christ and the Apostles, by his *Spirit.* Natural religionists look to nature for religious instruction. Spiritualists consult the Spirits of the dead. Christians "search the Scriptures." Naturalists trust in themselves, Spiritualists in ghosts, and Christians in God, for religious instruction.

But Spiritualism is very comprehensive. It can find the true religion in Paganism, Mohammedanism, and Christianity! In nature, in the Bible, and in Spiritual rapping, tipping, and writing! Natural inspiration has its perpetual and world-wide refutation in *Paganism,*. We will, therefore, turn our attention to

THE INSPIRATION OF GHOSTOLOGY.

Spiritualism teaches that "the Bible is a record of Spiritual communications, made through departed human Spirits!" The Bible would be a strange book if it read as Spiritualists interpret it. Shall we give a few specimens?

1. And he shall be filled with the Holy Ghost of a dead man, even from his mother's womb! Luke 1. 15.

2. A departed human Spirit shall come upon thee, and the power of a ghost shall overshadow thee: therefore also that holy thing which shall be born of thee, shall be called the Son of God! Luke 1, 35.

3. And his father Zacharias was filled with the Holy Ghost of a dead man, and prophesied! Luke 1, 67.

4. He shall baptize you with a departed ghost! Luke 3. 16.

5. And the ghost of a dead man descended in a bodily shape like a dove upon him. Luke 3, 22.

6. Howbeit, when he, the Spirit of some dead man is come, he will guide you into all truth! John 16, 13.

7. And they were all filled with departed human Spirits, and began to speak with other tongues, as the Spirits gave them utterance! Acts 2, 4.

How absurd is such an interpretation of the New Testament! If the Bible is a record of Spiritual communications, made by departed human Spirits, then Moses and the Prophets, Christ and the Apostles, must have been the "mediums!" Christ, the Son of God, degraded to a level with Davis, Dexter, Harris & Co.!

A ghost medium! Can any man believe it till he is mesmerized out of his common sense?

The Christian idea of inspiration is something worthy of God and man. The *Spirit* of *God* inspired the *Spirit* of *man.* The Bible is the glorious result. Thanks be to God for his unspeakable gift!

J. J. TROTT.

A New Catechism for Calvinists,

THE following epitome of absurdities, involved by Calvinists, is from Matthews and Franklin's Debates, pages, 396, 397, and 398. It is a glance at some of the more prominent passages of Scripture, that no man can reconcile with Calvinism.

1. Can a man "fail of the grace of God," unless he was *once in grace!* See Heb. xii, 15.

2. Can a man be "renewed to repentance *again,*" "unless he had once repented? Heb. vi, 6.

3. Can a man "destroy a brother for whom Christ died," without destroying one of the elect? Rom. xiv, 15.

4. Are not those whom the "Lord bought," elect persons, and if they bring upon themselves swift destruction, is it not bringing swift destruction upon the elect? 2 Pet. ii, 1.

5. Can a man have his part taken out of the book of life, unless he had a part in it? Rev. xxii, 19.

6. Can a man have his name *blotted out of the look of life,* if it was never *in it?* Rev. iii, 5.

7. Can a man "count the blood of the covenant wherewith he was sanctified an unholy thing," and do "despite against the spirit of grace," and not fall from grace? Heb. x, 29.

8. Could Esau have a birthright unless he was one of the elect, and if he was one of the elect could he have lost his birthright? Heb. xii, 16.

9. Could Judas, one of the elect, *fall by transgression,* and be *lost,* without diminishing the elect? Jno. xvii, 12.

10. Could Paul have "become a castaway" without diminishing the elect? 1 Cor. ix, 27.

11. If Christ came into the world, that "the world through him *might be saved,"* can it be true that he passed by any portion of the world, without giving the least opportunity to be saved? Jno. iii, 17.

12. Can it be true, that "God concluded *all* in unbelief, that he might have mercy upon *all,"* and that God passed by *a part of mankind,* without having any mercy upon them? Rom. xi, 32.

13. Can it be true, as the Scriptures say, that "Christ died for all;" that "in Christ all shall be made alive," and yet that Christ only died for a part? 2 Cor. v, 14, 15; 1 Cor. xv, 21.

BIBLE REVISION.

14. Did the grace of God appear to *all men,* and yet did God pass by a part of mankind? Tit. ii, 11.

15. Is it the will of God that all men should be saved, but did he nevertheless ordain some to wrath? 1 Tim. ii, 4.

16. Did "God command all men everywhere to repent," when he knew many could not repent? Acts xvii, 30.

17. Did the benevolent Jesus say, "Except ye repent, ye shall all likewise perish," knowing that many could not repent? Luke xiii, 3.

18. Did the holy Jesus say, "he that believeth not shall be damned," knowing that one part of mankind could not believe? Mark xvi, 15,

19. Did Paul tell the Hebrew Christians to "fear, lest a promise being left them, of entering into his rest, any of them 'should seem to come short of it," knowing all the time that they could not come short of it?

20. Is it true, as Peter says, that "God is not willing that any should perish, but that all should come to repentance," and that God never granted the privilege of repentance only to a part of mankind? 2 Pet iii, 9.

21. Is it true, that God has no pleasure in the death of the sinner, and yet that he unchangeably ordained a portion of mankind to wrath? Ez. xviii, 23.

22. How can the Gospel be good news of great joy to all people, when it contains not one particle of love, mercy, or salvation, only for a part of the race? Luke ii, 10.

23. How can it be that "God is no respecter of persons," as Peter says, and yet that he passed by a part of mankind, without offering to save them? Acts x, 34.

24. How are the holy attributes of Jesus to be sustained, when he says, "How often *would I have gathered your children, but ye would not,"* when he knew they were ordained to wrath all the time? Mat. xxiii, 37.

25. How can God judge the world according to the Gospel, when the Gospel never offered one blessing only to a part of the world? Rom. ii, 16.

26. How can the wicked "despise the riches of the goodness of God," unless God has been good to them? Rom. ii. 4.

When our Calvinistic friends have learned and fully digested this "Shorter Catechism," we may make them a "Larger Catechism."

-----o-----

THE GOSPEL ADVOCATE.—Such is the title of a well executed monthly pamphlet, of 32 pages, edited by our able and judicious brother, TALBOT FANNING, President of Franklin College, near Nashville, Tenn. Bro. FANNING is one of our soundest and ablest editors and preachers. His pamphlet occupies the same field as the Magazine which died in the hands of the fallen Jesse B. Ferguson, and we hope will be sustained according to its great merit. See Prospectus on cover.

THE CHRISTIAN AGE.—This, the only weekly now published by the brotherhood, has been transferred to Bro. Basworth, of Pittsburgh, and is now individual property, the same as any other papers. It will now be edited by our able brethren EATON and LOOS. We wish it a generous patronage. See circular, on cover.

WESTERN RESERVE ECCLECTIC INSTITUTE.—The catalogue of this flourishing young Institution is before us. The faculty consists of the following esteemed and highly accomplished gentlemen and ladies:

A. S. HAYDEN, Principal, and Teacher of Moral Philosophy and Sacred History; NORMAN DUNSHEE, Teacher of Mathematics, Hebrew and Modern Languages ; THOMAS MUNNELL, Teacher of Ancient Languages and Literature; S. L. HILLIER, Teacher of the Natural Sciences; J. H. RHODES, Teacher in the English Department; G. C. REED, Teacher in the English Department; Miss ALMEDA A. BOOTH, Preceptress in Languages and Mathematics; Miss SARAH UDALL, Principal of the Primary Department, Miss HANNAH S. MORTON, Teacher of Instrumental Music; Miss JENNIE A. CHALLEN, Teacher of Drawing and Painting; P. R. SPENCER and J. W. LUSK, Teachers of Penmanship.

From the Catalogue we learn that there are 235 male and 210 female students; from Ohio, 407; Illinois, 6 ; Minnesota, 4; Michigan, 2; Massachusetts, 1; Pennsylvania, 13 ; Canada West, 6; Indiana, 3; New York, 2; Kentucky, 1; making a total of 445.

This Institution is too well known to need any encomiums from us. Its excellence and desirable situation, with the great moral worth and well known ability, combined with the most amiable and lovely character of its Principal, commend it to all who become acquainted with it.

The winter session of 1855-6 will commence November 19th, and continue fourteen weeks.

-----o-----

BIBLE UNION REPORTER.—We call attention to this very cheap and valuable work. See Prospectus, on cover.

Editor's Table.

EDITOR'S OFFICE, NO. 60 west Fourth street, north side, up-stairs. Elder M. B. HOPKINS will also make this EDITOR'S OFFICE, NO. 60 west Fourth street, north side, up-stairs. Elder M. B. HOPKINS will also make this his reading room. Orders for any of our works, any published by the brotherhood, or any works for sale in this city, addressed to either the editor or Elder M. B. Hopkins, will be promptly filled, at the lowest prices.

CASH-IN-ADVANCE SYSTEM.—Our invariable rule is, *low prices, precisely the same to all, and cash in advance.* There will be no dunning for money in this pamphlet. *Every man's pamphlet is his receipt.* If any man should receive a number, who has not paid, it is only a specimen for him to look at and show to others, for which we charge nothing, unless he is pleased to subscribe.

GEORGETOWN FEMALE INSTITUTE.—We call special attention to this valuable Institution. We are well acquainted with the Principal, Bro. G. R. HAND, and know him to have been one of the best and most popular teachers we have ever had in this city. We -lament his loss from our schools, but wish him all possible success, in his new and flourishing Institution. For particulars, see advertisement on cover.

BACON COLLEGE.— We take pleasure in calling attention to this Institution, now under the charge of the talented and amiable brother John A. Dearborn. Prospects, we understand, are now fair, for greater prosperity than this Institution has enjoyed for many years. We wish Bro. Dearborn great success in his laborious undertaking. See the notice on cover, for further particulars.

ERRATA.—On page 5, right hand column, fifteen lines from top, for "obscenity" read *"obscurity."* By an oversight in "making up," the last two lines of the Introductory Address were changed, one in the place of the other.

THE NORTH-WESTERN. CHRISTIAN UNIVERSITY, has entered upon its career of usefulness, we trust, and prosperity. It was recently opened by able addresses from brethren O'Kane and S. K. Hoshour, in the presence of a respectable attendance of brethren and citizens, both from the city and from abroad. The Institution, as yet, is only in its incipiency, with but three professors, viz: John Young, R. A Benton, and J. R. Challen. With anything like good management, it is destined to be an institution of permanency, and that will tell for ages to come on the destinies of man. We wish the able and talented professors the highest degree of success and prosperity, in their great and good work. We shall give a more extended notice when we are furnished with more of the particulars.

BRO. DANIEL VAN BUSKIRK, mentioned in the article under the caption "Labors in the Gospel," has returned home from Bethany. The article was in type before we knew of his return.

ELDER WM. LANE, of Laporte, Ind., is an accredited agent of the *American Christian Review* in all his travels.

PRITCHARD AND TERRELL'S DEBATE.—We still have on hand a few copies of this spirited and interesting Debate on Baptism and the Operation of the Spirit, between Bro. H. R. Pritchard, of Columbus, Indiana, and Rev. Williamson Terrell, a Methodist minister of considerable distinction. Price fifty cents.

NEW ARRANGEMENTS.—The brethren meeting on the corner of Walnut and Eighth streets, have called the esteemed and talented CHARLES L. LOOS, of Pennsylvania, to take charge of the congregation. We shall expect him to fill this responsible place in a short time.

Elder D. S. BURNET has taken charge of the church meeting on Sixth street, between Smith and Mound streets. God grant that these churches may prosper under this arrangement.

ALL persons wishing general agencies for our work, will please address by mail for that purpose.

Obituary Notice.

Our venerable father-in-law, Mr. JAMES PERSONETT, born October 5th, 1774, died November 7th, 1855, at the residence of his son, Mr. John Personett, some four miles from Middletown, Henry county, Inch It being the place of our former residence, in company with Mrs. Franklin, we happened there on a visit, saw him a few days before his death, and were with him when he departed. He met death with the utmost composure. He said he had outlived his generation, and that the present generation was no company for him, and, as the Apostle had said, he must put off this tabernacle, as the Lord had shown him. His only anxiety appeared to be, to depart, to be free from his sufferings, and relieve his friends, who had been kind and attentive to him, of their care and solicitude for him.

He lived about eighty-one years, the last twenty years a disciple of Christ, if not entirely, almost without having an enemy on earth, and died in peace. If we are not mistaken, he never had a lawsuit, and never was a witness before a court, or even a magistrate. His advices to his children and grand-children, were all good, and many of them long to be remembered. The next morning after his baptism, having remained with us over night, and about to leave, he said to us; "Children, live near to the Lord." "Let me die the death of the righteous, and let my latter end be like his."

THE AMERICAN CHRISTIAN REVIEW.

THE MISSION OF INFIDELS. —NO. 1.

WHAT is skepticism or infidelity? So many references are made to infidelity, that one would suppose, at first thought, that it was some system, doctrine, theory or creed, embodied, carefully digested, and set forth in due form; but such is not the case. It is no system doctrine, or creed. It affirms nothing, believes nothing, has nothing, is nothing and promises nothing. It sets forth no law, no organization, no initiation, no principles and no characteristic requirements; and abounds with all manner of absurdities, incongruities, contradictions and irreconcilable inconsistencies. It is no fact, no truth—but merely the negation of all facts and all truths. It is not a doctrine, but the negation of all doctrine. It is no law, but the negation of all law. It negates all systems, all testimonies and all promises. It negates and ignores all authority and all government. It has no concern for consistency, for morals, for character, or for anything except to maintain an eternal negation—an eternal denial of all that is true. It is a chaos without form.

The mission of infidels is not to build anything, establish anything or defend anything. They come not to show a more excellent way,—a high way of holiness—but to turn us out of the old way, without guiding our feet into any other way. Their mission is to pull down. They have no mission to elevate, ennoble and organize, but one mighty to deteriorate, degrade and disorganize. They come not to save, but to destroy. The reason why their work is so easily done, is because it is all pulling down, deranging, disorganizing, spoiling, and spreading desolation. The common adage: "Those who live in glass houses should not throw stones," is not applicable to them. They do not live in glass houses or houses of any other kind. They have no house at all, or anything else to defend; but their work is simply to stand off and hurl fire-brands at the buildings of others. Their work is simply that of an incendiary—spreading destruction as widely as possible, and then, tantalizing the man of God, because they can pull down faster than he can build up; or because they can destroy faster than he can save; or that they can spread contagion more rapidly than he can cure. But there is nothing strange in all this, unless it be that a human being should follow such a calling. It is not strange that the old proverb of the Bible: "One sinner destroyeth much good," should be found literally true, in all things, both temporal and spiritual. One enemy can sow more cheat, cockle, Spanish needles, rag weeds, thistles and burrs than a thousand good farmers can weed out; or can sow more tares than a thousand can pull up. One enemy can tear up more railway, burn more bridges and do more damage than a million can restore.

The mission of infidels is not to build up anything, but to pull down churches, civil laws, governments, morals, the characters of men and women, peace, happiness, protection of home, property and life. They come with a mission of denials of the truths contained in the Bible—a mission of war upon the Bible, religion, and the friends of purity and mercy. They come not with a mission of peace and good will to man, but a mission of hatred towards the Bible and all it enjoins—a mission to pull down and destroy—to spread desolation among other men's labors and lay their work in ruins, leaving nothing but wrecks and devastation. They come to neutralize, paralyze and dishearten all efforts for the amelioration of man's condition—to discourage, enfeeble and ignore all efforts to rise. They come not into our midst, with a warm, kind and affectionate appeal to the attentive, thinking and reflective portion—the more spiritually minded; but appeal to the luke-warm, backsliding, or the apostate, who is beginning to stand at a distance, who already is descending upon the retrograde plane—not to rescue him or to prevent his retrograde movement, but to accelerate it. The appeal to him is not to give him confidence, but to destroy his confidence, in his Bible, his religion, his brethren, and fill him with doubts and distrusts. It is not to embolden him, but to intimidate him and fill him with fears, and discourage him from all good forever.

The mission of infidels is not to enlighten, civilize and ennoble the nations. They have never enlightened, civilized or elevated a nation or a people since the world was made. They have never organized society or established peace and order in any place on this earth. They have established no civil institutions, no system of morals, no code of laws, no system of education, and no institutions of learning that deserve the name. Even the literature of the country has almost entirely been left to the believers in the Bible. It is an easy work to pull down civil government, subvert the foundation of organization, condemn the means of enlightenment, and object to them. It is an easy matter to deny everything and prove nothing; to doubt, vacillate and fear. It is an easy matter to distrust, fill others with distrust, destroy confidence, throw everything into confusion and uncertainty. Some men have fallen so fully into this state, that they hardly will venture to say they believe anything, have confidence in anything, or know anything. One man, under the blinding, benumbing and stupefying influence of unbelief, when asked whether he knew that he existed, hesitated to say he did.

What ability, knowledge or learning, does it require to deny everything? The most ignorant, illiterate, and stupid can deny as stoutly as the most learned, enlightened and talented. It requires no strength of mind to stand and deny—to declare in the most pertinacious manner, disbelief, want of confidence, doubts, distrusts and uncertainties in everything. A man who never read the Bible once through in his life, nor ten other books, who has the most corrupt character, can talk of inconsistencies, incongruities, contradictions and absurdities, in the Bible, as stoutly as anybody any blockhead could leap over the Falls of Niagara, or from the Suspension Bridge below. In the same way, any man, with, or without much mind, learning or talent, can leap into the dark abyss of unbelief, rejecting, condemning and despising all evidence; but would it not be the part of prudence, of wisdom and discretion in such, to look before they leap? It is a fearful experiment they are making. If the step is a mistaken one, it can never be retraced beyond this life. He who makes the experiment, obtains nothing now, only the unbridled privilege of declaring the Bible false—religion priest-craft—that man will never be called to account, hence all men can do as they list.

The mission of infidels is to risk, and induce all men to risk, the loss of everything, without the possibility of gaining anything, in this world or the world to come. They have no worthy object—they can have no worthy object in opposing the Bible. They have no reason for opposing it, for they do not propose to make the world any better. They have no proposition to make the world more true, kind affectionate or

happy. Indeed, the very fact of their malignity towards the Bible shows that it is no fable. The land abounds with acknowledged fables; why are they not enraged at these? They are read by the million; but skeptics are no more enraged at them than other men. If they are satisfied the Bible is all fiction, false or human, why trouble us about it? Why not let it pass? We hear thousands contending about the "signs in the moon," but we care nothing about them, and do not even trouble those who believe in them; the reason is we are well and fully satisfied, that there is nothing in them; Why do they not let the believers in the Bible pass in the same way? The reason is obvious; they are in doubt, not fully satisfied, and feel that there is uncertainty in their position. They see and are constantly impressed with the fact, that if the Christian could be mistaken, that his mistake amounts to nothing—that he is as happy now, and has as high assurance in regard to all beyond this life, to say the least of it, as they; and that if the skeptic should prove mistaken, his mistake will be an irreparable one. They see that a mistake on the part of a Christ-tian involves no danger, no serious consequences in this world or the world to come; while a mistake on their part, involves eternal consequences. They are not constantly impressed, too, with the fact, that they are relying upon that which amounts to anything like certainty; for a large proportion who have occupied their position, before death have repudiated and renounced it—many of them in the immediate expectation of death,—and warned all their friends against it. They find on the other hand that all who believed the Bible when in health, also believed it when approaching death, and that no man who has contended for its truth till he was in the immediate expectation of death, has then denied it. They must, then, see that their mission is simply to fill the world with doubts and distrusts, involving all in darkness and uncertainty. B. F.

-----o-----

WHOSO loveth instruction loveth knowledge; but he that hateth reproof is brutish.—Proverbs, xii: 1.

Where is the safe ground?

THERE is one class of men among us that have given us more importance than we claim, for at least the last twelve years. We were in hopes that they would become convinced, that what we thought, or what we might say, was not of sufficient importance, on the subject alluded to, to disturb anyone much, if we should never say anything about it. We have never thought that what we have to say, was of very high importance upon any subject; but especially when not allowed to select such a subject as suits us. But some of our friends seem to think, that what we say is of such great importance, that we are not to be allowed the privilege of *silence,* without suffering a pretty heavy penalty. Some poor fellows that we are acquainted with, appear to suffer much from proscription—they are not allowed to speak. But we are not likely to be proscribed for speaking, that we know of, but for *not speaking.* We have been scolded, bemeaned, threatened, and called a "coward," a "timeserver," a "dumb dog," and "popularity seeker," not because of what we *have* said, but because of what we have *not* said—because of our *silence.* We have already rolls of documents, some for public edification, but mostly for our own benefit, demanding, peremptorily, that We "speak out" on the subject of *slavery,* or we shall be proscribed for our silence. One man interprets our declaration, that we "will ride no hobbies," to mean, that we will not discuss slavery; and kindly informs us, that if such is our meaning, he will oppose our publication, preach against it, and stamp it under his feet. We must, then, "speak out."

But what shall we say? Here is the hard place. Shall we introduce geographical metes, boundaries, and distinctions into the Church of God—the *Church North,* and the *Church South?* We have looked carefully over the subject for many years, to see what course its leading expounders would take. We have carefully noticed the workings of the whole question, but have never thought that we had anything of much importance to say. We could perhaps collect some long lists of opprobrious epithets; many insulting and abusive terms, of an inflammatory nature and apply them to all, indiscriminately, who sustain the relation of owner, or master, of slaves; long and black lists of cruelties, on the part of masters, and many vivid portraitures of the evils of slavery. On all topics of this description, we might be prolific, voluminous, if not fluent. This is an easy work, and amounts to but little good when done; the mere wind work; the lightest and easiest part; mere gazing; the mere throwing up hats and huzzaing, which may excite, irritate, inflame, infuriate, and madden men, but disqualifies them to hear, think, and reason. Such a course may be well suited to sunder ties, infuse discord, distract orderly and peaceful communities, set old and long-tried brethren at variance, pull down churches, and spread desolation; but it builds up nothing, frees no slaves, relaxes no bonds of oppression, and prepares neither Church nor State for emancipation. It sets forth no well-defined and digested plan for accomplishing its own ostensible work. Not an agitator, so far as known to us, claiming to be a brother, has exhibited any theory, for either Church or State. The brethren who have agitated this subject, leave us in the dark on the following important points:

1. They have never decided, as a party of men, or in what they have published, whether all fellowship should be withdrawn, indiscriminately, from all slaveholders. We have noticed some articles that squinted that way pretty strongly; but they are generally *non-committal* on that subject.

3. No definite ground has been taken in regard to preachers who preach to slaveholders, receive into Church, and fellowship them. Should such preachers be fellowshipped? They are *non-committal* here.

3. Though the terminology of *North* and *South* has been introduced into the church, yet no one, so far as we have seen, called a brother, has taken the position, that the Church of God should be divided North and South. Upon this they have been *non-committal.*

4. No well defined course of procedure has been set forth and agreed upon, by any respectable number of men, or publications, favorable to agitation in the church of Christ. They are wholly *non-committal* here.

5. These brethren have never yet decided, in their publications, or in their meetings, whether the slave should be exhorted to obey his master, or run away.

6. They have never yet defined themselves upon the question, whether, under any circumstances, a slaveholder can be a Christian. Upon these and many similar matters, they are entirely non-committal. We have only been able, with certainty, to collect the following items:

I. They are opposed to slavery.

II. They desire to speak upon slavery.

III. They think others should speak upon slavery.

IV. They think those who keep silent upon the subject, "time servers," "dumb dogs, that bark not," "popularity lovers."

Now, we have long since learned, that men can go for all this, and hate slaveholders besides, and not have much sympathy for the colored man, and not much more piety than those who differ from them upon some of these points. With all our sympathy for the poor colored man, no commendable sympathy can be elicited for the little band of colored brethren, who meet on Harrison street in this city. They are known to be a worthy little band of disciples, numbering about twenty-five, and, though poor, out of their hard earnings they have raised a large amount, and paid toward procuring a comfortable place to meet and invite their friends to meet with them. They understand the Gospel well, and are still, through all the discouragements that lie in their path, persevering firm in the faith. We have frequently preached for them, and called attention through the Christian Age to them. The most of the preachers in the city have preached for them, and all admit their moral and Christian worth. But, if we are not mistaken, not more than three or four hundred dollars, in four or five years, have been raised, with all the appeals that have been made, to meet a debt of some thirteen or fourteen hundred dollars. Now, we doubt the sympathy that consists wholly in hating slaveholders, without any feeling for colored people. If we intend doing anything for the poor African, why not help these people out of this

debt, and give them an opportunity to show what they are capable of doing. This we only give as one example out of many that might be given, to show how we are to take the war of words now filling the land.

The question of slavery, at this period, in this country, is not one for children, for experiment, or with which men should trifle. A question that convulses mighty political combinations, commands the attention, constantly, of the Congress of a mighty, rapidly growing, and prospering nation, and convulses churches, is not one to be tampered with, nor sported over, by any great or good man. If the minister of Christ has any sound philosophy, any solid reason, good Christian judgment, and correct Bible understanding, he needs it when he approaches this subject. We have known churches torn asunder, over this question; old brethren, who had lived in peace and walked in harmony for thirty or forty years, set at variance, and heart-burnings, indescribable, infused among disciples, where not one member of the church had, or ever expected to have, one dime of interest in a slave, in this world. Many scenes of a similar nature, are occurring in different places. An element producing such results as these, is of too grave a character to be trifled with, by men who fear God, and work righteousness. Such an element is well suited to those who only pull down, create confusion, and spread desolation; but feared and dreaded by him who *builds up*. It is distressing to the good man, who has labored in the Lord, and gathered loving disciples into the fold of Christ, to see them scattered and destroyed. It is an easy matter to spread desolation, but difficult to restore; it is easy to inflict wounds, but hard to heal them. Men can pull down, who were never known to build up; sow discord, who were never known to restore peace; inflict wounds, but never known to heal any. We exhort all the children of God to be careful how they tamper here.

There is but one sure foundation for the Christian—but one sure rock; that rock is Christ. If we, as disciples of Christ, or Christians, would stand, we must fix our eye upon him, not with self-will, as though we would show him how he ought to teach; but, with humility of spirit, and the highest degree of reverence, we must fall at his feet, and *be taught by him.* What he taught and did, was right—infallibly safe for this world, and the world to come. What his holy apostles taught, under the infallible guidance of the Holy Spirit sent down from heaven, is safe and *infallibly right.* The lord and his apostles lived, preached, practiced, and established Christianity in countries where slavery existed. They spoke of it, and acted in reference to it; the course they pursued in reference to slavery, to master and servant, is the safe, the only safe, the infallibly safe course for every man of God. Here we plant our foot. Here we take our stand. We stand upon the Lord's own course of action; his holy and infallible teachings; the action of the apostles and their teachings. We have more confidence in the wisdom, goodness, and benevolence of Christianity, as *it is,* than all modern notions of it. We will maintain and defend the Bible itself, as *it is,* and leave the results to God. If any man thinks he can make a Bible more easily defended against the aspersions of infidels than the one which God gave us; or that he can more successfully defend some perverted view of the Bible we have, than he can a straight-forward, rational interpretation and application, be it so; we shall stand square upon the Bible as God gave it; we shall stand by every man who will stand upon it, and strive to maintain peace and unity among all who love it.

1. Our first position is, that we are opposed to any "Mason and Dixon's Line," or *North* and *South,* in the church of God. We know no metes, boundaries, and distinctions, geographical, in the kingdom of Christ.

2. We are opposed to "dissolving the union" among the disciples of Christ, North and South, and would not, with our present convictions, be instrumental in producing such a desolation, for any State in the government.

3. Jesus Christ and his apostles never made any direct attacks upon the mere relation of master and servant.

4. The existence of the relation of master and servant was permitted among the primitive disciples, and in the church.

5. Both masters and servants entered by the same door into the primitive church, and were members of it.

Hence we find the following instructions: "Servants, be obedient to them that are your masters, according to the flesh, with fear and trembling, in singleness of your heart, as unto Christ; not with eye-service, as men-pleasers; as the servants of Christ, doing the will of God from the heart; with good will doing service, as to the Lord, and not to men; knowing that whatsoever good thing any man doeth, the same shall he receive of the Lord, whether he be bond or free. And ye masters, do the same things unto them, forbearing threatening; knowing that your Master also is in heaven; neither is there respect of persons with him." Eph. vi: 5—9. No matter how much our impulses, arising from education and custom may be against it; a candid man must admit, with this passage before him, that the relation of master and servant did exist among the disciples here addressed. But the following is more bold, showing how the name of God may not be blasphemed, and what kind of a man he is who would teach otherwise: "Let as many servants as are under the yoke count their own masters worthy of all honor, that the name of God and his doctrine be not blasphemed. And they that have believing masters, let them not despise them, because they are brethren, but rather do them service, because they are faithful and beloved, partakers of the benefit. These things teach and exhort. If any man teach otherwise, and consent not to the wholesome words, even the words of our Lord Jesus Christ, and to the doctrine which is according to godliness, he is proud, knowing nothing, but doting about questions and strifes of words, whereof cometh envy, strife, railings, evil surmisings, perverse disputings of men of corrupt minds and destitute of the truth, supposing that gain is godliness; from such withdraw thyself." 1 Tim. vi: 1—5. The doctrine contained in this extract, the apostle commanded Timothy, and through him all evangelists of Christ, to "teach and exhort," and assigned as his reason, "that the name of God, and his doctrine, be not blasphemed," and put his mark upon every man who would teach otherwise.

These things we must stand by, if we claim apostolic authority. Jesus Christ did not institute slavery, either ancient or modern. The slavery of his day existed when he came into the world. He did not institute the relation of master and servant. That relation existed when he made his appearance among men. The civil institutions of his time existed when he entered his abode among men in the flesh, and he was not consulted in their creation or character. Whatever evils there were in them, and whatever oppressions resulted from them, in their legitimate workings, were not chargeable upon Christ nor his religion. His kingdom is not of this world, but designed for any human beings, in any civil government on earth, in any of the relations, where, in the providence of God, they may have fallen, to show them how they may serve God, in those relations, if they cannot equitably and peaceably be relieved from them, and attain a better life in a better world. Christianity makes no direct attacks upon the civil institutions of the country, be they good or bad, but shows men how they may be the servants of God, and be loyal subjects to Christ, their Heavenly King, and, at the same time, placable and obedient subjects of any civil government on earth. It did not establish the civil institutions of any country, and is not chargeable with the evils resulting even from the worst of them. But where its holy precepts are regarded, expressly relating to the different conditions and relations sustained in the civil government, from the king to the peasant, all are improved, purified, made better, and their happiness and usefulness greatly increased.

Our duty, as the disciples of Christ, is to convert all men, both bond and free, master and servant, as far as in our power, to Christ; thus showing the power of the Christian religion, to regenerate, save, improve, and make happy, in all the varied relations in this world. If a man holding slaves, is given to oppression and cruelties toward them, the tendency of Christianity is, when he comes under its influence, to tender his heart, remove all feelings of oppression, and fill his heart with mercy and humanity. This is seen in all those slave countries where Christianity is promulgated. Men, whose hearts become largely imbued with the spirit of the Gospel, gradually relax the bonds; the converted servant becomes better, and the feeling of kindness, between master and slave, is increased, and, in thousands of instances, results in his emancipation. In this way, the peaceable, orderly, and legitimate workings of the religion of Jesus Christ, has *legally* emancipated more slaves in these United States, fourfold, than all the *illegal* and *unscriptural* stealing and running off of slaves, by means of all the facilities of the underground railroad, which, it is said, is doing a heavy business. Hundreds of good men, in the same manner as the venerable Alexander Campbell, yet living and suffering no little for what he has said on this subject, and the beloved and lamented B. W. Stone, gone to his rest with the fathers, did, upon the above-named legitimate and peaceful principle, yielding to that preference which the Bible gives freedom over slavery, in the emancipation of all the slaves that fell into their hands. Such men show their faith by legal, good, and peaceable works of righteousness.

In conclusion, we remark, to all whom it may concern, that if the evils resulting from slavery, as a system, or institution, were worse than the most horrific picture ever drawn by the most overheated anti-slavery man, or worse than they really are, Christianity is no more chargeable with them, than it is for the oppression of the poor in Cincinnati, Philadelphia, or New York— for it is a worldly and human institution, not founded by the Author of Christianity. It is no result or emanation from Christianity, but stands upon the same footing as the civil governments of the world when Christianity came into it. If men who have slaves abuse them, Christianity is not responsible for that neither—for it, with all the weight of its authority, forbids such abuse; and such men, if in the church, are accountable to the church, and to the Lord, for their individual conduct. Christianity has bettered the condition of all, both bond and free, in all nations, in all countries, and in all ages, wherever it has gone, preparing all for a better world, when they shall pass beyond the imperfect civil institutions of this life. In one word, having been born, brought up, and hating lived in a free State, without ever having any interest in a slave, and intending never to have any, we have no commission from Jesus Christ to upturn the civil institutions of slave States, whether good or bad, much less, authority for making the church of God a political engine for such a purpose. We are not amenable for their institutions, nor their consequences, either as citizens or Christians.

-----o-----

Our Position as a Religious Community.
No. II.

IN our previous article under the above head, we took a kind of general survey, mainly of our *Bible alone* position. In our present article, we propose defining the doctrine if possible, so that all men can understand us. Some of our contemporaries, both in their publications and sermons, have amused themselves, with their readers and hearers, by saying that they did not know where to find us—that they could not tell what we believed—that we set forth no abstract, no epitome, or brief of our doctrines, that they can apply to for information. It is true, however, that at other times they seem to know all about it—to understand it perfectly, and that it is the most dangerous of all errors—the most heterodox of all positions ever occupied by mortal man. This discrepancy, however, is a matter for which we care nothing, and leave it for those concerned to reconcile as they may be able.

That Christianity itself, pure and unmixed Christianity, as it came from heaven, is a definable doctrine, an intelligible, complete and perfect system in itself, no man of any intelligence, we think, could deny. That the doctrine of Christ is a distinct, intelligible and definable doctrine—a complete and perfect system of doctrine in itself, is one of the clearest and most manifest truths ever uttered. And that a man can be a Christian, a Disciple of Christ, and nothing else, is equally clear. Indeed, that all that is of any importance is to be a Christian—a Disciple of Christ—must be acknowledged by all candid persons in the end. But still, when a man is asked what he believes, for him simply to say, the doctrine of Christ—Christianity—the Christian religion—is thought to be wholly unintelligible —a mere evasion—a kind of sly Jesuitical dodge; or, if asked what he is, to reply—a Christian—a Disciple of Christ—is looked upon as a mere pun—a trick—a kind of eelish evasion; so true is it that the clear, explicit and intelligible designations both of the doctrine of Christ and its adherents, are unintelligible to the benighted, blinded and stupefied theologians of these times. Still they are learned, wise and talented—as much so, we most solemnly believe, as the priests and rabbis among the Jews in the days of the Redeemer's pilgrimage on earth. But the difficulty is, that they are wise in everything but the things of God. Their eyes are keen, and their discrimination of the finest and most penetrating kind, in perceiving and making the nicest distinctions in all the doctrines and commandments of men. Their ears are acute to catch any sectarian designation, either of doctrine or parties. Mention the doctrine of the *Trinity*, and see how quick you will wake up that man with the white cravat. Mention *Unitarianism, Arminianism, Calvinism,* etc., and you will find around you learned men in abundance, who know what you are talking about. Mention the Philadelphia Confession of faith, Westminster Confession of faith, the Methodist Discipline, the doctrine of total hereditary depravity, final perseverance, or the five points of Calvinism, and you will find plenty of learned doctors who will prick up their ears. They know what all these designations mean. Mention to them Lutheranism, Episcopalianism, Presbyterianism, Methodism, etc., and it will be perfectly intelligible to them. They know, perfectly, the meaning of all this. Or, if they meet a man, and he says —I am a Lutheran, a Calvinist, a Methodist, etc., they understand him perfectly, for they are alive to all these terms; or, if a man says to them —I hold the doctrine of the Westminster Confession, the Philadelphia Confession, the Methodist Discipline, etc., his language is perfectly intelligible to them. There is no evasion about it. All these, and a thousand other technicalities of the same category, are perfectly well understood by the learned doctors of these times, because they are awake to all these matters.

But when they find a man who will know nothing but the things of God, who will receive no doctrine but the doctrine of Christ, and who will be nothing but a man of God, they can see no sense in him! He is a perfect evasionist, a quibbler, and they know not where to put their hand on him! Neither would they know our Lord, or his doctrine, if he were here in their midst. If they cannot now recognize his doctrine as a distinct, perfect and complete system of doctrine, without prefixing or affixing some of their own human designations, they would not have recognized his doctrine or his person, as the image of the invisible God, and brightness of his glory, if they had met him in the streets of Jerusalem, and heard the gracious words that fell from his lips. He said of his followers, "My sheep hear my voice; but the voice of a stranger they will not hear." It is so to this hour; the Lord's people hear *his* voice; but the voice of a stranger they will not hear. That greatest and most important of all oracles—the only oracle of the New Testament, directly from the lips of the Almighty Father, should not only command the attention of all men, but cause the whole earth to tremble in profound awe: "THIS IS MY SON, THE BELOVED, IN WHOM I AM WELL PLEASED HEAR HIM." This is Jehovah's own introduction of his Son, the beloved, to the children of men— and his own requirement to "hear Him." Studying such human designations, distinctions and discriminations among the doctrines and commandments of men as alluded to above, though it requires much learning and talent to do it successfully, is no adherence to the above great oracle from God—is no submission to it, and not one step toward the Kingdom of God. That great oracle introduces the great Lawgiver—the Redeemer and Savior of men—the founder of the faith—and requires all men to hear him. Shall we hear him? Shall we look 'to him as the Author of the faith—the system—the doctrine? Shall we? Can we? Can all men come to him, receive him and be received by him—lean on him, be taught by him, have his doctrine, and let their everlasting trust be in him? Then there is still hope for the world. Otherwise we are enshrouded in eternal darkness.

Is there such a thing as Christianity? What is it? There is such a thing, and it is the system set forth by Jesus Christ, upon the pages of the New Testament; else there is no light from God in the world—no revelation from heaven, and the world is lost. All the hope any man has of pardon here, or eternal salvation hereafter, in any system beneath the skies, is drawn from Christianity itself, and not from some modern form of it, some man's views of it, or some system extracted from it. From it is derived every ray of divine light and life enjoyed by all the nations of the earth. In it is our eternal all, for time and for eternity. Let no man, then, scowl his face, or put on an air of derision when we speak of Christianity as a distinct, perfect and complete system in itself; or when we speak of a man being a Christian, or a Disciple of Christ, as a distinct, perfect and complete profession, without being anything else. There is such a profession, and there is such a reality as being a Christian, a Disciple of Christ, and nothing else superadded; and it is the only profession, and the only reality in religion, worth one moment's attention among all the sons of men. If a man believes the doctrine of Christ, or Christianity, whatever more he believes is a redundancy—a dead weight—which, if it does not neutralize his Christianity, at the very least, is useless. If a man is a Christian, a Disciple of Christ, in the Kingdom of God, anything added, religiously, is only an appendage, a trammel, a dead weight, which, if it were possible for it to do no harm, could do no good. Christianity itself, is all that is of any value to him, or to one soul of our race. Add Calvinism, Lutheranism, Methodism, or any other ism, and, to say the least of it, you add nothing divine, and nothing that can be of any use.

We will not have a modern *form* of Christianity, some man's views of Christianity, or a system that some man has deduced from Christianity, but *Christianity itself,* as delivered and developed by Christ and his apostles; the whole of it—nothing more—nothing less. We shall never be satisfied with anything short of being Christians, Disciples of Christ, in the New Testament import of these terms; and we are determined to add nothing to this. We desire the King of kings and Lord of lords for our Savior, our Redeemer and our everlasting trust. We desire all the faith, all the hope and all the love he imparts to the children of men. We believe in him, and all he taught; we believe in doing all he commanded, enjoying all he gives now, and hoping for all he promises, both in this world and the world to come. In one word, we desire to put ourselves under his guidance, to be wholly controlled by him, to be like him, to imbibe his spirit, die in the faith of him, and dwell with him forever.   B. F.

-----o-----

Labors in the Gospel.
No. II.

ON Monday after the fourth Lord's day in August, we took leave of the beloved ones in Cincinnati, at thirty minutes past six in the morning, and a few minutes past nine o'clock arrived at Dublin, Ind., ninety miles from here, where we found our young brother, and the beloved evangelist, Daniel Van Buskirk, with a buggy, ready to convey us on our way to Bentonville, Fayette county, some five miles from the depot. We reached the meeting-house before meeting time, and our heart was filled to overflowing on meeting so many old friends, among whom we had so frequently, from seven to fifteen years ago, preached the word of God. Here, too, we met the venerable and beloved Elijah Martindale, who was present, and preached on the night when we confessed the Redeemer and Savior of the world. He has lived to see the cause, then new in that country, with but few friends, well established and strongly defended. He preached many years, with very little pecuniary reward, but with great success, supported a large family, and is now comfortably situated in temporalities, and universally beloved. We believe, too, that almost, if not quite all his children are in the faith, and one son in the ministry. The Lord be with him, and comfort him in his declining years.

Here, too, the amiable and universally esteemed evangelist, S. K. Hoshour, and his excellent lady, to our great joy, met us. Bro. Hoshour has the advantage of a fine classical education, and no man has a more unblemished reputation, or is more deeply engraven in the affections of the brethren. Yet he contends against two constitutional impediments of a very serious nature. *First,* He has poor health —is constantly enfeebled and languid. *Second,* He lacks self-confidence. He is exceedingly modest and unassuming. He is really diffident, so much so that he frequently is not willing to speak when it is evidently his duty to do so. He appears, much of his time, when among his preaching brethren, as if laboring under the impression that almost any of them were, better, and could preach better than himself—which is by no means the case. We can refer to no man with more affection than to Bro. Hoshour; and we hope he will not shrink to occupy that prominent and conspicuous place to which his age, his superior ability and amiable deportment entitle him, and which his preaching brethren so cordially award him. He deserves largely of the sympathy and encouragement of the brethren, and we trust will receive that consideration which he so justly merits.

We addressed the large audiences which came out to hear us, four times during the two happy days we spent here among our old friends and acquaintances—but were compelled to leave them on Wednesday morning, to meet other engagements.

Our beloved brother and fellow-evangelist, James Austin, from Jacksburg, Wayne county, had arrived on his way to the district annual meeting, and gave us a seat in his buggy. We two, being old acquaintances and fellow laborers, meeting and laboring together during the last fifteen years, had a pleasant ride of some nine miles, through one of the richest and most beautiful sections of country. We arrived at Ben. Davis' Creek, Rush county, in good season, and met with most cordial and affectionate greetings from brethren, as they came in from different sections of country. The President, Elder B. F. Reeve, so favorably known, and universally esteemed as a faithful evangelist and teacher of the Word, was present, and ready to take his chair in due time. Bro. Reeve is one of the great and good men of Indiana. He is not a man of one idea, nor of fancy, but a real and practical man, ready for every good work. His liberality has been known in all the good works of Indiana, which have by no means been few. No church, we presume, is inspired with a larger liberality, or has prospered more, than the church at Little Flat Rock, of which he is an overseer. The beloved John P. Thompson, who was largely instrumental in establishing the churches in Eastern Indiana, and an overseer in the same congregation with Eld. Reeve, was also present, but from poor health and many afflictions he has gone through, he has become somewhat superannuated, though he remains firm in the faith. Both of these good men have contributed largely of their time and personal labors as evangelists, for some thirty years past—nor have they been behind their brethren when money was demanded for the work of the Lord; and yet they have a competency to lean upon in their declining years. The Lord requires us to esteem such men highly, for their work's sake.

We attempt not a report of the cooperation, or district meeting, but shall simply confine our observations to a few points, which we trust may be of practical interest for other occasions. The meeting was conducted by spending a short time in items of business, and then hearing an address from persons previously appointed to deliver addresses upon important themes. In addition to speakers appointed to deliver addresses, Elder H. R. Pritchard, from Columbus, Ind., appeared in our midst, and added much to the interest of the occasion, by an able address on the Revision of the English Scriptures. There were, however, a few circumstances that operated against the interest, usefulness and enjoyments of the meeting. Elder P. Wiles, one of the overseers of the congregation at Ben. Davis' Creek, was severely afflicted, on account of which he was unable to be in attendance. Elder J. Daubenspeck, the other overseer of the congregation, through some unexpected turn in an important business arrangement, was called away to New York, and did not reach home till a late period. His house, however, as has been the case for many years, was open for the entertainment of as many as were disposed to accept the kind invitations of his very pleasant and agreeable family. We could but feel the absence of these aged and experienced brethren and officers of the church.

Another incident that marred the interest of the occasion, was the same that we have witnessed at many other meetings of the kind. The impression seemed to be general, that the meeting, especially for several days, was to be merely a kind of business meeting among the delegates, with which the brethren in general were to have no concern, and in which they would have no interest. This should be avoided in time to come, at all similar meetings. It should be the determination of brethren who have the management of all such meetings, to make them interesting to all who may attend, whether members of church or not. By the delegates meeting one hour before the time for the popular address, they may attend to all items of business in due form—and by the time the people generally are assembled, they may be ready to hear a discourse from some brother, on some theme especially appointed for the occasion, or a sermon. In this way, the meeting may be made interesting and profitable to the public in general. The meeting at Ben. Davis' Creek was conducted in this way, but the people, not generally understanding that such, would be the case, did not attend during the first sessions.

The business of the meeting was disposed of during Wednesday, Thursday and Friday, and most of the preaching brethren left for their various appointments. We continued to address the large assemblies who resorted here to hear the word, Saturday and Lord's day; but the public mind had been too much divided by the number and variety of public men and themes, for proselyting. Although the interest was great and the attendance large to the close, none were added. Many great themes were discussed. Much fraternal friendship and affection prevailed throughout the meeting; and the usual liberality of the brethren here, was extended to us. Take the meeting all in all, we have enjoyed but few happier, more interesting or useful. These large meetings to form new acquaintances and renew old ones, afford the highest happiness and most sacred joys to the true lovers of Jesus, found upon the shores of time. But these joys are only momentary, and but a foretaste of the future and eternal bliss of the world to come. "This world is not our home "we have no continuing city here." We must, as oft as we meet, be torn apart, while we are strangers and pilgrims here—but, thanks to God, we shall meet where parting shall be no more.

After a refreshing night's rest, surrounded by all the comforts of life, in the interesting and agreeable family of Bro. Daubenspeck, who was now present, where we have so frequently been entertained in years past, we were conveyed in his snug carriage, by his son, Mr. Wesley Daubenspeck, to the Central Railroad at Louisville, Ind., some eleven miles distant. Though we passed through one of the most bleaching rains, we kept perfectly dry and comfortable, entertaining ourselves in a most agreeable manner, in the discussion of a rich variety of important themes. Though he is a young gentleman of fine literary ability and much valuable information, he is very modest and unassuming. We have met but few young gentlemen of such varied information, and just conception of men and things in general. To what purpose he intends consecrating his valuable acquisitions, we did not learn. Information is not merely for personal and selfish gratification, and should, no more than wealth, be acquired for that purpose. A gentleman with an extensive knowledge should not, indeed no person should, think of living for *himself,* but for those with whom we stand identified in the world. We know not how one with such just conceptions should remain out of Christ.   B. F.

Review of Dr. Shaffer on Baptism.
No. II.

MY worthy friend Dr. Shaffer, says, "throughout the New Testament, in every place where it speaks of baptism of water and the Holy Ghost, and the washing of persons and things with water, the water and the Holy Ghost are always put in the dative case; therefore, the preposition *en*, which is generally in connection, and is translated *with*, is a correct translation." Page 126. From this, one not acquainted with the New Testament, would be led to think there were many passages that speak of baptizing "with water and "with the Holy Ghost;" but there is but one expression of the kind, from John the Baptist, in reference to his own baptism in water, in contrast with that which Christ should administer in the Holy Spirit and in fire, and some few references to it, in the whole book. The expression of John is recorded, Mat., iii: 11; Mark, i: 8; Luke, iii: 16; John, i: 26, 31,33. The same thing is referred to, Acts, i: 5; xi: 16; xix: 4. The whole relates to the one expression of John, and so far as baptizing "*with* water," is concerned, to the one thing, viz: John's baptism. This shows that it has nothing to do with the practice of the apostles, but relates wholly to John's baptism. Then, when we turn our attention to the fact that we have no authority, even here, far the word "with," but the King James' translators, and that they, in the only nineteen occurrences of the word *en* from the beginning of Mathew to chapter iii, verse 11, have given us *in* seventeen times, *within* once, and *among* once, while they have not given us *with* at all, we can see that the most manifest consistency required them after giving us, "*in* Jordan," to have given us "*in* water." They have, speaking of the identical same baptism of John, given us "*in* Jordan," and "*in* the River of Jordan," and the Greek *patamos*, from which they have given us "river," here, they have translated "waters," 2 Cor. xi: 26. Here then, this same baptizing that they tell us was "*with* water," they tell us also was "*in* Jordan," "*in* the river, or *waters* of Jordan."

From the Doctor's remarks, many would think that *en* is generally translated with, in the common version. But this is not the case. As before stated, it occurs nineteen times before it is once translated *with*. Then in the words "with water and with the Holy Ghost," we have it twice translated "with." Then we have nine occurrences of it before we have "with," and but one instance then. Then we find twenty-nine occurrences of it before it is again translated *with*. It continues at about the same ratio through the New Testament.

But, for the sake of a little variety, as the Doctor is fond of a little innocent amusement, we will give him a little, to rest from this lesson on the Greek preposition *en*. He has given us his faith. He says: "We believe the mode of baptism, as taught in the Scriptures and practiced by the Apostles, was by *aspersion* or *affusion*"-p. 124. This expression gives us the scope of the Scripture, in which to find teaching, and the Apostolic practice for example. Let us follow the teaching of Scripture to find *where* baptizing was performed. Mat. iii: 6, the holy writer says, they "were baptized of him *in* Jordan." Mat. i: 9, we are informed that our Lord was "baptized of John *in* Jordan." Mark i: 5, we are informed in the common version, that "there went out unto him all the land of Judea, and they of Jerusalem, and were all baptized of him *in the river* of Jordan;" and "*in the river* of Jordan," here is in the *water*, or *floods* of Jordan. Where did Philip, an evangelist of Christ, with an especial message from an angel of God, go~ to baptize? The common version says, Acts viii: 36, "they came unto a certain water." Now Doctor, we are *at* the water, or *to* the stream, where shall we go next? We will see where Philip went to baptize. Verse 38, we are informed, by the common version, that "they went down both *into the water*," and as if the writer feared we would make some mistake about it, adds the words, "both Philip and the eunuch." These scriptures show that they "went down *into* the water" to baptize, baptized "*in* Jordan" and "*in* the river, or waters of Jordan." Now how did they baptize, after going into the water? How did they baptize in Jordan, or in the river? The Doctor believes it was by *aspersion* or *affusion*. Let us see how this will read in a few places:

REVIEW OF DR. SHAFFER ON BAPTISM.

"And they went down both into the water, both Philip and the eunuch, and he *affused* him." It does not make it say, affused water upon him, which could have been done, but *affused him.* Again: "I indeed *affuse* you with water unto repentance, but he that cometh after me is mightier than I, whose shoes I am not worthy to bear; he shall *affuse* you with the Holy Ghost and with fire." Mat. iii: 11. Again, Mat. iii: 6, "And were *affused* of him in Jordan," or Mark i: 5, "*affused* of him in the river of Jordan." "Buried with him in *affusion.*" Col. ii: 12. "One Lord, one faith, one *affusion.*" Eph'. iv: 5. "Know ye not, that so many of us as have been *affused* into Jesus Christ, were *affused* into his death? Therefore, we are *buried with him by affusion* into death?" Ro. vi: 3-4. How do you like it, Dr.? Do you sincerely believe the Lord was affused in Jordan—that John affused in the river Jordan—that Philip and the eunuch went down both into the water, that he might *affuse* him. Do you seriously believe the disciples were affused into Christ? But we let this *affusion* rest here for a time.

If we had not, once, face to face, called Dr. Shaffer's attention to his formidable array of Greek Lexicons, and seen his confusion, we might have thought he would desire us to approach them. But we know he dreads the mention of them. If he ever saw the Lexicons he professes to quote, he *knows* he has put an imposition upon his readers. If he never saw them, but has given the definitions from some irresponsible source, he is as guilty of imposition as if he had seen them. He professes to quote the following authorities: Schrevelius. Schleursner, Scapula, Hedricus, Ainsworth, Cole, Pason, Suidas, Conler and Stephanus. In his quotations, he represents these ten as giving *sprinkle* as one definition of *baptize.* In a few moments, I have found where seven of them have been quoted in the most important controversies ever held on the subject of baptism, in this country, and the word sprinkle is not found once among them. Whether he has taken the Latin definition, generally found in the Lexicons, to be something different from the English, and translated some Latin word *sprinkle,* or inserted the word *sprinkle* without thinking he had any authority for it, we presume not now to determine, but that the definitions he professes to quote are not found in the Lexicons, from which they purport to be quoted, every man knows that ever saw them. His pretended definitions are wholly unauthorized, and the attempt to impose them upon the good people of this country, is one of the boldest and most manifest impostures of our times.

But, for the sake of argument, suppose ten Lexicons could have been found, giving *sprinkle,* as a sixth or seventh meaning, while every one of them give plunge, dip, overwhelm, or immerse, as the first meaning of the word, what man of sense would suppose that it would occur more than one hundred times in one book, always with a sixth or seventh meaning, attached to it? We but seldom find a word used with a sixth or seventh meaning attached to it, and when it is so used, there must be something in the connection clearly showing such to be the sense in which it is used. But I ask Dr. Shaffer, or any other Doctor, when he found that every Lexicon, gives immerse, plunge, dip or overwhelm as the first meaning of the word invariably used by our Lord and his Apostles, what led him to pass the first, literal and obvious meaning, and seek some other? Can he give a reason why he did not, when he found the word used invariably in the New Testament, to express the consummating act of initiation, and found that there was a unanimous agreement that the literal meaning of that word is immerse, tell us why he did not receive that meaning? Why did he seek some other meaning? Especially, why did he seek *sprinkling,* or as he so politely and learnedly calls it, *affusion?* If the Lord meant sprinkling, there was no difficulty in finding a Greek word with precisely that meaning. The word *sprinkle* occurs frequently in the New Testament, and if that was what the holy writers meant, why did they not use the same word when they spoke of the ordinance. The word *sprinkle* or *sprinkled,* is found four times, as follows: Heb. ix: 13: v. 19; v. 21; 10; 22; but in the original, it is *rantize,* not *baptizo.* The word *sprinkling* is found, Heb. xii: 24; 1 Pet. i: 2, but in the Greek it is *rantismos* and *baptizo*. The word *sprinkling* is found, Heb. xi: 28, but the Greek word from which it is translated is *proskusis* not *baptizo*. These are the only occurrences of sprinkling in the New Testament, and from this, anyone can see that it has nothing to do either with *bapto* or *baptizo*. If the Lord and the Apostles meant *sprinkle* when they used the word *baptizo* or *bapto,* why did they not use the same words they did in these other places, where we all know they did mean *sprinkle?*

We proceed to inquire what the translators of the common version thought *bapto* meant. It occurs only three times and is never applied to the ordinance. Luke xvi: 24, it is translated *dip*. John xiii: 26, and Rev. xix: 13, it is translated *dipped*. Here then, is what they think *bapto* means, and what they have unhesitatingly translated it. Now, as *baptizo* comes from *bapto,* it would be singular if the latter should mean *dip* and the former *sprinkle*. What did the same learned body of men think *baptizo* meant? In 2 Kings v: 14, in the Greek Septuagint, we have *baptizo,* and, in the common version, it is translated *dipped*. This shows what they thought it meant. If Naaman *baptizing* himself, was *dipping* himself, as they have rendered it, or if Naaman *baptizing* himself in Jordan, was *dipping* himself in Jordan, as they have rendered it, why is not John baptizing in Jordan, dipping in Jordan? Here then, we have the authority of the King James' translators, that both *bapto* and *baptizo* mean *dip*. Will the Doctor be able to show that they ever thus sanctioned *sprinkle* as a meaning of *baptizo?* He certainly never will.

BEHOLD, how good and how pleasant it is for brethren to dwell together in unity! It is like the precious ointment upon the head, that ran down upon the beard, even Aaron's beard: that went down to the skirts of his garments; as the dew of Hermon, and as the dew that descended upon the mountains of Zion: for there the Lord commanded the blessing, even life for evermore.—Ps. cxxxiii.

A Sermon.
[BY ELDER M. B. HOPKINS.]

TEXT.—Tell me, ye that desire to be under the law, do ye not hear the law? For it is written, that Abraham had two sons—the one by a bond-maid, the other by a free woman. But he who was of the bond-woman was born after the flesh, but he of the free woman was by promise. Which things are an allegory—for these are the two covenants, the one from the Mount Sinai, which gendereth to bondage, which is Agar. For this Agar is Mount Sinai, in Arabia., and answereth to Jerusalem which now is, and is in bondage with her children. But Jerusalem which is above, is free, which is the mother of us all. For it is written, Rejoice thou barren that bearest not, break forth and cry, thou that travailest not—for the desolate hath many more children than she which hath a husband. Now we, brethren, as Isaac was, are the children of promise. But, as then, he that was born after the flesh persecuted him that was .born after the spirit—oven so it is now. Nevertheless, what saith the Scripture? Cast out the bond-woman and her son, for the son of the bond-woman shall not be heir with the son of the free woman. So, then, brethren, we are not children of the bond-woman, but of the free. Stand fast, therefore, in the liberty wherewith Christ hath made us free, and be not entangled again with the yoke of bondage." Galatians, 4th chap.

MY respected auditors, I ask your careful and prayerful attention to the consideration of the foregoing Scripture, from the pen of the great Apostle to the Gentiles —one whose whole life and energies were spent in an effort to bind with Christian bonds, in one fraternal society, both Jew and Gentile.

The topic, you perceive, before the mind of Paul, is the covenants. The two covenants considered, illustrated, and traced out, under the beautiful, striking, and impressive figure of an allegory, drawn from certain allegorical personages in the early family of Abraham. A correct and comprehensive knowledge of the two covenants here brought to view, is of the utmost importance to the Bible-student. No one can have an enlarged horizon of Bible information without it. As we explore the principles, promises, incidents, and attributes of these covenants, we explore the Jewish and Christian dispensations, the Old Testament and the New, the law and the gospel; and by their aid we are enabled to make the grand survey between the territories of Judaism and Christianity, and bound the authority of Moses and Jesus Christ. Ignorant of these covenants, and the Bible is in chaos—Judaism is Christianity, and Christianity is Judaism—a Jew is a Christian, and a Christian is a Jew. Darkness covers the Bible, and gross darkness hovers over the understanding. It knows no order. A stranger to all arrangement, it bids defiance to all efforts at classification. We would as likely look into the book of Chronicles for the way, the truth, the life, as into the book of the Acts of the Apostles; but with this knowledge the sun rises in the heart, the vail is stripped from the understanding, and we behold, as in a glass, the glory of the Lord, and while with admiration and rapture we gaze upon his transcendent glory, are changed into the same image, from one degree of glory to another, by the spirit of the Lord.

It is of the utmost importance that we have a clear and accurate definition of the word covenant, in this investigation. The literal acceptation is agreement. In its legal, and technical sense it applies only to such agreements as are under seal, the making of which is accompanied with greater solemnity. No circumstances of greater solemnity can be imagined than those that accompanied the making of the Sinaiatic covenant. Jehovah descends upon the pinnacle of Sinai. The pealing thunder announced his awful presence. Darkness and blackness enshrouded the mountain. It smoked as a furnace. The tempest howled to the storm. And the voice of the trumpet, exceeding loud, struck terror to the heart of Israel. God called Moses to the top of the mount, and in the midst of this terrific scene delivered to him the words of the covenant. He sketched before him what he had done for Abraham, Isaac, and Jacob, and for the present generation of their descendants. He further informed him of all that he purposed to do for that nation, and also what he should require of them. Moses having received these words descended from the mount, and came and told the people of all the words of the Lord, and all the judgments, and all the people answered with one voice and said, "All the words which the Lord hath said will we do." Here is the agreement. The mutuality of agreement, but no covenant. It must be reduced to writing, and sealed. Moses reascends to God, and wrote in a book all the words of the Lord, And after its reduction to writing, he took the book of the covenant, and read it in the audience of the people. Both parties, the covenanter and the covenantees, hear this written agreement, with all its propositions, stipulations, conditions, etc. And after the careful reading by Moses the people signify a second time their acceptance. But still the covenant is not perfected. It must be sealed. Moses, killing the proper animal, caught the blood in a basin, and dipping the hyssop in the blood, sprinkled both the book of the covenant and the people, accompanying it with the repetition of this solemn formula of words: "This is the blood of the covenant which God has enjoined upon you." The covenant is made. God and Israel stand in covenant relation to each other. He is no longer known as the God of Abraham, Isaac, and Jacob, only, but as the God of the Hebrews also.

Solemn, impressive, and melting, were the circumstances attendant upon the making of the new and better covenant. The covenanter descended upon our earth in the person of Jesus, the Mediator, clothed in our nature, and made the pilgrimage of human life, from the womb to the grave, that he, *experimentally,* might know us, in all our infirmities, ignorance, trials, temptations, sufferings, and death, that thus perfected, fully qualified, he is a faithful high-priest, and is able to have a right share of compassion on the ignorant, and them that are out of the way, *seeing he himself was encompassed with infirmity* — enveloped in humanity—the sins of a world upon him—baptized beneath the mighty wave of human suffering, and in the presence of a blushing sun, and bursting rocks, he sealed with his own blood the new covenant with the house of Israel and the house of Judah.

These two covenants embody within them all preceding covenants and promises made with the Jewish people. The covenant conveying the land of Canaan to Abraham, as an estate of inheritance forever, was merged into the legal dispensation. Gal. iii, 18-19. "For if the inheritance be of the law, it is no more of promise; but God gave it to Abraham by promise. Wherefore, then, serveth the law? It was added because of transgressions, till the seed should come to whom the promise was made." The law was added. Added to what? To the promise of the inheritance. The inheritance of Canaan, till the seed should come. The covenant of circumcision passed from the hand of Abraham to that of Moses, and became part and parcel of the Mosaic institution. John vii, 23. "If a man on the Sabbath day receive circumcision, that the law of Moses should not be broken." Acts, 15. "Except ye be circumcised, after the *manner of Moses, ye cannot be saved.*"

The covenant concerning the Christ, made four hundred and thirty years before the date of the law, maintained a separate and distinct existence, forming no part of the Sinaiatic covenant. Hence, in all the legislation of Moses, there is not one word of reference to this spiritual promise. The new covenant is but a development of this promise. The oak from the acorn. The great tree, in the branches of which all the fowls of heaven may lodge, from the mustard seed. Thus there arise before us the two great institutions, covenants, or testaments, in all their grandeur and glory. The old and the new—the Sinaiatic and Jerusalem—the temporal, and the spiritual, and eternal, all these covenants are thus contrasted in the sacred Scriptures, but never *identified.* A distinct agent was employed by the covenanter in the making of these covenants, called mediators, or middle persons. Moses stood as a middle person between God and Israel. Ex. xx. 21. "And the people stood afar off, and Moses drew near to the thick darkness where God was." Gal. iii, 19. "The law was ordained by angels in the hand of a mediator. The man Christ Jesus is the Mediator of the new covenant." Heb. xi: 15.

He is the mediator of the new testament, that by means of death for the redemption of the transgressors that were under the first testament, they which are called might receive the promise of an eternal inheritance."

But, my auditors, while we have thus clearly before us these two covenants, and their respective mediators, I am about to propound that the Bible also reveals, describes, and defines two churches, standing each upon one of these two covenants—a church upon the old covenant—another, not the same church, upon the new covenant. Here is the battlefield. Here I must break a lance with my Pedo-Baptist brother. For Pedo-Baptism, or infant Baptism, as the word Pedo indicates, stands upon four glass legs. They are as follows: The church before Christ, and after Christ—one and the same, identical. Second, Circumcision, the door into the Jewish church. Third, Circumcision done away under Christ. Fourth, Baptism, substituted for it. Upon these four pillars rests all the weight of the Pedo-Baptist temple. Shall I break one of them? I will try first the identity of the churches. The identity of the Jewish commonwealth with the church of Jesus Christ. It ought only to be necessary to state it, to disprove it. What can be the logic of this proposition of identity? Let us hear it. Well, here it is. Both and called by the name church. Both called the people of God. Both had ordinances of divine service. Both had the gospel preached. Both were under obligations to live a holy life, etc.; therefore they are identical. What a conclusion! Shall I expose the fallacy'? Men are called animals; so are the beasts. Both are called the creatures of God. Both live by eating. Both are subject to pain. Both are mortal, etc., therefore they are identical!! They argue from resemblances to identity. There is the breadth of the heavens difference between similarity and identity. But let us hear Paul on the question of identity. Eph. ii, 14-15. "For he is our peace who hath made both (Jew and Gentile) one, and hath broken down the middle wall of partition between us; having abolished in his flesh the enmity, even the law of commandments contained in ordinances, for to make in himself of twain *one new man,* so making peace." The terms, new man, are equivalent to new body, new society, or NEW CHURCH. Mark, a new church; but the expression new church associates with OLD CHURCH. Here we have it, then, an old church and a new one. The old church was the church in the wilderness—"This is he that was in the church in the wilderness with the angel." The Jewish church, standing upon the old covenant. The new church is the Christian church, standing upon the new covenant.

Let us hear Jesus upon the same topic, Matt. xvi—"Who do you say that I am?" Peter replies: "Thou art the Christ, the son of the Living God."

Jesus replies, "Upon *this rock* I WILL BUILD my church." Not, I have built, but, I will build it. There is a vast difference between *building* a house and *remodeling* it.

Connected with all bodies, societies, and churches, is the idea of a constitution. Without a constitution they are in chaos—with, there is shape, proportion, and strength. But may I inquire, what is a constitution? The constitution of a State is but the definition of the supreme authority of that State. If it be an absolute monarchy the constitution is very short. The Czar is supreme—is the constitution of Russia. The constitution of the Jewish church is, "Hear oh, Israel, the Lord your God is one Lord." Jehovah was the center and source of all power. Just before the ascension of Jesus into heaven, he informed his apostles, that the scepter had changed hands—"That all authority, in heaven and in earth, was given to him."—Math. He ascends to heaven, above all principalities, powers, might, and dominion, and every name which is named.

The apostles, assembled in constitutional convention at Jerusalem, promulged the constitution of the kingdom of heaven, in the following words: "Therefore, let all the house of Israel know assuredly, that God hath made that same Jesus whom ye crucified, both LORD and CHRIST." Thus, while we have one God and Father, we have also one Lord Jesus Christ.

It is a common saying—indeed, it is the outburst of common sense—that every church must have a law to govern it—a creed-book, church-ritual, or whatever name you may see proper to give. No sooner, therefore, had Moses organized the Jewish church, than a divine volume issues from the press, appropriately called the *Old Testament*. It is appropriately so called, because it was for the government of the old Church, standing upon the *old covenant*. This was the *creed-book* of the church for fifteen hundred years—the only authoritative book. Upon the organization of the new church, in Jerusalem, a new volume made its appearance, appropriately called the New Testament—a creed-book—the only creed-book of the new Church.

But who can think or speak of the church, without associating with it in his mind the proclamation of the gospel. The proclamation of the gospel is as essential to spiritual life as oxygen to animal. While, therefore, the church was in its pilgrim state, in the wilderness, Moses, Aaron, Joshua, Caleb, and other elders, preached the gospel to them. Heb. iv: 9. "For unto us was the gospel preached, as well as UNTO THEM, but the word preached did not profit them, not being mixed with faith in them that heard it." Here, you perceive, Paul affirms, the gospel was preached to them, as well as to us, but surely not the same gospel. McKnight says, it was the gospel of the earthly inheritance—the earthly Canaan promised four centuries before, to Abraham. And so says the context: whereas the gospel preached to us is the glad tidings of the heavenly inheritance—the celestial Canaan—that inheritance which is incorruptible, undefiled, and that fadeth not away.

Into every church there is an initiatory process, or rite, mechanically called a door. Into both these churches there are doors of ingress and egress—a door in and a door out. What was the door into the Jewish church? Ah! this is a most important question. Here I must break the second glass leg of infant membership. Was circumcision the door into the Jewish church?—the only door into said church? Then was the Jewish church composed of males only. *"Every man child among you shall be circumcised.* This is no pettifogging. It is a fair conclusion from the premises. It is inclusive and exclusive—including males and excluding females.

That circumcision was not the door into the Jewish church, is proven by another fact. It is impossible to pass from, the outside of a building through the door of the building, and not enter the house. If we pass through the door, we must enter the building; but whole tribes entered through this so-called door of the Jewish church, but never entered the church. There were the tribes of Ishmael, Esau, as well as the six nations descended from the six sons of Abraham by his second wife, Keturah, all were circumcised, and observed it in their generation for many years, but were they members of the church? The very law of circumcision shows most conclusively that that rite did not change the ecclesiastical relations of the recipient of it. "God said unto Abraham, thou shalt keep my covenants, therefore, thou and thy seed after thee, in their generations. This is my covenant which ye shall keep between me and you, and thy seed after thee: Every man child among you shall be circumcised. And ye shall circumcise the flesh of your foreskin, and it shall be a token of the covenant betwixt me and you. And he that is eight days old shall be circumcised among you; every man child in your generation, he that is born in thy house, or bought with money of any stranger which is not of thy seed. He that is born in thy house, and he that is bought with thy money must needs be circumcised. And my covenant shall be in your flesh for an everlasting covenant; and the *uncircumcised man child,* whose flesh of his foreskin is not circumcised, that soul shall be *cut-off* from his people; he hath *broken* my *covenant.*"—Gen., xvii, 6—14.

The uncircumcised man child, you perceive, was to be CUT OFF from his people. The branch cannot be cut off from the trunk unless it first be united with the trunk. No one can be cut off from the church unless first a member of the same. The uncircumcised Jew was to be cut off from his church for his neglect. He was a member of the church before his circumcision; circumcision, therefore did not make him a member. It was no door. It constituted no new relationship between the individual subject of it and the Jewish people. Let us, then, return to our former inquiry. What was the door into the Jewish church? I answer, BIRTH and PURCHASE. "He that is born in thy house, and bought with thy money, must needs be circumcised." All born of Abraham's flesh, and bought with Abraham's purse, were, by virtue of said birth or purchase, members of the Jewish church, and were circumcised, not to make them members, but because they were already members.

The ligament that bound the Jew to his church, was a fleshy one. The Jewish church was the Jewish nation, and *vice versa.* A man entered the Jewish church as, and when he entered the nation; yea. as he entered the world. Membership in the church was hereditary. All the sacred offices in the church descended from father to son, on hereditary principles. The crown floated down the channel of David's flesh and blood — the sacerdotal robes that of Aaron. Into the church of Jesus Christ, as the kingdom of heaven, there is also a door. What is that door? How do the sinner and the humble enter the church of God? I answer by BIRTH. Ah! that is only part of the truth—by a second birth, not by being horn, but by being BORN AGAIN; not a birth of flesh and blood, but of the spirit of God. The Lord for the first time laid the great naturalization law of the kingdom of heaven, before Nicodemus: "Verily, verily I say unto thee, except a man be born of water and of the spirit, he cannot enter the kingdom of heaven. The ligament of union to this church, is not Abraham's flesh, but Abraham's faith. "They that are of faith, are blessed with faithful Abraham." The preaching of John the Baptist was: "Say not among yourselves that we have Abraham to our father, but bring forth fruit meet for repentance."

Thus, my respected auditors, we have before your minds two covenants—"the Old" and "the New"—two mediators, Moses and Messiah — two churches, "the church in the wilderness, and the church of Jesus Christ—two gospels —two inheritances—two books, the Old Testament and the New—and two births, the one of flesh, the other of spirit—all and singular of which is beautifully, clearly and forcibly taught by Paul in the allegory before us. Let us hear him with care and candor. "For it is written that Abraham had *two* sons, the one by a bond maid, the other by a free woman; but he who was of the bond woman was born after the flesh, but he of the free woman was by promise—which things are an *allegory.*" What is an allegory? It is not a metaphor or simile, but a number of metaphors. It sustains the same relation to a single metaphor that a cluster of grapes does to a single grape. This allegory is a cluster of four metaphors. The two women and their two sons. The two women represent the two covenants—"These are the two covenants the one from mount Sinai, which gendereth to bondage, which is Hagar; the other from Jerusalem, which is Sarah." Sarah, the wife proper, represents the spiritual covenant made at Jerusalem; Hagar, the bond woman, represents the covenant made at Sinai. The two sons, Ishmael and Isaac, represent the children or churches of the covenants. Ishmael represents the Jewish church; Isaac the Christian church. Let us, therefore, examine the distinctive features of these two churches, as they were typified and adumbrated in the early family of Abraham, in confirmation of all that I have before said concerning them.

These two sons, although both the sons of Abraham, are so upon very distinct principles. Ishmael, the son of the bond woman, was born on principles perfectly natural. "He who was of the bond-woman, was born after the flesh;" but Isaac, the son of the free woman, was born on supernatural principles: "He of the free woman was by promise." Isaac was the offspring of faith: "Through faith, also, Sarah herself, received strength to conceive seed, and was delivered of a child when she was past age, because she judged him faithful who had promised; therefore sprang there even of one, and him as good as dead, so many as the stars of the sky in multitude, and sands of the sea shore innumerable." "And being not weak in faith, he considered not his own body, now dead, when he was about an hundred years old, neither yet the deadness of Sarah's womb. He staggered not at the promise of God through unbelief, but was strong in the faith, giving glory to God. Thus have we stereotyped in this patriarchal family, the radical distinction between Jewish and Christian churches, in the very nature of the births of these two sons. The Jewish church is the church of the flesh. Its members, like Ishmael, are born of the flesh, and according to the flesh. The principle of growth and increase, is natural generation. The Christian church is the church of the spirit, because born of the spirit, and filled with the spirit. *Its* principle of increase is supernatural regeneration: "Verily, verily I say unto thee, except a man be born again, he cannot see the kingdom of God."

The second point of difference in these two sons, illustrative of the difference of the two churches is, in their *condition,* considered in reference to the institution under which they lived. The one was slave—the other was free. In all slave countries, the offspring takes the character and condition of the mother. If she be slave the descendant is slave. If free the descendant is free. Ishmael, therefore, was a slave. Isaac a son, a free son. They appropriately shadowed forth the difference in the moral and spiritual condition of these two churches. The siniatic covenant "generates to bondage." The Jewish Church wore a yoke, a slavish yoke, that "neither they nor their fathers were able to bear." "They were entangled in the yoke of bondage," "all their lifetime; subject to bondage through fear of death." The Jerusalem covenant is free; she regenerates to freedom, "stand fast therefore, in the liberty wherewith Christ hath made us free." We brethren, as Isaac was, are the children of promise. "If the Son make us free, we shall be free, indeed. The church of God is freed from condemnation by justification, strengthened against temptation by the spirit of God, and has overcome death by faith in the resurrection." "Blessed be God who giveth us the victory through our Lord Jesus Christ."

A third and most important difference between these two sons, was in their relations to Abraham's property. Ishmael, because a slave was not the heir, he was entitled only to a slave's portion, "a bottle of water and a loaf of bread." Food and raiment are a slave's right. Isaac was the heir apparent to all the estate of Abraham, which was by no means inconsiderable. Isaac was a wealthy prince. How strikingly illustrative this of the comparative wealth and blessing of the two churches. The one limited to the earthly Canaan, its bread and water, its milk and honey, while the other as a joint heir with Jesus, anticipates a heavenly Canaan, an incorruptible, undefiled, and unfading inheritance at God's right hand. Paul's schedule of their property, is as follows: "Whether Paul pr Apollos, or Cephas, or the world, or life, or death, or things present, or things to come, all are yours." They wait "for a far more exceeding and eternal weight of glory."

But the fourth and last difference between these sons of Abraham, typical of a most important difference in these prospective churches, was in their *spirit*. There is a spirit homogeneous with the condition of man. The slave Ishmael possessed a slavish, low, mean and persecuting spirit, whereas, the free Isaac, was docile, humble, pious and a suffering man, elevated above the flesh—a spiritual man. This difference in their spirit is developed most strikingly at an early period of their lives, while both resident in their father's family, Isaac having reached the age of five years, a period at which patriarchal mothers removed their children from the breast, "Abraham made a great feast the day Isaac was weaned." Large numbers of happy guests surrounded the table laden with patriarchal simplicity; joy and hilarity covered the board. The young prince was the topic of conversation. Mother Sarah received many an honest compliment on account of her son. Many a heart breathed silently a sincere prayer to God for blessings upon a son of faith and old age, joy and gratitude filled each heart, with bare one exception—a feeling of jealousy and hatred, raged in the bosom of Ishmael. Ishmael mocked and persecuted Isaac. But what does this persecution mean? Would to God it had no *meaning*. Paul gives a solemn interpretation to this short piece of history, (twenty-ninth verse of text): "But as *then,* he that was born after the flesh, persecuted him that was born after the spirit, even so it is *now.*" These sons, in their spirit, and in the fruit of their spirit, represent the two churches. The one filled "with the spirit of bondage to fear," the other "with the spirit of adoption, whereby they cry Abba Father." Ishmael stands for a persecuting church, Isaac a persecuted one. No sooner were these two churches together in Jerusalem, than the church of the flesh opened the fires of persecution against the church of the spirit. The fire broke forth first at Jerusalem, spread to the cities around, and to all the Roman provinces wherever a synagogue was to be found. Here is the beginning of the cruel sufferings of the people of God, for conscience's sake; while Jerusalem has its tens of thousands of hallowed associations, it has at the same time many unpleasant reminiscences. From thence bloody and cruel edict after edict was issued against the disciples. There the first martyrs sealed their testimony with their own blood: while the Jewish church had power, blood ran from every vein of the church of Jesus Christ; but "the blood of the martyrs became the seed of the church." The arm of this Ishmaelitish church was at length broken by the Roman power. Peace and gratitude ensued for a season. About this time, infant membership had its rise; a wicked hand was lain upon the only naturalization law of the Kingdom of Heaven. "The birth of the spirit," "ye must be born again," and flesh was substituted for it. Flesh and blood, and not faith and a holy life became the passport to citizenship in the kingdom of God. The effect was, that tribes and nations moved right into the church of God, not by operation of the spirit of God, but by operation of the touch of a moistened finger in the name of the Trinity to the babe of hereditary flesh and blood. The church swallowed the world or the world the church, it is difficult to determine exactly which. The law of the spirit being, if not stricken from the statute of the Kingdom of Heaven, at least a dead letter; corruption now poured into the church. Whole nations of unregenerate men and women now crowded the gates of the kingdom, filled with pride, ambition, and a love of power. Modern Italy, Spain and Portugal, and I might say Mexico, are lamentable illustrations of the corrupt workings of the flesh rather than the spirit. In these countries, all belong to the church, from the self-denying monk to the plundering guerrilla party. Give to such a church as that civil power—and civil power they will have—and you may confidently look for the desolating scenes that disgrace the pages of sacred history. I solemnly look upon this plea of flesh rather than the spirit as the cause of the persecutions in the past. What else could be looked for from a church composed of flesh and blood, superstition and ignorance—a church without spirituality and even sound morality. History confirms my position here; all the persecuting churches have

been those who received far many more accessions on account of their flesh than on account of their faith. It is justly the boast of Baptists, that they never persecuted —they never drew the sword from the scabbard. They chose to suffer with the Lord themselves, rather than cause suffering to others.

But, my auditors, I must take you once more with me to Abraham's family, at the weaning of Isaac, and feast of Abraham. "We are there informed that the mocking of Ishmael was observed by Sarah. Displeased with the treatment of her son by her servant, she requested Abraham "to *cast out this bondwoman and her son, for the son of the bondwoman, shall not inherit with my son, even with Isaac."* Abraham was grieved. He *loved* his son tenderly, and whilst he stood reflecting, God spoke and said, Abraham, hearken to the voice of thy wife, *"cast out the bond-woman, and her son."* But this woman and her son are typical personages, typical of Jewish covenant and church. To cast out the bond woman and her son, is but a precept TO CAST OUT THE JEWISH COVENANT AND THE JEWISH CHURCH. But mark the reason of this repudiation of the bond-woman and her son. "The son of 'the bond-woman"—the son of the flesh, shall not inherit with the son of the free woman"—the son of the spirit. Here is a repudiation of *the fleshly principle,* and an endorsement of the spiritual—the children of the flesh are not heirs. It is, therefore, no matter of surprise that the Baptist said, "the axe is laid unto the root of trees," the tree that brings the *good* fruit, shall stand—the unfruitful tree shall be hewn down and cast into the fire—that flesh was about to give way for spirit—blood, for piety and a holy life. Wonderful revolutions in divine things are clearly taught by this allegory—the *old covenant* has given way for the *new.* The mediator, Moses, for the *mediator* Messias—*the Jewish church for the Christian church*—the *gospel* of the earthly inheritance for the *gospel* of the heavenly —the *earthly Canaan* for the *heavenly*—the *old testament* for the *new*—the *birth* of the *flesh* for the *birth of* the *spirit.*

That which now stands between the individual, whether Jew, Greek, barbarian, male or female, bond or free, and the Kingdom of Heaven with all the fullness of its blessings is the birth of the spirit. This is God's own naturalization law, made for the benefit of oppressed foreigners and strangers. Let no ruthless hand touch it, but let it stand from age to age as the door of the Kingdom of Heaven—and blessed is he that hastens to enter through this gate into the city. Amen.

-----o-----

The Temptation after Baptism.

[BY JAMES CHALLEN.]

THE ordinances of religion receive a blessing from above, and the appointed means of conveying it to the obedient believer, if followed by prayer, and a godly life. Jesus prayed immediately after baptism; and it would be well if all his followers would do the same. In regard to ordinances, it may be observed, that independent of God's authority, or Christ's name, they are of no value. It would have been the height of folly in Naaman,, the Syrian leper, to have attributed his cure to the waters of the Jordan, rather than to the Divine Agency which accompanied his acts of obedience. It does not derogate from the freeness of the Gospel salvation, that it is suspended upon the express conditions of its author. If he bids us "wash and be clean," and commands us to "ask that we may receive," we only comply with the means of God's appointment, and thereby show our proper estimate of the grace of God by availing ourselves of the use of the channels through which it flows. Thus baptism is called a "birth of water," "the laver of regeneration," "the answer of a good conscience," a "burial with Christ." These expressions show its importance, and indicate the necessity of obedience to it. For if it is a "birth of water," "the laver of regeneration," "a burial with Christ," etc., how can one be "born" in the sense indicated, without baptism, and how wash in "the laver," unless he comes to it, and how be "buried with Christ," without the baptismal grave? And how obtain a good

conscience if baptism is its answer? There is a "birth" then, a "washing," a "burial," which no one can have, who has not come to this ordinance! And here I would observe, that many of the exhortations to purity and a holy life, are predicated upon obedience to this institution. To whom then, do these exhortations belong, but to those who have submitted to it, and to no other? Ro. vi; Col., iii: 1—14; Titus, iii.

After the baptism of our Savior, the Holy Spirit, in the shape of a dove, descended upon him; like the dove which Noah sent out from the ark, bringing the olive branch of peace, to Him, the true ark of salvation, to all who are IN HIM. It was a symbol of God's purpose not to destroy those who had taken refuge in him.

No sooner was Jesus baptized, and the Spirit of God had entered into him, than he was led into the wilderness to be tempted by the devil. And is not this, in some measure, the condition of all his disciples. Not only has the world lost one of its subjects, but Satan one of his adherents; and it is not to be wondered at, if he would seek to recall him back. And therefore the many temptations to which young converts subjected. It is also to be remembered, that he who would commence a new life, and cultivate its virtues, will find his sensibilities greatly quickened, his conscience tender, so that the enemy will take especial pains to harass and annoy him. But it is said, that the spirit led him into the wilderness. Well, it is not safe to go of one's choice into temptation; and we should pray, not to be led into it, nor abandoned under it. But if, in God's providence, Or the leadings of his spirit, we are placed in circumstances of trial, it may be for wise and useful purposes, as on occasion of triumph and reward, and for the growth of new virtues, and new graces. "Blessed is the man that endureth temptation: for when he is tried he shall receive the crown of life, which the Lord has promised to them that love him."

It is of the Lord's mercy that we are not always subjected to temptation; that our table is not a snare; that sense should not open to us, in every object, something to allure and destroy. Our High Priest is so fully acquainted with our nature, and the might and malice of our enemy, that he not only intercedes for us, but throws around us the shield of his protection, to ward off the many darts which would inflame and torment us. Sin and temptation, like the remnants of the seven nations of Canaan, occupy the outworks and borders of the Holy Land, into which we have entered; and it is only when we neglect our duty, and are disobedient, that they make any incursions upon us, with success. Beware, lest we enter into any covenants with them, as they will prove thorns in our sides. Some seem to pass through life without any sore temptations; like the Israelites, who had rest, sometimes for seven, and once for forty years. Happy condition! how peaceful such lives! Christ armed himself against temptation after his baptism, by prayer and fasting; and how nobly he bore the shock, and overcame the enemy, by the word of God. Do we not need similar defense and preparation?

Satan's first temptation was addressed to the appetite of hunger—one of the first necessities of nature. See in this the skill and cunning of our adversary. He knows our weakest points. A good soldier always is on his guard here. The wall of stone is a good barrier, but the picketing is easily taken or broken. Place the strongest defense always at the weakest point. Christ was hungry: "Convert this stone into bread," "eat something, you will starve here in the wilderness, "if you be the son of God!" you can do it! He refused; because it would manifest distrust in the care of his Father. "God can take care of me here for forty days, as he did of Israel in the wilderness for forty years." And will not God take care of his own? He will defend us. and supply our wants in all the places in which he may lead us. He can either lessen the appetite, or open up new means for its gratification; or he can drown the sense of it by patience and resignation. "My grace shall be sufficient for you." Satan is not willing that we should live a life of self-denial, and therefore is he seeking to convert the stones of the desert into bread. If he can induce us to gratify our appetites in ever so little, he gains a mastery over us. See how this appears, in the life of the voluptuary, the dissolute, the intemperate!

Satan, foiled in his first attack, makes another, addressed to a higher and more refined element—reliance upon the uncovenanted mercies of God. "Cast yourself down from the battlement of this temple." For it is written "He shall give his angels charge of thee," etc. The tempter knew just how much of this scripture to quote. He left out the very life of the passage. Our Savior knew it. God has promised to keep us "in all our ways," provided they are his ways; but if we go out, to the right or left, then he has not made any provision for us. Sins of presumption are most grievous sins. We should not tempt God.

Foiled again, he renews the attack. In appealing to his ambition, his love of empire, he showed him all the kingdoms of the world, and the glory of them. "These I will give thee, if you will fall down and worship me." What an insult! What insolence! Avaunt, foul fiend! The only reply of the Savior was, "Get thee behind me, Satan." "It is written, thou shalt worship the Lord thy God, and *him* only shalt thou serve."

The temptations to which men are now subjected, are many, and among them these may be considered:

1. To the evils of poverty, the appetite of hunger, and all the necessities of such a state.

2. To the tendencies of our nature, to trust to a blind fatality, to the dogmas of predestination. "O, it will all come out right at last."

3. To love of empire, the taint of an ungodly ambition, the world and its glory, which are passing away. These are our great temptations, and the Savior has taught us how to overcome them.

-----O-----

HOOPS.—The Boston Bee says, that in some of the fashionable churches, where five could sit last year, only three ladies can be accommodated this year, on account of their hoops. The consequence is, that more pews must be hired, and the prices of available ones are increased. Fashion is costly and inconvenient.

Evangelizing.

WE are now at the private house of Bro. L. Davis, New Paris, Ohio. Being engaged in a protracted meeting, and it being the first day of the year, we awoke some time before day, and our mind is running upon the evangelical work. Indeed, we have been taking a general survey of the cause, and the field to be operated upon. If we are not sadly mistaken, here is where the attention of the brotherhood needs directing now. It is no matter how many schemes the brethren engage in, nor how good their object, if they neglect evangelizing, the cause will fall. In every city, town, village and neighborhood where evangelical labors are not enjoyed, the cause is languishing and suffering. The attention of the evangelists has been divided and distracted by unavailing and useless schemes, to the neglect of the great evangelical work. Schemes of organization have been commented upon, until the brethren have become sickened, and turned from the subject, at the first sight of the caption of an article treating upon it, feeling conscious that it will not afford relief. Long theories upon officers and their qualifications, and fine descriptions of the duties of the *pastorate appear* in the prints, but the churches fall soundly asleep under their fine theories. If we intend to save the cause, we, as evangelists of Christ, have something more to do than to seek good places, ease and earthly comfort. The Lord did not intend evangelists to open an office, and sit down in it and wait for sinners to come to them to be converted. But he intended the living preacher to go to sinners, with the living voice and preach to him the living word of the living God. The command is to *go, go* and *keep going,* while God shall give us life; *go,* believing in God, with strong faith—trusting in the Lord for a support now, and eternal glory in the world to come.

A little preaching on Lord's day will not do the work. The Word should be preached every day and every night, as far as possible. We cannot confine our labors to cities, towns, and villages, expecting preaching to be brought to us, as work to a tailor, hatter or shoemaker; but we must *go out* into the country, among *the people,* and be

among *the people,* and be *one of them,* as messengers sent from heaven to take them to God. We are not to confine ourselves to the fine meeting-house, but, when we can do no better, go to the court-house, the town or city hall, the old seminary, the school-house, or the private dwelling, and preach to the people. We must not wait for the large assembly, but preach to the few taw small, humble and unpromising congregation; we must not merely *pretend* to preach, while we are only complaining of them, telling how bad they are; whining over them, and murmuring—showing contempt to them and all their arrangements—but preach to them in the name of the Lord, remembering that in every human form you see, there is a living spirit, upon which Jesus looked when he died, and which is worth more than the great globe on which he walks. No matter how lowly, how humble, how poor and uncomely all their temporal arrangements, you will find on acquaintance, some who will love the Lord, turn from their sins, and become jewels in the Lord's, and also in the preacher's crown of rejoicing. Do not go into the work with a cant upon your lips, with disheartening words, but preach to them as for life; plead with them with their real danger spread out before your eyes, remembering the reward of him who shall save a soul from death.

In this great work we do not need to work up the imagination, but simply to enter into the *reality;* deal in solemn and awful *realities,* and keep the mightiest and grandest *realities* before the people all the time. Men well skilled, have been able to speak of fiction so much as if it were reality, as to give it the effect of reality. In direct contrast with this, some men speak of reality so exactly as if it were fiction, as to give it simply the effect of fiction. The religion of Jesus Christ is reality. He is a real, ever-living and divine person. Christianity is a real system, that really unites man with this glorious and real person. The salvation of the souls of men, of which it treats, is no fiction, but a real work, of higher importance to the happiness of man, than all the works ever performed through human instrumentality. It is our work to awaken men, arouse them from their slumbers, and induce them to open their eyes, minds and hearts to the realities in the Bible, in the world and in man; to the realities all above, around and beneath us. Our work is not to set the world to dreaming, or put men to sleep: or to induce them to imagine that they are talking with the spirits of the departed, ghosts, or *demons.* This we leave for those idle dreamers who have nothing to do but practice sorcery or necromancy. 'Our work is not to put men asleep, but to awaken them. The voice of our mission cries, "Awake, thou that sleepest, and arise from the dead, and Christ shall give you life." We must go with the kind and benevolent and warning voice, stirring men from their stupor, as you would the dying man, to have him take conscious cognizance once more, of his real condition. Our work is to *go out,* with this great cause burning upon the altar of the heart, moving our souls and quickening every energy into manly activity; and thus, to the extent of our power, turn men from their sins. Our hearts must be full of the great theme of Calvary; it must dwell upon our lips in the pulpit, and out of it. Our breasts must be swelled and animated by the expanded benevolence of the Redeemer, extended to all mankind. We lose ourselves in the great work to which we are called, and constantly look to and put our trust in Him who has called us, and honored us with an instrumentality in his great work.

We are not to stop on account of a man's condition in this world, whether he be rich or poor, bond or free, high or low; whether he lives in the fine mansion, or the humble cottage, we have a mission to him—a mission of love and mercy; a mission from God. Go to him, as holy men of old, not seeking *his,* but *him*—making an effort to save him, and make him instrumental in saving others—make him sensible that he is a human being, and of the same race with yourself, and that your work is with him and all such, to labor for their good, and bring them to the lamb of God who takes away the sins of the world. He will hear you, and, if won to the Lord, will send strains of gratitude to heaven forever, that he ever saw the day that you came to him with the good tidings of great joy to all people.

Brethren, turn your attention to your evangelists. See to their temporalities, and see to them well. This you can now do without any pressure, and it is but reasonable that you should do it. The Lord requires it; his cause demands it, and your own conscience approves it. Make it the first great item to secure and sustain faithful evangelists—keep them continually in the field, or the churches will die all over the land. Never let the preachers stop. God help them and keep them going! B. F.

-----O-----

Letter from B. K. Smith.

NEAR INDIANAPOLIS, Dec. 13, 1855.

BROTHER FRANKLIN: Your note of the 10th inst., accompanied by specimen numbers of your "*Review*" came to hand to-day. I will do the best I can with them.

Concerning the "long letter on important matters," for which you call, like Nebuchadnezzar's dream, "the thing has gone from me," and I know not whether I shall ever be able to call up the same train of thoughts that was then struggling for utterance. As well as I can remember, I wished to have given you a formal congratulation upon your resumption of tripod, as editor of a monthly Magazine of such respectable appearance as the specimen before me, and all under your own control. At any rate, this is what I *now* desire to do, and accordingly tender you my most sincere congratulation. May your most sanguine hopes be more than realized; and your *Review* attain a popularity, only equaled by its usefulness.

I have read, with a good deal of interest, your introductory address—in fact the whole number—and am free to pronounce it, on the whole, the cheapest publication of the kind, now in our ranks. My only fears are, that you will not be able to keep it up to its present promise, in size, matter, manner, and style of mechanical execution, and make it a *paying* enterprise at your present rates of subscription. But I presume you have your contract made for the year's printing, and knew what you were about.

It is certainly a great advantage to an ardent, zealous temperament, such as yours, to have such a medium of access to the attention of mankind, entirely under your own control: and to have arisen to a position enabling you to command such a medium, is, of itself, no mean acquisition. My congratulations are therefore, none the less cordial that this achievement is the result of your own indomitable energy and perseverance, and not of fortuitous circumstances, created and thrown around you by influential friends.

I trust I need say nothing to you, of the responsibility of the position you occupy—of the mighty influence you will exercise for good or for evil—for weal or for woe—to thousands, not only of the present generation, but perhaps, for ages to come. When I think of these things, I often feel an instinctive shrinking within myself, from the responsibility of the humble position I occupy myself; and it is nothing, compared with the responsibility of yours. I have an abiding confidence, however, that the Lord will give grace, equal to our day and trials—that He will give grace and glory, and no good thing will He withhold from them that walk uprightly.

You have certainly assumed the right ground in your introductory address—that of good will to all, and rivalry to none; and if you do not succeed in getting a favorable notice and cordial welcome by the corps editorial of our brotherhood, it will be an exhibition of illiberality on their part, that will eventually find its own end in the great heart of the brotherhood. But I will not suffer myself to doubt the hearty and *unanimous* welcome of our editorial brethren to your *debut*. Indeed, the "*Record*" and the "*Age*" have already spoken out—the former in anticipation of its appearance, and the latter announcing and hailing its advent, in the most flattering and fraternal terms. This is as it should be; and will be followed up, I trust, by others.

One word of admonition, and I will close this rambling letter: Be a little more merciful when you get after the like of poor Quinby again. I do not wonder at his desiring a little hell for your especial case. Be a little more forbearing next time.

In the bonds of Faith, Hope, and Love,

B. K. SMITH.

Mr. Quinby—the Star once more.

Mr. Quinby, the editor of the *Star in the West*, a Universalian sheet published in this city, in his issue of December 15th, favored his readers with three distinct and separate articles, avenging himself upon us, on account of the gentle flagelation administered to him in our first issue. But, though he labored the subject, it appeared impossible for him to satisfy himself, or at all to give vent to the bilious accumulations contained in his bitter soul. He abuses, vilifies, bemeans, and accuses us of lying; makes false statements touching the *Age*, is contradicted by the editor, and has to take back what he had said. Poor creature! he reminds one of a serpent, so enraged as to bite itself, except that he cannot bite to hurt, since we extracted his teeth. The champion of Universalism, and great oracle of his party, has cowed down, and is as tame as a young kitten! A few months ago, he was publishing Mr. Peters' challenge, and telling about Mr. Dearborn "backing out," and pouncing upon "Ben. Franklin," who was not saying *one word about debating himself,* and declaring that he would not debate the duration of punishment, when this same "Ben. Franklin" addressed him a letter, assuring him that he would debate that subject with him, or any man that he would indorse. Here our champion *fell.* Here he turned his tune, and began to talk about "bullies." Here the poor man got his eyes opened, to see that his system could not be sustained; that it is nothing but an apology for religion, the wicked man's excuse for not turning to God, a mere negative scheme, without piety, only suited to pull down, subversive of the whole force of the Gospel, ignoring all the ordinances of the New Testament, at war with all the principles of the whole government of God, as well as the manifest principles of the civil institutions of our own country. His work is to ridicule the most awful sanctions of the government of the great God, and continually sympathize with the lawless and disobedient. He sympathizes more with him who deliberately blew a man and his wife out of this life, without one moment's warning, than the laws of his country, which had sentenced him to be punished. He is on the side of sin. He feeds upon the corruptions of society. He stands ready to take the apostate by the hand and assist in his downfall, and then join him in exultation over the ruin and desolation occasioned by it.

But, not to trouble the reader further with this case, we shall just state, that we suspect the following to be a fabrication of his own, out and out:

He states that he was told, referring to myself, by one of my "brethren in the ministry, *that he had no confidence at all in the sincerity of the man; that he would not fellowship him, nor be seen in the pulpit with him.*"

Now, we do not believe he can product the brother in the ministry who said this; but if he will, we will give the public the benefit of his name, as soon as possible after we receive it.

He has not even had the honor to send us so much as the paper containing his abusive article, much less exchange.

We are on terms of most perfect good will with the *Christian Age,* and every man connected with it, and wish it the highest degree of prosperity, as we said before Mr. Quinby uttered a word of his low fabrications.   B. F.

Queries Answered.

1. Query.—*Brother Franklin:* What kind of baptism does the apostle speak of, 1 Cor., 12:13? I heard a man that is called a "big preacher," say that it is spirit baptism. I do not understand it that way, though I may be wrong.   Walter Moore.

This passage, unquestionably, referred to the ordinary immersion in water, which completed their initiation into Christ. The baptism of the Holy Spirit never initiated any persons into Christ. Those baptized in the spirit on Pentecost, were already in Christ, or in his body, when baptized in the spirit. Those at the house of Cornelius, were not in Christ when baptized in the spirit, nor did that baptism take them into Christ; but after their baptism in the spirit, the apostle commanded them to be baptized in the name of the Lord. This baptism, which is a command, in which man can be baptized at will,

QUERIES ANSWERED.

and man can administer, is water baptism and the initiatory ordinance. But the baptism of the spirit, which man cannot administer, which is not a *command,* but a *promise,* and in which man cannot be baptized at will, never was designed to, and never did initiate any person into Christ. But the baptism alluded to, in the query, is the one by which "we are *all* baptized *into* one body." This baptism is common to *all.* It introduces them *into* one body. .

By the way, it would be hard for our sectarian friends to prove that they have ever enjoyed this baptism, no matter whether it be spirit or water; for it introduced into *one body;* and they certainly have never been baptized into *one body,* by any kind of baptism.

2. QUERY.—If those under the law received a just recompense of reward, for every transgression and disobedience, in this world, will they be punished in the world to come for the same transgressions?

ROBERT EDMUNDSON.

The subject introduced by brother Edmundson, in the above question, is one that cannot be satisfactorily discussed and answered in a few words; yet we have but a small space for its elucidation now. We, therefore, cannot promise full satisfaction. The law of Moses neither could give eternal life, nor punish with eternal punishment. Its rewards and punishments were not spiritual, but worldly; not eternal, but temporal; not in the future, but in the present world. The law could not purge the conscience. By the deeds of the law no flesh could be justified in the sight of God. The law offered no heaven, and threatened no hell. A man could conform to the letter of the law all his life, so as to escape all its punishments; or, as in the case of Saul of Tarsus, as touching the law be blameless, and yet have no piety towards God, no purification of conscience, or not at all justified in the sight of God. A mere conformity to the law of Moses prepared no person for heaven, or guaranteed to no person anything in the world to come. A man receiving all its rewards—all its promises, its Canaan, its milk and honey, etc., etc.—in this world, was no reason why he should not enjoy heaven. On the other hand, the penalty of that law falling upon its transgressor, was no reason why he should not be punished in the world to come, any more than the penalty of the civil government falling upon a transgressor is a reason why God should not punish him.

The truth is, Abraham was justified by faith, in the sight of God, four hundred and thirty years before the law, even while yet in uncircumcision. His faith looked not to the law, its rewards or its promises, but to Him who was the end of the law, who is the resurrection and the life—the Lord from heaven. In receiving the promise, Abraham received Christ, was justified by him, and through him gained heaven. All the justification, from Abraham to the giving of the law, and from then to Christ, was through faith in the promise, or in Christ, the substance of the promise, and not through the law. Abraham, by faith, saw the day of the Redeemer; and through that faith reached beyond the law, beyond all its rewards and punishments, and above them, to a spiritual system, a spiritual life, and spiritual world. Upon this promise, and faith in it, rested the piety of Abraham, and all his descendants, to Christ; in it was their hope of heaven and the world to come; through it was justification, and without that faith there was no justification. Without this faith there was no purification of conscience, no purification of the heart, and union with God, though a man had kept the law all his life. But if a man lived without this faith, and died in his disobedience to the law, he certainly died without justification, without his soul being purified, and consequently without any preparation to enjoy God.

The mere circumstance of a man being punished for his sins in this life, has nothing in it to purify his soul, purge his conscience, or prepare him for the enjoyment of God. The Egyptians, the antediluvians, the Sodomites, and the Jews, had a just recompense of reward sent upon them in this world, but this only sent them down to *tartarus,* to be reserved, with the angels that sinned, to the judgment of the great day, where, we are assured, Sodom and Gomorrah shall appear . Some men appear

to think, that if men are punished, to use their own style, as much as their sins deserve, they must necessarily be happy then. But men cannot be happy—cannot enjoy God, without justification, purification of heart and conscience, and, unless thus prepared for the enjoyment of God, they cannot enjoy the world to come. This is a work that punishment cannot do. The hurling of angels, that sinned, down to hell, the drowning of antediluvians and Egyptians, the burning of Sodomites, and slaying of Jews, did not purify one of them; nor can we see that any punishment will ever purify, or justify one of them. If men live in unbelief, commit some capital offence, and are executed for it, though this may be a just recompense of reward, it will not purify their souls, and prepare them to enjoy God. When men pass the boundary line of life, they pass all the means, in the economy of God, for preparing them for heaven, and no punishment will ever do what the grace of God could not do.   B. F.

-----O-----

The Christian.

EIGHTEEN hundred and fifty years ago there lived in Judea a personage by the name of Jesus, the Christ. He was also called the Son of God—the son of man—the man of sorrows, who was acquainted with grief. He had many followers, known and recognized as his disciples. They were also denominated Christians, deriving their name immediately from him in whom they believed. How appropriate the title—Christian! Every believer loves and cherishes it. It is full of meaning. The associations connected with it are of the most pleasing, of the most endearing character. It is true, that sad memories are awakened by it; memories of him who had not on earth where to lay his head. It speaks of many melancholy scenes; of bitter, burning tears; of deep sighs, and convulsing agonies. While, however, it suggests a life of labor and sacrifice, of weariness and suffering; while it speaks of Gethsemane, the bar of Pilate, and Herod, and the dreadful summit of Calvary—it points to the grave from which the Redeemer of a ruined race arose in might, and majesty, and triumph; it points to the realms of infinite bliss, to which he has ascended, in order to intercede with his Father for all those who love him.

In days of pure and unadulterated Christianity, those only were called Christians who cordially received the religion of Jesus, the anointed of heaven. Such alone as came to God, not according to their own contracted views of righteousness, but according to the plan proposed by the Divine mind, were then deemed worthy the significant and solemn appellation of Christian. But in these latter days of free-thinking—of mental, not spiritual progress, many are called Christians who have only partially obeyed the high and holy commands of the Messiah. These exhibit not by word nor deed, a change of heart. Their minds are not in subjection to the will of God; their thoughts are wandering, their minds are light as gossamer, and their actions among men, directly opposed to the teachings of Christ and his apostles—to the spirit and genius of Christianity. Like the congregation at Ephesus, they have "lost their first love; or, if that holy passion ever warmed their hearts, ever filled their bosoms with rapture, they must have early lost it in the conflict against sin. If they ever had on the strong armor of God, their fellow-soldiers nor their enemies, have been able to ascertain the fact. They have a name to live, and are dead. They bear the name of Christ, yet emulate not his goodness, his resignation, or his fortitude. They become insulted if you doubt their honesty, or integrity, and yet wish you to approve their aberrations. They desire a place among the saints on earth, that they may have a place among the sanctified in heaven. They want to be citizens of the kingdom of Satan, and at the same time citizens of the kingdom of the most high God. They wish to be approved by the world, the flesh, and the devil, that they may enjoy the pleasures of sin, and at the same time to be associated with the followers of the son of God, that they may enjoy the benefits of Christianity. A Frenchman, an Englishman, or a citizen of the United States, may be distinguished by his language, habits, or manners, but it is almost impossible to ascertain from his words, or deeds, who is Christian, or who anti-christian, who is building up, or who breaking down the walls of Zion, who is proclaiming the unsearchable riches of Christ to a perishing world, or who is crushing the high purposes of the heralds of the cross. The conversation of the Christian of the nineteenth century differs but little from the conversation of the man of the world. The manners of the Christian are not much better than the sinner's. The habits of the Christian and not, perhaps, such as men would call wicked, but they and of no real advantage to anyone. His example, perhaps, is not considered a bad example, but it does little toward recommending to men the religion of Jesus, the Christ.

The Christian, the professor of Christianity, should at least be reminded of the confession he has made, in the presence of God and men, of the high position he has taken before the intelligences of earth and heaven, of the duties and labors he is called upon to perform, of the many obligations he is under to love and serve the living God, of the exalted motives which should lead him to persevere in well doing, of the crown of life which may be awarded him when this body shall have mouldered into dust, when mortality shall have put on immortality, when death itself shall be swallowed up in life everlasting. W. C. R.

-----O-----

The First Epistle of John.

I. WHAT was from the beginning, what we have heard, what we have seen with our eyes, what we gazed upon, and our hands handled; concerning the word of the Life, (and the Life was manifested, and we have seen, and do testify, and declare unto you that eternal Life which was with the Father, and was manifested unto us,) what we have seen and heard declare we unto you, that ye also may have fellowship with us; and, again, our fellowship *is* with the Father and with his Son Jesus Christ. And these things we write unto you, that your joy may be fulfilled.

And this is the message which we have heard from him, and report unto you, that God is light, and darkness in him there is none. If we say that we have fellowship with him, and walk in the darkness, we lie, and do not the truth; but if we walk in the light, as he himself is in the light, we have fellowship one with another, and the blood of Jesus Christ his Son cleanseth us from all sin. If we say that we have no sin, we deceive ourselves, and the truth is not in us. If we confess our sins, he is faithful and righteous to forgive us *our* sins, and cleanse us from all unrighteousness. If we say that we have not sinned, we make him a liar, and his word is not in us.

II. My little children, these things I write unto you, that ye sin not: and if anyone have sinned, we have an Advocate with the Father, Jesus Christ the righteous; and he is himself the propitiation for our sins; yet not for ours only, but also for the whole world.

And hereby we know that we have known him, if we keep his commandments. He that saith, I have known him, and keepeth not his commandments, is a liar, and the truth is not in him: but whoso keepeth his word, truly in this man hath the love of God been perfected: hereby we know that we are in him. He that saith he abideth in him, ought himself also so to walk, even as He walked.

Beloved, I write not a new commandment unto you, but an old commandment which ye had from the beginning: this old commandment is the word which ye heard from the beginning. Again, a new commandment I write unto you, which thing is true in him and in you: because the darkness passeth away, and the true light now shineth. He that saith he is in the light, and hateth his brother, is in the darkness until now. He that loveth his brother abideth in the light, and there is no occasion of stumbling in him. But he that hateth his brother is in the darkness, and walketh in the darkness, and knoweth not whither he goeth, because the darkness hath blinded his eyes.

I write unto you, little children, because your sins have been forgiven you for his name's sake. I write unto you, fathers, because ye have known him *that is* from the beginning. I write unto you, young men, because ye have overcome the wicked one. I write unto you, little children, because ye have known the Father. I have written to you, fathers, because ye have known him *that is* from the beginning. I have written unto you, young men, because ye are strong, and the word of God abideth in you, and ye have overcome the wicked one.

Love not the world, neither the things in the world; if anyone love the world, the love of the Father is not in him: for all that *is* in the world, the lust of the flesh, and the lust of the eyes, and the pride of life, is not of the Father, but is of the world: and the world passeth away, and the lust thereof: but he that doeth the will of God abideth forever.

Little children, it is the last hour; and as ye heard that the Antichrist cometh, even now there are many become antichrists; whence we knew that it is the last hour. From us they went out, but they were not of us; for if they had been of us, they would have abode with us; but *it was* that they might be made manifest that none of them are of us: And you, ye have an anointing from the Holy One, and know all things. I have not written unto you because ye know not the truth, but because ye know it, and that no lie is of the truth. Who is the liar, but he that denieth that Jesus is the Christ? This is the Antichrist, who denieth the Father and the Son. Every one that denieth the Son, neither hath he the Father; he that confesseth the Son hath the Father also.

You, therefore, let that which ye heard from the beginning abide in you; if that abide in you which ye heard from the beginning, ye also shall abide in the Son and in the Father. And this is the promise which he himself promised us, the life eternal. These things I have written unto you concerning those who would deceive you. And you, the anointing which ye received from him abideth in you, and ye have no need that anyone teach you; but as the same anointing teacheth you concerning all things, and is true, and is no lie, and even as it taught you, ye shall abide in him. And now, little children, abide in him; that, when he shall be manifested, we may have confidence, and not be shamed away from him, at his coming.

If ye know that he is righteous, ye know that every one that doeth righteousness hath been begotten of him. III. Behold what manner of love the Father hath bestowed upon us, that we should be called children of God! therefore the world knoweth not us, because it knew not him. Beloved, now are we children of God, and it hath not yet been manifested what we shall be, but we know that, when it shall be manifested, we shall be like him, for we shall see him as he is.

And every one that hath this hope on Him purifieth himself, even as He is pure. Every one that committeth sin committeth also violation of law; and sin is violation of law. And ye know that He was manifested to take away our sins; and in him is no sin. Every one that abideth in him sinneth not; everyone that sinneth hath not seen him, neither known him. Little children, let no one deceive you; he that doeth righteousness is righteous, even as He is righteous. He that committeth sin is of the devil; for the devil sinneth from the beginning. For this was the Son of God manifested, that he might destroy the works of the devil. Every one that hath been begotten of God doth not commit sin, for his seed abideth in him; and he cannot sin, because he hath been begotten of God; in this are manifest the children of God and the children of the devil.

Every one that doeth not righteousness is not of God, and he that loveth not his brother. For this is the message that ye heard from the beginning, that we should love one another; not as Cain was of the wicked one, and slew his brother; and wherefore slew he him? Because his own works were wicked, but his brother's righteous. Marvel not, my brethren, if the world hateth you. As for us, we know that we have passed out of death into life because we love the brethren: he that loveth not *his* brother abideth in death. Every one that hateth *his* brother is a mankiller; and ye know that no mankiller hath eternal life abiding in him.

Hereby have we known love, because He laid down his life for us: we also ought to lay down *our* lives for the brethren. But whoso hath the world's goods, and seeth his brother have need, and shutteth up his bowels from him, how abideth the love of God in him? My little children, let us not love in word nor with the tongue, but in deed and truth.

And hereby we know that we are of the truth; and shall assure our hearts before him. For if *our* heart condemn us, God is greater than our heart, and knoweth all things. Beloved, if our heart condemn us not, we have confidence toward God. And whatsoever we ask, we receive from him, because we keep his commandments, and do the things that are pleasing in his sight. And this is his commandment, that we should believe on the name of his Son Jesus Christ, and love one another, as he gave us commandment. And he that keepeth his commandments abideth in him, and he in him: and hereby we know that he abideth in us, by the Spirit that he gave us.

IV. Beloved, believe not every spirit, but try the spirits whether they are of God: because many false prophets are gone out into the world, Hereby ye know the Spirit of God: every spirit, that confesseth Jesus Christ come in flesh, is of God. And every spirit, that confesseth not Jesus Christ come in flesh, is not of God; and this is that *spirit* of the Antichrist, whereof ye have heard that it cometh, and now it is in the world already. You, little children, are of God, and have overcome them; because greater is he that is in you, than he that is in the world. They are of the world; therefore *what is of* the world they speak, and the world heareth them: we are of God; he that knoweth God heareth us; he that is not of God heareth not us. By this we know the spirit of truth and the spirit of error.

Beloved, let us love another; for love is of God, and every one that loveth hath been begotten of God, and knoweth God. He that loveth not knoweth not God: for God is love. In this was manifested the love of God in us, that God hath sent his Son, the only begotten, into the world, that we might live through him. Herein is love, not that we loved God, but that he loved us, and sent his Son a propitiation for our sins. Beloved, if God so loved us, we also ought to love one another. No one hath at any time seen God: if we love one another, God abideth in us, and his love hath been perfected in us. Hereby we know that we abide in him, and he in us, because he hath given us of his Spirit. We also have seen, and do testify, that the Father hath sent the Son as Savior of the world. Whosoever shall confess that Jesus is the Son of God, God abideth in him, and he in God. We also have known and believed the love that God hath in us. God is love, and he that abideth in love abideth in God, and God in him. Herein hath love with us been perfected, that we should have confidence in the day of judgment, because as He is are we also in this world. There is no fear in love, but perfect love casteth out fear; because fear hath punishment: but he that feareth hath not been perfected in love. We love him, because he first loved us. If anyone say: I love God, and hateth his brother, he is a liar; for he that loveth not his brother whom he hath seen, how can he love God whom he hath not seen? And this commandment have we from him, that he who loveth God love also his brother.

V. Every one that believeth that Jesus is the Christ hath been begotten of God; and every one that loveth him that begat, loveth him also that hath been begotten of him. Hereby we know that we love the children of God, when we love God, and keep his commandments. For this is the love of God, that we keep his commandments; and his commandments are not burdensome. For all that hath been begotten of God overcometh the world; and this is the victory that overcometh the world, our faith. Who is he that overcometh the world, but he that believeth that that Jesus is the Son of God?

This is he that came by water and blood, Jesus the Christ; not with the water only, but with the water and the blood; and the Spirit is that which testifieth, because the Spirit is truth. For there are three that testify, the Spirit, and the water, and the blood; and the three agree in one. If we receive the testimony of men, the testimony of God is greater; for this is the testimony of God which he hath testified concerning his Son. He that believeth in the Son of God hath the testimony in himself' he that believeth not God hath made him a liar, because he hath no believed in the testimony which God hath testified concerning his Son. And this is the testimony that God gave to us eternal life, and this life is in his Son. He that hath the Son hath life; he that hath not the Son of God hath not life.

These things have I written unto you that believe in the name of the Son of God, that ye may know that ye have eternal life, and that ye may believe in the name of the Son of God. And this is the confidence that we have towards him, that, if we ask any thing according to his will, he heareth us: and if we know that he heareth us, whatsoever we ask, we know that we have the petitions that we have asked from him. If anyone see his brother sinning a sin not unto death, he shall ask, and shall give him life, *even* to those who sin not unto death. There is a sin unto death: not for that do I say that he shall pray. All unrighteousness is sin; and there is a sin not unto death.

We know that every one that hath been begotten of God sinneth not; but he that been begotten of God keepeth himself, and the wicked one toucheth him not. We know that we are of God, and the whole world lieth in the wicked one. But we know that the Son of God is come, and hath given us understanding that we may know the True One; and we are in the True One, in his Son Jesus Christ. This is the true God, and the Life eternal.

Little children, keep yourselves from the idols.

-----o-----

EDUCATION IN ENGLAND.—The Edinburgh Review says, it appears to be proved that more than one-half of the adult population of England and Wales cannot write their own names! And this state of things is in a fair way to continue; for according to the census of 1851, out of 1,394,188 children in England and Wales, between 7 and 14 years of age, only 701.345—about 50 per cent.—were at school. Could England adopt the Common School system of this country, such a state of things would soon cease.

-----o-----

THE tongue of the just is as choice silver: the heart of the wicked is little worth.

Editors' Table.

WM. JARRETT is an accredited agent for the *American Christian Review,* in all his travels.

To CORRESPONDENTS.—Several valuable articles are received, but not till the February number was in type, which will account for their non-appearance.

THE SERMON.—The valuable Sermon in this number, from Elder M. B. Hopkins, is printed in a tract by itself, also, and can be had at this office, at the following rates: Ten copies and under, 5 cents per copy; over that number, 3 cents per copy. Postage paid by publishers.

Success of the Gospel.

BRO. A. E. MYERS, of Bethany, Va., writes, under date of November 30th, that he, in company with Bro. T. Berry, formerly of Boston, Mass., but now of Bethany, recently held a protracted meeting, at which 7 were added. By an oversight, he did not say whether the meeting was at Wheeling or Bethany. He says, "The cause is gradually rising in this region.".

Bro. Wm. Jarrett, of Williamstown, Ky., called upon us on his return from a tour in the southwestern part of Indiana, and southeastern part of Illinois, and informed us that some 30 were added to the Lord through his labors, at the several points visited on this trip.

MIAMI COUNTY, IND., Dec., 22, 1855.
BROTHER FRANKLIN:—I have just closed my evangelical labors in Miami county, with the following results, since the third Lord's day in August:

At Mud Creek convention, 3 by baptism and 2 by commendation. At Pleasant Grove convention, 5 by baptism and 5 by commendation. At Pipe Creek convention, 1 reclaimed. At Manna convention, 1 from the United Brethren and 1 by confession. At Wesaw convention, meeting lasted ten days—Bro. Thompson principal laborer; 9 by baptism and 7 by commendation.—34 in all.

The cause in Miami county is on the advance. To the Lord be all the praise. The coming year, Fulton county is to be the principal field of my labors.
Your fellow-laborer in the Gospel,
BENJ. WHARTON.

Literary Notices.

WE call special attention to the advertisement of Elder Challen, on cover. No one can fail to see the importance of such a work as he proposes to publish; nor will anyone doubt that he is the man to publish it. He has been with us, coming in and going out, from the beginning, and is, in every way, competent for the work. We anticipate a treat when we receive his new book.

His *Ladies' Christian Annual* has become too well known to need any commendation from us. Suffice it to say, that he is constantly laboring to improve it, and make it still more and more attractive to Christian ladies. We have just received volume one, in beautiful embossed binding—a splendid ornament for a center table.

His new book will be for sale at this office, and we will cheerfully order any of his works.

-----o-----

UNIVERSAL MUSICIAN—We also call attention to the advertisement on the cover, of this valuable music book, by the well known and gifted A. D. Filmore. Its rapid sales, and high commendations from the most distinguished teachers, are a sufficient guaranty to all who desire to purchase such a work. For sale at this office.

-----o-----

DEBATE BETWEEN ORVIS AND MAGRUDER.—This debate was held at Aquinta church, King William. county, Va. The subject was the Punishment of the Wicked and the Kingdom of God. Mr. Magruder affirmed the utter extinction of the wicked. Mr. Orvis denied. Mr. Orvis affirmed the establishment of Christ's kingdom on earth since his first advent. Mr. Magruder denied. We have only read the discussion of the first point. Mr. Orvis has argued the question ably, and sustained the truth. Mr. Magruder assumed his definitions, and refused to use words in their ordinary sense, and evaded the main issue throughout. The main argument for the *immortality* and *eternity* of the soul remains unanswered.

-----o-----

OBITUARY.

SISTER MANSFIELD, consort of Wm. Mansfield near Luray, Henry county, Ind., died in the faith of God's elect, January 4th, and now rests with the spirits of the just. She had reached the age of 60 years and 7 days, and walked with the Lord about 36 years, being a constant reader of the Bible, and a pious and devoted Christian. Her trust was in the Lord to the end; and to him she committed her soul in death. She leaves a kind and affectionate husband, six children and a large circle of friends and brethren to lament her loss. We have been personally acquainted with this interesting family for many years, and baptized some of the younger members into the church of Christ, some ten years ago. The Lord be with them.

THE AMERICAN CHRISTIAN REVIEW.

Vol. 1.] CINCINNATI, MARCH, 1856. [No. 3.

ELDER CHALLEN'S NEW WORK.

THE following is from advance sheets of a new work, styled "*The Gospel and its Elements.* By Eld. JAS. CHALLEN, Pastor of the Disciples Church, in Philadelphia, Pa." The work is now ready, and for sale at this office. We put in an urgent plea for this book, that it may have an extended circulation; that the rising generation may have the result of the mature thoughts, in a very concise and condensed form, of an able and faithful man of God, who has devoted some thirty years to the study and proclamation of the word of God. This valuable article, originally and really a sermon, though not as extended as we intended the sermon for each number, must occupy that place this month. Several sermons from distinguished brethren, are promised, and some of them upon the stocks, but none finished. ED.

"THE GOSPEL OF CHRIST IN OPPOSITION TO THE GOSPEL OF THE SECT.

"This subject is one of no ordinary importance, and deserves our particular attention. Other topics may claim a passing notice, as they stand related to the things of earth and of time, but this is one which relates to the soul and to eternity. And as we have but one message sent to the nations, called the gospel, it is of the highest moment that we know what it is, and attend to its authoritative commands.

"The gospel, in promise and in prophecy, has enlisted the attention of the wisest and best men of all past ages, and cannot be unworthy our enlightened consideration. It was the great subject with reference to which God was pleased to make special and abundant revelations, during not only the infancy of the race, but in its more advanced state under the patriarchal and Jewish institutions.

"It was with reference to this, that after the fall a medium of communication was opened between heaven and earth, and angels ascended and descended upon the Son of Man. Silence for ever would have remained over our heads, unbroken by a single word from the Father of Light, had it not been for the anticipated relief to be brought to us by the gospel of Christ. Our race, having forfeited every claim upon the justice of heaven, would have been doomed to the darkness of an eternal night, but for the hope which the glad tidings of great joy have brought to us.

"The chains of darkness which bind the angels who sinned to their prison-house, in penal fires" to the judgment of the great day, would have been used for us, but for the grace which has been revealed therein. Sword in hand, insulted justice would have summoned us to appear before its dread tribunal, without redress and without relief, but for the blood of atonement, which had set its red seal on this message of mercy to man.

"For the introduction of this 'golden age,' the reign of Heaven, a long list of holy men were raised up, reaching from the gates of Eden to the wilderness of Judea, connecting the altar of Abel with the baptism of John, and both with the blood of Christ. 'Through faith the just subdued kingdoms, wrought righteousness, obtained promises, stopped the mouths of lions, quenched the violence of fires, escaped the edge of the sword, grew strong from sickness, became valiant in fight, overturned the camps of the aliens; and the women, emulating the courage of the men, were made valiant in weakness; others were tortured, not accepting deliverance, that they might obtain a better resurrection; others had trials of mockings and scourgings, of bonds and imprisonments. They were stoned, they were tempted, they died by slaughter, they went about in sheepskins, being destitute, afflicted, maltreated; of these the world was not worthy: they wandered in deserts, and mountains, in caves and holes of the earth.' Now all these ancient worthies, though commended on account of their faith, did not receive the promise,' did not enjoy its fulfillment, 'God having provided something better for us, that they without us should not be made perfect.'

"The gospel then is both the faith and hope of sin-oppressed humanity, and in comparison with which, wealth and fame, earthly rest and peace—all that renders life and country dear, are as nothing. 'Seeing the promised good, the ancients confessed that they were strangers and pilgrims in the land.'

"Without the gospel we should have had

'No patron, intercessor none; now past
The sweet, the clement, mediatorial hour;
For guilt no plea, to pain no pause, no bound,
Inexorable all—and all extreme.'

"From these considerations, may we not say that no duty is so imperative as that which demands our devotion to its claims. But before we can do so, we should first ascertain—'What is the gospel?'

"The gospel is glad tidings to all creatures; a proclamation from the Prince of Salvation to the guilty and the lost, and proceeding from the highest authority in the universe.

"Many have been the proclamations sent of God, on special occasions, to man; and all of them contain a distinct and clearly-ascertained message, leaving the mind in no doubt in regard to the objects proposed, or the duties required. These are characteristics of all messages proceeding from authority, whether human or divine. The gospel, under the commission given to the Apostles, implies an official announcement.

"There are several proclamations to be found in the Old Testament scriptures, which indicate the nature of such acts; and to a few of them we invite your attention.

"God said to Moses, 'Speak unto the children of Israel, concerning the feasts of the Lord, which ye shall proclaim to be holy convocations;' 'six days shall work be done; but the seventh day is the Sabbath of rest; ye shall do no work therein." Lev. xxiii, 1.

"This is one of God's proclamations; and what can be more specific? Surely, no Israelite could mistake its meaning, or fail, through ignorance, to attend to the duties required therein. Six days they might work; on the seventh they should rest, and do no work on that day.

"In the Prophets, the word proclaim frequently occurs, and always with reference to a distinct message. Thus, Isaiah speaks concerning the mission of the Messiah: 'He hath sent me to proclaim liberty to the captive, the opening of the prison to them which are bound,' etc. Isaiah lxi, 1.

"Among all nations, the solemn acts of war and peace are announced by proclamation; and they are always designed to be of a most definite and specific character. Many things may be said in the public press, and in conversation, and even in the halls of legislation, on the subjects of peace and war; but none of these amount to a proclamation. Even the ruler of a nation may threaten to chastise a foreign foe, and make all necessary preparations for war; but this is not a proclamation. It is something that proceeds in due form from the sovereign authority of the State. And so is it in relation to the gospel. It is a proclamation of mercy, sent to the nations, by the Prince of Peace; a direct and specific message, couched in few words, so that he who runs may read. It should be placed on the corners of the streets, on the public highways and great thoroughfares of the nation. It is seen and read of all men. Such a proclamation must of necessity be made in few words, that all may understand it. It must be made in the language of those who are chiefly interested in it; and by heralds and messengers, by the voice and the public press of the nation, brought within the reach of all classes of men—to every creature. Such, then, is the nature of the gospel message, proclaiming peace by Jesus Christ, to those who are nigh, and to those who are afar off.

"Thus no historical records of the Old Testament, no biographical notices of the ancient worthies, no prophetical announcements, none of the sacred songs of the Psalmist of Israel, none of the wise sayings of Solomon, no moral precepts, none of the parables of the Saviour, no expositions of scripture, no letters sent to the churches, no apocalyptic visions of John in the Isle of Patmos, no moral lecture, no essay upon any of the elements of the Christian religion, no system of theology, however true, can be dignified by the name of the gospel as proclaimed by the Apostles of Christ, no more than the discussions in the Senate or the House on the subject of war, and the ten thousand allusions to it, or conjectures about it, can be called a proclamation. Much is taught on every Lord's Day, and faithfully taught out of the scriptures, which is dignified by the term gospel, in the common acceptation of the word, but which deserves not the name. To teach is one thing, to preach another. Our Saviour both taught and preached, and so did the Apostles.

"We shall now call your attention to several portions of scripture, in which the word gospel occurs, in order to ascertain the precise meaning of the term, and the uses to which it is applied.

"The first of these references will be found in the letter to the Galatians: 'And the scripture foreseeing that God would justify the heathen through faith, preached the gospel unto Abraham, saying: In thee shall all nations be blessed.' Gal. iii, 8.

"Here we have the gospel—the gospel preached to Abraham, and the announcement also that the scripture preached the gospel to him. And why is it said that the Scripture preached it? Simply because it was first announced by God to Abraham, and afterward it went to record, and became a portion of the inspired scripture. It was thus proclaimed to Abraham, and afterward written in the divine oracles, that in him, and in his seed, which was Christ, all the families of the earth should be blessed. This is what we simply call the gospel in promise.

"Again, we have another application of the word, as used by Paul in his letter to the Hebrews: 'For unto us was the gospel preached, as well as unto them.' Heb. iv, 2. But what does the writer here mean to indicate by the gospel, as preached to the Israelites? He means simply, a distinct announcement to them of the entrance into the land of Canaan, after the toils of their desert life should be past; or at farthest, their entering into that rest of which Canaan was a type. For the same Gospel, concerning a rest for the people of God, is announced to the Christians, as was announced to the Jews.

"The gospel then proclaimed to the Israelites, primarily had reference to their entering into Canaan. But as David had spoken of another rest, which the Jews did not obtain when they entered into Canaan; and, as this was spoken many centuries after the possession of the land of Canaan, the Apostle concludes that it still remains for the people of God. In a more extended meaning, therefore, as given by Paul, the gospel here spoken of is simply a promised rest, in that land of which Canaan was a type.

"So fully did the Jews understand the nature of this proclamation, in its primary application to Canaan, that they trod the wilderness for the space of forty years in hope of its fulfillment. Some did not enter into that rest, through unbelief, but this was not owing to any want of distinctness in regard to the proclamation, but in consequence of their obstinacy and wickedness—their unbelief.

"The announcement was plain and simple, but they did not believe it; and, therefore, failed of enjoying the blessing that it promised them. This is equally true in regard to the spiritual and eternal rest, proclaimed to us in respect to another world. To those who, by patient continuance in well doing, seek for glory, honor, and immortality—eternal life shall be. To such, an abundant entrance will be administered into the everlasting kingdom of our Lord and Saviour Jesus Christ.

"And again, we have another use of the word, as given us by one of the Evangelists: 'Jesus came into Galilee, preaching the gospel of the kingdom of God; and saying, The time is fulfilled, and the kingdom of God is at hand.' Mark i, 14, 15.

"Here Jesus is said to have preached the gospel—the gospel of the kingdom—the gospel of the kingdom of God. And you will observe how specific that gospel was which he preached: he preached, saying, 'The time is fulfilled.' The time spoken of by the prophets for this event to occur—'the kingdom of God is at hand.' It was now at their very doors.

"The language could not be more specific than if the superintendent of a railroad should stand at the depot and say: 'The hour is now twelve, and the train is coming; it is at hand.' It is important to apprehend fully the nature of this proclamation of Christ, or we will not be able to distinguish between the gospel as announced by him in person, and the gospel as announced by the apostles, subsequently, in his name.

"If the gospel, as proclaimed by the apostles under the last commission, is a distinct message, and we are called upon to believe it; if it presents certain commands, which we are called upon to obey, and promises, designed to operate as motives to action; then it is plain, if we receive any other message in its stead, obey any other commands not specified, or are moved by any other considerations not known in the proclamation, we may fail of receiving the gospel altogether, and deprive ourselves of that salvation which it announces.

"Suppose, now, I should believe the five points of John Calvin—or what is familiarly styled the doctrines of grace—or the articles of the Westminster Confession—or the liturgy and thirty-nine articles of the Protestant Episcopal Church—or the twenty-five articles of the Methodist Episcopal establishment—or the six articles, more or less, of the Friends' Meeting—or the ten articles of the Free-Will Baptists—or the entire body of the faith, as contained in the Philadelphia Confession, on which the Baptist Churches are founded. Is it certain that I shall, by so doing, believe the gospel in matter and spirit, as preached by the apostles of Christ?

"Certainly, if the gospel is in Calvin, it is not in Wesley. If in the Friends' Meeting, it is not in the Episcopacy. If in the Free-Will Baptists, it is not in the Bound-Will Baptists: unless it can be demonstrated that two things, essentially different, are one and the same thing; that sweet is bitter, and bitter sweet; that light is darkness, and darkness light.

"It is most certain that, with all the apparent charity existing among the so-called Evangelical parties, if we take their respective creeds as the true exponents of their faith, it is more in name than in fact, as the faith of the one sect destroys the faith of all the rest. If anyone of them is true, then all others which differ from them must be false.

"There are no sects in heaven; there will be none in the millennial age. They will be saints, disciples, Christians, then; and why should they not be so now? What they expect to become when the darkness is past, we aim to be now; and as they affect not to know us by the scriptural names of disciples or Christians, but would wish us to assume some earthly badge of distinction, so they may, in a future day, so effectually change their creed and name, as hardly to be able to know themselves or one another!

"If the names of the respective parties in existence are not in the Bible, then there is no need for them; and if the creed contains nothing but the Bible, why is it adopted? And if contrary to it, or not exactly in conformity with it, it ought to be rejected. As well might we call a planetarium representing the solar system, the universe, and substitute it for that system, as to adopt the creed as a better symbol of the faith than for that system, as to adopt the creed as a better symbol of the faith than the scriptures of truth. Will the planetarium give us day and night, seed-time and harvest, summer and winter? Will it furnish us with the elements of fire and air, earth and water, or light? Will it impart and sustain life in the vegetable or animal kingdoms? No more can the creed!

"Far easier would it be to give us a material structure by human hands, to take the place of the solar system, than a moral one to supersede the spiritual organism found alone in the Bible. It is here, and here alone, we find our spiritual universe; our sun, moon, and stars; our light and fire; our earth, air, and water. Here we find all religious truth arranged in due order, and in the nicest proportions, by a hand that understands the wants of man. He "who hath measured the waters in the hollow of his hand, and meted out heaven with a span, and comprehended the dust of the earth in a measure, and weighed the mountain's in scales, and the hills in a balance:' He has given us His Word, and 'magnified it above all His name.' 'Who hath known the mind of the Lord, that he should be His counsellor?'

"But, says one, the creed is but an epitome of the Bible. The gospel of the sect, then, is only the gospel in epitome, and not the true gospel of Christ.

"Give us the gospel as it came from the hands of the Author. This will make us wise to salvation and perfect us in love.

"The gospel, as preached by the apostles, was not from men, neither by men, but given by the command and revelation of Jesus Christ. 'And if we,' said Paul, 'or an angel from heaven, (as now among the spiritualists), declare unto you a gospel different from what you have received, let him be anathema!' This is Paul's decision and judgment, not ours.

"The gospel of Christ—what is it? It is **a** great Evangel—glad tidings to all people. It is called the gospel of peace—the gospel of the grace of God—the gospel of your salvation.

"Many are the references found in the New Testament, concerning the facts and principles of the gospel. We call your attention to a few of them. God so loved the world, that he gave his only begotten Son, that whosoever believeth in him, should not perish, but have everlasting life.' 'This is a faithful saying, and worthy of all acceptation, that Christ Jesus came into the world to save sinners, of whom I am chief.' 'This is the record, that God has given to us eternal life, and this life is in his Son.' But Paul gives us several brief compends of the gospel, from which we select the following, as being the most perfect and complete:

"'Moreover, brethren, I declare unto you the gospel which I preached unto you, by the which also you are saved, and in which also you stand. How that Christ died for our sins, according to the scriptures, and that he was buried, and that he rose again the third day according to the scriptures.' 1 Cor. xv, 1, 2, 3, 4.

"On this formula we would observe, that Paul reaffirms the gospel that he originally preached to the people of Corinth. He declares that they received this message from his lips, and that they were saved by it, and now stood in it. In his proclamation to them he announced the following facts,—That Jesus died; that he died for their sins; that he died for their sins according to the scriptures; and that he was buried, and that he rose from the dead on the third day according to the Scriptures. These facts then as announced by the Apostle, he calls the gospel, which saved those who received it.

"But in the Acts of the Apostles we have three discourses recorded, which exhibit most faithfully the manner and matter of the Apostolic preaching.

"The first is the discourse of Peter in Jerusalem, on the day of Pentecost: Acts ii. The next is the discourse by the same Apostle, to Cornelius and family, when 'God first visited the Gentiles, to take out a people for his name:' Acts x. And the other is Paul's sermon to both Jews and Gentiles, at Antioch of Pisidia, in which he repeated to the Gentiles what he had preached to the Jews, making no distinction between them, but preaching to them alike, the same gospel: Acts xiii.

"These discourses contain a few plain facts with reference to Jesus of Nazareth: that he sprung from David according to the flesh—the royal seed promised to him; that he was approved of God by miracles, signs, and wonders; that he suffered the death of the Cross; was buried and raised again from the dead on the third day, and exalted to the right hand of the Father, as Prince and Saviour; made both 'Lord and Christ,' and constituted the Judge of the living and the dead; and that to those who should believe on him, repent, and be baptized, their sins should be forgiven them on account of his name.

"Such then is the faithful account of the gospel of Christ, as given us in these discourses. Those who received it as such, and complied with its requisitions, were saved by it. They are spoken of in the Acts of the Apostles, and in the epistles, as converted, pardoned, justified, sanctified, adopted, reconciled, redeemed. They are called Saints, chosen of God, sons and daughters of the Lord Almighty, kings, priests, heirs of God, and joint heirs with Christ.

"What need have we then for any other Gospel of salvation from angels or men?

"Let us hold fast the form of sound words, as announced by the Apostles, in faith and love.

"'I charge you,' says the Apostle, 'therefore, before God and the Lord Jesus Christ, who shall judge the living and the dead at his appearing and kingdom,—Preach the word.'"

-----o-----

Our Position as a Religious Community.
No. III.

WE never could feel that any man who spoke of our position, in taking the Bible as our only rule of faith and practice, as a *dangerous* position, or as an unevangelical position, spoke seriously, or could really and conscientiously believe what he was saying. To speak of a man who receives the whole revelation from God to man, as spread upon the pages of the Bible, and cherishes it as the pure word of God—who will not give up aught of it, but holds on to it all as precious—the man who receives the whole of Christianity, as portrayed in the predictions of the Old Testament prophets, fully revealed and developed in the New Testament—who receives the law of God, the only law the Church of Christ had for the first three hundred years of its existence; and insists upon doing all the great Head of the Church requires in that law, enjoying all its blessings, and looking for a gracious fulfillment of all its rich promises, as occupying *unsafe ground,* has the least appearance of a sincere objection of anything we ever heard. What have those who oppose that position, not contained in it? Have they anything more than what God has revealed to man in the Bible? Have they anything more than Christianity, the whole of Christianity, as God gave it? Are they doing anything more than God commands? If they have something more than God has revealed to man—something more than Christianity—and are doing something more than the law of God requires, that makes them *safe,* or *evangelical,* while those who have nothing more are upon dangerous ground, and not evangelical, we move that they get out, in a book, precisely what it is that is not in the whole revelation from God to man, not in Christianity, nor required in the law of God, that makes them safe and evangelical, that others may avail themselves of the advantage of it.

Or does the revelation from God contain too much? Does Christianity contain too much? Does the law of God extend too far? Are human creeds an abridgement, in which the unessential, and consequently unnecessary, part of the law of God is left out? And is it necessary that a man subscribe to such an abridgement, thus leaving out what wise and learned divines have ascertained not to be essential, in order to stand upon *safe* ground, be *orthodox* or *evangelical?* After we have received the Bible, Christianity, the whole law of God and its glorious Author, and submitted to him from the heart, body, soul and spirit, if we still stand upon dangerous ground, would it make us safe, orthodox, or evangelical, to submit to a human creed? Surely it would, in the estimation of our opposers. From the day we would subscribe to some popular human creed, forward, without one particle of any other change of heart or life, we would be safe, orthodox and change of heart or life, we would be safe, orthodox and evangelical. So potent is a human creed, made by uninspired men! But, in the name of common sense, how much safer, or better in any respect, would we be in the eye of God? If it would not make a man safe to believe with all the heart in the God of his existence, in the Redeemer who died for him, in the whole revelation of God to man, in all Christianity, in the whole law of the Lord, and submit himself solemnly to his Creator—is it credible—could the greatest dupe of human and uninspired creeds believe, that it would place him upon the sure rock to receive a human creed? A grander absurdity never entered into the human brain.

Or is the difficulty that, in order to stand upon safe ground, we should adopt a human creed to explain the Bible, Christianity, or the law of God? Is it so, that the Infinite One, in addressing his intelligent creatures, has failed to come down to their capacities, and that we need a few human creeds, written by uninspired men, to make the revelation of God to man intelligible to the common people? Is it true, that in order to stand upon safe ground, be orthodox, or evangelical, we should have a human creed, written by uninspired and fallible men, to explain what the inspiring Spirit of the Living God meant when he spake to the children of men? And if we, being uninspired, cannot understand what the Holy Spirit of God means, how can uninspired human creed-makers understand it, or set forth its meaning in their creeds? "But they are learned and wise men." Yes, and they, in their different *orthodox* or *evangelical* creeds, have set forth a mass of learned and wise contradictions, absurdities and unintelligible dogmas, which would throw an impenetrable cloud over the last blessed hope of man, if he had to understand them or be lost. But, thanks to God, we do not have to understand them. The merciful Lord does not require an impossibility. It is an impossibility, in the very nature of things, to understand a writer who not only did not understand himself, but whose writings are wholly inexplicable.

But I maintain that all the human creeds in the world are founded in a mischievous, wicked, ruinous and false assumption; or. rather, we should have said, in two assumptions, of this description:1. It is assumed that the law of the Lord is insufficient for a rule of faith and practice. 2. It is assumed that uninspired and fallible men can make a creed that can accomplish what the law of God, delivered by infallible inspiration, could not do; or, rather, that uninspired and fallible men can supply the deficiencies of the infallible inspiration of the Spirit of God. No man who insists upon having a human creed, can avoid, in all his attempts to sustain himself, basing all his arguments upon these two assumptions. No argument, in favor of a human creed, ever was made, or ever can be made, that is not founded in a supposed inadequacy or insufficiency in the law of the Lord. All who admit the law of God to be a sufficient rule for our faith and practice, have no argument, no reason, to offer, and no motive to try to frame any, for another law. The very first dictate of common sense says, if the law of God is sufficient, we need nothing more. But if the law of God is not sufficient, an anxiety may arise to have the deficiency supplied. And what a modest assumption, after assuming a failure on the part of the wisdom of God in making a perfect law, after assuming that the law of God is insufficient to do the work assigned it, to assume that *man—uninspired man—*can supply the deficiency, by adding a human creed to accomplish what the word of the Lord could not do! How singular, too, that assuming such an incompetency in the law of God—such a deficiency in the Bible, in Christianity, in the divine system God has given, and meekly adding to this the assumption that uninspired creed-makers can supply this defect in the word of God, should make a man *safe, orthodox,* or evangelical! According to this view of the subject, all that a man needs, to place him upon safe ground, make him orthodox and evangelical, is to think a little less of the Bible, Christianity, the law of God, and a little more of the works of uninspired men, in their pious efforts in supplying the deficiencies in the law of God; to have a little less confidence in the wisdom and works of God, and a little more confidence in the wisdom and works of men.

But, on this score, we are diverging farther from safe ground, orthodoxy or evangelicity, every year. Every year's reading and meditation upon the Bible and. the history of the Church, gives us more and still more confidence in the perfection of the Bible, its perfect completeness for a rule of faith and practice, just about in the same proportion as our confidence diminishes in the capacity of man to supply deficiencies, if any existed, in the Bible. If any man of reading and thought lacks evidence of the weakness, insufficiency and utter incapability of man—not the common herd, but the most wise and learned; not the most vicious and corrupt, but the best and most pure—to make a creed, a rule of faith, or a law to govern the Church, and thus supply the supposed deficiencies in the law of God, we think the efforts of the last three centuries, in making creeds, formulas, rules, laws, disciplines, adapting them to the churches, enforcing them, governing the churches by them, with all their conflicting doctrines, practices customs and forms of government, should afford a full satisfaction. Look at their Babel language! See their contradictory doctrines! Notice their warring elements! See the organizations under them splitting asunder! Sec the new ones springing up, and declaring all the old ones wrong! Then talk about a man being safe, orthodox or evangelical, because he has subscribed to a human creed! Which one shall a man adopt? "The one he likes best," says one. Which one does God like best? Does He approve those men who assume that His law is defective, and that they have supplied the defect? Does He approve those creeds which are based upon these assumptions, and those people who adopt them, and disapprove all those who deny these assumptions, and maintain the perfection and capability of the law of the Lord, for the accomplishment of the designs of God? Which one of all these human creeds, assuming insufficiency in the "perfect law of liberty," and man's capability to supply this insufficiency, shall an honest man adopt, to put him upon safe ground, make him orthodox or evangelical? We say, and would say it with our last breath, *none of them*. It can only involve a man in error—in inconsistency—induce him to assume the insufficiency of the law of God, and fallible man's ability to supply it—set him in an everlasting antagonism with many as good as the world affords, and diminish in his mind the value of the word of God. B. F.

-----O-----

Review of Dr. Shaffer, on Baptism.
No. III.

THE Doctor says, "We now affirm, that the word '*baptize,*' when used in a sacramental, or theological sense, *never means immersion, but pouring and sprinkling,*" p. 155. Now, Doctor, what do you mean by "sacramental, or theological sense?" Have you a sacramental or theological dictionary, in which *baptize* is defined differently from the definitions found in other dictionaries? Come, my dear sir, I am afraid you are about to play a trick upon us. Were the dictionaries in your formidable array "sacramental or theological?" If they were not, why did you quote them, in giving us the "sacramental, or theological sense" of "baptism?" Did you intend to deceive us, and induce us to receive the common for the "sacramental, or theological sense?" Or, if these are "sacramental, or theological" dictionaries, and give the "sacramental, or theological sense," how do you harden your face, quiet your conscience, and put on the assurance, to stand before them, after quoting them as authorities, and so palpably contradict every one of them? Not less than nine or ten of the authorities he professes to quote, in his own garbled and false quotations, give *immerse* as the primary meaning of the word *baptize*. Yet he proceeds not more than twenty-five pages, after giving these definitions, and in one affirmation contradicts and sweeps them all away. He quotes their definitions, or professes to do so, in discussing the meaning of the word *baptize*, in a "sacramental, or theological sense," as he calls it, and some nine or ten of them give *immerse*, not as *a* meaning, but *the* primary meaning. He then faces them and says: "We now affirm, that the word '*baptize,*' when used in a sacramental, or theological sense, *never means immersion,* but *pouring and sprinkling!!!*" He does not believe his own authorities, and even his own garbled and distorted quotations from them!

But we must bring the Doctor to a more serious account. He must now stand before father Wesley, whom he quotes and professes to believe. He says: *"Buried with him,"* (alluding to the ancient manner of baptizing by immersion). His note, Rom. vi, 4. Mr. Wesley is here speaking of what the Doctor calls the "sacramental, or theological sense," and says, it alludes to the ancient manner of *baptizing by immersion.* His son in the Methodistic faith, Dr. Shaffer, says, we affirm that it never so means. Here, the father is at variance against the son—in a palpable and direct contradiction. What shall we do in this dispute between the father and the son? Let us call in Dr. Clarke, and see if we cannot convince this bold son of Methodism that he is wrong. Page 131, of Dr. Shaffer's own book, we find the following:. "Dr. Adam Clarke says, 'Were the people dipped or sprinkled? 'for it is certain, *bapto* and *baptizo* means both.'" He is here speaking of what the Doctor calls the "sacramental, or theological sense," for he is speaking of the ordinance, and having just mentioned both dipping and sprinkling, he says, "It is certain, *bapto* and *baptizo* mean both." Both what? Both *dip* and *sprinkle.* Dr. Shaffer may now sit down, for both Wesley and Clarke are against him, and in the most palpable manner contradict him. He affirms that baptize *never means immerse*; they both declare, with his lexicons, that it *does mean immerse.* But we are not through with Dr. Shaffer on this sweeping denial, that baptize ever means immerse, when used in a sacramental, or theological sense. While father Wesley and Dr. A. Clarke are fresh in his memory, we call his attention to his discipline, p. 112. Here we find this little book giving directions to such men as Dr. Shaffer, how to baptize. How does it say it shall be done? It says, he "shall sprinkle or pour water upon him, or, if he shall desire it, *shall immerse him in water."* Now, reader, bear in mind that Dr. Shaffer is a presiding elder, and on page 44, of his discipline, we find the following requirement enjoined upon him: "To take care that every part of our discipline be enforced in his district." Now, how does the Doctor obey this requirement of his office? His book requires him, when candidates for baptism shall desire it, to *immerse them;* and he is bound, by all the solemnities of an ordination, to take care that every part of the discipline be enforced in his district. He is not only bound to enforce every part himself, but to see that the preachers under his charge do the same. How then, does he enforce the requirement, if the candidate desires it, to *immerse him?* Why, he affirms that baptize never means immerse, when used in a sacramental, or theological sense, though this is precisely the sense in which it is used in his discipline! Not only so, but he declared, in the presence of hundreds, in our discussion with him, that the discipline was wrong on that point, and that he had not obeyed it in thirteen years, by immersing any person himself. But when pressed for violating his ordination vow, in failing to enforce every part of the discipline, he said he did enforce it, by enjoining it upon some other preacher, when a person desired to be immersed, to administer, who believed in it!!!

Such is the elastic conscience of the man who writes against immersion. In opposition to the lexicons quoted by himself, in opposition to Wesley, Clarke, and his own discipline, he affirms that baptize never means immerse, and when shown that his solemn ordination vow required him to enforce *every part,* not excepting to *immerse* those who desire it, he refuses to administer, because he does not believe in it, but enjoins it upon some other man to do what he affirms there is no authority for! If this is not Jesuitism, none can be found on this earth. Having now shown the Doctor where he stands in making his unfounded assertion, we shall proceed to take him through the *washing* process.

On pages 144 and 145, we find the following: "Having our hearts sprinkled *(baptized)* from an evil conscience, and our bodies washed *(baptized)* with pure water." Now, one fault we have for years found with sprinklers is, that they find *too much* baptism. The

Doctor is one of this class; he finds baptism where there is none in Greek or English. The figurative expression, "Having our hearts sprinkled from an evil conscience," though it contains the precious word *sprinkle,* has no Holy Ghost baptism or any other kind in it. The Doctor had said, preceding the above remark, "The soul is to be baptized with the blood of Christ, by the Holy Ghost; the body is to be baptized with water, by a proper administrator." Now, we find nothing about baptizing "the soul" in the word of God, and therefore think this baptism of the soul is only a figment of the Doctor's loose method of thinking. But, after introducing the novel notion of baptizing the soul, the Doctor proceeds to quote a passage setting forth his new doctrine, that has neither of the words, *baptism* nor *soul,* in it. His passage is simply the expression, "Having our *hearts* sprinkled from an evil conscience." It is not the *soul* here mentioned by Paul, but the *heart,* and he does not say anything about its being *baptized,* but *sprinkled.* It is not *baptizo* that is here translated *sprinkle,* but *rantizo.* These two words do not belong to the same family at all, and are "no kin" to each other. Nor is this any less an imposition of the Doctor, than the latter part of the quotation: "Our bodies washed (baptized) with pure water." "Washed," in this passage, is not *baptizo,* but *lotto,* which is only found six times in the new testament,...as follows: John xiii, 10; Acts ix, 37; xvi, 33; Heb., x, 22; 1 Pet. ii, 22; Rev. i, 5. We admit, however, that it expresses the result of baptizing, though not baptizing itself. As *baptizo* is not *louo,* so *immerse* is not *wash*; but if you immerse a man in clean water, the result is that his body is washed; but it does not, therefore, follow that immerse is wash, or a man could not be immersed and not washed. A man baptized in the Holy Spirit, in fire, or in sufferings, is not washed. This shows that baptize is not wash, or a man could not be baptized and not washed. When it is stated that a man is baptized, if we learn whether he is *washed,* it must be from some other word or words besides baptize, for it has no wash in it. If it is said he was baptized *in clean water,* we learn that he was washed, from the words, "in clean water" and not from the word baptize. If we should see an account, that a man had been baptized *in fire,* we should learn that he was burnt, not from baptize, for it does not mean *burn,* but from the words "in fire." The same is true in regard to dying. Some of the lexicons give *dye* as a definition of *bapto* and *baptizo.* But there is no such meaning in either of these words as dye. Baptizing in fire, in the Holy spirit, in sufferings, in clean water, etc., never dyed anything. The idea of *dye* is not in *baptize,* or you could not baptize and not dye. If we read that anything is baptized *in ink,* we know that it is dyed, not from the word *baptized,* but from the words "in ink." To stain, dye, cleanse, wash, drown, purify, etc., may follow as the result of baptizing in certain substances, but the idea is not in the word baptize. This is evident, from Acts xxii, 16, where both *baptize* and *wash* occur in one sentence, or Greek *baptizo* and *apolouo.* "Arise and be *baptized* and *wash* away thy sins." The Holy Spirit here uses two words, and expresses two ideas, or two distinct things. The one follows after, and is the result of the other. The first is to be baptized. Then something follows, in these words: "And wash away thy sins." It may be said, the words, "wash away thy sins," are figurative, and mean pardon. We are perfectly aware of that, but the figure shows that *washing* is a result that follows baptizing in water, or no such figurative expression could arise from it.

We will dismiss the Doctor, for the present, with the single remark, that his practice has neither immersion, pouring, sprinkling, washing, cleansing, purifying, dying, staining, tinging, sinking, or drowning, about it. It is entirely out of the catalogue. As he simply lays moistened fingers upon the forehead, his must simply be *slightly wetting.*

-----o-----

HE that tilleth his land shall have plenty of bread; but he that followeth after vain *persons* shall have poverty enough. Prov. xxviii, 19.

The Christian Ministry.
No. I.

THE Church of Christ was not made for the preachers, but the preachers of Christ were made for the world and the Church. The Church of Christ does not belong to the preachers of Christ—it is not *their* property—but they belong to the Church—are *its* property. The Church is not the servant of the preachers, but preachers of Christ are servants of the Churches. The Church of Christ is not called and sent by preachers, but preachers are called and sent by the Church. Preachers in the kingdom of Christ are no more dignitaries, kings, and priests, than any other members. They are the Lord's instruments, put forth through the Church to do his work, and mighty instruments too, while the Lord is with them, but the poorest, most useless and miserable creatures on this earth when forsaken of God. Or, in other words, when they are doing *the Lord's work,* with an eye single to his glory, there are no such instruments for good among men; but when they become selfish, engage simply in their *own work,* or that which they can turn to their own personal aggrandizement, their usefulness ceases, and they are dead weights upon the cause. Our Lord's own life is the model of all perfection in human character, both public and private. No community need look for any permanent good from any preacher who does not imitate the character of his Lord and Master. He may be much of a gentleman, very fine, pleasant and interesting to worldly minded persons, and not do anything or say anything that would remind anyone of the Saviour of the world. But to come under the name of a preacher of Christ, a disciple of Christ, and not be like him, not make men think of him, love him, and desire to come to him, is a deception upon the Church and the world.

No saying of our Lord needs enforcing upon us in all its amplitude, at the present period, more than his declaration: "My kingdom is not of this world." Paul says: "The wisdom of this world is foolishness with God." "The Lord knoweth the thoughts of the wise, that they are vain." Again, he says, "He taketh the wise in their own craftiness." The holy John says, *"Love* not the world, nor the things of the world; and again, "If any man loves the world, the love of the Father is not in him." Our lord says, "Blessed are the meek, for they shall inherit the earth." The New Testament abounds with the same sentiment, and no man that heeds it can fail to be impressed with its anti-worldly character throughout. But what is the legitimate deduction from all this? Is it not, if the kingdom of God is not of this world, and its subjects not allowed to love the world, but a spiritual kingdom, a divine institution, that its interests cannot be promoted by worldly means and appliances? The kingdom of Christ being a spiritual kingdom, not of this world, not of the nature of the kingdoms of the world, it cannot make conquest by the sword—by the arm of flesh. It is unlike all the kingdoms of this world; is separate and distinct from them, and does not make any direct issue with them, and its subjects may be good citizens and peaceable subjects in any civil government in the world, and indeed are required to be such. But it is as probable that the citizens in the kingdom of Christ could take the sword and with the arm of flesh go forward, build up and propagate his kingdom among men, as that it can be done by resorting to worldly policies, appliances, and appeals to the flesh—to the lusts of the eye, and the pride of life. The holy apostle says, "I came not to you with excellency of speech or of wisdom, declaring unto you the testimony of God." What reason does he assign for this? His reason follows: "For I determined to know nothing among you save Jesus Christ, and him crucified." He did not come among the Corinthians with a flourish of excellency of speech and of wisdom, that might dazzle the eyes, elate the mind, and prevent the cross of Jesus from appearing, but he determined to make known nothing but Christ and him crucified. His own soul was under the power of the cross of Christ; his Redeemer was uppermost in his mind, was his all, and he had counted all things but dross that he might win Christ. He believed that the power to attract, convert and save men was in the cross, or in HIM who hung upon the cross, and not in the excellency of his speech, or the wisdom of men's words, and he desired all men to know that the work was of God and not of man.

By calling illiterate men of Galilee to the apostleship, without worldly wisdom and accomplishments, and placing them before the world as the Lord's instruments to speak to man, a full assurance was given that the work **was** not of man, or of the wisdom of man, but of the wisdom and power of God. The excellency of their speech, the attraction of their personal appearance, and all that pertained to them merely human, it was manifest to all men, could not have moved the souls of men and produced such a revolution in the hearts and lives of such vast multitudes. The work done was too great, too opposite to all movements known among men, too little like this world to be attributed to a human, and therefore must be ascribed to a divine cause. The apostles had no worldly influence upon the masses of society upon whom they operated; they had no worldly attractions needed none, desired none, and used none. But when they approached men, it was with strong confidence in that prime article of their creed: "The gospel is the power of God unto salvation to everyone that believeth." Their confidence was in the grand, transcendently great and stupendous fact that "Christ died for our sins according to the scriptures, that he was buried, and that he rose again the third day according to the scriptures." They spoke of these great facts as sufficient in magnitude to move heaven and earth, and doing so, spoke of them as they really are. But in speaking of them, they were not contriving how they might round off a pretty period, make an oratorical display, or show their eloquence. The story they had to tell was so vast in itself, so vital to all the best interests of all nations and people, and so perfectly filled their own hearts and absorbed their whole powers, that it only appeared necessary to them to tell it in the plainest, simplest and most artless manner, which is always the best, most powerful and effectual way of telling anything great in itself. Nothing appears more contemptible to one who realizes the transcendent glories and majesty of our glorious Redeemer and his gospel, than to see some poor, feeble worms of the dust, with a few fine words, flowery speeches, and well rounded periods, trying to paint the gospel of Christ, to commend it to the children of men. Some flowers are so infinitely exquisite in all the perfections of beauty, attractions and loveliness, that an effort of the finest artist to paint them would only spoil them, obscure their beauty and attractions. The same is true of any attempt to paint the glorious gospel of the blessed God. A human artist would not appear more ridiculous in attempting to add to the beauties and attractions of the hues and symmetry of the rainbow, than he who would attempt to paint, polish and beautify the gospel of Christ. Such a man may show himself, may show his fine skill, what a workman he is in his art; and spectators may see him and his fine painting, and admire both, but they will not see the Redeemer, his word, nor his glories, nor will they worship him. All this kind of thing is of the world, and shows that the preacher's own soul is not filled with the glories of his Lord, and the power of his gospel; that he has no confidence in the attractions of his Lord, who is lifted up to draw all men to him, and in his gospel, his power to salvation to the believer. Hence men listen to such efforts and are frequently highly pleased, while their hearts are not in the least touched with the power of the Lord, and their souls are no more moved to cry out, "what must we do to be saved?" than if they had listened to a fine lecture on astronomy or anatomy. The reason is obvious: The Lord is not in it. His cross is hid by the fine painting, flourishing and display of the mighty man. The Lord is kept back, that the man may appear; the gospel of Christ is not seen nor felt, but the mere show of a poor mortal that would have served a better purpose at a school exhibition, than to have strayed into the place of a gospel preacher, is all that appears.

"But do you intend to discourage classical literature, learning, and refined, elevated, liberal attainments?" Not when consecrated to God; but when used for mere worldly show, and as a means to bring men into notice ignorant of God, there is no greater injury to the Church. If a man's learning is combined with piety, devotion, and consecrated to Jesus Christ, and he is possessed with the humility and meekness inculcated in Christianity, and his learning enables him to unfold the unsearchable riches of Christ, with the simplicity, sincerity and devotion necessary to commend it to the hearts and consciences of men, it is of great value. If the Lord dwells in a man, if the great matters of the kingdom of God fill his soul, and if his learning is used in presenting the simple gospel of Christ in meekness, it may be of great service to him; but it requires much care to keep the Lord in front of it, so that the hearers will see nothing but him. The more gifted the man, the more learned and powerful, the better, if all his powers are engaged in setting forth and honoring the Lord—sanctifying *Him* in the eyes of the people. At the same time, he should rely upon no learning, no talent, or power that he possesses, but upon the Lord, upon his gospel, the power of God unto salvation to everyone who believes. He must look to heaven for the means to move men to repent; he must appeal to God, and keep God and his works before his audience, and in this way show that his confidence is in Christianity itself and the Author of it, and not in himself, not in man. "Whether men have what the world calls learning or not, they must know God, and have the love of God in their hearts, if they would induce others to love him and turn to him. B. F.

-----o-----

Mission of Infidelity.
No. II.

IN our previous article, under the above caption, we confined our observations mainly to the deteriorating tendencies of Infidelity, without attempting any description of its various methods of accomplishing its work. In this article we propose to enter upon its methods of operation. It is not confined to anyone method or form of operation. It proposes no system or plan of action. It is confined to no rules of warfare, has no laws of argumentation, no definite mode of attack, nor laws of honor in conducting the battle. It is perfectly unscrupulous, and will adopt any stratagem that can be invented to oppose and defeat the truth.

The mode of warfare adopted by Paine, Hume, Volney, Bolingbroke, Voltaire and their cotemporaries, was manly, noble and honorable, compared with many of the methods employed in these times, in opposing divine revelation. They made a direct, fair and palpable issue with believers in the Bible. They openly denied the divinity of the Bible and the Lord Jesus Christ. Even Robert Owen, in his discussion with Mr. Campbell, openly and boldly affirmed that " all religion is founded in ignorance." But it has been discovered, in this *inventive* and *progressive* age, that this bold, manly and candid issue with Christianity, did not succeed well. It has been found too direct, plain and palpable for success, and that something more circuitous, indirect and stealthy would succeed better. Hence the citadel of truth is now approached almost invariably by a circumlocution, under some kind of a garb, cloak or pretense of faith. The worst attacks upon the Bible, religion or morality, mow made, are under some pretense, form and name of religion. Let us then look at some of these wily and insidious methods of attack.

1. The first one of these side-issue schemes that we shall mention, goes under the name of *Universalism.* It is frequently called " a system of faith," but we hold it to be a deadly enemy of all faith; inimical to the Bible, to piety and even morality. But it makes its attacks by a circumlocution, indirectly, all the time professing to believe. It infuses its neutralizing influences so stealthily and insidiously, that many of the unwary mistake it for a system of faith. But we invite men of reason, candor and cool reflection, to stop and take one deliberate look at it. "When the faith of Christ was preached by the Apostles, it led men to repent of their sins, turn to God, confess Christ, be baptized, unite as disciples in the Church organization, meet for prayers, exhortation, celebrating the Lord's death and sufferings; continuing steadfastly in the Apostles' doctrine, etc. In our own time, when religious men preach the faith of Christ, those who receive it, are led to most solemn repentance, abandon-

ment of their sins, union with the Church, regular attendance upon divine ordinances, prayers, exhortations and unremitted attendance upon the worship of God. The preaching of the gospel led men to inquire, "what must I do to be saved?"

But who is there that does not know that preaching Universalism leads no man to inquire, "what shall I do to be saved?" It leads no man to repent. It has no repentance in it. Indeed, it ignores and subverts the very basis of all repentance. It induces no man to say, as he leaves the preaching, "I intend doing better and being more conformed to the life of Christ." It leads no man to confess Christ. Paul says, "with the heart man believeth unto righteousness, and with the mouth confession is made unto salvation." This is something unknown to the whole scheme of Universalism. Those who collect around him who preaches Universalism, and swallow it down, never confessed the Lord Jesus with the lips in their lives, unless they made a profession of the faith of Christ in some other Church, from which they have apostatized. The solemn institution of baptism, to which the Lord himself submitted, which he enjoined in the same commission containing salvation for every creature; which was practiced by the Apostles and submitted to by all the first converts, is almost if not entirely ignored and set aside by the artful and evasive scheme to which we refer. All the Bible says on this subject, is nothing in the system here spoken of. This insidious scheme subverts all remission of sins, hides and shuns all divine appointments for that important object. It knows nothing of all divine influences, all piety and devotion to God. What has it done with the Lord's supper? that significant and solemn appointment of the Savior, to place his sufferings before us and keep him in remembrance? It has set it aside, subverted it and turned it out of the assemblies. Where are their meetings for prayers? Where are their Sunday Schools? Where are their Church Organizations? Where are their Meeting Houses? What have they done with all the solemn and sublime institutions and worship of the meek and lowly Redeemer?

After preaching and debating through this country for thirty years, how many churches have they organized and meeting regularly to worship? They boast of great numbers, numbers equal to some of the most popular parties; but where are their organizations? We all know that largo numbers may be found who talk this system, in many towns, with wealth and every facility for meeting and worship; and yet they do not meet once in three months. Look at their rallying points, where they have numbers and wealth, and have had for years, such as Knightstown, Dublin, Philomath, Ind.; Oxford, O.; Warsaw, Ky., etc., where they have been battling orthodoxy for many years, and tell what they have done. They have "strengthened the hands of the wicked, that he should not return from his wicked way, by *promising him life."* See Ez., xiii, 22. They have opposed and pulled down other men's work; but what have they built up? What have they built up, and what are they building up generally throughout this country? It is manifest as day, that they are not building up anything but unbelief. The mission of the doctrine, and of the party, is to weaken faith, weaken obedience, weaken all incentives to repentance, harden men's hearts, and lead them to laugh over the sins of the world. It leads men to laugh over the most solemn things the Almighty has ever said, and induces them to descend to the lowest sophistries, quibbles, and duplicity possible for a human being.

That the obvious tendency of Universalism is irreligious; that it is opposed to holiness, to reformation of life; that it is in eternal hostility to all efforts to make the world better; that it paralyzes and neutralizes the efforts of men to serve God—is one of the most manifest impressions upon the mind, both from the theory itself, and from the history of its practical workings among men. No pretended system in our time has been characterized by such daring and unblushing effrontery. It comes forward under a pretense of faith, but ridicules the most awful and fearful things which that faith reveals. It discards the eternal discriminations which the faith of the Lord Jesus maintains between the righteous and the wicked—between those who serve God, and those who serve him not—

between vice and virtue—except the reward of the one and the punishment of the other, received in this life. It proposes to believe the Bible, and would have men believe that it teaches that he who was an atheist, a deist, and a scoffer at all that God has said, and a blasphemer of the name of God till he breathed the last breath, shall be received up into glory, and seated down with the holy martyrs of Jesus, and enjoy God forever! No other system has so far imposed upon the credulity of mankind as to face the world, as well as the heavens, and declare that the lake of fire prepared for the devil and his angels, where the beast and the false prophets shall be tormented day and night, forever and ever—the *gehenna* of fire, where the worm dieth not, and the fire is not quenched—is in this world, and that the wicked we see are actually enduring its punishments!

No infidel desires any better opposition to religion than this. No man who hates the Bible, and wishes its influence upon the world counteracted, desires any more effectual method of doing it than this, so far as men will receive it. Those who fall under its influence will neither worship God nor keep his commandments. Atheism itself has all the incentives to a righteous life found in this system, and may be trusted just as far. Its influence is to harden the heart, and fill the world with impenitence and indifference.B. F.

Organization—No. II.

We suggested, some months since, that those favorable to some kind of clerical organization should go into the work, and give us a practical demonstration of the excellencies of their theory. It is an easy matter to concoct and detail a fine theory upon paper, or in the pulpit; but to put it in practice, and show that it can achieve what its friends think, is a different matter. Some nine churches in Kentucky have given evidence that they are in earnest in the matter, or at least enough to make a representation have given this evidence. If the cause of "decline among the churches in Kentucky" is in our want of organization, we may expect a new era to dawn upon us, now that this work of organization has commenced. It has commenced, too, in a good place, and in good hands, to make a fair trial. But we reserve our comments till the reader shall see for himself the whole of what the first effort, aided by the talented, learned, and excellent brethren, H. T. Anderson and S. Ayres, has brought forth. The following is the document:

Proceedings of a Convention of Delegates from Christian Churches, of Garrard, Lincoln, Casey, Mercer, and Boyle Counties, held in Danville, on Thursday and Friday, the 13*th and* 14*th of December, 1855.*

According to an arrangement made during the months of October and November, a meeting was held in Danville, on Thursday and Friday, the 13th and 14th of December, 1855, for the purpose of forming an Association or Union of the Christian Churches of the counties of Garrard, Lincoln, Casey, Mercer, and Boyle; when the following churches were represented by their delegates:

County of Garrard—Lancaster and Pleasant Grove.

County of Lincoln—Stanford, Hustonville, McCormack's, and Givens'.

County of Casey—Green River Church.

County of Mercer—Cane Run.

County of Boyle.—Sycamore and Danville.

After much discussion, conducted in a kind and brotherly spirit, the following constitution was unanimously adopted:

Having considered the state of the cause within our bounds, and being convinced that the condition of the churches is not such in all respects as the will of our Divine Master, made known through the Holy Oracles, requires; and perceiving that we have hitherto confined our labors too much within ourselves, and that we have not sufficiently cultivated a spirit of association and of joint action; convinced, also, that the various members of the body of Christ are mutually dependent on one another for aid, strength, counsel, and support, and being fully persuaded that in our being brought into more intimate union, and being bound together by one common interest, we shall be able to effect much good for ourselves, and for the common cause of truth; to secure these ends, we, the delegates of the churches above named, do form the following

CONSTITUTION:

ARTICLE 1. There shall assemble, annually or semi-annually, as may be determined, a meeting which shall be styled "*The Central (Kentucky) Christian Union,*" and which shall be composed, first, of all the ministers of the gospel in good fellowship with, and residing within the bounds of, the churches composing this Association; *second,* of one Elder from each church, to be chosen by the church; and *third,* of representatives from each church, in the proportion of one for each church of one hundred members or less, and one for each additional hundred members, which representatives may be either Deacons or private members.

ART. 2. The *Union* may receive from the churches composing it, letters of information concerning their condition, the number of members, increase, deaths, their spiritual health, etc.

ART. 3. The *Union* shall have the right to hear any case which may be laid before it, by any church or churches composing it, and shall consider such case, and express their judgment upon it.

ART. 4. If there shall at any time arise any who shall teach things tending to the injury of the churches and the cause which we plead, such person or persons shall be subject to the discipline of the *Union.*

ART. 5. The *Union* shall take into consideration the subject of education, both general and ministerial. It shall consider and act upon plans for Bible distribution, missionary objects, tract distribution, Sunday schools, and upon whatever else may tend to the welfare of the cause of our Divine Master.

ART. 6. The *Union* may cooperate with any other association of our brotherhood, whether district or State meeting, or general convention, and may appoint delegates to them.

ART. 7. The *Union* shall have power to pass all necessary by-laws for carrying out its objects, as expressed in this Constitution.

ART. 8. The officers of the *Union* shall be a President, a Secretary, and such others as may be considered necessary.

ART. 9. Delegates from a majority of the churches composing this *Union* shall be a quorum-for business.

ART. 10. This constitution may at any time be altered or amended by a majority vote of those who compose the *Union.*

The foregoing articles were separately considered and adopted, and afterward, as a whole, on motion of Bro. G. C. Riffe, and by a rising vote, were unanimously adopted.

H. T. ANDERSON, *Pres't.*
S. AYRES, *Sec'y.*

NAMES OF THE DELEGATES COMPOSING THIS CONVENTION.

Lancaster Church —Jesse Embry, Jacob Robinson, Albert Herndon, Wm. H. Pettus.

Pleasant Grove—W. B. Middleton.
Stanford—N. G. Tevis.
Hustonville—Elder W. L. Williams.
McCormack's—Marcus Helm, Z. Hughs, W. Helm.
Givens—.Jas. Warren, Jas. Crome, G. W. Givens.
Cane Run—Elder H. T. Anderson, T. Bergen, J. G. Lipscomb, J, B. Bowman, A. H. Bowman.
Green River—G. C. Riffe.
Sycamore—J. G. Phillips, N. H. Elder.
Danville—J. Smith, S. Ayres, J. Harlan, P. B. Mason, C. T. Worthington.

A number of brethren, not delegates, were present, who, by resolution inviting them, participated in the discussions.

RESOLUTIONS.

The following resolutions were adopted by the Convention:

On motion of Bro. J. Embry,

Resolved, That we, the delegates present, will urge upon our respective churches the adoption of the foregoing constitution, and will also use our earnest efforts to bring the subject before other churches not here represented.

Adopted by a rising vote, unanimously.

On motion,

Resolved, That brethren H. T. Anderson, W. L. Williams, and G. W. Givens be a committee to prepare a preamble, to be prefixed to the Constitution.

Resolved, That the Secretary have printed a sufficient number of copies of the proceedings of this Convention, for distribution among the churches within our bounds.

Resolved, That the Saturday before the third Lord's day in February, 1856, be appointed for the first meeting of the *Central (Kentucky) Christian Union.*

Adjourned with prayer.

H. T. ANDERSON, *Pres't.*
S. AYRES, *Sec'y.*

To the Churches in the counties of Garrard, Lincoln, Casey, Mercer, and Boyle: DEAR BRETHREN—

Please give the subject of *organization,* as presented in the foregoing Constitution, a calm, dispassionate, and thorough examination, and, in connection with your investigations, carefully read certain articles entitled *"The Nature of the Christian Organization,"* in the *Millennial Harbinger* of 1841 and 1842, especially that in the volume of 1842, which commences on page 59.

For the truth's sake,
H. T. ANDERSON.
DECEMBER 16, 1856.

This meeting makes no reference to the Bible, nor its authority, except to assert in a general way that the churches are not in such a condition, in all respects, as our Divine Master requires; but the president refers us to the *Millennial Harbinger* for authority! Now we have quite a distinct recollection of some heavy complaints against the *Christian Baptist,* for circulating improper sentiments on this very subject; but it appears now that authority is to be drawn from the *Millennial Harbinger* to counteract the *Christian Baptist*. But, passing this, we proceed to notice their move more carefully.

We are truly sorry that this controversy has come up. It appears that schism among men is becoming so rife, that no great and good work can he prosecuted with general unanimity. Our power must constantly be weakened by jarring and opposing elements. I am truly sorry these brethren have made the move they have; because I esteem them, love them, and desire the most fraternal feeling between us, and I fear that I cannot make the objections I solemnly entertain without producing unpleasantness. We object to their movement in the following particulars:

1. The object of the meeting—"for the purpose of forming an association OF union of the Christian Churches," etc. A meeting for such a purpose as this is wholly unknown to the New Testament. There is not a hint of the kind in the Christian code.

2. This meeting calls into existence a new set of officers, wholly unknown to the New Testament. The New Testament knows no president or secretary,—no delegates, either of preachers or private members—of an association of churches.

3. The New Testament knows nothing of meeting annually or semi-annually, in the "Central Christian Union," "which shall be composed 1st, of all the ministers of the gospel in good fellowship," "one elder from each Church" and "one representative for one hundred members." This is wholly a new order of things, and throwing wide the gates for all kinds of mischief.

4. The fourth article of the Constitution makes this Union of preachers, elders and delegates an umpire to decide upon the doctrine that shall be preached in the Churches and to exercise discipline over men who shall teach erroneous doctrine. The private members in the nine Churches composing the Central Union, from this time forth, may receive the doctrine preached to them with implicit confidence, as they have committed the guardianship of the faith to their spiritual guides, who have power to judge for them and exercise discipline.

5. Indeed, this Union seems to pretty much dispense with Churches and such officers as the New Testament recognizes, for, after enumerating several things which it is to do and act upon, it adds, "and upon whatever else may tend to the welfare of the cause of our Divine Master." This comprehends the whole.

6. God has constituted the *Church* the pillar and support of the truth, and it is the duty of the Church, the whole Church, in every place, as the only organization having any authority from God, to act for itself and do its own business. No officer in the kingdom of God, has any authority over Churches or preachers except the officers of individual congregations. The New Testament knows no jurisdiction of any office beyond the individual congregation, except where an evangelist is building up and establishing new congregations.

7. Let the Churches go into such a Central Union as these brethren have, and the first difficulty that shall arise among the leading men, will infuse confusion and distraction throughout all the congregations combined in it. A general division cannot take place while the individual, congregational, and, as we are confident, the scriptural organization obtains. Combine the Churches in an Association, and let some difficulty occur among the leading men, and they will sunder the Churches from one side of the country to the other.

B. F.

-----o-----

The following came to hand, after the foregoing was in type, and as it comes from a full grown man—one of mature years, extensive reading and experience, We let it speak for itself.—ED.

NICHOLASVILLE, KY., Feb. 12th, 1856.

DEAR BRO. FRANKLIN: I cannot furnish you a discourse for your March number, but I hope yet to write some for you. I have just been to Pleasant Grove, between here and Danville, where I have engaged to preach, once a month, the present year.

You will see by the document I send you, that some of our Churches, in the Counties of Garrard, Lincoln, Casey, Mercer and Boyle, held a Convention by delegates, at Danville in December last. The result of the deliberations of said Convention was the formation and adoption of a Constitution of ten articles, among which the third and fourth deserve especial notice. They read thus:—

"ART. 3. The Union shall have the right to hear any case which may be laid before it, by any Church or Churches composing it, and consider such case, and express their judgment upon it."

"ART. 4. If there shall at any time arise, any who shall teach things tending to the injury of the Churches, and the cause which we plead, such person or persons shall be subject to the discipline of the Union." That our brethren who formed the Constitution of which the above articles make a conspicuous and ominous part, were actuated by the best of motives, and really believe that its practical adoption by our Churches, will cure very many of the evils they are suffering, I do not doubt. But I must be allowed to express the overwhelming conviction, that so far from curing these evils, its adoption will make *bad, infinitely worse.* That we have here the outlines of a Court of Appeals distinct from the Congregations and above them, with badly defined, but great powers; and one too, which from its very nature, must be quite tardy in its operations; and worst of all—one which has no countenance from the word of God—are positions, to my mind, most palpable. Let us look a little narrowly at article third. What is meant by the right of the Union to hear and decide upon any case brought before it, by any Church or Churches? Does it mean no more than that it may give advice, which may be received, or rejected, by the Churches with impunity? If this is all, we have little to object. But we apprehend that Brother Anderson, who I understand wrote it, and Brother Ayers, and perhaps others who adopted it, mean more. If these brethren then, who were prominent in this movement, meant only this, or more than this, they owe it to themselves, and the Church to define their position. This is all we have to say at present on this article. A word or two in regard to article fourth. This article, as you will see by reading it, makes the Union the supreme judge of sound doctrine. And though it designates no particular Teachers, I suppose it means Elders, or Bishops and Evangelists. Suppose, then, a Bishop or a Pastor of a Congregation, arise and teach things "tending to the injury" of the Church to which he belongs, must that Church allow him to occupy their pulpit, until the next session of the Union?! Or, may that Church try him, and reject him as a heretic?! If you say they may not, where is the independence of the Church?! And if you say they may, then by your own decision, your Court of Appeals is a nullity. Or will the advocates of this article maintain that the Union would have a right in such a case, if they found evidence satisfactory to them, to reverse the decision of the Church, and send back their Pastor, whom they had unanimously excluded, and require them to support him and receive his doctrine as orthodox?!

A beautiful engine this, to promote the peace, purity and spiritual progress of the Churches!

But I have done—I intended to say but a word. I wish you to publish the document I send you, or at least the Constitution, which is now being submitted to the Churches in the bounds of the "Central (Ky.) Christian Union," and make such remarks upon it, as you may think the interests of our cause require. I think it demands prompt attention. Please show the document to the Editors of the *Age*, and request them to notice it in their next issue. Yours truly,

JOHN ROGERS.

-----o-----

The following is the decided voice of another of Kentucky's ablest and most experienced men. It speaks for itself on the foregoing subject.—ED.

PARIS, (KY.) Jan. 15th, 1856.

BROTHER FRANKLIN:

Dear Sir: Yours came to hand by due course of mail. I also received the first number of your *Review*. Accept my thanks, both for your letter and your periodical.

I have read, I think, nearly all that you have written, from the beginning, and I am glad to see you again on the arena, with a broad space, within which to battle it for the truth, and I trust a good supply of ammunition. You are, in my estimation, *one* of the *few* suited to the editorial chair. Clear, cool, strong, discriminating, balanced!—without these characteristics, a writer cannot succeed, to any great extent, in the advocacy of Apostolic Christianity. Hence, many have made such havoc, both of themselves and the cause of truth.

One special reason, however, why I rejoice to see you again before the public, is, not only that I consider you sound in the faith, and able to vindicate it, but sound also in *organization*. This question may be destined to produce much perplexity among our brethren, and to do some harm. It will probably be thrust upon us from time to time, so that we shall be compelled to discuss it. In that case I shall greatly calculate upon you as a host upon what I consider the scriptural side of that question.

And since I have named organization, it may not be improper for me to say that I go against all Church organizations that are *above, below* or *beyond* the scriptures. Victory perched upon the banner of the cross, only under the apostolic organization. So soon as the "mystery of iniquity" destroyed the simplicity of this organization, and in the ratio in which other organizations became paramount, the Church became not only corrupted, but enfeebled, and unfitted for its high vocation. With full faith, therefore, in the Christian organization, as the apostles left it, call me *ultra, fogy,* or what you please, I say, sink or swim, live or die, survive or perish, I go for that old organization, now and forever!

Truly,   A. RAINES.

Please find two dollars enclosed. Anna Lee $1,00, N. Middletown, Bourbon Co., Ky.; and

J.M. Berry, $1,00, Clintonville, Bourbon Co., Kentucky.

Trine Immersion.

WE have been requested from several sources of the highest respectability, to write an article on Trine Immersion. We intended complying with this request sooner, but, owing to pressing engagements, have not been able to do so. Nor can we now devote a large space to it.

Trine Immersion, is three immersions, or immersing three times. Triune God, is "three one God," or three persons in one Godhead. Trine Immersion is an adjunct of Trinitarian-ism, and consequently was unknown to the whole Church till the dispute touching the Trinity had been introduced. When the Church introduced the learned nonsense of three Gods in one God, the doctrine of three immersions was invented, introducing into the three Gods in one. We write from home, having no access to authorities, but from memory, we believe Trine Immersion existed as early as the fourth century. Nothing but immersion is mentioned for baptism in any writing of the first or second century; and long after the introduction of Infant Baptism, infants were not only immersed, but, in many instances, immersed three times. No period of the history of the Church, or of the world, gives clearer evidence of the inclination of man to corrupt the institutions of heaven, than the second and third centuries. While one party was maintaining the most speculative theories of the three persons in the Godhead, and hence maintaining the necessity of three immersions, another set of visionaries were contending that infants were sinners and must be baptized to save them from the Adamic sin. Another class, about the same time, were mystifying the minds of the people with the notion, that if a person should sin after baptism, he could not obtain pardon, and consequently that baptism should be deferred till a late period in life, that no sin should be committed after baptism. But we shall not go into the examination of the doctrine of these parties further now than simply to state our objections to Trine Immersion.

There is a party sparsely scattered in some sections of the United States, called Tunkers or, as some call them, Dunkards, who pertinacious and invariably practice Trine Immersion, or literally *three immersions*. The people here alluded to are a kind, friendly and generally peaceable order, and, in many respects, practice the religion of Christ with much humility and simplicity. But in the matter of this article, we think, they make a very serious perversion of the gospel. We object to them on the point in question, as follows:

1. Trine Immersion destroys and entirely defeats the symbolical or emblematical design of the ordinance. As Christ was buried in the tomb, so are we "buried with him in baptism." As he rose from the dead, so we rise from our burial in baptism to walk in a new life. See Rom. vi, 1—8. Christ was buried *once,* and we are buried with him, in baptism, *once,* not three times, to represent his *one* burial. He rose from his burial *once,* and, in imitation of his rising from the dead *once,* we rise *once* from the baptismal grave, not three times. As Christ died *once,* we die to sin *once.* As he was buried *once,* we are buried *once,* in baptism. As he rose from the dead *once,* we rise *once* from baptism. This beautiful and divinely designed analogy, is subverted and entirely destroyed, in an administration, that buries the person *three times* and raises the candidate *three times.* Christ died but once, was buried but once, and rose from the grave but once; so we die to sin but once, are buried in baptism but once, and rise from the baptismal grave but once.

2. In the same passage, the same verse and the same sentence, where the word of God affirms that, "there is one Lord" and "one faith," it also affirms that there is "one baptism." See Eph. iv, 5. When this whole passage is translated, so as to give us, in the place of the Greek *baptizo,* immerse, it affirms that "there is one Lord, one faith, and one immersion." That the Apostle here affirms, that "there is but one Lord and one faith," no one who understands the force of language denies. It is equally clear, that with precisely the same force, he affirms that "there is but one baptism," or when *baptizo* is translated, that "there is but one immersion." It would be equally as good doctrine, and do as little violence to the sacred canon, to contend for three Lords and three faiths, as to teach and practice, as the Tonkers do, three immersions. It is an evident violation of the manifest intention of the Apostle, and tends to schism—the identical thing that he was guarding against. In inculcating unity among the children of God, he exhorts them to endeavor to keep the unity of the spirit in the bond of peace, and as a reason for this, gives them an epitome of the units of Christianity. This divine epitome contains seven units, which every man of God is bound to maintain throughout Christendom, in these days of schism. These units may be regarded as articles of faith in the Christian code. The man who is not sound here, is unsound in the "unity of the spirit" and is not orthodox, in the true import of that term.

3. The first unit, or article of faith; in this epitome, relates to the Church or body of Christ. All creeds have an article concerning the Church. This one is not like that in other creeds. It is very short and concise, but inflexible. It affirms that "there is one body." He who denies that there is one body or one Church, or affirms that there is more than one body, is not sound in the faith—a heretic.

4. The second relates to the spirit, and is unlike any article of faith, upon the spirit, in any other creed in the world. It simply affirms that "there is one spirit." He who denies that there is one spirit, or affirms that there is more than one spirit, is not sound in the faith, but advocates a heresy.

5. The third unit, or article in this epitome, relates to the Christian hope, and is not found in the articles of faith in most creeds. The Apostle affirms, that "there is one hope." He who denies that there is one hope, or affirms that there is more than one, is not sound in the faith, but maintains a heresy.

The fourth unit, or article, relates to Christ, and differs from any article we ever saw concerning him, in any other creed. It affirms of him, that "there is one Lord," He who denies that there is one Lord, or affirms that there is more than one,

maintains a heresy and should be dealt with as a heretic.

5. The fifth unit, or article, in this epitome, affirms, that "there is one faith." He who denies that there is one faith, or affirms that there is more than one faith, is at war with the whole force and intention of the passage, is unsound in the faith—a heretic.

6. The sixth unit, or article, in this epitome, affirms, that "there is one baptism," or one immersion. He who denies that there is one, baptism, or affirms that there is more than one, is at issue with the whole force and intention of this passage, and consequently advocating schism in the body of Christ.

7. The seventh and last unit, or article in this epitome, relates to the Deity, and differs from the article of faith concerning him, in any book, except the Bible. It affirms that "there is one God and Father of all." He who denies that there is one God, or he who maintains that there is more than one God, is at war with the whole force of this passage.

Here is briefly Paul's epitome of the units embodied in the one system of Christ. We maintain, that it is as sound reason, sound theology, and sound adherence to the obvious import of language, to teach that there are three bodies, three spirits, three hopes, three Lords, three faiths and three Gods, as that there are three baptisms. It is as manifest as noonday, that as there is one body, one spirit, one hope, one Lord and one faith, there should be but one baptism into the one body, one spirit, one hope, one Lord, one faith and one God, the Father of all, above all, in all, and through all.   B. F.

-----O-----

JANUARY, 17th, 1856, HARRISON, O.

DEAR BROTHER FRANKLIN: I have received the first number of the *Review,* and am well pleased, with everything in it except one, but of that, I am undecided, and, unless you can explain it to my understanding, I must remain so. In No. 11 of your Prospectus, you say, "but the editor will ride no hobbies, countenance no one-ideaism, and his pages shall be used for no such purpose." Now, Sir, I am utterly at a loss to know what you intend to exclude from your pages as "one-ideaism."

Units make up the sum of millions, trillions, etc.; ones make up the 900,000,000 of human beings who people the earth, and the great "body of sin" is made up of single sins; the incalculable sum of ideas that now fill the minds of earth's myriads, are capable of being numbered, from one almost to infinity, and each single idea is the image of a single *thing;* and there is a word expressive of, or the representative of that idea. All the ideas that compose the mighty whole, are single and count but *one;* but each idea has a number of kindred ones that cluster around it and in the mind are inseparable from it. For example, we have the word *drunkenness,* expressing one idea only, that idea is the image of a *thing.* Who can think of the *thing* without thinking of every-*thing* connected with it? its cause, character, good or bad, and its effects on the countless millions of our race; and if its character and effects are adjudged *bad,* what philanthropist can refrain from pondering in his mind the best means of removing the cause, that the effect may cease. We also have the word *Slavery,* representing *one idea,* and that idea the image of a *thing;* who can think of the *thing* without thinking of many *things* inseparably connected with it; its origin and character, and its effects on the slave and his master. And if its effects on both are decided to be evil and only evil, and that continually, who can refrain from reflecting on the means of its removal from the world, and particularly from the Churches.

I might multiply examples, but these are sufficient. I now ask for information, which of the "*one-ideas*" that compose the mighty whole, are you going to exclude from your pages; or do you intend to say that you will not devote your whole time and energies in discussing one single subject. No, you don't mean that, for you say "the truth, the whole truth, and nothing but the truth," will be maintained by you; and surely the whole truth has more than one idea. Now my dear brother, let me say that whether you intended it or not, the No. 11 of your Prospectus will be taken for Benj. Franklin's *pledge,* that on a certain subject, obnoxious to some, your mouth shall be padlocked, and that though your mind be allowed to range in the mighty ocean of ideas, good and bad, and to commend the one and reprove the other, on that one idea, you will be dumb as the dogs in Egypt If this has for a moment been your intention, throw that padlock into the pit where the old Serpent, the Devil and Satan is ultimately to go, and walk forth in the true dignity of a son of God, disenthralled from every encumbrance, and interdict nothing from your pages connected with truth, *the whole* truth, reproving and rebuking with all long suffering and doctrine wherever it is necessary, and though the human heart, in regard to some darling sins, may be as hard to melt as an iceberg, yet the full warm beams of the sun of righteousness can, and will, effect much that to man seems impossible.

Give this a place in the *Review,* and respond to suit yourself.

Your brother in the good hope.

W. M. IRVIN.

REMARKS.

We have never penned a little sentence that has occasioned so much uneasiness, called forth so many letters, and brought down upon our head such unmerciful strictures, as the one alluded to above, viz: "The editor will ride no hobbies, countenance no one-ideaism, and his pages shall be used for no such purpose." Through respect to an elderly brother, one we love and whose intentions we think, are good, and who writes in a good spirit, we have given the foregoing space, as a kind of exponent of those upon the same subject, only that others are scarcely, any of them, so well tempered. Those that are abusive, as some of them are, with those who have nothing new to offer, with a long list of hobby-riders, who have sunk the last vestige of influence they have, and only appear grieved that they cannot induce others to act as foolishly as they have done, we must let pass in the most profound silence. But a respectful answer to candid men we think due, and shall strive to give. Men who have but one idea, and probably that a mistaken one, which they have stereotyped, adopted as their creed, before which they stand and adore, bending reason, politics, religion, the Bible and world, and if they could, would bend the heavens to it, are beyond the precincts of our mission. We do not believe the Almighty has put it in our power, or made it our duty to convince such. There is a soundness in the great mind of mankind; there is reason and an appreciation of what is just and right, and to that soundness, reason and appreciation, we shall make our appeal in all those matters, and leave the event with God. But we proceed to Bro. Irvin's troubles.

He seems a little alarmed at our declaration, that we will ride no hobbies and give countenance to no one-ideaism. Now, what is the trouble here? Does he desire us to ride hobbies and give countenance to one-ideaism? But he finds two sins, viz: Drunkenness and Slavery, which he understands and thinks others understand, us to mean by the declaration above, that we "sing dumb" upon. He must then, think these subjects hobbies, one-ideaism, or that we did not mean what we said, or else did not understand what we were saying. Not only so, but in that same sentence, we promise that "whatever is lovely, of good report, pure, peaceable, tending to the good of man and the glory of God, shall be maintained and defended"—that we "will maintain *the truth, as it is in Christ—the whole truth, and nothing but the truth."* Now does he understand the subjects of which he speaks to be hobbies, one-ideaism, not included in whatever is lovely, of good report, pure, peaceable, for the good of man and the glory of God, the truth as it is in Christ—the whole truth and nothing but the truth? He must think so, or that we did not mean what we said, or that we did not know what we did mean. We think the scope given, in this eleventh item sufficiently ample for any good man.

But our brother wishes us to define what we mean by one-ideaism, and explains to us how the universe is made up of atoms. With this request we will cheerfully comply. It is to be carried away with one idea. The idea may be a good one, or it may not; but one-ideaism, is giving an idea an undue importance. A man addicted to one-ideaism, can no more cover it than a leopard can change his spots. If he attempts to pray, he will commence with something else as a stepping stone, regularly paving the way and unmistakably

making his way to his favorite idea. When it is put forth and he is delivered of it, he is relieved for the time being, especially if he finds that it annoys someone. If you call on him for an exhortation, a sermon, or if he writes, he may wind round and round, trace back and forward, but it will, in spite of himself, in all his efforts to conceal it, be manifest to all, that he takes no interest in all he is saying, only as it subserves his purpose, in paving the way to the one idea, the center around which the whole man revolves, and to which his entire existence is subservient. If that one idea is not dragged in, the man is not relieved, his burden is still upon his soul, and he is in travail waiting to be relieved.

You will see this class of men at meetings, and conventions, both political and religious, without the most distant idea of promoting the objects of the meeting, convention, etc., as the case may be, but with no higher aim than introducing their idea to notice, making the meeting an engine, and men, met under other obligations, and with the ostensible object of the meeting before them, instruments to carry the *pet idea* on the high road to fame. Sometimes this class of men, because other men have other objects in view, are actually engaged in some good and great work, have not time, will not be annoyed nor turned aside to hear them nor dispute with them, or if they do, give them but a passing notice, think all the world afraid of them. But they need have no fears on this score. An idea that has not force enough to burst its way forth into the world in defiance of all fogies and conservatives, would die a natural death, if the parent of it could get someone to bring it forth.

In our remarks, relative to hobbies and one-ideaism, we were not confined to anyone class of hobbyists and one-ideaists, but to all classes. A man who makes one-idea the center of his life, or makes it his hobby, we care not what that idea is, unless it be the great idea of Christianity itself, will never do anything more than perplex and annoy others. We should make the Lord Jesus the supreme idea, and make everything bow to him. Let the pure and holy religion of the Lord and Saviour be the supreme idea, and let everything in us and about us bend to it. It is divine; it is safe, or there is nothing safe in this world. God parted the heavens to reveal his Son to man, made all nature yield to his mandate, the earth to tremble when he died, and graves to open when he rose, to evince his Divinity, that the great remedial system might have a common center upon which for the soul of man to rest "If I be lifted up," said this great Sun and center, "I will draw all men unto me." Let no side-issue, no irrelevant question; let no question, no matter how great, draw our attention away from Him who is the way, the truth and the life. Many of the disputes of these times, are started by the enemy to detract attention from Him who is the center of all spiritual light and life. B. F.

-----o-----

The many "Human" Creeds, Disciplines and Confessions of Faith vs. The one "Divine" Creed, Discipline and Confession.

CHAPTER I.
OF FAITH.

IN investigating and contrasting the various human systems of religion, confessions of faith, forms of discipline, and creeds, with the *one* Divine, I shall permit them to speak, if not always *verbatim*, in *substance* for themselves. In the sequel, it will appear evident that they not only contradict themselves and each other, but that they are inconsistent in their various theories, and inharmonious with the Bible. But we shall hear them speak for themselves, from their standards of orthodoxy:

Presbyterian—Faith is the *alone* instrument of justification.

Methodist—Yes, sir; the doctrine that we are justified by faith *only* is most wholesome, and very full of comfort.

Christian—But, my dear brethren, do you not perceive how that by *works* we are justified, and *not* by faith *only?* But, will you be so kind as to give me a definition of faith?

P. and M.—It is the gift of God.*

---

* A proper rendering of Eph., chap. 2, v. 8, would be: "For by favor are you saved through faith; and this salvation not of yourselves; *it* (the salvation) is the gift of God;" not *it,* the faith, is, &c.

C.—"Faith is the confidence of things hoped for, and the conviction of things not seen; it comes by hearing, and hearing by the word of God." You both say that we are justified by faith *only*, but the Bible says "we are *not* justified by faith *only*; that faith, *without* works, is dead, being *alone!*" Hence, your faith, being *alone*, is *dead* faith, and can never save anyone. This is one essential difference between your doctrine and the Bible. One must be untrue! Which shall we say it is, the one of divine origin, or the ones of human invention?

What would you think of me, if some fatal malady was preying on the vitals of both of you, and I had a panacea for the distemper, but withheld it from one, and let death do its work, and gave it to the other? Would not you say,, and justly, too, that I was an inhuman and partial wretch? The sinner has a fatal malady preying in his heart. God has the panacea—faith, the gift of God! He refuses to give it to the sufferer, and the consequence is, he dies. This is a true representation of your system of justification by faith *alone*—the gift of God, and it represents him in no enviable character to us—a respecter of persons!

CHAPTER II.
OF THE WILL.

C.—Well, brethren, shall we speak of the *will?* If so, define it.

Pr.—Yes, of *free will.* Man has wholly lost *all* ability of will to any spiritual good whatever.

M.—Yes, our condition is such, that we have no power to do good at all.

C.—I conceive the will to be "that faculty of the mind by which we determine either to do or forbear an action; the faculty which is exercised in deciding, among two or more objects, which we shall embrace or pursue," or which we shall reject.

Your definition of the will would be, that it is that dormant faculty of the mind whereby God determines for us, that we *shall* do either so and so, or not; that it is the faculty of *our* minds that *He* exercises in deciding for us whether we shall pursue good or embrace evil: hence, upon this hypothesis, He would be responsible for all our acts, and not ourselves. If we do good, it is because He determines that we shall; if evil, He controls our actions to that end, and, consequently, is the author of evil in us. Such are the legitimate conclusions of your human theories.

I affirm that man's *will* is directed or influenced by HIS *judgment!* This you deny. I affirm that man's *understanding,* or *reason,* compares different objects, which operates as matter for good or evil. You affirm that he acts under *restraint. I* say the *judgment* determines, from the evidence before it, which is preferable, and the *will* decides which to pursue! You say the *judgment* is *passive,* and the *will* acts only as it is *acted* upon!

You admit that man, primeval, had power to *will* and to *do* good, and the fall of our first parent demonstrates that he, also, had power to *will* and to *do* evil. Hence, he had unlimited restraint of will! But by his fall, you teach, he lost at least one-half of his freedom of will —the ability to do good —and, consequently, if he had not the power to do good, he must, by restraint, do evil; thus logically depriving him. of all liberty of action—yet, strange to say, you hold him accountable for the deeds done in his body by another!

I presume you will admit that it would be a *laudable action* for the sinner to turn to God; but what solemn mockery it would be for the Messiah to say, "Come unto me, all ye that are heavy laden, and I will give you rest *"if* any man thirst, let *him come* unto me, and drink," when the sinner had not, neither could have, the *will nor* the power to comply with the request!

It is the Messiah's *will* to have *all* men saved, (1 Tim., chap. 2, v. 4); and if man's *will* was subject to his, all would be saved. But it is evident that all *will not* be saved, though all may, if they *will.* Hence, *the creature has power to resist,* or to *comply* with the Creator's *will* at pleasure, and this places man in his proper position—that is, makes him responsible for his own acts.

It is true that, in some sense, everything that we have may be called a gift; "for," as the Athenian poet sang, "in him we live, and move and have our being." But among these gifts may be enumerated the power of emotion, liberty of conscience, and freedom of will, which make us accountable beings.

Man either has the power to control his acts, or he has not: if he has not, he cannot, in justice, be held accountable for them, nor can there be, in *equity,* a general judgment; if he has, he must, of necessity, have power to control his will, and can, in justice, be held accountable for his deeds, and, in equity, be judged for the acts done in his body.

A. APPLEGATE.

-----O-----

Affairs About Indianapolis.

On Saturday, Jan. 26th, through extreme cold and storm, we hastened to the Cincinnati, Hamilton and Dayton depot, to take the six o'clock A. M. train for Putnam county, Ind. Reaching the depot in time, we took a seat in a car of the lightning express train, in full confidence that the iron horse, who had taken us through the same route so frequently without a failure, would pass us, via Richmond and Indianapolis, to Greencastle, Indiana, in the usual time. But, alas! we found that he proceeded with extreme caution, as though he feared some of his limbs would be dislocated every bound he made. Nor were his fears without just grounds, for, soon after crossing the bridge over the Great Miami, above Hamilton, about twelve inches burst out of one of the rims of a wheel under the tender. After a few minutes hesitation, the brakes were pressed upon the broken wheel and its mate tight enough to lock, and in that situation they were slid through (some forty miles) to Richmond, some two hours behind time. This left us to wait for the evening train, at six o'clock. It finally arrived, a little behind time, and was hindered by snow all the way to Indianapolis, whence the train had left for Greencastle about an hour before our arrival. We hastened to the Farmers' Hotel in company with Mr. Aspenwall, who lives near neighbor to us in the city, and whom we found on the evening train, and with whom we enjoyed a very comfortable night's rest.

On Lord's day morning, we made our way through the snow to the house of the well-known and beloved brother, L. H. Jameson, who has for many years had charge of the church in Indianapolis. He informed us that the term of his engagement was about closing, and that he did not expect to keep the charge any longer, but that he had engaged as secretary for the N. W. C. University. Through his kind invitation, we addressed the small congregation, in the morning and at night, who came out through the snow. In the course of the day, we visited brethren J. M. Telford, J. B. New, and O. Butler, and thus spent the day very pleasantly. We also saw brethren A. R. Benton and Dr. Egan, formerly of Wilmington, O., and J. R. Challen, and had much important conversation in regard to the great matters upon which our future prosperity largely depends. We were also introduced to several young brethren already in the ministry, and preparing for a more extended usefulness.

The brethren have been appealed to, more generally and effectually, by the able, energetic and industrious John O'Kane, but also by others, throughout the State of Indiana, and in several adjoining States, to contribute of their substance for the establishment of a valuable institution of learning. To this appeal a noble response has been made, and, through the excellent management of the valuable brother, O. Butler, who has had the main charge of the finance and business, an edifice has been reared up which is a credit to the brethren, the State, and the capital. It is situated about one mile north-east of the State House, in the suburbs of the city, on one of the most beautiful sites in the environs of the city. Many brethren from different parts of the State, and from other States, have visited this noble structure, and reported favorably of it. Public expectation is now pretty well elevated in regard to what is to be accomplished, which may all be realized by a judicious, cautious and persevering effort on the part of those connected with this noble undertaking; and we 'hope and pray that their most sanguine expectations may all be more than realized.

The incipient steps in organizing a faculty

have been taken, and brethren John Young, L. H. Jameson, R. A. Benton and J. R. Challen are actively employed, with about eighty students, and the way is opened to a great work. But this great work is only commenced; the road is simply opened to it, and the fortune is yet to be made. We know of no position occupied by brethren, where a greater responsibility rests than at this point. The time has now come when brethren expect to see some fruits from their liberality, and if some is not seen, good is not done, and the Institution is not managed so as to meet the expectations of the brethren abroad, and gain for itself a good reputation, in vain may a further endowment be expected, or other works of the kind be supported in time to come. Not only does this responsibility rest upon the faculty, but, to a considerable extent, upon other leading brethren about Indianapolis. It will not only be expected that education in general be promoted, but that the Christian ministry receive a special benefit from this institution. This will be expected from the fact that a main plea in soliciting funds was based upon the education of young men for the ministry. This is certainly a great and good work. But those who undertake the education of young men for the ministry take upon them an immense responsibility, which, no doubt, will be felt by the brethren in this instance.

We do not presume to be able to instruct the brethren engaged, or that may be engaged in this work; but some things strike us with so much force that we can but give utterance to them. There must be harmony among the Professors and those who have the immediate management of the institution. There must not only *appear* to be, but there must be, the fullest confidence throughout, and unanimity, making everything bend to the supreme object of the institution. Every young man should feel that the faculty and principal managers compose a unit—that they are *one,* and their aim *one.* Partiality should not be any place, but, by all means, it should have no place here. Selfishness and worldly ambition should not have the least countenance any place, but especially among those who stand as instructors and an example to young men preparing for the highest and most important calling on this earth. If the Christian ministry would command the respect of the private membership, and of the world, the individuals of that ministry must not only *appear* to, but must *really respect* each other. If the professors in a college would command the respect of the students and those without, they must not only *appear* to, but must, in *reality, respect* each other. Selfishness is as sure of its reward as any weakness in human nature. A selfish preacher will lose the respect of his preaching brethren as sure as he is a living being—of the brethren generally, and certainly of young preachers. There is no place, that we now think of, where it is more important that men show generosity, nobleness of heart, enlarged and expanded feelings of kindness and regard for all around them, than among the professors in a college.

When we look for distinguished men, the matter is not simply whether they are men of learning, of talent, and ability to teach; but, have they nobleness of mind, an extended horizon and the good of the world at heart? Are their lives models of goodness, of expanded benevolence, and enlarged efforts for the good of mankind!

There is one more point we must notice, before we close. In Indianapolis there are some fifteen or eighteen preachers—some of them old and experienced men, some in the prime of life, and others young, aiming to perfect their education and knowledge for a more useful life. In a place like this, where the professors in the college are all preachers, where there are other able and eminent men, and where the characters of young men are forming for the ministry, those from abroad will expect to find a model Church. Here, where the brethren from abroad have contributed means for erecting a good meeting-house and a college, and where the most distinguished men in the State are spending the energies of their lives, brethren from abroad will expect to find the Church flourishing. Such an expectation is natural and right. In view of it, there should be an effort, as far as possible, to show forth Christianity in this Church. At present, the

Church has no preacher whose business it is to look after its interests and take the special oversight. It certainly cannot succeed in this way. At such an important point, it is utterly out of the question for the Church to maintain its position, unless represented by about as good talent as the country affords. Here, where strangers are frequently present from all parts of the Union, where the Legislature of the State assembles, and where the first order of talent is employed in every other department, it is certainly in accordance with the dictates of reason and common sense that the Church place a man before the people, as a public exponent of the cause, equally gifted, and commanding the respect of the people. B. F.

-----o-----

Circles.

The universe is one great circle. It is composed of myriads of myriads smaller ones—some smaller, but all comprehended in, and serving to make up this one.

"All are but parts of one stupendous whole,
Whose body nature is, and God the soul."

All of nature's matter exists in globes, revolves on axles, and in circular orbits. There are no squares, no triangles, or other regular cornered bodies in all, as it comes forth and moves from the hand of God.

God being the soul, the center of the universe, He is also its circumference, its all animating, vivifying Spirit, permeating, pervading, upholding and sustaining all. In Him and from Him is all motion, all life. "In Him we live, and move, and have our being." O the height! O the depth! O the extent, on every side, of illimitable space! Height without top, depth without bottom, and extent in all directions without bounds!

THE CIRCLE OF HUMANITY.

This embraces every human being, of all races, of every tribe, and every tongue. God is our common Father, and all we are brethren. This is a great circle, as the earth we inhabit is a great body; but we see many that are larger and many that are smaller. The earth is not large when compared with her sister planets—much less when compared with the center of our system, the sun. So the circle of humanity is not large when compared with the circles above it, with principalities, with powers. Nor is it small when compared with those below, with circles of other genera and species, and the circles within itself.

THE FAMILY CIRCLE.

This is the beginning and the smallest of all the circles of humanity. At the head of this stands the husband and father; at his left, joined hand in hand, stands the wife and mother; and ranged around these, and indissolubly joined to them, stand the children. Everyone is grasped and held tightly by the father's right and the mother's left hand. He has a right hand and she a left for every-one. She could not give them her right hand, nor he them his left, her right hand belongs to him and his left belongs to her. With these they hold on to one another, and with the others to the children, that the circle be not broken.

With marriage begins within another family circle—yes, two others, one in that of the new husband, and the other in that of his wife. The husband steps in between the father and mother and daughter. He gives his right hand to the two former, and becomes by adoption their son; he gives to their daughter his left hand, and becomes her husband. A new relation is formed in two families. She, the new wife, becomes now the daughter of his father and mother, the sister of his brothers and sisters.

The principle, the *bond* of the universe and of all its subordinate circles, is one and the same; it is LOVE. God is love. Love, therefore, is the bond of humanity, and the bond of the family. Thou shalt love God, to bind thee to Him, and to his system of things; thou shalt love thy neighbor, to bind thee to him.

No son or daughter can be adopted, constitutionally and happily adopted, without love; and in adopting, all the members of the family, the families of both contracting parties, so far as practicable, should be consulted, and all should be pleased. The father and the mother first, and then the son and the daughter to be married, and then the others. With the parents should be the beginning, or the first, after God. To Him first, and to them next, should the unmarried apply—for "a good wife is from the Lord;" and parents have property and an interest in their children which places them next to Him. With them is to be settled all preliminaries; and without a good and perfect understanding here, obtaining their free consent and approbation, not another step should be taken. With these he may advance, proceed properly, safely, surely, and gain the heart and hand of the daughter. In gaining her hand thus, he takes it from her parents, at the same time giving a hand to them. He steps in between them and her. But, *verbum sat.*

Other circles, composed of parents, children, and other relatives, may be noted in another article at another time. B. F.

-----o-----

OBJECT OF THE BIBLE UNION.—As to the *object* of the Bible Union, I submit the question:—Is there anything *here* to call forth the opposition of Christian men? It is *to procure and circulate the most faithful versions of the sacred Scriptures, in all languages, throughout the world.* A *formal* defense of such an object before a *Protestant* tribunal, would seem not only to be gratuitous, but a serious impeachment of their intelligence and honesty. It is a fundamental principle of evangelical Christendom, that the sacred Scriptures, in the languages in which they were originally written, not only contain, but *are,* the *only* revelation of the mind and the will of God in respect to our apostate race. They communicate to us all the *certain* knowledge we possess of the God who made us, of the Saviour who redeemed us, of the Spirit who sanctifies us, of the duties enjoined upon us, and of the destiny that awaits us. They alone exhibit to us the character of that God, and the mutual relations subsisting between Him and us. They unfold to us the wondrous work of redemption wrought out for us by that Saviour, through the efficacy of which "God can be just and yet justify the sinner that believeth in Jesus." They disclose the agency of that Spirit by whom we are regenerated, sanctified, and "made meet to be partakers of the inheritance with the holy ones in light." They point out and define the nature and the obligations of those duties we owe to our Creator and to our fellow-creatures, and reveal to us the awful solemnities and eternal duration of the destiny beyond the tomb. They only can furnish an *answer* to the most momentous question relating to human welfare, "How can man be just with his Maker,"—"*Relating* to human welfare," did I say? This question involves the *whole* of human welfare for time and eternity. But why attempt to exalt the unspeakable value of God's revelation to man? His lips must be touched with the hallowed fire from off the eternal altar, and his hand skilled to sweep an angel's lyre, who would adequately extol those living and soul-satisfying streams that flow from the eternal fountain of truth and consolation.

Now this revelation from God imposes, among its highest obligations, upon those who possess the inestimable treasure, that of imparting it to those who have it not. This can *be fully* discharged only by *faithfully* transferring the contents of the Inspired Original into the *vernacular* languages spoken by the different nations, peoples, and tribes of the earth. And it is as much our duty to impart it with the *fullness* and *clearness* commensurate with *human ability,* as to give it at all. Better, far, to allow imperfections in anything else than in such a work as this.—*B. U. Reporter*

-----o-----

THE BIBLE UNION, A SCRIPTURAL SOCIETY.— Though not claiming to be considered a *denominational* society, the Union *does* claim to be a *Christian,* nay, pre-eminently, a *Scriptural* society. Whether presumptuous or not, it *does* claim to have ascended and taken its firm position upon the sublime heights where the cloudless orb of revelation may reach and illumine, with its holy light, *every* object from mountain to mote. It has emblazoned upon its front, "the Bible, the *whole* Bible *and nothing but the Bible,* and this Bible, in its unveiled, divine meaning, *just as God has given it.* I have my own views of the teachings of the Bible, and I hold them on strong convictions and with firm tenacity, and am ready, on all fitting occasions, to defend them, and show the *reason* of my faith, but as a "Bible Union" man, and standing on this platform, I do not feel at liberty to protrude my *peculiar theological* views, to the offense of honest men of a different way of thinking, who stand side-by- side with me in a sincere desire, and a single-eyed aim to secure for all men a *faithful* transcript, in their own tongue, of the *whole* teachings of the "Oracles of God." Nor will I allow others, thus associated with me, without unmistakable marks of my disapprobation, to avail themselves, in anywise, of our common relation to the great enterprise, to hold forth and inculcate their *special* views of

Bible doctrine, and commit me to a seeming endorsement of, or acquiescence in, sentiments which I repudiate. I hold that it would be the saddest perversion of the noblest aim—the most lamentable degradation of the grandest enterprise which can' animate the zeal of Christian men—to use the "Bible Union" to subserve the partisan and sectarian interest of any sect of Christians, merely *as such.—B. U. Reporter.*

THE GREAT HERESY OF THE AGE.—I have a word of admonition to utter. I would kindly warn those who oppose the Bible Union, against a *heresy* more pernicious and fearful, far, than any misconstructions and unwarranted inferences which the weak and perverted understandings of men may put upon, and draw from the *plain readings* of God's word. It is *that* which dares to lay its hand upon any portion of this word and say, it *shall not,* or even that it *need not,* be given to those for whom it was designed by its gracious Author. THIS IS THE GREAT HERESY OF THE AGE, and of all ages since a revelation from heaven has been given to sinful man. Other heresies may be mistakes, grievous mistakes it may be, as to the true import of the voice of God, which all have the same right and means to interpret for themselves. But this dares to *stifle* the voice of God itself. With blasphemous presumption, it *intercepts* the messages of Heaven to dying man, sits in judgment upon the wisdom of Jehovah, and decides what is fitting and necessary of His message to give to man, and *suppresses* the remainder. This heresy in all its forms, whether it suppresses the *whole* or *part* of God's word, is the genuine mark of the "man of sin." Its sits in the place of God, and teaches for his doctrines the commands of men. It is the *true* mother of the whole "damnable" brood of heresies which in all ages have cursed the Church of God. Beware, my dear brethren, you who have so keen a scent for heresy as to snuff it where it cannot be found, of the polluting touch and stench of this *heresy of heresies.* Better that your hands be withered and your tongue palsied, than to give, in any way, "aid and comfort" to this child of hell. No, my brethren, look in the direction of real danger, and be entreated to join your voices with ours, and with united cry, in God's name, let us say to the abettors of this enormous heresy, Presumptuous men! *Stand aside,* and let God speak out *all* the words of His messages of life and salvation to a dying world.—*B. U. Reporter.*

THE BIBLE UNION IN GERMANY.—It will gratify the friends of Brother Oncken to know that we were able to transmit to him more than one thousand dollars, during the last month. This amount was made up of small sums, from one to five dollars, very rarely more than five.

There is not a more inviting field of Christian toil on earth than that in which Brother Oncken and his fellow-laborers are engaged. We have already contributed largely to aid him; and, in the future, much will be expected from us, to assist in the circulation of the Sacred Scriptures, in thousands of copies. Those who would contribute for this cause should express their desire at the time of sending their remittances.—

B. U. Reporter.

PROTESTANTISM, THE HOPE OF HUMANITY.—In the light of history and of a true philosophy, we affirm *that the only solid hope for humanity is in Protestantism.* Protestantism affirming the *divine inspiration,* and the *divine sufficiency* of the Scriptures, can point with confidence to many of the brightest pages of history, to the mightiest and best nations of the earth, to almost numberless monuments of science and art, benevolence and piety, as the fruit of her principles. All this, too, while enfeebled and crippled by a thousand internal strifes, springing from the seeds of superstition which she still nourishes in her bosom. We ask then, what may not these principles work out, when their advocates cease to strive with each other, and turn their forces against these two great foes? Into what fair forms may humanity then rise! what stateliness, what majesty, nay, what glory, in the uprisings and outflowings of mind, and heart, and life, illuminated, converted, and sanctified by the Spirit of God!

The union of all who acknowledge the divine inspiration and sufficiency of the Scriptures, we, look to as one of the most desirable of all consummations. The true philanthropist cannot but long, and pray, and labor for it; for he can see no prospect of millennial peace and glory without it. And to this end, a catholic movement, in a catholic spirit, such as the American Bible Union can claim, must be hailed with unfeigned delight by all the pure in heart, as they come to understand its character and designs.

It used to be argued that the asteroids were fragments of a once mighty planet, broken by internal convulsions into many portions; the fragments still held by the sun's attraction, and becoming each a planet by itself. Even their fragmentary grandeur is attractive; yet it is hard to discern it. It has required long searching to discover their scattered beauties; and one cannot but think how superior the magnificence of the original planet, as it swept in its orbit around the sun! So these numerous sects have but a fragmentary grandeur. That they are still held by the power of the Sun of Righteousness, and still reflect His light, is matter of rejoicing. But how dim and pale is this radiance, compared with that of the primitive church, when the glory of the Lord had risen upon her? It is a beauty still, but a beauty hard to find, and, to the eyes of the multitude not discoverable.

The spiritual astronomer, with powerful telescope, may discover and make known to the multitude many charming facts, and unfold a very charming philosophy; but could the real friends of Jesus be brought together into one again—and be bathed in the pure light of God, with what power would that light be reflected to every eye—filling all the world with gentle and peaceful illuminations, and driving away the gloom and the watery darkness! To labor for this is a most philanthropic and pious aim of life; and none can tell what even a feeble instrumentality may be made to accomplish, by steady perseverance.

Once when a large congregation of worshipers were engaged in singing, the devotion of the occasion was greatly marred by almost countless discords. Each worshiper had a tune of his own—or at least his own version of an original tune—which was just near enough like the tune the others were singing to give it a common claim; and enough unlike it to destroy all harmony and melody. It seemed as if the hymn must be dragged on through all these torturing discords to the end. But there was *one voice* which sung correctly the original tune. It was not very loud—not at all boisterous—but it was *correct*—it was *faithful*. One by one, other voices fell in with it. Slowly but surely the original tune gained strength. Its sweetness, its truthfulness, its superiority gained its way from ear to ear, and from heart to heart, until the whole congregation sung in unison, and the closing strains were marked by great strength and delightful harmony. Is it too much to hope that the American Bible Union, advocating the pure word of God in faithful translations, though it seems like a very feeble instrumentality, may by gentleness and perseverance, prevail against a thousand discordant tongues, and gather round it steadily the sympathies and prayers, and lives of those who fear God, until all the harsh and grating sounds of sectarian strife shall be drowned in the rich, full, swelling harmonies and melodies of the united children of God? Surely, if this may be, earth has never yet heard so glad a song; heaven has not yet been addressed in strains so triumphant as shall then go up from the one body. It will be like Milton's "seven-fold chorus of hallelujahs and harping symphonies." May God hasten it in his time.—

B. U. *Reporter*.

The Second Epistle of John.

THE elder unto an elect lady and her children, whom I love in truth, and not I only, but also all who have known the truth, for the truth's sake, which abideth in us, and with us it shall be forever: There shall be with you grace, mercy, peace,, from God the Father, and from the Lord Jesus Christ, the Son of the Father, in truth and love.

I rejoiced greatly that I have found children of thine walking in truth, as we received commandment from the Father. And now I beseech thee, lady, not as writing unto thee a new commandment, but that which we had from the beginning, that we love one another. And this is love, that we walk according to his commandments. This is the commandment, as ye heard from the beginning, that ye should walk in it. For many deceivers have entered into the world, who confess not Jesus Christ coming in flesh: this is the deceiver and the Antichrist. Look to yourselves, that we lose not what things we have wrought, but receive a full reward. Every one that transgresseth, and abideth not in the doctrine of Christ, hath not God: he that abideth, in the doctrine of Christ, the same hath both the Father and the Son. If anyone cometh unto you, and bringeth not this doctrine, receive him not into the house, neither bid him hail: for he that biddeth him hail shareth in his wicked works.

Having many things to write unto you, I would not with paper and ink; but I hope to come unto you, and speak mouth to mouth, that our joy may be fulfilled. The children of thy elect sister salute thee.

PROPORTION OF FOREIGNERS.—Of the 305,000 inhabitants of Wisconsin, about 35,000 are Germans, 19,000 English, 21,000 Irish, 4,000 Welsh, and 3,500 Scotch. In Louisiana, the foreign is to the native population as one to five; in Texas, as one nine; in Virginia, as one to forty; in North Carolina, as one to three hundred; in South Carolina, as one to thirty-three; in Georgia, as one to one hundred; and in Florida, as one to twenty-four.

Editors' Table.

Office of the *American Christian Review,* West Fourth street, No. 60, on third floor, open stair way from outside. Signs will be seen at the entrance.

Postage on this Magazine, when paid quarterly in advance, *six cents* a year.

Plenty of Elder M. B. HOPKINS' Sermon, seen in the February No., in a neat tract, for sale at this office.

-----o-----

Prospects of the American Christian Review.—No doubt many of our friends would like to know what our prospects are. To all such we would say, that they are of a very encouraging character. No enterprise of the kind, known to us, by any brother, has met with anything near the same success. Truly are we thankful to the Lord, and to his people, for thus opening our way to such a promising field. May we have strength, wisdom, and discretion to discharge the trust committed to our hands, acceptably to the Lord, and to the good of man. We can supply two thousand more subscribers with back numbers.

We have been engaged almost incessantly at protracted meetings during the last five months. Within the last four weeks we have had some thirty-five additions in the several meetings where we have been engaged, viz: at Carthage and White Oak. At Bowerville, though we had a most interesting meeting, none were added.

Pamphlets to Give away.—Any person desiring one copy of the "American Christian Review" and two copies to give away, by sending us $2, shall have three copies sent to any address.

WE have just closed an interesting meeting at Bethel, Wayne Co., Indiana, with a number of valuable additions. The large house was filled to its utmost capacity all the time, and the deepest interest prevailed to the close. Nor did the brethren fail to extend to us a liberal hand in token of their esteem. At the close, we laid before them the case of our colored brethren, on Harrison street, in this city, when they cheerfully contributed $2,690 toward liquidating the debt on their church property.

Revision Meeting.

[For the American Christian Review.]
LOUISVILLE, KY., Feb. 15th, 1856.

The annual meeting of the Bible Revision Association, will be held at Louisville, Kentucky, on the Thursday before the 2nd Lord's day in April next, the 10th of April, 1856, at 2 o'clock, P. M. All the friends of pure versions of the word of God, are invited to attend. Ample provisions will be made for the accommodation of the delegates and members from a distance. Eminent speakers from various States are expected to be present. Let all our friends be prepared to speak and to hear, that all may be edified and the cause we advocate may be advanced.

JAMES EDMUNDS.
Corresponding Secretary.

-----o-----

Success of the Gospel.

DEAR BROTHER FRANKLIN—The glorious cause of our blessed Redeemer is still onward in southern Michigan. I have just closed an interesting meeting near Paw Paw, where I delivered ten discourses to large and attentive audiences. *Eleven* persons put on the Lord by baptism, and *two* were added who had been previously immersed—one from the Methodists, the other from the Baptists. At other recent meetings some half dozen were added to the congregation of the Lord—to whom be all the praise.

Yours, fraternally, Wm. M. Roe.

BUCHANAN, January 18, 1856.

LOUISVILLE, KY., January 22, 1856.

DEAR BROTHER—I have just closed a ten days meeting at Memphis, Ind., resulting in five immersions. All the immersed are young men.

In haste and truly, G. W. LEONARD.

-----o-----

Literary Notices.

The Family Companion, or a book of Sermons on various subjects both doctrinal and practical; intended for the private edification and comfort of Christians; and to aid the sincere seeker after truth in finding the true church, and the law of induction into the same; and in understanding the gospel doctrine of Election, Conversion, Justification, Satisfaction, etc.

By ELIJAH GOODWIN.

Such is the title of a new book, now in press in this city, to be ready for distribution by the first of April next, and for which we bespeak a liberal patronage, believing it will be a useful auxiliary in the cause of truth. Orders for this work should be addressed to Elijah Goodwin, Bloomington, Monroe County, Indiana, or to this office. Price $1.00, single copy.

"The Christian Sentinel."—Such is the title of a monthly pamphlet, 32 pages, double column, conducted by W. A. Mallory and the Faculty of Eureka College, and published at Springfield, Ill. The February No. is the first we have received, which is put up in good style, arranged with much taste, and filled with valuable matter. We wish it much success.'

"The New York Chronicle."—Such is the title of a large, and ably conducted sheet, published in New York, and edited by Pharcellus Church and Jay S. Backus. This valuable paper has been the principal

organ and defender of the great Bible Union and Revision movement. It is one of the most valuable weekly religious newspapers in the world. We think it is what it professes to be: "The largest and best printed Baptist paper in America." Address P. Church & Co., New York Chronicle office, New York.

"*Man of War Life; a Boy's Experience in the U. S. Navy.*" 1 volume 16mo., illustrated—"*The Merchant Vessel; a Sailor Boy's Voyages to See the World.*" 1 volume, 16mo., illustrated. By the same author.

A writer who is destined to cheer the family circle in many thousand houses, on many a winter night. He writes well—admirably. * * * He tells the story of the vicissitudes as well as the pleasures of the life of the boy or man before the mast.—*Washington Star.*

Full of variety, and adapted to awaken the interest of young people in traveling adventure, while it must greatly extend their geographical knowledge.—*New York Times.*

Very striking and graphic pictures of life at sea, evidently authentic and very instructive. * * Has adventure enough to please, yet truth enough to dissipate the charm of a sailor's life.—*N. Y. Evangelist.*

There is in them a vast amount of information respecting the commerce of the world.—*Presbyterian Witness.*

Will take captive the young.—*Journal and Messenger.*

There is no affectation in them.—*Dayton Gazette.*

These books are not for mere children, but for lads of some years and discretion. They are remarkably well written.—*N. Y. Independent.*

The reader is only left to wonder why one who can write so remarkably well, had ever anything to do with the rigging.—*Boston Traveler*

Has a fine eye for observation, and excellent descriptive powers.—*Louisville Courier.*

Multitudes of young readers will delight in these books.—*Presbyterian Banner.*

Since Dana's "Two Years Before the Mast" we do not call to mind any more admirable descriptions of a sailor's life. Herman Melville's nautical narratives are more highly spiced with piquant descriptive scenes, it is true, but for quiet, absorbing and. as far as a landsman can judge, faithful accounts of life on shipboard, commend us to this anonymous author.—*N. Y. Tribune.*

Published by Moore, Wilstach, Keys & Co., Cincinnati.

"The Voice —An Essay to Extend the Reformation." By F. W. EMMONS. 18mo., pp. 250, neatly bound in sheep, price 50 cents; or 60 cents, postage prepaid by mail.

Cheap enough.—*J. T. Johnson.*

Now, in all conscience, this last piece [on "The Fellowship is, to any church, or to any man who wishes to know God's will on a most important matter, worth double that sum. The brethren, in my judgment, ought not to leave unpurchased one of the volumes in which is found said discourse. Brethren, let me prevail with you to send for a few copies of the Voice.—*Walter Scott.*

How can funds be raised? I do verily believe, that if the views of brother Emmons on the *koinonia* were carried out, they would furnish us with all the funds necessary for the poor saints, and the poor sinners too—money for the one, and the gospel for the other. My dear brother, call the attention of the brethren to the "Fellowship."—*James Challen.*

I accord with the above. B. F.

A few copies for sale at this office.

OBITUARY.

CHICKASAW, Mercer co., O., Feb. 3, 1856.

BRO. FRANKLIN—Last week I sent you four subscribers and four dollars; to-day I send you three subscribers and one dollar.

Since I last wrote you, Bro. War. P. LONG (January 30th), died of a short but severe attack of typhoid fever. He had been a resident of Hamilton county but has been a resident of this county (Mercer), for the last eighteen years —had been a member of the Christian connection but, upon a confession of his faith, was immersed, and became one of the Elders of the Church of Christ at Chickasaw, near sixteen years ago.

Bro. Long was a straight-forward, plain man, and a true Christian. I was with him one night and part of two days, before he died. During the night we repeatedly heard such expressions as these fall from his lips—"The blessed Son of God:" "Blessed are they that do his commandments:" "We must take the Bible for our guide." Although he suffered much, he bore it with Christian fortitude and patience, and calmly fell asleep as an infant falls into an ordinary slumber. Bro. Long was about sixty years of age, and left an aged companion and numerous relations to mourn his loss.

A funeral discourse was spoken by the writer to a crowded and weeping house on the occasion, upon the text, "Blessed are the dead that die in the Lord."

J. D. WEIGHT.

Sister STOUGHTON, consort of Bro. John L. Stoughton, of Madison county, Ind., departed this life January 14th, 1856, in the thirty-seventh year of her age.

She died in the hope of an immortal crown, having proved "faithful until death." She had been a member of the Christian Church sixteen years, and was highly beloved by all who knew her. She left many sorrowful hearts in her neighborhood, to mourn her departure. But we sorrow not as those who have no hope.

WASHINGTON FRANKLIN.

THE AMERICAN CHRISTIAN REVIEW.

CINCINNATI, APRIL, 1856.

A SERMON: BY ELDER A. RAINES, PARIS, KY.
REMISSION OF SINS IN THE NAME OF JESUS.

"THUS it is written, and thus it behooved Christ to suffer, and to rise from the dead the third day; and that repentance and remission of sins should be preached, in His name, among all nations, beginning at Jerusalem."—Luke xxiv, 46,47.

THE remission of sins is a boon superlatively, excellent. It is an act of God, dwelling in the Holy of Holies, in light unapproachable. It is an emanation from the mercy of God, through the redemption that is in Christ Jesus. It is conferred freely, and richly, upon all who obey, from the heart, the gospel of the Son of God.

The wages of sin is death. Death temporal, and all our physical ills, are the fruits of the first sin of the first man. Eternal death is the fruit of our personal sins. If, therefore, we would, to any extent, learn to appreciate the value of pardon, we must first obtain adequate conceptions of the turpitude of sin; and, in order to do this, we must contemplate it as it exhibits itself in its bitter and burning fruits—all the miseries of this life, and the weeping, and wailing, and gnashing of teeth—the worm that never dies, and the fire that shall never be quenched, in the dark world of woe to come.

But the most vivid exhibition of the malignity of sin is to be seen on the cross, in the bleeding agonies of the crucified Lamb of God. He was an impersonation of perfect virtue. He was the brightness of the Father's glory, the express image of his person; and yet sin, in the persons of those whom he came to bless and to save, put him to a most cruel and ignominious death. Thus we perceive, that sin, had it the power, would destroy God. Horrid as is the thought, it would drag from the eternal throne the Father of mercies, the God of peace and love, the creator and preserver of all, and put him to the most cruel death. Its having done this to the Son, who is the express image of the Father, is demonstration itself, that it would do the same to the Father if it possessed the power. Let none marvel, then, that sin should sink the soul of the impenitent into the blackness of an everlasting darkness—into the fathomless depths of that fiery abyss, which is the second death.

There is another aspect in which the cross of Christ may be viewed, by which the malignity of sin is indicated. Without the blood, the sacrificial death of Jesus, there could have been no remission. The costliest creature sacrifice would not suffice. The death of Michael, the Prince of the heavenly hierarchies, would have been an offering too mean. Nought but the blood of

God's only begotten and well-beloved Son would avail as a ransom for sinners. The blood is the life. Man's life had been forfeited by sin; and, therefore, blood for blood, life for life; and that, too, his blood and life "who thought it not robbery to be equal with God," in order to man's redemption. If sin be that trivial thing which some represent it to be, would Christ have died in order to redeem sinners? Would not a God of perfect wisdom and goodness have chosen a less expensive method of redemption? As, therefore, he has not, and never uses inappropriate methods, or a superfluity of means, it follows that the ratio of the demerit of sin must be measured by the depth of the humiliation, and the intensity of the sufferings of Christ; and if so, as lofty as are the heights from which the Saviour descended, so profound are the depths into which sin will plunge the sinner, who dies without redemption through the blood of Jesus.

These remarks are preparatory. The grand Subject which we wish to develope, as God may give us, or may have given us ability, is the remission of sins in the name of Jesus. And may we not be permitted to ask, Whether or not, as God has been good enough to grant remission, he has not also been good enough to grant remission upon such terms, as that those who understand and obey the gospel shall have satisfactory evidence of it. Christian joy is made, in the Christian scriptures, a Christian duty. "Rejoice in the Lord always, and again I say rejoice." But must not dubiety as to whether or not our sins are pardoned, greatly mar, if not totally destroy or prevent our Christian joy? How can a considerate man be happy, who doubts, or is a skeptic in regard to the pardon of his sins? Suspense is always painful. How many restless days, and sleepless nights, have men spent, with respect to the loss of a few hundreds or a few thousands of dollars. And when life is involved, suspense is often productive of intolerable anguish. But what is life—what is the loss and gain of the whole world, compared with the salvation or the loss of the soul? All temporal interests dwindle, in the comparison, into insignificance. We perceive, therefore, that it is of vital importance that a Christian, in order to permanent joy, shall have permanent assurance of pardon; and reason would dictate that the amount of divine goodness necessary to the granting of pardon, in order that we might be saved, would also grant the means of satisfactory assurance that we might be happy.

There is, also, another reason why the christian should have full assurance of pardon. It is, in a good degree, his strength. Doubt is, in this case, not only misery, but feebleness—a cankering skepticism which will corrode and debilitate the soul in all its religious struggles and aspirations. "Am I pardoned?" the troubled soul will say! Let the answer be, "perhaps." "Only perhaps!" "Then," says the soul. "perhaps I am an heir of perdition. Perhaps I am deceived, and the victim of a delusion! Perhaps! O! these enfeebling doubts—these chilling, damning damps of death!" Thus he who doubts, as it respects pardon, may be as effectually paralyzed as he who doubts the sonship of Jesus, or the verity of the Divine existence. To be strong, therefore, in the grace that is in Christ Jesus, we must have a satisfactory assurance that God, for Christ's sake, has pardoned our sins.

This assurance the primitive Christian had. In no part of the New Testament do we find a Christian doubting the pardon of his sins. We have obtained redemption through his blood, the forgiveness of sins, is the language of unadulterated Christianity, in its hale and undegenerate days. And hence they were exhorted "not to forget that they had been purged from their old sins,"—evidently proving that they had full assurance of pardon, unless it be admissible to affirm, that as man may forget what he never knew! they never hoped that they were pardoned. They hoped for eternal life, and all good things to come. Their hope was set before them, but never behind them, as is the case with many modern Christians. They had not learned to make doubting meritorious; nor to feed each other with stale crumbs of comfort, by a rehearsal of their doubts. This dolorous skepticism was reserved for the dark and cloudy day of sectarianism—for the murky atmosphere of those "who are ever learning, and never able to come to the knowledge of the truth!"

No mortal priest—either Romanist or Protestant—can give me this assurance. As forgiveness is an act of God, so my conviction of that act must be by the word of God. Those inner lights, which may be darkness, or satanic delusions, and which have not the demonstration of miracles, or the seals of a Saviour's blood, will not suffice. Give me the rock and I will build upon it,—thus saith the Lord, and I will believe and rejoice. But away with the fluctuating quicksands of human feelings and imaginations as evidences of pardon, "To the law and the testimony; if they speak not according to this word, it is because there is no light in them."

We shall proceed, to the words of our text: "Repentance and remission of sins should be preached in his name among all nations, beginning at Jerusalem." In the discussion of this subject, we shall consider the following particulars:

1st. The name of Jesus.
2d. The place where.
3d. The time when.
4th. The person by whom preached.
5th. General remarks, and conclusion.

1st. *The name of Jesus.* The word name, in this connection, indicates the radix, the axle, the hinge of the whole gospel system. In Christianity all things were to be done in the name of Jesus. Col. iii, 17. Under the former dispensation, and under the personal ministry of Jesus, religion had been administered in the name of the Father. The gospel was to be administered in the name of the Son. He was crowned Lord of all—the prophet, priest and king of the church, and head over all things to the church. His image and superscription, his seal and signature should give life, and efficacy, and authority to the whole Christian institution. "All power [authority] is given unto me in heaven and in earth. Go ye, therefore, and teach [disciple] all nations, baptizing them in [into] the name of the Father, and of the Son, and of the Holy Spirit; teaching them to observe all things, whatsoever I have commanded you. "Matt. xxviii, 18, 19, 20. Hence, the apostles spoke and acted in the name, that is, by the authority, of Jesus. Through this commission the mantle of Christ's authority, as a teacher, fell on them. They were thus divinely authorized to teach all that the "one law giver," the "King of Zion," commanded them to teach and to do all he commanded them to do. They preached in his name; they prayed in his name; they sang in his name; they baptized in his name; they administered the Lord's Supper in his name; they wrought miracles in his name; and, in one sentence, "whatever they did, in word or deed, they did all in the name of the Lord Jesus, giving thanks to God and the Father by him." Col. iii, 17.

The point upon which we would concentrate is, the power, the efficacious and saving power of the name of Jesus. "There is none other name under heaven given among men, whereby we must be saved." Acts iv, 12. Hence, as the name of Jesus has saving efficacy in it, so this efficacy connects itself with the gospel preached in his name; with the ordinances administered in his name; with singing and prayer presented in his name; with miracles enough in his name; and with all things that are truly done in the name of our Lord Jesus Christ. Faith, filled with the gospel, is faith filled with grace and truth, and is the connecting link between Christ and the soul—the spiritual conductor through which passes into the mind and heart of the believer all Divine and saving influences. And the name of Christ just as naturally connects itself with his nature, divine and human; with his bloody passion and cruel death; with the whole of his redemption work; with all that he has promised to do in the salvation of men; with the perfections of his nature and character; with his eternal glory and renown; so that "he is wisdom, and righteousness, and sanctification, and redemption," to all who "put him on," Gal. iii. 27, or upon whom "his name is called." Acts xv. 17. "God has highly exalted him, and given him a name which is above every name; that at the name of Jesus every knee shall bow, of things in heaven, and things in earth, and things under the earth; and that every tongue should confess that

Jesus Christ is Lord, to the glory of God the Father." Phil. ii. 9, 10, 11.

Our readers will perceive that we are not teaching a form of godliness, while we deny the power thereof. There is power in the name of Jesus. Hence, there is power in the gospel, in faith, in repentance, in confession, in baptism, in the Lord's Supper, in prayer, and in good works—the power of the name of him who said, "All power is given to me in Heaven and on earth."

Thus through the name of Jesus do we find saving virtue in the appointments of God. Therefore, "man does not live by bread alone, but by every word that proceedeth out of the mouth of God," Matt. iv. 4-. Hence, if the Saviour has said, "He that believeth and is baptized shall be saved," Mark xvi. 16, it follows, that baptism, in the name of Jesus, for the remission of sins, is the appointment of the Sovereign Lord and Lawgiver; and hence, in pursuance to this commission, the apostle said, "Repent and be baptized, every one of you, in the NAME of Jesus Christ, for the remission of sins." Acts ii. 38; for so, according to our text, "repentance and remission of sins were to be preached in his NAME, among all nations, beginning at Jerusalem." And who art thou, O! man, that repliest against God? Shall the culprit condemned to death, chaffer with the Governor of the Universe, as to the terms upon which he shall be delivered from death?

Permit us to illustrate the subject now under consideration. Two persons purpose to unite themselves with each other in matrimony. They have mutually loved. They have mutually declared their love. They have obtained license. All things are ready. They stand up in the presence of a person legally authorized. They listen to a simple ceremony from his lips. They assent to it. He pronounces them, in the name of the commonwealth, husband and wife. They are no more twain, but one flesh! Is this a great mystery? It illustrates the gospel process by which we are married to Christ. Rom vii. 4; Eph. v. 25, 26. Christ loved the sinner—wooed him by all his overpowering charms revealed in the gospel. The sinner loved Christ in return—confessed—put him on in baptism—his state is changed, from condemnation to justification—as in the illustration, the state of the parties was changed from celibacy to matrimony—in the name of him, whose name is Saviour, and the legitimate appropriation of whose name is salvation.

Take another illustration. I pass along the street and behold a giant outlaw committing depredations on the persons and property of the citizens. I command him to desist. "In whose name," says he, "do you presume to command me?" In my own name, I reply! He dashes me against the earth, and puts his foot upon my neck. But suppose the case changed. Suppose that I am an officer of the Commonwealth, legally authorized to make this outlaw my prisoner. The Commonwealth is pledged—stands, with all its power, at my back, to execute the law. The analogy is obvious. Were I to baptize, in my own name, it would be inefficacious—it would be sinful! But the authorized administrator baptizes in the name of Jesus; and therefore, around him and the believing penitent, who submits to this appointment, all Divine power and authority stands pledged for the fulfillment of the promise, "He that believeth and is baptized shall be saved." Scoffer! art thou not afraid of the power? Do that which is good, obey the gospel, and thou shalt have praise of its author!

There is a difference, wide as the poles apart, between baptizing *in* the name, and *into* the name. *In* the name, means by the authority of; *into* the name, implies a change of states. Thus persons are said to enter *into* matrimony, or *into* partnership, to go *into* debt, to plunge *into* ruin, etc. Persons entering into matrimony, pass from the single *into* the married state. Persons going into debt, pass out of a state of un indebtedness *into* a state of indebtedness, etc. Hence, we baptize *in* the name, that is, by the authority of Jesus, *into* the name of the Father, and of the Son, and of the Holy Spirit. In this ordinance, therefore, the believer passes out of the state of condemnation, *into* the state of justification. Thus the commission as given by Matthew, harmonizes perfectly with that given by Mark: the one affirming that the baptized believer is pardoned; the other implying the same by his use, when the passage is correctly rendered, of the word *into*.

We shall conclude our remarks, under this head, by a quotation from Hodge, a modern writer, and a learned Pedo-Baptist. On the words Rom. vi: "As many of us as were baptized into Jesus Christ, were baptized into his death," he says, "In the phrase to be baptized into anyone, the word *into* has its usual force as indicating the object, design, or result for which anything is done. To be baptized into Jesus Christ, or unto Moses or Paul, therefore, means to be baptized in order to be united to Christ, or Moses, or Paul, as their followers, the recipients of their doctrines, and expectants of the blessings which they have to bestow. See Matt. xxviii. 19, 1 Cor. x. 2, 1 Cor. i. 13. In like manner, in the expression, baptized into his death, the preposition expresses the design and the result. Thus baptism unto repentance, Matt. iii. 11, is baptism in order to repentance. Baptism unto the remission of sins, Mark i. 4, that remission of sins may be obtained; "baptized into one body," 1 Cor. xii. 13, that we might become one body. The idea of the whole verse, therefore, is, that as many as have been baptized into Jesus Christ, have become intimately united with him, so that they are united with him in his death, conformed to its object, and participate in the blessings for which he died."

Having now, we trust, made apparent the difference between the phrases *in* the name, and *into* the name, and having also shown, to some extent, the meaning of each of these phrases in the several instances referred to, we pass to our next proposition, which is,

2nd. *Where was remission of sins, in the name of Jesus, first preached?* Our text says, "at Jerusalem." And Christ says, also, "thus it is written." For proof, read the following: "The Lord shall send the rod of thy strength out of Zion: rule then in the midst of thy enemies." Ps. ex. 2. "And many people shall go and say, come ye, and let us go up to the mountain of the Lord, to the house of the God of Jacob; and he will teach us of his ways, and we will walk in his paths; for out of Zion shall go forth the law, and the word of the Lord from Jerusalem." Isa. ii. 3. "For the law shall go forth of Zion, and the word of the Lord from Jerusalem." Mic. iv. 2. These passages harmonize precisely with our text; and show, incontrovertibly, that Christ's gospel was first fully developed, and preached at Jerusalem. Remission, in the name of the Father, had been proclaimed through every bloody offering from Abel's altar to the granting of the apostolic commission, but was first announced, in the name of Jesus, at Jerusalem. Had the gospel been first—I mean Christ's gospel—preached at Rome, at Corinth, at Athens, at any other city or place, these prophecies would have been falsified; but, in this case, as in all other cases, the prediction is unerring, because uttered by "the Spirit, who searches all things, yea, the deep things of God:"—holy men, committing them to record, "as they were moved by the Holy Spirit." 3d. When was this gospel first preached? We answer, on the day of Pentecost. Hence, Christ says, immediately after having commissioned his apostles, "and behold, I send the promise of my Father upon you; but tarry ye in the city of Jerusalem until you be endued with power from on high." Luke xxiv. 49. "The former treatise have I made." says Luke, "of all that Jesus began both to do and teach, until the day in which he was taken up, after that he through the Holy Spirit had given commandments to the apostles whom he had chosen."—"He commanded them that they should not depart from Jerusalem, but wait for the promise of the Father, which, saith he, ye have heard of me. For John truly baptized with water; but ye shall be baptized with the Holy Spirit not many days hence." Acts i. 1-5. Hence, "when the day of Pentecost was fully come, they were all with one accord at one place." Acts ii. 1. The Holy Spirit descended upon them, and filled them, not only with all the fullness of the gospel, but endowed them also with the gift of tongues, so that they could preach it in all the languages of man, whither they might be sent to preach the gospel. We are safe, therefore, in the conclusion, that Jerusalem was the place where, and the day of Pentecost the time when, the remission of sins, in the name of Jesus, should first be preached, since the world began! But by whom should this doctrine first be preached? We answer:

4thly. *By the Apostle Peter.* "And I will give unto thee," says Christ, to Peter, "the keys of the kingdom of heaven; and whatsoever thou shalt bind on earth, shall be bound in heaven; and whatsoever thou shalt loose on earth, shall be loosed in heaven." Matt. xvi. 19. A steward, who should receive from his lord the keys of certain apartments, would, in the reception of those keys, receive also, both *authority* and *ability* to open and enter, legitimately, all the apartments, the keys of which he had received. This was figuratively, or spiritually fulfilled in Peter, so soon as the Holy Spirit came upon him. He possessed authority and power to open the temple of Christianity, and all its magnificent apartments, to both Jews and Gentiles. This he did, for the Jews, on the day of Pentecost, and for the Gentiles, at the house of Cornelius! We say Peter did this, and no other man! Jerusalem, by an irreversible decree, was to be the place, and Peter the man. Hence, not James, nor John, nor Thomas, but "Peter standing up with the eleven, lifted up his voice and said," etc. Acts ii. 14. The apostles all spoke, one in one language, and others in other languages; but Peter had the precedence! The preaching of the others was but translations of Peter's discourse. "Unto *thee,*" in the singular, "will I give the keys." Not to all the apostles—of course not to the popes! "And whatsoever *thou,*" in the singular, "shall bind"—"shall loose"!! To no other man, than Peter, has this power ever been imparted. Nor has it been necessary. The door of the gospel kingdom being once opened, no man can shut it! The pope may open, and shut, the door of his kingdom, at his own option; and others may do the same, in regard to the doors of *their* petty kingdoms! But we rejoice, that "the happy gates of gospel grace, stand open, night and day." None, but Prince Messiah, can shut them; and this he will never do, until "he shall come a second time, without a sin-offering unto salvation."

5 th. *General remarks and conclusion.*—

The characteristics of Peter's preaching were, 1st. Pre-eminent fitness to excite faith in the minds of those to whom it was addressed. He preached Christ, crucified, buried, risen, glorified. He presented to the minds of his hearers such proofs as were directly fitted to convince them that Jesus was the Messiah, the Son of God, the Saviour of sinners, the Lord of all; and, consequently, to put them into the possession of faith in Jesus, the cardinal first principle of the gospel, without which not even the first step can be taken toward either the kingdom of grace or of glory.

2ndly. It was pre-eminently fitted to produce in the minds of those that believed it, deep and bitter convictions for sin. "He," says Christ,—the Spirit—"shall convince the world of sin." Peter preached "as the Spirit gave him utterance," Acts ii, 4, and therefore, the Spirit,—the gospel being then, as it is now, the word of the Spirit—wrought faith and conviction in the minds of those who were converted on the day of Pentecost. They were made to feel the enormity of sin, in that they had been instigated to nail the innocent Son of God to the accursed cross, and put him to a most infamous and cruel death.

3rdly. It was fitted to excite penitence, deep and bleeding penitence, for having sinned against a Saviour superlatively kind. "O! thou bleeding Lamb! thou who hast said, "Father forgive them for they know not what they do,' is there forgiveness for us." This, or something like this, must have been the language of their hearts. They loved Jesus, seeing that he had first loved them, and had given himself to die for them, that through his blood, and in his name, they might obtain the remission of all their sins.

4thly. It was fitted to produce reformation. The exemplar was most upright, the motives comprehensive and omnipotent: motives, high as Heaven, deep as hell, comprehensive as the universe, and durable as eternity! Being "pierced in their hearts," "they were dead to sin," and through faith in a risen Savior, "alive to righteousness"—prepared, therefore, to serve God "in newness of life."

5thly. It was fitted to administer immediate relief to believing penitents. "Men and brethren, what shall we do?" "Repent and be baptized, every one of you, in the name of Jesus

Christ, for the remission of sins," &c., Acts ii. 37,38. "Then they that gladly received his word were baptized; and the same day there were added to them about three thousand souls." The manacles and fetters of their sins fell, broken, to the ground. They could now go on their way rejoicing. They had believed and been baptized, in the name of him who had died for them, and who had said "he that believeth and is baptized shall be saved." They could not doubt the veracity of Jesus; and hence, felt a rejoicing freedom, a renovating emancipation. How unlike to this are the gospels of modern sectarianism!

This gospel, this and no other, was, by the command of Christ, to be preached in his name among all nations. "If any man preach any other gospel to you, than that which we have preached unto you, let him be accursed," Gal. x. 9. The gospel as preached by Peter contains the terms of reconciliation—the conditions to be complied with on the part of sinners, in order to reconciliation with God,—the terms which the Son has authoritatively propounded through the Apostles. Any person, therefore, who shall propose other terms, or conditions of pardon, than those first preached at Jerusalem, and to be preached among all nations, perpetrates a forgery—does that, in the name of Christ, which he has never authorized. Hence, the malediction of Paul. O! it is a fearful thing, willfully to pervert the gospel! Ye haughty men, take care! Your clerical robes will not shield you when this globe shall be sheeted in flame! Away with party pride, and denominational selfishness! We shall be judged by the word which Christ has spoken, at the last great day.

It has often been objected that Peter, himself, did not, at the house of Cornelius, preach baptism for the remission of sins! Let us for a moment examine this case. "He shall tell thee what thou oughtest to do," Acts x. 6. "Who shall tell thee words, whereby thou and all thy house shall be saved." Acts xi. 14. Thus spoke the angel to Cornelius. Now what are the saving words? Why, Peter, with great brevity, preached Jesus to him, that he might believe, and commanded him "to be baptized in the name of the Lord." This, in so far as Peter's preaching is concerned, is positively the whole case. How accurately this tallies with the commission, "He that believeth and is baptized shall be saved." But Peter also in this discourse says: "to him give all the prophets witness that through his *name,* whosoever believeth on him shall receive the remission of sins." Now if Peter commanded them to be baptized in his *name,* and if in his name they received the remission of their sins, does it not follow that they received remission in baptism? Faith, baptism, and the name of Jesus, being all connected in this discourse, which contains the words by which Cornelius and his house should be saved, as they are connected in the commission, as given by Mark, and in the discourse on the day of Pentecost, and in the obedience of Cornelius and his house, the remission of sins in baptism is the necessary result. Nor does the descent of the Spirit militate against this position. The Spirit imparted to the converts the gift of tongues, Acts x. 48, and was a miraculous demonstration that God had granted to the Gentiles repentance unto life, Acts xi. 12, but the *gift of* faith came through the mouth of Peter! "God made choice among us, that the Gentiles by my *mouth,* should hear the word of the gospel and believe," Acts xv. 7. Believing therefore, by the mouth of Peter, and being baptized, in the name of Jesus, as Peter commanded, they were saved, or pardoned, as Christ promised. Their hearts being "purified by faith," and being "baptized *into* Jesus Christ," and "into his death," they obtained redemption through his blood, the forgiveness of sins.

If we are right, in our position, that remission of sins, in the name of Jesus, was never preached until the day of Pentecost, it follows that those who quote cases of pardon which transpired previously to that day, are guilty of an egregious blunder. As well might we, of Kentucky, consult our old State Constitution to ascertain our constitutional duties and privileges under the new. The new covenant was not sealed or ratified until after the death of Christ, and Christ was not crowned until forty days after his death, and ten days before the Pentecost! How, then, could the new covenant be in force anterior to the death and coronation of Jesus? But Jesus having died and sealed the new covenant with his blood, and being crowned Lord of all, on the memorable Pentecost, after his death, the administration of the new covenant began! There, "beginning at Jerusalem," we find the gospel terms of pardon; then fully developed, and never before since the world began.

If those who assume to be evangelical preachers, would practically regard this fact, it would save them, in communities enlightened by the gospel, from many blunders, and some shame, and those led by their teaching from much blindness! We should hear no more, for instance, of the thief on the cross, as a reason why persons need not obey Christ in the ordinance of baptism. The thief on the cross! a worthy exemplar of a worthy cause!! During his life he robbed men of their property, and now, that he is dead, he is ready to rob Christ of his glory, and men of their souls!! The thief! why, sir, the thief himself would reprove you! He was nailed to the cross. Baptism with him was an impossibility. Is it so with you? You are not a thief nailed to the cross! You may, indeed, be nailed to a stubborn orthodoxy, and I will not judge you. But I can give you a better model than the thief! Take Jesus for a model. He performed a laborious journey to receive water baptism at the hands of John, and when he had received it, said: "Thus it becometh us to fulfill all righteousness." Is not this a better model than your thief on the cross? Besides, your thief case proves too much! He had never joined the church. Does this make it unnecessary that we should join the church? He had never partaken of the Lord's Supper. Does this make it unnecessary that we should partake of the Lord's Supper? He had never given his goods to feed the hungry and to clothe the naked. Does this make it unnecessary that we should have that charity, without which we are nothing? In short, he had been a dishonest man Does this make honesty a non-essential, in regard to pleasing God, and ultimately obtaining a place in Heaven? Let us hear, then, no more of the thief on the cross, as a reason why the sinner need not obey the Saviour in the ordinance of baptism.

Every intelligent reader of the scriptures knows that there are many instances in the interim between John the Baptist and Pentecost, in which Christ, being personally present, pardoned sinners. But are the terms upon which they obtained pardon precisely those upon which we are to obtain it, under the New Covenant? A woman washed Christ's feet with tears, and wiped them with the hair of her head? Are these conditions of Gospel salvation? Zachaeus, who was rich, said: "The one-half of my goods I give to the poor, and if I have taken anything from any man, by false accusation, I restore him fourfold." "This day," said Jesus, "is salvation come to this house." Take also the case of the rich young man: "What shall I do to inherit eternal life?""Thou knowest the commandments," said Jesus; preached the law instead of the gospel! "All these have I kept from my youth up." "Yet lackest thou one thing: sell all thou hast, and give to the poor!" Why not preach these cases as models, rather than the thief on the cross?

But I must close. Reader, "begin at Jerusalem." Make this your stand-point. From this beginning corner, you may run, with accuracy, all the lines of the plantation of Grace. The favor of our Lord Jesus Christ be with you!

-----o-----

Revision Meeting in Louisville, Ky.

We were not a little interested and amused with an article which appeared in the *Louisville Courier* some four or five weeks ago, in anticipation of the Revision Meeting announced for the 10th of April. The announcement of the annual meeting of the Revision Association awakened from their quietude the following formidable array of names and churches, as appended to a labored document, extending over nearly two columns, closely printed matter, in the *Courier:* "W. L. Breckenridge, of the Presbyterian church; H. M. Denison, of the Protestant Episcopal church; Samuel Lowry Adams, of the Methodist Episcopal church

South; E. C. Trimble, of the Cumberland Presbyterian church; and G. Gordon, of the Associate Reformed church." What a flourish of names and churches is here made, to bear up, give force to, and press forward the warning voice, so benevolently tendered and lifted upon the walls of the several little Zions here mentioned, and so deeply interested in opposing all the dangerous efforts to obtain pure versions of the word of God, for all nations, now about to be made by the Revision Association! How these pious men and churches tremble at the impious and dangerous efforts of the Bible Union, to give every word which God has spoken, *correctly* translated, to the *whole people!* They are sufficiently acquainted with history, are men of sufficient understanding and forecast to see the dangers attending the ruthless erasure of all error from our translation of the Sacred Scriptures! We doubt not these men feel as indignant at the attempt to give the whole people, not even excepting the *English,* a correct transcript of the original Scriptures in our Vernacular, as the conscientious, learned, and zealous young Saul of Tarsus did at the apostles and first Christians, for writing, publishing, and preaching the same Scriptures in the language of and to the people in ancient times. No doubt their spirits burn with a vehement zeal in opposition to the great and good work of revision. They are unquestionably in trouble—deep trouble; it is no empty pretence; they are seriously in deep, heart-felt anxiety, and great concern. They feel intense solicitude, and their souls are burdened with the magnitude of the subject upon which they have lifted the kindly warning voice.

Reader, do you inquire what all this deep solicitude is about? If so, we will try and develop it to you, in some brief observations upon the main points in their article, objecting to the Revision movement, as follows:

1. They are opposed to the Revision effort because it is *sectarian.* This is truly a singular objection for them to make! Every one of them belongs to a sect, with a sectarian name and creed, and the entire religious benevolence of each one of them, is now, and has always been, circumscribed within the narrow limits of a mere partisan human sect, and his entire life has been engrossed, absorbed, and literally swallowed up, in the maintenance and up-building of sectarianism. Not one of these men know how to do a single act, religiously, in any other way, only as a *sectarian.* Even in their present array and display of names, each one sails under his partisan sectarian designation; and yet, objecting to the Revision movement under the pretext that *it is sectarian!* This is the most ridiculous pretext we have ever known! This caps the climax! No; the trouble is not that the move is sectarian. The work of revision is Protestant; it is catholic. All who love the truth, the whole truth, and nothing but the truth, are in for this great common-ground and truly Protestant move. The real difficulty with the gentlemen whose names, and the *sectarian* names of whose churches, are arrayed against revision, is that the Revision work is not sectarian; it is catholic; it is Protestant. They know the door is here barred against all sectarianism. Their high-sounding sectarian names all go for nothing in the Bible Union. It is neither Baptist, nor Pedo-Baptist; Trinitarian, nor Unitarian; Arminian, nor Calvinistic. All, in this great work, stand upon the same common level. Their partisan peculiarities find no place in the Bible Union. It knows no man after the flesh, nor after sectarianism; nor is it in any way responsible for the doctrine of its members, upon any subject, except faithfully translating the word of God. If the man is right on revision, the Bible Union pays no regard to his doctrine on other points.

2. The second point introduces the main trouble, viz. translating *baptizo.* They say the Bible Union will translate the Greek word *baptizo,* immerse. How have they arrived at this conclusion with so much certainty? They appear certain that *baptizo* will be translated *immerse.* We think so too, but why? For one reason, and one only, viz. one of the general rules governing the revisions is, that "the exact meaning of the inspired text, as that text expressed it to those who understood the original Scriptures at the time they were first written, must be translated by corresponding words and phrases, so far as they can be found in the vernacular tongue of those

for whom the version is designed, with the least possible obscurity or indefiniteness." No wonder these gentlemen express themselves with confidence touching the translation of this word; they have good reason so to do; not because the Bible Union has made any special arrangement for that word; but because it has a general requirement for *all words,* that will certainly reach *that one.* The requirement to translate *all words* into corresponding words in English, as far as possible, they know, will translate *baptizo,* immerse. They have no fears that the Bible Union will translate that word *wrong;* but they know that it *will be translated,* and translated *correctly,* and that a correct translation of it will not suit them. Here lies the trouble. If *baptizo* means *sprinkle,* the Bible Union rules require it to be so translated. The Bible Union has no special rule for that word; it is under precisely the same rule as all other words. The Bible Union simply requires that that word, and all other Words, be translated *correctly.* These men are opposed to having that word correctly translated; they want to leave it in Greek, where the learned King James' translators left it.

Their third objection is, that there are so few connected with the Revision movement. But, we inquire, why are there so few connected with it? if indeed the number be few, but which we do not believe. Have not others been solicited as strongly as those engaged in the work? If there are many men of great learning and standing not engaged in the work, or not favorable to it, why did they not come forth and watch over it? Even if they thought the common version good enough, and the move uncalled for, when they found that it would go on—the Bible would be revised—why did they not take hold of it, and see that it was done right? Or, if they thought the move uncalled for, why did they not attend the meetings, oppose the move, and show that it was uncalled for? All the Bible Union aims at is, to translate the whole Bible right—to give the people—the whole people, the whole Bible, with every word correctly translated.

If the errors in translation in the common version be few, the fewer changes will be demanded. The friends of the Bible Union desire every word *translated precisely right.* That is all they want. We have long been satisfied that there are some men who do not desire every word in the Bible translated precisely right; but we did not think there were five clergymen in Louisville, who would voluntarily come out, giving their names and the names of their churches, and place themselves in so awkward a position before the world.

The truth is, whether the number in favor of revision be many or few, the precise issue between them and their opposers is simply this: The friends of revision are determined to have every word in the Bible correctly translated—to have all errors, be they many or few, removed. Their opposers are determined that every word shall not be translated; that the errors in the common version, (and all admit that there are errors in it), be they many or few, shall remain in it. This is the exact issue, and if there are but few favorable to having every word in the Bible correctly translated; having all error removed from it; and if the number opposed to translating every word in the Bible correctly—to removing all error from it, be great, so much the more lamentable the state of the case. With us, it matters not how many great names of men, nor how many high-sounding names of sectarian churches, nor how many high-sounding human titles are arrayed in opposition to translating every word of the Living God correctly—to removing all error in translating, and in favor of leaving the people to read manifest errors, and having the preacher read from the pulpit most palpable errors, in translating, as the *word of God;* we know they are wrong—on the side of error—in favor of darkness, and consequently anti-Protestant. If the errors are ever so few and insignificant, in the common version, no man living ever did, or ever can offer a good reason for retaining them, and reading them as the word of the Living God. No set of men can present themselves in a more unfavorable attitude than the men have done whose names with the names of their churches, are paraded in the *Courier.* They came out of their own choice and free will, arraying their names and the names of their churches against correctly translating every word which God has spoken, and removing all errors in translation from the common version. They oppose themselves to a meeting, the object, and the only object, of which is, to promote revising the English scriptures—translating *every word* in the Bible—removing *all error from it.*

The plea is made that many distinguished and learned Baptists are opposed to revision. This is true; but what would it prove if ten times as many were opposed to it? opposed to correctly translating every word of the Bible, and to removing all error from all translations, and would succeed in their opposition; it would only prove that error had prevailed—had gained a victory; that darkness had gained a temporary triumph; light had been repulsed and betrayed—that the Lord had again been betrayed and forsaken by professed friends, and that the enemies of light had gained a temporary triumph. But these gentlemen may set their hearts at rest on this score. Light has a few friends yet. The Bible has friends yet. God has friends, and his word has friends, who will never rest while anything is mutilated, obscured and incorrect, or covered in dead languages. The time has come for searching everything to the bottom, bringing out everything in its purity. Those human structures, holding doctrines and practices not found in the Bible proper, but simply favored by erroneous translations, must take care of themselves. The friends of truth can do nothing for them.   B. F.

-----o-----

Our Position as a Religious Community.
NO. 4.

WHY should our maintaining the all-sufficiency of the Bible, as a rule for the faith and practice of all Christians, prove so obnoxious, so offensive and antipodal to the numerous religious combinations of these times? When this position was first shown to us, we thought all the good would greet it with joyfulness. It was so self-evidently just, right in itself, and manifestly the will of God; it so honored the Saviour of the world; the wisdom, goodness and benevolence of God; it so elevated Christianity, the Bible, the law of the Lord; maintained its perfection, dignity and glory; its supreme adaptation to the conversion of the world, the edification of saints, government of the church and guidance of the children of God to heaven; opened such a beautiful, safe and Godlike way for the escape of all the good, the pious, those who love Jesus and one another, to unite, in one community, one holy communion, one precious band of sons and daughters of the Lord Almighty, in the unity of the spirit, the bond of peace and love, and thus escape from all the bickerings, contentions, strifes and religious feuds that now mar the peace and comfort of the followers of the meek and lowly Jesus, that we thought it would be received with acclamation. We thought the main body of professing Christians would delight to speak of our Heavenly Father, as having given us a perfect, a complete system; to speak of our gracious Redeemer as the author of the faith; a perfect system of faith; complete in all its parts; adapted to man in a world of sorrow and sin, and as having given us the glorious gospel—the power of God to salvation to everyone that believeth. But how sadly we were disappointed here! Nothing appeared more repugnant to the great majority!

It is true, we found many who bless the Lord for the prosperity of their party, and ascribe the honor of it to him. We found many who would honor the Lord for raising up Methodists, Baptists, Presbyterians, Episcopalians, Lutherans, etc. Many praised God for Trinitarianism, Unitarianism, Calvinism, Arminianism; for Methodism, Presbyterianism, Baptistism, etc., but men who would honor God for the Bible, in all its divine perfections; who would honor and praise God for Christianity, as a complete, perfect and independent system; honor and praise God because he had raised up Christians, followers of Christ, children of God, heirs of the eternal inheritance, but who would be nothing more, were comparatively hard to find! Why is this? How can it be that anything so manifestly right, so perfectly consistent, and so perfectly in accordance with all the authority of heaven, should find an opponent among all who possess goodness of heart and a desire to do the will of God? The same question may be asked in regard to all those who refused Christianity when it was first proposed to mankind. Why did so many, not merely of the low and vicious, pagans and such like, but religious people, learned doctors, scribes and priests, the most refined, noble and great, reject it at the beginning? Was it because it was not a complete, perfect and infallible system? By no means; but rather the opposite. It was mainly because it claimed to be a perfect, complete and infallible system. Nay, more; it was because it claimed to be *the* perfect, complete and infallible system, that they hated it. It left no room for the wisdom of man to amend, complete or perfect. It left no room for uninspired and fallible man to prefix or affix. It left no possible room for any compromise with any other system. It left no possible ground for any other religious system to stand upon. It claimed infallibility. It rose up to the highest summit and claimed perfection. It came clothed with all the authority of the Divine Throne; and claimed to fill heaven and earth with the authority of the ineffable Jehovah, and left no authority for any other law or any other system. It came with all the glory of the Infinite One, and left no glory for any other system. It came filled with all the fullness of the incommunicable Spirit of God, with the only power to bless and save man. The power of the Almighty was in it. It called not upon man for favors, for assistance, and a position among other systems, but held out to man the only hand of mercy, of deliverance, of salvation, or pardon. It claimed the whole habitable earth as its rightful territory; the whole family of man as the extent of its mission, leaving no room for anything else.

But all this exclusiveness was not the extent of its offense. It did not stop here; but proceeded to set aside, as null and void, all other systems. To the Jew it said, "The law is abolished." "The handwriting of ordinances is taken out of the way"—"nailed to the cross." "Christ was the end of the law for righteousness." "By the deeds of the law, no flesh can be justified in the sight of God." To the pagan, it said of all their gods, that they were no gods—that they were powerless and could not save. To all, both Jew and Gentile, it declared them all sinful—in unbelief; gone out of the way and in a state of condemnation before God. It made no distinctions of men in high stations or low, but condemned sin in both king and subjects, rich and poor, priest and people. It waged an open, an unmitigated and uncompromising war upon every species of sin, vice and corruption. It unhesitatingly upbraided the hypocrisy and ostentation of the popular Pharisee, in his affected prayer upon the street, and gave the preference to a poor unpopular publican, who could do no more than smite upon his breast and say, "God be merciful to me, a sinner!" It boldly and firmly set forth the character of the popular priest and Levite, who passed the suffering man who fell among thieves, and honored the unpopular and, we may also add, the heterodox Samaritan. It approached the reveling, drunken and profligate Felix, regardless of his civil power, popularity or wealth, and set forth to him, "temperance, righteousness and a judgment to come." It boldly condemned every lust of the flesh, the pride of life, the love of the world. It faced every sinner, high or low, rich or poor, in church or out of it, and demanded in the most commanding and authoritative manner of him, in the name of the Lord, to repent—to break off his sins by righteousness, and bow implicitly to its claims—that Almighty God " commands all men everywhere to repent, because he has appointed a day in which he will judge the world." It faltered not, feared not, hesitated not one moment to declare to the incorrigible, the persistent in sin, and finally impenitent, that God would punish them with the devil and his angels.

Is it to be wondered at, that a system thus meeting and condemning all evil, sin and wickedness of every description; setting aside all the religious systems in the world as null and void, and setting itself forth as infallibly right and the only infallibly right way to please God here and attain heaven hereafter, should meet with opposition among misguided, ignorant and worldly men? Surely it is not; nor is it any more to be wondered at, that the same Divine system, claiming still to be the only divinely authorized religion, setting aside everything else as human, fallible and unauthorized, and still condemning all the sins of the world, should still be opposed. If we had came forward with another *form* of Christianity; another system that some man had extracted from Christianity, from scripture, and simply claiming that we could prove it by scripture, thus standing upon a level with the parties around us, we would have been orthodox enough by this time, and could have been tolerated well enough. This could have been understood without any trouble. But to come forward with the Bible, not as the proof-book, to prove *our* doctrine, but *the doctrine itself;* not referring to Christianity to show that *our* religion is like it; but presenting Christianity itself as our religion; having no religion but the religion of Jesus Christ itself; no faith but the pure faith of the Son of God; being nothing but Christians, disciples of Christ, followers of the Lamb, and doing nothing only what God requires, is a most intolerable heresy. It shows no favor to anything, but seems to engross all in its grasp. It literally subverts everything else, sets aside all isms, doctrines and commandments of men of every grade, as the most insignificant childish play. It comes to men, claiming the right to have the attention of all as though all beside were undeserving of any note or any regard whatever. Not only so, but it gives no chance to assail, expose and refute, for it maintains nothing but the Bible, but Christianity, but what God has given by inspiration and proved by supernatural signs and wonders, accompanied with gifts of the Holy Spirit, which all its assailants have to admit true! Can we expect to present the only true religion: the religion of Jesus Christ itself; the only true system: Christianity itself; the only revelation from God: that contained in the Bible; the only authority of God: the authority of the word of God; the only true doctrine: the gospel of Christ itself; and declare everything else unauthorized—null and void; hindrances to the progress of truth and righteousness; to the edification of saints and the conversion of the world, and meet no opposition? Not rationally. The watchmen on the old party walls of their little Zions will see the tendency of all this. They will see— they cannot help seeing—that precisely in proportion as we succeed in fixing the attention of the people upon God, his authority, his Son, our gracious Redeemer and Saviour, his word, his law, his religion, as a distinct, complete and perfect system, with all the power, grace, wisdom, mercy, benevolence and authority of the Almighty in it, calling the attention of man to it as the only medium of salvation, all their systems must necessarily lose their attraction, their command and influence, and hasten to ruin. Many of these watchmen are pledged for life, too bigoted to look if they may be mistaken, too obstinate, and self-willed to yield, and will oppose to the last. B. F.

-----o-----

Evangelizing, No. 2.

For the last five months we have been almost incessantly in the evangelizing field. During this period, we have been taking extensive items. The proper place to make a preacher is by the side of an old, a well-tried man, who is a preacher, in the field, where the work is to be done. In the same way, the proper place to find out the real state of the cause, is to go out into the evangelizing field. Men who merely read theories upon preaching, and theorize upon it themselves, know but little about it. They are like men who sit in a pleasant room and read fine theories upon farming, but never farm any; they know but little about it and practice none. The work cannot be done by *thinking* alone, no matter how well a man thinks, nor theorizing, no matter how good the theories; but reading, thinking and praying the Lord's blessing upon his labors, he must go forth into the field and put his hands to the work. No young man will ever become a farmer by sitting in the house and reading fine theories upon farming, no matter how good and true they may be; but let him read some, consult others who have experience, and ply his hands daily to the practical use of what he learns, and he will become a farmer. Going through the theory with his hands has a tendency to inscribe it indelibly upon his mind. He must have a practical use of tools, as well as the theory about them.

In the same way, the young man who would become a preacher, while he is receiving knowledge, or obtaining the theory, must ply himself to the work, making a practical use of what he learns. A man may study for years and acquire an immense amount of knowledge, but having no practical use of it, he is as helpless as an infant. In precisely this predicament are thousands who have gone through the manufacturing process of making preachers, without any practical use of all they have learned. Indeed, many of them have learned nothing of consequence, of one of the most important chapters in a real preacher's learning, viz: "The ways of the world." The knowledge of the Bible—general "book-learning," is all right. It is indispensable. But to *know man,* is equally important. Man must be studied to be known. We must converse with him face to face. We must know the world by actual contact with it. We must know the church by actual observation. We must know the obstructions in the way of truth and righteousness by actual contact with them, with actual and personal efforts to remove them.

Not only so, but the people must know the preacher—see him, hear him, and have personal interviews with him. His work cannot be done by proxy. He must go *himself* and put his own hands to the work. He must be with them and give them a personal example of deportment and religious conversation, read the Bible to them, pray with them, in their families, give thanks at their tables, go with them to the place of worship, preach to them and persuade sinners to repent. A man who does not do this, is really no preacher of Christ, and will accomplish nothing for his name. But we have strayed from bur purpose. We must return to speak of the state of things abroad.

We find many things far from being favorable, and that demand a mighty effort, on the part of all who love the Bible. We find things within and without, that he who would promote the interests of the cause, must encounter as . impediments of a very serious nature. Indeed, the days are decidedly evil, while the opposing and malignant influences are almost innumerable. He who wars against the opposing elements around us, must certainly add to his faith courage, and take to himself the whole armor of God, that he may be able to stand, having done all to stand. Never, since the Lord ascended to heaven, was it more difficult to present, enforce and maintain the pure faith of Christ, distinct from everything else, and keep it so, than at the present time. We therefore beg leave, under the head of "Evangelizing," to notice some of the evil influences around us.

1. The public mind is so completely bewildered, confused and confounded on the whole subject of religion, that anything clear, pointed and tangible, is thought to be almost out of the question. To meet this confused state of things, apologize for it and excuse the people in making no effort to extricate themselves from it, as well as resist all that any man may say in favor of something better, a kind of conventional agreement has been entered into that "it is no difference what road any man travels to heaven,"—that "whatever a man thinks right, that is right to him,"—that "there are good and bad among all"—that "if the heart is light, that's all,"—that "it is no difference what church a man belongs to," &c., &c. All who talk in this way, look upon any man who attempts to define the gospel, the church of Christ, the Christian doctrine, or Christianity, as a distinct system, complete and perfect in all its parts, as a simpleton, **a** bigoted, uncharitable and narrow-minded heretic. Here lies the battle-field. Here is the point for discussion. Is Christianity itself in the world, in a definite, tangible and explicit form, so that a man can receive it in an intelligible manner, as a distinct system? Has the Lord revealed Christianity to man, so that he can receive it and be a Christian, a servant of Christ and child of God, and nothing else? or is the world left in the dark, so that the best that can be done, is to make a mere imitation of Christianity, of our own, allowing others to do the same, maintaining that the imitation the nearest like the original is the best, but that any imitation will do? But in the same way, the young man who would become a preacher, while he is receiving

anyone can see, that we cannot tell whether an imitation is good, unless we know what the original is; and if we do know what it is, there is no excuse for not taking it, instead of any mere imitations.

2. The worst difficulty there is to encounter is the general state of indifference. There is a general state of don't-careitiveness. The Galio feeling abounds. Of all the opponents the preacher of Christ has to contend with, there is none that we so much dread as the man who cares for nothing—who is wholly indifferent—who scarcely has vitality enough to sit up in his pew, unless he can sleep sitting. There are men in these times, who by custom, mere habit, indifferently float along with the current to the place of worship, and sit, lean down, lie down, or lounge in an audience before a preacher, who seem to say, by every motion, every cuticle of the face, expression of the countenance and move of the eye, in thunder tones, to the discerning preacher, *I do not care what you say—whether your doctrine is true or false.* This discomfits the preacher. What can be done for a man who does not care? What can a preacher do for a man whose spirit is so calloused and numbed as to be incapable of giving attention to a single discourse? What can be done for men who have so lost the love of the truth, all interest in it, and so unfeeling to all its appeals, as to sit before him Who pleads its holy claims with earnestness, wholly inattentive? To such men the whole appears idle tales, a kind of dream or kind of dim vision. Many in this description, in church and out of it, cannot be aroused from their stupor, awakened from their slumbers and brought out from the almost impenetrable spell of thick darkness that envelopes them, by the efforts of any preacher. The thunders of Sinai would not do it. The melting strains of gospel love will not do it. Heaven's beneficence to man is all nothing to them. Many in this generation will never be awakened from this deep and awful slumber and the thick darkness that surrounds them, till the voice of the archangel from heaven and the trumpet of God shall summon them to the judgment of the great day.

An effort is demanded, such as we, as a people, have never made, such as man has rarely made, in any age, and equal to anything in the power of man to make, to awaken our cotemporaries from this terrible and fearful state of death. None but men who are in earnest can do anything in this work. Men who have no concern themselves, or who are nearly in the same predicament, may deliver their little, dry and lifeless harangues, but they make no impression. Men must be fully alive, have the benevolence of God at heart, enter the work with the whole soul, and labor mightily for the Lord. We must feel the need of a great effort, to save man, maintain righteousness and restrain the world from sin, and our efforts must make men feel the necessity of such an effort. It is not necessary that the imagination should be wrought up, but merely that the people be made conscious of the reality, to move those in the reach of reason and argument. But we defer approaching any other point, for a month.

-----o-----

Review of Dr. Shaffer on Baptism. No. IV.

Dr. Shaffer says "The baptism of the Holy Spirit had the appearance of cloven tongues of fire, which sat upon them. This was the visible sign or emblem of the Holy Spirit. It was not a large flame of fire, that they might have been plunged or immersed in it; but it sat upon them, just as we pour water upon a person to baptize him. It was in the form of a tongue, to represent that the *gift of tongues* was connected with the baptism of the Holy Ghost." (Page 150).

There is about as much stupid confusion of terms in this short extract as we ever saw in the same number of words. The truth is, his baptism is the most difficult thing to know anything about we ever saw. At one time he affirms, with much dogmatism, that the mode of baptism, as he expresses it, is affusion. He soon forgets this, and tells us that it is like cloven tongues sitting upon persons. Soon, however, he is off from this, and we hear him say, "We pour water upon a person to baptize him." Again we hear him speak of washing for baptizing. But, finally, we see him administer without sprinkling, pouring, washing or immersing, by laying his moistened fingers

gently upon the forehead, with the solemn words upon his lips, "I baptize thee in the name of the Father, and of the Son, and of the Holy Ghost." If we could believe him, his moistened fingers, laid gently upon the forehead, represent cloven tongues, like as of fire upon persons, affuse, pour, wash, purify, cleanse and "bury in baptism!" If this is not the climax of mystification, we know not where it will be found.

The Doctor allows the cloven tongues, like fire, were the visible sign or emblem of the Holy Ghost. Now where the Doctor learned this, we pretend not to say, for there is no such intimation in all the connection. The tongues, though probably upon the head, almost where the Doctor lays his moistened fingers to baptize, were no *sign,* or *emblem* of the Holy Spirit, nor were these cloven, or divided tongues, the *Holy Spirit itself,* but Heaven's emblems of the different tongues or *languages* spoken by the Apostles of the Lamb. But the Doctor was anxious to find a baptism *on the head,* and he guessed that the cloven tongues, not emblematical of the Spirit, nor like it, but *like fire,* were upon the head. He then guessed that they represented the Spirit. He next reasoned as if they were the Spirit itself, informing us that the flames were not large, that they might have been plunged or immersed in them. But the Doctor as well as the reader, must keep things which are in themselves distinct, equally distinct in their reasoning. The tongues were not the Spirit, did not represent the Spirit, but were *like fire,* and represented the different languages spoken. No one was baptized *with,* or *in* the tongues, but they *sat upon* the Apostles. The tongues, like as of fire, were not *poured out,* did not fill the house, nor represent any kind of baptism. It was the Holy Spirit that was poured out, and not the tongues. We invite the Doctor to keep his eye upon this fact, that it was the Spirit that was poured out, and he can soon determine whether *poured out,* here means *baptized.*

On page 149, he undertakes to find the mode of the baptism of the Holy Spirit. After quoting the prophesy of Joel, he remarks: "Here we see the baptism of the Holy Ghost was clearly performed by *pouring;*" and then, as if to make his work doubly strong, he says: "And, to put the matter beyond doubt, Peter, rehearsing the matter, says, He hath shed forth this which you now see and hear" and then, after thus proving, as he professes, that baptism is *pouring,* he only proceeds six pages till he affirms that it is sprinkling, or, as he politely and learnedly expresses it, "affusion!" With him, "shed forth" is *pour,* and this is "fell on them," and this is affusion," and this is "wash," and this is "purify," and this is "cleanse." Now, there is nothing more evident than that Dr. Shaffer did not know what he was about when writing his book. If he says he did, we ask him what was "shed forth?" what was "poured out" on Pentecost? The Lord says, "I will pour out my Spirit." It was the *Spirit,* then, that was poured out, not the tongues, not the people. It was the *Spirit* that was "shed forth," or "fell on them." Now, Doctor, who were baptized? The spirit was "poured out," then, does mean baptized, for it was the people that were baptized, and the Spirit that was poured out. But if you will have it, that "poured out" means baptized, then the Spirit was baptized, for it was "poured out" The pouring out was not the baptizing, but something that preceded it. We pour the water into the baptistery, and then baptize the people in the water, and thus the *water* is *poured,* and the *people* are baptized. On the day of Pentecost the Spirit was "poured out," but the people were baptized. The original word from which we have "poured out," (Acts ii. 17), and "shed forth," (verse 33), is not *bapto* nor *baptizo,* but *ekkeo,* and is never applied to the ordinance. If we could induce the Doctor to take one independent thought, we would mention to him with emphasis, that the people were baptized, but if there was any pouring for baptism, the water was poured, not the people. The people were baptized of John, *in* the river Jordan, but they were certainly not poured of John, in the river Jordan. Neither the river Jordan nor the people were *poured* of John, but the people were baptized.

REVIEW OF DR. SHAFFER ON BAPTISM.

But if the Doctor will have it that baptize is pour, and inclines to his favorite method of baptizing *with* water, we should feel no little surprised to see him pouring the people *with* the river Jordan!

The Doctor (page 148,) gives us the following quotation: "And suddenly there came a sound from heaven, as of a rushing, mighty wind, and it (the sound) filled all the house where they were sitting." The reader will perceive here, that my friend, Dr. S., infers that it was the *sound* that filled the house. If it should appear that the house was filled with the Spirit, the Doctor himself sees that there is no avoiding immersion. Let us look at the facts in the case. It was the *Spirit* that was "poured out," "shed forth," and "fell on them," was it not, Doctor? Your Bible says it was. Do you believe it? Well, your own witness says "He hath shed forth this which you now *see* and *hear.*" What was it that was "shed forth," which they *saw* and *heard?* It was the Holy Spirit. It was the Holy Spirit that Jesus promised, that John said they should be baptized in, that was poured out, that was shed forth, that they saw and heard, and that filled the house and the disciples. To raise a quibble about the *sound* is as unworthy as it would be to say that it was not Mr. Shaffer that I heard in the discussion, but the *sound* of his voice. It is true that they heard a sound from heaven, but it is equally as true that they heard the Holy Spirit, who made the sound. He was the author of the sound, of the tongues, the gifts bestowed and the words uttered, and those who saw the figurative representation of tongues, heard the sound and the words uttered, saw *and heard him,* who showed himself in gifts and tongues visible, and made himself audible in a mighty sound, as a rushing wind. But the Doctor turns grammarian, and says "the pronoun *it* has for its antecedent *sound."* Yes, and it has also, and equally as grammatically, for its antecedent, the Spirit who made the sound, who was shed forth, whom they "saw and heard."

The Dr. decides that there is but one real baptism, which is that of the Spirit. The baptism in water is only to represent it. He has also decided that in this baptism of the Spirit the soul is baptized.

According to this when were they baptized, and how, on Pentecost? Was the soul baptized by the appearance of tongues *upon the head,* or when they were all *filled with the Holy Spirit?* If it is, as the Doctor affirms, the *soul* that is baptized in Holy Ghost baptism, it is no "affusion" nor "pouring," but took place when they were *filled* with the Spirit, when the soul was overwhelmed with the Spirit. There was no sprinkling here. To talk of representing this glorious and miraculous display of the power of the Spirit of God, by a slight sprinkle, only shows that a man has never appreciated, in any degree, this illustrious event, and fulfillment of one of the most notable prophesies in all the Bible. Such notions lead to as unworthy love and groveling conceptions of the great, supernatural and stupendous work of the Holy Spirit, on the memorable Pentecost, as sprinkling is below and short of what God requires for baptism. How absolutely low, unworthy and utterly contemptible, to be led by the stupefying, blinding influence of a system, that would turn the coming of the Holy Spirit of God from heaven, the visible representation of tongues, the sound as of a rushing, mighty wind, with all the wonderful work of the Spirit on that day, overwhelming and filling the apostles, into a mere *affusion!* The Spirit of the living God was poured out, shed forth, seen, heard, and the house and people were filled, overwhelmed with his Divine presence and power, This was no sprinkling, nor is any sprinkling on this earth any representation of this stupendous work. It is the most ridiculous thing we have ever found, to see a man trying to represent the grandeur, power and majesty of the works of that day, or to hear him speak of doing it by sprinkling a few drops of water upon the face. The Holy Spirit, on that occasion, put their whole beings under his overwhelming power; their entire bodies, souls and spirits were controlled by him. Even their tongues, their vocal organs, and their very breath, used in the utterance of words, were under the absolute command and made the infallible instrument of the Spirit of all wisdom, in delivering Heaven's message of salvation to man.

the work done on it the most grand and sublime ever known since the sun first rose, and sent forth his rays upon the face of the newly created earth, and the imagery that would represent it must be no insignificant and unmeaning ceremony. Dr. Shaffer, therefore, need not look here, while trying to find a *sprinkling* mode of baptism, nor while trying to *avoid immersion*. They were not *sprinkled* in the Holy Spirit, but immersed, overwhelmed. It filled all the house, and filled them.   B. F.

-----o-----

Clerical Organization.

NEAR INDIANAPOLIS, March 6, 1856.

BRO. FRANKLIN—On reaching home last night, from the trip on which I was starting when I saw you last Friday at the Union Depot, I found the March No. of the *Review,* with which, as a whole, I am well pleased.

Like Brother Rogers, I have not been able to furnish a discourse for the March, and I cannot certainly promise one for the April No.; but still I hope to find time to do something of the kind before a great while.

My attention has been attracted to the doings of those ten congregations of our brethren in Kentucky, whose constitution and proceedings I saw first in the *Age,* and now in the *Review*. I was rather meditating some anim-adversions on the movement myself, or, rather, on those obnoxious features of it, when your March No. came to hand with such a crushing avalanche of condemnation from yourself, Bro. Rogers and Bro. Raines, in addition to the little sketching it received in the *Age,* that really my sympathies, always inclining to the weaker party, are becoming enlisted in their behalf. I beseech you, therefore, to hear me a few words.

It is known to the most of your readers that I have written considerably within the last few years, upon church organization, cooperation, missionary societies, &c., and in all these I have endeavored, like Job of old, to "sin not, neither to charge God foolishly." In other words, I have been actuated by a sincere desire for the *advancement*—not the *retrogression*—of this reformation, esteeming it, as I yet do, the last hope of a sin-ruined world. And I still say, if it be true that we cannot resort to *any* measures by which our aggregate strength, numerical, moral and pecuniary, can, in some good degree, be brought to bear upon the world around us, without involving a departure from New Testament ground, it is a melancholy comment upon the frailty of poor humanity, and no very flattering eulogy on the wisdom of the Divine Author of the system.

But so it is. As yet *every* effort of our brethren, East, West, North or South, having for its object the accomplishment of the aforesaid purposes, has either utterly failed through its own inherent inefficiency, or, unfortunately, fallen under the anathemas of some of our leading brethren, who have seen, or thought they saw, something dangerous, or *horn-like,* on its cranium.

Is it possible that he who "upheld all things by the word of his power," either could not, or would not give us a system *capable* of being *lawfully* worked to any better results than we have, as yet, seen under the *disciplinary* training and *cooperative* machinery of the "Current Reformation?" Is any brother, whose heart is fired with the love of God, and a realization of the work the Master has given us to do, willing to sit down contented, and see churches depopulated by the apostasy of their members, for the want of a well-digested and faithfully executed system of church edification, in the hands of a competent and *Scripturally* constituted eldership? And is he *satisfied,* moreover, to see sinners perishing on every hand for want of more energetic and efficient efforts to bring them under the saving influences of the Gospel?

I cannot believe the former of these double interrogations, and I trust I never shall become willing to sit down and submit to the latter. Indeed, it may be my mishap to live to see this reformation encrust itself in a shell too hard to admit of any growth; but I shall not cease to *pray* and *hope* for better things; yea, and *labor* for it, too.

But how, it may be asked, is a better state of things to be induced? I see no way of bettering it, we may finally get out all the details of the Lord's plan, if, indeed, he has given us a *detailed* plan of operation and cooperation, or otherwise, become satisfied that he has left the *details* of his plan to be settled by conventional arrangements, from time to time, as the exigencies of the cause may demand, and the improvements of the age may warrant.

Whenever we become fully satisfied of this fact, as all must be, sooner or later, we will be prepared to receive with greater patience, the imperfect effort at detailed plans submitted by the brethren, and instead of demolishing, by a single blast of indignation, the whole fabric reared by the united wisdom of *ten* churches, and that, too, before it has had time to have done either good or evil, we will be disposed to suggest such amendments as we may think calculated to *improve,* if not to *perfect* the plan; and if we cannot succeed in getting our own views adopted entirely, we will be willing to see the practical working of it, before we entirely repudiate it.

Such is my feeling in relation to this Kentucky move. I decidedly disapprove of the 3d and 4th articles of their Constitution, and would earnestly recommend their speedy repeal ; still, I am not disposed to annihilate the whole proceeding, on account of that error of judgment, if it be an error, as I honestly think it is.

Let them give their plan a fair trial, and if it succeeds, well; if not, unite your wisdom with theirs, in making such amendments as will give it efficiency and success.

It is much easier to pull down than to build up, and I fear what you and others have already said may have sealed the fate of the whole enterprise.

You should not have taken it from them, unless you had given them something better in its stead. Understand me, I agree with you and Bros. Rogers and Raines, in the specific objections offered to the concern; but like the old man in the anecdote, I think it too " big a *boo* for so young a colt." B. K. SMITH.

-----o-----

REMARKS.

We are from home, as we are a large share of our time, engaged in a protracted meeting. We aimed to have had the foregoing article of Bro. B. K. Smith with us, but on opening our port-folio, find that we have not got it. His remarks, however, from our memory, from a single reading, are general, and we can respond as far as necessary now, while we have opportunity. He laments that we should have laid hostile hands upon the first-born clerical organization, without giving it time to bring forth fruit, and thinks that an effort should have been made simply to strike out objectionable features and amend it. He also deplores the idea that our power cannot be brought to a focus, and made to bear upon the world; that so soon as an effort to do this is made, the alarm is raised by someone, and the effort is strangled in its infancy, and the same deplorable state of things must continue.

Now we have noticed for a year past, that our brethren favorable to some such scheme as the one set on foot at Danville, Ky., have assumed that the " downward tendency," which they maintain exists, results from our having no such organization as they plead for. But here we take the issue with them; the thing they assume is the identical thing to be proved. Our mind is made up on this point. If preachers lament that the cause languishes, let them cease scheming about some organization unknown to the New Testament, and go into the field and labor for the Lord's sake, and for the Lord's name, as brethren did years ago, and as we are doing now, and, as certain as God is the author of the Bible, we shall prosper. Preaching is what is needed, fervent, soul-stirring preaching, exhortations, entreaties and impressive persuasions with the people to turn to God, and be saved.

We are told that "preachers are not supported." Be this as it may, one thing is certain, *viz:* that such an organization as plead for, will give no better support to *working* men. There are men in all communities that never did and never will work, unless it be to work their way into the fat places of some ecclesiastical machinery, where they can skim off the cream, and leave the skim-milk for working men. We do not intimate that any among us are aiming at this, but to this it comes in all the contrivances in the world, of the kind, and you will find men ready for it among us, as soon as the opening is made. No, if good men, industrious, laboring men, desire a support, and we all know they must have a support, let them go out among the people, where their lives and labors are known, eating the fruits of their *own labors;* if they cannot get a support in this way, they cannot in any way. We would rather trust to the Lord for a support, through his people, where we are known, and where we do the labor, as we have done now for fifteen years, than to any ecclesiastical organization, such as alluded to, in this world. This principle works right. The apostle says: "If any work not, neither shall he eat." Why should not this apply to preachers as well as to other men? Let every man who can preach go into the field and work mightily for the Lord, and while the work will progress, the preacher will find a support.

We object to the organization formed by our brethren in Danville, not merely because it is not done to *suit us,* but because the entire move is uncalled for, unwise, and wholly unauthorized. The thing is wholly unknown to the New Testament. The New Testament records inform us of the organization, or, rather, the institution of individual communities, or churches, and the appointment of officers in them. But these records know nothing of any organization of the churches in any given district into one body, under a new set of officers, who are officers not of the churches but of the district. While we were generally satisfied with the simple New Testament organization of individual communities, with full power and authority to do their own business, and the preachers went forth to build up, strengthen and sustain these communities, as well as convert sinners; we prospered throughout the land; but the moment we began to try to ape the parties around us, in scheming at things beyond the simplicity of Christ's own order, our success began to abate. The principal difficulties which have caused the most distressing controversies among us, have grown out of attempts, one way or other, to combine, concentrate and organize the Christian communities into some kind of a body unknown to the law of God.

We are perfectly aware that if we wish to put the Christian communities into the power of men, to control them, wield them, and make them engines to honor man, we need some kind of an organization, beyond the simple organization of the New Testament; but the simple, independent church, for keeping the ordinances, religious instruction, and saving the world, is all-sufficient for the good of saints and the glory of God. Indeed, one of the principal reasons why this question of organization has perplexed the minds of so many, is, that they are looking for, and trying to make out something unknown to the whole New Testament. They overlook the simple, easy and common-sense arrangement of the New Testament, and complain that we have no arrangement. The way of the Lord is so perfectly simple, easy and natural, that they do not regard it as a way at all, and think we must supply the deficiency, or do what the Lord has left undone. It is amusing to see the different routes by which brethren have attempted to arrive at the same conclusion, on this point. One brother sets out gravely to show scripture authority for such an organization as is desirable, and claims that he finds abundant authority for it. Another looks over the matter, and is satisfied that he has failed. He throws all that plan aside, and claims that the whole matter is left to human prudence and discretion, and that we need no authority for it, any more than to build a house of worship, or send out a missionary to a certain field of labor.

It is no matter what way brethren attempt to arrive at the thing, whether by authority from the Bible, or merely as a prudential and discretionary arrangement, it is wrong, and will only result in evil, and only evil continually. All history shows that the first foothold that Anti-Christ obtained, was in making a man an officer, giving him official power and control over a district of churches. As soon as this principle had obtained in the primitive churches, the power of this *Bishop of churches* grew with wonderful rapidity, the one-man power increasing, the districts enlarging, and human power taking the prerogative of divine, until the Bishop grew into a lord, both political and ecclesiastical, and the concentration never ceased, till it embodied and centered all power in one earthly head, the Pope. When power was thus concentrated, they could bring it to bear upon a heretic, in the form of an anathema, or upon his neck, if they wished, to cut off his head.

The kingdom of God has no use for any such schemes. Christians desire to serve God, save themselves and those around them. They have no vain glory to build up some great system for the world to admire. Their ambition is to spread righteousness in the earth, peace and good will among men. Their mission is to make men personally better, and prepare them for a better life.

There can be no objections to churches cooperating in any great enterprise that may come before them, such as employing an evangelist either to preach among them, to send out in their own country, or go to a distant land, or in sending means to the poor saints at Jerusalem, in Ireland, or wherever they may be found. There can be no objection to churches cooperating in such a work as the Bible Union; but in doing so, they give the Bible Union no authority over them; nor do they give any other churches or men authority over them. They only unite their efforts with other churches in accomplishing what they both Relieve to be a good work, but not to obtain assistance from others to govern them, or dictate what kind of doctrine or preachers they shall have. B. F.

-----o-----

A Serious Difficulty.

Our attention has been directed to an article in *The Presbyterian of* Feb. 9th, published in Philadelphia, written by a clergyman in a very serious difficulty. The article is headed "The Baptism of Children of Unbelieving Parents." The writer says: "I have been called upon to-day to baptize a child, neither of whose parents are members of the Church, and I have evidently given offense by refusing to do it." He then proceeds: "How can I administer baptism in such circumstances?" Here you see, is a serious matter. In the midst of this trouble, he says: "Our Confession of Faith is most explicit on this point." It says: "Not only those that do actually profess faith in, and obedience unto Christ, but also the infants of one or both believing parents, are to be baptized." What makes the matter more singular still is, that he adds: "And even more explicit, if possible, is the word of God." Why need he be in such a strait, when the Confession is so very explicit and the word of God even more explicit? But the reader is anxious to know where the word of God says anything about it, and he will be no little surprised when he learns where baptism was instituted. He says: "Going to the first institution of this precious sacrament, God's covenant with Abraham is in these terms: 'And I will establish my covenant between me and thee, and thy seed after thee, in their generations, for an everlasting covenant; to be a God unto thee, and to thy seed after thee.'"

Now that the Confession is explicit on the subject we cheerfully admit, but that the Bible says one word as to whether the parents of children to be baptized shall be believing or unbelieving, we most unhesitatingly deny.

We go further, and promise that if any clergyman in America will show that infant baptism is mentioned in the Bible, in any shape or form, we will stand pledged before the world, to show that the children of unbelieving parents are as much entitled to it as anybody. If any man will show that anyone person, without faith, repentance, and personal preparation of heart and life, or one single thought or divine impulse, is entitled to baptism, we will show that all men are. Or if any man will show that a fleshly relation ever entitled anyone person to baptism, we will show that it entitles all men to the same privilege. We stand pledged to prove that a fleshly relation entitles no person to either faith, repentance, baptism, prayers, the Lord's supper, or any other spiritual blessing in Christ. No blessing in Christ is promised to any fleshly relation, or to any because they are in any certain fleshly relation. Fleshly relations secure fleshly blessings; but spiritual relations secure spiritual blessings. It is a spiritual relation to be in Christ; but a fleshly relation is to be in a father's family. One relation obtains by being born of the flesh, and the other by being born of the Spirit. The one obtains by being born of an earthly father, and the other by being born of the Heavenly Father.

What a ridiculous idea, that any man professing to be a minister of Christ, should go back to the covenant with Abraham to find the institution of baptism! If we go there to find "the first institution of this most precious sacrament," we not only find not one word about it, but find the very man with whom it was instituted entirely ignorant of and failing even to observe it, and all his descendants for near two thousand years. A man to speak of "this most precious sacrament" being instituted this great length of time before the most pious people knew it, or even observed it, is ridiculous in the extreme! But why go back to the covenant with Abraham to find the institution of baptism, where there is not one word about it? Why not go directly to our Lord's own commission which he gave to his apostles, where we do find baptism? For the good reason that there is not only nothing about children here, but prerequisites that put infants out of the question. Here it is, "Go *teach* all nations, baptizing them," &c. "Go into all the world, and *preach* the Gospel to every creature," &c. Not only so, but it is added: "He who *believes* and is baptized shall be saved." This does not suit, because it places *teaching, preaching* the gospel, and *believing*, before baptizing. The matter sought by the advocates of infant baptism, is something to base baptism upon besides *teaching, preaching,* or *believing*. But all the preachers in the world cannot produce, from the Bible, an instance of baptism, not preceded by teaching, preaching Christ, and faith in him. For the sake of preachers in the same difficulty, we make the following observations:

1. Baptism is a command from God to the person to be baptized. No one but the person to whom a command is given can submit to it. An infant is not a subject of command, cannot submit to a command, and, therefore, is not commanded in the scripture to be baptized, or do anything else.

2. No person ever was commanded to have another person baptized by our Lord; nor did any person ever do such a thing, under his authority. It is not, therefore, the duty of any person to have an unconscious infant baptized.

3. Baptism is always preceded by hearing and believing. An infant cannot hear the gospel, and believe it and therefore, cannot scripturally be a subject for baptism.

4. Baptism is the answer of a good conscience. An infant can have no conscience, either good or bad, and therefore cannot be a subject of baptism.

5. Baptism is the visible form of making a profession. An infant can make no profession, and, therefore, cannot be a scriptural subject for baptism.

6. Baptism must be preceded by a preparation of heart. "With the *heart* man believeth unto righteousness, and with the mouth confession is made unto salvation." "When they heard this they were pricked in the *heart,*" etc. An infant can have no heart in it, and, therefore, cannot be a subject for baptism.

We will try and define, as near as possible, in a few words, the precise difference between us and Pedo-Baptists on this subject. We hold, that hearing the word of the Lord, believing in Christ as the Redeemer and Saviour of the world, solemn and sincere repentance for all sins, a divine change in the heart, purposes, or designs, and a personal submission of a person's own soul to the divine authority, requiring man to be baptized, are the pre-requisites to baptism—that he who has these is entitled to the ordinance, no matter of what nation, tribe, or tongue, or whether his parents are believers or unbelievers. Our friends of the Pedo-Baptist order hold, that the infant of one or both believing parents, without ever having heard the word of God, without any faith in, or knowledge of, the Redeemer, without any repentance, any preparation of heart, or any recognition of the divine authority, or even any knowledge of what baptism is, or what it is for, and without any will or consent in it, by virtue of a fleshly birth, or a fleshly relation to its earthly parents, is entitled, to, and a proper subject for, baptism. The whole question turns upon the single point, are the antecedents to baptism fleshly or spiritual? If the antecedents to baptism are simply, that one or both of the parents shall be believers, then all the Baptists in the world are laboring under an important mistake, and depriving many proper subjects from this divine appointment. But if the antecedents required in the word of God are spiritual, such as being "begotten by the word of truth," "pricked in the heart," "believing with the heart," "repentance unto life," "confessing with the mouth," having "the heart purified by faith," etc., all Pedo-Baptists are making a most fearful mistake, in baptizing so many in the awful "name of the Father, and of the Son, and of the Holy Ghost," who have not the first antecedent required by the Author of the Christian faith.

The simple matter is, whether we shall have some process of proselyting infants, before they can have any will in the matter, any choice of their own, make any decision for themselves, before they have a single impulse upon the subject, a single thought, or any heart in it—thus disciplining them without reason, without scripture, without the spirit of God, without Christ, and without their own consent or knowledge, by virtue of a fleshly relation to believing parents, or wait till their own hearts and spirits are susceptible of divine impressions, till they can hear the Lord themselves, believe in him, repent of their sins, love him, adore him, and submit in their own persons to him, in baptism, and everything else he has appointed. We are for the latter—we have no confidence in proselyting unthinking and unconscious infants; but if any do it, we recommend the Romish plan for it, viz: baptize every one you can lay moistened fingers upon, whether the parents believe or not. B. F.

-----o-----

Even a fool, when he holdeth his peace, is counted wise; and he that shutteth his lips is esteemed a man of understanding.

The Ministerial Calling—Its Support.

THE subject above named, is one to which the attention of the brethren has been called, and no doubt the reflecting portion of them is well posted in regard to the nature and importance of the subject under consideration. It is not my object on the present occasion, to endeavor to throw any new light upon this subject; that would be a vain effort for one of my humble ability to make. Still, a subject so important cannot be too familiar to our minds. Without attempting to investigate the nature and importance of the "ministerial calling," I shall endeavor rather to call attention to the conceptions which some men have of this calling and those engaged in it, and my own ideas of these things.

1st. I will notice that the calling is considered by some as being disreputable, and ought not to be encouraged.

The mind of any individual must indeed be much more conspicuous for moral obtuseness, mental dullness, and gross impiety, than for moral acuteness, mental penetration, and spiritual piety, that entertains any such preposterous ideas as the above, concerning the ministry. Such minds are extremely narrow and unjust, for they cannot take a broad view of this subject, and unjust, because they regard all men as disreputable who are engaged in this calling, from the fact that they have known some engaged in this calling to be bad men. Now, it is unfair to condemn any calling as disreputable simply because a person engaged in it dishonored it, or was a base individual. If we are allowed to condemn all professions because someone engaged in each did wrong, then we might condemn not only every profession, but also every vocation in which men are engaged, for there are none but that has some base persons engaged in them; and what man can say, with any semblance of truth, that all vocations are dishonorable?

We have seen that the ministerial calling is not to be considered disreputable simply because some persons engaged in it are bad men. If it is disreputable, then there must be something in it to make it so. In order to find the truth of this matter, we must inquire into the nature of this calling, (which we had not intended to do in this paper); but we shall be brief. What is there in the nature of this Calling to make it disreputable? Nothing. Why? Because this is a holy calling; it is so because ordained by the Lord Jesus Christ, and nothing ordained or originated by Him is wrong or unholy. For he is altogether reputable, holy, just, and good. Therefore everything ordained or originated by Him must be of the same nature. It is very clear then, that, instead of this calling being disreputable, it is just the reverse. Then it is not disreputable.

But the objector farther says, that it ought not to be encouraged. Of course, if it is disreputable, it ought not to be. But we have clearly shown that it is not so, but on the contrary, that it is something reputable. If this be so, I cannot see why it ought not to be encouraged. Anything that is of good reputation, is certainly calculated to make him so, who lives in accordance with its nature. Then, if for no other reason, it ought to be encouraged on the ground that it makes him who engages in it of good character. Now, a good character is more to be desired than much riches, says the "wise man." But this is only one reason why it should be encouraged; there are others more weighty; and, 1. The mission of that man who engages in the "ministerial calling," is to preach the purest, soundest, and sublimest morality that ever entered ino or proceeded from the mind or heart of man. 2. But still better, his mission is to preach and teach the most sublime, soul-redeeming and enlightening and meliorating system of religion ever taught by man or angel. 3d. His mission is to preach and make peace in this world of strife and contention. 4th. In one word, his mission is to teach and encourage everything good, and repudiate and deprecate everything evil. If these be the objects of the "ministerial calling," (and who dare deny it?), why not encourage it? There is no reason why we should not; but there are certainly very weighty ones why it should be encouraged. There is no calling in which man engages, that promises and will do more for the amelioration, both in the present and future state, of the race of man, than this. And yet, strange to relate, there is no honorable calling in which a man engages, that does not receive more encouragement than this! Even those who profess to love and encourage the ministerial calling, do but little, comparatively, to encourage those who would enter upon it. If a young man engages in the profession of law, (which, in these days, is to teach men how to take advantage of the law in order to get the advantage of their neighbors), he is liberally encouraged. * * * If a man wishes to become a politician, and learn to dupe the people by making political hobbies, he is encouraged to his heart's content, and into office he rides on his own hobby. But now, here comes along a young man of fervent piety; he loves his God; he loves the immortal souls of men; he sees the broad road that leads to eternal ruin wide open, and thousands rushing onward to it. This causes his manly, his Christian heart to throb with strong emotions of pity and love. He says to himself, "Perhaps I may be an humble instrument in saving some of these poor souls." The resolution is no sooner made than entered into. But, hark! What do I hear, both in the church and world? "He is a fanatic!" "A zealot!" "Madcap!" "He's crazy!""He wants to render himself conspicuous!" And a thousand other remarks too hateful to mention. Why all this tirade of epithets? Because he is going to be a preacher.

But notice this young man a little farther. He applies himself to his work; ardently, zealously, and faithfully does he plead with souls, and warns them by everything sacred, to be reconciled to God. Night and day, like Jacob of old, wrestles he with his God for the souls of men. He becomes the humble instrument of converting many to God. His heart is full; joyous emotions swell his bosom! But, alas! his purse is empty and his family reduced to poverty.

Brethren, is it right thus to treat earth's noblemen? Is it right that we should indulge in such harsh epithets toward one who loves God and his fellows? Is it right that we should suffer our young and old preachers to come to want?

You know it is not. God will hold us accountable for it. For every privation which they have endured, the brethren who can and will not relieve them, will, in my humble judgment, be held accountable. But, oh! say some, these things only serve to develop the man. How? By killing him? Strange way we have of developing men! Preachers have enough privations to endure, without our wantonly adding to them.

The time has come when the honest and sincere preacher of the gospel should cease to be called or considered a "pauper." I am heartily sick of it, and so I think every friend of truth and righteousness should be. I am not for pampering preachers; I am for feeding and clothing them and their families, and have enough over to educate their children. This I beg not, but this I contend for, and the Bible and justice says it is yours. Should there be any who entertain any doubts as to the truth of this matter, I refer them to Luke x. 7, 1 Cor. ix. 1-14, Gal. vi. 6. May the Lord help us all to do our duty more faithfully.

A FRIEND OF PREACHERS.

LIBERTY, Clay co., Mo., Feb. 10, 1856.

-----o-----

Wars and Rumors of Wars.

ON Friday night before the third Lord's day in March, we commenced a series of discourses, in Florence, Ky., which we continued over Lord's day, with large and interesting audiences. An arrangement had been made for a discussion, between Messrs. J. W. Bidgell and J. D. H. Corwine, commencing on Monday night, and to continue five successive evenings, in the Christian chapel. The former of these gentlemen is a circuit-rider in the Methodist Episcopal Church. The latter has occupied the same position, but has seceded, and now protests against the economy of the M. E. Church, and dispenses with the ordinance of the New Testament. The points for discussion are the following:

1. Ministerial affairs and prerogatives, as held and exercised in the Methodist Episcopal Church, are unscriptural and detrimental to Christianity. Mr. Corwine affirms.

2. Water baptism was designed to be perpetuated in all ages of the Church. Mr. Bidgell affirms.

3. Water baptism is the cause of schism, and carnal security in the Christian Church. Mr. Corwine affirms.

At the appointed hour the house was filled to its utmost capacity, and the debatants were on hand with stacks of books. Mr. Corwine is a grave man, in appearance, candid and unassuming, modest and gentlemanly, well acquainted with the political structure of the Methodistic system, but certainly but poorly posted up in the New Testament. His antagonist is entirely a different man. His very first appearance announces, to a discriminating observer, that he is saying to himself, "Stand aside here; *I* think *I* know all about it." He is small, sharp-countenanced, tonguey, and rather a keen man; but Mr. Corwine is the better scholar.

Mr. Corwine rose and opened the discussion with a few very appropriate and respectful observations. He then, very deliberately, though kindly and respectfully, proceeded into the oppressive, tyrannical and despotic features of the Methodist system. We took no notes, and shall not attempt anything more than to give a few points, from memory, without being particular as to the order in which they were presented. He maintained that a general principle is abundantly set forth in the scriptures, condemnatory of supremacy in office, in such passages as the one where our Lord reprimanded those who desired the preference of his right and left hand in his kingdom. Such as those who inquired who should be the greatest in the kingdom. That the declaration that "we -are all kings and priests," clearly intimates equality of rights, and is subversive of all grades of ministerial authority and prerogatives. He contrasted this with the grades of authority and power conferred upon the different officers in the Methodist Church, beginning with the class-leader, the lowest officer in the Church, and passing up through the steward, circuit-rider, presiding elder, in regular grades up to the bishop, the highest officer in the Church. He referred to many passages in the discipline, setting forth gradation from inferior to superior in office, such as the ordination vow, in God's name, amounting to the same as an oath, to "reverently obey them to whom the charge and government over you is committed, following with a glad mind and will their Godly admonitions." Dis. p. 128.

He walked into the self-created, self-authorized and self-empowered ministry, showing that the people have no voice who shall he their ministers, what pay they shall have, nor what their qualifications shall he; that the court to try them is created by ministers, conducted by them; that the whole arrangement is a perfect despotism—that the whole Church property belongs to the preachers—that the people cannot sell a house which they have built with their own money, etc., etc.

Mr. Bidgell opened with some pleasantry, and the declaration that he was "in for war," and in his first speech challenged "any man between the poles, who had not been as high as Paul, or deep as the deluge, to debate with him the twenty-five articles of his Discipline." This challenge, as generally understood, was for us, but we stood it without the least notice, except the single observation, at the close of one of our discourses, that we came not there to interfere with either of the disputants, or their debate, in any way, and that certainly we should accept no challenge from either of them.

He then set out, with great earnestness, to prove different grades of ministers. This he proved in a summary way, in appealing to the Aaronic priesthood, and the Levitical of the Old Testament, to the apostles, evangelists, pastors and teachers of the New Testament. He seemed to think that all would see at once that the grades of office in the M. E. Church, were precisely the same as those referred to in the Old and New Testaments. But, if we are not much mistaken, there were many there convinced, as we have long been, that there is not a New Testament office, nor officer, in the M. E. Church.

His method of proving the call to the ministry was alike summary. He showed that Aaron was called of God, and that Paul said of the Apostles, "How can they preach except they be sent?" He then inferred from this that Methodist preachers are called and sent. Mr. Corwine could not see the connection between the premise and the conclusion. B. F.

-----o-----

Nicholsville, March 20th, 1856.

DEAR BROTHER FRANKLIN: It may afford you some gratification to know that I occasionally, in my travels, come across your periodical, and that I am greatly delighted with its contents. I can most cordially take you by the hand and bid you onward, praying the Lord's blessing on your labors. We greatly need a paper in Kentucky, and you could be most liberally sustained, as well as aided by a host of good writers.

At this time we have on hand several most worthy, Christian enterprises. 1st. The orphan girl school at Midway. It still needs about $20,000 to complete its endowment. It would be a great blessing, and a high honor for some one or two persons to step forward and cap it.

2d. We are raising a large fund to be placed in bank stock, independent of any institution of learning, the interest of which is to be devoted to the education of pious youths for the Christian ministry. We have obtained already about $30,000 in subscriptions, and we are educating several young men, of great promise, on the interest.

3d. We are attempting to endow Bacon College with $100,000, and have obtained already about $50,000 of the amount.

These enterprises have developed a new feature in this reformation, and the sterling worth of the brethren is manifesting itself in a manner worthy of themselves, and the cause in which they are engaged.

All will acknowledge that a vast deal more might have been accomplished in the last twenty-five years; but a nobility of soul has characterized the brotherhood from first to last. Proper appeals, properly explained, have been responded to in a worthy, Christian manner. We have been for co-operation from the beginning, and we have been for liberality in giving.

I could give proofs in abundance. When we first started we formed a co-operation of several counties, and engaged Elders John Smith and John Rogers for three successive years as our evangelists, and they accomplished a mighty work. They were paid for their services; and, more or less, co-operations have existed ever since; and the other parties, the Baptists in particular, are under peculiar obligations to us, for the advantage we have been to them in regard to co-operation and liberality. We have personal and party defects, and who calculates on perfection? We should, all of us, labor to cure these defects; but great care and prudence should be exercised in all our labors. Love should be the ruling passion in all that is done or attempted.

Some seem to imagine that tight lacing and a rigid discipline would heal all the difficulties that beset us. What a grand mistake. A love for the cause must exist. The heart must be in it. Love to God and man—the salvation of our race, must predominate. A self-sacrificing disposition on the part of preachers and people is indispensable. Personal piety and devotion springing from a heart leavened by the gospel needs not much tight lacing, watching or rigid discipline. A fatherly watch and care on the part of shepherds of the flock is needed. A visiting of the families, urging them into family worship, alluring the members to the regular meetings on the Lord's day—at prayer meetings and Bible classes. These are the things that are needed, and to be urged by the elders; and, to cap the climax, the overseers leading the way, let each member endeavor to imitate the Saviour in relieving the wants and woes of our unfortunate race.

We are associated with a mighty host of worthies, for which we ought to be thankful. May we all abound in good works, a thousand fold more, is my prayer in the name of Christ, my Lord.

Most affectionately,   J. T. JOHNSON.

N. B.—Bro. Rice and myself are here for a day or so. My home is now in Lexington, with my youngest daughter. My post office is there. J. T. J.

Is Man Capable of Self-Government?

Facts.

1. God placed Adam and Eve in the garden. He gave them law. Their destiny was committed to themselves. They disobeyed; they fell, and ruin was the consequence.

2. A remedial system was presented; the Patriarchal Age was subjected to it. Its blessings were personal, and depended on obedience. The grand consummation in consequence of disobedience, was concentrated in the deluge.

3. The Legal Age was introduced and submitted to a nation at Mt. Sinai. The voice of the nation was appealed to. God was chosen as their King, and Moses as his servant. Disobedience ruined the nation.

4. All this was preparatory to, and introductory of the Christian Age; and the great question is still before man, Will you choose God as your ruler, or the Devil? This question is at the very door of the Church of God. "If thou shalt confess with thy mouth, that Jesus is Lord, believing in thine heart that God has raised him from the dead, thou shalt be saved."

This is the greatest question that was ever submitted to man, and each one has to decide it for himself. It involves one's eternal destiny. If God has so highly honored us, who will cast it away, or surrender it into the hands of another? If God has submitted this grand question to every man, and consequently considers him capable of deciding it, what question belongs to the Christian system from a participation in the decision of which anyone of its subjects is to be excluded?

The Great God has committed all power into the hands of his Son. Christ is, emphatically, our King and Sovereign. He is to be confessed, he is to be obeyed in all things. Having voluntarily become his subjects, we are under every obligation to honor him by an implicit submission. His citizens are required to band themselves together, in the fear of God; to choose their officers; to submit to them, and to aid them in enforcing the laws of Christ, as well as to be ready to every good work for the good of the body, and for the conversion of the world. Neither is independent of the other. There must be a concurrence. It cannot be otherwise. But all must be done agreeably to the will of our Great Law-giver. Those who depart from this are responsible to him. The minutia of conducting matters to a proper issue, is another and different question. The body must be consulted. It must act. It has been active in submitting. Its continued loyalty must be tested by constant appeals, and constant action. Every member of the body has a duty to perform; and the officers who fail to call into requisition the talents, the influence, and the resources of the members, are either ignorant of their duty, unacquainted with the genius and spirit of Christianity, or they are grossly and culpably negligent. We must cultivate love to God, love for man, love for the cause, love for the' Bible, love for the prayer meeting, for the Bible class, for Sunday schools, love for the poor and needy, the widow and orphan, love for the salvation of the world.

When we love one another with pure hearts and fervently, there will not be much need for discipline. The army will present a front to the world more terrible than an array of glistening bayonets. Each congregation, and each member of each congregation, will then be seeking out objects to relieve, and the cry will be from thousands of the purest hearts, what can I do to advance the cause of salvation? Young and old, rich and poor, male and female, will, with one mind and one heart, march to the rescue.

It will not be, How small is the sacrifice that will be received at my hands, but How much can I bear? May the Lord speed us in such a result! Then our coffers will be supplied, and overflowing for every good work, and our State meeting enterprise will be worthy of a great and good people, engaged in the best cause in the world.

Oh! the vast difference between the present time and twenty-five years gone by! Matters have settled down into something like permanence, congregations are established, preachers are settled and sustained, evangelists and preachers are being educated, and they are now received and heard, just so far as they are known and commended by a *responsible* congregation. It is not now, as is the case in every revolutionary movement, that responsible and irresponsible men and boys are running to and fro, as they list. Things have cured themselves. Let time do her work. We cannot force her faster than she chooses to travel.

Having some experience and age on my side, with the love of Christ and his cause, the ruling passion of my soul, *the Lord knoweth,* I modestly think I may say to my brethren, *think of these things.*

Let us make a fresh start; let us love one another more, and strive to emulate each other in good works. We now have enterprises before us that will try us all to the bottom, and some of us will not live to see the glorious results. We can work faster and do more as our time is short. Grace, mercy and peace to the brotherhood. As in all my epistles, my own name, J. T. JOHNSON.

-----o-----

The many "Human" Creeds, Disciplines, and Confessions of Faith *vs.* The one "Divine" Creed, Discipline and Confession.
CHAPTER III.
INCONSISTENCIES.

I SHALL now proceed to contrast some portions of your doctrines with others, and also with scripture, and show their inconsistency.

Here is a book—the production of fallible men; as such, it cannot claim divine authority for its precepts; yet you require all officers in your church to "adopt it, as containing *the* system of the doctrine taught in the holy scripture."

Now let us look at its origin. We find that it was first adopted by the Presbyterian churches of America, in May, 1821. At the time of its adoption, it must have been either perfect or imperfect; if it was perfect, it must be imperfect now, since it was "*amended* "in 1833; if imperfect, then you compelled your officers to receive and adopt an untrue system of doctrine, as that taught in the holy scriptures.

Thus we see, from the very first page of your excellent summary of the Bible, that you have compelled your members to subscribe to a false doctrine either for twelve or twenty- three years. But, as it was mere humanity that decreed their orthodoxy or heterodoxy, the same corrupt source may yet invalidate that which is now sound.

---

* Presbyterian Confession of Faith.

Whoever heard of an "amended" Bible? For more than eighteen hundred years it has remained unchanged, while your summary of it has changed twice in less than twenty years.

Here is another little book,* of no higher origin than the one we have just glanced at. The very first sentence, and second word in it, stamps imperfection on its contents, and warns us to beware! "The DOCTRINES!" We read nowhere in the Bible of the doctrines of Jesus Christ. It is always styled the *doctrine*—in the singular! But in the Bible we *do* read of the *doctrines* of *men* and of *devils*—in the plural! And it would seem, that this book, true; to its origin, treats of "the *doctrines* of men;" and if it treated only of united societies, conferences, circuits, class-meetings, love feasts, band societies, and other human figments, I should not notice its doctrines of men for man. But, in the very outset, it treats of "Articles of Religion," and lays pretensions to be also a DISCIPLINE sufficient for the perfection of man!

Now I shall contrast portions of their contents, and see how harmonious they are.

In the book first mentioned we read, that God has predestined some men and angels to everlasting life, and has fore-ordained others to everlasting death, and that these angels and men, thus predestined and fore-ordained, are particularly and unchangeably designated; and their number is so certain and definite that it cannot be either increased or diminished. Thus it unalterably fixes the future destiny of all mankind by the fore-ordained decrees of God.

But when you come to speak of the last judgment, you predicate that all persons who have lived on the earth shall appear before the tribunal of Christ, to give an account of their thoughts, words, and deeds, and to receive according to what they have done in the body, whether good or evil.

In the first passage cited, you make man's eternal destiny dependent on unconditional election. In the second, you make it contingent on the *quality* of his thoughts, words, and deeds. These conclusions conflict with each other. One *may* [is] be true! One of them *must* be *false*!

---

*Methodist Discipline.

I shall now contrast several specimens of your doctrines, which you teach are to be received "as being an ordinance of God," with scripture.

You teach, "there is no sin so great that it can bring damnation upon those who truly repent." The Bible teaches, "whoever speaketh against the Holy Spirit, it shall *not* be forgiven him, neither in this world, neither in the world to come."

You say, the elect "can neither totally nor finally fall away from the state of grace, but shall certainly persevere therein to the end, and be eternally saved." The Bible reads, "they have forsaken the right way, and have gone astray." "It had been better for them not to have known the way of righteousness, than, after they have known it, *to turn away!*" "Demas has forsaken me, having loved this present world!" Where died our father Adam, who was created in the *image* of God, in Eden, or out of it?!

You both affirm, that man is justified by faith *alone!* The apostle James affirms, that man is *not* justified by faith only.

But, I presume, you will not both affirm to this question: Can a Christian fall from grace?

P.—A Christian can neither totally nor finally fall away from the state of grace, so as to be eternally lost!

M.—Ah! brother, you are mistaken there; a Christian may depart from grace given him, and fall into sin, and you are to be condemned for saying he can no more sin so long as he lives here, so as to be totally and finally lost!

C.—I presume it will be granted, that if a witness in giving testimony contradicts himself in the important parts of his evidence, that at least a part, if not all, of his testimony, is *untrue*. This is precisely the position of P.'s testimony, as to man's future destiny. *First,* he fixes it by - unconditional *election. Second,* by the *quality* of his thoughts, words, and deeds.

Again, if the evidence of two witnesses disagree in its essential parts, either one or the other must tell that which is *untrue!* This is precisely the case with P. and M., when one testifies that a Christian *cannot* totally and finally be lost, and the other that he *can!*

Again, if the evidence of both disagree with the known facts in the case, that of both must be *untrue!* This is the case with P. and M., when they both testify, that "Faith is the *alone* instrument of justification"—"We are justified by faith *only!*" when the truth in the case is, "that by works a man is justified, and *not* by faith *only—alone!*

ABNER APPLEGATE.

Little Heart's Ease.

Did you ever read the story of *Little Heart's Ease?* When all the other flowers in the garden were discontented and wishing they were situated differently, the Heart's Ease looked cheerfully up into the nobleman's face; and when he said, "How is it, Little Heart's Ease, that you look so bright and happy, when all around you are withered and discontented? She said, "Because I think that if the nobleman did not want me in his garden, he would not have placed me here; so I am determined to be just as good a Little Heart's Ease as ever I can be." This Little Heart's Ease has read a lesson to me, and I do not intend to be unhappy or discontented any more.

The Third Epistle of John.

The elder unto the beloved Gaius, whom I love in truth.

Beloved, in all things I pray that thou mayest prosper and be in health, even as thy soul prospereth. For I rejoiced greatly, when brethren came and testified to thy truth, how thou walkest in truth. Greater joy than this I have none, to hear of my children walking in truth.

Beloved, thou actest faithfully whatsoever thou doest toward the brethren, and toward the strangers; who have testified to thy love before the church: whom thou shalt do well to set forward on their way in a manner worthy of God: for in behalf of the name they went forth, taking nothing from the Gentiles. We, therefore, ought to receive such, that we may become fellow-laborers for the truth. I wrote unto the church: but he who loveth to be foremost among them, Diotrephes, doth not admit us. Therefore, if I come, I will bring to remembrance his deeds which he doeth, prating against us with wicked words; and, not contented with these, neither doth he himself admit the brethren, and those who would he hindreth and casteth out of the church.

Beloved, do not imitate what is evil, but what is good. He that doeth good is of God; he that doeth evil hath not seen God. Unto Demetrius testimony hath been borne by all, and by the truth itself; but we also testify, and ye know that our testimony is true.

I had many things to write, but I will not with ink and pen write unto thee; but I hope straightway to see thee, and we shall speak mouth to mouth. Peace *be* to thee. The friends salute thee. Salute the friends by name.

Gems of Thought.

KNOWLEDGE is power, in the pulpit as well as out of it. To bless mankind, God does not indeed require man's wisdom, neither does he require man's ignorance. As he graciously condescends to work by means, the more appropriate the means, the more abundant will be his blessing, without which all means will be alike in vain.

IT is our work to *cast* care—God's work to *take* care. Distrustful care is a canker that doth waste and dispirit. Care adds much to our grief, nothing to our comfort.

LET US not take on too much for them whom God hath taken away; let us not trouble ourselves for them that are at rest; let us not shed over-many tears for them who can now shed tears no more forever; let us not grieve too much for them who cannot grieve, because sorrow and sighing are fled away.

LOVE is happiness; he who grows in love, grows therefore in happiness. God is love; and love is his image within us. If I would resemble him, let me strengthen love, never allowing a degrading selfishness to reign in my heart.

GOD made for some of the martyrs a prison sweet as a garden of flowers—what then will be heaven? If afflicting mercy be so great, what will be crowning mercy?

MEDITATION on death gives a grand and mellow tint to our habits of thinking—as a great ocean exposed to the rising sun borrows from its edge to the farthest bound of waters a celestial glow of light.

Life is the day of salvation, the golden season when grace may be obtained, the period when the ship of the gospel lies in our harbor, bound for Immanuel's land. Never to be remeasured, never to be recalled, never to be redeemed, let us improve it by applying our hearts unto wisdom.

If the sun is going down, look up at the stars ; if the earth is dark, keep your eyes on heaven. With God's presence, and God's promises, all may be cheerful.

Grace humbles while it elevates; and the more we are loaded with divine benefits, the deeper should we sink under a sense of our unworthiness. The lowest valleys are the most fruitful; on them the gentle dew descends from the surrounding hills, and the boughs that are laden with fruit bend toward the earth.

Where the heart has been opened by the power of God's grace, the mouth will be opened in the celebration of his glory.

The love of Christ is unparalleled in its nature, intense in its ardor, immense in its extent, and glorious in its purpose and issue.

He that is not against his sin, in a lively resistance, is for it in his affection. He that does not oppose the tempter, invites him. He that hinders not the occasion of his sin, tacitly wishes the event.

-----o-----

A Good Sentiment.—It is better to go to the house of mourning, than to go to the house of feasting. Sorrow is better than laughter, for by the sadness of the countenance the head is made better.

So spake Solomon, the wise man, and surely he had a right to speak on this subject, for he had tried both feasting and mourning ; he had experienced sorrow, and had enjoyed the pleasures of mirth, and spake from the heart, when, in old age, he uttered this sentiment. He knew that all the purposes of the heart formed in the house of mourning are of the purer and better kind.

Editor's Table

Office of the *American Christian Review,* West Fourth street, No. 60, on third floor, open stair way from outside. Signs will be seen at the entrance.

Postage on this Magazine, when paid quarterly in advance, *six cents* a year.

Eld. John A. Sidener, is located in Chillicothe, Livingston county, Mo., where he desires all communications for him addressed.

Errata.—Page 108, nineteen lines from the bottom, for " incommunicable," read *infallible.* How we failed to notice this improperly used word, we are unable to tell.

Eld. A. Raines' Sermon.—The valuable Sermon found in this No., is also printed in a tract by itself, and is for sale at this office. Price, 5 cents, single copy, or three dollars a hundred. We still have plenty of the Sermon of Eld. M. B. Hopkins, found in No. 2 of Review.

North, Western Christian University.—We have just received assurances that the University is in a prosperous condition ; that everything is working well; the utmost unanimity, harmony, and good feeling among all, both professors and students. The Lord grant that such may be the continued report from that important point.

The Communication of Eld. J. T. Johnson.—The voice of this distinguished man of God is very different from many we now hear. Look over it and see if brethren are not aiming to do something noble in Kentucky. This comes from one who has traveled over a large portion of the State, and who knows what he is talking about. It is not mere theory with him.

-----o-----

Success of the Gospel.

Bro. K. Wilson wrote of his evangelical labors, and of some splendid success that had attended his efforts. By some means the letter is mislaid, or we would insert the item of news.

Brother T. Bernaw, of New Paris, who was at our meeting at Bethel, when we left, says, " I have just got home from Bethel, where I preached two sermons each day, Friday, Saturday, and Lord's day. The result was, twenty additions—eight before you left. It was truly a refreshing time from the presence of the Lord. Uncle Elisha made one of his big exhortations.

Brother R. A. Bowermaster, of Bowerville, Ohio, speaking of our late visit in his place, says, "The work of the Lord is going on here. Two have united with us from the Methodists, and one has been restored since you were here, and all desire to know when you will be here again."

DEAR BROTHER:—At a meeting near Paw Paw, on Lord's day evening, the 2d inst., *one* young gentleman confessed his faith in Christ. Also, during a series of meetings in Hamilton, held in conjunction with our beloved brother, and fellow-laborer, Edward Barnum, two persons bowed allegiance to the Prince of Life. I have just closed a meeting of unusual interest in Pipe-Stone, Berrien county. Much prejudice was removed, sinners were led to rejoice in the glorious liberty of the children of God, and the disciples of Jesus were comforted and greatly encouraged in the divine life. *Six* were reclaimed, *two* added from the United Brethren, and *six* were received by confession and baptism. A deep and general interest was awakened, and an impetus given to the cause of primitive Christianity in this region, which we trust will bear it onward, despite the frowns and anathemas of sectarian bigots, and the vile sneers and maledictions of the infidel world. Praised be the name of the Lord, who giveth us the victory through our Lord Jesus Christ.

WILLIAM M. ROE.
Buchanan, Mich., March 16th, 1856.

-----o-----

Literary Notices.

"*Campbellism: its Rise, Progress, Character, and Influence,*" by the Rev. N. L. Rice, D. D. Such is the title of a pamphlet, of 140 pages, numbered 170, published by the Presbyterian Board of Publication, Philadelphia. We sympathize with the Rev. Dr. in his labors of love, and propose to aid him and the Presbyterian Board of Publication, by giving the public a pamphlet of like dimensions, affecting all he has said, and furnishing like information touching the rise, progress, character, and influence of Presbyterianism. We pledge our self to give him a dose that shall fully satisfy his utmost curiosity. There is no necessity that such a braggadocio as he should go unrebuked.

The Pastorate.—Such is the title of a discourse by Eld. D. S. Burnet, now pastor of the church on Sixth Street, ordered by the State Meeting, in Harrods-burgh, Ky. This discourse contains many fine thoughts, well expressed, and will well repay a careful reading. Price 5 cents, single copy; 25 cents, six copies; $1 for thirty copies; $3 for one hundred copies. Address Eld. D. S. Burnet, Cincinnati.

Christian Sunday School Library.—We learn from a notice on the cover of the Pastorate, that "more than forty volumes of the Christian Sunday School Library are stereotyped, and that the balance will soon be out It is now wholly in the hands of Elder D. S. Burnet The statement is, that this leaves him involved in a debt, without means to print the first 1000 copies. In view of this, he asks for the speedy payment of Life Directorships, and Life Memberships, remaining unpaid.

In press, and will be published in April, "The Memoirs of *Rev. Spencer H. Cone, D. D."* Prepared by his Sons.

Dr. Cone was President of the American Bible Union, correspondent and friend of Adoniram Judson, the eminent Missionary, and one of the most remarkable men of the present age.

The *Bible Union Quarterly* thus speaks of him:

"Whose heart is not heavy with the swelling emotions of Borrow, as he seeks in vain in *his* wonted place for that beloved form, whose very presence in our meetings was a strength and a joy; and the thought rises that he shall 'see his face no more,' no more hear that familiar voice which ever rung like a clarion-peal in defense and advocacy of the highest and holiest truth, and in cheer and encouragement to its faithful friends, and whose very name was a guaranty of success to every enterprise and principle to which he gave his heart and soul. May God have mercy on the man who can cherish aught but honor, love, and gratitude for the character and services of Spencer H. Cone."

Dr. Cone's life was full of romance and incident, as well as a bright example of Christian virtues; and the volume is one which should find a welcome at every fireside and a place in every family library.

It will contain 450 or more pages, printed on fine white paper, bound in muslin, and embellished with a steel portrait, engraved by Buttre, whose reputation as an artist is unapproachable. 12mo; price $1.25.

Agents wanted to canvass every town and county in the United States, who will receive a liberal commission, and to whom a specimen copy of portrait, style of type and binding, will be furnished in advance of publication.

TERMS—Cash on delivery. Sample copies sent by mail to any part of the country, (post paid), on receipt of $1,25.

Supplied by Thomas R. Harris &, C. H. Farrell, American Bible Union Rooms, 350 Broome St., N. Y.

OBITUARY.

DAN WEBSTER, Henry co., Ind.

Bro. Franklin—Our beloved sister, SUSAN SMITH, consort of Bro. Ira Smith, is no more. She calmly and triumphantly fell asleep in Jesus, on the 27th of December, 1855, in the 35th year of her age. She had been a member of the church of Christ about three years; and she had, previous to uniting with the Christian Church, belonged to the regular Baptist Church some ten years, and by the spotless purity of her life and character she exhibited the highest evidence that she had learned of Him who is meek and lowly in heart. In fervent piety and entire consecration to God, she had few equals. She lived the life of the righteous, that her latter days might be like theirs. She exhorted her friends and relatives to prepare to meet her in the blessed mansions above, where there shall be no more parting, and where the weary shall forever be at rest.

SAMUEL S. CANNADAY.

THE AMERICAN CHRISTIAN REVIEW.

Vol. 1.]   CINCINNATI, MAY, 1856.   [No. 5.

THE KINGDOM OF MESSIAH.

BY W. C. ROGERS.

31. Thou, O king, sawest, and behold a great image. This great image, whose brightness was excellent, stood before thee; and the form thereof was terrible.

32. This image's head was of fine gold, his breast and his arms of silver, his belly and his thighs of brass.

33. His legs of iron, his feet part of iron and part of clay.

. 34. Thou sawest till that a stone was cut out without hands, which smote the image upon his feet that were of iron and clay, and brake them to pieces.

35. Then was the iron, the clay, the brass, the silver, and - the gold, broken to pieces together, and became like the chaff of the summer threshing floors; and the wind carried them away, that no place was found for them: and the stone that smote the image became a great mountain, and filled the whole earth. * * * *

44. And in the days of these kings shall the God of heaven set up a kingdom, which shall never be destroyed: and the kingdom shall not be left to other people, but it shall break in pieces and consume all these kingdoms, and it shall stand forever.—DANIEL, ii.

ONE of the strongest evidences in favor of the authenticity of the Word of God, is its purity, simplicity, and moral grandeur. The purposes of God, manifested in the old and new covenant, are of the most benevolent character, the means employed for the accomplishment of these purposes simple, and the consequences resulting there from in the highest degree beneficial to mankind. In all that God has said and done, nothing can be found unworthy the character of the moral governor of the universe. Not only is there no antagonism existing between the principles and objects proposed in the sacred Scriptures, but the most perfect harmony. The combined wisdom of the past, neither could have projected nor executed such a work as the Bible. It is beyond the conception of the finite mind. Its origin is higher than earth, and its projector loftier than him whose days are as a "shadow that declineth." A proud monument it stands in the midst of ruins and desolation. The subversion of governments, and the crashing fall of empires disturb not the fixedness of its deep and broad foundation. It was built by the Most High, and is by him sustained. We are not only astonished at the inimitable beauty and simplicity of the word of God, but are subdued in contemplating the exactness with which the prophetic declarations come to pass. The inspired prophet looked through the thick darkness of coming ages, and saw the rise, decay, and final destruction of tribes, nations, and monarchies. But he lived not to see fulfilled what he declared should transpire hereafter. He died, not comprehending the full meaning of his own predictions. The Christian student of the nineteenth century, does not, of course, understand all prophecy; but enough of its fulfillment is exhibited in the past and present to demand an acknowledgment from all, of the greatness and goodness of Him who doeth according to his will, in the armies of heaven and among the inhabitants of the earth.

For the purpose of seeing what God has done for the salvation of a lost race, and what good thing is yet reserved for a perishing world, I propose to consider the time when the God of heaven designed setting up that kingdom which shall never be destroyed. Nebuchadnezzar, king of Assyria, had dreamed a dream. Daniel, the captive prophet, came into his presence and commenced the revelation of his dream. "Thou sawest, and behold a great image. This great image, whose brightness was excellent, stood before thee, and the form thereof was terrible. This image's head was of fine gold, his breast and his arms of silver, his belly and his thighs of brass, his legs of iron, his feet part of iron, and part of clay, * * * Thou art this head of gold." Daniel spoke with remarkable definiteness. There is no evasion in his remarks. Thou art this head of gold, settled at once the position of that power ruled by Nebuchadnezzar. The Assyrian empire was a vast and mighty empire. Its capital was Babylon. Its walls, gates of brass, proud temples, beautiful gardens, and inexhaustible treasures, spoken of by historians, and sung by many a bard, proclaim the magnificence and power of this renowned city. This empire ended B. C. 538, and was succeeded by another kingdom, in accordance with the words of Daniel. "And after thee shall arise another kingdom, inferior to thee." This language was addressed to Nebuchadnezzar. He was assured, that on the ruins of his kingdom should arise a kingdom of inferior character. The Assyrian empire surpassed the Medo-Persian empire, alluded to by Daniel, in splendor and treasure, and power. It was well represented by the breast and arms of silver. It is a settled fact that the Assyrian empire was represented by the head of gold. The only kingdom arising immediately after it, was the Medo-Persian. Therefore, since this is the case, and since the Medo-Persian was not equal to the Assyrian empire, the prophet could have meant no other empire. It continued only for a short period of time. It terminated B. C. 331, and was followed by a kingdom whose characteristic features were faithfully sketched by the inspired prophet. After the destruction of the second kingdom, "a third kingdom, of brass, should arise, which should bear rule over all the earth." The Macedonian empire bore rule over the then-known world, extending from the Adriatic sea to the Indies, embracing the most, powerful and warlike nations of that time. The Greeks, from the character of their armor, were called "brazen-coated." In the days of their glory they were invincible in war, unsurpassed in the love of science, and the cultivation of literature. These facts are sufficient to identify this empire with the third kingdom —the kingdom of brass. Alexander the great, who had at least extended and strengthened the Macedonian empire, died B. C. 323. After his death his empire was divided among his four generals. Their possessions were soon embraced in the fourth kingdom. "And the fourth kingdom shall be strong as iron: forasmuch as iron breaketh in pieces and subdueth all things; and as iron, that breaketh all these, shall it break in pieces and bruise." Thus is the Roman empire delineated. The Romans were brave and death-defying. They were indefatigable in whatever they undertook, and usually accomplished their purposes. They were tough as iron. The Roman empire was emphatically the iron kingdom. No empire more justly merited that appellation.

Thus far have we seen the kingdoms, or empires, represented by the gold, the silver, the brass, the iron, of that terrible image, beheld in a night vision by Nebuchadnezzar. In the changing fortunes of these four empires we see the hand of God. He is not an idle spectator of the affairs of this world. Individuals, communities, and nations, cannot elude this sleepless eye. His searching glance penetrates the deep fountains of the heart, and all the machinations of good and bad, great and small, are known to him.

Daniel ii, 44, makes the following significant declaration: "And in the days of these kings shall the God of heaven set up a kingdom, which shall never be destroyed; and the kingdom shall not be left to other people, but it shall break in pieces and consume all these kingdoms, and it shall stand forever." "These kings," and "these kingdoms" are employed in this verse as synonymous. Nebuchadnezzar is addressed as if he were the kingdom of Assyria. "And after thee shall arise another kingdom." Such language is not inappropriate, since the king is guaranteed supreme authority. But the question to be determined is, *in the days of what kingdoms did God purpose setting up that kingdom which shall never be destroyed?* Some say, in the time of the four great empires above named; others say, in the time of the ten kingdoms which arose phoenix-like from the ruins of the Roman power. Hence it is believed by some, that the kingdom of God is already set up; others are of the opinion, that it is not yet set up, but will be in the future. The ten kingdoms represented by the ten toes, are not alluded to in the second chapter of Daniel as kingdoms. They are not once mentioned by him under the appellation of kingdoms. But the four empires which we have noticed above, *are* called kingdoms. It is therefore more probable, that God designed coming generations to understand, that he would rear his kingdom in the days of the four kingdoms, mentioned as such, than in the days of the ten kingdoms, not mentioned as such. The little stone cut out of the mountain without human agency, and the kingdom which should destroy all other kingdoms, are descriptions of the same divine power; because the little stone was to be cut out of the mountain during the existence of the image, was to strike it on the feet, prostrate it, and grind it to powder. And the kingdom of the Most High was to be reared in the days of the four kingdoms, as will be seen hereafter—symbolized by the wonderful image beheld by the Assyrian king. It is worthy of notice, that this little stone, before becoming a great mountain and filling the whole earth, struck the image and crushed it. Not before, but after this event, did it embrace the area of the whole earth. In connection with this sketch, notice that the kingdom of the God of heaven should break in pieces certain kingdoms, and should stand forever—should exist when all powers shall have decayed and faded from the earth. But before the erection of this kingdom, it will be perceived, by reference to the Old Testament, that a personage of glorious character, of celestial endowments, must make his appearance among the Jews. Jacob in blessing his sons, remarks: "The scepter shall not depart from Judah, nor a lawgiver from between his feet, until Shiloh come; and unto him shall the gathering of the people be." Thus faithfully did the venerable patriarch speak of the coming of the Son of God, and what should follow. The scepter did not depart from Judah until Messiah came. When he appeared the people did gather to him. This prophecy can refer to none, save Jesus Christ. Isaiah beheld the advent of the blessed Saviour, and was enraptured in contemplating the peace that should attend his reign as king, and the immunities to be enjoyed by his happy subjects. "For unto us a child is born, unto us a son is given, and the government shall be upon his shoulder; and his name shall be called Wonderful, Counsellor, The Mighty God, The Everlasting Father, The Prince of Peace. Of the increase of his government and peace, there shall be no end; upon the throne of David, and upon his kingdom to order it, and to establish it, with judgment and with justice from henceforth forever. The zeal of the Lord of hosts will perform this."

Jeremiah, looking forward, doubtless, to the appearing of the same great and good One, alludes to the covenant which God will then make with the house of Israel. "Behold, the days come, saith the Lord, that I will make a new covenant with the house of Israel, and with the house of Judah. Not according to the covenant that I made with their fathers in the day that I took them by the hand to bring them out of the land of Egypt, which my covenant they broke, although I was an husband unto them, saith the Lord. But this shall be the covenant that I will make with the house of Israel: After those days, saith the Lord, I will put my law in their inward parts, and write it in their hearts, and will be their God, and they shall be my people.' But before the coming of the Redeemer, a herald must appear among the inhabitants of Judea, and prepare them for receiving him. Isaiah describes him as the "Voice of one crying in the wilderness, prepare ye the way of the Lord, make straight in the desert a highway for our God." These things are written as the canons of prophecy, by the finger of God. The shade and coloring, the characters and scenes are all executed by him who is "mighty in strength and wisdom."

Opening the New Testament we are introduced, by the four sacred historians, to John the Immerser, the harbinger of Messiah. He appeared among the Jews before it was publicly announced that Jesus was the Son of God. With boldness and fidelity did he accomplish the work assigned him. He died a martyr; but, before he finished his career, Jesus of Nazareth was declared to be the Son of God. It was made known that He, of whom the prophets and bards of Israel had spoken, tabernacled in Judea. The time, place, and circumstances of his birth proved, that he was the "Desire of all nations." He lived, and taught, and suffered; he died, was buried, and rose from the dead, as was affirmed of him, hundreds of years before his coming.

The Bible student is aware of the fact that John the Harbinger, the twelve apostles, and the seventy evangelists commissioned by Jesus Christ, proclaimed the kingdom, or the reign of heaven as at hand. This was the burden of their proclamation, be it remembered, before the ascension of Messiah. After his ascension, we read of those that "God had delivered from the power of darkness and translated into the kingdom of his dear Son." John, on the isle of Patmos, declared that he was in the "kingdom and patience of Jesus Christ." When, at Caesarea Philippi, Peter acknowledged that Jesus was "the Christ, the Son of the living God," Jesus affirmed that he would build his church on that confession, and in giving Peter the keys of his kingdom, he showed that his church and kingdom were identical. It should be carefully noted, that in this conversation Jesus affirms that he *will* build his church. Had it been reared, he would not have said this. After the ascension of the Son of God, we read in Acts of the Apostles that "the saved were added to the church." "Church of Christ" and "Church of God," are expressions of frequent occurrence in the Epistles. Christ remarked, before going to his Father, that the "beginning" of the proclamation of the law of his church or kingdom should be "at Jerusalem." "Out of Zion shall go forth the law and the word of the Lord from Jerusalem." After his departure, Peter, rehearsing the conversion of Cornelius and his household to the brethren of Jerusalem, said: "And as I began to speak, the Holy Ghost fell on them as on us at Jerusalem." All things were in readiness for setting up the Kingdom of the Son of God. He had vanquished the belligerent powers of earth and hell. He had passed the portals of the grave, entered the confines of Satan, grappled with him, and wrested from him the keys of death and the invisible world—had broken and cast aside the fetters that bound him, and ascended in triumph mightier than the proudest heroes of the past. Attended by a multitude of angels, he directed his course toward his Father's abode. The gates were lifted up, the everlasting doors flew open wide, the King of glory, the Lord strong and mighty, the Lord mighty in battle, entered into the Palace royal of the Universe—sat down at the right hand of the Majesty on high, received from the Father the crown and scepter of universal empire, angels, powers, and authorities being subjected to him. He sent down the Holy Spirit according to promise, to the Apostles, according to the command of Jesus, waiting at Jerusalem. They were immersed in it. They were endowed by it, with power for a special work—a work which was not to be commenced until they were capacitated for it from on high. Peter, to whom the keys of the kingdom of heaven had been committed, arose, and in the strength of Israel's God, proclaimed the law of induction into the kingdom of Messiah. "Go ye therefore and teach all nations, baptizing them in the name of the Father, and of the Son, and of the Holy Spirit." "Go ye into all the world and preach the gospel to every creature; he that believeth and is baptized shall be saved, but he that believeth not shall be damned." "And he said unto them, Thus it is written, and thus it behooved Christ to suffer and rise from the dead the third day; and that repentance and remission of sins should be preached in his name among all nations, beginning at Jerusalem." Peter, armed with celestial might, fearless as David among the Philistines, determined to obey his risen, exalted and glorified Lord. He declared that Jesus was the anointed Son of the living God—that he was reigning on high—full of power to forgive their sins and heal their maladies. He spoke, that the multitude, hearing and understanding and appreciating his words, might believe on the Son of God, and live. If he did not proclaim these facts for this purpose, for what purpose did he utter a word on that momentous occasion? Christ had said, "Neither pray I for these alone, but for them also that shall believe on me, through their word." Convicted of having crucified the Lord of Glory, convinced of their awful and fearful condition, pierced to the very heart by the startling, overwhelming facts adduced by Peter, the multitude exclaimed, "Men and brethren, what shall we do?" "Repent and be baptized, every one of you in the name of Jesus Christ, for the remission of sins; and ye shall receive the gift of the Holy Ghost," said the faithful ambassador of Jesus. They that gladly received the word were immersed— about three thousand. These three thousand believed that Jesus had died, had been buried, and had risen from the grave, because they gladly received the word of Peter. They reformed—changed their conduct, because Peter would not have given a command that might be slighted with impunity. They professed their faith in the Son of God, because Philip required of the Ethiopian Eunuch a profession of his faith before he would immerse him. The conditions of pardon are the same everywhere, under the same dispensation. They were immersed into the name of the Father, and of the Son, and of the Holy Spirit, unless Peter was unfaithful in proclaiming his Lord's will. They were immersed for the remission of sins, according to the Christian philologist— according to the full meaning of the word of God. They received the remission of sins, because it was declared they should, in submitting to the command of Jesus Christ. They received the gift of the Holy Spirit, because they were promised it, on certain conditions with which they complied. They became living members of the Church of Messiah. They became living stones in the temple of the living God. They became obedient subjects of the glorious King of Saints. Builded on the Rock of Ages, nothing could move them. Flood and roaring tempests could not jostle the sure foundation of that storm-defying Rock. It will stand the shock of the leagued forces of earth and hell. The fierce armies of Satan will ever recoil from the dreadful attack, maddened, confused, and distorted. The Kingdom of the Son of God was founded in the days of the iron Kingdom—the Roman Empire. However much this may be denied, it will forever remain a fact. Daniel had said that in the days of certain kingdoms, or kings, the God of heaven would set up a kingdom. In the days of the last of the four kingdoms above mentioned, God did set up a kingdom. It may be supposed, that unless all the kingdoms were existing at the time of the setting up of the kingdom of God, the conclusion arrived at is not legitimate. In the book of Ruth, it is said, "in the days when the Judges ruled," evidently signifying in the time of some, or of one of the Judges. So we say an event occurred in the days of the twelve Caesars, meaning in the time of some, or of one of the twelve Caesars. Those who abjure this law of interpreting the words of prophecy, will find a difficult task in accounting for the fact that the gold, the silver, the brass, and the iron of the Assyrian king's image were crushed together by the little stone. The magnificence of the first, the inflexibility of the second, the dauntless invincibility of the third kingdom were in a certain degree found existing in the fourth kingdom. The little stone cut out of the mountain without hands, in destroying the malignant enemies of the Roman empire, showed its ability to overcome all obstacles, of whatever character they might be. The little stone and the kingdom of Christ are the same power. The apostles compared themselves to earthen vessels—the Gospel to treasures within these vessels—that the excellency of the power might be of God. Had not God, his Son, and the Holy Spirit presided over, directed, and sustained the work, the Kingdom of Jesus Christ had never been reared. This Kingdom began its progressive march in the days of Tiberius Caesar. It steadily, firmly, proudly moved on, increasing continually in might, until in the days of Constantine the Great, it paralyzed the energies of the Roman empire. Constantine, by an imperial edict, A. D. 331, prohibited the worship of idols, and announced that Christianity should henceforth be the religion of the Roman people. Idols, altars, and temples were devoted to destruction. In Antioch find Corinth, in Ephesus, Athens, and Rome, in the most populous and enlightened cities then existing, the Gospel had been successfully proclaimed, and meek submission rendered to the King of kings. In the wilderness, on the mountains, in the caves of the earth, and on the distant islands of the sea, the Sacred Scriptures were read, prayers were offered to the living God, and the songs of Zion sung by the ransomed sons and daughters of the Lord God Almighty.

III. When the Son of Man makes his second personal appearance among the inhabitants of the earth, he will find that kingdom existing which was organized by his authority on the day of Pentecost. If this position can be established, it cannot successfully be maintained that the God of heaven will set up a kingdom between the present time and that period, or that he will set up a kingdom at that time differing from that kingdom which is now standing and will then be standing, of which his Son is now King and will then be King. If the above proposition can be sustained, the time when God purposed founding that kingdom which shall have no end, or shall never be destroyed, is forever settled, and all opposing argumentation ineffective. In Luke, we are informed that a nobleman went into a distant country to receive for himself a kingdom, or to procure for himself royalty. The nobleman went abroad to receive a kingdom; Christ went to his Father and was crowned Lord of lords. The nobleman, before his departure gave to his subjects talents to be increased; Christ has committed to the citizens of his kingdom abilities to be improved. The nobleman returned and reckoned with his subjects. The Son of God, at his appearing, will demand of his followers an exact account of their stewardship. From this narration and others, it may be inferred that there will be no change in the divine government until the conclusion of all things. In Matthew, Christ is represented as coming in glory, accompanied by the holy angels, seated on the throne of his glory. All nations are before him. The good are separated from the bad. The righteous are addressed by the King, "Come ye blessed of my Father, inherit the kingdom prepared for you from the foundation of the world." Of this kingdom, the Son of Man is represented as then being King. It has already been stated that Jesus became King of a particular kingdom on the day of Pentecost. Of that kingdom he is still the King, and since it has not been authoritatively announced that there will be a change of rulers, until the grand drama of redemption shall have been closed, he will therefore, at that fearful period mentioned by Matthew, be King of the same kingdom.

Corroborative evidence is found in the first letter to the Corinthians. It is remarked that in the resurrection of the dead, every one shall come forth in his own rank, or character. "Christ the first-fruit, afterward they that are Christ's at his coming. Then cometh the end, when he shall have delivered up the kingdom to God even the Father; when he shall have put down all rule, and all authority and power. For he must reign till he hath put all enemies under his feet. The last enemy that shall be destroyed is death." From these citations it is manifest that Christ will reign as King until having subdued all enemies, until having ended his glorious work, he returns the crown and scepter to his Father, that God may be all in all. But previous to the end of the reign of the Son of God, the destiny of the living and the dead shall have been decided and forever fixed. Because all nations shall appear before him, and being separated, the wicked shall go into everlasting punishment, but the righteous into life eternal. Those who affirm that God will rear a kingdom in the future—in the days of certain kingdoms, contend also that this kingdom will destroy all other kingdoms. This cannot be the case, since we have just seen that Christ must reign until he has put under his feet all enemies—the last enemy being death. Therefore, could it be proved that God would set up a kingdom hereafter, and could this kingdom be identified with the kingdom described by the prophet Daniel, taking into consideration that this kingdom must break in pieces all other kingdoms, it could not possibly fulfill its mission, inasmuch as there would be no kingdoms to bruise—none to destroy.

IV. The King of this Kingdom is the Son of the Most High, the chiefest among ten thousand, and the one altogether lovely, the Alpha and Omega in Redemption, the loftiest, purest, and most glorious being that ever tabernacled among men, or communed with the invisible and unsearchable Jehovah. Heroes, philosophers, and poets, the great, the royal, and the mighty have passed away, and now sleep that sleep which "knows no waking" until the morning of the resurrection. But Jesus the Christ, the Son of the living God, though once dead, now lives and will live forever. Seated at the right hand of the everlasting Father, clothed with plenary power, he intercedes in behalf of all who approach the Lord God Almighty in accordance with his will. He remembered a fallen world while in the midst of the iniquitous, and though absent, forgets not the deplorable condition of the sons and daughters of Adam. In all that he said and did, in Gethsemane, on the cross, and while the shadows of death encompassed him, he remembered the high purpose of his mission, to seek and to Save the lost. He is now our prophet, priest, and king. Would you, sinner, be happy? Then obey this King.

The privileges of this kingdom have no end. In this kingdom the blind are enabled to see, the weak are made strong, the diseased receive health, the dead are made alive. In this kingdom the captive is set free, the faltering is encouraged, the innocent protected, the humble exalted—the weary find rest. In this kingdom new joys are continually springing up, bright prospects are ever opening in the distance, and the future is gilded with fadeless hues of beauty and loveliness. Here the voices of the just of all ages, falling on the ear in sweet cadences, speak words of consolation. Here communion is enjoyed with the Father, the Son, and the Holy Spirit. Here a peace is enjoyed the world cannot give and which the world cannot take away. Friendship decays not, and the light of hope never departs.

The subjects of this kingdom will enjoy everlasting life. They fear not the sullen mutterings of hostile powers. Storms may gather round them, lightnings wild and fierce may blaze in awful grandeur above them, thunder-bolts of wrath may fall about their pathway, they stand firm and fixed as the everlasting hills of God, for an arm omnipotent is outstretched for their protection.

Under the broad banner of Prince Messiah, gemmed with the star of Bethlehem, are they marshaled, a blood-washed army, going from conquest to conquest, from conquering to conquering, and onward will they proceed until the thunderings of victory and triumph ascend from every land to him that sits upon the throne and to the Lamb forever. Soon the portals of the great city of our God will be opened; crowns, honors, and royalties will soon be given the holy and faithful conquerors, who will, during the ages of eternity, be happy, in a world in which there is no separation, no suffering, no night, no death.

-----o-----

[For the American Christian Review.

Beecher's Conflict of Ages.

BROTHER FRANKLIN—You will remember, that while we were together at the State Meeting at Indianapolis, last October, we stayed one night at Bro. Jamison's. The conversation turned on the subject discussed by Edward Beecher, D. D., in his late work entitled the "Conflict of Ages."

My curiosity was excited, and I borrowed the work of Bro. J., and brought it home with me. Since then, I have perused it as opportunity offered; but from my frequent, and often protracted absence from home, the reading has necessarily been by snatches. I think, however, that I have gathered his main positions; and though I am convinced he is mistaken in the idea that he is a chosen instrument to re-adjust the machinery of the gospel, so as to cause both wheels of his figurative steamboat to run together; I hail the work, coming from the quarter it does, as a favorable omen, foreshadowing an ultimate abandonment, by theologians generally, of those old fundamental errors, based on mere deductions from assumed attributes of Jehovah; and from which has arisen almost every form of error, from the most iron-bound election and reprobation of Calvin, to the most ultra universalism of Hosea Ballou.

I allude to the dogma, That the moral relations, actions, and ultimate destiny of both angels and men, are bound by the eternal decrees of the infinite Jehovah; so that nothing can occur, either in the natural or spiritual world, but in pursuance of those decrees. I say both Universalism and its great antagonist, Calvinism, take their rise from this assumption; and I am truly glad that one of those schools has furnished a man of sufficient candor, as well as boldness, to face the dogma square up, and endeavor to avert the dishonor which he sees necessarily attaching to the character of Jehovah, on the supposition that his creed is correct; even at the expense of resorting to the ridiculous, expedient of pre-existence.

I read, with intense interest, that part of the work which should have contained the proof of his main position—viz: "that man is not an original creation, but a second edition of a pre-existent fallen race;" but I confess I found nothing that, to my mind, came within a thousand miles of meeting the necessities of the case. For laying aside, for the present, that insurmountable objection to his theory, growing out of the fact—universally obtaining—*that we have no recollection of a pre-existent state, in which we individually sinned, and thus forfeited those inherent rights of new created minds,* of which he speaks so much; I say, waiving this objection for the time being, I would ask him for the first shadowy intimation in all the Bible, that man is but a second edition of a pre-existent, sinful, fallen race?—!

And if these two insurmountable difficulties were obviated or withdrawn, I would ask how his theory relieves the character of God of the dishonor and injustice he seems so aware that by his favorite Augustinian—alias Calvinian—theory it is involved? It is manifestly but a shifting of the difficulty from one shoulder to the other. For if the spirits of men existed in a former state, and there fell, in accordance with an inexorable previously existing decree; they were as effectually denuded of those inherent *rights of new created minds,* of which he speaks, as they could be, on the hypothesis of inherent moral depravity through the fall of Adam.

If their previously incurred guilt was *not* the result of *decree,* but the *apostasy* of moral agents, possessing the power to stand or fall, and actually exercising the latter, where is the necessity of going back to a pre-existent state, to locate this moral agency? Why not just let go the old dogma of total hereditary depravity at once; and contemplate man, as the Bible does, as a moral agent in his present state; and, though greatly deteriorated in his moral faculties by the corrupting influence of long continued evil associations, yet, possessing the capacity, by availing himself of the "abundance of grace, and the gift of righteousness" provided in the gospel for all, to arise to a participation of the "divine nature" here, and of eternal glory hereafter.

This not only starts both wheels of our author's steamboat to running in the same direction, but it agrees with our own consciousness, and impresses man with a just sense of his individual responsibility to God. Or, to adhere strictly to his figure, this gives a *new wheel* instead of his old crazy one—*Total Depravity*—which never did, and never can be made to run in harmony with the other— his self-evident principles of *honor and right,* by which, as he alleges, God is bound to give to every new created mind such a moral constitution as, at least, to render it possible for him to accomplish the ostensible object of his creation.

This view, I say, furnishes a wheel which works in beautiful harmony with the above, and teaches man to regard the Divine interposition in "redeeming him from death, and ransoming him from the power of the grave," as having placed in a measure, his eternal destiny in his own hands; so that if he does not "reign in life by one, Jesus Christ," it will be because he did not —*i. e.* would not—"receive [the] abundance of grace, and the gift of righteousness" so bountifully provided for him.

I incline to the opinion, though he does not actually avow it, that our author has conceived the idea, that the race of man is but an incarnation of the fallen angels — a kind of purgatory, in which the less guilty of them may expiate their crimes, and be restored to their former position as holy angels; while the rest, becoming still more and more confirmed in wickedness, shall be remanded back to their "chains of everlasting darkness," at "the judgment of the great day."

Now this is a pretty theory, (though it can never be reconciled with his Augustinian theory of the eternal decrees, without subverting his principles of "honor and right," and thus setting his wheels to going in opposite directions). *My* whole objection to it, however, may be expressed in the following words: *It is impossible for it to be true;* and that for the following reasons:

1st. It would present Satan as the tempter of the infant race of mankind, in the attitude of a cool conspirator against himself and his adherents.

2nd. It is wholly unsupported by the word of inspiration, and,

3rd. It is actually testified against by that word, Heb. ii, 16: "For verily he [Christ] took not [hold] on angels, [to redeem them]; but he took [hold] on the seed of Abraham." I presume the Dr. will not seriously question the correctness of this paraphrase; the whole context so obviously requiring this construction to be put on that passage.

"The angels that sinned," then, are not the subjects of redemption; while man is. The reason of this is obvious to the attentive student of, and believer in, the Bible; but to a mind blinded by any of the mere theories, recognized by our author as contributing to the age-lasting conflict of which he writes, it is utterly incomprehensible. Let. us examine it a little.

Man was originally created "a little lower than the angels," but with the avowed object on the part of the Creator, of ultimately exalting him above them. See Gen. i, 26, 28; Ps. viii, 5, 6; Heb. ii, 5 — *passim.*

In what did the difference between man and angels consist, originally? Chiefly in this: that the former was *capable* of becoming subject to death, while the latter were not. Both were constituted moral agents, and as such, were under law to God. Now a law without a sanction, or penalty, is of no force whatever. What then, were the penalties respectively, of the laws governing these two classes of beings? I answer, on the part of man, Death and the grave, or more properly *Hades;* on the part of angels, that *"Everlasting Fire"* mentioned (Mat. 25, 21) by our Lord as having been prepared for *Diabolo* and his angels.

What were the workings of these laws? Part of the angelic, and all the human race, became involved in the penalties respectively. How did the angels become involved? By individual participation in the sin, whatever it was, to which the penalty was annexed. How did man become involved? Not by individual participation, but by a kind of Metonymy, as existing seminally in the first pair. How, then, can we be justly held responsible for a transgression in which we individually took no part? If the penalty affected our *moral* relations to God, we could not; but as the results are, to us, simply physical, we can. How is this? Death, is to us, simply the physical result of our being descended from Adam, who begat all his offspring *after having incurred the penalty of the Adamic law*; and as it is a law of physical science, that a stream cannot, without the application of a foreign power, rise above its fountain, so Adam, being mortal, could not impart immortality to his offspring.

Then, if the fallen angels were capable of propagating their species, their progeny would *inherit* the eternal misery of which their parents have become the subjects, as the mere physical result of their parentage—would they? Exactly so; and for this reason, if for no other, the angels are incapable of marriage, as well as of death. And so, our Lord tells us, it will be with mankind in the resurrection state.

But to return to the question, "Why could not the angels be redeemed as well as men? You see, that in the very nature of the case, capital punishment inflicted on beings incapable of death, must be eternal in its duration. Such being the character of the angelic existence, the penalty for capital offenses, whatever may be the kind, or intensity of the punishment expressed by the term *fire* in the passage (Matt. xxv, 41) it *must* be everlasting, or, eternal in its duration; consequently, to redeem them from it, would be to compromise the *truth* of Jehovah, which is just as immutable and infinite as any other of his attributes. The penalty being necessarily—as applicable to imperishable beings—eternal in its duration, precludes the idea of "Mercy and Truth" meeting together, and harmoniously co-operating in their redemption; hence, "He took not hold on angels," as already quoted.

But the case was entirely different with regard to man. It will be recollected that he was made *lower* than angels, but with the capacity, if true to himself, of rising above them—indeed this was the avowed object of his creation. His low estate capacitated him to suffer *death* as the penalty of his law, or the law of his being, and so it was arranged. Now, had he been a father before he sinned, and the children had not partaken with him in the transgression, he might have been left to perish in his transgression, and the original purpose of God with regard to man—his glorification at the right hand of God—been accomplished in his offspring. But the whole race existed in the guilty pair at the time of the transgression; and God must either abandon his original design, create another race, or redeem this — an alternative of three choices, so to speak. He chose the last, bless His Holy name!

But how can he interpose to redeem man without compromitting his *truth* as in the case of the angels? Why, if the old theory of a threefold death in the Adamic penalty, be true, he cannot. If any part of that penalty was *necessarily* eternal in its duration, *truth* would necessarily oppose *mercy* in every effort to abridge that duration. But I rejoice to know that *truth* was vindicated to its utmost demand, and still left room for *mercy* to interpose a Redeemer. Hear the united voice of "mercy and truth" now "met together" in the person of our gracious Redeemer. "I will ransom them from the power of the grave; I will redeem them from death: O death, I'll be thy plagues; O grave, I will be thy destruction." Hos. xiii, 14.

In all this, you discover no allusion is made to the moral agency of man as an individual being; but his physical condition is contemplated as the subject of the Divine compassion and this physical inability, which separated between him and the accomplishment of his destiny, is removed by providing him a resurrection into a state of being, similar to that of the angels, in two particulars at least—*i. e.,* they will be incapable alike, of marriage and of death.

But our entering upon, and enjoying that everlasting inheritance, "prepared for us from the foundation of the world," involves some moral and spiritual qualifications, only attainable through the exercise and discharge of the functions of moral agency. Hence, in the communication that informs us of our redemption from death, we are told that *conditional* redemption, even from our individual iniquities, entered into, and formed a part of the remedial system; that *He died for our sins* as well as to redeem us from the penalty of the Adamic transgression. We are therefore invited, nay urged, to renew our moral and spiritual intimacy with God; and as *individuals,* are thrown upon our moral responsibility to Him, with a sanction, or penalty, corresponding to the imperishable existence to which we are destined by the resurrection—even a portion with the "devil and his angels." Matt. xxv, 41.

The children of men, who shall incur this penalty, will be, like the fallen angels, beyond the reach of mercy or redemption, inasmuch as Mercy cannot interpose, only at the expense of Truth—which is inadmissible.

In view of the before mentioned great deterioration of the moral faculties, not so much the effect of the Adamic sin, as the result of long association with evil, the gospel proclamation is admirably adapted to man in his comparatively helpless condition. It commences by bespeaking his attention to the wonderful love of God in giving his Son to die, the just for the unjust, to bring us to God. It appeals to the best feelings of his soul; causing an involuntary gush of grateful emotion to spring up in his heart, promopting the inquiry, "what can I do to manifest my gratitude for so much benevolence shown to me?" It answers, "If thou shalt confess with thy mouth the Lord Jesus, and shalt believe in thy heart that God hath raised him from the dead, thou shalt be saved," etc. He answers, "I believe [with my whole heart] that Jesus Christ is the Son of God; what more must I do?" It answers, "Repent and be baptized, in the name of Jesus Christ, for the remission of sins, and you shall receive the gift of a Holy Spirit."

In obedience to these simple elementary principles of the oracles of God, he enters *into* the Father, Son, and Holy Spirit, as a covenanted child of God; fully authorized and empowered to "work out his own [eternal] salvation with fear and trembling"—God working in him "to will and to do of his own good pleasure."

Thus, his moral relations are restored. He walks with God, the Father and Son dwelling in him; and though he is still liable to the penalty of the Adamic law—death, on account of [the Adamic] sin, yet the "spirit is life, because of righteousness" and if he continues to entertain that spirit, which it is his privilege and duty to do, his mortal body shall be quickened by *it* eventually in the resurrection, and the result will be, not only an imperishable body—this *all* shall have, both saints and sinners—but a glorious holy body, like that of the glorious Redeemer, in which to enjoy that eternal existence on which he will have entered.

On the other hand, those who reject this abundance of grace and the gift of righteousness, will nevertheless experience the *physical* results of the redemption from death, but failing to renew their moral relations to God—not receiving his spirit here—they will not be raised in his image there; consequently they will not be capable of enjoying His glory in the eternal world. Not only so, but being found transgressors against a law, the penalty of which, is eternal punishment, they alike, with *Diabolo* and his angels, will be made partakers of that hopeless perdition into which their own sins, in despite of the goodness and mercy of God, will have plunged them.　　　　B. K. SMITH,
Near Indianapolis, March 12, 1856.

-----o-----

Our Position as a Religious Community.
No. 5.

Is it not desirable, that debating, disputing, and all the unhappy religious wars and strifes should cease? All the good answer, Yes. How, then, can they ever cease, until some one system, one institution, one doctrine, or one faith, claiming the attention of all, having a mission to all men, clothed with all authority, and one that all admit true, shall be presented and received? Never, till such a system shall be presented and maintained, can there be an end to strife among the people of God. But are we in reach of any such system, institution, or faith? We maintain that we are, and that it is the duty of all good men to make a mighty effort, at this particular crisis, to extricate it from the encumbrances, trammels, fetters, and shackles, that men have hung about it. There is, in the midst of all the errors and confusions of these times, something that all parties talk about, that they call "the truth." There is something they call "Christianity." They speak of "the church of Christ." There is something they call "the gospel." They speak of "the religion of Jesus Christ." They all speak of "the doctrine of Christ." They also speak of "Christians," "Disciples of Christ," "Saints," etc. Now what do they mean by all this? What do they mean by *the truth, Christianity, the church of Christ, the gospel, the religion of Jesus Christ, the doctrine of Christ, Christians, Disciples of Christ, Saints, etc.?* If the speaker be a Methodist, what does he mean by "the truth"? He does not mean his doctrine, for he does not claim that it is *the truth,* but simply that it is according to truth, that it is taken from the truth, and may be proved by the truth. When he speaks of *the gospel,* he does not mean Methodism, for he does not claim that Methodism is the gospel itself, but a system founded upon the gospel, taken from it, according to it, and that may be proved by it.

When he speaks of the religion of Jesus Christ, he does not mean Methodist religion, for he does not believe that any man can be saved who does not receive the religion of Jesus Christ, but he admits that persons may be saved and not receive Methodist religion. He only claims for Methodist religion, that it is like the religion of Jesus Christ, that it is taken from it, founded upon it, and may be proved by it. When he speaks of Christians he does not mean Methodists, as such, or you would not hear him say, "Christians of all denominations." The name Methodist, designates, simply, those who have subscribed their discipline, and united with the church bearing that name. But the word Christian designates an entirely different class. It takes in many not included in the term Methodist.

In the same way, when you hear the Presbyterian speak of the truth, the gospel, the doctrine of Christ, Christianity, etc., he does not mean Presbyterianism; for he does not claim that it is the truth, the gospel, the doctrine of Christ itself, but a very wise system deduced from the gospel, founded upon it, and that may be proved by it. Hence, he admits that persons may receive the truth, the gospel, the doctrine of Christ, and be saved, who are not Presbyterians. When he speaks of Christians, Disciples of Christ, Saints, etc., he does not mean Presbyterians, as such, for he says, " Christians, Disciples, Saints, etc., of all denominations." Hence, too, you hear all parties speak of "Christians, Disciples, Saints, etc., of every faith and order."

There is not a party, with a human creed, beneath the skies, when it speaks of " the church of Christ," that means simply those in its own communion, or its own body; they do not claim that they are the church of Christ, but like it; sometimes identical with it, or as near like it as any other; nor is there one of these parties that claims that their doctrine is the doctrine of Christ, the gospel, but deductions from it, founded upon it, and that can be proved by it. Hence, you constantly hear them declaring, with great earnestness and confidence, that " we can prove *our* doctrine by Scripture." " We can sustain *our* doctrine by the truth of heaven." " I have proved *my* position by the unerring word of God." "I can prove *my* creed by the Bible," etc., etc. Can any man fail to discover here, the continual distinction made between *our* doctrine and *the* Scripture ? *our* doctrine and *the truth of heaven ? my* position and the unerring *word of God? my* creed and *the Bible?* This distinction runs through almost all the preaching and writings of our day. You will hear **a** continual stream about our doctrine, our creed, our church, our way, our views, our faith, our religion, as well as your doctrine, your creed, your church, etc., and both *your* doctrine and *our* doctrine, *your* creed and *our* creed, *your* church and *our* church, must be sustained and well proved by Scripture. This, of course, will be the work of *your* preacher and *our* preacher. Here is a clear distinction made between three systems; 1. *Your* doctrine. 2. *Our* doctrine. 3. The *Scriptures.* Here the continual concession is kept up, that your doctrine and our doctrine, are not Scripture, but something we are trying to prove by Scripture.

Now, where is the necessity for all this? Did the Lord give us the truth, the gospel, Christianity, the Scriptures, that we might deduce systems of our own from them, found them upon them, and prove them by the Scriptures? Surely not; but in all this there is **a** continual concession of a departure from the Lord; and we are just as well assured, as we are that God has revealed himself to man, that a return is indispensable to our acceptance with-God. All these systems, that they call " our systems," and doctrines that they call " our doctrines," that they are trying to prove by Scripture—no matter how near like the Bible, or how far from it—are not the gracious system itself, given us by our glorious Lord and Saviour Jesus Christ, but departures from it, substitutes for it, and innovations, such as men cannot maintain and appear guiltless before the Lord of hosts. The holy apostle says, "all Scripture, given by inspiration of God, is profitable, *for doctrine."* 2 Tim., iii., 16. He does not say, "all Scripture is profitable to *prove* doctrine," but "it is profitable *for* doctrine." The Scripture is the doctrine itself; not the mere proof-book to prove *our* doctrine. It is the truth itself, and not merely a book to refer to when we are trying to show that something else is true. While men talk about *their* doctrine, their creed, their church, their religion, their way, etc., etc., the great Master of Assemblies speaks of *his* doctrine, his religion, his truth, his church, his people, his way, etc., etc., and He demands the attention of all men to Him, as the way, the truth, and the life; and says, "no man cometh to the Father but by me." John, xiv., 6. If men know what the truth is, what the doctrine of Christ is, what Christianity is, so that they can appeal to it to prove *their* doctrine, they know what it is so that they might receive it *itself,* enjoy it, and be saved by it, and consequently they will be left without excuse. There can be no apology for a man who knows what the truth is, what the doctrine of Christ is, what Christianity is, who will use it merely as a proof to sustain, prove, and impose something else upon himself and others, for he might just as easily have received, the truth, the doctrine of Christ, Christianity itself, enjoyed it, and been saved by it, as to have trifled with it, in trying to prove something else by it. But if a man does not know what the truth is the doctrine of Christ, Christianity is, and adopts something else, he is simply guessing at it, and is not to be relied upon. He has no foundation.

We are as well convinced, as we are that there is a glorious heaven for the righteous, and a hell for the wicked, that no man now living, who knows what the Lord's truth is what the gospel of Christ is, what Christianity is, and what the Bible is, and has appealed to it to sustain something else, and now continues so to appeal to it, could, if his life were at stake, give a good reason why he did not receive the truth itself, the gospel, Christianity, the Bible itself, rely upon it, as his only hope for life, his only guide, as the only divine system, the only divine institution, in the place of perverting its glorious influence and power to sustain and prop up something else. And we are equally certain, that no man can answer to God, when the actions of all men shall be spread out in the last judgment, for such a course. If Christianity is a system, if it is a divine institution, if it is the religion of Jesus Christ, if it is from God, and now binding upon the human family, as almost all the religious parties of these times admit, and as cannot be denied, the sin of departing from it is great enough; but to have the assurance to try to make it sanction any other system, to testify in support of any other, to try to divert its influence, power, and authority from its own work, to sustain and prop up some human system not mentioned in it, when it has expressly, under the most fearful and awful penalty, forbidden any perversion, addition, or subtraction, is a species of daring and aggression upon the institution of heaven and government of God, such as one would suppose no believer in the Bible would risk. Still it is done—almost daily done, in the pulpits all over the land; and those who will not do it, who condemn it, who receive the Bible, Christianity, the gospel, the religion of Jesus Christ, all that God has revealed to man—all that has the name of God upon it, keep it distinct from everything else, and will have nothing more, are opposed everywhere, sneered at and branded as *heretics.* Be it so. We look not to man for reward. We look not to sectarian parties to honor God, our Lord Jesus Christ, the Bible, Christianity, or the gospel. We do not expect them, as parties, to come to the Bible, unless to draw support for their own schemes. But we regard not this ; we know we are right; and it is not the great number that will stand, but those who are right. "Truth is mighty above all things, and will prevail." Brethren, push on the war, on this great question. The Bible will prevail in the end. Its enemies will all fall. B. F.

-----o-----

He that regardeth the day, regardeth it unto the Lord: and he that regardeth not the day to the Lord, doth not regard it. He that eateth, eateth to the Lord, for he giveth God thanks; and he that eateth not to the Lord, eateth not, and giveth God thanks. For none of us liveth to himself, and no man dieth to himself. For whether we live,- we live unto the Lord; and whether we die, we die unto the Lord: whether we live therefore, or die, we are the Lord's.—Romans, xiv., 6-8.

The Mission of Infidels, No. 3.

In our No. 2, under the above head, we showed the practical workings of unbelief, in its mission, of destroying the work of righteousness, and paralyzing the word of God, through the vain and empty pretences of Universalism. This led us into a field too inexhaustible for anything like a full elaboration in a single article. We, therefore, enter the same field again, with the following proposition:

Atheism furnishes all the rewards and punishments that Universalism, does, and has all the incentives to a righteous life.

We, of course, are now speaking of that class of Universalists who deny any rewards and punishments after death, which comprises an overwhelming majority of all who wear the name. But though they deny any rewards or punishments after death, they say that they believe in rewards and punishments as firmly as any of their opposers, but they are all in this world. They believe in a hell for the wicked and a heaven for the righteous, but all in this world; they hold that the wicked shall not go unpunished; that every man shall receive according to his works, but he must receive it in this life. We call upon the Universalist to find this heaven for the righteous in this world. He commences expounding such passages as, "Lay up for yourselves treasures in heaven," etc. "They who do his commandments shall enter by the gates into the city"—"Straight is the gate and narrow is the way that leadeth to life," etc., and he finds the heaven, where the treasure is to be laid up, here in this world, precisely where the Atheist finds his heaven, and the enjoyments of it to consist of the natural results of a correct life, such as a good name, the friendship of the world and worldly prosperity, such as would have been the result if Jesus had never lived nor died, and such as any Atheist will admit to be a legitimate result of a correct life. Such a religion as this, has no God in it, no Saviour, no Holy Spirit, nor piety. But he proceeds to expound, "They who do his commandments shall enter by the gates into the city," etc. The city here, he says, is New Jerusalem, or the church. The church consists of all the children of God, and all men, he says, are the children of God. To be a human being is to be a child of God, and to be a child of God is to be in the church or city, and the consciousness of having lived a correct life, is the enjoyment of the holy city, New Jerusalem. Here again, the Atheist gives him the right hand of fellowship, and says, that he believes in this holy city and all its enjoyments, though he does not believe in the existence of a God. But our expositor proceeds: "Strait is the gate and narrow is the way that leadeth to life," etc. The life spoken of here, is in this world, and consists in the satisfaction a man feels in having done what he believes to be right. "This is the life you are seeking, is it?" says the Atheist; "I believe in seeking this life too," says he.

In one word, all the reward a righteous man finds, is not only confined to this life, according to this system, but it consists in the natural and legitimate results of a man's conduct. For instance; if a man is temperate, he is apt to rest well, feel well, have a clear head, good appetite, and good health. If he speaks the truth, is honest in his business transactions, benevolent, moral, and genteel, he enjoys the confidence of those who know him, has good credit, is loved and esteemed, as a legitimate and philosophical result. This reward, as a general thing, we all admit, a man will receive. But all this would have been so if God had never loved man, if Jesus had never died, and if Christianity had never been preached. An Atheist may believe in this class of rewards, and can consistently appeal to them as reasons for a righteous life. So can a Christian appeal to all the natural, legitimate, and philosophical results, tendencies and advantages of a righteous life, as a reason for conformity to correct principles, with as much force as either of them, and then, rise transcendently above them both, and present the additional, superlatively grand and overwhelming reward promised to the good, the pure, and the holy, of an unperishable and eternal crown in the world to come. But now we turn our attention to look for the punishment—the hell threatened for the wicked,

"*I* never denied that there is a hell, but then it is in this world." Well, where is it? "It is remorse of conscience." Well, an Atheist believes in this hell. "Hell is the valley of Hinom, where criminals were executed and their bodies consumed." Atheists believe all that. "Jerusalem was destroyed." Atheists believe that too. "Men who are immoral, corrupt, and dissipated, bring disgrace upon themselves, subject themselves to fines and imprisonment." Atheists believe all that too. "But men who dissipate, degrade and abuse themselves, destroy their constitutions, impair their health, and become wrecks of humanity." Atheists believe all that and much more of the same kind. But Christianity admits that all calamities of these kinds have fallen upon men, in this world; admits all the natural evils that follow, as legitimate or philosophical results; that they have resulted, and do result, from transgressions; and urges them as a reason for a righteous life, with as much force and power as either of the parties mentioned, and then rises infinitely above them to the last resort for the incorrigible—the eternal punishment of the world to come.

We are perfectly aware, that the unbelieving sophists, to whom we refer, tell the people that they do not believe in such long credit, as the orthodox hold to; that they believe in the man being punished for his sins, as he goes along. But what punishment do they believe in, not admitted by all the orthodox, as they style their opposers? Do they believe in the lashing of conscience? All others believe it, and certainly *feel* it, when they do wrong, as much as they. Do they believe that transgressors will be fined, imprisoned, or hung? All others believe it as much as they. Do they believe that transgressions will destroy character, bring poverty and disgrace; that dissipation, corrupt habits, and gluttony, will destroy the physical man? All others believe it as much as they. Do they believe that all transgressions of physical laws are followed by certain fixed and unalterable penalties? All others believe in all these penalties, or more properly, consequences; that they are as severe, speedy, and certain as any Universalist; but the Universalist makes this *the hell*; the *only hell* of the Bible; the lake of fire prepared for the devil and his angels; while the Christian looks above all this, to a judgment after death, followed by an eternal punishment and banishment from the presence of the Lord, and the glory of his power.

The mission of unbelief, in this direction, is

1. To force the Bible to agree with the Atheist, in theory, that a man's conduct in this life, no matter what it may be, cannot destroy his happiness in another life.

2. That there shall be no reward in another world, for virtue, righteousness and obedience rendered to God in this life.

3. That there shall be no punishments in the world to come, for disobedience, corruption, and crime, committed in this life.

4. That the death of Christ amounts to nothing, as the consequences of sin all follow now, and fall upon man just as they did before he died.

5. That repentance amounts to nothing, as the punishment of sin is simply the natural result of a violation of a natural law, and must follow its violation whether you repent or not.

6. That there is no pardon of sin—that as you put your hand in the fire the burn must follow—as you spend your money, you must become poor—as you dissipate, your physical energies must be impaired; so, as you sin, in all cases the penalty must follow.

7. All this being conceded, the grace of God is at an end. There is no such an attribute as mercy in the government of Jehovah.

8. No love of God is manifested either in the life or death of. Jesus, nor has his death produced any change in the world.

No wonder that infidels hail this theory with joyfulness, flock around the Universalian preacher, and call him "brother." His operations are fatal to the Bible, to the mission and divine authority of the Lord Jesus, and better calculated to turn the whole subject of religion into ridicule, than any open infidelity ever advocated in the world. By this kind of circumlocution, the Bible is now sought to be subverted, and its influence upon the world destroyed. But all men of discernment can see, that this is only a scheme to pull down and destroy—that it has no efficacy to save, to make good or improve mankind

—that it can do no good, in any event, to one soul of our race, either in this world or the world to come. It is only an instrument, one of the most effectual instruments of unbelief, in destroying all good, all virtue, and all piety.

-----o-----

"The Central (Ky.) Christian Union."

BROTHER FRANKLIN: *The American Christian Review,* No. 3, has by chance just fallen into my hands; and I see, beside two letters from Kentucky, relating to the same general subject, in your No. 2, on "Organization," you have published at large the proceedings of a convention held in Danville, Ky., on the 13th and 14th of December last. From my past intercourse with you, I have no reason to suppose you are to be included in the suspicion, becoming quite prevalent, that the question of Organization is to receive no fair and impartial treatment at the hands of our editors. Nevertheless, I will ask, that you may declare your purpose in the outset: Do you intend to be governed by what was in the beginning deemed the peculiar honor of "this reformation" in its original pleadings, viz.: *a full and fair hearing of both sides?* For the present, I will presume it, and trust I may always have reason to say, in the language of the Apostle, "even as it is meet for me to think this of you."

First then, in reference to the convention. A brother happened without previous arrangement to meet, during an appointment at Lancaster, Ky., the remnant of a "District Cooperation meeting," which had struggled for a year or two to maintain a feeble existence, and was now on the eve of going the way of all the numerous attempts in the same territory before it. Finding them about to disband in discouragement, he proposed to them to invite their respective churches to send delegates to Danville as a convenient point, for the purpose of consulting with other delegates on the propriety of forming an association of the churches on a plan embracing certain ecclesiastical elements. They readily consented. Another "Co-operation" met the week following, at Hustonville, under circumstances of the same character, and the same proposition was made to them, and was met with the same response. This was all done without the knowledge of the Danville church; but as soon as they were informed of it, letters of invitation to most of the churches in the counties named in the proceedings were sent out. The first meeting was held in November, and after a few hours' deliberation, adjourned to meet in December. At, the latter meeting, the constitution which had been presented at the first meeting, was still further considered, and the discussions were free and brotherly. It was found, on the evening of the second day, that it could not be adopted, and the present one was written by the chairman in the course of a few minutes, while the discussion was going on. It was designed to embody the principles upon which an agreement had been expressed during the debates, and with but little amendment it was adopted as the minutes report.

There was no time for trimming and polishing, nor was it deemed necessary, as it was regarded but a preliminary act of a free people, which could be altered or abolished at their pleasure. It does not claim perfection, but it asserts the right of free and sovereign bodies to form alliances for mutual defense, and the promotion of the general welfare. Like all the productions of a feeble brotherhood, it must be judged with a charitable judgment.

Thus far the opposition has availed itself of appeals to the prejudices of men, and they have uniformly turned away from the Bible, the dictates of common sense, and the sad lessons of our experience, as a body, and have judged it by something they call "the principles of this Reformation," at the same time not knowing whereof they affirm. And this may be a sufficient explanation of our appeal to the *Millennial Harbinger,* of 1842, page 59. I am one who suffered decapitation at the hands of your beloved system of *congregational* government, so called. In those days, we preached the untrammeled investigation of the Scriptures, Faith that cometh by hearing, Baptism, with its pre-requisites, for the remission of sins; and with the Bible *alone,* the opposition were confounded, and went backward and fell to the ground; but they arose and brought *"Baptist customs"* against us, and we were led to execution. We thought, in appealing from the Bible to "Baptist customs," they were judging us by a "human creed;" and it would be well, we think, for brethren who talk so much about "the principles of this Reformation," to show wherein their position differs from that of the Baptists at the period referred to. A neighbor editor, in remarks upon our document, in a tone of solemn warning, says, "it is new among us."

The old Baptist cry, "It will split the churches," has been revived and much used already; and I am sorry to see that some of your remarks tend in that direction. Should a stroke be made at the foundation of Christianity, an attempt to destroy any vital principles in its doctrine or polity, I recognize in such cases, as a last resort, the right of revolution. But is it such an assault upon Christianity—indeed, any assault upon it at all, to deny the divine right of *Congregationalism, Isolation,* and *Independency,* either, or all of them? If so, then such men, pioneers in this reformation, as Hall, Pinkerton, Anderson, Burnett, Scott, and last, but first of all, Alexander Campbell, with a host since risen up, whose number God is daily increasing, are culprits before you. These named, were once the advocates of Independency. They were as sincere, and likely more able in that advocacy than any that now appear in its behalf. But experience and a clearer understanding of God's word have taught them better. The most eminent in the above list thus speaks:

"V. When, then, any particular congregation offends against the constitution of Messiah's kingdom, by denying the doctrine, by neglecting the discipline, or by mal-administration of the affairs of Christ's church, essentially affecting the well-being of individuals or other congregations, then said church is to be judged by the eldership of other churches, or by some other tribunal than her own, as an accused or delinquent member of a particular congregation is to be tried by the constituted eldership of his own congregation." *Mill. Harb.* 1841, p. 45.

Again: "The experience of every day, added to the great principles propounded in both Testaments, especially in the New, and to the positive precepts and examples of the Lord and his apostles, more and more impress all of us who feel our responsibilities, who have some influence in the church of Jesus Christ, and to whose hearts the peace, purity, and happiness of Christ's kingdom are paramount, all-absorbing, and transcending concerns—that *our organization and discipline are greatly defective, and essentially inadequate to the present condition and wants of society."*

"But as I intend this only for an introduction to some essays on *the importance of a community organization, more homogeneous with the nature of the kingdom of Christ than any yet developed among us,* I hasten to the following melancholy disclosure." *Mill. Harb.* 1841, pp. 532, 536. Then follows a dark picture, rather blacker than any contained in my "Signs of the Times No. 6."

Again: On the delicate question of *ministerial communion,* the same able expounder thus speaks: "I lay it down as a maxim not to be questioned, that where there is Christian communion of any sort, special or common, there must be an amenability of the participants to some common *tribunal,* and a mutual responsibility to watch over, and nourish, and comfort one another." *Mill. Harb.* 1842, p. 63.

Again: That Independency is of *modern* origin, is declared at the close of a brief abstract of church history by the same writer, as follows:

"Soon as a disrespect [arose] for hereditary office, or, what is the same thing in effect, under another name, for bishops by succession from the apostles, the partiality for what we have called *lay bishops,* or those chosen without regard to such hereditary ordination, gradually increased, and Independency was born. [Mark that! "INDEPENDENCY WAS BORN!"] This among many Protestants became a popular theory, and they undertook to reform the church by making every congregation a sort of kingdom of Christ within itself. This view, under various new modifications and accidental new attributes, has obtained among Congregationalists—much improved and enlarged, however, by the experience of its supporters." "

Our Baptist brethren have been partial to

it, especially in all the branches and derivations from Welsh and English organizations. In this they have much improved upon the plan of the Associations, State and Federal Conventions for general and great objects and undertakings. Still, in the fierce democracy of their congregational movements and disciplinary proceedings, they have been the most disputatious, feeble, and fractional people on earth. They are, in the most important and essential of all the ends and uses of government, under the chances of a *gunarchy." Mill. Harb.* 1842, p, 61. But enough for once. These are the origin, the workings, and tendencies of Independency under all its improvements, as drawn by a master hand.

With this before us from the ablest, and most highly authorized expounder of "the principles of the reformation," the threat to "split the churches," if we unionists do not desist from an advocacy of, and our attempts to establish the *real* "principles of the reformation," the apostolic union and dependency of the churches—comes with rather a bad grace from you all. Cases have already occurred where these *true* "principles of the reformation" as seen in the above extracts, have been waived, through the super-abounding forbearance of our friends, on account of the clamor of a small minority with their cry of "split the churches," when the union movement could have been carried by an overwhelming majority. In other cases, persons have been intimidated by this behavior, and induced to vote against the clear convictions of their judgment. This may be set down to the account of the tyrannical nature of Congregationalism, which, when even in a lean minority, must *"rule* or *ruin."*

You file seven objections to our movement. They are very curious. I had thought "this reformation" had long since passed the period which some were wont to call its childhood. But you put forth said objections so seriously, that I must treat them accordingly. Time was when such a mode of setting forth the claims of "the Bible alone," was common among us; but latterly, or within fifteen years, we have had but little of it in central or southern Kentucky. As I need not occupy space to notice them all, I will take the first two as a fair specimen of the whole, and give their counter-parts as a sufficient answer for the present.

Objection 1. "The object of the meeting—"for the purpose of forming an association or union of the churches," etc. A meeting for such a purpose is wholly unknown to the New Testament. There is not a hint of the kind in the Christian code."

Answer 1. The object of the meeting—for the purpose of forming the South Western District Co-operation of Ohio; the Kentucky State Meeting; the American Christian Missionary Society; the American Christian Publication Society, (you so zealously defended); the American Bible Union; the Revision Association, (in advocating whose aims at Nashville you spoke so ably); etc. A meeting for such purpose, or purposes, is wholly unknown to the New Testament. There is not a hint of the kind in the Christian code.

Objection 2. "This meeting calls into existence a new set of officers, wholly unknown to the New Testament. The New Testament knows no president or secretary—no delegates, either of preachers or private members—of an association of churches."

Answer 2. The above meetings have called into existence new sets of officers wholly unknown to the New Testament. The New Testament knows no president or secretary, or board of managers of the American Bible Union Publication Society —no delegates, either of preachers or private members—of a District or State Co-operation of Churches—knows nothing of a hymn book, family prayer, periodical, preaching of Evangelists, sometimes called "our teaching brethren," either in their monthly or semi-monthly diocesan visitations; knows nothing of "The American Christian Review," edited by Elder B. Franklin.

As to the sixth objection, with its sweeping assumptions, I would suggest the importance of giving the points embraced in it a closer examination. Very truly, S. A.

DANVILLE, Ky., Mar. 20, 1856.

REMARKS.

I. We do intend to "give a full and fair hearing of *both sides,"* but we may not always agree with brethren about what is a *"full* and *fair* hearing." Our readers must decide whether we do this. "The peculiar honor of this reformation" is nothing with us; the simple matter is to *do right;* to learn *the will of the Lord and do it.* "This reformation" is not the criterion, nor "the principles of this reformation," nor "Baptist customs." We are just as free to-day as ever the *Christian Baptist* was, or the *Millennial Harbinger,* to look at the naked question, *What is right?* or what does the Bible mean? or what is the true course of action? or what is Christianity? We say not this because we desire to except to the teaching of brethren, for we have never been among that class who have advanced so fast as to be likely to suffer martyrdom from conservatives a half century behind the times; but because we are not willing to adopt an erroneous principle, in directing the mind of the brethren to mere traditional authority. We must not only think and act for ourselves, but try and induce those who may follow after to do the same.

II. Our brethren, in this new organization, must recollect that they are in the affirmative. We are in the negative. We have nothing to prove; they have everything to prove. We are not expected to quote Scripture against something not mentioned in the Bible; but he who affirms that something, is expected to show Scripture for it; or in default of doing so, loses his case. He who affirms infant baptism, must show primitive practice, or Scripture for it, or he who denies it defeats him. The organization we contend for is all found in the New Testament, but the one in question, we presume, has no countenance there. Such a system must be found in Scripture, or it must be conceded that it is not only not there, but that there is *no system there,* and it must then be proved that we have authority to make one to suit ourselves, and bind it upon the disciples. This is involving matter of too much moment to be dashed off hastily. It involves the following absurdities:

1. That the great Protestant proposition, or article of faith, that "The Holy Scriptures contain all things necessary to salvation, so that whatever is not read therein, or may be proved thereby, is not to be required of any man," or, as Paul expresses it, that the Holy Scriptures thoroughly furnish the man of God to all good works, is not true.

2. That the simple church organization, which we now have, is no organization, no system, no arrangement, hence "our decline."

3. There is no system, no organization, no arrangement, or plan of government set forth in the New Testament.

4. We must have a system, organization, or plan of church government.

5. Finding, therefore, that we have no adequate organization, that none is set forth in the law of God, and that we must *have one,* it becomes our duty to make one.

6. As this organization is to take the oversight of preachers, doctrine, and the discipline of the churches, the individual members and churches must reverently obey the rules set forth by this organization.

Upon this quicksand every creed and every human system of church government on this earth is built, viz: A supposed insufficiency in the divine system found in the New Testament. This insufficiency we deny, and claim that the New Testament gives us the only organization we need, the only officers, and the work to be done.

III. The cry about splitting churches has not been hinted at by me, in such a sense as alluded to in the foregoing. I have no fears that brethren in writing and preaching on this subject, "will split the church," as pressing gospel principles did the Baptists. I do not believe the new-organization doctrine has power enough in it to split the churches. The main fears we have are, that brethren will become wearied with it, that they will die off; and that those brethren favorable to such an organization, will become disaffected towards and wounded by those who are not favorable. Our allusion to division, was not that the dissatisfaction occasioned by pressing it upon us, would divide us; but if the thing could be carried into effect, and some disagreement should occur among the leading men in it, they would have a power, with such an engine, to sunder us, as other similar bodies have been severed.

IV. If such a host of men—pioneers—are

favorable to such an organization as is in question, it is strange that the public sentiment should be so strong, fixed, and general against it, that the *Christian Baptist* should have been condemned, as it has been, in some communications. This thing of gleaning a few scraps from a writer, that may appear favorable to a scheme, and from them announce that the *writer is for it,* is the way Bro. Campbell has been made favorable to many things that he certainly is not for. He is able to speak for himself, and when he and the other brethren sanction your organization, we will dispose of the case.

V. My denial of Scripture authority for forming the Kentucky organization, is all set aside, and the thing shown to be right, by simply referring to another organization that has no authority! Singular positions require singular proof. The simple circumstance of brethren meeting and co-operating in sending out a missionary, or doing any other benevolent work, admitted by all Christians to be right, without any express authority from Scripture, is not precisely the same as organizing a district of churches into a body unknown to the New Testament, with a complete set of officers, not only unknown to the law of God, but to whom those mentioned in the law of God are amenable; who are to judge preachers and doctrine for the churches, as well as administer discipline! The benevolent societies mentioned by Bro. Ayres, are only formed by individuals voluntarily, for a certain object, without having any control over churches, preachers, or doctrine. They are not church organizations at all, but merely voluntary; and a Christian could act in reference to them as he would to schools or any good arrangements in society, which do not claim to be church organizations. The officers in the Bible Union are not church officers, nor have they any authority over churches, preachers, or doctrine. The same is true of publications, prayers in the family, etc., etc. These are all individual works, and form no system to be bound upon others, nor do we ask the church to regard them as standards or authorities. Not only so, but evangelists not only preached anciently, but wrote and published their writings. But there is a mighty difference between writing and publishing our writings, with the consent of all who subscribe for them, and forming organizations to govern the churches and preachers of Christ, and sit as *censors* over the doctrine of the Lord Jesus Christ.   B. F.

-----o-----

Tour to Michigan, No. 1.

ON Wednesday, April 2d, we took our leave of the dear and loved ones in Cincinnati, and took cars at the depot on Sixth street, at seven o'clock and thirty minutes A. M. In two hours and a half, passing up the most beautiful valley in the world, the Great Miami, by Hamilton, we passed through Dayton, sixty miles distant, and soon began to see some spots of snow. Our swift-winged train fleeted on rapidly, passing Springfield, Hebron, Bellefountaine and Tiffin, finding still more and more snow and ice, till we reached Sandusky city, at five o'clock P. M., 218 miles from Cincinnati. Here, upon Sandusky Bay and lake Erie, we saw the immense surface of ice spread out as far as the eye could extend, and some two feet thick. Here we waited till twenty minutes before seven, P. M., for the western train for Toledo, which made its appearance in due time, and a mighty train it was, consisting of seventeen passenger cars, well filled. In five minutes after our magnificent locomotive started, we were crossing Sandusky Bay, where, for miles, in the twilight, we could see but little except the broad surface of the ice, out of which the red clouds, beautifully crimsoned by the rays from the setting sun, appeared to be rising on our left, and in which they appeared to be setting on our right, as our giant-like locomotive steered on westerly across the bay. In two hours we passed smoothly along the lake shore and, crossing the immense bridge over the great Maumee Bay, we entered Toledo, where the cry was, "change cars." We hasted down in the midst of the greatest swarm of living and moving humanity we ever saw at any railroad depot. The cars for the west were all filled in three minutes, and hundreds of passengers yet running to and fro, fearing that they would be left. Car after car was added to the great train, till all were on no information that we should be in this place, nor did the brethren know that we were to be there until we were in their midst. Finding, however, that we should remain over one night, the suggestion was made that we should speak at night, but the incessant snow and rain through the day, the darkness of the night, with our weariness after the tumbling we had had the night before in the cars, abated our usual zeal so much that the appointment was declined. We, however, learned that the Baptists were engaged in a protracted meeting, under the labors of a preacher from New Albany, Ind., by the name of Johnson. Accompanied by Bro. E. Bender, we repaired to the Baptist meeting, where we were introduced to, and kindly received by the preacher, who invited us to participate in the exercises. At his request, we prayed with them, and at the close of his short discourse upon the words, " The end of all things is at hand; be sober and watch unto prayer," we spoke for a half hour, maintaining that there is no repentance beyond the boundary line of time, and consequently that all repentance must be in this world. The small audience in attendance listened with the utmost attention, but we thought the prospect for a prosperous meeting rather unpromising.

South Bend is a beautiful town, situated on the St. Joseph river, in St. Joseph county, bearing all the evidences of enterprise and improvement. It is, however, smitten with that blasting, desolating and degrading system of despotism and ignorance which has ruined the fair prospects and brightest hopes of so many great countries, cities and towns both in the old world and the new— subverted so many civil governments, shedding so much blood, and deluding so many of the inhabitants of the earth during the last thousand years of the world's history, viz: *Romanism.* A college is here erected for beguiling the brightest flowers, both male and female, of the whole country into subservience to the law duplicity, that requires a man to believe the priest contrary to his own senses, when the priest tells him that the consecrated bread which *he sees,* is the real flesh of the Lord Jesus Christ. Are Protestant fathers and board, and off our majestic train moved at a few minutes past nine o'clock, P. M.

But now a new part of the drama commenced. The fatigues of the day, the dull monotony, the jar of the cars, and lateness of the hour, began to operate upon the crowded passengers. In a few minutes heads began to hang, and pretty much all that could be seen was sleeping masses of humanity. We too, weary and overcome, committed our safety to the hands of the faithful and gentlemanly conductor and engineer, all under the supreme protection of Him who has promised that the everlasting arms shall be underneath, who will never leave nor forsake us, and to whom be praises forever and ever, we fell into the embrace of Morpheus, first twisting thi way, then that; now the circulation stopped in an arm, then all sensibility had departed from a leg; now a cramp in the side, then a twitching in the limbs, half awake and half sleeping, now dreaming, then beyond the boundary line of consciousness, etc., etc. Thus, in this half conscious state, we passed over almost two hundred miles, first across a corner of Ohio, then a long route through southern Michigan, and then into northern Indiana, down the beautiful St. Joseph river, passing Mishawaka, and getting off at South Bend, at daylight, making at least 440 miles in twenty- two and a half hours. What was more singular than anything of the kind we have ever witnessed, amidst the vast multitudes we saw on the whole route, we saw only one human face that we recollected ever having seen before. That face was the face of an Indian, a Baptist missionary, to whom we had been introduced a short time previously, but whose name has escaped our memory.

Arriving so early, though we knew brethren in South Bend, we made our way to a hotel to await the opening day, rather than disturb a family so early, though public hotels are loathsome places to us. After getting a hearty breakfast, and some two hours rest, we hasted to the residence of the distinguished and well known stenographer, A. E. Drapier, where we were introduced to his intelligent and interesting lady, and also his son, where we received every attention and kindness. We had given mothers determined to go stupidly, blindly and willfully along, encouraging their sons in going into a most profligate, licentious and corrupt priesthood? Will they see their fair daughters, and encourage them in entering those dens of wickedness, Romish nunneries, where they are thrown into the power of Romish priests, whose whole history is but little short of a history of debauchery and the very lowest corruptions? If they do, God will give them tears and sorrow, mourning and grief, that will bring them to their sensibility, when it will be too late to save their daughters or themselves. Such truckling to this lowest and most debasing of all the religions of this earth, would be despised by such a man as Luther, or any true American, unless all history is a farce.

We enjoyed a most refreshing night's rest at the residence of Bro. Drapier. At an early hour on Friday, April 4th, according to agreement, Bro. Wm. M. Roe met us here with his buggy to help us on our way some twelve miles to Buchanan, his place of residence, where an appointment was made for us at night. Bro. Roe is a young preacher of much promise, who has arisen from obscurity, and mainly by his own efforts, educated himself, and entered an extended field of usefulness. He has made himself more thoroughly master of the bewitching, exciting and speculative obstacles which lie in the way of the progress of the cause, than any other person we saw in the bounds of our tour. He has an untarnished reputation, and is now justly looked to as the most substantial defender of the faith in this large and interesting country. Bro. David Miller, who formerly did noble service in this country, has gone to Ohio. Bro. Wm. Theodore Horner, who has also done the cause much creditable service in this section, is also about leaving for Ohio. Elder Corbly Martin, who did great service in planting the cause in this country, with whom we have spent some of our happiest and most profitable days, has gone to his rest with the fathers. Elder Reuben Wilson, another faithful pioneer in sowing the good seed in this extended region, and who deserves great credit for his ardent devotion and untiring labors in the cause, has gone to Indiana. Elder John Martindale, another old soldier, who stood side by side with the latter mentioned two, in the main struggles for primitive Christianity, has gone to Iowa. We pretend not to give the reason why these good men have left this country. There is a reason, and we hope the brethren will philosophize upon it till they find it. Bro. Wm. Roe is the only preacher, so far as we could learn, who is to be wholly devoted to the evangelical work in a large section of country. From what we could learn, we thought the brethren generally were sensible what such a young brother is worth, and we trust they will see well to his temporalities, and keep his path clear for the highest usefulness of which he is capable. We hope also that some other enterprising preaching brethren will find their way to this country, and aid in this great work.

Leaving South Bend, we faced the cold wind, passing snow banks more than three feet deep, and several places found solid ice in the middle of the road; in some five miles we reached the residence of Bro. Roe's father, on the edge of Portage prairie, where we met old friends, good and true, of whose hospitality we partook, and with whom we spent some three joyful hours. In the evening we crossed the prairie, and in a short time reached the residence of Bro. Roe, in Buchanan, where we were introduced to his amiable lady, his brother and brother's lady, enjoying their kind hospitality. Buchanan is a pleasant little town, which we saw in its incipient state, some eleven years ago. The meeting-house belonging to the United Brethren, was opened to us, and well filled at an early hour. The audience gave us the most undivided attention, while we discoursed to them for an hour and a half upon the foundation of the kingdom of God. We were informed that several preachers were present, who gave heed to the things that were spoken. Several brethren were present whom we saw several years ago, and who are yet persevering for eternal life.

On Saturday, the 5th, in company with Bro. Roe, we took cars for Paw Paw, some thirty miles northeast of Buchanan, and passed on to Decatur, where we met Bro. Abbot, who conveyed us to his residence, some five miles distant from the railroad, where we were kindly received and entertained in his truly Christian and pious family. In a short distance from his residence we found quite a respectable congregation assembled in one of the commodious school houses with which this country is thickly dotted over, where we discoursed at length on the necessity of regeneration. At the close we were introduced to Bro. Edwin Barnham, who occasionally labors in word and doctrine, and enjoys the esteem and confidence of the brethren. We were also introduced to several others, whose names we cannot now recollect. We returned to Bro. Abbot's, where we enjoyed a very comfortable night's rest. Here we found a family in the habit of worshiping God daily, the worship, as we think, conducted in a profitable manner. Each member of the family capable of reading, has a copy of the Bible, and they read in a class, verse about, till the passage is read, when a familiar and profitable conversation follows upon what has been read. We have conducted family worship the same way a large portion of time in our own family, except that we use as many translations as we have readers, where we can have them, that the family may see the variations.

On Lord's day morning, by private conveyance, we, in company with many brethren, passed on to Paw Paw, the county seat of Van Buren county, Mich., and were introduced to many brethren who were collecting at the neat and pleasant court house, where we were to speak. By some inattention, the key was not secured, and the house was not opened in time, on account of which, we were informed, many left. The house, however, was pretty well filled in a few minutes, with about as orderly, attentive and respectful an audience as we have seen. Never have we seen an audience listen with more apparent interest for an hour and a half than this one did, while we discoursed to them upon the establishment of the kingdom of God. At the close, the announcement was made that in an hour and a half we would address them again. When this period arrived, the commodious court house was completely filled with people of all religious parties, not excepting Destructionists and Spiritualists, when we again addressed them for an hour and a half, on the adaptation of the new institution to man. At night we again addressed a large audience, upon the divine character and mission of Christ and his kingdom, making an effort against skepticism. We were truly delighted with the country, town and people. The buildings have a neatness of appearance. The town is pleasantly situated, and the evidences of enterprise are manifest on every side.

-----o-----

Evangelizing, No. 3.

ONE main difficulty in prosecuting the evangelical work is, that the preaching of these times has molded the public mind into a false shape, demanding something entirely different from apostolic preaching. The public expectation and demand now is, that the preacher make a strong effort to indoctrinate the people—that he make an effort to explain " our views," elaborate them, defend them, and show that we are nearer right than others around us. Much of the preaching is simply aimed to meet this demand, and amounts to but little more than an effort to plead "our cause" and ingratiate *us* into favor with the people. Hence we have long sermons *about* Christ, *about* the gospel, *about* faith, *about* repentance, *about* baptism, *about* the influence of the Holy Spirit, etc., but many of these sermons lead no one to love Christ, to believe on him, to receive him, confess him, be baptized, and, under them, we have no influence of the Holy Spirit. It is a continuous theorizing about Christianity) while they have but little Christianity; theorizing about faith, while they really have but very little faith; theorizing about repentance, but have but little genuine repentance; theorizing about the work of the Holy Spirit, while very little of the genuine work of the Holy Spirit is done. Indeed, it is one of the most common things for a preacher, who is in a cold and lifeless state, to preach about coldness and lifelessness in the church ; for a preacher, almost without faith, to preach a long theoretical sermon on faith, or a man without the Spirit to preach a long, learned and theoretical sermon on the work of the spirit, but such preaching scarcely ever inspires more warmth, life, faith or work of the Spirit, though the theorizing be very correct.

Theorizing upon faith, no matter how correct or philosophical the theory, never made a believer since the beginning of time. Theorizing upon repentance, no matter how correctly and philosophically, never led any man to repentance, nor did theorizing upon spiritual influences ever impart the influence of the Spirit of God to a living soul; nor does all the theorizing, explaining views of men, in these times, ever convert one soul to Christ, or save one human being from perdition. It converts men to certain views, theories, doctrines, or systems—sometimes to men, but never to God. Indeed, their conversion to these views, theories, systems, doctrines, or men, as the case may be, in the place of being any advantage to them, or bringing them any nearer to God, is the most insuperable obstacle in the way of their conversion to the Saviour of the world. How different the procedure of the Almighty in his approaches to an unbelieving world, to inspire within man faith to the salvation of the soul. He comes not with long theories upon faith, but reveals the thing to be believed, surrounding it with the evidences that prove it true. The great revelation which he makes—that which is called "the faith"—the creed upon which the sinner is to be received is, that "Jesus is the Christ, the Son, of the Living God." This is God's own revelation of his Son, the glorious person in whom we are to believe, confide and trust, as well as to whom we are to look for the salvation of our souls. At the Jordan, when the Lord was baptized, the Almighty Father of heaven and earth revealed and introduced his Son to man, in the following words: "This is my Son, the beloved, in whom I am well pleased." This great oracle reveals the creed to man, which he must confess with his mouth, believing it in the heart, before he can be baptized or received into the church of Christ. The burden of the apostolic preaching, to the unbelieving, was to disclose to them the mighty center of the whole spiritual system—to reveal, or, as they expressed it, to make known him who when lifted up should draw all men unto him. After they had introduced him in any place, and their writers or speakers had occasion to refer to it, they expressed the whole matter in such terms as the following: "Preached Christ unto them"—"Preached unto him Jesus"—"Preached the faith which once he destroyed"—"Preached the word"—"That the Gentiles by my mouth should hear the word of the gospel and believe," etc. But how few, comparatively, in preaching to the unbelieving, can confine themselves to the preaching of Christ; making him known; simply striving to convert men to him. Still, the entire effort, with the unregenerate, should be to make known and commend the Lord Jesus Christ to them—to impress their souls with his name, his love, his goodness, his mercy, his compassion and his glorious power to save man from sin now and from perdition in the world to come.

The work to which God has appointed the preacher is not to indoctrinate the sinner, but to convert him—not to a party, a creed, a theory, or system, but to the glorious *person* of our Lord Jesus Christ—to identify himself with him—commit himself, body, soul and spirit, to him—commit his all for time and for eternity—his entire interests to him forever and ever—to enter with all he has, or is, or ever expects to be, into an eternal identification with him, and put his everlasting trust in him. "But must not Christians have doctrine?" Most assuredly; but when they have committed themselves into the hands of the Lord, been converted to him and taken him for their Leader, Master, Ruler, and Lawgiver, it is their duty to apply to him for doctrine, or, as he expresses it himself, to "learn of him." In entering the covenant, or in conversion, we "take his yoke upon us," or receive him, and, having received him, it is our duty to turn to him as our Teacher, and learn of him, receive the doctrine from him— look to him for doctrine, for instruction, and for all things, both for this world and the world to come. Thus, you perceive, in the place of our having no creed, we have *two;* one for the sinner, the other for the saint; one for the man to confess before baptism, or before he can be received into the church, and upon which he *is received,* and the other for him after he is received, to be the rule of his conduct in all after life. The first creed reveals to him the great Teacher, whom he receives in his conversion, and his adoption identifies him with this great Teacher and Saviour. The second creed is the revelation which the great Teacher puts into his hands after his conversion, and would be of no use to him if he had not been previously converted and prepared for it.

In the place of preaching Christ to the world; setting forth his death, his sufferings, his burial, his resurrection, ascension, coronation, being crowned Lord of all, and reigning King of kings, and Lord of lords, before men to lead them to love him, receive him and place themselves under him, to be his forever and ever; we say, in the place of this, many preachers give the sinner long expositions of what he calls "our views," "our doctrine," or explanations of faith, repentance, baptism, the work of the Spirit, or some fine theories upon regeneration, the new birth, or some other kindred themes, which simply leads the hearer to notice the skill of the mighty man, in making nice distinctions and minute discriminations, which lead none to love God or adore the Saviour of the world. Thousands of the speculations now being preached to sinners, upon conversion, regeneration, faith, repentance, baptism, the work of the Spirit, etc., only perplex and confuse the mind of men of the world, and leads them to think that they can never know anything about it. It leads the minds of the people from the Lord, and, though many of them think the preaching good, the effort able, and suppose all right, they neither love God nor repent of their sins. We must cut ourselves loose from all this speculation—free ourselves, the cause, and people, from the perplexing and confusing mystifications and entangling influences of these times, by simplifying, defining and presenting in a tangible form precisely what is to be believed, how it affected those who believed it, what they inquired, how they were answered, what they did and what it was for. We must preach Christ, the Saviour and Redeemer of man—keep him before our own eyes and the eyes of the people, love him ourselves and induce those who hear us to love him, to worship and adore him forever.

Is it not possible to rescue the people from the pernicious and blinding influences of speculative theories and theorists, and induce them to receive the simple faith of Christ, become his disciples love him and serve him? Have the leaders of the people, in these times, as they did in the days of the Lord's pilgrimage on earth, stolen away the key of knowledge, and fastened them down with such an impenetrable spell of thick darkness that they are unwilling to be rescued from this servile slavery to human speculation, to the rejection of the sun of righteousness? Or is the world so lost, the mind of the people so bewitched, the delusions around us so enchanting, that it is impossible to attract the attention of the people, arrest their affections or impress their hearts, by the love of God to man, by the sufferings of Christ, by all the divine sanctions of the blood of the everlasting covenant, by the glories of heaven, or the terrors of hell, to turn to the Lord and follow him who loved us and gave himself for us? Is the public mind so distracted, and are the people so confused and lost to all that God has said and done, that they cannot be induced to love Christ better than all human theories, regard him and feel the force of all his love to our lost and ruined world? Are the people so set upon gnawing the bones of contention, keeping up sectarian feuds; disputing upon the lifeless, soulless and profitless controversies thrust upon them, that they will neither hear the Lord nor be interested in the word of his grace? Must the public mind be wholly occupied with the useless distinctions between the views of men, the useless comparisons of doctrines and commandments of men, the comparative merits of different human systems, and an eternal train of customs unknown to the primitive church, thus bewildering the people and blinding their minds that they may neither see the Lord nor regard his authority? Is it impossible to bring the authority of the Almighty again to bear upon the world, to lift up the Lord before the people, that he may draw all men unto him, convert them to the Lord and place them under him? Is it impossible to rescue the people from the blinding influences of these times—from being merely followers of men, and believing human theories, which have no power to save, in the place of believing the great truth, that Christ died for our sins, according to the scriptures—that he was buried, and that he rose from the dead? Is it impossible to interest the public mind with the things of God—with the revelation from God to man, with the religion of Christ itself? Is the love of God gone from the world? Has the Holy Spirit of God abandoned the church? Is the human race mad, insane and ruined, so that all pleadings and entreaties to turn to God must fail? Must the holy religion of Christ be set aside for the silly disputes of these times? Shall that holy religion that saved such vast multitudes in the days of the apostles, fired the hearts of the missionaries of the cross and supported the holy martyrs in passing through all the cruel scourgings, tortures and privations for the name of the Lord, be contemned, despised and rejected by the people of our day? O, that God would enable us to arouse the people of this generation from the awful stupor and deep slumbers of carnal security to prepare to meet God!   B. F.

-----o-----

Catching and Scattering the Sheep.

Our Lord admonishes us to "Beware of false prophets, who come to you in sheep's clothing, but inwardly they are ravening wolves; by their words ye shall know them." Matt. vii. 15, 16. Again he says, "He who is an hireling, and not the shepherd, whose own the sheep are not, seeth the wolf coming, and leaveth the sheep and fleeth; and the wolf catcheth them and scattereth the sheep." John x. 12. In this holy teaching of our Lord, we have much in little. He here explains to us, 1st.' That the wolves in sheep's garb are false prophets, or false teachers; 2d. That they may be known by their fruits, or works; 3d. That their work is to catch and scatter the sheep. The good Shepherd, and all true teachers, come not to destroy, pull down, and spread desolation; to catch, scatter, and devour the sheep, but to gather, unite, build up, and save. Whatever scatters, destroys, and devastates, but never gathers, builds up, or saves, is manifestly only the work of false teachers—devouring wolves, not sparing the flock—"they who separate themselves, sensual, having not the Spirit"—devilish. The time has come for those who love the Lord, who love the brethren, and who love the cause of Christ; those who have labored many years in turning men to God; who have gathered many into the fold of Christ; seated them down in heavenly places in Christ, in love, peace, and harmony, should fix their eye on a class of men, who never convert anybody, never build up any congregations, never settle any difficulties, restore peace, or promote happiness any place, but who are perfect leeches upon the churches; annoying them, eating out their vitals, creating dissention and distraction wherever they have the least power or influence. This class of men must be called to account, and the churches must be made to feel their pernicious influence, that their work of ruin and desolation may be called to a halt.

We have one branch of this kind of men in view especially now, and would that there were not other branches equally ruinous in their work and influence upon the church, to which we now invite especial attention. We mean that entire class of teachers, both male and female, whose central idea is, and whose principal efforts are aimed to prove, that man is wholly a material being, or that man consists wholly of matter. What there can be in this to inspire man with the least zeal, anxiety, or concern to propagate it, we never could see; but so it is, some men, and some *women,* have traveled aid preached it with the zeal of apostles. We do not mean that they go out, like the apostles, to preach to every creature. We have never known them to go out among men of the world and build up a church any place. We have never known them to heal a division, or reconcile alienated parties, or promote peace, in any instance. Their work is among churches, built up, and loving disciples gathered by the labors of other men. Here they must be permitted to preach, or they are proscribed, gagged, and persecuted! But when they preach, who is made any better? The people, to say the least of it, do not pray more, love God more, or do more in anything that is good. Peace, love, and joy do not follow. Sinners are not converted, the community is not reformed, nor the saints strengthened. Not one change in the practice of the whole community, for the better, is seen. What does follow? Why, probably some of the members begin to argue that man consists wholly of matter—that he is nothing but a thinking lump of clay—that after he dies, he no more exists than before he was created—that all who have died, both righteous and wicked, no more exist than before their mothers conceived them—that the second death is taking apart the second time the materials of which man is composed—unmaking him a second time, thus throwing him into an eternal non-existence, to suffer the eternal punishment of an eternal impossibility of ever suffering or being punished at all. With this single idea, the church, on every meeting for worship, the social circle, on all occasions, and almost all private interviews, must be incessantly annoyed. It becomes the Alpha and Omega, the beginning and the end, the center and the circumference. But what is the result? Probably, through the good influence of some faithful men, the disciples are not immediately scattered. But all improvement ceases; all devotion gradually declines; prosperity terminates, love waxes cold, and religious obligations begin to be neglected.

But suppose they succeed in scattering, or dividing the flock, do they build up a party and prosper? Suppose they carry the majority with them, do they even then prosper? By no means, in a single instance known to us. Dr. N. Field, of Jeffersonville, Ind., a man of fair talents, once drew a respectable portion of a flourishing church after him; but where are they and the doctor now? Has not a regular and deathly decline attended both him and his church? His labors have amounted to comparatively little, while others with less talent have built up many strong churches and turned large numbers to God. Dr. Field does not, however, make the effort to sow the seeds of his deathly theory that some men do. For another example, look at Dr. John Thomas. Here is another man of fair talent, who has had a fair opportunity, if there had been anything but *destruction, death,* and *ruin* in his doctrine, to have built something up; but where are the churches established by him, flourishing and extending? He can look back to the ruins, which he has pulled down; but where has he built up and established anything that is growing and promising any good to man? We can point to the divisions that this class of men have made, to the desolations of their career; the contentions, heartachings, feuds, and bickerings they have occasioned— the divisions they have produced and churches they have pulled down, but where are they building up anything? If they organize a church, having no soul either in the church or members, except a material one, of flesh and blood, it falls quietly *asleep,* as soon as the contention that created it is over. Just in proportion as this soulless thing is maintained and prominence given it, must religion die, and the usefulness of all who fall into it must also die. Its unblushing inconsistencies are so egregious that they counteract and neutralize all efforts to rise above its inherent antagonism to the great vital principles of the religion of Jesus Christ, and render them entirely nugatory. The absurdity of the eternal punishment of the wicked being precisely the same as before we were created, viz. *non-existence,* and that both righteous and wicked are in the same punishment from death till resurrection, *i. e. non-existence,* is so utterly preposterous and antipodal to all contained in the Bible, that it must neutralize and counteract all efforts to do good on the part of those under its influence. The idea of a spiritual system, from the spiritual world, given by the great Infinite Spirit, for beings having no spirits, or consisting wholly of *matter,* is so manifestly self-condemnatory and absurd, that its force upon most men is but little better than Atheism. That inscription upon the tomb-stones in France, during the reign of terror, which French Atheists applied to *all men,* Materialists apply to only a *part,* viz.: "*Death.— an eternal sleep."* Indeed, Materialists maintain that all men will sleep, but that this sleep will not be eternal, except to the wicked. The that this sleep will not be eternal, except to the wicked. The "eternal sleep," the heaven dreamed about by French Atheists, which all men were to enjoy, is now metamorphosed, by Materialists, into the hell in which the wicked shall be punished!

We have no confidence in men and theories that have no power except to scatter, tear down and destroy. The time has come when the brethren should put their mark upon all this description of men, we care not what their idol may be, who are simply prating, whining, complaining, and murmuring among loving disciples gathered by the labors and sacrifices of other men, but who never built up a church, healed a difficulty, or promoted peace any place in their lives. Nothing is so ridiculous as for such men to go grumbling round the country, finding fault with everything, pulling down other men's labor and building up nothing, all the while prating about *progression* and *reformation.* Tremendous progress, that miserable prating, whining, and grumbling that never builds up anything, but always pulls down, catches the sheep and scatters them! Mighty *reformers* they, who never reformed anybody since God made them, who never built up a church or gave any prosperity to the cause, any place, or did anything more than scatter and devastate! Atheism has done this much, and will do it again. If men have found any new light worth anything, and are themselves men of any force, improvement will appear; fruits will follow their labors. But nothing can be more manifest than that God did not send those men who only spread desolation, who only pull down, scatter, and kill, we care not what fine theories they propagate, nor how prettily they may talk. We want men who will preach the Lord Jesus Christ, who will regard him, adore him, and obey him, and not a set of self-willed men, who idolize their own notions, and are determined to have them and propagate them, if the Lord's name is forgotten, his ordinances disparaged, his house forsaken, and the fold scattered asunder. Mercy and peace upon the Israel of God. Mark them who cause divisions and contentions.

Review of Dr. Shaffer, No. 5.

FOR the sake of widening our scope a little, we introduce to the reader the following, from the *Nashville Christian Advocate* of January 10th:

"INFORMATION WANTED.—Will Immersionist, who knows, be so kind as to give an unpretending, conscientious pedo-Baptist a little information? I want to know if the *familiar* passage in Ephesians—'One Lord, one faith, one baptism'—means, when rightly understood, 'one Lord,' the Lord of the *Baptists;* 'one faith,' the faith of the *Baptists;* 'one baptism,' *immersion;* or does it mean that one Lord is the Lord of all—one faith, confidence in the Lord—and one baptism, in the name of the Father, the Son, and the Holy Ghost? And when Paul said that there was but one baptism, was he speaking in reference to the *mode,* and endeavoring to prove that sprinkling and pouring were not valid? Furthermore: In Acts xi, 15, 16, Peter says: 'And as I began to speak, the Holy Ghost *fell* on them, as on us at the beginning. Then remembered I the word of the Lord, how that he said, John indeed baptized *with* water; but ye shall be baptized *with* the Holy Ghost.' The Holy Ghost *fell* upon them; Peter called that baptism. Now, what would a similar application of water be called? If a torrent, sufficient to *overwhelm* the candidate, were poured on, would it be baptism? And I want to know if *immersed* ought to be substituted for *baptized* where the latter occurs in the last example? *How does the 'new version' read?*

INQUIRER."

While we are endeavoring to enlighten Dr. Shaffer, we will try to furnish the "information wanted" for the above "unpretending, conscientious pedo-Baptist,"

1. He desires to know whether the "one Lord" of Paul, Eph. iv, 5, "means one Lord, the Lord of the *Baptists."* We answer, by no means is he the one Lord of Baptists, Methodists, or Presbyterians, but the one Lord of Christians, disciples of Christ, or children of God. He is not the foundation of the Baptist church, the Methodist church, or the Presbyterian church, but he said, "Upon this rock I will build my church." Mat. xvi, 18. This church, built upon this rock, which He calls *"my* church," the "church of

of God," the "one body," "one new man," the "building of God," "temple of the Holy Spirit," and "household of the faithful," is the one of which he is the "one Lord," and the only one which has any authority from him for its existence. He dwells in it, his Father dwells in it, the Holy Spirit dwells in it. The "one Lord" is the head of it, as the husband is the head of the wife, and he is the head of no other. He is the foundation of no other.

2. Inquirer wants to know whether the "one faith," Eph. iv, 5, is the "faith of the *Baptists.*" We answer, no; nor the faith of Methodists, Presbyterians, etc., but "the faith once delivered to the saints," the "faith of Christ," the faith of Christians, disciples of Christ, and the only faith ever authorized since the Lord ascended to heaven. The dispute about Baptist faith, Methodist faith, Lutheran faith, etc., all amounts to nothing, only to keep men wrangling and disputing about mere fruitless leaves. The time has come when good men are lifting their eyes above all this — far above it, to the ancient faith, the one faith that gives life through the Redeemer. See John xx, 31. This faith is the medium through which life is given to the children of men. This faith opens the way to become sons of God. "As many as received him, to them gave he power to become sons of God, even to them who believe on his name." This faith makes Christians, disciples of Christ, children of God; but it makes no Baptists, Methodists, etc. It is confidence in the one Lord, the Redeemer of the world, and enables a man to lift his eyes above all the little party disputes between Baptists and Methodists, relative to their comparative merits, or which are the nearer right, and shows that nothing avails anything short of that which *unites a man with God.*

3. He wants to know whether Paul's "one baptism" is one *immersion.* Without the least hesitation we answer, it is. He knew what the word baptize, or *baptizo,* meant, and when he said "there is one baptism," it is precisely "one *immersion,*" no more nor less. If the Greek *baptizo* means sprinkle, then Paul affirms that there is but *one sprinkling;* or if it means pouring, then he affirms that there is but *one pouring.* But the truth in the case is, that there is but one immersion, emblematical of the one burial, of the one Lord, who died once for all, which introduces the proper subject into the one body, the habitation of the one Spirit.

4. Inquirer wishes to know if Paul was speaking in reference to the *mode* of baptism. We answer, no. He never said one word about the mode, nor did anybody else in his time. This dispute about the mode is of more recent date, a trick of modern times. The whole Bible is as silent as the grave about all *modes* of baptism. All books written in the first two centuries are silent about *modes* of baptism. The preachers of that age knew what baptism was, and were in no disputes about it, and in all the references of both the preachers and writers of those times, they have nothing to say about *modes of baptism,* but in speaking of baptism itself, they have frequently expressed themselves in such a way as to show what it was that they called baptism. But all this was, apparently, incidental, and not in view of any dispute about it. This, too, is an important point, for men of reason must see that if there had been different ways of baptizing, it could not have escaped attention for two hundred years. Yet it is a fact that no book written in the first two centuries gives the remotest hint of any difference about the manner of baptizing.

Our "Inquirer" now unites *teacher* with "Inquirer," in his person, and quotes the words, "As I began to speak the Holy Ghost fell on them as on us at the beginning," and informs us that Peter calls this baptism. Now, so long as he continued simply in his office of *inquirer,* he did well, but his very first effort at teaching is wrong. Peter never called "fell on them" baptism, nor any other man who knew what he was about. What was it that "fell on them?" The Holy Ghost fell on them. Does "fell on them" mean baptized? Let us try the passage. "As I began to speak the Holy Ghost was *baptized* on them," etc. How utterly ridiculous. "Fell on," or *ekkeo,* the Greek word from which it comes, does not mean baptize any place in the New Testament. *Ekkeo* is translated *runneth out,* Mat. ix, 17; *spilled,* Mark ii, 22; *poured out,* John ii, 15; *pour out,* Acts ii,

17, the same, verse 18, *hath shed forth,* verse 33, and in a similar manner in the dozen remaining occurrences of it in the New Testament; but it never means baptize, nor did any holy writer ever call it baptism. No' two things are more distinct, in a clear mind, than the "pouring out," "shedding forth," or "fall on," as the common version renders *ekkeo,* and baptizing in the Holy Spirit. It was the *Spirit* that was poured out, shed forth, or fell on them, but the *people* were baptized. Pouring out the Spirit preceded the baptizing of the people. Baptizing the people followed after pouring out the Spirit. The pouring out was in order to the baptizing. The water is poured out of the clouds, but the people are baptized in the river. The pouring out of the water, and baptizing in it, are two distinct things.

As we are a little pressed for room, we shall be compelled to dismiss the Dr. with a shorter lesson than common this month. B. F.

-----o-----

Letter from J. T. Johnson.

LEXINGTON, April 8, 1856.

DEAR BROTHER FRANKLIN:—I have just closed a most interesting meeting at Leesburg, assisted by Bro. Gano. We had eight additions, and a most favorable impression was made on many persons who had previously misunderstood our teaching, and of course were prejudiced. The brethren were generous and liberal. They contributed $175 to the Orphan Girl School at Midway, $25 to the evangelical fund, and two persons subscribed $150 to the educational fund. The church, I judge, will hereafter act liberally in respect to this fund. Previous to this, I had assisted Bro. R. C. Rice at Nicholasville, until he had four valuable additions also, and I learn he gained twenty before he closed. Thanks be to the Lord for all his goodness. In haste I have written and sent you a sermon for publication. It is in its first dress; excuse blunders in polish.

Yours, J. T. JOHNSON.

N. B. While some of the leading Baptist preachers are castigating, and endeavoring to pronounce Bro. Campbell and us little fry, they might find themselves better employed in correcting the errors of some of their young, beardless evangelists; and a little castigation might be of service to some of the more aged.

I was informed, the other day, at Leesburg, by several of the most respectable Baptists, whose names are furnished below,* and can testify if desired, that on the trial of a highly respectable and intelligent member of the church, at Silas, on a charge of contempt of the church, got up on the spur of the moment, he at the same time denying, and just at the moment of putting the question, a respectable minister rose and placed one hand on the Bible and the other on the church book, asking which was the authority by which they were acting in the case. The Preacher, Mr. Barbee, as I was informed, replied that the church book was the authority. Several of the members then asked for letters. The member was excluded, protesting his innocence.

Again, one of their young preachers, I think a graduate of Georgetown college, whose name can be given if demanded, in a conversation with me a few years past, on the subject of the operation of the Spirit in conversion, and in answer to a question propounded to him, remarked that Jesus Christ never converted a person on earth, and could not if he were here, by *his word*; that the operation of the Spirit was necessary. I replied that I would sooner assume the responsibility of denying divine honors to my Saviour, than to deny him the power to convert a sinner; at the same time referring to Paul in the 5th ch., and 2d letter to the Cor., "Who hath reconciled *us* to himself by Jesus Christ," in allusion to all the apostles.

Again, one of their more aged men, in the pulpit, in reference to our teaching, amused himself and the congregation with the following, in substance. That, on a baptismal occasion, a preacher, or someone else, desired to know if they were about to baptize, and upon what principle. He was answered in the affirmative, and upon the faith of the candidate. He desired to know the design of baptism. It was replied, for the remission of sins. Then, very gravely the that he knew an old man that not only believed,

---

* Messrs. Milton Chinn and wife, Hearn, Joseph Hawkins and wife, and others.

but trembled, and would be glad to be baptized. He was asked, with some anxiety, who the person was. It was replied, that Beelzebub was the old man.* What horrible blasphemy. He ought to repent in sackcloth and ashes. The gentleman who heard it, observed that it was too low for a politician, and he left.

Yours truly,   J. T. JOHNSON.

---

*Mr. Metcalf heard Mr. Helm, at Mayslick, tell this anecdote, this spring.

Editors' Table.

Office of the *American Christian Review,* West Fourth street, No. 60, on third floor, open stair way from outside. Signs will be seen at the entrance.

THE valuable article from Bro. A. E. Myers, of Bethany, Va., which was in the hands of the compositor, was unavoidably crowded out. It will appear next month.

-----o-----

The Voice.—We noticed this work some two months ago; a few copies were left with us, which have been sold. A few copies more have been left, so that any orders can now be filled. This book contains the discourse on *Order,* and the *Weekly Contribution,* which attracted much attention and occasioned much investigation, many years ago. Price 50 cents. See notice in *Review* No. 3.

-----o-----

MANY, who know that we have made an effort to reconcile the brethren in Noblesville, Ind., are anxious to know the result. This we now have in writing, from the parties themselves, but it is not satisfactory, and, as we do not wish to do anything rashly, we wait one month longer, hoping that some change for the better will take place, when the result *shall appear.*

-----o-----

WE are still able to furnish back numbers complete, to about 1,500 new subscribers. We will thank any correspondents who will furnish us names and address of persons to whom we may send specimen numbers of the *American Christian Review,* who probably would subscribe. Some two or three hundred of the January number were sent out as specimens, which leaves us about the same number of extra copies on each of the succeeding numbers, which we should like to send out to persons who have not seen the *Review,* to induce them to subscribe.

Success of the Gospel.

Bro. J. C. IRVIN, of Bowenville, O., writes under date, April 11, that, "A Bro. Cathell, who has faithfully battled with the warring elements of partyism and manism in religion, has sustained himself for years as a Christian, has stood aloof from the sects, striving to find the way of the Lord more perfectly. He has united with us, is preaching and contending earnestly for the faith once delivered to the saints."

Bro. R. Edmunson writes, that under his labors six were baptized, eight miles south of Noblesville, Ind., fourth Lord's day in March; at Sugar creek, Hancock county, four more added, and one, who had been baptized, also united. The first Lord's day in April, in company with brethren Bennet and Lowe, six more were added, at Buck creek, Hancock Co.

Queries Answered,

Q. 1. What are we to understand the *gift* of the Holy Spirit to be, as promised by Peter on the day of Pentecost?

Q. 2. What *promise* did Peter allude to on the day of Pentecost?

Q. 3. When is an individual born of the Spirit?

G. W. THOMPSON.

ANSWERS.

1. The gift of the Holy Spirit, promised to those who received Christ, was the common indwelling comforter, sent forth into the heart, by which we call God Father, enjoyed by all the children of God.

2. That which Peter called "the promise," or Pentecost, and which is emphatically called *the promise,* in the Bible generally, if not always, is the promise made to Abraham—"In thee and in thy seed shall all nations be blessed." This is the gospel in promise.

3. An individual is born of the Spirit when he is converted, or when he obeys from the heart the form of doctrine delivered to him.

Q. What is meant, John x, 12?—"But he that is a hireling and not the shepherd, whose own the sheep are not, seeth the wolf coming and leaveth the sheep and fleeth, and the wolf catcheth them and scattereth the sheep." What does the wolf catch? Be particular.

AARON HARLAN.

Our article upon this passage was in type, when this came to hand. We answer the query, that the wolf catcheth the *sheep.* The pronoun *he,* the hireling, is singular, but the pronoun *them,* caught, is plural. There was but one hireling, but more than one in *them,* the caught. Besides, the sense of the whole passage shows that the wolf catches the sheep.

The Right Sentiments.

Editor Christian Review:

DEAR BROTHER:—Being in the city of Rochester, N. Y., and having a copy of your April issue to glance at while journeying, let me express my hearty approbation of the following sentiments from your pen:

"The New Testament records inform us of the organization, or, rather, the institution of individual communities, or churches, and the appointment of officers in them. But these records know nothing of any organization of the churches in any given district into one body, under a new set of officers, who are officers not of the churches but of the district. While we were generally satisfied with the simple New Testament organization of individual communities, with full power and authority to do their own business, and the preachers went forth to build up, strengthen and sustain these communities, as well as convert sinners, we prospered throughout the land; but the moment we began to try to ape the parties around us, in scheming at things beyond the simplicity of Christ's own order, our success began to abate. The principal difficulties which have caused the most distressing controversies among us, have grown out of attempts, one way or other, to combine, concentrate and organize the Christian communities into some kind of a body unknown to the law of God."

Will the beloved brethren, who earnestly desire to think, resolve, speak and act as the faithful disciples of old, read the above words again, and lay them up for safe-keeping in their own book of remembrance? A grand pity, brother Franklin, that some devout men, apparently zealous for reform, will not allow themselves to be satisfied with the instructions of the Holy Book relative to all social, congregational, and general duties which pertain to the saved in Christ. Some good people talk as though the Lord had given his friends power to pass resolutions and create organizations to save men!

My brother, allow me to ask you a question that may be answered for the benefit of many. In what part of your New Testament do you find either the word "organization," or the idea expressed by this pretty modern word?

In the love of the pure truth of God, yours,

D. OLIPHANT.

ROCHESTER, N. Y., 13th April.

Please address me, as usual, at Brighton, Canada West. D. O.

REPLY.

We do not find the word "organization" any place in the New Testament, applied in the modern sense, or used in any way; nor organize. The term employed by the Lord, in reference to establishing his church, is "build"—"upon this rock I will *build* my church." Mat. xvi, 18. This term is applied to the establishing of churches by Paul, Heb. iii, 3-4. Acts xx, 32, we have "*build* up;" 1 Cor. iii, 15, we have "*build* thereon." Eph. ii, 20, the apostle says, "And one *built* upon the foundation of apostles and prophets," etc. Could we not change some of our *organizers* into *builders?* We need builders, who will fitly frame the house and erect a holy temple for the Lord. Let us keep building, but let every man take heed how he buildeth thereon, for every man's work shall be tried by fire, of what sort it is. B. F.

-----o-----

CHICKASAW, Mercer Co., April 9, 1856.

BROTHER B. F.—Inclosed you will find a copy of a letter, addressed by me to Dr. Shaffer, shortly after your debate with him, and his response, which I desire you to publish in your review of his book on Baptism. They will show, to a demonstration, the estimation the doctor places on his own efforts as a disputant, when the arguments on both sides are presented in a tangible form before a discerning public. JOSHUA D. WRIGHT.

"CHICKASAW, Mercer Co., July 2, 1854.

BRO. DR. H. M. SHAFFER—*Dear Sir:* I embrace the present opportunity of dropping you a few lines, requesting you to write your speeches of the Cold Water Debate. My reasons for this are—

First. It was the desire of some of our citizens that it should be done.

Second. The partial agreement that we entered into, on Cold Water, last January, when we arranged our propositions and time of debate, of having a discussion at Piqua, with yourself and some man that we might select, and have it published.

Third. You, and your brethren utterly refusing to have you write your speeches of your discussion with B. Franklin, commencing June 20th, 1854. at the Wesley Chapel, Darke county, Ohio, which we doubt not was the wish of a large majority of the audience, and your opponent.

I wish you to respond to my request at your earliest convenience, affirmatively or negatively.

Yours, with respect,

JOSHUA D. WRIGHT.

P. S.—As a matter of course, if we write our speeches, in order to make a book for the people, our correspondence, with your first proposals, should precede the discussion. J. D. W.

BELLEFONTAINE, Ohio, July 20, 1854.

Dear Sir: Yours duly came to hand. You ask me to furnish you a copy of my arguments at our debate on Cold Water. I followed my book on Baptism in the argument. You can take them as printed, chapter by chapter, and publish any argument you may think best to meet them. As for my speeches, I did not even take notes of them, so my speeches I cannot give, but my arguments I can, as I followed the plan and arguments in my book, and would be glad if you would copy them and put your arguments by them, and publish them in a book. 1 think it would subserve the cause of truth.

Yours, respectfully,

H. M. SHAFFER.

Rev. J. D. WRIGHT.

THE AMERICAN CHRISTIAN REVIEW.

SERMON BY ELDER J. T. JOHNSON.

Rom. v. 10: "For if when we were enemies, we were reconciled to God by the death of his Son, much more being reconciled, we shall be saved from wrath by his life."

1. THE doctrine of Reconciliation is fundamental in our holy religion, as it regards both God and man, and as respects the thing itself, and its benefits and influence on man. This is the theme of my discourse; and after I shall have laid down several leading and fundamental truths in connection with it, it shall be my pleasure to make the subject manifest in all the fullness and clearness of the Divine volume.

2. The Book then is the infallible rule, and to it we make our first and last appeal. It must settle all questions. So respond all Protestants.

3. We have redemption through the blood of Christ. His death is that without which no man can be saved. To repudiate this, is to cast away the *only* ground of *hope* of living again, and of Heaven. Without the shedding of his blood, there is no remission. Here we stand upon the Rock of eternity. Col. i, and Eph. i.

4. Jesus Christ is the Son of God. He is a Divine personage—the Son of Mary, and the Son of God—the Head of the body, the congregation—vested with all power in Heaven and upon earth. We are complete in Him, the head of all principality and power—the only Lawgiver Judge in his Kingdom.

5. Reconciliation to him, restores peace and unity among his disciples, without which there is no peace, purity, or happiness, but desolation and death. Union, then, is a great land-mark never to be lost sight of.

6. The Christian system is Divine—it is spiritual—it is perfect; and whatever it accomplishes is Divine, is spiritual. Every religious conviction, emotion, impression, or impulse, is the result or offspring of this divine, spiritual system or science. It is God's power to convert, to heal, to save, to sanctify, and finally to fit a man for Heaven. It is most gratifying to know that these grand truths are generally admitted, and that the labor of their discussion is at an end. We have fought our way through all the fiery opposition of licentious, and unbridled, malignant babblers, and satisfied the world of our scriptural correctness.

7. Let us now proceed to the examination of *"The Reconciliation."* "God *so loved* the world, that he gave his only begotten Son," etc. The Son died to reconcile the *sinner* to God. If God so *loved* the world as to give his Son to die for us. how much better could he love us after the death of his Son? There can be no question but what he loves his obedient children better than the

rebellious. The one he loves with pure delight; the other he loves with pity. He delights in the saved. He delights to save, and in the offer of salvation. The Christian religion is a system of reconciliation. And that the meanest capacity may understand the proposition and proof, it is stated as follows: Whenever a sinner is reconciled to God, his heart is changed, and he is in a saved state. That this desirable change may be accomplished, it is indispensable that we ascertain the power that accomplishes it. In other words, the power that changes the heart, reconciles the sinner to God—and *vice versa.* And inasmuch as *the Book* is the infallible guide and rule, we will make our appeal there, knowing that we cannot be misled.

8. We first make our appeal to the law and the testimony. Then we may look at, appreciate, and enjoy its philosophy—its adaptedness to the object to be accomplished.

In the first place, I ask your attention to the clear, explicit declaration of Paul to the Colossians, 1st ch., 20th, 21st, and 22d verses. "And having made peace through the blood of his cross, by him to reconcile all things unto himself," etc. "And you that were formerly alienated and enemies in your minds by wicked works, yet now hath he *reconciled* in the body of his flesh through death," etc.

Again: Paul to the Romans, 5th chapter and 10th verse, "For if when we were enemies, we were reconciled to God by the death of his Son, much more being reconciled we shall be saved by his life," etc.

Again—Paul to the Ephesians, 2d chapter and 14th, 15th, and 16th verses: "For he is our [i. *e.* Jew and Gentile] peace, who hath made both [i. *e.* Jew and Gentile one in Christ] one, and hath broken down the middle wall of partition between us [i. *e.* Jew and Gentile], etc., and that he might *reconcile* both [same as above] *unto God* into one body by *the cross,* having *slain the enmity thereby,"* etc.

Here Paul comes down upon us like an avalanche. "God forbid that I should glory save in the cross of our Lord Jesus Christ, by which the world is crucified to me, and I to the world." Gal. vi, 14.

These proofs are conclusive. What more power is needed to change the heart or reconcile the sinner to God, than that which crucifies me to the world and the world to me? Paul says the Cross accomplishes this. On the Cross Jesus died—on the Cross he shed his blood—on the Cross it was "finished"—our stripes were healed, our redemption was secured. Was ever love like this? Let rocks and hills their lasting silence break; and all harmonious human tongues. their Saviour's praises speak. All-conquering love! Enough to subdue the stubborn Jewish heart, and tame the wily Greek—to turn the raven to a dove, the lion to a lamb.

"The Gospel is *the* power of God unto salvation to everyone that believeth." Rom. i, 15,16. How God-like in authority! It is clothed in all the authority of God. It convicts, converts, heals, saves, and sanctifies. How powerful in its motives! How cheering, consoling, and soul-inspiring in its promises! How soul-subduing, purifying, and redeeming! It prepares and lifts a man from earth to Heaven! It gives victory over death, and a crown of glory in Heaven!

What mighty, what sudden changes are wrought in this life, in the minds and hearts of men! See two men, with their seconds, on the field of honor, falsely so called; filled with deadly hate, and murderous purpose; they take their stand; the word is given; they fire. One falls; the other sees the ruin he has accomplished; a wife robbed of an affectionate husband; children deprived of their only support; a soul ushered into eternity! He is overwhelmed; anguish seizes his heart; a gush of penitence impels him to his bleeding victim; forgiveness is sought; it is granted; the mutual embrace. Who can describe the change in heart of these men? The regret, the pain, the anguish; the love, the gratitude of both parties, and all together at the reconciliation!

Again. See that interesting couple, confiding, loving, making their escape to consummate the most sacred of human pledges against the will of their parents. What is it that impels them? Their hearts have been changed! Love for love! unquenchable love! never dying love! See these same parties on a steamer, dashing along, anticipating the moment with ecstasy that shall pronounce them *one!* The father is in full pursuit, supposing the young man to be faithless; an impostor, a coward; seeking *his* fortune, rather than the daughter, as the prize. At the moment when he heaves in sight, he sees the steamer on fire; he sees the couple on deck, and the fire advancing with almost lightning speed towards his beloved daughter. He sees the young man, in great haste and apparent trepidation, pass a few words with her and retire! Great God! what must be the father's feelings, to see his loved one abandoned at that perilous crisis by the one with whom she had staked all that is dear! Not an effort to save her. He is confirmed in the dastardly, base purpose of the youth. At that moment she leaps overboard to risk her life in the waves, rather than perish in the flames. Just as she sinks, the young man leaps overboard, and as she rises to the surface, he grasps her in his arms, resolved to save or perish. With gallant spirit, a brave heart—a love as glowing and unconquerable as the love of the Saviour—he bears her safely to the arms of that heart-broken parent. Who can now describe the joy of that father? his outburst of gratitude to the youth who had so gallantly saved his daughter from a watery grave? What a change of heart! Unless a fiend, he would respond, "Sir, you are worthy of my daughter, and all the fortune I can give you!"

Again. See those men on a journey, returning home. The one is anticipating, and in the fullness of his heart, painting to his young associate the joys of his meeting and embracing that loved wife and children of his, in a few hours more. The wife and children, however, have been informed, and are laboring under the impression, that the young man is a deadly enemy of theirs, and is seeking an occasion to take the life of the husband and father. Under these circumstances, they reach a stream most difficult and dangerous to ford, in consequence of the swell from heavy rains. The young man resolves to take the lead and risk his life, rather than that of the man and family that he loves. They both enter, and make their way cautiously along; just as the youth nears the shore, he hears a noise behind; he looks around; he sees his friend plunged headlong into the stream, struggling for life and death. He dashes out; leaps from his horse; plunges into the stream, and at the moment when he is sinking for the third and last time, he grasps him in his arms and lifts him up. No sooner are they up, than they are dashed under the waves. He rises again, resolved to risk his life; he seizes him again; no sooner are they up, than the violence of the stream again washes them under. A third time he risks his life, resolved to save or perish with his friend. With giant grasp and struggle, he bears his friend safely to the shore Who can describe the feelings of the wife and children? What a change of heart! They would be the veriest fiends of Hell, if other feelings than love and gratitude could find a place in their bosom. They are conquered, overcome by love!

What is all this? What are a thousand such cases, to the case in hand? Man, lost, ruined, bankrupt, and undone; doomed to misery, disease, mortality, death, and Hell in consequence of sin; crushed in heart at the loss of friends, parents, brothers and sisters, sons and daughters, and, most painful of all, the loved partner of his bosom! In such an awful condition, and at such an awful crisis, the Son of God leaves the Heavens, comes to seek and save the lost and ruined sons and daughters of Adam. He led a life of suffering, and sorrow, and grief in ministering to our race. He suffered every indignity and insult, while teaching the way to Heaven. He suffered, he bled, and died; patient like a lamb he endured the cross; despised the shame. He went to the grave; rose a conqueror; ascended to the Throne of his Father. He redeemed a ruined world! Is there no power in all this? Is there no power in death? Was the nation in mourning at the death of a Washington, a Jackson, a Clay, a Webster? Did you ever lose a kind father, an affectionate mother, a fond and doting wife, a loved son or daughter?

Is there no power in burial? On taking any of these to the grave, did not the first shovel-full of earth that struck the coffin, pierce you to the heart? But, oh! the relief, the comfort, the gratitude, that the Saviour had gone there before them—had warmed and animated it; had made it a door to that house not made with hands, eternal in the Heavens!

10. How may we be assured that we are reconciled to God? To the law and to the testimony. We know that we have passed from death unto life, because we love the brethren. Surely such a person is reconciled; has a changed heart or affections. Again— "He that hath my commandments, and keep- eth them, he it is that loveth me." Again— "This is the love of God, that we keep his commandments."

What are the terms? Faith, Repentance, Immersion into the name of the Father, Son, and Holy Spirit for the remission of sins. Then a seeking for glory, honor, etc.

But there are thousands who are waiting for something that has never been promised, having been led by teachers as blind as themselves, ignorant of the great facts now made as clear as a sunbeam, that the Gospel is the power of God for salvation to all who believe. Thus for instance, as has often occurred, ask persons, Why are you not a Christian? With a cloud of despondency, the response is, I am waiting for a change of heart! Then interrogate them—Do you believe in the Son of God? I do. Do you love him? I do, with all my heart. Do you love Christians? I do, and desire to love them more. Do you hate sin? I do, and have been striving against it for many years. Do you desire to be a Christian and go to Heaven? I do. Such a person has a changed heart, and prepared for obedience, if they had not been mistaught, and waiting for some other power to come down from Heaven to convert them. What a dreadful condition! What blundering preachers!

There are others, however, most evidently not reconciled to God. They manifest themselves in various ways. They are afraid of immersion. Some are too proud, and say, I will risk Hell before I will be plunged under the water, and come up dripping out of the water, under the gaze of mockers and scoffers. Others again, are afraid of husbands, and wives, and parents, and of the abandonment of friends. But when fully recognized, there is a cheerful surrender of body, soul, and spirit, with a desire to be immersed under the gaze of a world, whether of mockers or scoffers, or of friends.

Oh! what a trial we have witnessed on dying beds! I can never forget the conflicts of a most interesting, lovely young man on giving me and his wife the parting hand, at the same moment! he would have given the world to have lived, while there was a convulsive struggle to be reconciled to die. He had sung; he had prayed; I had sung for him; I had read and prayed for him. What a scene! What a parting! He took me by the hand, while he grasped his wife's hand by the other. Says he, My uncle, I heard you preach often; I believed your preaching; I ought to have obeyed the Gospel; but a *little false pride* kept me from it. The hardest trial I ever had is to say farewell to my wife! If ever a being made a noble sacrifice on a dying bed, for fifteen or twenty days to honor his Saviour and redeem all the past, he did. May the Lord be merciful to him in the great day!

Sinners, be ye reconciled to God! Wait not for a storm cloud nor a dying bed! Life's journey will soon be over with us all—and the Christian will meet with loved ones in Heaven, fathers and mothers, brothers and sisters, husbands and wives, and children; and the blood washed throng will be there! Oh! the riches of Heaven! The plaudit, Well done! Delay not, delay not! Be ye reconciled to God, and bathe in the ocean of love.. Amen.

J. T. JOHNSON.

-----o-----

Tour to Michigan.—No. 2.

ON Monday, April 7th. by the kindness of Bro. M. Merriman, accompanied by Bro. Roe, we were helped on our way from Paw Paw, some fifteen miles distant, to Wayne, where we were kindly received and entertained by his very orderly Christian family. At night, or "in the *evening*," as they call a night meet in that country, a crowded audience assembled, to whom we discoursed at considerable length, on the simplicity, perfection and moral excellence of the Gospel of Christ and its adaptation to the human family. Marked attention was given to the things that were spoken. We noticed some young people who appeared to feel it a little burdensome to keep still and orderly during so long a discourse. They, however, came near keeping still, which seemed to be such an effort on their part that we enter no complaint. On Tuesday morning, by urgent solicitation, we turned a little aside from our day's travel, of some twenty miles distance, to speak at a funeral. Here, in the humble log school-house, we found the coffin, containing the remains of a Baptist gentleman, by the side of which sat the bereft, weeping widow, with her helpless infant in her arms, and friends around. We addressed this mourning group at an hour's length, upon Man's Spiritual Nature, the Immortality and Eternal Existence of the Soul, and left many of them in tears, in the house of mourning, in all probability to see their faces no more in this world. We hastened on to Dowagiac, where we met Bro. Ephraim Alexander, whom we saw eleven years ago, and again three years ago, by whose kindness we were conveyed to his residence, where we partook of his rich and bountiful supplies of the comforts of life, enjoying every attention and kindness desirable. By the industry of Brother Alexander, during the short space of some two hours in the evening, an appointment was circulated, and quite a respectable congregation assembled in a school-house nearby, to whom we discoursed for an hour upon the' Reconciling of both Jew and Gentile in One Body, under Christ, though much wearied and dull. Here we were on Young's Prairie, one of the most beautiful and fertile prairies in the State. Here, April 9th, we saw snow banks more than two feet deep, though the weather was quite warm and pleasant. Up to this time we had seen no mark of the plow.

On the 9th, by the kindness of Bro. Alexander, we were conveyed some five miles distant across the prairie, to the residence of Bro. John Alexander, in Vandalia, where we were kindly received, and enjoyed every attention desirable from Bro. Alexander, his excellent lady, and venerable mother-in-law. Vandalia is a small town, of some 200 inhabitants, which has sprung up pretty much in the last two or three years. The brethren have erected a neat house for worship, have a good influence and are in a prosperous condition, and, we trust, will make a permanent effort to maintain the cause. We discoursed to those who resorted here to hear the Word, on Wednesday night, on Thursday, at two o'clock, and night; Friday, at two o'clock and night; Saturday, at two o'clock and night; Lord's day, at eleven and at night.

On Lord's day, at 3 o'clock, Bro. Roe relieved and gratified us very much, in an affectionate, kind and able presentation and advocacy of the claims of Jesus of Nazareth. On this happy day, in the presence of several hundred people, we immersed six, who made public confession of their faith in Christ, among whom was a gentleman who was a Presbyterian, who gave up a church membership, secured by a *birth of the flesh,* without any consent or knowledge, on his part, for a church membership, secured by being born again—"born of water and of the Spirit," into which he entered by his own choice, in his own personal submission to the authority of Christ, to whom *he yielded himself* to be a servant. One gentleman, a Baptist, and two ladies, who had previously been baptized, with the six baptized on the occasion, to the great joy of the brethren, united with the church. Many others were seriously impressed, and much good for the cause, we trust, was done here.

At night, while we were speaking, a man made his appearance, first in the door, but afterward, through the kindness of Bro. Nicholson, was conducted to a seat near the pulpit, whom, from his broad-brimmed hat, which he kept on for some time, the cut of his coat, the drab color and other external appearances, of which his religion, as well as that of his party, mainly consists, we perceived to be a Friend, or, as generally called, a Quaker. At the close, we were informed that this man, who was still stationary at his seat, desired to speak with us. We approached him kindly, to know what he desired, when he inquired, "Did thee say, in thy discourse to-day, that Friends are all infidels?" We informed him that we did not, but that we said the tendency of the doctrine of Friends is to infidelity, that many of them are running into Universalism, some into open unbelief, and that Elias Hix is quoted in the late editions of Paine's Age of Reason, as strengthening infidelity. He admitted that many Friends in his country were running into Universalism and open infidelity, but insisted that neither Friends nor their doctrine should be blamed for it. We ascertained that he was a preacher, a kind and good citizen, and a man of good character; but he is certainly the most completely deluded, confused and blinded man we ever undertook to talk with upon the religion of Jesus Christ. That saying of the Lord, respecting Israel, is certainly true of Friends, that "blindness in part is happened to them," but if the passage be applied to this unfortunate man, the words, "in part," should be stricken out. No clear ray of the light of the gospel can ever penetrate the thick envelop of darkness that enshrouds him. Unless the vail be taken from the hearts of that people, called Friends, they are gone.

Our here spoke of the "outward ordinances." We informed him that Friends had no ordinances of Christ, either *outward* or *inward*. He mentioned the baptism of the Holy Ghost. We informed him that they had no baptism, of either the Holy Ghost or water—that their church has not a gospel ordinance, officer, psalm, hymn, or Spiritual song, and that the Bible is literally turned out of their assembly—that their whole body is turned away from the teachings of the Spirit of God, as found upon the sacred pages of the Bible—that they are looking to the blind and stupid imaginations of a class of ignorant and deceived men, claiming to be inspired, as the apostles, without the first evidence of any inspiration, any more than Ann Lee, Swedenbourg, or Joseph Smith. Such blind leaders must, with those whom they lead, fall into the ditch. Such blind guides must, as certain as that the Bible is from God, both ruin themselves and those who adhere to them. God will confound the stupidity of any people who leave the holy and infallible teachings of the only authorized and divinely established revelations from Heaven, no matter what they turn to, whether the divinations of modern soothsayers, sorceries, unclean spirits, now called "spirit manifestations," "spirit communications," or from pretended inspirations, but manifestly under no supernatural guidance, and many of them simply under the influence of a self-willed, unenlightened and unregenerated human spirit. All such systems must ultimately and inevitably land those influenced by them in some of the meshes of unbelief, and this is where Friends are going as fast as the wheels of time can carry them on.

On Monday, we took our leave of the brethren, who had shown us so much kindness and liberality, and, through the kindness of Bro. Hull, were conveyed through quite a rain some five miles, to Brownsville, and introduced to a few brothers and sisters, who came out with the faint hope that we might arrive, notwithstanding the rain. We spoke at two o'clock, for an hour, upon Love. At night, only a moderate congregation had assembled, the people doubting our arrival, owing to the rain. On Tuesday, 15th, we addressed a respectable congregation on the Coming of Christ and the End of the World; and were introduced to many brethren, good and true. At night we spoke again, on the Orthodoxy of Our Position, and, at the close, six persons came forward, four to confess Christ, one a Baptist, and one lady who had been baptized. The latter two were joyfully received by the Disciples; and on the next morning, at eight o'clock, we met at the water and immersed the four who made confession the night before, and left them in tears, with exhortations to be true to the Lord, who had called them to glory and virtue. Some complaint was made here, as in several other places, of Know Nothings, Republicans and Democrats, but we advised the brethren to keep all these out of the church—to have nothing but *Christians* in the church; to know nothing but Christ, nothing but Christianity. No man, who understands anything of the Spirit of Christ and his religion, will think of such a thing as erecting the church into a political tribunal, to decide upon the political creeds of men. Men have a right to then political creeds, but no right to push them into the kingdom of God. We know no know no law there but the law of God, and no king but Jesus.

Taking an affectionate leave of the dear friends here, by the kindness of Bro. Hull, we were brought on our way to Dowagiac, where we took cars and soon landed safely at Buchanan, where we spoke to a respectable audience at night, on Conversion to Christ. By request of brethren, we remained one day to make an address, on Friday night, on the Eternal Existence and Immortality of the Soul and the Work of Materialism. We made a speech of some two hours length on this question, which was listened to with deep interest to the last word, and which, we trust, will not soon be forgotten. The destructive influences of Materialism have been much felt throughout this whole region of country; but it has had its day, and has well-nigh run its race. The disciples here are doing well; and, we trust, will prosper and do honor to the cause.

Weary and anxious to reach home, we lay down to try and sleep a little before starting on the train, due at three o'clock and twenty- five minutes, on the morning of Friday, the 18th, with the kind proposal that Bro. Roe would rouse us from slumber in time for the cars. But our anxiety was too great to sleep- much, and we arose, without any person awaking us, and took our leave of our dear and esteemed young brother, Wm. M. Roe, who had been with us all the time while in Michigan, his kind lady, his brother and brother's excellent lady, and repaired to the cars, and waited from three o'clock till five, before the train appeared. About sunrise, we stepped on board the great train, consisting of some fourteen passenger cars, and passed on some thirty miles, to Michigan City, before seven o'clock, and found that we were destined to wait till ten o'clock. This we think rather a hard fate, these times, when we measure distance by time, where four hours stand for one hundred miles. Thus losing two hours in the morning before starting, and three hours in Michigan City, we looked upon as being hindered one hundred and twenty-five miles, in our aim to get through the world. This is almost intolerable! We were, however, partly compensated, for it afforded us time to go down upon the dock, and, for the first time, take one fair look at the beautiful Lake Michigan. At the hour, the cars arrived, and we were off, whirling through the immense prairies of Northwestern Indiana, by Lafayette, to Indianapolis, thence by Greensburg, Lawrenceburg, and reached home at twelve o'clock at night; making more than nine hundred miles travel, and delivering some twenty-two sermons, in a little over two weeks. Blessed be the Lord who has been with us and preserved us.

B. F.

-----o-----

Infidelity.

WEST LIBERTY, Va., March 31,1856.

BRO. FRANKLIN—I have just arisen from a perusal of the February No. of the *"American Christian Review."* I am much pleased with its contents. It breathes forth a spirit of piety and devotion that must give it a commanding influence if persevered in, and speaks out boldly in favor of the Bible and our holy religion. There is a false squeamishness that sometimes takes possession of preachers and editors, so that they are unwilling to call things by their proper names, and to represent Bible things by Bible terms; this, I am happy to see, is not a defect of your monthly, but where either Heaven or Hell, life or death, salvation or damnation, or any other Bible doctrine is introduced, you speak of it in the language of inspiration. Following this rule, you cannot fail to accomplish much for the cause of truth and righteousness. God has not only communicated to us certain ideas, but he has even furnished us the vehicles in which those ideas rode down from Heaven to earth; hence we hear the great Apostle to the Gentiles saying, when speaking of the things received from God, "Which things also we speak, not in the *words* which man's wisdom teacheth, but which the Holy Spirit teacheth; comparing spiritual things with spiritual," 1 Cor. ii, 13. Calling Bible things by Bible names is certainly a safe rule. The first piece in this No., "the Mission of Infidels," is certainly well conceived to expose their babbling; for to talk about Infidelity as a system, is to have no respect for the use of language. Its beginning, middle and end is this—you may call it a syllogism if you please—Infidels doubt everything. The Bible says, "he that doubteth is damned," or condemned; therefore, every Infidel is condemned. This they all know and feel, hence their uneasiness about the Bible doctrine. But if condemned now, when shall they be acquitted? by whom? by what law? how? These are solemn questions to the man who opens his heart to this damning legion of doubts, and says, curse me here and hereafter, and as many others as you can! I received and read a little work last year, entitled, "The Evidences of Christianity, as exhibited in the writings of its Apologists down to Augustine," being the HULSE-AN PRIZE ESSAY of 1852, by W. J. Bolton, Professor in Gonville and Caires College, Cambridge, and republished in Boston in 1854, by Gould and Lincoln, 59 Washington street, which I would commend for perusal by everyone who is the least affected by the modern phases of skepticism either in the old or new world. Solomon very appositely declared, about three thousand years ago, that "The thing that hath been, is that which shall be; and that which is done, is that which shall be done; and *there is no new thing under the sun.* Is there anything whereof it may be said, see, this is new? it hath been already of old time, which was before us." Ec. i, 9. This is certainly true of every objection that is now urged against Christianity by the doubting and wavering minds of this country and of Europe. Hear what this learned author says on page seventeen, when alluding to the effect an appeal to the Patristic writings must have on our age. "A further result of the discussion before us must be to deprive the modern skeptic of the claim of *originality.* I think that it will appear in the sequel that most of our present popular objections to Christianity have been anticipated centuries since. With the exception of a few sophistries and transcendentalisms, which destroy themselves, I scarcely know of an infidel position that we do not find taken up and exploded by such writers as Origen, Arnobius, Eusebius. Perhaps the exposure of such a circumstance, considering what a sharp spur notoriety is may serve to lower the value of rash opinions, even in the eyes of the inventor himself; or, the bloom of freshness being lost, more certainly in the eyes of others also."

Bolton is not the only man of letters who has thus spoken and written of modern Infidelity. Andrew Michael, called also the chevalier Ramsay, a learned Scotchman, in his Essay on Pagan Theology, annexed to his Cyrus, tenth edition, page 341, after tracing the identity between the ancient and modern systems of philosophy, says:"Modern freethinkers have only revived the ancient errors, disguising them under new terms. The history of former times is like our own. The human understanding takes almost the same forms in different ages, and loses its way in the same labyrinths." And Dr. Hundeshagen, of the University of Heidelberg, very justly observes, when speaking of the Infidelity of Germany, that "The first age of the Christian Church is rightly called the Apologetic, for the Christian religion had then to win its right to existence by its struggles. We of this age are in this respect carried back to the commencement of Christianity, for the forefront of the battle of parties relates to the very existence of the Christian religion. So that without doubt we are called upon to apply our Christian attainments to the same Apologetic task which engaged the attention of the first centuries." This seems necessary, since the human mind, after making a few evolutions and counter marches, is returning to the same stand-points from which Celsus, Porphyry, Lucian, Herocles, and others of the first centuries of the Christian era, hurled their' poisoned javelins. The first, attacking Christianity as a *new* religion; the second, denying everything but *nature;* the third, classifying Christianity with *every kind of fanaticism, and fraud;* the fourth, besides contrasting the pretended miracles of Apollonius with those of Christ, and the first Christians, wrote a book to prove the Scriptures guilty of falsehood and contradiction. Is there an observant eye, either in Europe or America, that does not see that those scenes are being acted over again? What means that German Neology, that says that 'Christianity as it now is, is new, being a tree of that German Neology, that says that 'Christianity as it now is, is new, being a tree of gradual growth and ever changing?' Or that English Deism, with which many of her ablest statesmen, philosophers and poets is tinctured, which says, 'I believe in Nature and in Nature's God?' Or worse still, that motley something in America—what shall I call it? I cannot call it either German Neology, English Deism, or even French Socialism. What is its name? Ah! it has no name—it can have none! I might express some of its characteristics by saying that it is a neologistic, deistic, socialistic, uncontrolled, individual self-willedness—believing nothing, quibbling at everything, doubting everything. I sometimes think, in looking at this hydra-headed monster, that we need another satirical Hermias. You will no doubt recollect this Christian philosopher, a contemporary of Tatian, and his great work, called *Irrisio Gentilium Philosophorum,* exposing the absurd and contradictory opinions of the Greeks on nature, the world, God, the human soul, etc., and thus proving by their discrepancies how worthless and useless they are.

It may not be amiss for me to give an extract from this author, since something of the kind seems needed in our age to expose the babbling of would-be philosophers. In chapter one, and onward, he says:

"Some of the philosophers assert that the soul is fire, as Democritus; some air, as the Stoics; some motion, as Heraclitus; an exhalation or emission from the stars, furnished with motion, as Pythagoras; some, generative waters, as Hippon; or harmony, as Dimarchus; or blood, as Critias; or breath, or unity, etc. Behold the variety of opinions entertained by the sophists, each of them pretending to the truth.

"Again, one calls pleasure the chief good; another calls it an evil, and a third places it between the two extremes. Some assert the immortality, some the mortality of the soul. Some reduce it to a bestial level, or dissolve it into separate bodies, or give it a migratory circuit of three thousand years. What else is this but fiction or madness, or both together? And being at such a loss with regard to their own nature, is it any marvel that they should fall short when they begin to investigate the nature of God? Nevertheless, they have had the boldness, not to say stupidity, to attempt it. They who know nothing about themselves, freely discuss God. They who are ignorant of the construction of their own bodies, undertake the fruitless task of explaining that of the world. But at the very outset they oppose one another. Anaxagoras differs from Melissus; Parmenides and Anaximenes from Empedocles; Protagoras from Thales and Anaximander; and Archelaus from Plato and Aristotle. Even those who are more ancient yet, as Perecydes, (who said that the gods were only natural principles), and others, exhibited the like rivalry. Leucippus, Democritus, and Heraclitus, all think differently from Epicurus and his followers, while Pythagoras concludes that the beginning of all things is unity, from whose figures and numbers the elements were made—thus dissenting from all. These things I have related, that the contrariety of philosophical opinions may be made manifest, and the endlessness and inutility of their theories exposed." As Hermias has exposed the Greek philosophers, and shown that there is no unity among them, so ought someone to take up every modern skeptic of any note and place him in contrast with his brother skeptic. This would certainly be a benevolent work.

Yours, &c., A. E. M.

-----o-----

Baptismal Repentance.

Mr. BELOVED BRO. FRANKLIN: It gives me pleasure once more to address you in your editorial capacity. I feel like thanking God for opening a door of usefulness in the editorial rank, all your own, where you do not have to build upon another man's foundation; but the field being your own, the responsibility of your position is between God and your own conscience. May God make you an able instrument in his hands for much good in the world. It gives me pleasure to witness the readiness to aid you, manifested on the part of the brotherhood, in giving the fruits of their reflections on the great subject pertaining to our blessed Master's kingdom. I would be a co-worker with them, and would here present you with a few reflections on the above subject, for which I am chiefly indebted to William Sherlock. Should these pass the editorial ordeal, I may present you with a second number on Repentance after Baptism.

By baptismal repentance, I mean that repentance which is necessary in persons, in order to their receiving Christian Baptism. This is the repentance which is most frequently mentioned in the New Testament, and to which the promise of remission and forgiveness is annexed; this our Saviour preached, *"repent, for the kingdom of heaven is at hand,"* Matthew iv, 17. This he gave authority to his apostles to preach, *"that repentance and remission of sins should be preached in his name among all nations,"* Luke xxiv, 47.

Now, this repentance, both as to *Jews* and *heathens* who embraced the faith of Christ, was renouncing all their former sins, and false, superstitious or idolatrous worship; and this qualified them for baptism, in which they obtained the remission of all their sins in the name of Christ. And for this reason remission of sins is promised to repentance, because all such penitents are received to baptism, which is the washing of regeneration, which washes away all their sins, and puts them into a state of grace and favor with God; as Peter tells the Jews, *"Repent and be baptized every one of you in the name of Jesus Christ, for the remission of sins,"* Acts ii, 38. And much to the same purpose Ananias told Paul, *"arise and be baptized, and wash away thy sins, calling on the name of the Lord,"* Acts xxii, 16. And I know not anyone text in the *New* Testament, wherein the remission of sins is absolutely promised to repentance, but what must be understood of this baptismal repentance; and then repentance and remission of sins are inseparably annexed; because such penitents wash away all their sins in baptism, and come pure and undefiled out of that mystical fountain, which is set open for sin and for uncleanliness to wash in, and to be clean.

Now I grant, should any person who comes to baptism rightly qualified and disposed, with a sincere repentance and steadfast faith in Christ, die soon after he is baptized, before he has time and opportunity to exercise any of the graces of the Christian life—such a man shall go to Heaven without actual holiness; the remission of his sins in baptism, upon his repentance, will save him, though he have not time to bring forth the fruits of repentance in a holy life; and this is the only case I know of, wherein a penitent can be saved without actual holiness; viz.: by baptismal grace and regeneration.

A baptized Christian must not always expect to be saved by such favor as saves and justifies in baptism; baptismal favor is inseparably annexed to baptism, and can be no more repeated than baptism.

The favor of baptism washes away all the sins of our past lives, how many, how great soever they have been, only upon our profession of our faith in Christ, and repentance of all our sins, and vows of obedience to the laws of Christ for the future; but whosoever, after baptism, lives a wicked and profligate life, and hopes to be saved at last only by faith in Christ and sorrow for sins, and vows of living better when he is just a dying, will be miserably mistaken; for this is only the favor of baptism, the grace that meets us at the outset of our Christian profession, therefore not the rule and measure whereby God will judge baptized Christians, who have had time and opportunity of exercising those Christian graces which they vowed at their baptism.

A man who retains the faith of Christ, though he lives wickedly, does not forfeit his baptism, but shall be forgiven whenever he repents and forsakes his sins, and lives a holy life. But if he delays this so long 'that he has no time to amend his life, that he can do nothing but be sorry for his sins and vow a new life, it cannot be promised him that this shall be accepted at the hour of death, because the gospel requires a holy life, not merely a death-bed sorrow and remorse for sin.

Sorrow for sin, and vows of a new life, will be accepted at baptism, as the beginning of a new life; but that is no reason why they should be accepted at our death, when they are only the sorrowful conclusions of a wicked life. God will receive us to grace and mercy at baptism, upon our solemn vows of living to Him, but He has no where promised to accept of our dying vows instead of holiness and obedience, as a recompense for a whole life spent in wickedness and folly.

If you ask why faith and repentance, without the actual obedience of our lives, should not as well be accepted by God on our deathbed as it is at our baptism, I shall ask another very plain question, why a husbandman who hires laborers into his vineyard in the morning, receives them into his service, protection, and pay, only upon their promise to be faithful and diligent in his work before they have done anything? I say, when these men have loitered away the day without working, why should not he reward them at night, because they then also profess themselves very sorry that they did not work, and make a great many promises and vows, that if they were to begin the day again they would? A promise of faithfulness and diligence was reason enough why he should take them into his service, but their sorrow for not working, and their resolution of working, when the time of working is past, is no reason why they should be rewarded, or escape the punishment of loiterers.

This is the very case here; we are saved by the mercies of God, and the merits of Christ, which we partake of by our union to him. This union is made in baptism, which incorporates us into the body of Christ; and from the very first moment of our union, we are in a state of grace and justification, our sins are washed away in His blood, as water purges away all bodily defilements, and the Spirit of Christ dwells in us to renew and sanctify us. Now all that is required by God, or that seems in the nature of the thing necessary to this union, is a general repentance of all our sins, renouncing our former wicked course of life, professing our faith in Christ as the Son of God and Saviour of the world, and vowing obedience to His laws; for this qualifies us to be His disciples, and to be received into His service, and into the communion of His body and church, and therefore this faith and repentance justifies in baptism, because those who thus repent of their sins and believe in Christ, are received to baptism, and in baptism have all their sins forgiven, and are put into a state of grace and favor with God.

But now, though faith and repentance, and the vows of obedience are sufficient to make us the disciples of Christ, and to put us into a state of justification, yet they are not sufficient to save those who are the disciples of Christ, without actual holiness and obedience of life; for to be a disciple of Christ does not signify merely to believe in him, and to vow obedience to him, but to obey him. It is reasonable enough that upon our vow of obedience we should be received into his service, but it is not reasonable that we should be rewarded without performing our vows; for it is as ridiculous a thing to think that our repeated and fruitless resolutions of obeying our Saviour, should pass for obedience, as that the son should be thought to do his father's will, who said, *I go, sir,* but went not; especially when, after our vow of baptism, we live a very ungodly life, and never think it time to repent, and to renew our vows again until we come to die. If we consider the difference between what is necessary to make us disciples of Christ, and what is required of us when we are disciples, we shall see a plain reason why faith and repentance, as that signifies sorrow for sin and vows of obedience, will justify us in baptism, but will not be accepted upon a deathbed, after a life spent in wickedness; for when a baptized Christian comes to die, he is not then to be made a disciple of Christ, and to be baptized again, but to give an account of his life since he has been Christ's disciple; and mere faith in Christ, sorrow for sin, and vows of obedience, without actual holiness of life, though with the ordinance of baptism it will make a disciple, yet it will not pass in a disciple's account, especially when the sum total of his life is nothing but sin, and sorrow, and fruitless vows; for this is not the holiness of life which Christ requires of his disciples.

May the Lord bless these reflections to the souls of all who read them.

Affectionately yours in the Lord,

CHAS. D. HURLBUTT.

WABASHTOWN, Wabash Co., Ind., April, 1856.

Conclusion of the Noblesville Matter.

ABOUT three years ago difficulties arose in the church in Noblesville, Ind., resulting in division, since which they meet and worship separately, one party keeping their former house, the other in a new house which they have built. As each of these parties frequently invited preachers from abroad, brethren who know nothing of the merits of their difference were embarrassed, not knowing which party, or whether either, should be recognized. To meet this difficulty, Bro. J. M. Mathers drew up the following document and sent it, with the names annexed, to each party:

To the Disciples of Christ at Noblesville, greeting;

DEAR BRETHREN:—The undersigned have learned, with sorrow, that a serious difficulty exists among you, which has resulted in disunion. Now, brethren, will you permit us to make a few suggestions? 1. Taking for granted that you cannot settle your difficulty among yourselves, we recommend you to call a committee of experienced brethren from other churches, who shall meet at Noblesville, and investigate the matters of complaint, to the satisfaction of all concerned. 2. The question of laying on of hands, in ordination, being a doctrinal question, cannot, of course, be a matter of adjudication by the committee. 3. The parties to pledge themselves to abide the decision of said committee and agree to conform their action to it. 4. The object of the investigation to be, the restoration of peace, harmony, and Christian fellowship among you, that our preachers and brethren, in visiting Noblesville, may not be embarrassed with the difficulty, and that the cause of the blessed Saviour may no longer be crippled with it. And we suggest that said reference be made at an early day. A copy of this paper is also sent to the other congregation.

C. GR. BERRY,	JOHN O'KANE,
J. M. TILFORD,	ELIJAH
BENJ. FRANKLIN,	GOOWDIN, JOHN
B. K. SMITH,	BRAZLETON, J.

Indianapolis, Oct. 15th, 1855.

This proposition, made by brethren at the State meeting, Oct., 1855, was generally known and considered proper. The demand from abroad was to know, *which party had refused, to comply with this proposal.* Many preaching brethren knowing that we would be there about the first of March, desired us to ascertain and make known which party had refused. On arriving, we addressed a note to brethren A. B. Cole and H. St. John Van Dake, each the authorized correspondents of the respective parties, precisely alike, inquiring what answer they had given to the document sent them from brethren at the State Meeting, and whether they were now willing to agree to the proposal contained in it. Each party furnished a copy of their answer, which we now have—Bro. Cole proposing to make an effort among themselves first, and not agreeing to the proposal; but Bro. Van Dake agreeing to the proposition, with the specification, that the procedure should be according to Scripture. Bro. Cole, in reply to my note, still did not agree to the proposed reference. Bro. Van Dake, in his reply to my note, did agree to the reference. We urged upon all, with all kindness, both publicly and privately, the necessity and importance of agreeing to the reference as proposed by brethren at the State Meeting, but failed to induce the party with which Bro. Cole is identified to agree to it, though he frequently said he desired it. We saw Bro. Cole after we returned home, and continued the correspondence; and to bring the matter to an issue, addressed each party the following:

CINCINNATI, O., *March 21st,* 1856.

BRO. COLE—*Dear Sir:* Yours, of the 17th inst., is received, but with specifications that make it no agreement to the proposed reference to a committee. To make short of the whole matter, please answer me, either affirmatively or negatively, whether you agree to the reference to a committee, as originally proposed, without any specification.

I am now satisfied that the only course to cut off all evasion, on both sides, is to insist upon a direct answer to the above, from both parties; and if they do not agree to the reference, publish the result, to show where the fault lies. I shall write to Bro. Van Dake the same as above.

With kindest regards,

I am respectfully yours,
BENJ. FRANKLIN.

MY DEAR BRO. COLE—I concur with Bro. Franklin in the above suggestions and question. This meets my design when I signed the document referred to above.

ELIJAH GOODWIN.

Bro. Goodwin saw the whole correspondence, and knows the principal persons of both parties, and was fully posted up in the state of the case when he appended the above note to my letter. In reply to this, I received a letter referring to a previous letter, which appears below, stating that, "as we now view things, we can give no other answer than that already in your possession." Here follows the answer alluded to:

NOBLESVILLE, Ind., *March 17th,* 1856.

DEAR BRO. FRANKLIN—Our congregation, on yesterday, authorized me to make the following answer to your last inquiry in your note of the 3d inst.: That we accept the proposition of yourself, Bro. Mathers and others, as contained in your letter of the 15th Oct. last, with our understanding of said communication, that your object and design is not that such committee shall inquire or decide as to the Scriptural existence of us as a church of Jesus Christ. But that they are to investigate fully and impartially as to the causes, and the causes only, which led to the difficulties and division now existing among us, and that they are to embrace in such investigation the conduct and action of individuals and parties, so far as the conduct or action of any individual or individuals, party or parties, may have been instrumental in producing such difficulties and division, or in perpetuating and continuing the same, such investigation being made with the desire and aim to restore peace, harmony and fellowship among the Disciples at Noblesville. The elders of the church are directed to confer with you as to the choosing said committee, and the time and place of meeting.

Your brother, in the good hope,
A. B. COLE.

The following is the reply of the other party:

NOBLESVILLE, Ind., *March 30lh,* 1856.

BRO. FRANKLIN—The church, to-day, passed the following resolution:

"*Resolved,* That the church approves, unanimously, the affirmative answer, in Bro. Van Dake's reply to Bro. Franklin's interrogatory of the 21st inst."

Yours, in the Lord,
H. ST. JOHN VAN DAKE.

The publishing of this can do no party any injustice. If Br. Cole and those connected with him, desire to relieve and place themselves in a proper position, let them remove the words, "with our understanding;" take off the restriction, also, forbidding an inquiry into their "Scriptural existence as a church," and commit their cause, as the other party has done, and as we urged and entreated them to do, unreservedly to a committee of good brethren from other churches.

B.F.

-----o-----

Our Position as a Religious Community.
NO. 6.

AMONG those religious structures founded upon human creeds, there is a kind of general understanding, viz: That as they all occupy a similar position, a similar foundation, and are about alike vulnerable, they will mutually concede to each other the right peaceably and unmolestedly to enjoy their positions. Hence, the main point of attack—the most vulnerable point, is not touched. The point we allude to is the unrighteous, untenable and arrogant assumption of *deficiency in the law of God, and that human creeds can supply this deficiency,* which is the foundation of every creed in the world. The great position we have taken, are maintaining and pushing throughout the land, is that all creeds are wrong, and should be rejected, as rules of faith and practice, whether the doctrine contained in them is true or false. We reject a human creed as a rule of faith and practice, without looking into it, or regardless of the doctrine contained in it, whether true or false, because *it is a human creed.* We put them all upon a level here, put them all upon the defense, and demand of them before the holy law of God and before God who gave that law, to give a strict account of themselves. If one of them stands up and says, "I contain nothing but true doctrine," we reply that "the charge against you is not—the *main* indictment is not for containing. or preaching false doctrine, but for impiously impeaching—at least by implication, the law of God, in asserting that it is *insufficient,* and that you are a substitute, *sufficient* to accomplish what it could not do, and thus attempting to set aside the Law of God and occupy its place. This charge we maintain and can sustain against all human creeds, wherever used as authoritative rules of faith and practice. They assume the authority of the throne of the Lord, set aside the law of the Great King, occupy the place of it, and demand the homage and submission due alone to the law of God.

This point all the parties founded upon a human creed slide over. This charge they never make. No one of them can make it, because all the balance would reply, "Physician, heal thyself." In this way, all being alike criminal on this point, there is a mutual agreement to let it alone, as all live alike in glass houses, it shall be the mutual understanding not to throw stones. They make some slight attacks upon each other, but not upon vital points, and consequently but few wounds are inflicted, or deaths caused. Their attacks upon each other are such as distillers make upon each other. They frequently allege against each other that, you do not make a good article of brandy—that we produce a better article, &c., but in all these charges the admission is made, that it is perfectly right to make the article, but it should be a *good article.* But the genuine temperance man approaches and takes a deeper hold on them. He assails them at another point that they kept entirely quiet about. He gives himself no trouble about what kind of an article they make. He cares nothing about the comparative merits of the article they make, but assails the business, without any regard to the article, whether good or bad, as a public nuisance, injurious and detrimental to all the great interests of society, and insists that the whole business should be thrown aside. He insists that the article they produce, whether what they call good or bad, is evil, and only evil, continually, in all its tendencies. As a matter of course, they will all drop their frivolous disputes about the comparative merits of the article they produce, and unitedly meet the common assailant, who questions and denounces their entire operations, and seeks to have them set aside. In the same way, when we assailed the whole family of creeds, without any respect to their comparative merits, as a nuisance, injurious in all their tendencies, usurpers of the place of the law of God, destroyers of peace and union among Christians, and insisted that they should be rejected and set aside bodily, their adherents ceased all their little disputes about the comparative merits of their creeds, and united against the common enemy, united and combined, with all the talent, learning and prejudice they can command, to stand up, defend and maintain, not the doctrine contained in their creeds, for in this there is but little agreement among them, but the *right to have a human creed at all of any description.* They maintain the right, and we deny it.

The issue is between the bible and human creeds. We are for the bible, they for creeds. Having thus far defined and defended our position, we proceed to notice some of the excuses, or apologies, for human creeds, as offered by their devotees.

Apology 1.—It is not necessary to make such an incessant war upon our creed; it is just like the bible; it is all scriptural." In this case, admitting, for the sake of argument, what is not true of any human creed, that it is "just like the bible," we reply, that it is useless, and will do no better than the bible itself. If it is just like the bible it will accomplish nothing more than the bible, and be just as deficient. Nothing can be gained by it; nothing can be accomplished by it which the bible itself could not accomplish, so that it must be utterly useless. In that case there can be no excuse for having it—not only so, but the person holding on to and contending for such a creed, is inexcusable on another account. To give up a creed just like the bible, and take the bible itself as a rule of faith and practice, a man would lose nothing, for

OUR POSITION AS A RELIGIOUS COMMUNITY.

he would find all his creed in the bible. We insist, therefore, that one of the most inexcusable, unreasonable and unjustifiable positions a man can occupy, is to hold on to, contend for and insist that he cannot do without a creed which he insists is just like the bible, though he can have the bible itself! The bible will certainly accomplish all that any creed just like it can.

Apology 2.—"It is useless to be contending against our creed. It contains nothing that is not in the bible. It is simply an abstract, epitome or abridgment of bible doctrine, so arranged as to be convenient and show at a glance what we hold." This is quite a specious apology, and has succeeded in deluding and deceiving many persons, and silencing their consciences, and is therefore more especially deserving of attention. This apology is dangerous because it acknowledges that the creed contains and sets forth what the party believes—its faith. Now, we assert, without hesitation, that any man who believes no more than is set forth in any human creed on earth, and will do no more than any human creed requires, has neither faith nor obedience enough to be acceptable with God. There is not a human creed on earth that contains the *whole Christian faith.* Their faith is too narrow. We have no confidence in epitomes, abstracts or abridgements of the faith. Nothing less than the faith, the whole faith of Christ, is sufficient to meet the divine approbation. No man's faith not as broad as the bible is broad enough for us. His faith must contain Moses and Jesus, the prophets of the Old Testament and the apostles of the New. There must be no abstracting, no epitomizing, no abridging. The man not willing to receive Christ, and the whole Christian faith, as God has set him and the faith forth, in the holy scriptures, is not a Christian, and had better make no pretence to Christianity. We do not wish a man to come describing how he *views every point of doctrine.* We do not desire him to come declaring that he receives Christ as a Trinitarian or Unitarian, a Calvinist or an Arminian, but to come with a contrite spirit, avowing it as the desire of the heart, and his full determination, to receive Christ with all his heart, as God has revealed him in the prophecies of the Old Testament and the Apostolic preaching of the New.

The advocate of a human creed says, he wants his creed to "show at a glance what we hold." I Look over your creed, then, right carefully, and see *what you hold,* and look over the New Testament with the same care, and see what an amount it contains that *you do not hold,* or that is not in your creed, and you will see that your creed is not a respectable skeleton—that it not only lacks the flesh, blood, muscles, arteries, veins, &c., of the body, but it lacks many of the bones, and, what is vastly more, it lacks the life, the soul, the spirit. If it contains *what you hold,* much as precious as any part of the Christian faith, and as binding as anything God has revealed, clearly and explicitly laid down in the New Testament, is not contained in what you hold at all. Much of as precious truth as is contained in the bible, a vast amount as clear to the children of God as anything contained in the Christian faith, an immense deal as consoling to the dying saint as anything in the word of God, as any man who has ever looked must admit, is not found in any human creed. We say again, and can prove at almost any length, that there is not a human creed in the world that is a respectable skeleton, that is even a perceptible shadow of the Christian faith. Indeed, no creed appears to have been intended simply to set forth the *Christian faith.* It does not appear to be the object of any human creed to set forth the simple faith of Christ or Christianity. None of the creeds claim to be the *Christian faith, the Christian confession, Christian discipline or Christian system,* but one is "The Philadelphia Confession," another "The Westminster Confession," and a third "The Methodist Discipline." The object of these books, and all of the same kind, appears to be more to set forth the views their authors had of certain points of doctrine, or their notions of these points, than to set forth the whole Christian faith itself. Their object is much more to show how the parties adopting them held certain points of doctrine, and to distinguish their views from some others, than to set forth the

Christian faith. The creeds, then, are but little more than epitomes of men's views of certain points of Christian doctrine, their abridged understanding of these points. Now, the belief and reception of *men's views* of the Christian faith will not save any man, much less the belief and reception of *their views of a few points* of doctrine; but, to be saved, a man must believe and receive the Christian faith—*the whole Christian faith itself.*   B. F.

-----o-----

Review of Dr. Shaffer on Baptism.
NO. VI.

It is important in reviewing a book, to notice the supreme object of it, its main bearing, and what its probable effect will be. We have, therefore, made an effort to gather the supreme object of *Shaffer on Baptism*, its spirit and tendency, so far as it shall have an influence. We inquire then, what the main design of the Doctor was "on the mode," as he calls it. Was it to enlighten any person? Was his design to rid the public mind of any difficulty, relieve it from any bewilderment, open the path of duty and make it clear to anyone seeking the way of the Lord? Has he brought a clear precept or example from the Bible, showing any established rule by which we may know precisely what the Apostles did when they baptized? Not in a single instance, from one end of his book to the other. At one time he is talking about sprinkling, at another time pouring, then washing, now wetting then dying, &c., &c., but nothing is established, and we declare solemnly, that he seriously attempts to establish nothing. His aim, in writing his book, and in all his boasted debates, as well as his sermons, has not been a serious, solemn and manly effort to establish anything. He did not hope to establish anything, nor labor for it. No; his supreme object, and only object was to unsettle the public mind in regard to immersion. His effort was to darken counsel, raise a fog, mystify and confuse the public mind. Precisely as far as his book has any influence, will it be to unsettle, blind and confuse. This is the utmost that all sprinklers think of. The sum total of their reasoning amounts to about this "Baptism is unimportant, a mere external ceremony, not essential. It is not certain how the apostles baptized; therefore, it is a matter of no consequence how it is performed. Sprinkling is convenient, decent and easy; therefore, we will practice it." This is about the sum of the matter. Against this we offer the following:

1st. Most words have different meanings, and may be used in different senses, but no word used twice in reference to the same thing can have different meanings. If a word is used in different senses, it must be when used in reference to different things, where it may be allowable to use the word in a different sense. For instance, the word *preach* may have different meanings, and be used in different ways; but if used a thousand times, in reference to the public proclamation of the gospel, it always means precisely the same thing. The word *gospel* may have different meanings, but if it is used a million of times to express what the apostles preached, it always means the same thing. It must be applied to something else, before it can possibly mean anything else.

2d. The Lord and his apostles used but one word, when they spake literally of the divine appointment for initiation. On all occasions when they spoke literally of the divine appointment—of that same thing, they used that same word, *baptizo*. That *same word* applied to that *same thing*, must have the *same meaning*. No man who understands himself can deny this. If *baptizo* means sprinkle in one place, when applied to the divine appointment for initiation, it means sprinkle in every instance when applied to the same divine appointment; or if it means immersion in one place, it means immersion in every place.

3d. The thing done for baptizing in one place, was the same done in every place, in apostolic times. They did not pour in one place, sprinkle in another and immerse in another. If such had been the case, allusion to the different performances would have been found in the New Testament and other books written in the first two centuries. Disputes about the comparative merits of the different things done would be found; but no things done would be found; but no allusion to any but one way, no debate about it, nor intimation of any but the one practice. No such thing as mode is mentioned at this period. Mysticism had not then introduced any confusion and darkness upon the subject.

4th. History testifies that the one thing practiced during the first two centuries *was immersion*. From this there is no appeal. There is not an intimation to the contrary in the Bible, nor any book written in two hundred years after the birth of Christ.

5th. There is not a Lexicon in the world, that gives *sprinkle* as the primary meaning of *baptizo*. Its meaning cannot be sprinkle, when not a Lexicon in the world gives sprinkle as its primary meaning.

6th. The principal Lexicons do not give sprinkle as a definition, either primary or secondary, of *baptizo*, at all. Did our Lord and his apostles use a word invariably to express the divine appointment, in a sense different from all the definitions given by all the principal Lexicons in the world? Surely not.

7th. If it be maintained, as it is by a few extravagant men, in their maddened rage against immersion, that some two or three Lexicons, of but little authority, have given sprinkle as a seventh or eighth meaning of *baptizo*, how can they feel any confidence that our Lord and his apostles used *baptizo* in that sense, when every one of them gives immerse as the first, or primary meaning?

8th. When we read of baptizing in a certain place, "because there was *much water* there," is not the natural, clear and fair conclusion, that they did not need "much water" to sprinkle or pour, but to immerse? We are not prepared to hear the old cavil, that the "much water" was for the beasts and other purposes. The sacred history does not say that "John *repaired* to certain places because there was *much water*, or that he *preached* in certain places because there was *much water*," but he was at a certain place *baptizing* because there was *much water* there."

9th. When we read of their going "*down into the water*," and "coming up out of the water," is not the plain, natural and unavoidable conclusion, that they did not go down into the water to sprinkle or pour, but to immerse? They certainly were not so silly as to go "down into the water" and come "up out of the water," to sprinkle or pour.

10th, When we read of "John baptizing in Jordan," our Saviour being baptized of John "in Jordan," and "baptizing in the river of Jordan," is it not irresistibly clear, that John was not *sprinkling the people in Jordan*, or that he did not sprinkle our Lord in Jordan, but that he immersed the people—immersed the Lord, in Jordan.

11*th*. When we read, Rom. 6:1-6, of their being "buried with him by baptism," and Col. 2: 12, of being "buried with him in baptism," is it not as manifest as anything can be to an honest man, whose eye is single to know what they did, that they did not bury them by sprinkling or pouring, but by immersion? Men may cavil as they please, but there is nothing in these passages that can lead an unbiased mind to think of sprinkling or pouring.

12th. When we read in connection with being "buried with him," of being "risen with him," is it not as evident as noon-day, that they were not risen from sprinkling, in which they could not have been buried, but from immersion, in which they had been buried?

13th. It is natural, when the church apostatized, that they should have forsaken the more laborious way, and adopted that which is more easy and convenient. This is precisely what men of reflection would expect a proud and indolent clergy, seeking pleasure, pride and fashion, to do. How natural that such men should dispense with immersion, and resort to that easy, simple and convenient way of *sprinkling*. This would suit both them, their proud and unchanged members and infants all much better, and the whole matter can be apologized for by a few words, simply saying, "If the heart is right, that's all," or "baptism is not essential."

14th. But can any man in his right mind believe, that when the church became corrupt, the clergy became proud and indolent, they would have given up the easy, convenient and pleasant practice of sprinkling, for the more laborious, unpleasant and inconvenient practice of immersion? We are not aware that the clergy tice of immersion? We are not aware that the clergy have ever apostatized from the more convenient, easy and pleasant, to the more inconvenient, laborious and unpleasant, in anything *they had to do themselves.*

15th. How many can the Doctor find who have been solemnly immersed, upon a confession of their faith in the Lord, "into the name of the Father, and of the Son, and of the Holy Spirit," that afterwards became dissatisfied and desired to be sprinkled or poured? We presume that the Doctor could not produce a dozen well authenticated cases of this kind if his life were at stake.

16th. How many can he find who have been sprinkled or poured, and afterwards became dissatisfied and never could be made to believe that sprinkling or pouring would do, and who never could rest till immersed? He can find plenty of this class in almost every neighborhood he ever saw in his life. We find numbers of this class wherever we go.

17*th*. It is a fact that sprinkling and pouring have always been in dispute, ever since their earliest mention for baptism in the history of the church. They have both always been in debate and doubt, and are at the present time. How is it, Doctor, that you are laboring to practice that upon the people, which has always been suspicious, doubtful, and in dispute? Is there not something wrong in this?

18th. Immersion has never been in doubt, suspicion and dispute, among any considerable number of men of knowledge and candor; has never gone through debates and disputes to any considerable extent, but has been admitted valid by almost all even of those who practice something else.

19th. Now, Doctor, show us where the conscience can be, in view of these considerations, in inducing good, well-meaning people, as you are trying to do, to receive the doubtful, the questioned, disputed, which is constantly failing to satisfy in thousands of instances, where it has been imposed upon honest, sincere and candid people, in the place of practicing that which is admitted, even by its opposers, to be safe, and always satisfies those who receive it.

20th. Dr. Shaffer, my dear sir, you know that many of the members of your own church are not satisfied with the sprinkling or pouring that has been imposed upon them, and that many people lament at death that they have not been immersed. This is a solemn matter! We are doing work for eternity, and there can be no apology for practicing that which is doubtful, fails to give satisfaction to thousands in health, as well as many in their dying moments, in the place of that which your own Wesley says was "the ancient manner," which your own Discipline requires of you, if the candidate desires it, and which always satisfies those who receive it. What apology can you offer to those whom you have thus involved, to your own conscience or to God the judge of all?

-----o-----

The Contrast Fairly Stated.

THE Presbyterian Board of Publication, in Philadelphia, has recently issued a tract, numbered 175, styled "Campbellism, its Rise, Progress, Character and Influence. By Rev. N. L. Rice." A promise was made, in the *American Christian Review,* a short time since, of a tract of similar size, in return for the Doctor's kindness. To the Presbyterian Board of Publication, therefore, but especially to Rev. N. L. Rice, are the following pages dedicated, hoping that they may be received in the same spirit of kindness in which they were written, and prove a blessing to all concerned.

1. What is *Campbellism?* This has been a puzzling question. It is hard to find out precisely what it is. Not a man yet, of all who have been engaged in fighting this monster, has defined it, explained it, or told what it is. It has been called a dangerous *heresy,* and so many hideous warnings have been given against it, that the hair would almost stand upon a man's head to hear about it, and yet no one has told what it is. The reason no one has defined *Campbellism* is simply, that *there is no such thing in existence,* except in the imaginations of some misguided doctors. As near as any man can now come at what they

mean by Campbellism, it is *Christianity itself,* unmixed, unadulterated, and without any other name. This is evident, for when they hear a man preach who preaches nothing but Christianity, nothing but Christ, simply aiming to convert men to him, and induce them to receive him as their only Leader, they call it *Campbellism.* It is nothing but a nick-name they have given the gospel to keep men from hearing it. In the same way, they call the preacher a *Campbellite,* who will preach nothing but the gospel, nothing but Christianity, to raise prejudice against him and prevent people from hearing him. In precisely the same spirit, here comes Rev. N. L. Rice, of heresy-hunting memory, in a tract of forty pages, against Campbellism, which the reader may think as he pleases about, but which is as much against the religion of Christ, and those trying to receive it, practice it and maintain it, and it *alone,* as was in the power of Dr. Rice to make it, without, in so many words, saying so. No man in this country, at this, time, can preach simply the gospel of Christ in the name of the Lord, under no other name, and maintain the law of God, as the only rule of faith, without being called a Campbellite, and branded with preaching Campbellism. This is precisely what Dr. N. L. Rice has spent a large share of his life in opposing. This will be fully developed in the following pages. The first point of contrast between him and those he opposes, or the Disciples of Christ, as here instituted, is, that they think Christianity itself, as the Lord gave it, sufficient—that to receive it in all its fullness, be a *Christian* in the Bible sense, governed by the law of God alone, is sufficient. This the Doctor opposes, and insists upon sundry human appendages, as will be seen. Here is the real issue.

2. On page 1, the Doctor says, "It was no ordinary work which he (Mr. Campbell) and his friends proposed to themselves; it was a *radical reformation* of the church throughout the world." Here is the head and front of the offence. Here is the issue, as stated by himself: The Disciples proposing to reform the church throughout the world, but Dr. Rice opposing it. Strange if bad men should propose a radical reformation of the church throughout the world, and good men oppose it. Here is the issue, or *contrast, reformation* and *opposition* to reformation.

3. He quotes from Millennial Harbinger, vol. 3, p. 362, the following question and answer: "And what of the apostasy? —do you place all the sects in the apostasy? Yes, all religious sects who have any human bond of union, all who rally under any articles of confederation other than the apostles' doctrine, and refuse to yield all homage to the ancient order of things." This the Doctor looks upon as horribly reprehensible. With him, it amounts to nothing—or rather it is necessary, to have a "human bond of union," "articles of confederation other than the apostles' doctrine," and "refuse to yield all homage to the ancient order of things;" and to call a people who do this "apostate," is, with him, almost sacrilege. Let candor be appealed to; let solemnity and honesty be appealed to; let every sincere man tell what could make an apostasy, if having a *hitman,* in the place of a *divine* bond of union, other articles of confederation than the apostles' doctrine, and refusing to yield all homage to the ancient order of things, would not do it. The contrast here is very striking. The Disciples maintain the *divine* bond of union and reject the *human.* The Doctor holds on to the *human* to aid the *divine* bond of union, in accomplishing what it could not do without the *human!* The Disciples oppose all articles of confederation other than the apostles' doctrine. The Doctor maintains other articles of confederation than the apostles' doctrine. The Disciples maintain that we must yield all homage to the ancient order of things. The Doctor opposes yielding all homage to the ancient order of things, and maintains that those who refuse such homage are not apostate.

3. The Doctor says, "Christ and his apostles effected a radical reformation in the church, but it was when tradition had been substituted for the Bible." It would be truly interesting to know what church it was, in which Christ and his apostles effected a radical reformation! They certainly never effected any reformation in the Jewish church, for it instigated the crucifixion of Christ and persecuted the apostles till its

overthrow. The "one *new* man," or church, which the Lord made of the twain, of which he said, "Upon this rock I *will* build my church," had not apostatized, so as to demand a radical reformation, in the apostles' time. It did not during this period adopt any "human bond of union, any articles of confederation other than the apostles' doctrine, nor refuse to yield all homage to the ancient order of things," and consequently had not become an apostate church. Christ and the apostles never effected, nor tried to effect a radical reformation in any church. They let the old apostate church, as the Lord accused them of, keeping doctrines and commandments of men, and disobeying the law of God, go, as beyond the reach of reformation, and built a church upon Christ, the rock, laid of God, for a holy temple—a habitation for the Lord through the Holy Spirit.

4. The Doctor informs us, that "Luther, Calvin and their co-laborers effected a glorious reformation; but it was when both clergy and people had long been ignorant of the Bible, and oral tradition, expounded by pretended infallibility was their rule of faith." But, he says, "Mr. Campbell undertook a radical reformation among those who took the Bible as their only rule of faith and practice." This statement is made upon page 2, and he only proceeds to page 7, where he gives as one of the two principles, upon which, to use his own peculiar style, "the Campbellite sect is organized, the rejection of all creeds, and union upon the Bible alone." According to his account of the matter, Mr. Campbell came among a people "who took the Bible as their *only* rule of faith and practice, and undertook to produce a radical reformation by inducing them to "reject all creeds, and unite upon the Bible *alone*. If the Bible was their only rule of faith and practice, it is strange that they should have opposed Mr. Campbell, who undertook to persuade them to unite upon their only rule of faith and practice—the *Bible alone!*

Why did not the Doctor say that Luther, Calvin, &c., "effected a glorious reformation *in the church,*" as he said Christ and the apostles did? He says, Christ and the apostles effected a reformation *in the church,* but when he gives an account of Luther's reformation, he leaves out the words, "in the church." He knows how to look out for danger. With him, Christ did not build a Church, establish a new building, or make "a new man," a new church, but merely reformed an *old church.* But he saw that it would look ridiculous to speak of Luther effecting a glorious reformation *in the church,* that he came out of, separated from, that never was and never will be reformed. Luther and Calvin found many opposers in effecting this glorious reformation, and the glorious work of reformation had to be done in spite of them, precisely as it now has to be done in spite of Rev. N. L. Rice.

5. The Doctor says, "The success of this movement was, for a number of years, remarkably rapid." He then proceeds to file in order five reasons for this remarkable success. These reasons must have a brief notice, in the same order in which they are stated.

1. "Mr. Campbell's zealous advocacy of *immersion* as the only valid baptism, and his opposition to infant baptism, gave him great fame among the Baptists." Both these points had been maintained with as much zeal and pertinacity by all Baptists as they ever were by Mr. Campbell. He had no new advantage in advocating these points. The Baptists had always had the same advantages, but had not been able to make so good a defense on these great points. But it is entirely natural that Dr. Rice should think of these points, when he mentions Mr. Campbell. He tried him on these questions, and is aware of the force his noble energies would have on the public mind. Why does not Mr. Rice gain large numbers to the Presbyterian church by maintaining infant baptism and opposing immersion? He has been as zealous and determined in maintaining infant baptism and opposing immersion, as ever Mr. Campbell was on the opposite side, but it does not appear that any remarkable success has attended his efforts. How is this to be accounted for? Zealous efforts result in remarkable success in advocating immersion and opposing sprinkling, but in no remarkable success on the opposite side! How is this? It is a clear matter to a man who candidly reflects. It is now generally known that

infant baptism is not mentioned in the Bible, nor in any book written in two hundred years after the birth of Christ. For this to be revealed and commented upon by a man of Mr. Campbell's ability, must in the very nature of things, make headway among all classes of opposers. It is also known that immersion is admitted to be *valid* baptism by all men of all parties of any considerable degree of respectability, and that sprinkling or pouring, for baptism, is not mentioned, or even hinted at in the Bible, or any book written in two hundred years after the birth of Christ, and has been held in dispute and doubt by a large number of learned and pious men, ever since introduced. It is known too, that every Greek Lexicon in the world defines *baptizo,* immerse, or something equivalent. When this is shown and commented upon by a man of Mr. Campbell's ability, with the expressions of the common version, such as "went down into the water," "came up out of the water," "baptized in Jordan," "baptizing in Enon, near to Salim, because there was much water there," "baptized in the river of Jordan," "buried in baptism," and "planted together," it must tell upon the minds of candid men. Success must attend the effort; but the most that can be done in the opposition is to retard; no remarkable success is expected.

2. The Doctor's second reason for the "remarkable success of this movement," is, that "The apparent zeal of Mr. Campbell for the union of all Christians, misled many well meaning people." The Doctor is wide of the mark here; it was not Mr. Campbell's "apparent" nor his *real* zeal for the union of Christians, that was so much the secret of the success of this movement, as the sacred doctrine of union enforced by the authority of the Almighty, not that "misled many well-meaning people," but *led them rightly,* into one fold, under the one great Shepherd and Bishop of souls. It was the holy prayer of our Lord and Savior, that believers should be one, as he and his Father are one, not that "misled so many well- meaning people," but *led them rightly,* to unite upon the foundation of the apostles and prophets, Jesus Christ being the chief cornerstone, under the "faith once delivered to the saints." It was the divine mandate of the Holy Spirit, speaking through Paul, with all the authority of the eternal throne, beseeching them in the name of the Lord Jesus Christ, all to speak the same thing, be perfectly joined together in the same mind and in the same judgment, and that there be no divisions among them, not that "misled so many well- meaning people," *but led them rightly,* to unite upon the law of God, under the name which the Lord gave his people, discarding all human laws and names. This righteous appeal, from these premises, not only reached the "well meaning," but the *good,* those who love God and his people, and was a mighty means, under God, in leading them to discard the silly and unlearned disputes of the clergy, and unite under Christ; and this holy sentiment and requirement of the Spirit of God, and the prayer of Jesus, is what Dr. Rice not only resists, but teaches men to resist, and fights against with every power of his soul. The Disciples are laboring and praying for this union, and he is opposing it. All heaven and all the good on earth are in favor of union, while all the powers of darkness are opposed to it.

3. The Doctor's third reason for this remarkable success, is that "many were drawn into this movement by the extremely easy and simple way of becoming a Christian, proposed by Mr. Campbell." The Doctor is partly right here, but only right in part. The way of becoming a Christian proposed by Mr. Campbell, or the way in which persons became Christians under the teaching of the apostles, was extremely simple and easy; and what was in its favor more than any system ever approved by Dr. Rice was, that it never failed to make a *Christian,* and made something else with another name. The prophet, looking down through more than seven centuries at this system, said, the "way shall be so plain that the wayfaring men, though fools,' need not err therein." The Lord said of it, "They who seek shall find." In divine encouragement, he said to those whom he would invite, "My yoke is easy, and my burden light;" and, at the close of the holy volume, he says, "Who-soever will, let him come." It being entirely of grace, of mercy, is,

of course, free. So simple is the way, so easy to find, and admission so accessible, that on the day the Lord was seated upon the throne, and sent forth the Spirit to guide the apostles into all truth, on hearing the first announcement of the gospel from their infallible utterance, three thousand inquired the way, and, without a single exception, found it. Not one of them went from the place seeking, or was put off till another day. This never could have been the case without clearer instructions than Dr. R. ever gave seekers. Not a single case is mentioned upon the sacred record of persons seeking the way to the Redeemer, or the way to pardon, who did not find it on the first interview with the minister of Christ, and on the same day on which they came in contact. All the tedious processes, such as that called confirmation, that at the anxious seat, or mourner's bench, which result in keeping people seeking, mourning, agonizing and grieving for weeks, months and years, in the midst of doubts, sometimes driven into despair, or insanity, are as un- scriptural as Romish penance, and as unreasonable as unevangelical or unscriptural. Who could have believed that the holy, the plain, the easy and infallible way of the Lord should be spoken against, on account of the very fact that should commend it to our respect, viz: *that it is adapted to the whole people and made accessible to them,* and not like some of those blind systems that keep men groping in the dark!

But simple and easy as the way of the Lord is, it made Christians anciently and does the same now, and nothing else. It never made a Presbyterian since the world was made, nor was one ever heard of till many long centuries of the Christian era had passed away. But Dr. R. is one of the last men who should ridicule any system about an *easy way.* The easiest way yet heard of is, to sprinkle a few drops of water upon the face of an unconscious infant, in the name of the Trinity, without any faith, any change of heart, experience, spiritual influence, holy impulse, or feeling, to initiate it into Christ, or into his church! Yes, this is the *easy way,* not to make *Christians,* for no one was ever made a Christian in this way; but to deceive people into the belief that they are in the church of Christ, when they are not; to introduce them into the Presbyterian church; to deceive them when they come to the years of responsibility, making them believe that that has been done for them, which none but themselves can do—to *"yield themselves"* to be servants of God. This is the *easy way* not to make *Christians,* but to get them into the Presbyterian church, without being Christians, without regeneration, the new birth, conversion, or any knowledge what it is. This "easy way" has involved more people in difficulty, in doubts, dissatisfaction and perplexity, and hindered them from making an intelligent and personal profession of the Christian religion, than all the other errors in doctrine in the world combined. Still Dr. Rice is for it and doing his utmost to "draw" as many, not "well-meaning people," but unconscious infants, before they mean anything, or know what those mean who have this unmeaning ceremony performed upon them, into it as possible. How can any man who thus "draws" unconscious infants into a church, before they know there is a church, a Holy Spirit, a Redeemer, or even a Deity, have the assurance to speak of men *drawing* well-meaning persons into a movement, when they make their appeal openly and to the intelligence of those who have attained to the years of accountability? Those operating through a mother, already in the church, as deeply prejudiced and misguided as the preacher, to "draw" infants into the church, before, they know anything, are the persons who "draw," not "well-meaning," but infants without *Weaning,* into the church, and who have the *easy way.* This honor no man taketh to himself more than Dr. N. L. Rice.

4. The Doctor's fourth reason is, that "The popularity of this reformation was greatly increased amongst a large class of men by the zeal with which Mr. C. assailed the clergy and denounced all the benevolent enterprises of the age. The clergy of all denominations he represented as corrupt men, influenced wholly by ambition and the love of money." That Mr. C, handled the clergy without gloves, no one is disposed to deny. Indeed, his lash must have

THE CONTRAST FAIRLY STATED.

cut keen and left an abiding sting which Dr. R. feels sensibly to this day, seeming only to increase in intensity in the place of abating, though the main work was done almost as long ago as the birth day of Dr. R. The Doctor, like young Saul, being exceedingly mad against the Disciples, seems destined to signalize himself in defense of the traditions handed down, and being so constituted that he can learn nothing, and feel the force of no reason till public sentiment forces him, he receives many severe cuts that a little prudence would have relieved him from. Whether Mr. C. applied the rod too severely is a question of but little consequence now; but, if Dr. R. is anything like a fair exponent of the clergy, and his temper, spirit and general bearing represents theirs —it is exceedingly doubtful whether they ever received one stripe amiss. As to the representation that the move for reformation gained numbers by appeals to avarice, it is confronted, wherever success has attended the effort, by the numerous houses for worship built, the institutions of learning erected, the preachers supported, contributions to the Bible Union, and other good works. Who were they that left other religious bodies and united upon the Law of God? Were they the more penurious, the miserly, the narrow hearted? or were they not as noble, free, liberal and whole hearted as any they had? Have they not built more meeting houses in several States in the last twenty years than the Presbyterians have since the settling of the country? Dr. R. knows they have, and more in the very country where he has fought them most than any place else.

i. The Doctor says, "This reformation gained popularity, too, because it made every immersed person, however ignorant a *preacher,* and every little church wholly independent of all others." This reason amounts to nothing. The Disciples stand upon the primitive practice, and will maintain it though it should give a rapid increase. They are willing to throw all the restrictions found in the New Testament around preachers and preaching, but no others. But the truth is, the Doctor is under a grand mistake about it being so easy to become a preacher among the Disciples. He has not tried preaching yet where he was opposed by all parties, and had to learn to ward off blows from every direction—from the Atheist, Infidel, Universalist, and through all the ranks of sectarian partisans. He has not tried preaching yet where he had to increase the numerical strength of his church by solid appeals to the intelligence of thinking men and women, exhorting them to repent of their sins, turn to God, and personally seek the salvation of their souls. He has never tried this yet; but if he does, he will find it a different work from persuading mothers, who belong to his church, and are already under his influence, to bring their infants to be sprinkled, and that it will require a different kind of talent. Many men with a little literature, whether regenerated or not, can read sermons, say prayers, hear an organ and sprinkle infants, who never could convert a soul to Christ, or build up a saint in the most holy faith. Such men are the last who should open their lips about it being easy to enter a ministry where the entire increase of the membership depends upon the efforts of the ministry, appealing to the judgments and to the hearts of those capable of thinking and acting for themselves, inducing them to repent, believe, and turn to God, in person, and *yield themselves* to the obedience of faith. The easy ministry is that which operates upon infants, *drawing them in* before they can think or know anything about it. Such are the Doctor's five reasons for the remarkable success of this movement.

4. The Doctor now approaches a little more closely to "examine the principles that lie at the foundation." He says, "The Campbellite sect was organized, if it can be said to have an organization, upon the two following principles: 1st, The rejection of creeds and union upon the Bible alone. 2nd, Asking but one question of candidates for baptism, whether they believe Jesus Christ to be the Messiah." Dr. R. appears so averse to what is right, so determinedly, perpetually and inevitably disposed to the wrong, that if there is any wrong way in his reach to state a thing, he is certain to find it. Both the points here stated as laying at the bottom of the "Campbellite body," how it shuts out heresy— and if he makes a convert, which is not often the case, he is merely a convert to *Presbyterianism,*

the Presbyterian church, doctrine and ministry. In this case, as a matter of course, it is necessary to ask many questions, take the applicant through a rigorous examination, to know whether there is soundness in the intricate matters of an unintelligible catalogue of doctrines, many of which the preachers themselves never did and never can understand or agree upon. The minister of Christ simply labors to convert men to Christ, and when the hearer believes in his heart that God raised him from the dead, and confesses him with the mouth, and bows his whole being in personal submission to him, receives him according to the gospel, he receives *in him* all he has for man, and binds himself to observe it; or, in other words, he receives the whole system and takes its obligations upon him, when he confesses and receives him who is the head of it. But this, as a matter of course, does not suit Dr. R., for it leaves Presbyterianism out—*the whole of it*—including nothing but Christianity—*the whole of it.* The ancient evangelist received those who confessed and submitted to Christ; Dr. R. receives two classes, viz: 1st, Those who receive Presbyterianism, as set forth by the ministry and the Confession; 2nd, Those unconscious infants brought to him that he may sprinkle water upon their faces in the name of the Lord, who never answered even "one question," or had one thought upon the subject. What do these know about the doctrine of the church they are thus "drawn in to?" or what do nine-tenths of those who bring them know about it? Not one out of ten of them know what is in the Confession of Faith, or what is not in it, and all the infants are brought in without knowing anything about it! Yet he who would continue this system, nine-tenths of whose members know no more of their entrance into the church, and had no more to do in it than they know of and had to do in entering this world, would oppose and ridicule the precise practice of the holy apostles and first evangelists of Jesus Christ, because they simply labored to save men—to convert men to their Lord and Master—receive which he appears to think himself called and sent to tear up, root and branch, are about as awkwardly stated as they could be in the same number of words. He, as a matter of course, places the point which naturally and scripturally comes first, last. He has so long been in the habit of preaching church polity to men of the world to convert them, or so addicted to presenting and preaching his creed that they may give their assent to it, and be converted to it, that he can conceive of no other mode of procedure for us than preaching "union upon the Bible alone," first, and then preaching the confession of Christ next. Never, in any pamphlet, were there clearer evidences of confusion of mind, or the absence of a clear appreciation of the structure of Christianity than in this. If there is anything clear in Christianity, or in the evangelical procedure set forth in the New Testament, it is that preaching Christ and confessing him go before church discipline or rules of Christian practice. The difference between such a preacher as Dr. R. and the primitive evangelists of Christ, is as wide as heaven and earth. They went out with hearts overflowing with the love of Christ, with minds overwhelmed with the glories of Him whom they were sent to preach, who was lifted up to draw all men to Him. They gloried in Him, preached Him, and labored to convert men to Him, and induce them to identify themselves with Him. When persons were won to Him, loved Him, were sorry for having sinned against Him, and demanded of the preacher "What doth hinder me to be baptized," the preacher responded, "If thou believest with all thy heart thou mayest." The penitent man responded, "I believe that Jesus Christ is the Son of God." The evangelist took the man down into the water and baptized him, and he went on his way rejoicing. Having thus placed himself under a new Leader, a new Lawgiver, with all confidence in him, he applies to his new Master, his Lord and King for law, for the rule of faith that is to guide him as a man of God, through the journey of life. How different this from Dr. R. He preaches the Presbyterian doctrine, Presbyterian Church and Presbyterian ministry, and tells how wisely and scripturally the whole system is arranged, them when they would confess and receive him! He also would sneer at and prejudice all men, if it were in his power, against all those who now insist that we must preach precisely what the apostles preached—no more, no less—those who become his now must believe precisely what those believed who were converted under the apostles preaching, and that converts now must make precisely the same confession they did then and render the same obedience! This he opposes with every power, and would improve upon the wisdom of the infallible Spirit that guided the apostles and first evangelists, by adopting a few of the appendages devised by Presbyterian *divines!*

4. The rejection of all creeds—all *human* creeds, and union upon the Bible, the *divine* rule, and the *only divine* rule. What Mr. Wesley calls "the sufficient and the only infallible rule both for faith and practice," the Doctor thinks a most dangerous and ruinous step. He then proceeds to make war upon those receiving the Bible as their only rule of faith, and presents the following proposition: *"The body possesses no unity of faith, but errors of every shade find a home in it."* He then sets out with almost the zeal and madness of young Saul on his way to Damascus scenting heresy. But there is one thing which he fails to do, viz: to find any error in the rule of faith adopted by those who take the *Bible alone.* This people have no error in their rule of faith. If the preachers do commit blunders, they are not in the rule of faith bound upon the disciples. But Dr. Rice, and his preaching brethren, commit as many blunders and show as many imperfections as other men, and have a creed, abounding in errors, bound upon them and all their brethren into the bargain. Let us open the Confession, almost at random, and see what will turn up. See the following: "By the decree of God, for the manifestation of his glory, some men and angels are predestined unto everlasting life, and others foreordained unto everlasting death. These angels and men, thus predestinated and foreordained, are particularly and unchangeably designed, and their number is so certain and definite that it cannot be either increased or diminished."—Con. p. 23. Now, granting the truth of this, the conduct of men in this life has no more to do with eternal life than the volition of an infant has to do in its baptism or initiation into the church. The predestination and foreordination of God, and not the actions of men or angels, fixes immutably their eternal state, whether it be life or death, and all the preaching, prayers, tears and repentance of all the men in this universe cannot change the eternal condition of one human being or angel, or in any way affect it.

Let us hear this little book again: "To these officers (the officers in the Presbyterian church,) the keys of the kingdom of heaven are committed, by virtue whereof they have power respectively to retain and remit sins, to shut that kingdom against the impenitent, both by the word and censures, and to open it unto penitent sinners, by the ministry of the gospel and by absolution from censures, as occasion shall require."—Con. p. 156. Now, if the officers in the Presbyterian church had claimed the keys of that church, no reasonable man would have doubted the claim; but that they have "the keys of the kingdom of heaven," can "open and shut" it, or "remit and retain sins," will not be believed by many well informed people. The Presbyterian church is not "the kingdom of heaven," the door of it is not the door of "the kingdom of heaven," and the keys to it are not the keys to the kingdom of heaven. This same book, notwithstanding all Dr. R.'s noise about the heathen, teaches that they cannot be saved. It says, "They who having never heard the gospel, know not Jesus Christ, and believe not in him, cannot be saved, be they never so diligent to frame their lives according to the laws of nature, or the laws of that religion which they profess; neither is there salvation in any other, but in Christ alone, who is the Saviour only of his body, the church." Con. p. 208. This speaks for itself. But since Dr. R. speaks of "all sorts of doctrines," he shall rest a little from this lesson in the Confession and hear John Calvin. Calvin says, "And therefore even infants themselves bring their own condemnation into the world with them, who, though they have not produced the fruits of their iniquity, yet have the seeds of it within them; even their whole nature is, as it were, a seed of sin, and therefore cannot but be odious and abominable to God."—Institutes, vol.

2, p. 483. What if these sinful infants die? The Confession answers: "Elect infants, dying in infancy, are regenerated and saved by Christ through the Spirit, who worketh when and where and how He pleaseth."—Con. p. 64. Such is a slight sprinkle of the *sorts of doctrine* taught under the wise and prudent arrangement of Presbyterianism, and this is not a tithe of what may be selected from their standard works. Look, too, where a number of the strongest and most influential men they have ever had in this country have strayed to, with all their synods, presbyters, learned ministers, aided by the Confession! Look at the Beechers, disciplined in Presbyterianism, and their minds confused with the perplexing and unintelligible questions that form the main features in the system! Where is it leading these to? Look at Finney, who was one of the most distinguished men in the Presbyterian church! What does he now think of it? Let us hear him speak of these wise presbyters and synods. He says:

"These things, in the Presbyterian church, their contentions and janglings, are so ridiculous, so wicked, so outrageous, that no doubt there is a jubilee in hell, every year, about the time of the meeting of the General Assembly; and if there were tears in heaven, no doubt they would be shed over the difficulties of the Presbyterian church. Ministers have been dragged from home, up to the General Assembly, and there heard debates and witnessed a spirit by which their souls have been grieved, and their hearts hardened, and they have gone home ashamed of their church, and ashamed to ask God to pour out his spirit upon such a contentious body."

This is the language of a man who was well acquainted with this system and the ministry. He speaks from personal knowledge. Look at the debates, strifes and divisions in this body, and then ask the question—Have Presbyterians developed the wisdom, prudence and necessity of having a *human* creed to accomplish what the Law of God could not do? Have they shown that all those who have taken the Bible as their only rule of faith, are "drawn in," deceived and led astray? and that they would do wisely to abandon the Bible-alone position, and come under the Presbyterian Confession?

The truth is, Barton W. Stone and A. Campbell, being both perplexed, in their younger days, with the unintelligible language of Presbyterianism, involved in its perplexing disputes, but brought up in different countries, ran considerably apart on some points; but when they resolved to relinquish all unscriptural doctrine, and even unscriptural style, and give supreme honor to Christ, they united without regard to difference of opinion. After this the difference vanished, and the fruitless disputes of their younger days disappeared to a great extent; and that B. W. Stone honored our Lord Jesus Christ more than Dr. N. L. Rice ever did is susceptible of the clearest proof, though he refers to him as contemptibly as if he had been an Atheist. But he knew what was in Presbyterianism, and so did A. Campbell, and both renounced it for the Bible, as their only rule of faith, of which they have no reason to be sorry either for time or for eternity. There is not one ray of light from heaven that has ever reached the abodes of men, in any creed, or any book, or any man, that is not in the Bible. Mr. R. may, to the day of his death, as most probably he will, try to create distrust in the minds of those who look upon the Bible as their only rule of faith, and unite upon it; but it will amount to nothing at last, for every man must be as conscious as that he is a living being, that if the man who honestly reads the Bible to know his duty, or the will of God, and does it to the best of his ability, praying daily for the divine aid, both in understanding and doing, is not safe, infallibly safe and right, no man in' this world is safe. Suppose, for the sake of the case, the step in receiving Bro. Baines, with the avowal that he did not renounce Universalism, was wrong, it is no argument against the Bible-alone position, but simply an error in their procedure upon the position. It is manifest enough that those who hold Universalism do not hold it as an opinion, but make it the prime article in their faith. But Bro. Raines, true to his profession to take the

Bible, the whole Bible, and nothing but the Bible, soon found that it was no system of Universalism, and from that day to this he has been as sound on the whole question of future punishment as Dr. R. himself. Indeed, Dr. R. holds and maintains, with the utmost pertinacity, the main error of Universalism, viz: "That all that Christ died for will be saved." He is also involved in that other fundamental error of Universalism, viz: That nothing that a man can do in this life can in any way affect his condition in the eternal state, that before the world, God, by an immutable decree, determined the precise number and persons to be saved and lost; and, according to this, all the Bibles, missionaries, preaching, praying, with all other efforts, has never saved one soul, and all the sin on earth has never damned one. Such is the position of the man, such the absurdities in which he is involved, who would ridicule the effort of all sincere and good men who are trying to escape from the delusions of this age, and return to pure Christianity as it came from heaven, men who believe and maintain all that is divine, all that is from heaven, and escape all that is human. Can men lead the people astray by insisting upon their adhering strictly to the law of God, the whole of the law of God?—uniting upon it, living in peace and love? Let the Lord reign. Let his law be the supreme authority. The Bible is right, if anything is right. All led by it are led rightly; all under its influence are under proper influence; all opposed to it are wrong—all the way wrong. Dr. R. stands in the opposition, and there we must leave him for another month, when we shall finish his pamphlet. B. F.

-----o-----

Letter from Elder B. F. Hall.

VICTORIA, April 28, 1856.

B. FRANKLIN—*Dear Brother:* Yours of the 31st ultimo, together with the two copies of your American Christian Review, came duly to hand, for which 1 thank you. I have shown your paper to a few brethren, and obtained the following subscribers: M. M. Jones, A. Allee, Nancy Lovelady, Andrew Prather, J. Kuyerkendall, all to be sent to Yorktown, Derritt county, Texas. Enclosed please find the pay for all for one year. I hope to be able to send you other names and the money soon.

I like you and your paper very much. I have my own views of organization and church polity. They are different from yours, but this does not make me love you the less. On the subject of church government, I have no quarrel with my brethren. In matters of expediency and church polity, if they will not agree with me, I will co-operate with them. We must harmonize and labor in concert. Where no vital principle is involved, we must "learn to bear and forbear." We must be united. There must be no schism in the body.

You may be aware that, owing to a diseased condition of my throat (laryngitis), I have not for several years been able to preach as constantly as formerly. With the hope of improving the condition of my throat and of making a living, I last fall removed to Texas. I have settled in Goliad county, on the Cavesa, some twelve miles from the county town, in a sparsely settled neighborhood; a high, healthy, rich, but rather undulating country. I have literally pitched my tent at a point which has been christened "Hallonian Mott." It overlooks pretty much the whole country around for many miles. The Cavesa is a beautiful, clear stream, abounding in fish, with a sprinkle of alligators. Here I fondly hoped to live secluded, and unsolicited to preach until my throat became well or better; but in this, I already find myself mistaken. My "Rancho" has already been discovered by many persons, and I find myself on a direct line from the town of Goliad to San Antonia. I am quite near to many excellent brethren, and not over four miles from one of their preaching places, and some eighteen miles from a church of about ninety-five members! I think them to be clever people, and generally well to live. Among them are some four acceptable preachers of good report. I have been at one of their monthly meetings, and addressed a congregation quite respectable in numbers and behavior. Moreover, in appearance they will compare favorably with country congregations generally.

They are to have a District Co-operation

meeting at Shilo, some four miles from Yorktown, the second Lord's day in next month. The churches in Western Texas have an Evangelist, Brother Strictland of Georgetown, and another, Dr. Jourdan, of Yorktown, whose labors are confined to a more limited district. These both are good, intelligent brethren, whose hearts are in the work. They are now together in this section. They have opened the spring campaign, and have already made some conquests to the Redeemer's cause.

If you know of any good brethren who wish to raise stock and farm it in a good country, with fine climate, rich soil, and a salubrious atmosphere, send them out here. Land and stock are cheap, and plenty for sale. They can reach here by way of New Orleans; thence to Indianola in regular steamers; thence to Victoria by stage, and perhaps soon by steamboat. From here to my rancho on the Cavesa is thirty-five miles, where I will be glad to see them, and will take pleasure in showing them the country. Yours, truly,

B. F. HALL.

-----o-----

A Word to the Brotherhood.

AFTER the labors and experience of twenty-six years, in the cause to which we have pledged ourselves, I am confirmed in the judgment which I formed at the commencement, that we must rely upon our own efforts for success, and that it is vain to ask or expect to receive favors at the hands of any of the existing parties. Notwithstanding all our efforts to conciliate the Baptists, who are supposed to be more nearly agreed with us in doctrine and practice than any other party; and notwithstanding our co-operation with them in some of the noblest enterprises of the age, many of their leading men seem to take pains and enjoy a peculiar delight in holding us up as an odious party, and as just objects of suspicion and avoidance. The fact is not only so, but it is done at the expense and in direct contradiction to the Word of God.

As evidence of this, you have only to look at the works that have recently made their appearance. There is a vast deal of worming and twisting to nullify the plainest Scriptures upon the most important topics, to accomplish our condemnation, and subject us to the odium of the world, and thus destroy our influence. Some of them, in their attempts to explain away a plain statement, have involved themselves in the most glaring contradictions and inconsistencies. Labored attempts are made to prove that remission is before obedience, notwithstanding the following lucid, positive, unambiguous Scriptures are *staring* them in the face: "He that believeth and is baptized shall be saved," "Repent and be baptized, every one of you, in the name of Jesus Christ for the remission of sins," " Whosoever shall *call on the name* of the Lord shall be saved," "Arise, and be baptized, and wash away thy sins, *calling on the name* of the Lord," etc. etc.

Not willing, however, to ignore the doctrine entirely, they *shy* around it, and without intending it, admit the whole matter.. For instance, where one says "the clement of obedience is *in*, or *part* and *parcel* of saving faith," how upon earth can the man himself know that the element of obedience is in his faith, until he has obeyed? It is an utter impossibility as long as it is true that a man may flinch at any moment before obedience.

Again: when another says, "The man that believes and is baptized is most certainly a saved man, for the Saviour says, "he that believeth and is baptized shall be saved," to prove that salvation is somehow or other connected with baptism, when administered to a penitent believer, is it not a full and unequivocal surrender of the question? If you approach the subject of the Gospel, you will find the same blundering inconsistency. While Paul positively, without qualification, asserts that the Gospel is the power of God unto salvation to everyone that believeth, they will attempt to pare it down and obscure it by a dogma that has no existence in philosophy or fact, that it is powerless unless the spirit of God takes it and imparts to it a peculiar power that it does not inherently possess, as the power of God to save the believer provided he obeys it.

Again: some of their prominent preachers will contend that a sinner is both saved when he believes, and is in the Kingdom; and yet they refuse to commune with their loving pedo-Baptist friends, who are in the Kingdom, if they are right!

Again: at a recent proselyting meeting, such was the desire to keep up the party lines, that the candidates for baptism were asked, "Has God for Christ's sake forgiven you?" The answer being in the affirmative, the vote was taken whether the person should be admitted to Baptism. The response being favorable, the persons were immersed. But before and at the immersion, lest the great congregation should suppose they were relying too much on immersion, and that perhaps it might be esteemed too Campbellitish, the immerser would distinctly announce that he "did not immerse for the remission of sins, but *unto* remission of sins—or the answer of a good conscience."

A distinction without a difference, and not to know it! What torturing of the Word of God! How severely put to the *rack to* make it speak the dogmas of the merest partisans! The fear of man makes mighty havoc of the Christian religion. We will learn in the great day who it is that ought to be feared.

Brethren, we must march out on the field of battle, armed and equipped for the mighty conflict. There is a mighty host at our doors. We have to fight the battle alone. You need not expect favors. The world's salvation is before us. A crown of glory awaits the conqueror. The motives for action and self-sacrifice are as lofty as the Heavens. They span the Heavens and the earth—time and eternity.

In proportion to our labors and success will the world and the parties be benefitted. If we fail, they will be more confirmed in their schisms and denominational enterprises. If we succeed, they will see the folly of their partisan warfare, and fall into the ranks of the grand Union army. This being accomplished, the world would lie at our feet an easy conquest. May the Lord help us on, and speed the day. Affectionately,

J. T. JOHNSON.

-----o-----

BOAST not thyself of to-morrow, for thou knowest not what a day may bring forth.

For the American Christian Review.
Letter from Texas.
PALESTINE, Texas, March 28, 1856.

DEAR BRO. FRANKLIN: The third number of your *American Christian Review* has just reached me. Nos. one and two have not arrived. Most heartily do I unite with brethren Raines, Rogers and others, in rejoicing that you are again at the helm of so good a vessel. The times demand such men. I mean not to praise you; but you have given evidence of good common sense (a rather rare commodity now), industry, and faith in God so strong, and so intelligent, that you can afford to speak "the truth, the whole truth, and nothing but the truth," without fearing what man can do to you. You seem, too, to look all around a question, and from one end to the other of it, before speaking; to consider its bearings, general and special, in connection with its comparative or its absolute importance. Hence, you are not a *hobby rider.* If you have not so much literary lore, a fancy so rich and poetic, or a manner so suavity and bewitching, it may be well, for the same reason it was well for the apostles of our Lord to be men of your kind. They were never much tempted to go far beyond the Word of God, to deal in the fanciful, to strive to be eloquent, learned or great, except Paul, and he most happily resisted the temptation.

But I am especially glad to see the stand you take touching the "*Union,*" "made and provided" by brethren Anderson, Ayres, etc. I need scarcely tell you that I feel a deep interest in the cause in the counties composing this "Union." You may remember that I lived and labored there several years—in one of which I witnessed near one thousand additions to the churches.

These brethren have made—I hardly know what to call it; a *thing,* might be imprudent, because disrespectful; a *creed,* it is not, because it does not tell us what to believe; a *discipline,* would not be exactly expressive of it, for it only assumes that it *will* discipline the unruly, without giving us the rule by which it will do it. This leaves us in a very awkward position. Suppose I should visit my old friends, in Danville, Stanford, or elsewhere in the consecrated boundary;

would I not be in danger of the discipline of the "Union?"—and the more so, not only for this article, but because they have not said what shall be preached or done. Before I knew it, I might have exposed myself to their "Union discipline."

Now, I may make this visit, and it does seem to me that both consistency and simple justice require them so to define their faith and rules of decorum, discipline, etc., that we may know when we are obnoxious to their displeasure, and when we may expect their smiles and favors. I might return to Texas with my Christian character utterly mined, because I did not know what they desired me to preach or to do. I used to understand them when we took the Bible alone as a rule of faith and practice—as a creed and discipline; and if they will just publish, at length, what we must believe, and preach, and do, and what we must not believe, or preach, or do, and the rules by which they will try the disobedient, then, if I cannot comply, I will prudently keep out of the hands of that "Union." I am not afraid of the Bible and its rules of discipline, but human creeds and disciplines, ever changing, and ever needing to be changed, I am afraid of.

Yes. this Danville Union *requires* a full and specific creed and discipline; and, perhaps, a vigilance committee, to make special rules for special cases between the regular sessions of the body. What would be thought of a teacher who would chastise a pupil for violating a rule never made known to the school?

This Union has grown out of the "signs of the times." It is the legitimate offspring of the significant "signs of the times." The assumption was, that the churches are not as pious, not as happy, harmonious, and useful as they should be. We all plead guilty. This was nothing new. We had all discovered and deplored it before. But the assumption goes farther; it says that the *cause* of these errors and deficiencies is, the want of organization— *human* organization—such an organization, I presume, as the Danville "Union!" I never thought this latter assumption worthy of argument, and was by no means pleased with the manner in which it was managed. I presume but few were. I was at too great a distance to take part in it,—and was too much engaged otherwise; besides, I could not presume that my mite, trifling as it must have been, was needed. Still, I have read this controversy with deep interest, and have always felt like bearing my testimony for the truth—especially in that region of country— in all such matters. I think I could show, that human creeds and disciplines were at first, are now, and ever will be, designed to *supply the place of Christian piety.* Want of piety gave rise to them. They exist neither in heaven nor in a pure state of the church. And, instead of curing, they increase the cause which produced them. All this is proved by the history of the church and of the humanism in it. As they increase the evil, so must they be increased in force, in volume, and in severity, till they arrive at the inquisition, the gibbet, the dungeon and the rack!

I would say more, but before this reaches you the case will, doubtless, be argued by others, and more fully and ably than I would likely do it. Let me say these things to my old friends, however: I am not away from the *cause,* if I am away in Texas. Let us speak kindly—*plainly,* to be sure; but the case is bad enough, and need not be made worse by severity of style. If I could put the paragraph in brackets, or somewhere else, so that others would not read it; or if I could get these brethren to *lean over this way* till I could speak to them without others hearing, I would tell them how ashamed I am of their "Union."

Believe me ever, most affectionately, and in the deepest earnest, your co-worker in the vineyard of the Lord. C. KENDRICK.

-----o-----

LET another man praise thee, and not thine own mouth; a stranger, and not thine own lips.

FAITHFUL *are* the wounds of a friend; but the kisses of an enemy *are* deceitful.

OPEN rebuke is better than secret love.

Editor's Table

Office of the *American Christian Review,* West Fourth street, No. 60, on third floor, open stair way from outside. Signs will be seen at the entrance.

MANY important communications, obituaries, items of news, queries, etc., were unavoidably left out.

ELD. E.E. Orvis, King William Court House, Va., has discontinued his monthly pamphlet. Arrangements have been made to send the *American Christian Review* to his subscribers, in place of the *Christian Union and Review.* All who have paid him for the current year, will be credited for Vol. I., of the *Review.* Those who have not paid him, will please forward $1 each to us at this office, which will make all square to the end of this year.   B. F.

WE have been informed that our remarks, appended to Bro. B. K. Smith's article, on "Clerical Organization," in the April No., have been unfavorably applied to him. When we spoke of men who would not work, except to work their way into fat places, we did not think of such a thing as Bro. Smith being one of that kind. He is precisely the opposite—one of the *working* men who would be *harnessed* and *worked* in such a clerical contrivance as some think we need, while men who would not do half the amount of labor, would get double the money and then make out that they were living upon a mere pittance.

The Social Revolutionist.—Such is the title of a monthly of sixteen pages, edited and published in Greenville, Darke county, Ohio, by John Patterson and Wm. Denton; L. A. Hine, of this city, corresponding editor. It caps the climax of all the vagaries of these times of delusion. It is as void of sense as piety; the most complete mass of confused and crude notions ever printed upon so much paper; the very scum of all the errors advocated by the stupid dupes around us. There is manifestly no cure for such brainless drivellers, of unbelief, sorcery, free love, and sensuality. They despise the Bible, marriage and the civil government about alike. Their ignorance is their bliss; their glory is their shame.

Elder Joel Hume in Trouble.

THE attack of Eld. Hume upon us, at Florence, Ky., a few days since, is without any provocation; and the statements made, discreditable to us, without the least foundation. I wrote my speeches according to our *written agreement,* and passed them all through the hands of Judge Green, the gentleman mutually chosen to inspect our speeches, and decide whether they were written according to agreement, with authority to strike out anything added, or insert anything left out. Not one of my speeches received the slightest change from him. Nor did I have anything to do with the printing, not even so much as the reading of the proof of my own speeches, on account of which many typographical errors are found in them.

The truth is, Mr. Hume would stand up before my face and say that *I* had said things which I had not said; and, I am informed, that he wrote his replies, in part, if not altogether without reading what he was replying to. People show him these statements, alleging that I have said what I have not said, and he is simply trying to excuse the matter. I did not reply to his speeches at random, but had every one before me, and looked to see what was in it before writing my reply. Not only so, but numerous low, uncouth and ungentlemanly expressions, by my permission, granted to his face, were left out of his speeches. He called himself "Hume," "old Hume," and "old man Hume," hundred of times in the debate, with other ridiculous things, of which I spoke to him kindly, showing how it would look in a religious discussion, and advised him to leave such expressions out. But for the present I leave him to writhe in his agony, and shall probably attend to him in a more documentary way before long.

Success of the Gospel.

ELD. John Rogers, of Carlisle, Ky., May 15th, says; "We have had six immersions here within a few days."

Bro. Finley Oakes, writing May 7th, from Mount Morris, Greene county, Pa., says: "I have devoted the most of my time, since last September, to traveling as an evangelist, and have organized three new congregations, added forty-seven to the army of the faithful—thirty-one by baptism—the balance from the sects."

We are just from a meeting at Salem, Green Co., Ohio, commenced by Bro. M. B. Hopkins,' and up to Saturday, May 23, when we left, eight had been added.

WEST MIDDLEBURY, Logan Co., Ohio,
April 24, 1856.

BRO. FRANKLIN—*Dear Sir:* As an item of church news, I would say, Bro. Henry Dixon, of Huron, Co., Ohio, closed a meeting of some sixteen days on last Lord's day evening, for us, with a most glorious result. Twenty souls, in all, joined us, for mortality; thirteen by confession and immersion; two from other churches; one by letter, and five reclaimed. To God give all the praise.

Your brother,   W. M. HELLINGS.

MIDDLETOWN, Henry Co., Ind., March 17, 1856.

BRO. FRANKLIN: We are carrying on a meeting here with some success. Four additions thus far, with prospects of still further success. Of the four already joined, three were by baptism, and one immersed, Methodist,

Bro. J. B. Cobb, of Franklin, is with me. If any further success attends, we will report.

As ever,
   B. K. SMITH.

DAYTON, Ohio, April 23, 1856.

-----o-----

DEAR BROTHER FRANKLIN: Since the first of February I have immersed ten persons, upon their professing faith in the Messiah. We are getting on here more prosperously than at any time since my labors commenced in this city. We must soon commence our appeals to the brotherhood at large for aid to pay for our meeting house. Pray for us. I hope to see you in New Salem in May, third Lord's day, or on Monday after. I hope, Bro. Franklin, you will make all effort necessary to be there.

Fraternally yours, in the Lord,
   J. M. HENRY.

CINCINNATI, May 16, 1856.

BRO. EDITOR—I have held the following meetings, at the times and places specified, viz.: Including the third Lord's day in March, at Warsaw, Ky. Effected a re-organization of the church at this place.

Including the fourth Lord's day in March, at Germantown, Ky. One confession.

Of an evening between the first and second Lord's days in April, at Falmouth, Ky.; one confession.

At Dover, including the third Lord's day of April; two confessions, three who had been baptized.

At Warsaw, Ky., on the fourth Lord's day in April; one confession.

At White Oak, on the first Lord's day in May; three confessions—two who had been baptized.

Yours, M. B. Hopkins.

THE review of the Tract, by Rev. N. L. Rice, found in this number of the *Review,* is put up separately in a neat tract, and can be had at this office, or sent by mail, for five cents single copy, or three dollars for one hundred copies.

-----o-----

OBITUARY.

MOUNT HEALTHY, April 25, 1856.

ELDER FRANKLIN—At the request of the friends of the deceased, I send you an obituary notice for publication in your periodical. If it is too lengthy, make such an abstract as you think proper.

Died, at the late residence of his father, Aaron Lane, deceased, on Monday, the 21st of April, JOHN SUTPHEN LANE, in the 39th year of his age. He died of that fatal scourge, the "small-pox." He was a young man of great moral worth and integrity, and in his last illness drew round him a large circle of devoted friends, who, together with the family, have been exposed to the contagion. What awaits us, as the consequence, is known only to God. With earnest prayer for deliverance from evil, we humbly resign ourselves into the hands of Him who has control of all things. In his decease, Mr. Lane leaves a devoted wife, with whom he had but just entered upon the stage of life—a widowed mother, who looked hopefully and trustingly upon him in her declining years—together with brothers and sisters and a large circle of relatives and friends, to mourn his *apparently* untimely loss.

Mr. Lane was not a member of the church militant, but we trust he is of the church triumphant. We believe he *desired* a place among the professing people of God, but the *force of circumstances* kept him from enjoying it. A few evenings previous to his death, he called his friends around his bed, and requested them to read a portion of the Word of God. After which he desired us to pray. In much weakness, we engaged with him in supplicating the Father of our spirits to be merciful to him, and to us sinners, for the sake of Jesus Christ. After which, we conversed with him in relation to his probable change. He expressed a willingness to depart, and a submission to the will of God; confessed his short-comings, neglect of duty, and unworthiness, but trusted in the Saviour. We cannot sorrow as those having no hope, for we feel that our loss is his eternal gain.

Thus died one of the most worthy of men, beloved and esteemed by all who knew him, professing indeed no other creed than confessing with his mouth the Lord Jesus, and believing in his heart that God had raised him from the dead. N. H. HUNT.

Every Day.

EVERY day there is groaning and crying,
Every day there is weeping and sighing,
Sickness and sorrow, and delving and dying.
   Every day.
Every day there is happiness brewing,
Every day there are mercy deeds doing,
Faith, hope and love their work are pursuing,
   Every day.
My little daytime hath sorrow and gladness,
Merry-toned joy, and the music of sadness,
Dottings of goodness, and circles of badness,
   Every day.
Let there be ebbing and let there be foaming,
Let there be resting, and let there be roaming,
Somewhere'll be sunshine, somewhere the gloaming,
   Every day.
And when breathings of evil the strife-flames are Fanning,
Holier spirits are angel-deeds planning,
Rainbows of promise the heavens are spanning,
   Every day.
    Bugle

THE AMERICAN CHRISTIAN REVIEW.

Vol. 1.]   CINCINNATI, JULY, 1856.   [No. 7.

DISCOURSE ON ELECTION, BY ELDER SMITH.

PETER, an apostle of Jesus Christ, to the strangers scattered throughout Pontus, Galatia, Cappadocia, Asia, and Bithynia.

Elect according to the foreknowledge of God the Father, through sanctification of the Spirit, unto obedience and Sprinkling of the blood of Jesus Christ: Grace unto you, and peace, be multiplied.—I. Peter, i: 1,2,

THE subject of election is one that has engaged the tongues and pens of theologians more or less for the last fifteen centuries. It is not my purpose, in this discourse, to even refer to the various theories that have been woven in the intellectual looms of those who have tilted, polemically, on the Calvinistic and Arminian sides, respectively, of this subject; but to treat of it as though nothing had ever been said or written upon it heretofore.

I am strongly impressed with the idea, that if its discussion had been left for the present generation of free-born Americans to commence, or had the ancient Greeks and Romans, in the days of Augustine—who commenced it—understood and enjoyed the blessings of true republican liberty, as we do now, the subject need never have been mystified as it has been. Let us then approach it in the light of the Bible, and of common sense, without any reference to what the ancient or modern fathers have said on it.

The noun *election*, with the verb *to elect*, from which it is derived, are very familiar terms to Americans, and need no labored definitions to make their *political* signification known to this audience. All understand the verb to mean *to choose*, and the noun, *the act of choosing* one or more individuals, to serve their fellows in some specific office or capacity, to which they are called by such election. The *service of the public*, and not the personal aggrandizement of the elect individual, is the avowed object of the election. It is also equally well understood, that to say a man is elected simply, does not convey any distinct idea to the mind as to what particular office he is elected to. It may be as supervisor of the road, or fence-viewer; or it may be to the senate, or even the presidency of the United States. The word applies, with equal propriety, to the choosing of persons to fill these, and all the intermediate offices in this republic, or confederation of republics.

The word also involves the idea of a sovereign electing power, from whose, choice the election proceeds. This power may be vested in the people at large, in electors chosen by them, in the legislature, in the executive and senate, or in the senate alone. The choice is neither more nor less an election, because made by many, by few, or by a single election. The good of the whole is, however, *always* the avowed object of the choice, unless the sovereign authority is corrupt, and turned away from the legitimate objects of its existence.

The idea of eligibility is likewise involved; the conditions of which are prescribed by the constitution, or supreme sovereign authority. In some governments, the faithful performance of the duties of one office is made the condition of eligibility to another; as, under the old constitution in Kentucky, the oldest justice of the peace was the only eligible candidate for the sheriffalty.

Now these remarks apply, in all their various bearings, to the subject of election as taught in the Bible. There are a great variety of callings to which men are, and have been, chosen or elected, mentioned in the Bible. There is also some variety as to the location of the elective franchise; also in the conditions of eligibility. All, however, is supremely adapted to promote the best interests of the race of mankind.

We propose, however, in this discourse, to speak only of those kinds of election in which Jehovah is the Elector. Of these there are several, which, for the sake of distinction, we will classify as follows:

I. National;
II. Particular, or Personal;
III. Conditional; and
IV. Universal.

These terms are admitted to be somewhat arbitrary; but it is hoped we shall be able to illustrate each class with sufficient clearness to make the subject entirely plain to every attentive mind.

I. OF NATIONAL ELECTION.

Of this class, it is sufficient for our present purpose to remark, that the Jews, as a nation, were elected, or chosen of God, as the depository of the Divine Oracles, to preserve the knowledge of the true God, during the working out of the problem whereby it was demonstrated, that "the world by [human] wisdom knew not God."—I. Cor. i: 21. "To whom pertained the adoption, and the glory, and the covenants, and the giving of the law, and the service of God, and the promises; whose *were* the fathers, of whom, as concerning the flesh, Christ came, who is over all, God blessed forever. Amen.—Rom., ix: 4, 5.

Other nations were, from time to time, chosen of God, to minister to this *emphatically elect nation:* sometimes as a scourge, to punish them for their sins, as the Midianites, the Philistines, and the Assyrians; sometimes to deliver them from captivity, and protect them from surrounding dangers, as the Medo-Persians; and, finally, to destroy their nationality, when they had filled the measure of their national sins, by crucifying the Messiah, as the Romans.

In all these cases of national election, the wisdom, propriety, and benevolence of God will not be questioned, I presume, by anyone who will make himself acquainted with all the facts. On the contrary, he cannot but see the goodness, and universal benevolence of Jehovah in the whole proceeding.

II. OF PARTICULAR, PERSONAL ELECTION.

We come next, to speak of particular, personal election. I use these terms, not so much because of their peculiar fitness to distinguish this class from some others, as because they have long been appropriated to express the idea of sovereign choice between individuals, such as the choice between Jacob and Esau.

Of this class, we may remark here, as well as anywhere, that, while it is clear that such a class of election is taught in the Bible, no person was ever elected to everlasting life under it. All the cases recorded, or supposable under this head, are of individuals chosen—doubtless on account of their fitness, either possessed or foreseen—to occupy some position, or to perform some important work *for the benefit of the non-elect.* Their election to salvation, and to eternal life, depended upon precisely the same conditions upon which others received them.

At the head of this class, as supremely the elect of God, stands our glorious Redeemer, the Lord Jesus Christ, who, of all the beings in the universe was alone found capable and worthy, and was consequently chosen, or elected of God to redeem a world from ruin, and to introduce everlasting righteousness. In this case—the election of a Redeemer, who, by the grace of God, should taste of death for every man, and thus bring eternal life within the reach of all—the wisdom and benevolence of God shines with unparalleled splendor; and the non-elect—the whole race of man is non- elect in this sense—are laid under everlasting obligations to God in this behalf.

Of this second class, but infinitely below this case, in point of importance and sublimity, stand all the cases of particular, personal election, recorded in the Bible. A few cases, only as specimens, can be named here. Abraham, of all the descendants of Noah, was selected—doubtless on account of his peculiar fitness for the service, either seen, or foreseen by the Lord—to be the father of the faithful, the first depositary—in the post-diluvian world at least—of the distinct promise of a blessing to all the families of the earth, and to be the progenitor of the holy seed through whom the blessing should come. And this seed, through a succession of forty odd generations, is caused to pass through a line of elect persons—some more, and some less conspicuous on the pages of Jewish history.

Beside these, under the head of particular, personal election, may be named Noah, Moses, Joshua, Gideon, Barak, Sampson, Jephtha, Deborah, etc.; not forgetting Pharaoh, Baalam, and Judas, who were all chosen instruments— chosen on account of their fitness for the service they were to render,—and all exhibit the wisdom and goodness of God in the admirable adaptedness of each instrument in working out his benevolent purposes in behalf of poor fallen man. In addition to the above, all the prophets, apostles, evangelists, pastors, and teachers of both Old and New Testament times, were variously chosen to the performance of special services, and as media for communicating certain portions—each his respective part— of the benevolent counsels of Jehovah to the world of mankind. And *all* demonstrating the universal goodness of God to the world.

III. OF CONDITIONAL ELECTION.

The third class, as we have them arranged, would seem to come more properly after that which we have named as the fourth class; but we have chosen this arrangement as more agreeable to our proposed method of discussing the subject.

By *conditional election,* we mean an election that is attainable by complying with certain conditions which render the individual eligible; without which none can attain it; and with which, all may. Of this class, there are two kinds of election in the gospel economy,— one to salvation, or pardon of past sins; the other, to eternal life. The conditions of the former of these are expressed in a single sentence, thus: "God has from the beginning chosen you to salvation, through sanctification of the spirit and belief of the truth."—II. Thess., ii: 13.

The other,—to eternal salvation,—Christians are commanded to "work out * * with fear and trembling."—Phil., ii., 12; or to "make their calling and election sure; for if [they] do these things, [they] shall never fall; for so an entrance shall be ministered unto [them] abundantly, into the everlasting kingdom of our Lord and Saviour Jesus Christ."—II. Pet., i: 2.

This must suffice for the present, on these two kinds of conditional election. We will dismiss this class (for the present), with this remark: Eligibility to the election unto eternal life, is dependent on the attainment of the election unto salvation; and eligibility to this, is based on the fourth and last class named in this arrangement, to which we will now direct your attention.

IV. OF UNIVERSAL ELECTION.

The election alluded to in our text, is evidently of the fourth class, *i. e.* universal. Let us read it again:

"Peter, an apostle of Jesus Christ, to the strangers scattered throughout Pontus, Galatia, Cappadocia, Asia, and Bithynia, elect—according to the foreknowledge of God the Father, through sanctification of the spirit— unto obedience, and sprinkling of the blood of Jesus Christ: Grace unto you, and peace be multiplied."

Now, it will be seen at a glance, that the election here mentioned, is not of either of the classes already spoken of. That it is universal—which is my assumption—we will see how far Scripture and facts will go to establish.

What is this election unto? Not to the service assigned any of the elect nations spoken of; not to the office of Redeemer; nor is it to that of patriarchs, prophets, nor apostles; neither is it an election to eternal life; nor yet unto salvation from sin. What is it then? Simply an election *"unto obedience and sprinkling of the blood of Jesus Christ."*

Then if it be true that "God commandeth *all men, everywhere,* to repent," and obey the gospel, and thus partake of the "blood of sprinkling, which speaketh better things than that of Abel," he has certainly made them eligible to obedience, etc.; and this Peter calls His choice, or election in this passage.

One remark I will here drop, for the benefit of theorizers as well as for the better understanding of the subject before us. Every *act* necessarily presupposes a *time* when the act was performed. Election involves the idea of an act; therefore the idea of a *time* when the election took place: hence, "eternal election" is a palpable absurdity. For if we date the act, no matter how far back—say millions of ages before Adam was created—eternity runs infinitely back of that; and that point in the infinite duration of eternity, at which the act was performed, is the *time* of the *act.* Eternity is but the infinite extension of time.

From this, it follows, with the force of a demonstration, that every election mentioned in the Bible, implies a *time* when such election took place. We propose showing, not only the *time,* but the *place* and *manner* of this universal election of *all men, everywhere,* to obedience, and sprinkling of the blood of Christ.

The language of the passage itself, furnishes a good clue, which, if well followed, will lead to very satisfactory results in this particular. It says, the election was "according to the foreknowledge of God the Father, through sanctification of the Spirit."

What is the foreknowledge of God here alluded to? Certainly not that infinite omniscience by which everything past, present and future—here, there and everywhere—is open and known to Him. All things are according to that; but the very fact that Peter says this election was *according* to His foreknowledge, implies that something of the kind might occur, *not* according to this foreknowledge, the validity of which would be vitiated by such *non accordance.* How, then, did Peter know that this was in accordance with it? Evidently because the foreknowledge here alluded to was a matter of revelation, and Peter could speak with confidence of a matter so manifestly in accordance with what God had *before made known*—the obvious meaning of the term as here used.

From Peter's language here, we learn that not only the election, but the *manner* of it, was foreshown, or predicted; that it should be "through [a] sanctification of [or by] the [Holy] Spirit." Let us now examine the foreshowing of Jehovah — comparing facts with it—for a little while, and see what the result will be. A single quotation, out of many that might be made from the Old Testament prophets, will suffice, I think, to render this matter plain to every one:

"And it shall come to pass afterward, that I will pour out my Spirit upon all flesh; and your sons and your daughters shall prophesy; your old men shall dream dreams, and your young men shall see visions; and also upon the servants and upon the handmaids in those days, will I pour out my Spirit. And I will show wonders in the heavens and in the earth; blood, and fire, and pillars of smoke. The sun shall be turned into darkness, and the moon into blood, before the great and terrible day of the Lord come. And it shall come to pass, that whosoever shall call on the name of the Lord, shall be delivered; for in Mount Zion and in Jerusalem shall be deliverance, as the Lord hath said, and in the remnant whom the Lord shall call." Joel ii: 28, 32.

Here is a specimen of the foreshowing of Jehovah. It tells us that God intended to pour out his Spirit upon *all flesh*; and when certain phenomena then described should be witnessed, it should *come to pass, that whosoever should call on the name of the Lord, should be saved.* Well, are there any facts fulfilling this prediction? Read the second chapter of Acts, and see how signally, and to the very letter, it was fulfilled on the day of Pentecost. Hear the inspired Peter reading and commenting upon this very prophecy, and saying, "This is that which was spoken by the prophet Joel," etc.

Did it actually come to pass, that *whosoever* called upon the name of the Lord, was saved?

"Then they that gladly received his word, were baptized; and the same day there were added unto them about three thousand souls." v. 41. "And the Lord added to the church daily, such as should be saved." v. 47.

Who are the characters that "should be saved?"

"Whosoever shall call on the name of the Lord," says the *foreknowledge of* God.

How were they to call on His name, and obtain salvation?

Peter tells them, verse 38: "Repent and be baptized every one of you, in the name of Jesus Christ, for the remission of sins, and ye shall receive the gift of the Holy Spirit."

Do you pretend that this out-pouring of the Spirit was "upon all flesh," and that it actually sanctified, set apart, or "elected" unto obedience, and sprinkling of the blood of Jesus Christ," all mankind, even those strangers to whom Peter wrote?

No, sir. There was a "remnant" not called, or elected, on that day; and I presume these "strangers throughout Pontus, Galatia, Cappadocia, Asia and Bithynia," were of this Gentile "remnant;" but if they were, they also 'were "elected" in precisely the same way, at the house of Cornelius, when God extended the "call" to the Gentile world. The same facts occurred and the same results followed throughout the Gentile world. The apostles proclaimed everywhere the new oracle—the twelve to the circumcision, and Paul and his co-laborers to the Gentiles—that "whosoever shall call on the name of the Lord shall be saved."

Not a single instance of out-pouring upon any *individual,* as such, to qualify him for obedience and sprinkling of the blood of Jesus Christ," is upon record. All the "flesh" of Abraham received it, metonymically, on the day of Pentecost; and all the "remnant" at the house of Cornelius. All mankind, therefore, are elected, or set apart to obedience— made eligible thereunto—and that in exact accordance with the foreknowledge of God, the Father, through sanctification of the Spirit.

Hence, as Paul tells the Athenians, God *"now* commands *all* men, *everywhere,* to repent." And he will hold no man guiltless who slights the gracious privilege conferred by the election "unto obedience." This must be gladly embraced, and used as a stepping-stone to the election "unto salvation," which, "from the beginning," has been attained only "through sanctification of the Spirit," or election to obedience on the part of God, and "belief of the truth" on the part of the creature. Dying sinners, will you not, at once, improve the privilege you enjoy, and by obedience, secure the election to salvation, and thus become a candidate for eternal life? For I tell you, plainly while you reject obedience and the blood of Jesus, to which you are now elected, you can neither be saved from your past sins, nor become a candidate for the immortal joys at God's right hand. You are ineligible by the divine constitution for any such aspirations; and it is folly to expect the Divine Sovereign to alter the constitution for your accommodation, when he has taken such pains to make the path to eligibility "so plain, that the wayfaring man, though a fool, need not err therein."

Much more might be said in illustration of the subject. Enough, however, I think, has been said to make the subject sufficiently plain to the *thinking* mind. Those who will not think, there is but little hope of benefiting. A brief recapitulation is all, therefore, that I shall detain you with now, leaving the obviation of objections, and the further elaboration of the positions taken, to a future occasion, should such a work be found necessary.

We have seen that the subject of election, when stripped of the sectarian garb in which it has generally been clothed by theologians, whether they have been assailants or defenders of it, — I say, when looked at in its Bible dress, it is found a very plain, and by no means a repulsive subject. In contemplating it *Scripturally,* we are led to admire the universal benevolence of Jehovah in every phase of it.

In choosing a nation from among the nations of the earth, as the depository of his will, the exponent of his mighty power, and the medium through which a Redeemer should be given to the RACE, he exhibits wisdom, propriety and benevolence to the race at large.

In selecting the BEING on whom he was pleased to lay the redemption of the race, could men, or angels, have suggested a choice that would have done higher honor to the wisdom or benevolence of God?

In the selection of patriarchs, prophets and apostles, the good of mankind is manifestly the leading motive consulted, and the choice always demonstrates the wisdom of the Great Elector.

In arranging the conditions of salvation and eternal life for the race at large, how benevolent in him to enfranchise the whole race, by an election to obedience, and sprinkling of the blood of Jesus; and thus put it in the power of every one to enter upon a career of grace here, to be terminated in glory hereafter!

Language fails to give utterance to the admiration his boundless goodness inspires.

"Come, then, expressive silence
Muse his praise!"

-----o-----

Letter from J. T. Johnson.

NICHOLASVILLE, March 22, 1856.

DEAR BROTHER FALL: Entertaining for your person the highest regard; confiding, to every reasonable extent, in your knowledge and judgment of the science, the genius and spirit of Christianity; and conscious that independence is part and parcel of your education and character, I have taken the liberty of presenting you some of the conclusions to which I have been conducted in my investigations of the Christian Scriptures.

1. That God has ever had a government in and over this world. It was developed in the Patriarchal age; in the Legal age; and the Gospel age.

2. God has ruled the world by his Son ever since he was enthroned, some 1820 years since.

3. The government established is perfect, as regards both the naturalization of the alien and the government of the citizen.

4. That love is the element and cement for happiness and strength; and this feeling and sentiment is to characterize all that is said and done.

5. This singular community, overcome by love, and voluntarily coming out of the world, must band themselves together, in the fear of God, for his worship, and to labor for the accomplishment of all that is required, as expressed in his code.

6. This Body is required to select its officers for the purposes of government; who, in conjunction with the Body, are under supreme obligations to keep the Body pure and active in the discharge of every duty.

7. These officers are overseers, or bishops and deacons. They, together with the members, are subject to Christ, their Head; and these officers are subject to appointment and removal, at the pleasure of the congregation, subject to our Supreme Lawgiver, who is able to save and destroy.

8. In our view of the subject, each congregation is independent of every other. Its internal concerns are subject to no tribunal on earth. Its external fellowship with others is another matter entirely. It may seek benefit from every quarter.

9. These congregations, as such, owe obligations to each other, in extending the Redeemer's kingdom, and in imparting the blessings of his government to every living thing.

10. These congregations, with the aforementioned officers, are the highest religious tribunals on earth. They are responsible to the Supreme Head for all internal and external duties, and to no one else.

11. The Bishops, or Overseers, are *now* the highest and most important officers belonging to the Body. And whenever it is practicable, a plurality is necessary to each congregation for its perfection and purity, and any assumption, that more than one will work an injury, is based on the untenable ground, that Christian Bishops cannot rule in harmony and love. May the Lord save us from ambitious, envious and jealous Bishops.

12. The congregation, with its officers, have the power to select and ordain Evangelists, to sound out the Gospel and extend the boundaries of the reign of Christ, and to establish congregations, subject to the appointing power. He is the head, subject to the control of his Head.

13. In general movements and enterprises,

either for the spread of the Gospel, the endowment of a college or school, the relief of the orphan boy or girl, or the education of pious persons for the Christian ministry, the necessity of a general concert, general consent, and general action is apparent and self-evident. Yet who can find, in the New Institution, a power in this general assemblage to select and ordain Elders, Deacons, or Evangelists?

14. The best system on earth will work badly with bad men. An imperfect system will work very well with good men.

Each congregation is more wisely and benevolently organized by the Lord's arrangement, than human wisdom ever conceived. Yet many seem not to see it. Who can be more interested than the congregation itself, in its own edification, purity and happiness? We may need helps, and are at liberty to call them in. If we reject their advice, if the Lord approves, well; if he does not, we pay the penalty.

Personal piety proceeding from a heart overflowing with love to God and man is the thing to be aimed at. What a mighty revolution could be accomplished in 12 months, if every disciple of Christ would become imitators of the apostles, and emulate each other in doing good. To feel for the miseries of others, and to relieve them, is pure and undefiled religion.

For the present, yours truly,

J. T. JOHNSON.

-----o-----

Our Position as a Religious Community. No. 7.

WE closed our article under this head last month, in considering some of the common apologies offered for maintaining and holding on to human creeds. In that article we considered apologies 1 and 2. In this we proceed to

Apology 3. One of the most common excuses offered for human creeds, is that, "We want something to keep us together—something to bind us in union." This apology is based virtually upon the same two preposterous assumptions we have before mentioned. It assumes, with great apparent innocence, that the Bible cannot keep us together, that it cannot bind us in union. Then it assumes, with much modesty, that a human creed *can* keep us together—bind us in union—*can do* what the Bible *cannot do*. This, it appears to us, should startle any good man at once. These assumptions are arrogant in the extreme, and not only arrogant, but made without any regard to facts. Do human creeds keep churches together? We assert, fearless of successful contradiction, that the whole history of human creeds proves that they do not keep churches together. Let us take one look at three of the most popular creeds in this country, and see what they have done in keeping churches together. How has the Baptist creed succeeded? Has it kept the Baptists together? By no means. From the one original Baptist stock we have now not less than nine or ten parties of Baptists. How has the Presbyterian creed succeeded in keeping its adherents together? It is thought to be a very wise and powerful document. Has it kept Presbyterians together? It has succeeded no better than the Baptist creed. With all its adhesive power, Presbyterians, within the last century have sundered into some eight parties. This needs no commentary. How has the Methodist Discipline succeeded? It is itself nothing but an offshoot of the Episcopalian creed, which did not prevent the Methodists from stranding off from the Established Church. The Discipline has not been in operation more than one hundred and twenty years. How has it succeeded in keeping Methodists together during that period? During that time Methodism has stranded into some eight or ten fragments. What a comment this furnishes upon the efficacy of human creeds to cement together. Other creeds have done no better; and yet, in the face of all this, men want human creeds to *keep them together!*

But now we lay along side of this another fact. While the inspired apostles were in the church; while the Holy Spirit, not merely as a Comforter, as he is and has always been in the Church, but inspiring men, delivering revelations through them, performing miracles to confirm them, and displaying many spiritual gifts, the church had no creed but the law of God. Nor did they have any other creed for more than two hundred years, in the days of the church's greatest prosperity, her greatest unity and greatest glory, than the word of God. Nor did they, while there was no creed but the law of God, have but one church or one order. Not only so, but we are not aware that the church ever did divide, where there was no law, no rule of faith, no creed but the Bible. We do not doubt but trivial factions took place in individual congregations, but anything like a general division in the whole body, resulting in two distinct orders or denominations from the time of the division forward, has never taken place, that we are aware of, where they had no creed but the Bible. All history shows, beyond all dispute, that wherever human creeds have prevailed, divisions have abounded, partyism has increased, and unity has been diminished. But where the people had confidence in the Bible, the law of God, the "perfect law of liberty," union has more widely extended, and peace has more generally prevailed. Why then, in the name of reason, hold on to human creeds to keep churches together, when they have so universally failed, and refuse the Bible, which has never failed?

Apology 4. "We simply want our creed to distinguish us from other denominations. How could we understand and discriminate between our doctrine and the doctrine of other denominations, if our doctrine were not set forth definitely in a creed?" But why do you wish to distinguish between yourselves and other Christians? The very circumstance of keeping up these distinctions, and perpetuating divisions, which, we know, is the work of human creeds, is a strong argument against them. No distinctions in doctrine should be kept up among the people of God; and the apology we are considering admits that these distinctions would be lost sight of, if we had no human creeds. If we had no creeds but the Bible, we would have nothing to believe but the Bible, and nothing else to describe our faith, and, as a matter of course, would have no faith but Bible faith. We would have no names but Bible names, no doctrine but Bible doctrine, no churches but Christian churches, and no law but the law of God. We would have no authority but the authority of God. The submission would be to him, and not to man. Men would trust in him, rely upon him, and honor him, and not trust in, rely upon and honor some human contrivance, and forget him. It is no honor to any Christian man to distinguish his doctrine from that of some other man, or even to show that he is more orthodox than another; but it is an honor to any man to distinguish his Saviour from every other teacher or head in the universe, and to distinguish his doctrine from every other doctrine, and hold on to him and his doctrine with the utmost pertinacity. This, too, is easily done, if any man will set himself about the work. There is no teacher like him, or that a man may mistake for him; nor is there any head of church or state that bears the least similitude to him. The main body of clerical teachers, the great bishops, archbishops, cardinals and the pope, are as unlike him as heaven and earth. No one acquainted with his character, as delineated upon the pages of the New Testament, would ever mistake the pope or a vast majority of the clergy for him, or their works for his. Nor would any man acquainted with his doctrine, as set forth by his apostles, mistake any of the other doctrines of these times for his. There is not a sufficient similitude to lead to any such mistake on the part of any man who is on the lookout, or as the Lord commanded, who is *watching*. There is, therefore, no excuse for keeping creeds to enable parties to recognize distinctions between parties, for the very recognition of these distinctions is an assistant in keeping up partyism, and a mighty hindrance to the union for which our Lord prayed.

Apology 5. "Why assail our creed? We do not receive nor expel members by the creed. Many of our members never saw it." In such cases as this, and there are many of them, we admit the creed does but little harm compared with one in lively operation and full force. But the reason of its doing less harm is, that in such a case they are approaching what we are pleading for. A creed partially dead is not as bad as one fully alive. But still, in such a case as mentioned in this apology, the idea is kept up that we have a creed and it contains *our doctrine*. It is true one who never saw his creed, as a matter of course does not know what is contained in it, or does not know what his own doctrine is, and really does not know whether he believes it or not. But still when his mind reverts to his doctrine, it turns to his creed. Thus the creed, though he never saw it, calls his attention when he does happen to reflect upon religion, and diverts it from the bible. In the place of having it fixed in his mind that his doctrine is in the bible, that when he would examine it he should go to his bible, the preposterous idea is settled in his mind, that his doctrine is in his creed, which he never saw, and if he would consult it, he must go to the creed.

But we ask any man, in the name of common sense, what use a creed can be which is not read in the church, which many of the members never saw, and which is used in no way in the church or private families? The faith of a church should not be laid away in a creed in some safe drawer, but should be alive in the hearts of the members, producing fruits of righteousness. What strange freaks we find in the religious world! There are thousands of people in this country who never saw their creed, the book containing their own articles of faith, their own faith and order; who have taken so little interest in it, that they have never tried to see it, nor to get to read one line in it, and who, of course, know nothing about what is contained in it; but who will be offended in one moment, when we tell them that their creed is useless. And yet, what man of understanding can fail to see that in all such cases the Koran, the Book of Mormon, or a last year's almanac, would have done just as well! How strange too; in all the creed-making assemblies, the utmost pertinacity is seen to have every word exactly so. The doctrine must be expressed in just so many and just such words, without the omission of the cross of a *t* or the dot of an *i*. When this system of doctrine is complete, it must be sacredly regarded and defended. But how many of the members ever know anything about it? What proportion of them can ever be said to believe it? Not one in fifty of all in the parties now under the domination of human creeds. The people in general have never read their own creeds, and have never heard them read, except some particular portions of them. They do not know, and are not any the worse of it, what is contained in them. But still they cannot do without the creed! They would be ruined to set it aside! We should like to know wherein? That creed, that they never read, of the contents of which they know nothing, did not make them Christians. Faith in that creed did not convert them, or bring them to God. If they are Christians at all, faith in God, in the Redeemer and Saviour of men, in the word of God, in the gospel of Christ has made them such, and to God and the word of his grace, they should commit themselves, their everlasting trust, and not allow themselves to be divided by human creeds.   B. F.

-----o-----

The Contrast Fairly Stated.
No. II.

ON page 8th, the Doctor says, "The body possesses no unity, but errors of every shade find a home in it." This is not only untrue in itself, but it contains one of the most malignant, premeditated and willful misstatements ever contained in the same number of words. The true state of the case is as precisely the opposite of this as language can express it. There is no such unity among anybody of people on this earth; nor is there anybody of people in the world among whom errors of every shade find so little repose, or are so far from finding a home. Every preacher and writer is entirely free and untrammeled, with the most perfect liberty to attack, assail, expose, and refute every error of every shade that makes its appearance. Their motto is *the truth, the whole truth, and nothing but the truth.* Every preacher is under the most solemn obligation, to "contend earnestly for the faith once delivered to the saints" — to "preach the word," —"preach Christ"— to "make known nothing but Christ and him crucified"—to "glory in nothing but the cross"—to "stop the mouths of gainsayers," and "put to silence the foolishness of ignorant men." Not only so, but every private member has "the right of private judgment," and the privilege to express it, even to a preacher, and this right is exercised.

No man among the Disciples has any right, or privilege, to preach any doctrine but the doctrine of Christ. The doctrine of Christ, the whole of it, and nothing else, is the length and breadth, the height and depth, of the faith of a Christian. Every man among the Disciples that oversteps the bounds of the doctrine of Christ, or stops short of it, is not only liable to be assailed, but certain to be exposed, both publicly and privately, by both preachers and private members, as far as he is deemed worthy of notice. If he is a popular and influential man, the public journals lay their hand on him and his career is soon checked. This is not only the best means of securing the truth to a religious body, but the only divine means for keeping the faith uncorrupted and pure to the day of Jesus Christ. But Dr. R. has the honor of belonging to a church and preaching for it, that not only is a home for some of the worst errors in the world, but these errors are canonized, sanctioned and maintained by the highest ecclesiastical authority in his church, and he dare not touch them; and as to unity, the Disciples have maintained their unity, without any division of any importance, or any general division in the body, while Presbyterians are wrangling about church government, New School and Old School, some maintaining the most ultra fatal Calvinism, and others, as the Beechers, like wandering stars, seeking an escape from Calvanism, in Unitarianism, or pre-existence, or transmigration of souls. Look to the disputes of Dr. Wilson, of Finney and many others, within the last thirty years; and the later disputes on Slavery, of which the debate between Dr. N. L. Rice and Blanchard, is a fair illustration, and behold the *unity* of Presbyterians, and how beautiful it is for brethren to dwell together in unity! Here, if it were desirable to dwell upon the frailties of human nature, or the imbecility of human systems, a subject might be found not only for a tract, but for many volumes, showing that the legitimate tendency of the works of all such men as Dr. R. is to prevent anything like harmony, unity and love, from ever obtaining among the children of God. How different where Disciples have been preaching the word of God! They have entered communities where the people were divided into parties and commenced preaching peace by Jesus Christ, who is Lord of all, and collected men from all these parties, united them upon the foundation of apostles and prophets, Jesus Christ being the chief corner stone—seated them down together in heavenly places in Christ, having destroyed the enmity that was between them and made them one. This is the work that troubles Dr. R.

On page 14, Dr. R. proceeds to speak of "some of the acknowledged evils of the system." Here we find pettifogging in abundance. Here the Dr. enters his old trade of *sophistry*. Where does he look to find "some of the acknowledged evils of the *system?*" He gravely proceeds to quotations from Mr. Campbell, in which he speaks pretty freely of *mistakes in practice,* or of men having failed to carry out the system. As a matter of course, the errors in practice, in the estimation of a deceived man, or one who would deceive others, are to be made an objection to the system itself. So sophistry teaches, so sophistical doctors think, or, at least would make others think. The logic is this: Some men, who have received Christianity as their only system, Mr. Campbell acknowledges, have failed to teach and practice it correctly; therefore, there are acknowledged evils in the system. Dr. Rice may extend his reasoning still more widely. By the same sophistry, the same system might have been condemned in Paul's time. He confessed that there was division in the church at Corinth—that a corrupt man had his father's wife—that brethren went to law with brethren—that the Lord's Supper was turned into a Pagan feast, and that many in that church denied the resurrection of the dead. Some enemy heads an article, "Acknowledged Evils of the System," and then proceeds to quote the apostle, where he makes these godly and candid admissions, that certain men had failed to practice the holy system which the Lord had given. Look here! exclaims our pettifogger, what a list of "acknowledged evils" I have collected from Paul's own pen! This same sophistry is used by infidels against the holy religion of our Lord and Savior. They point us to the defections, unloveliness and perverseness of such men as Dr. R.; to their bitterness of spirit, proneness to misrepresentation, selfish and partisan course, and make such men an objection to the religion of Christ and to the Christian ministry. The only reply that can be made, is the one that must now be made to Dr. R., viz: That we must distinguish between the *system* and the *practice*. The system is divine; the practice is human. The system is perfect; the practice is imperfect. God made the system; man practices it, or *professes* to practice it, but sometimes comes far short. His failure in the practice, in the place of being an "acknowledged evil in the system," is only an evil *in the man,* a departure from the system. The wayward course of such unlovely, opposing and averse men, under a profession of religion, or in the ministry, is no evidence against the system, religion, or the ministry, but an evidence of the weakness and imperfection of such men. They would be perverse under any system. They are not exponents of the religion they profess, nor the system they have adopted. The system is not to be judged by the men, but the men must be judged by the system.

"The system examined and its errors exposed," is the next head. Under this head, the Dr. attacks, demolishes, kills and buries "Baptismal Regeneration." If he only could invent some way of keeping it *killed,* so that it would not have to be killed over again every new moon, it would save an immense amount of hard labor. But no method has yet been invented to kill it, so that it will *stay* killed. It is impossible to tell how many times Dr. Rice has killed, buried and cast into oblivion this horrible doctrine of Baptismal Regeneration; but still, if we could believe him, it is alive, and efforts must be made to kill it. Now, that Dr. N. L. R. knows that the Disciples no more believe in Baptismal Regeneration than he does, is just as certain as that he is a man of common sense. But, since he is haunted with Baptismal Regeneration, and determines to keep telling that the Disciples believe in it, he shall have a little baptismal regeneration from that pure and, with him, almost infallible source, John Calvin.

"From our faith derives three advantages, which require to be distinctly considered. The first is, that it is proposed to us by the Lord as a symbol or token of our purification; or, to express my meaning more fully, it resembles a legal instrument properly attested, by which he assures us that all our sins are cancelled, effaced and obliterated, so that they will never appear in his sight, or come into his remembrance, or be imputed to us. For he commands all who believe to be baptized for the remission of their sins. Therefore, those who have imagined that baptism is nothing more than a mark or sign by which we profess our religion before men, as soldiers wear the insignia of their sovereign as a mark of their profession, have not considered that which is the principal thing in baptism, which is, that we ought to receive it with this promise, 'He that believeth and is baptized shall be saved.'" Calvin's Institutes, vol. 2, p. 477.

"Nor must it be supposed that baptism is administered only for the time past, so that for sins into which we fall after baptism it would be necessary to seek other new remedies of expiation in I know not what other sacraments, as if the virtue of baptism were become obsolete. In consequence of this error, it happened in other ages, that some persons would not be baptized except at the close of their life, and almost in the moment of death, that so they might obtain pardon for their whole life—a preposterous caution, which is frequently censured in the writings of the ancient bishops. But we ought to conclude, that at whatever time we are baptized, we are washed and purified for the whole life. Whenever we have fallen, therefore, we must recur to the remembrance of baptism, and arm our minds with the consideration of it, that we may be always certified and assured of the remission of our sins." Calvin's Institutes, vol. 2, p. 478.

Here is baptism not only for past but future sins, and baptism, by implication, a "remedy of expiation" for sins. But let the doctor hear Calvin again:

"I know the common opinion is that remission of sins, which at our first regeneration we receive by baptism alone, is afterward obtained by repentance and the benefit of the keys. But the advocates of this opinion have fallen into an error, for want of considering that the power of the keys of which they speak, is so dependent on baptism that it cannot by any means be separated from it." Calvin's Inst., vol 2, p. 479.

Commenting upon the expression of Paul, "So many of us as were baptized into Jesus Christ, were baptized into his death: therefore we are buried with him by baptism into death, that we should walk in newness of life," Calvin says: "In this passage he does not merely exhort us to an imitation of Christ, as if he had said that we are admonished by baptism, that after the example of his death we should die to sin, and that after the example of his resurrection we should rise to righteousness; but he goes considerably further, and teaches us that by baptism Christ has made us partakers of his death, in order that we may be engrafted into it." Calvin's Inst., vol. 2, p. 480. On the same page, he says: "Thus we are promised, first, the gratuitous remission of sins and imputation of righteousness; and, secondly, the grace of the Holy Spirit to reform us to newness of life." Again, on page 481, he says, "Thus John first, and the apostles afterward, baptized with the baptism of *repentance,* intending regeneration and, by *remission of sins,* absolution." Here Calvin teaches that John the Baptist and the apostles taught "the baptism of repentance, intending *regeneration,*" and that this was for "remission of sins, or absolution." But Dr. R. must be well instructed, by his venerable father Calvin, on this subject He says again, on the same page: "John and the apostles agreed in the same doctrine; both baptized to repentance, both to remission of sins; both baptized in the name of Christ, from whom repentance and remission of sins proceeded." Still further, same page, he says: "For who will attend to Chrysostom, who denies that remission of sins was included in the baptism of John, rather than to Luke, who, on the contrary, affirms that John came preaching the baptism of repentance for the remission of sins. Nor must we admit that subtlety of Augustine, 'that in the baptism of John sins were remitted in hope, but in the baptism of Christ they were remitted in fact.' For as the evangelist clearly testifies that John, in his baptism, promised the remission of sins, why should we diminish this commendation, when no necessity constrains us to it?"

Let the doctor have patience, and he shall be well enlightened from Calvin. Hear him in regard to infants: "And therefore even infants themselves bring their own condemnation into the world with them, who, though they have not yet produced the fruits of their iniquity, yet have the seed of it within them; even their whole nature is, as it were, a seed of sin, and therefore cannot but be odious and abominable to God. By baptism, believers are certified that this condemnation is removed from them; since, as we said, the Lord promises us by this sign, that a full and entire remission is granted, both of the guilt which is to be imputed to us, and of the punishment to be inflicted on account of that guilt; they also receive righteousness, such as the people of God may obtain in this life; that is, only by imputation, because the Lord, in his mercy, accepts them as righteous and innocent." Institutes, vol. 2, p. 483. Hear Calvin again: "Ananias, therefore, only intended to say to Paul, 'That thou mayest be assured that thy sins are forgiven, be baptized. For in baptism the Lord promises remission of sins; receive this and be secure.'" Institutes, p. 487. Again, page 488, he says: "By baptism God promises remission of sins, and will certainly fulfill to all believers: that promise was offered to us in baptism; let us, therefore, embrace it by faith: it was long dormant by reason of our unbelief; now, then, let us receive it by faith." Please hear Calvin yet again: "The virtue, dignity, utility and end of this mystery, have now, if I mistake not, been sufficiently explained. With respect to the external symbol, I sincerely wish that the genuine institution of Christ had the influence it ought to have, to repress the audacity of man. For, as though it were a contemptible thing to be baptized in water according to the precept of Christ, men have invented a benediction, or rather incantation, to pollute the true consecration of the water." Institutes, vol. 2, p. 490. Be not surprised at the mention of being "baptized *in water,*" here, for on the next page, Calvin says: "The very word *baptize,* however, signifies to immerse; and it is certain that immersion was the practice of the ancient church."

But to close up these quotations from Calvin, let us hear him once more, urging the necessity, not only of infant baptism, but infant regeneration: "For if they pretend that infants do not perish, even though they are considered as children of Adam, their error is abundantly refuted in Scripture. For when it pronounces that in Adam all die,' it follows that there remains no hope of life but in Christ. In order to become heirs of life, therefore, it is necessary for us to be partakers of him. So, when it is said, in other places, that we are 'by nature the children of wrath,' and 'conceived in sin,' with which condemnation is always connected, it follows, that we must depart from our own nature to have any admission to the kingdom of God. And what can be more explicit than this declaration, that 'flesh and blood cannot inherit the kingdom of God '? Let everything of our own, therefore, be destroyed, which will not be affected without regeneration, and then we shall see this possession of the kingdom of God. Lastly, if Christ speaks the truth when he declares himself to be 'life,' it is necessary for us to be engrafted into him, that we may be rescued from the bondage of death. But how, it is inquired, are infants regenerated, who have no knowledge either of good or evil? We reply, that the work of God is not yet without existence, because it is not observed or understood by us. Now, it is certain that some infants are saved; and that they are previously regenerated by the Lord, is beyond all doubt. For if they are born in a state of corruption, it is necessary for them to be purified before they are admitted into the kingdom of God, into which 'there shall in no wise enter anything that defileth.' If they are born sinners, as both David and Paul affirm, either they must remain unacceptable and hateful to God, or it is necessary for them to be justified." Institutes, vol. 2, p. 508.

Now, if the Doctor please, he will turn to the Confession of Faith, page 144, and read as follows: "Baptism is a sacrament of the New Testament, ordained by Jesus Christ, not only for the admission of the party baptized into the visible church, but also to be unto him a sign and seal of the covenant of grace, of his engrafting into Christ, of regeneration, of remission of sins, and of his giving up unto God, through Jesus Christ, to walk in newness of life; which sacrament is, by Christ's own appointment, to be continued in his church until the end of the world." Now, the reader will bear in mind, that it is here stated that baptism is "for the admission of the party baptized in to the visible church." Please compare this with the following from Confession, page 394: "Baptism is not to be administered to any that are out of the visible church, till they profess faith in Christ, and obedience to him; but the infants of such as are members of the visible church, are to be baptized." This cuts off all children whose parents are not members of the visible church, and debars them from admittance into the visible church, and from the "sign of regeneration and remission of sins." Now what becomes of all these infants, who die out of the visible church? Let the following answer: "They who having never heard the gospel, know not Jesus Christ, and believe not in him, cannot be saved." Con., p. 208. If we would be certain, in regard to all children,—those not in the church, with the whole pagan world, look at the following: "The visible church is a society made up of all such as in all ages and places of the world do profess the true religion, and of their children."—Con., p. 209. Here is the body of Christ, or the visible church, consisting of those who *profess the true religion, and their children.* Of whom is Christ the Saviour? "He is the Saviour *only of his body, the church."* According to this, Christ is not even the saviour of those infants whose parents are not in the visible church and, consequently, if they are saved, it must be *without a Saviour.* This is no forced construction, but evidently the plain and obvious import of the Confession, hence, on page 64, we have the following; "Elect infants, dying in infancy, are regenerated and saved by Christ through the spirit, who worketh when, and where, and how he pleaseth." But what of *non-elect* infants, who die in infancy? for if there be any non elect, they must have been non-elect when in infancy, and "from all eternity." What of all these infants, of parents not members of the true church, who are here decided out of the body, of whom Christ is not the Saviour? Dr. R. Says: "None of these die in infancy!" *No* matter when they die; they always were non-elect, always will be, and cannot be saved, for they never had a Saviour! Here we have, not "all sorts of doctrine," for then we should find some good, but the most pernicious doctrine, not only of water regeneration, regeneration of elect infants, but of infants without a Saviour! Not simply preached by some ignorant and irresponsible preacher, but put forth and bound upon the unenlightened by a learned and powerful tribunal of Presbyterian *divines!* Nor is this even a tithe of the preposterous absurdities contained in this book.

Would it not be a brilliant move for the Disciples to yield the scripture doctrine of regeneration, which they hold and teach—that we are begotten not of corruptible, but of incorruptible seed, the Word of God—that we are born, not of blood, nor of the will of man, nor of the will of the flesh, but of God—that except a man be born again he cannot see the kingdom of God—that ye must be born again—that if thou shalt believe in thine heart that God raised our Lord from the dead, and confess with the mouth, that thou shalt be saved—that to whomsoever a man *yields himself* a servant to obey, his servant he is—to yield the doctrine of personal submission to Christ, in personal confession, with *the whole heart,* in personal and willing obedience, under the divine influence of a previous change and purification of heart by faith, in which the entire being bows to the authority of the great King, for an empty, lifeless, spiritless, system of infant regeneration, baptism and membership, in which the subject has no will, no heart, does not yield to God, and about which it has no more personal knowledge than it has of being born into the world? No, Doctor; while the Disciples believe there is a God, a glorious Saviour, in whom dwells all the fullness of the Godhead bodily, a Holy Spirit, sent to reprove the world; that man is an accountable being, and that the gospel of Jesus, the Christ, is divine,—never, NEVER, NEVER, while they recollect their confession of the name of Jesus, and the solemn covenant into which they entered with him, voluntarily, in penitence, trembling and tears, dare they, can they yield for the poor, empty, and unmeaning ceremony of infant church-membership? No, sir; nor can you have any heart, good feeling, nor pious emotions in your warning and entreaty with the people not to unite with the Disciples. You know, or, if you do not, the fault is your own, that you do not hold a truth of heaven, a holy impulse, act or thought not held by the Disciples of our Lord Jesus Christ. You know, or might know, if you would inform yourself, that if all the truth held by the Disciples were stricken out of your church, that not one scrap of anything divine would remain in it. What is the meaning, then, of your warning, other than the struggle of a determined partisan, to maintain a system that cannot stand the test of gospel light and truth?

Dr. R. says, "The only other doctrine of Mr. Campbell which claims particular attention, is his denial of the influence of the Holy Spirit in regeneration and sanctification." p. 30. Now, if Dr. R. does not know that Mr. Campbell does not deny, but has always admitted and asserted the influence of the Holy Spirit in regeneration and sanctification, he is certainly much more blinded by determined partisan zeal than even the most enlightened thought possible. The very first quotation he makes, to prove that Mr. Campbell denies the influence of the Holy Spirit in regeneration, asserts that the "Holy Spirit puts forth *moral and converting power."* The question of which Mr. Campbell was speaking, was not whether the Holy Spirit put forth converting and sanctifying power, or influence; for Mr. Campbell constantly asserted that he does put forth this influence; but whether he puts it forth *through his word,* or *abstractly from, it.* Mr. Campbell asserts that the Holy Spirit puts forth power, or influence, in conversion and sanctification, in the following quotation, made and italicized by Dr. R.: "As the spirit of man puts forth all its moral power in the words which it fills with its ideas, so the Spirit of God puts forth all its converting and sanctifying. power in the words which it fills with its ideas." This expression of Mr. Campbell, asserting that the Holy Spirit puts forth power in converting and sanctifying, is quoted by Dr. R. to prove that Mr. Campbell denies the power, or influence, of the Holy Spirit in regeneration and sanctification! As if to show his blindness and stupidity more fully, he quotes the following from Mr. Campbell, to prove the same thing: "We plead that all the converting power of the Holy Spirit is exhibited in the Divine Word." Here Mr. Campbell is speaking of the "converting power of the Holy Spirit," and how it is exhibited, in the very words quoted by Dr. R. to prove that he denies the influence of the Holy Spirit in regeneration and sanctification! The Holy Spirit not only *influences* men in their conversion and sanctification, but all converted and brought to God, are *converted by the Holy Spirit.* By one Spirit are they all baptized into one body. The Holy Spirit as certainly puts forth his influence, exercises his power, and the work of regeneration and sanctification is done by him, and is as much his, though he does it through the word of truth, the ministry, ordinances, and acts of obedience, as if he had done the same work without the use of any instrumentalities. Dr. R. has been challenged for ten years, and so have all who believe with him, to produce an instance, where the Holy Spirit has converted and sanctified one person in the absence of the gospel, declared by Paul to be "the power of God unto salvation to everyone that believeth;" but an instance of this kind neither he nor any man has or ever can produce. But instances numerous are recorded upon the sacred pages, where men were converted by the power of the Spirit of God, put forth through the gospel. The Holy Spirit of God now puts forth his influence through the gospel and the ministry, his divinely chosen means, and converts men in numerous instances. In the face of all this, Dr. Rice comes forth and publishes, and Presbyterians circulate, in a tract, that those who believe that the Holy Spirit operates through the gospel in converting men, deny the influence of the Holy Spirit in conversion and sanctification! The apostles, under the infallible influence of the Holy Spirit of God, preached the gospel, to convert men, to turn them from darkness to light, and by the power and authority of the Spirit converted thousands. All the ministers sent of God, in our time, preach the gospel to convert men; and all those converted by the Holy Spirit, so far as yet informed, have been converted through his own divinely appointed means, the gospel, the ministry, etc., nor is there one scrap of authority for any man to preach, that men can be converted, or try to convert men, without the gospel. And to allege that he who believes, and teaches, that the Spirit of God operates through the gospel, and the ministry, in conversion and sanctification, denies the influence of the Spirit, is as wicked as it is illogical and untrue. Such manifest misrepresentations may serve to prejudice, mislead and darken the minds of those whom a good ministry of Jesus Christ should enlighten and save, but will involve him who practices it, in an awful predicament to stand the final decision of the Judge who knows what is in man. Dr. R. says, "Indeed, if the doctrine of Mr. Campbell be true, prayers for the conversion of sinners, and the sanctification of believers, are wholly unavailing and useless. Are they not solemn mockery?" What is here called "the doctrine of Mr. Campbell," is the doctrine of the New Testament, that the Holy Spirit converts sinners and sanctifies believers through the word, or through the truth. David says, "The word of the Lord is perfect, *converting the soul."* Here, doctor, follows the seed sown by the Holy Spirit, which springs forth in the new birth, or regeneration. The Spirit says, "Being born again, not of corruptible seed, but of incorruptible, by the word of God, which liveth and abideth forever." 1 Pet. i: 23. Here is the seed which the Spirit of God sows in the heart, to produce the new creation, the new birth, or regeneration. All born of this incorruptible seed, the *word of God,* are born of the Spirit. It is the work of the Spirit, just as much as if he had seen fit to perform it without the incorruptible seed, the word of God. Now will Dr. R. face these holy and infallible teachings, and declare that he will not henceforth pray for the conversion of sinners, because "the law of the Lord is perfect, *converting* the soul," and the Spirit of God itself, speaking through the holy apostle, declares, that we are "born again not of corruptible seed, but of incorruptible, by the *word of God.* Now will he refuse to pray for the conversion of sinners, and call it mockery thus to pray, simply because the Spirit of God has seen fit to make the word of God the seed of regeneration, or the new birth, or because he regenerates or converts men through the word, and not without the word? As well might he refuse to pray for his daily bread, because the Lord does not give it to him by an abstract operation of the Spirit, without the tedious process of tilling the ground.

But there is something a little more serious still for the Dr. to reflect upon here. If sanctification of believers is through the Word, as Mr. Campbell teaches, the Dr. asks, "is not prayer solemn mockery?" All the disciples of Christ answer, No; for our Lord and Master prayed the Father, for believers, "Sanctify them *through thy truth: thy Word is truth."* Dr. R., do you call that prayer, "solemn mockery?" No, sir, you know it is not. Then, take back that rash and unchristian expression, and join with our gracious Lord in most solemn and fervent prayer to the Almighty Father, to sanctify believers *"through thy truth."* It is sanctification of the Spirit, though through the truth, just as much as if it were without the truth. Come Dr., take back all this rashness, and remember that the whole is the work of the Spirit, both in regeneration and sanctification, and it is just as important that we should pray that it may be done, if the Spirit does it through the truth, as if he did it separate from, or without the Word.

The limited space allotted to this tract is now near filled, and a very few words must close it.

1. The cause of the tract, penned by Dr. R., no doubt, was his mortification arising from so many people being converted from sectarianism in reading the Lexington Debate. He has come to the conclusion, that his productions, touching the positions of the Presbyterians and Christians, in a tract, circulated among his brethren without Mr. Campbell's replies, will prove more effectual.

2. Many Presbyterians will hear the Disciples preach, become awakened, and exchange their birth-right membership, conferred upon them without their choice or knowledge, for the membership proposed by the Saviour, into which they choose for themselves to enter, in personal confession and submission to God. This annoys Dr. R. exceedingly, and this he hoped to avert, in some degree, by sending a tract, prejudicial to the Disciples, to be circulated and read privately by his brethren.

3. Dr. R. knows, that a large majority of the members of his church, never decided for themselves to become members, did not choose the Presbyterian doctrine, church, or creed, or know anything about it when inducted into the church; and that when the consciences of honest persons of this kind, are awakened by the plain preaching of Christ among the Disciples, and they act for themselves, choose and decide the course they will take, they choose to go with the Disciples. This he hoped to prevent, in some degree, by prejudicing the minds of his brethren, so that they would not hear the Disciples preach.

4. Dr. R. knows, that a large majority in the Presbyterian church, well-meaning and honest-hearted, have no baptism, but infant baptism; and that they did not, as a matter of course, *choose this for themselves,* but somebody else *chose it for them,,* decided that they should have it, and imposed it upon them, without their consent or knowledge. Many of these, when they come to mature years, and hear for themselves, see that baptism is an act of obedience, which requires the person's own will, consent and action, and, on hearing the gospel, will decide to yield a personal and voluntary obedience to God, in baptism. This also, the Dr. desired to counteract.

The Dr. knows, that a large number of his brethren, as honest and well-meaning as any they have, without their choice, consent, or knowledge, and before they could decide any question, in their infancy, had sprinkling imposed any they have, without their choice, consent, or knowledge, and before they could decide any question, in their infancy, had sprinkling imposed upon them for baptism; and that when they became capable of thinking and deciding for themselves what God requires them to do, on hearing the Disciples preach, insisting upon all reading the Scriptures and deciding for themselves what is right, conclude that their sprinkling, in which they had no choice, consent, or heart, could be no obedience to God, and chose to be immersed, thus carrying out the convictions of their own consciences. This Dr. R. dislikes, and this he aims to prevent, by keeping his brethren from hearing.

6. Dr. R. knows that his church is governed by a human creed, which the members must believe or be excluded; and yet that this creed admits that "the Holy Scriptures contain all things necessary to salvation," and that these Scriptures themselves declare that "He," Christ, "hath given all things necessary to life and godliness"—are "able to make us wise unto salvation"—to "perfect the man of God for every good work," and that "they are for doctrine," and that many of the best members in his church, on hearing the Disciples preach, prefer to take these Holy Scriptures as the man of their counsel and guide to a better world, and lose their reverence for the Confession, and go with those who love and follow the Lord Jesus Christ. This mortifies Dr. R., and this his pamphlet is aimed to prevent.

7. Dr. R. knows that many in the Presbyterian church are separated, by sectarianism, 'from their nearest and dearest friends on earth, division walls running between husband and wife, parent and child, brother and sister, neighbor and neighbor, &c., and that the pious have all along prayed that the time might come when these unhappy divisions might cease, when all who love God would "see eye to eye," and unite in the holy bands of Christian love. He knows that the Disciples come preaching peace by Jesus Christ, the Lord of all, urging his holy prayer, that *all who believe may be one as he and his Father are one,* that the world may believe—urging that exhortation of the holy apostle, "that you all speak speak the same thing, be of the same mind and of the same judgment, and that there be no divisions among you." He knows that this union can never be brought about among the pious, the good, those who love God and His people, the only ones who desire it, under any other rule of faith but the law of God, and that this is just what the Disciples are urging, and that all the better portions of his brethren will know this, when they hear for themselves; hence his effort to keep them from hearing. Why does he not exhort his brethren to go, with their Bible in hand, and hear what unscriptural doctrines they preach? Because he knows that all their prejudice would soon vanish in this way, and, therefore, he prefers giving them garbled extracts, which, he knows, do not fully nor fairly exhibit the minds of the writers quoted.

8. Dr. R. knew, when trying to prejudice the minds of his brethren against the Disciples, on Baptism, that his own dear Calvin and his Confession express the very doctrine he was battling, stated in more objectionable terms than in his garbled quotations; and the reader of this will agree to the same, when the quotations contained in this tract are examined.

9. Dr. R. knows, that he does not know, or hold a truth, of all that God has revealed to man, not held by the Disciples; nor is there a revealed truth of the Bible in all Christendom, not held, sacredly held, by the Disciples. We trust the day is dawning when the Lord, lifted up to draw all men to Him, will be honored, regarded and followed, and when men, not having His spirit, will cease to control those who desire to do the will of God. The Lord hasten that day!

-----o-----

BLESSED is he that considereth the poor; the Lord will deliver him in time of trouble.

The Lord will preserve him, and keep him alive; and he shall be blessed upon the earth; and thou wilt not deliver him unto the will of his enemies.

The Lord will strengthen him upon the bed of languishing.

Preliminary Address on Infant Baptism.

Dr. Shaffer—*Dear Sir:* Having reviewed your book on what you call "the mode of baptism," so far as we think demanded, and being about one hundred miles from home, and no copy of your book with us, but unwilling to neglect you for a month, we shall proceed to address you this kind letter preliminary to a brief review of your book on infant baptism.

If you please, then, we invite you, sir, to come and let us take sweet counsel together. You are aware, that you and myself have come to that time of life, when, if ever, we shall make an impression, for good or for evil, upon those in the reach of our influence. Neither of us desires that impression to be pernicious and condemned by the great Judge of the living and the dead. It is therefore important that we lose sight of all worldly ambition, selfish feeling, and carnal influences, and fix our eye as singly as possible upon the *will of God and the good of man.* The simple question for us to look at should be, Is it the will of God that infants should be baptized? If it is, we cannot be true and faithful servants of God, and good ministers of Jesus Christ, without advocating and practicing it. If it is not, we would be incurring the charge of imposition in advocating and practicing it. Thus, you perceive, the matter assumes a very serious aspect. Let us, then, humbly sit down before the question and take a serious look at it.

Is it the will of God that infants should be baptized?

1. It is certain there is no commandment in the word of God, given to any, either preachers or private members, to baptize infants. This you know, Doctor, as well as any man. Well, sir, you know that your book of Discipline says, "The Holy Scriptures contain all things necessary to salvation. So that whatever is not read therein or may be proved thereby, is not to be required of any man." How then can it be the will of God that any man should baptize an infant, when no man is commanded to do it, or in the absence of any such command contained in the Holy Scriptures?. and why should it be required of any man to do it? If you and myself, Doctor, were about to baptize an infant, and the Lord were suddenly to stand before us, and inquire, "Who hath required this at your hands?" what could we answer? that we had inferred it from Scripture? Would he not respond, "Where and when did I ever leave men to infer my positive requirements? When I positively required Adam and Eve to abstain from the inhibited fruit, I gave them positive commandment. When I placed before Abraham the positive requirement to offer his son, I gave him positive commandment. When I sent the apostles, with the positive requirement to baptize believers, I embodied that requirement in a positive commandment. But you claim that it is a positive requirement to baptize an infant; yet you know that there is no positive commandment to do it! How do you get a positive requirement without a positive commandment?" What could we say in reply? Would we not stand speechless? How, then, shall we answer to him in the day of Judgment?

2. No person, it is certain, is commanded in Scripture to have an infant baptized. Now, my dear sir, can it be a positive divine requirement for a parent to have an infant baptized, when it is set forth in no positive divine commandment in the Bible? Is any parent divinely required to attend to a positive institution not positively and divinely commanded? No man, by any reason or philosophy, can ever show, in the absence of positive divine commandment, that it was right, or a divine requirement for Abraham to offer Isaac. Indeed, all reason, in the absence of the positive divine commandment, declares that it was wrong. In itself, or without the divine commandment, it was wrong. But the Supreme Ruler of the Universe, being above all right and wrong, abstractly, or in itself considered, by the force of supreme authority, put forth in positive divine commandment, made that which was wrong in itself, right; and on account of Abraham's respect and subordination to the divine authority, set forth in the divine commandment, the Almighty honored his name and will honor it in all ages to come. In the same way, though no human reason can show that baptizing an infant, in itself, or abstractly considered, is right, is necessary, if we had positive divine commandment to have our

children baptized, and would obey, we should be walking in the illustrious steps of Abraham. This is precisely what parents lack, in having their infants baptized, of attending to a positive divine institution—the *positive divine commandment.* If infant baptism had a positive divine commandment, it would be a positive divine institution; in the absence of this, where it must stand, it is a *human tradition.*

3. It is certain that infants themselves are not commanded to be baptized, for they are not capable of receiving and obeying the command, "be baptized." Commands are only for accountable or responsible beings. The institution, therefore, cannot be a positive divine institution, for there is no positive divine command to administer baptism to an infant, to the parent to have it done, or to the infant itself to be baptized.

4. We are not informed, in all the Bible, that any prophet, apostle, or holy man ever baptized an infant. If infant baptism is a divine institution, it must have been the universal practice in the primitive church. Could it have been the universal practice of the whole church during the period that the Scriptures were being committed to record, and not one holy writer have mentioned a single instance of anyone ever baptizing an infant? When they brought young children to our Lord that he might put his hands on them and bless them, the holy writer made it an item worthy of record. Did these holy writers witness the baptizing of thousands of infants, and never think it an item worthy of note, under any circumstances, that they saw some man baptize an infant? Do you believe, Doctor, that these writers saw men in numerous instances baptizing infants and never mentioned it?

5. We are not informed in all the Bible of any person bringing an infant to baptism, or having an infant baptized. Did they see thousands brought to baptism and baptized, and never mention a single one? Could they have seen multitudes brought to the church for baptism and baptized, as they must have seen if such was the universal custom, and never have thought it a matter of sufficient importance for an item in all the sacred records. Such a supposition is preposterous in the highest degree. No man can believe that such was the universal or even the general custom, and not made an item by one single sacred historian. The way to account for their making no mention of any person bringing an infant to baptism, or of one being baptized, is to be found in the fact that they neither saw nor knew of any such custom.

6. Could it be possible that infant baptism was practiced in the ancient churches, and not mentioned or alluded to in any way in all the Sacred writings? Such a thing would be an impossibility; yet it is true that it is not mentioned or in any way alluded to in the whole Sacred record. All will see, from a moment's reflection, that if the practice existed at all it must have been general, and that such a practice could not have generally prevailed, and the Sacred writers, in so minute a narrative as they have given us of the procedure of the apostles, the building of churches, and many incidental matters, have failed to make a single mention of it.

7. It is not mentioned in any book, by any writer, approving or disapproving, or indifferently, in any way, among all who wrote in the apostolic age, or within a century of that time. All the writings of the first two centuries leave us wholly in the dark on the whole subject.. All that is known about the whole practice must be gathered from books written this side of the divine Fountain and Source of all light and all spiritual knowledge.

8. Doctor, who authorized you, or any parent, to choose infant in place of adult baptism, and impose it upon any child before it could, make any choice, or know anything about right or wrong in the matter, thus depriving it of the right of private judgment?

9. Doctor, who authorized you, or any parent, to decide in favor of sprinkling, and impose it upon any infant before it could decide for itself or know anything about it? How do you know but the infants you sprinkle, when they become capable of deciding for themselves, will prefer adult baptism and immersion? How can you thus deprive them of the right of private judgment in these two important points? B. F.

Five Arguments Against Union.

Union among all the children of God is a dangerous project, on account of the following considerations:

1. Many poor printers would suffer for employment. No creeds but one, at most, would then be needed, which would take off a large amount of printing, thus depriving many poor printers, book binders, paper-makers, book-sellers, etc., etc., of a large share of their regular employment, now obtained, under the wise and beneficent system of many creeds and parties. But the mention of the many creeds, of which the book-makers get the manufacturing, is but a small item compared with the whole advantage, accruing to this honest and laboring class, by the multiplication of many sects and creeds. For, no sooner are these printed and put in circulation, than some man is displeased with some of them, and is conscientiously moved to write a book against it. This done, and some friend of the creed must write another book in defense of it. This makes much more work for the printer. Then, a new sect arises, and as a matter of course, many new books must be printed, setting forth and defending the new doctrine. Then, as a matter of course, the old parties, which are *orthodox*, must publish a few books against the new party, which is a *heresy*, until it is strong enough to stand and live in spite of all the old parties, when it, with the same doctrine, becomes *orthodox!* This all augments the work of the printer. But the benevolent work of this wise arrangement stops not here. Each party must have a hymn book suited to its own doctrine, which furnishes a new job for stereotypers, printers, paper-makers, binders, book-sellers, etc., etc. Then each party must have commentaries, periodicals, Sunday school books, tracts, etc., etc., not contaminated with the errors of other parties. What an amount of work of this kind would be cut off from all these poor mechanics, if the uncharitable doctrine of *union*, maintained by some men, should ever be generally received. The people then, would read the Bible, use the same hymn book, the same periodical, the same Sunday school books, without any works *of* controversy, expositions or defenses of partisan peculiarities. Who can fail to see how disastrous this would be to printers. Their "craft would be in danger."

2. My second argument against union, is found in the injury that would result to another class of mechanics, *viz:* Those in any way employed in the erection of meeting-houses. Any man, at a glance can see, that about five-sixths of all this kind of employment would at once be taken from the poor mechanic, by the union of all the children of God. The little town now with six or eight hundred inhabitants, requires about six meeting houses, which is quite an item with the builders. But if the parties were all one in faith, communed at one table and worshiped in one house, they would have no use for the other five. Thus the doctrine of the union of all Christians, would endanger the craft of another class. At about the same rate would it diminish this kind of employment throughout the country. Is it not uncharitable for men to propagate a doctrine thus endangering the craft of so many honest laboring men?

3. This ruinous doctrine of the union of all Christians, against which I am contending, is dangerous and to be detested, in the third place, because if it should ever go into effect generally, which, I think, it cannot, it will deprive so many preachers of employment and take the support from their families. If the people in the little town of six or eight hundred inhabitants, now paying six preachers, were united, meeting and worshiping in one house, they would, as a matter of course, need but *one preacher*. Thus, any man with half an eye can see, that the dangerous doctrine here argued against, would throw four out of five, or five out of six of all these good men out of employment, and out of support. Thousands of them now supported, and really needed to keep up the churches and defend their doctrines, in their partisan state, would neither be needed nor supported, if this uncharitable doctrine of union should prevail. Who will favor a doctrine, endangering the craft of so many good men?

4. My fourth argument is, that union would endanger the employment of many good

religious editors. We could think of no kind of use of more than one editor in that case where we have ten now. If the old apostolic doctrine of one body, one spirit, one hope, one Lord, one faith, one baptism, and one God and Father of all, should prevail, all those editors now defending parties, keeping up-distinctions, maintaining peculiarities, and warding off blows from others who disagree with them, would be deprived of their employment. Who can fail to see, that if the people should ever learn to love one another, and *all be one,* as Jesus prayed, simply loving their Saviour and following him, they would have no more use for editors whose occupation it is to maintain and perpetuate partyism among their fellow-creatures. All these good men would be thrown out of employment and their scanty support taken from them, leaving no need of any editors except a few to maintain the one faith once delivered to the Saints. Can any man be so hard-hearted as to advocate a doctrine endangering, as this would, the craft of so many good men?

5. My fifth argument is, that this doctrine of union, being now advocated by so many, would rob many great and good men of their honor, as leaders or heads of parties. If that dangerous doctrine should ever become general, calling no man master or leader, for we have but one Master, Leader, or Head, the Messiah, all these great and highly honored men, now called leaders, masters and heads, would be called, simply *brethren,* and no more honored than other good men. The people would greatly lose their reverence for all these, be looking to, reverencing and loving their only Leader and Head, the Lord in Heaven. The people would cease to worship the creature and worship the Creator. They would linger around the cross, the Lord's table, the place of prayer and the Bible, with their affections on things above and not upon things on the earth, looking upon each other as brethren; and all the honor of human leaders and human heads would disappear, eclipsed by the glory that excelleth, the great Leader in heaven. Who will have the assurance to advocate a doctrine thus dangerous to the *honor* of men?

Thus we have given five arguments in favor of the present divisions among Christians. If any man shall offer five more, or five better arguments on the same side, we will certainly give them space. B. F.

-----o-----

Letter from Brother Wharton.

PLEASANT GROVE, Fulton Co., Ind.)
May 6, 1856.)

BROTHER FRANKLIN:—As you have proposed giving to your readers a sermon in each number of the *Review,* I have concluded to write a short article for your numerous readers; not as a sermon, to appear as the frontispiece in the *Review;* but if you think it will advance the cause of our Divine Master; you may put it in some corner of your paper. I propose offering some thoughts on our position as a people, and the obligations arising from it. Our stand, and our Basis, is the Bible, for everything in Christianity. And while all religious orders have made out their theories of Christianity, we, as a people, have made out none. While they have made their Creeds and Disciplines, we still have made out none. While they profess to believe these, adopt them, and practice according to them, we profess to believe, adopt, and practice according to the Bible. While the sects take the Bible to prove their theories, creeds, and disciplines to be right, we take the Bible as our only theory, and creed, in Christianity, and the New Testament as our only book of discipline, with all its facts, commands, promises, and threatenings. We have professed before heaven and earth, that all the Lord our God has commanded, we will do. The profession we have made, the position we occupy, as a people, make us, like unto a city, set on a hill that cannot be hid. The eyes of the world are now turned toward us, and they ask, will this people revolutionize the world? Will creeds be put down? Will party names be lost? Will the Bible, and only the Bible, be the basis on which all the discordant parties in the religious world will unite, and harmonize? Are they not looking at the practical tendencies of our position? May they not justly inquire, are these people more just, upright and holy than the sects? are they more humble, pious, and devotional? are they filled with the Spirit of the Divine Master, and bearing all the fruits of the Spirit? In a word, are they better Christians than others? Does not our position enable us, and our position require of us, that we exhibit in our lives the pure principles of the gospel, with its practice? They will answer all these questions in the affirmative. Does not God require all this at our hands?

But there is one point more, to which especially I wish to invite attention. The gospel must be preached, for it has been demonstrated before our eyes, that churches will not exist without preaching, and that sinners will not be converted to God without it. God has ordained, by the foolishness of preaching, to save *even* them that believe, as well as to convert the sinner to himself. The preacher, to preach profitably, must not entangle himself with the affairs of this life; but give himself wholly to the work of the ministry. In order that he may do this, God has ordained that they who preach the gospel shall live of the gospel. This is as clearly taught in the New Testament, as is baptism for remission of sins. But alas! our brethren don't keep all the commandments and ordinances of the Lord, to do them. If our brethren would have contended as zealously for this, as they have for baptism for remission, and have shown their faith by their works, we would not have found so many preachers, eminently useful, laboring in their shops, and on their farms; some on rented farms, others, in school houses—for the support of themselves and families; and when they preach, making nearly all the sacrifice that is made for the gospel. We would not have witnessed the fall of churches, that has taken place among us. On the contrary, the cause of our Divine Master would have been triumphant in Ohio, Kentucky, Indiana, and elsewhere. I think we would not have heard so much about "our downward tendency," as we have. The Lord knew about this matter. He knew just how many preachers he wanted in his vineyard; and apportioned them according to the wants of his people. He knew how much wealth would be necessary to place in the hands of his people, to accomplish his purpose in the Divine arrangement; and has done it. And if our brethren will only keep the law of the Lord, the Lord will bless them a hundred fold in this life; and in the world to come, give them life everlasting. It will not do to say that God works without foresight or arrangement; neither will it do to say he is a hard master, imposing heavy burdens grievous to be borne. Nor yet, that there are too many preachers. Nor yet, that there is too little wealth. God looked through time; He saw all the necessities of the case, made out his own plan, understood his own arrangement, and then made out the Law; and when made, it is a perfect Law. Did God work without foresight or arrangement, when he selected the twelfth tribe of Israel to minister before him, and gave them none inheritance, among their brethren? Did he bind too heavy a burden on the eleven tribes, when he exacted the truth? And was it too grievous to be borne, when he laid additional claims on them, to bring their trespass offerings; the first born of their flocks, with the first fruits of their ground; and all to support his ministry? He certainly understood his own arrangement, and then required what was just and right in the premises, with promises of great blessings (temporal) if they would walk, in all his commandments and ordinances, to do them. These were the palmy days of Israel. But when they forsook the Law of God, the glory departed from Israel. And, has not God provided some better things for us under the gospel? Most assuredly he has. And shall we be permitted to enjoy these good things under the reign of Prince Messiah, and he make no demands on us. Nay, verily. The churches of Christ must have regular preaching; sectarianism, which is anti-Christianity, must be put down by the proclamation of the glorious gospel of Christ. Sinners, that are slumbering on the brink of an awful hell, must be converted. And every enemy, that stands opposed to God's moral, spiritual, and divine government, under the reign of his son, must be destroyed before Christ will sit in judgment on the world. And shall Christians have no instrumentality in this glorious work? If we don't, God will have a people that will, and to whom he will say, when he determines the fate of the world, well done, good and faithful servant, enter into the joys of thy Lord.

Brethren, our course is onward and upward. Heaven is our destination; all that is pure, lovely and good, and eternal life also, are objects of our hope in Christ. May our love to each other abound. May our good works be multiplied, that sects may see the all sufficiency of the holy scriptures, as a rule of life and conduct: and sinners see the purifying and sanctifying influence of the gospel of Christ, and all be made to confess to the glory of God and the Father. Amen. BENJ. WHARTON.

-----o-----

Correspóndanse.

BUCHANAN, MICH., June 7, 1856.

DEAR BRO. FRANKLIN:—Amid all the opposing influences of these times, the glorious cause of our blessed Redeemer is still on the advance in this section of country. There has recently been *one* accession from the Methodists to the Christian congregation in this village; also in Paw Paw on the Lord's day, May 25th, a young gentlemen, the son of a president in the Methodist Protestant church, yielded to the high mandates of Heaven's eternal King, exhibiting his loyalty to Jesus Christ by being buried with him in baptism. In Wayne, there have been *five* accessions to the church within a few weeks past. *Two* were received by letter, *one* restored, and *two* were immersed by Bro. Loyal Crane, of Paw Paw. On last Lord's day morning, at the same place, after a discourse on the *action* of baptism, a young lady who had been *sanctified* by some good orthodox divine of these times, came forward, renounced Methodism, and was planted in the likeness of Christ's death. Also, in the afternoon of the same day in Dowagiac, after a discourse on the power and sufficiency of the gospel, *two* persons, who constituted an *entire household,* confessed the Savior, and put on the Lord by baptism. These were the first fruits to primitive Christianity in Dowagiac. Bro. E. Barnum was the Baptist on this occasion. To the Lord be all the praise.

WM. M. ROE.

MADISONVILLE, May 14, 1856.

DEAR BRO. FRANKLIN:—Enclosed you will find the amount for another subscriber at this place, Eld. O. Collins.

I have been laboring here for about twelve days. The resident preachers are brethren O. Collins, W. C. Dimmitt, and Evangelist Geo. Heverin—men who can be trusted anywhere, and invaluable to the cause.

I had a fine hearing from first to last, with the best feelings of the community. Yet we had but few additions, only eight, and three of these by letter. It is confidently believed that much more good has been accomplished, and that the harvest is almost ripe for a great ingathering.

The world, however, has taken a firm hold of the people, and it is most difficult to free them from it.

In the good hope, J. T. JOHNSON.

EATON, OHIO, May 19th, 1856.

DEAR BRO. FRANKLIN: We are again called to mourn the loss of a most dearly loved child. Our dear Johnny V. was taken from us on Monday, May 12th, 1856, of an inflammation of the kidneys, resulting probably from whooping-cough. He was 22 months and 10 days old. This is the second trial we have suffered of parting with an only child, our oldest having died on the 7th of January, 1853. We are deeply and doubly afflicted, yet we trust in the Lord for strength to endure our trials, hoping through his mercy to be able to meet them in that happy morning when they shall be freed from the power of death, and live to die no more. May the Lord help us to meet them there. ENOS ADAMSON.

BRO. FRANKLIN: Your visit to this country has done immense good by way of removing prejudice, and some whom you left crippled, have since obeyed the truth. Your discourse on Materialism here was just the thing needed. Its advocates here are in the same predicament with the old gentleman in Cincinnati to whom you proved the immortality of the soul. The "Review" for June has not yet made its appearance. I fear something is wrong about the mail. I have the mail. I have disposed of some of those books you left, and shall do the best I can with them. More anon.

Yours, in hope of eternal life,

WM. M. ROE.

-----o-----

Where is the Safe Ground?

Our article, under the above head, has been before the people five months, and has received a far more general approval than we expected. In these times of excitement, side-issues and sophistical declamation, with little regard to consequences, we doubted how many might still remain disposed to calm, deliberate, and dispassionate reason and Scripture. There are times in the progress of human events, of upheavings, convulsions, and fomentings, when the mind cannot be arrested with anything sober and reliable, and when there is no determining where the landing place will be. From the signs of the times, we doubted whether our country were not hastening to such a crisis. But we are satisfied that there is a soundness in the heart of the Christian brotherhood, as well as in the judgment, that *can,* and *will,* still be reached, by rational appeals to the only rule of all Christian faith, love, and union. No more gratifying assurance of this has come to our notice, than the manner in which our article on the much agitated subject of Slavery has been viewed by the great body of the Disciples.

It is true that a few brethren, whom we have esteemed good and true, have taken offense, some refusing to support us, and, we doubt not, have deprived us of many subscribers. Indeed, some few have declared that they would do their utmost against us; but, we trust, all of this description will feel better and actually *be better,* after a little cool reflection; and probably they may yet be convinced that they are not doing much for the glory of God, or the good of the cause, in their war upon us. If, however, the brethren, after a fair exhibition of their labors, find that they are building up the cause, promoting peace, union, and love among the Disciples, and that their war upon our influence, and against the circulation of the *Review,* all tends to good, be it so; we murmur not, complain not, and entertain not an unkind feeling towards any human being, but submit the case to Him who judges righteously. But one thing all may rely upon, who threaten to diminish our beautiful and rapidly increasing subscription list, |viz.: That we are not *writing for subscribers,* but the brethren are subscribing very rapidly *for our writings.* We shall write what *we believe*—what *we consider Scriptural, safe,* and *for the good of the cause,* and shall try and find readers; but if we should at any time fail to find subscribers, we shall not change, and write or publish what *we do not believe* for the sake of subscribers. We are not writing for the success of our publication, but for the success of *the cause,* and we say not what we say on this subject, for *our own* sake, but for the sake of *Him* who died for us, *his cause* and *those for whom he died.*

As far as we have seen, not a man among all those who have attacked our article on the Safe Ground for a Christian, has assailed and shown a single sentence or word contained in it to be erroneous. Indeed, no man of any note has formed a direct issue with it. It has been called "pro-slavery," an "apology for slavery," a "defense of slavery," the "weakest document we have ever written," and we have been called an "apologist for slavery," a "popularity-seeker," a "dough-face," "worse than a slaveholder," etc., etc.; but these expressions only come from men who *talk about* our article, without forming any issue with it, and, no doubt, in some instances, without having read it with sufficient care to know what is in it. But we have seen nothing yet that needs any reviewing from this class of writers. To think now of correcting all the false issues, evasions, misunderstandings, quibbles, personal allusions, sneers, and *ad captandum* slang is out of the question. There is no obscurity in our cause nor writings, that needs an everlasting train of explanations. What we have said, is what we *mean,* and it will not be misunderstood by those making an effort to understand. We shall, therefore, let all these things take their course; they will find their level. But we are looking beyond this, to see where the cause is to be during the coming political campaign. Are we, as disciples of Christ, citizens of a kingdom not of this world, a religious community, to be distracted, disconcerted, and thrown into confusion? or are we drawn to a common center, by an attraction so heavenly, commanding, and binding, that no side-influence can divert us from our course? The Lord is about to test us, prove us, and show whether we are true, sincere, and men of integrity to the great principles which we profess and have been inculcating, or will turn traitor to them, despise them, and trample them under our feet. We have been preaching union upon the Bible and the Bible alone to our neighbors; but the time has now come to test us practically and compel us to apply our philosophy in an instance of the greatest moment and best calculated of all others to show its power—its moral and spiritual efficacy among ourselves.

What course shall we take, then, during the coming campaign? Shall preachers of the gospel of Christ enter the pulpit, with exciting political news in their heads and hearts, and make Kansas-Nebraska and anti-Kansas-Nebraska, Slavery and anti-Slavery speeches? Shall their themes be the Constitution, Liberty, Popular Sovereignty, North, South, Fillmore, Buchanan, Fremont, American, Democratic, and Republican? Shall these be the themes that consecrate the house of God during the coming months, while thousands are perishing for the word of God and dying in their sins? We say, and would, if we had a voice louder than the seven thunders of the Apocalypse and more immutable than the oath of the angel of God, standing with one foot upon the land and the other upon the sea, say No, by NO MEANS, for the following reasons:

1. Jesus and his apostles, in all their official acts, never attempted to correct the political institutions of the country, no matter how corrupt they were, but left them, and those who made them, to take care of their own responsibilities. We must follow their precedent, or we are not the disciples of Christ.

2. Our Lord and his apostles, in all their official procedure, never made a decision, or gave even an opinion, upon the merits or demerits of any form of civil government, republican, monarchical, either limited or absolute. They left all these matters to take their course, and lifted their thoughts above them to a spiritual kingdom that shall endure when time shall be no more. We must do as they did, or forfeit our claim to be one with them.

3. The Lord and his apostles never made a decision, or gave an opinion, on any system of slavery, though slavery existed in some form or other in every country where they preached and wrote, in all their official career. We must humble ourselves to the same limits.

4. We have the infallible directions of the Spirit of God, to believers connected with slavery, both masters and servants, and these directions we must give when we speak on the subject at all, or depart from the faith because we are opposed to it. Every man who does not do this, manifestly repudiates the practice and teachings of the holy apostles.

5. Jesus and his apostles did not found slavery of any kind, and neither our Lord nor his religion can be responsible for any system of slavery or its results, no matter how good or how bad. Slavery is an institution of the world, as all other political institutions are, and neither the kingdom of God nor its subjects are responsible for its results.

6. Our Lord and his apostles never formed an issue between the kingdom of God and the kingdoms of this world. How utterly preposterous and absurd it is, to the mind of one who has noticed that our Lord never made an issue between his kingdom, or his religion, and any civil government or kingdom of the world, to see some misguided creature trying to form a direct issue between the kingdom of God and whatever political institution he may chance to fall out with, and trying to set the citizens in the kingdom of Christ in battle array with the citizens of the civil government! Such a man has no use for a church only as a kind of battering-ram to beat down some sinful institution that he has just perceived is to ruin the nation. He would have the kingdom of God a convenient engine, properly adjusted and poised, himself commander-in-chief, so that he can now bring it to bear upon Masons, then upon Odd Fellows, anon upon Sons

of Temperance, then upon Slavery, or any other monster that may rise. But the man who stands upon an eminence lofty enough to discern the kingdom of God, beholds an institution with an aim transcendently higher than deciding upon the rights and wrongs of the political governments of the world, amending, correcting, and perfecting them; the superlatively noble, grand, and beneficent object of translating *individuals,* whether high or low, rich or poor, bond or free, whether their political institutions are good or bad, out of darkness into light, and out of the kingdom of Satan into the kingdom of God, and in their few remaining days here, no matter what their earthly condition, prepare them for guests of the redeemed hosts who have washed their robes and made them white in the blood of the Lamb, in the house not made with hands, eternal in the heavens.

7. Christianity is *the thing* to be promoted, and not to be used as a mere *instrumentality,* by men who care nothing about *it,* and who are doing but little to advance *it,* to promote some object of their *own worldly ambition. We* must promote Christianity *itself,* and not employ it as a mere means to promote something else.

"Well, sir, what would you have a Christian do in regard to rulers and civil governments?" says one. When acting as a citizen in the kingdom of God, or in the house of God, "Pray for kings and all that are in authority, that we may lead a peaceable and quiet life, in all godliness and honesty." "Be subject to the powers that be," remembering that "we have no continuing city here," and that "this world is not our home." When acting as a citizen of the civil government, be candid, quiet, peaceable, and kind, and do just what *you think right,* allowing every man the same privilege, as Christ has left us all free here, and leave the event with God.

Brethren, from present indications, this year will be a glorious opening for the cause of Christ. There are spiritual-minded persons in almost all the parties around us; and if we determine to know nothing but Christ, nothing but pure Christianity, and confine ourselves strictly to the clear revelations of heaven— preach the pure gospel of the grace of God—preach Christ, and determine to know nothing else, while a mere carnal and worldly priesthood harangue their assemblies on politics, mix up church and State, law and gospel, turning their religious organizations into mere political engines, the very thing we have condemned the Romish priesthood for, thus wounding the feelings of all the more spiritual-minded members, and splitting their parties asunder, thousands of them will seek a church where the name of Jesus has charms, where the Lord is loved and worshiped, and where the true worshipers worship the Father in spirit and in truth. Let us keep the way clear for such, receive them to the fold of Christ, and show them how they can serve God and get to heaven, whether they can ever understand the slavery question or not.

Many of us have labored long and hard and sacrificed the main energies of our lives in gathering the many thousands to the fold of Christ that now throng places of public worship, and we cannot remain silent and see them scattered by the indiscrete and imprudent course of brethren, in thrusting upon them, and seeming to think that their souls' salvation is suspended upon their rightly understanding, the question of American slavery. We admonish the brethren to have nothing to do with any such question in the church. The Lord has not required the church, the preachers, or religious editors to make any decision, or to hold any particular class of opinions on the subject, nor can any man be blameless and push any such question into the kingdom of God. *We will stand square upon the Bible, by the Lord, the apostles, and every man who will stand by them.* The Lord direct us!

B. F.

-----o-----

THE days of our years are three-score years and ten; and if by reason of strength they be four-score years, yet is their strength labor and sorrow; for it is soon cut off, and we fly away.

He that rebuketh a man, afterwards shall find more favor than he that flattereth with the tongue. A man that flattereth his neighbor spreadeth a net for his feet.

Letter from Wales.

PERRYGLADFA, Newtown,
Montgomeryshire,
Wales, April 8th, 1856.

TO ELDER B. FRANKLIN:

Beloved Brother: Will you have the kindness to forward by first steamer *Hume and Franklin's Debate,* also one copy (paper covers) of *Bro. Challen's new work.* Send both to my address as above, and accept the enclosed postage stamps in payment.

The first three numbers of your *Review* have recently come to hand, for which I tender my best thanks. Your publication makes a very creditable appearance, and is filled with sterling matter. As no doubt you receive all the British intelligence of interest, I need not enlarge on that head, but will merely add that we are now anxiously looking toward America for Evangelists. Our number, as a community here, is small; our means limited; the habits and institutions of our country stereotyped; hence we find the work of *Restoration* an uphill, and, sometimes, disheartening enterprise, and reiterate our cry—COME OVER AND HELP US!

With Christian affection, I remain, in the blessed hope, yours most respectfully,

JOSEPH R. ROTHERHAM

[The subject of sending Evangelists to England has been noticed in several of our American publications, but we are not aware that any brethren have proposed to go. Indeed, we know of no brethren capable who could well be spared from their present field of operations. If some two brethren, good and true, having the confidence of the brotherhood generally, would go, there would be no difficulty in raising the means to support them. Can the men be found for this great work? or shall our brethren on the other side of the great water cry "Come over and help us," without any response? Is there no good man ready to say, "Here am I, send me?"]

HAPPY is the man that findeth wisdom; she is more precious than rubies.

Her ways are ways of pleasantness, and all her paths are peace.

For the Am. Christian Review.

BRO. FRANKLIN:—We have just closed a four days' meeting in Tipton, Ind., with fourteen accessions to the church there, (eight by baptism). An unusual degree of interest in regard to Christianity was effected. Our brother, D. R. Van Buskirk, (now a student in the N. W. C. University), did nearly all the preaching. His amiable deportment and Christian eloquence endeared him to the Disciples, and his labors in the gospel were highly appreciated by the church and people.

H. L. JOHN VAN DAKE.

May 24th, 1856.

COAL CHEEK, Ind., May 14, 1856.

BRO. FRANKLIN:—At our last monthly meeting at this (Cold Spring) church, I had the pleasure of introducing five individuals into the kingdom of Jesus Christ by baptism. A very good feeling pervaded the whole church. At a meeting held at Jacksonville in this (Fountain) county, including fourth Sunday in March, there were fourteen additions to the church. Speakers, Bro. Wm. Evers and myself. To the Lord be all the praise.

ELISHA SCOTT.

Repentance after Baptism.

BRO. FRANKLIN: In the article on Baptismal Repentance, we conditionally promised one on Repentance after Baptism, and are now seated to make good the promise.

You will permit me here also to fulfill a precept our Christianity enjoins upon us, viz.: that of giving honor to whom honor is due, in acknowledging my indebtedness to the same noble servant of our Lord whom I mentioned in my last.

Repentance after baptism requires not only a sorrow for sin, and some good purposes and resolutions of a new life for the future, but the actual forsaking of sin and amendment of our lives. In baptism, God *justifies the ungodly,* (Rom. iv, 5), that is, how wicked soever men have been, whenever they repent of their sins, renounce their former wicked practices, and believe in Christ, and enter into covenant with him by baptism, all their former sins are immediately forgiven, are washed away, without expecting the actual reformation of their lives. This was plainly the case both of Jewish and heathen converts, who upon the profession of faith in Christ, and renouncing their former wicked lives, whatever they had been, were immediately received by baptism; as Peter exhorted the Jews to 'repent and be baptized, every one of you, in the name of Jesus Christ, for the remission of sins, and ye shall receive the gift of the Holy Ghost (Acts ii, 38), and the same day they were three thousand baptized. This is gospel favor, which is the purchase of Christ's blood, that the greatest sinners, upon their repentance and faith in Christ, are received to mercy, and wash away all their sins in baptism.

But when they are in covenant, they shall then be judged according to the terms and conditions of that covenant, which requires the practice of an universal righteousness; such persons must not expect, as Paul reasons, that if they *continue still in sin grace will abound;* the very covenant of grace which we enter into at baptism confutes all such ungodly hopes. For how shall we, that are dead to sin, live any longer therein? Know ye not, that so many of us as were baptized into Jesus Christ, were baptized into his death? Therefore are we buried with him by baptism into death, that like as Christ was raised from the dead by the glory of the Father, so we also should walk in newness of life, Rom. vi, 1, 2, 3, 4. This is the difference Paul makes between the grace of the gospel in receiving the greatest sinners to baptism, and justifying them by the blood of Christ; and what the gospel requires of baptized Christians to continue in this justified state; in the first case, nothing is required but faith and repentance, upon which account we are so frequently said "to be justified by faith, not by the deeds of the law; to be justified freely by his grace, through the redemption that is in Christ Jesus; to be saved by grace through faith, not of works, lest any man should boast." Rom. iii, 20, 21, 22, 24; Rom. v, 1; Eph. ii, 8, 9. And I believe, upon inquiry, it will be found that justification by faith always relates to this baptismal justification, when by baptism we are received into covenant with God, and into a justified state, only for the sake of Christ and through faith in his blood; which one thing, well considered, would put an end to most of the disputes about justification, and about faith and works, which I cannot explain now, but shall only observe, that the constant opposition between justification by the faith of Christ, and justification by circumcision and the works of the law, (Gal. v, 2, 3), to the observation of which they were obliged by circumcision, is a manifest proof that justification by faith is our justification by the faith of Christ in baptism, which is our admission into the Christian church, makes us the members of Christ, and the children of God, which is a state of grace and justification; as circumcision formerly made them God's peculiar people in covenant with him, which is the covenant of circumcision; and justification by faith and justification by circumcision would not be duly opposed, if they did not relate to the same kind of justification; that is, that justification which is the immediate effect of one being in covenant with God.

But now, when we are justified by a general repentance and faith in Christ at baptism, we also vow a conformity to the death of Christ, by dying to sin, and walking in newness of life; that is, we vow an universal obedience to all the laws of righteousness, which the gospel requires of us, as circumcision made them *debtors to the whole law,* (Gal. v.), which is the reason why the works of the law and that evangelical righteousness which the faith of Christ requires of us are so often opposed in this dispute; the one the righteousness of the law, or of works, the other the righteousness of faith; and therefore, as circumcision could not justify those who transgressed the law, no more will faith justify those who disobey the gospel; but the righteousness of the law must be fulfilled in us, who walk not after the flesh but after the spirit. Rom. ii, 13, 25, 26, 27, 28, 29; Rom. viii, 4.

Now, the necessary consequence of this is, that mere sorrow for sin, and the mere vows and resolutions of obedience, without actual holiness and obedience of life, according to the terms and conditions of the gospel, will not save a a baptized Christian; for mere sorrow for sin and vows of obedience will be accepted only in baptism; but when we are baptized, we must put our vows in execution, or we fall from our baptismal grace and justification; and therefore, when we relapse into sin after baptism, no repentance will be accepted but that which actually reforms our lives; for baptismal grace is not ordinarily repeated, no more than we can repeat our baptism.

It seems to me that the above, together with the preceding article, above alluded to, ought to satisfy all candid inquirers as to our true position on the subject of baptism, as disciples of Jesus Christ.

In the hope that good may result to all who candidly exercise their reflection, I abide affectionately yours in the Lord,

CHAS. D. HURLBUTT.
QUINCY, Ill., June 18.1856.

-----o-----

Gleanings from a Sacred Field.—No. 1.

Nevertheless, I have somewhat against thee." Rev. ii, 4.

THE seven letters to the seven churches of Asia, are lasting memorials of God's long-suffering and inflexible justice toward his adopted children. He, that held in his right hand the seven stars, and walked in the midst of the seven golden candle-sticks, is the Son of God, the author and finisher of our redemption. In executing his Father's will, he appeared to John on the desolate isle of Patmos, and spoke of the existing condition of things and of what should follow. His first letter was written to the church at Ephesus. In addressing that church he spoke of things known to him. The Works of the Ephesian brethren were before him, from the least to the greatest. The labor, and patience, and long-suffering of these brethren he was well acquainted with. He knew that they could not bear those who were evil—had tried those who professed to be apostles, and found them liars—had labored for his Name's sake, and fainted not, in the midst of the unnumbered dangers and perils of the way.

From the foregoing statement of facts it may be inferred, that the congregation of disciples at Ephesus was, according to appearances, without reproach. "Nevertheless,' remarks the Son of God, "I have somewhat against thee, because thou hast left thy first love."

Therefore it is presumable that it required the omniscient vision of the Son of God to detect the sin, that was corroding the character of these Ephesian brethren. Had they been judged by the world, they would, not only have been pronounced righteous, but worthy a place in the mansions of rest. But he who knows the heart, and whence actions proceed, said that their labors were not superinduced by a pure and unadulterated love of Him from whom they received life and strength, and to whom they had plighted their faith and vowed allegiance.

Nothing is alleged against the labors of these brethren. On the contrary they are commended for their persevering and strict observance of the commands of the Most High. In the present day, however, there are many congregations whose *behavior* is not in accordance with Christian character. They have lost their zeal, their patience, their energy, their self-sacrificing disposition. Judging from what they say and do, the inevitable conclusion arrived at is, that they have a name to live, but are dead. True, "as is the fruit, so is the tree." Yet in the days of Paul, while some preached Christ of good will, others preached him through strife, envy and contention. While we are to judge of the character of our fellows, by their words and deeds, it is the province of the Son of God, to stamp with indelible fixedness the signet of good or bad upon the character of all. Being the omnipotent and omniscient King of the Universe, he surveys with an all-searching glance the unnumbered multitudes that throng the high-ways and by-ways of life. His penetrating gaze is fixed on each person, as though he were the only one that had a being. The motives that lead to action are all set down. All the proud boastings, evil machinations, and flattering unctions springing into birth within the chambers of the heart, are carefully noted by our vigilant, heart-searching and rein-trying King. Since this is the case, and since a very grave accusation is brought against the Ephesian brethren whom we would have considered altogether faultless; it becomes the disciples of Christ not only to do these things commanded in the perfect law of liberty, but to inquire on bended knees, with humbleness of mind, the motives that lead them to obedience. This is necessary that the Christian may not be deceived. Many are self-deceived in this day and generation. They cannot give a good reason, perhaps, why they are serving the Most High God.

The disciple of Christ does not serve him because a profession of Christianity is popular, because wealth can be amassed, honor obtained, a high position secured among the great of earth. He does not serve him because his neighbors do, because the religion of Jesus is recommended by the intellectual and influential of society. From no such considerations will he render homage to God the father. His thanks giving, his adoration, his supplications, and continued and arduous labors in the vineyard of the Lord flow from a consciousness of his lost, degraded, and miserable condition, and from a supreme love toward Him who so loved the world as to give his only and well-beloved son for the present and eternal well-being of the human family.

The Christian should inquire at the beginning of his race to the better world, and during his dreary and perilous pilgrimage through life, the purpose of every thought, of every word, and of every action. This must be done that he may know his true position, the relation he sustains to earth and heaven, that he may enjoy Christianity and be prepared for the solemn change which awaits all living,—for the great and terrible day of final adjudication.

"Remember therefore from whence thou art fallen, and repent and do thy first works; or, else I will come unto thee quickly, and will remove thy candle-stick out of its place, except thou repent."

Although the brethren at Ephesus appear free from actual transgression, even when closely scrutinized, yet Christ commands them in positive, direct, and poignant language, to reform. This is a serious lesson, to be read and studied by all Christian congregations. Christ did not charge them with not having labored—patiently enduring afflictions. No such accusation is filed against them. But they had not mingled love with their works— they had not rendered service to God from a full purpose of heart,—their affections had not been enlisted in obedience. They had brought into action only a part of their powers and capacities. Inasmuch as Christianity addresses the whole man, the body, soul, and spirit, must be surrendered a living offering to the living God. The Ephesian brethren had done well so far as they had observed the requirements of the almighty Father, but their actions—their service—proceeded not from the proper source. Jesus affirmed that unless they reformed he would remove from among them, the light of divine truth. They heeded not his admonition, and therefore have they fallen from their high position. They are no longer led by the lamp of life. Having abandoned the principles of Christianity, nothing could save them. The bread of heaven was rejected and death ensued. Darkness settled down upon them, and desolation and ruin brooded over them.

"The Christian history of Ephesus may be said to have ended with the sixth century; since that period it can hardly be said, that the church has existed there at all; and now there is neither angel nor candle-stick in the once flourishing city. From the ruins of the theater, the scene of noble martyrdoms, from the broken columns and scattered sculpture of her temples, from the desolation of her once peopled plain and terraced hills, a voice audible enough to those who will listen, proclaims, 'He that hath an ear let him hear what the spirit saith unto the churches.'"

W. C. R.

-----o-----

LOOK not upon the wine when it is red, when it giveth his color in the cup, when it moveth itself aright. At the last it biteth like a serpent, and stingeth like an adder.

Buy the truth, and sell it not; also wisdom, and instruction, and understanding.

Editor's Table

Office of the *American Christian Review,* West Fourth street, No. 60, on third floor, open stair way from outside. Signs will be seen at the entrance.

New Proposition.—As the current year is now half gone, and seven numbers of the *Review* published, we propose that any two new subscribers who will send us three dollars, shall each have the present volume, with all the back numbers, and the second volume in full. We have yet about one thousand back numbers. Beside these we have a large number of odd copies, containing articles highly esteemed, and that have been circulated as tracts, with much profit. Twenty-four copies of any number can be had for $1.

New Charge.—Our much esteemed, talented and deservedly popular brother, ELIJAH GOODWIN, has consented to accept the invitation to take charge of the first congregation in Indianapolis, and consequently desires all communications, for him, addressed to him at that place, instead of Bloomington, his former residence. We trust this will be a good arrangement, and that, with the hearty cooperation of the church, the talented and influential preaching, brethren of that young and growing city, and harmony with the new congregation there, which his amiable, humble and fraternal course will tend to secure, will prove a great blessing to the cause The brethren need not think of success without many and spirited efforts, cooperating with him who speaks in the name of the Lord. We do hope that the brethren in that city may combine their influence and make one mighty effort in the Lord's name. We know of no place where more responsibility rests upon brethren, and especially upon public men.

Endorsement—Rev. Baserman—The Star.—We simply desire to say, that we knew nothing of the endorsement in the *Age,* to meet Rev. Baserman, a Universalian, lately a Lutheran, in debate, till we saw it in print; and that we do not think we need any endorsement, to meet any Universalist in this country. If we did, we could find it in the *Star.*

Why did Mr. Quinby, and the whole posse of Universalists here, back out from the fair and honorable proposition of Eld. John A. Dearborn? As published in the *Star, the reason was, that we would be the man selected by the Disciples in this city!* Immediately on the back of this, the brainless editor of the *Star* commences trying to make his readers believe that even our own brethren here had no confidence in us. The very thing that troubled him was, that he thought our brethren had confidence in us, and would put us forward to meet them, and this oozed from his pen and found its way into the *Star.*

Christian Record.—Brother J. M. MATHES, who has so long been the safe, judicious and successful editor and publisher of this magazine, is now located at Bedford Lawrence county, Ind., and desires all his correspondence addressed to him at that place, instead of Indianapolis. We should have given this notice of our worthy brother and co-laborer sooner, but it still escaped our attention at the proper time. The *Record* has been so long and favorably known to the brethren, as a safe, judicious and reliable advocate of the cause, that nothing that we could say could add anything to its deserved popularity. We have no better man than Brother Mathes, none more generally and deservedly beloved. We wish all such men success in their laudable efforts to promote the cause.

"Making Melody in Our Hearts to the Lord."—In **a** fashionable city, not many hundreds of miles from here, a Christian congregation conceived the idea of advancing the cause and thus glorifying God, by aping the worldly and carnal establishments around them. Accordingly, the pews in the church, (meeting house) were cushioned and sold, an organ obtained, and a choir arranged in the gallery. On a certain occasion, soon after this scheme was adopted, several preachers and brethren being present who were not initiated, the little man who performs on the organ was seen ascending the gallery. One of the strangers inquired, "What is Bro.——— going up there for?" One sitting by responded, *"To make melody in our hearts to the Lord."*

"The English Bible.—History of the Translation of the Holy Scriptures into the English Tongue, with specimens of English Versions. By Mrs. H. C. CONANT, author of Translations of Neander's Practical Commentaries." Such is the reading of the title page of the most valuable new book with which we have been favored for several years. This ably and impartially written work begins with Wickliffe, the distinguished man of God, who first gave the English nation the Word of God in their mother tongue, furnishing a rapid and instructive outline of the life of this great man and the opponents with whom he had to contend, and the persecutions which he suffered, making the most grand and important chapter in the English history of the fourteenth century. Then carrying us, with a master hand, through the life, labors and martyrdom of Wm. Tyndale, with his noble assistant, young Frith, who attested his sincerity and devotion to the Word of God and the happiness of man in the midst of the flames that consumed his flesh at the stake, some time before the strangling and burning of Tyndale. The work from this proceeds down, giving the most complete and perfect information upon the procedure both of translators and their opposers, ending with the common version, of any book known to us. We most heartily recommend this invaluable work, not only as the most ready source of

information in regard to the whole work of giving us the Word of God in English, but the most illustrious example of female authorship of the nineteenth century. This is one of the books that will live, and be read by men and women of sense—the great and the good, when the writer shall have entered her rest.

-----o-----

Success of the Gospel.

Bro. H. St. John Van Dake, of Noblesville, Ind., writing under date June 11, says: "I have just returned from an interesting meeting at Boxley Town, Ind., we received sixteen; by baptism twelve."

Bro. Israel Howard, Fall Creek, Hamilton county, Ind., June 17, says: "Since March, eleven more have been added to the church here, all by baptism, under the labors of Bro. R. Edmondson-"

Bro. Aaron Hubbard, of Little York, Ind., June 11, says: "Our meeting resulted in twenty-three additions, ten after you left. We would be glad to see and hear you again. You must try and come again this fall. I am sure that your meeting made a better impression than ever was made before in this community. Our hearts are open to receive, and our hands are open to sustain you whenever you can come."

Bro. Wesley Hartley, June 18th, says: "We have just closed an excellent meeting at Lexington, Ind. three made the good confession."

Bro. Asa Hollingsworth, Indianapolis, June 17, says: "We have had some success in our field of labor."

Bro. W. M. Tandy, Carrolton, Ky., May 17, says "Bro. Wm. Tharp and I closed a meeting at the Hickory Flat, Henry Co., Ky., last Tuesday evening, which commenced the Thursday afternoon previous. At this point there had been a church constituted, and arrangements partially made to build a meeting house, but all seemed likely to fall through. The result of the meeting was, the brethren seemed to be awakened to a sense of their high obligations; we raised, by subscription, enough to build the meeting house, got the house under contract, and left the workmen commencing the job. The good Lord added two noble young ladies to the church, by confession and baptism. The prospects are good for many more. To the Lord be all the praise."

Bro. P. K. Dibble, Canton, Ohio, June 17, says:

Bro. Lockhart and I have been holding a meeting in Sparta, Stark county, Ohio, and, so far, there have been six additions, four immersed and two from the Methodists. The meeting still continues."

Bro. R. R., Cannelton, Ind., June 9, says: "There were three persons buried with their Lord in baptism into death, by a Christian minister."

Bro. Dan. Franklin, Rushville, Ind., June 5, says: "We have just closed a very fine meeting here, having obtained some thirty-five additions—thirty-one immersed, one from the Baptists, two reclaimed. Among the immersed was my first-born, Milton Franklin, whose dying mother, five years ago last April, took him by the hand, bade him farewell, and told him to 'be kind to everybody, obey his father and meet her in heaven.'"

Bro. Joshua D. Wright, Chickasaw, O., April 29, says: "We have had some additions lately to our congregation in Chickasaw."

Bro. P. K. Dibble, Canton, O., June 2, says, "I preached here on Lord's day, Monday, and Tuesday nights. The result was three additions to the church, one Baptist, one by baptism and relation."

Bro. B. Wharton, Rochester, Ind., May 8th, says, "I have had nine additions to the good cause the past month, all in this county, six by immersion, and three by relation. Prospects in this county are encouraging. We thank the Lord and take courage.

Our venerable brother Crane and lady, from Paw Paw, Mic., who were present when we were there in April, were in Covington, Ky., on the third Lord's day in June, visiting their son, Prof. Crane and family. At the afternoon meeting, Mrs. Crane communicated to her husband her intention to be baptized. At the close of the discourse at night, she came forward and made public confession of her faith in Christ, and we proceeded to the river "the same hour of the night,", and buried her with the Saviour of the world in baptism. She had been a Methodist twenty-five years.

OBITUARY.
Peru, La Salle Co., Ill., May 15, 1856.

Dear Bro. Franklin:—For the information of numerous friends in Ohio and elsewhere, I wish you to publish an account of the death of my long afflicted and beloved son, James A. Irvin.

He, in company with his mother, left Harrison, Hamilton county, Ohio, on the 7th of April and arrived in La Salle county, Ill., on the 9th, in as good health as he had enjoyed for a month before leaving. On the 17th April, my son A. R. and I arrived at Cedar Point, and found them at the house of a dear brother (John Vandevort). In a few days, however, he was confined to bed, but we were not apprehensive that his end was so near. He got up in a day or two, and on the second day of May we removed him two miles to our present residence, where he lingered until May 9th, ten minutes before one o'clock P. M., when, without a struggle or a groan, his ransomed spirit left its clay tenement to return to God who gave it.

"Let me die the death of the righteous, and let my last end be like his."

As ever, your brother,

W. M. Irvin.

THE AMERICAN CHRISTIAN REVIEW.

Vol. 1.] CINCINNATI, AUGUST, 1856. [No. 8.

THE BEGINNING CORNER, Or The Church of Christ Identified.

BY DR. .J. R. HOWARD.

Thou art the Christ, the SON of the living God:—upon this rock I will build my church; and the gates of Hades shall not prevail against it.— Matt. xvi: 16, 18.

SUCH were the words of the Lord Jesus Christ, in reference to the foundation and perpetuity of his Church—the kingdom he came to establish on earth—and which is destined ultimately to supersede all other dominions, and to become the last universal empire of the world; for "the kingdom and the dominion, and the greatness of the kingdom under the whole heaven, shall be given to the saints of the Most High, whose kingdom is an everlasting kingdom, and all dominions shall serve and obey him." These words of Christ, above quoted, were spoken by him in reference to the reply of the apostle Peter, who had anticipated the other apostles in assenting and confessing the great cardinal truth, that JESUS CHRIST IS THE SON OF GOD. It was upon this grand, comprehensive truth, that Jesus declared he would build his CHURCH; and that the powers of the unseen world should not prevail over it; but that it should continue to exist through all future time, amid the origin progress and decay of all other systems and organizations, whether civil, ecclesiastical, political or philosophical; and amid the rise, existence and fall of republics, kingdoms and empires.

VOL. I, No. 8—15.

In accordance with this prophetic declaration of the Messiah, his CHURCH was founded upon this ROCK by his apostles—his inspired and divinely authorized ambassadors and ministers plenipotentiary to the world; and they left it pure, uncorrupted, undivided and in unity. It was at first *a unit*—but *one*—"one body," animated by "one spirit," the Holy Spirit; and of which body Christ was the great head, and "Lord of the Spirit," and his disciples the members. But how is it now? Corruption and disunion have been doing their sad work for thirteen long centuries, or more; and reverse and disastrous change, schism and division have been the lamentable result!— Instead of the *one* church of Christ, there have been and are now, more nearly *a thousand and one* sectarian churches!

This is indeed an age of "churches," all claiming to be orthodox, and founded on the Bible, and appealing to its authority; and all busily engaged in making proselytes to their different systems, and in rivaling each other in power, influence and numbers. The sincere inquirer after truth is frequently perplexed, and at a loss to know to what church or denomination to attach himself; and generally aims to find the church which he conceives to be *nearest* to the Bible. Why not endeavor to find the TRUE church at once—the one founded *on* the Bible, and enter into that?—since there must be a true church somewhere, as Jesus declared "the gates of Hades should *never prevail* against it;" and as that alone is to triumph, and all *others* are destined to be utterly destroyed and annihilated! But a question of great importance may arise here, one involving a most interesting inquiry, and that is—*where* is the true church *now* to be *found?*—and how shall we be enabled to know it?—to *identify* and recognize it?

Now there were certain *marks* by which that church could be known and identified in the days of the apostles. These marks are now to be found in the New Testament as plain and distinct as they were then; and where they will apply, that is the *true* Church of Christ, and *all other* churches are spurious, mere counterfeits of the genuine, and not to be found in the Bible—or only predicted there as emanations from the great apostasy—the harlot "*mother* and mistress of all" apostate "churches," and as her daughters, granddaughters and their progeny. It is impossible for *all* the different sects, or even the self-styled "evangelical denominations," to be *the* Church of Christ, as there are *many*—"their name is legion," and that is a *unit*—but ONE, nor are they *"branches"* of it, for it never had, and cannot have any of these sectarian branches. *Branches* they may be and no doubt are, but not of the Church of Christ—branches of some other body from which they have originated—of the parent trunk that sprung up at Rome —or at least the most of them. But let us examine the different *marks* of the Church of Christ, in order that we may *identify* it, and ascertain where it is *now* to be found. There are several of these, and among them we will begin with

Its Origin and Perpetuity.

The Church of Christ originated, as we have shown, in the days of the Apostles, and was founded by them; while all others began in after ages, and were founded by uninspired men. It was founded by the apostle Peter under a special commission from the Lord Jesus Christ—the other Apostles "standing up" and concurring with him—and began at Jerusalem on the first Pentecost after the resurrection and ascension of Christ; while all other churches were originated by other and uninspired men—without any divine influence or authority—and began at other places, and in after ages, most of them in modern times, and some of them even in our own day. But such were the corruptions of the Christian Religion for ages—such was the influence of false systems, pretending to derive their authority from the Bible—such the perversion, misapplication, suppression and obliteration of its truths—that these *marks* were well nigh lost sight of, particularly those by which the primitive gospel is to be recognized and identified as that preached and taught by the Apostles. These marks were *faith, repentance,* and *baptism* in order to the remission of sins, in the original and scriptural import of these terms, and with their true object and design. But we can perhaps better illustrate this by the following anecdote of the "Beginning Corner:"

In early times, and before the settlement of the western country, many thousands of acres of land were taken up in it under authority of Congress, by various individuals, in compensation for services rendered the country. The manner of doing this was as follows:—a *corner* was made, called the *"beginning* corner," on some tree, by making *three* chops through the bark with a hatchet, one above the other facing some one of the four cardinal points; and then another row of three chops made on the same tree facing another one of the cardinal points, so as to be at a right angle with the other row. If one faced east, for instance, the other must face north, or south, as might be desirable, so as to form a right angle. Or, if one faced north, the other must face east or west—and so on, so as to form the tract of land from the angle made. Lines were then run, in the directions facing these chops, to certain distances each way, and then right angles again made, called corners; and lines run again, facing these, so as to meet or "close" at another point called a corner, diagonally opposite the first or beginning comer—including within the angles or lines a tract of land of a given amount of acres, in a square or oblong, as might be most eligible. But none but the first, or "beginning corner," was marked as above—which was done in order to identify the tract at a future day. The "survey" or tract had always to call for a certain tree, with these marks or chops upon it, as the *beginning corner*; and to render the finding and identification of it certain, the trees around this "corner tree" were also marked with chops facing it, called "pointers," because *pointing* to it; and the finding and *identifying* of this corner tree, was necessary to the identification of the land, and the consequent possession of it. Sometimes another tract of land was run out, or called for, calling for this particular tract and its beginning corner; and then perhaps several others calling for this, or for each other as connected with that.— These were called a *chain* or connection of "grants" or surveys; and the beginning corner of the first tract, the *key corner,* as when found, as it were, unlocking or opening to the whole—or as a *key* or clue by which to find and identify all the others. Sometimes, and in some cases, where many years had elapsed, the *beginning corner* was very difficult to find, and required much searching for, and close examination; and sometimes the aid of someone acquainted with it when made, was necessary, in order to find and identify it. Such was the case before us, which we have selected for our *illustration,* and in order to understand which we have made the preceding remarks.

An old Revolutionary soldier in Virginia held a claim for one of these tracts of land, or "old surveys" as usually termed, somewhere in the western country. He had neglected it for a long time, until the country became settled up, and covered over with other claims and tracts, made by entries, when at length he came out west to search for, find it, and take possession. But it could nowhere be found! The whole country in which it lay, was covered over by other tracts or claims—no room was found for his—and no one could inform him where it was. What was to be done? After searching long and in vain, he was about to sit down in despair, when he heard of a man, who knew where the corner was, and could point it out to him. Joy and hope fill his bosom, and he immediately goes for him, engages his services to show it, and brings him to the section of country. They commence the search. A particular tree is called for, in the grant, in a certain location; and a similar one is found in a corresponding situation. But vines, and parasitical growth have so grown, and twined, and wound around the trunk, and covered it over, that no marks can be found! They go to work, and tear off and strip it of these, when, behold! there are the identical marks, the original chops in the bark, as made there at first; and joy springs up in the old soldier's breast, and animates his heart, at the glad discovery! The *beginning corner* is found, the land identified, and his claim established. But his land is all covered over by other and subsequent claims. One man has made himself a beginning corner, and run off a tract to suit him—another had made himself a corner, and run off a tract—another had taken the first as a *key* corner, and run him off one—and another—and another—until the whole of the original survey was covered over! What is to be done?— Here is the original and real claimant—his corner found—and his land clearly identified—but all claimed by others! Will they now surrender their claims as false and untenable, and purchase of the rightful owner, and settle. or live upon his tract? By no means.—They all rise up in arms against him—call him all sorts of hard names—vilify and abuse and slander him—and contend against the clearest evidence that *they are the rightful owners!* There is a general combination against him, to put him down and oust him! The cry is, that he is trying to take our land from us—that *his* claim is a false one and *ours* the genuine—and all this. They say that he is mistaken about the beginning corner—that these marks on it won't do—that they are not the same made there at first, &c. They all go to law with him, in the vain hope of gaining and establishing their own claims, by perversion, misrepresentation, or in any other way, that will offer them, and their *well-paid lawyers* any hope or chance. But the testimony is produced in court, that these old chops are the true and genuine marks and this the original beginning corner; and suit after suit goes against them—their claims are invalidated—and the old grant is established to their complete discomfiture!

We come now to the application of this illustration, to the restoration of the primitive Gospel and primitive Christianity. In that part of the commission recorded by Luke, we read; "Thus it is written, and thus it behooved Christ to suffer, and to rise from the dead the third day; and that repentance and remission of sins should be preached in his name, among all nations, *beginning at* JERUSALEM." Here, to use our illustration, is the BEGINNING CORNER of the Christian Dispensation. It was made by the apostle Peter, at Jerusalem, on the first Pentecost after the resurrection and ascension of our Saviour, by the authority of the Lord Jesus Christ, and in accordance with the general commission here quoted, given to all the Apostles, and the special one given to Peter, to set up, or open the kingdom of heaven. He made the *three* marks necessary for a legal corner, on the old Jerusalem trunk:

1. Faith, produced by his discourse, and evinced by his hearers being "cut to the heart" by the words of the Holy Spirit spoken by or through him, and the question, "What shall we do?"

2. Repentance, when he commanded them to "repent."

3. Baptism for remission of sins, when he commanded them to "*be baptized* in the name of Jesus Christ *for* the *remission of* sins."

These marks were plainly and visibly made, so that all could see and understand them; and none then disputed them, or the validity of this beginning corner. But in the lapse of ages they were well nigh lost sight of, and came near being entirely obliterated. The parasitical growth of error, superstition, and mysticism. and the traditions, inventions, and corruptions of men, crept by slow degrees, and twined and wound around the old Jerusalem trunk, and covered and matted it over, until the old marks were obscured, and almost entirely lost sight of and forgotten!

Some, taking advantage of this state of things, and others, having made fruitless searches for the old corner, began, each one, to make a *new corner* for himself, and to run out a corresponding tract on the old survey, to suit their own notions and opinions. In process of time other tracts were run out, in accordance with new corners, or in correspondence with preceding ones, until, tract added to tract, they had almost entirely covered the old survey!

The *Roman Catholics* were the first trespassers on it, and made the first new corner, and run out a very large tract. This trespass on the old grant, opened the way for others; and the corner they made became a *keg corner,* for a chain or connection of chains.

The *Episcopalians* then made a corner, from the Roman Catholic, and run out a tract—the *Presbyterians* made one in connection, and run out at first one tract; and then this became a key corner, from which they ran out several other tracts, and then divided their first tract between the Old School and the New School—the *Methodists* made a corner from the Episcopalian, and at first ran out one tract; and then from this as a key corner, ran out several other tracts; and then divided the old tract between the Church North and the Church South—the *Baptists* made one, but "ran past Jerusalem,", not to Jericho, but to John the Baptist in the river Jordan, and *thought* they had made their corner there, but were mistaken, as they made it in modern times and somewhere else; and then ran out one, and afterward several tracts. And thus on, with all the other sects or denominations. But none of these began at the right corner.

The *beginning corner* of Roman Catholicism, was made at Rome—the beginning corner of Episcopalianism, was made at London—that of Presbyterianism, in Scotland—that of Methodism, at Oxford in England—of Baptistism, in Germany—of Lutheranism, there at Wittemburg—of Calvinism, at Geneva—and so on through the long catalogue of sects or denominations and religious parties. None began at the right place. But the beginning corner of the Gospel—of pure, apostolic, primitive Christianity—was made at JERUSALEM—"beginning *at Jerusalem."*

Justinian made the beginning corner of Romanism—Henry VIII. of England, made that of

THE CHURCH OF CHRIST IDENTIFIED.

Episcopalianism—John Wesley, that of Methodism—Menno, of Baptistism—John Knox, of Presbyterianism—Martin Luther, of Lutheranism—John Calvin, of Calvinism—and thus on to the end of the long catalogue of religious sects or parties in Christendom. But the *apostle* PETER made the "beginning corner" of the Christian dispensation—of pure, uncorrupted Christianity; and, as we have shown, by special commission from the Lord Jesus Christ himself. (See Matt. xvi: 19, and Acts ii: 14, 38: x. ch. xv: 7).

The *apostle* PETER, and *not Alexander Campbell*, made the beginning corner of the Christian Church. A. Campbell only acted the part of the man who *showed* the beginning corner of the old survey. He exposed and tore away the human additions and appendages, the traditions, mysticism, and error with which the marks on the Jerusalem trunk—the corner of primitive Christianity—had been covered over, obscured, and hidden from the view of men; and *identified* it, by the *original marks,* to be the *same one* made by Peter. And this is the reason why there is such an outcry against Alexander Campbell; and why he is so much opposed and abused by the various religious parties, who have made their new corners, and run out their tracts on the old survey! They well know that the *identification* of the *old* corner for which he is contending, will be *fatal* to all their old claims!—that if that stand, (and it *will* stand), they will have to give them all up, and "abandon the *ground*" which they have *taken*—the men-made systems they have espoused! Hence the great excitement and contention throughout the length and breadth of the land!—the opposition to this identifier of the old corner, and those associated with him—the debating and the declamation everywhere!

Had Alexander Campbell made a *new corner,* and run out a *new tract* on this old survey, according to the chart and compass of "orthodoxy," (as so self-styled), so as not to have *interfered* with the *claims* of *others,* he would have been hailed as a good, orthodox neighbor, and welcomed into the sectarian community. But he *identified* the *old corner;* and in this consists the great "head and front of his offence!"

And, as finding and identifying the original corner of the old survey, did not constitute the man who found it the locator or owner of the land, so the *identification* of the old Gospel—of the Church of Christ—does not make Alexander Campbell the *inventor* of a *new system,* or the *founder* of a *new party.* This he has always disavowed or disclaimed, in the strongest terms. He has been only the humble *instrument* in the hands of God, in the *restoration* to the world of apostolic and primitive Christianity, as it was left uncorrupted by the Apostles, and as it came completed and perfected from their hands.

The sectarian occupants of the new tracts, made and run out on the old Gospel survey, have tried, in various ways, to show that these marks made by Peter are not the *true marks* of the *old corner.* Some have endeavored to prove that "*faith alone*" is the *only* mark; and they accordingly made but *one chop* on their tree. But this would not do—would not constitute a *legal* corner. Others contended that there were but *two* marks necessary—*faith* and *repentance;* and they accordingly put *two* marks only on their tree.

But neither will these do, as the law requires *three chops* in all cases, all the country over, to constitute a genuine and legal coiner; and to be a *lawful* and acceptable one, it *must have* these *three.* Hence *one* chop will not do, and *two* are no better than one. These three marks were necessary; and accordingly the Apostle made *three* on the old Jerusalem trunk:—1. FAITH; 2. REPENTANCE; 3. BAPTISM "*for remission of sins.*" "And as every corner must have its *pointers,* to point to it, and show where it stands and is to be found, and that it is the true corner, so this has its pointers. It has *thirteen* pointers, the thirteen Apostles, who always point to it as the genuine corner—to this alone, and never to any other. The genuine corner must have *these three* marks; and every other corner that lacks them is not the right corner. To begin at such a one is to *begin wrong;* and there is great danger, in such a case, of *running wrong* and *ending wrong!* "Take heed." "Be not deceived." "So *run that ye may obtain.*"

4. PERPETUITY.—"On this rock," said Jesus,

"I will build my church, and the gates of hades shall *never prevail* against it." Nor have they ever done so, nor will they ever be able to do it. The powers of the unseen world, persecution, corruption and division, opposition of every kind and character, have been arrayed against it; and have all been unsuccessful in attempting to put down and destroy it! And though it was predicted concerning it, that it should be twelve hundred and sixty years in a state of depression, and perhaps of corruption or partial corruption, yet it has never been extinct. It has always continued to exist in some place, and in some state or condition. It was at first in a state of purity, as represented by the emblem of the *"white* horse," of the first seal in the Apocalypse. But this state did not continue long, for even in the days of the Apostles, "the mystery of iniquity had begun to work." It was then, or after that, for a long time in a state of depression, and perhaps partial corruption, as remarked, from the influence of that corrupted state of things represented by the *"black* horse," the Roman Catholic apostasy, in the third seal. Then, or afterward, atheism prevailed, and the French infidel philosophy, growing out of the abuses of religion by Romanism, and represented by the *"pale* horse," when true religion became nearly extinct in the heart of the civilized world. From these conditions, it is now emerging, and shall again be in a state of *purity,* as indicated by the "*white* horse," the second time, (in Rev. xix: 11,) and in a state of universal prevalence and triumph, consummated after the great battle of Armageddon, as indicated by the events predicted as then to follow, (in that chapter,) and to result in the introduction of the Millenium. Hence Satan attempted at first to destroy the church, by *persecution;* but "the blood of the martyrs became the seed of the church," and he failed. He then attempted to destroy it by *corruption;* and the long, dark night of the Roman Catholic apostasy came on. But Luther sounded the trumpet of reformation, the light of the truth began to dawn upon the benighted world, and the true church began gradually to emerge from that long, gloomy, dark night, but she did not get entirely out. Seeing her emerging, Satan then attempted to destroy her by *division;* and then "a thousand and one" sects arose, one after another, or really more than six hundred! But he is destined to be foiled and fail here, for the full blaze of divine truth is now shining in all its pristine purity, by the influence of the current reformation in restoring the ancient gospel; and the church, again in her primitive apostolic purity, is destined to go forth in the strength and power and irresistible might of the Lord of Hosts, and to achieve a universal triumph, and Satan is to be bound down in the bottomless pit for a thousand years, and a seal set upon him, so that he "shall *not* go forth to *deceive* the nations." Here, then, we have the first mark of the true church of Christ—ORIGIN and PERPETUITY. The church now, which can establish a claim to these marks, is THE *church of Christ,* all things else being equal, or if not otherwise defective.

II. NAME.—The church of Christ is known and recognized in the New Testament, by such appellations as these: "Church of God," and "Churches of Christ." Jesus calls it: "MY CHURCH." Hence we may with propriety call it the "CHRISTIAN CHURCH," or "CHURCH OF CHRIST." In fact, we are not authorized by the Bible, or in the New Testament, to call it anything else than according to the *divine* nomenclature. The New Testament recognizes no *party* or *sectarian names* whatever. The names, "Roman Catholic Church," or "Episcopalian Church," or "Presbyterian Church," or "Baptist Church," or "Methodist Church," and so on, are nowhere to be found there, and are not recognized by it; nor are the names "Roman Catholics," "Episcopalians," "Baptists," "Methodists, "Presbyterians," etc. All such names, as party appellatives and distinctions—or as distinctive appellations—are *condemned* by the Apostles in the most unreserved and unqualified terms, and ranked by them among the "*works of the flesh."* Says Paul to the Corinthians, in reference to this: *"Ye are carnal* [fleshly]: for whereas there is among you envying and strife, and *divisions,* are ye not *carnal,* and *walk as men?* For while one saith, I am of Paul; and another, I am of Apollos; are ye not *carnal."*

THE CHURCH OF CHRIST IDENTIFIED.

Will the Lord Jesus Christ, when He comes the second time, own as HIS churches those wearing any other names than *His?*—or than those names in the New Testament, authorized by Him to be worn? Most assuredly NOT! For illustration: Suppose a man was to leave his wife and family, to make a visit to a distant foreign country, necessary to be made, and to be necessarily absent for some long stated or indefinite period of time, but, at the same time, with the promise and assurance of *returning again,* to receive her again, and live with her as his bride, and to be again united to his family: and suppose that, during his absence, she was, with a perfect *knowledge* of all these things, to throw away *his* name, and take some *other* name, and be found, when he returned, *wearing* that other name—think you that he would own and take her as his bride? By no means! He would most assuredly refuse and reject her! Now, the church is called the bride or wife of the Lord Jesus Christ; and He is called her husband: "The *bride,* the Lamb's *wife.*" "Prepared as a *bride,* adorned for her *husband.*" "I have espoused you to *one husband,* that I may present you as a *chaste virgin* to Christ."

Now, the Lord Jesus Christ left the world about eighteen hundred years ago, ascended to heaven, was crowned King of kings, and took his seat on the throne of the Universe "at the right hand of the Majesty on high;" and has left in his WORD the *promise* and *assurance* of returning again to earth, to receive His bride, the Church, and be united to her, to reign on earth with her a thousand years, of sinless happiness and Millennial glory! But what has taken place since he ascended? As we have shown, corruption, division, and apostasy have done their evil work; and His Church, which his Apostles left pure, undivided, and uncorrupted, wearing *His name alone,* and observing his ordinances, worship, and commandments, has *apostatized* from Him, "left her first love," and become an abominable sectarian organization, called the Roman Catholic Church, full of loathsome corruptions and cruelties and evils and abominations; and has persecuted and tortured and evil-treated and put to death His faithful followers, until their blood has flowed in rivers and oceans, and cried to Heaven for vengeance upon this apostate church! Nor is this all. She has "committed *fornication* with the kings of the earth," and has, by this illicit intercourse, played the harlot, and become the mother of a numerous progeny of illegitimate *daughters, wearing other names* than that of Christ, as "Episcopalian church," etc., full of the spirit and corruptions of the old "scarlet" "mother and mistress of all" such "churches." And these daughters have "played the harlot" too, and produced a brood of illegitimate *grand-daughters* to the old mother, as the "Episcopal Methodist church," and others in the same category, with the blood of the old grandmother in their veins, and full too of her spirit, traditions, and corruptions! Hence the Lord Jesus Christ, when he comes the second time—to be united to his Bride, the Church—will *disown* every one of these corrupt, unauthorized religious organizations remaining—will REJECT *every one* of them—and will recognize but the *one* true Church, wearing His *name* to the exclusion of all others. And fearful will be their destiny then! It will be that of great Babylon herself—that of "the beast and false prophet," in Rev. xix: chap., where this union with her, and their destiny are fully and vividly portrayed.

Here, therefore, is the second mark of the true Church. The Church that wears the *"Christian"* NAME, to the exclusion of all *party* or *sectarian* names; and whose members do not own or wear any name but those of "Christian." "Disciple of Christ," etc., as found in the New Testament—is the Church of Christ, all other things being equal, or having all the other necessary marks.

III. CREED.

Such documents as human "Creeds," "Confessions of Faith," "Disciplines," "Articles of Faith," "Abstracts of Doctrine," etc., were totally unknown to the Apostles—never permitted by them—and have no authority whatever, not the least shadow of authority, anywhere is the Bible or New Testament; but are subversive of its authority, full of evil tendencies, and supplant that volume by their uninspired, unauthorized human legislation, and usurping and nullifying the ordinances and commandments of God, by their assumed authority over the minds and consciences of men. "In vain do they worship me," says Christ, "teaching for doctrines the *commandments of men.*" "Full well ye *reject* the *commandment* of God, that ye may *keep your own tradition,*" "Making the word of God of *none effect through your traditions.*" These written and published Creeds virtually "add to" or "take from" the Bible; and incur the Divine malediction for so doing, pronounced there against all such conduct. They create and continue parties, foment disunion, and keep up and perpetuate divisions!

The primitive Christians had no other creed than the Bible, nor did those who lived for ages after them. This alone kept them united for three hundred years—kept out heresy— and was all-sufficient to perfect them in holiness and character. And if the Bible was sufficient then for all these purposes, it is amply so now; and we have no need of human creeds.

The Church now which has no creed but the *Bible*—which owns and recognizes no other—whose motto is, "The Bible, the Bible alone, and nothing but the Bible"—is, all things else being equal, the true Church of Christ.

IV. UNITY AND CATHOLICITY.

Another mark of the genuine Church of Christ, is its UNITY and CATHOLICITY.

1. Its Unity.—It was but *one*—a *unit.* Jesus calls it "MY *Church,*" thus implying that it could be but *one*—a unit—and not "churches" in the plural. Wherever it is mentioned in the New Testament, in the general or abstract, it is only as *one:* "There is *one body* and one Spirit"—"THE *Church,* which is his *body*"—"by one Spirit we are all baptized into *one body*"—"we have *many members in one body*"—"now they are *many members,* yet but ONE *body*"—"Ye are THE *body* of Christ, and *members in particular.*" Hence the Church is composed of *one* general body, and not many "sectarian bodies;" and had no sectarian "branches." How would a cedar tree look, with here an *apple* branch, there a *peach* branch, yonder a *pear* branch, and yonder a *cherry* branch? How odd, unnatural, and grotesque would it appear! And how would the old Jerusalem trunk look, with a Roman Catholic branch, an Episcopalian branch, a Baptist branch, a Presbyterian branch, a Methodist branch, etc? What an odd, unnatural, and heterogeneous appearance would it present! But it neither has, and never had any of these sectarian branches growing from it. Its branches are all homogeneous with itself—of the same nature—and nothing more than its members, or the organizations composing the true Church of Christ.

2. Catholicity.—The Church of Christ is *catholic:* not *Roman* Catholic nor *Greek* Catholic, but CHRISTIAN *catholic.* The word catholic means *universal,* and the Church of Christ is the only true *catholic* or universal Church; all others are only sectarian parties—partial and imperfect in every respect, and destined to fall and perish—to be utterly overthrown and annihilated; while this is to prevail universally and everywhere, in every land and clime and part of the world—where "all shall see eye to eye, and hear ear to ear"—when "all shall know God from the least to the greatest"—and when "righteousness shall cover the land as the waters do the deep."

Where this UNITY and CATHOLICITY are to be found, that is the church of Christ, all things else considered being equal.

V. TERMS OF ADMISSION.

A fifth mark of the true church of Christ, is its TERMS OF ADMISSION. These are *Faith. Repentance, Confession,* and *Baptism,* in the order here presented, and in their Biblical import and application.

1. Faith in the Lord Jesus Christ, as the Messiah, Son of God, and Saviour of the world.

2. Repentance, or reformation, toward God.

3. Confession, with the mouth, before men, that "Jesus Christ is the Son of God." "These [miracles] are recorded," says John, "that ye might *believe that Jesus is the Christ, the Son of God.;* and that believing ye might have life through His name." And says Jesus himself: "Whosoever shall *confess* me *before men,* him will I also confess before my Father which is in heaven. But whosoever shall *deny me before men,* him will I also deny before my Father which is in heaven"—including him who *refuses*

THE CHURCH OF CHRIST IDENTIFIED.

thus to confess Him. Hence He says: "Whosoever, therefore, shall be *ashamed of me* and of *my words* in this adulterous and sinful generation; of him also shall the Son of Man *be ashamed,* when he cometh in the glory of his Father, with the holy angels." This *confession* must be made with the *mouth:* "If thou shalt *confess with thy mouth,* that *Jesus Christ is Lord,* and *believe in thine heart* that God hath raised Him from the dead, thou shalt be *saved."* It is first in the heart when believed—then comes out of the mouth when confessed; which is the evidence of its being believed: and hence, "Whosoever believeth on Him *shall not be ashamed;"* that is, to confess him. This was the confession made by the Ethiopian eunuch to Philip the Evangelist, when he demanded baptism of him: "If thou *believest* with *all thy heart,* thou mayest," said Philip to him. "I believe that *Jesus Christ is the Son of God,"* replied and confessed the eunuch. 4. *Immersion* "into the name of the Father, and of the Son, and of the Holy Spirit," for, or "in order to the remission of sins." (See Acts ii: 38, xxii: 16, etc.; and compare Romans vi; 3-7, with 17 and 18, and Colos. ii: 10-14.)

Where all these are not expressed *together* in the New Testament, in the order here presented, they are *understood;* and hence persons were addressed with one or more of them, according to the various situations, conditions and circumstances by which they were surrounded. 1. If infidel, or perhaps never having heard of Christ, as the jailor at Philippi, they are addressed, as he was, by Paul and Silas: *"Believe on the Lord Jesus Christ, and thou shalt be saved."* When there is faith enough to *change the heart,* and lead to *action* or *obedience,* then it is strong enough, and sufficient in degree or measure. 2. If already *believing,* as were the Jews on Pentecost, who inquired what to *do,* and evinced their *faith* by the question they asked, people must be addressed as Peter addressed them: *"Repent,"* etc. He did not command them to be *sorry* for their sins, to grieve, mourn, etc., on account of them, for "they were *cut to the heart"* by his words, and had already evinced their deep contrition and penitence by the question they asked; but he commanded them to "reform"!

When an individual is sorry enough for his sins to *forsake* them, then he is penitent, or has repented enough; he has mourned or sorrowed sufficiently, and his penitence is sufficient in degree or measure. So anyone may always know when he has *believed* and *repented* enough— when the measure of his faith and repentance is sufficient—when they are deep enough and strong enough. 3. *(Confession,* as in the case of the eunuch, and as spoken of and referred to elsewhere, according to the quotations already made.) 4. Where persons had both *believed* and *repented,* as in the case of Paul, they are not enjoined to do either, but merely to *"be baptized."* As Ananias said to him: "Arise, and *be baptized,* and *wash away thy sins,* calling on the name of the Lord." And hence it must be *for, or in order to the remission of sins,* as we have already observed. Hence the expression in Acts ii. 38:—"Be baptized for [in order to] the remission of sins;" and in various other places, as Rom. vi: 3-7, compared with verses 17th and 18th of same chapter; Col. ii: 10-14; Heb. x: 22; 1 Cor. vi: 11; Mark xvi: 16; 1 Peter iii: 21; Tit. iii: 5; etc.

The church now that requires all these, in the order here presented, in their Biblical import and design, and for the purposes here named, is the true church of Christ, all other things being equal; that is, if she has all the other marks required. Such a church, according to the declaration of our Saviour, shall never become extinct; but shall prevail and triumph universally.

VI. ORGANIZATION AND INDEPENDENCE.

Another mark of the true church of Christ is its ORGANIZATION and INDEPENDENCE. Persons thus admitted into the church of Christ— or according to the preceding *terms of admission*—were constituted into different distinct and independent bodies, called "churches," or more properly, *congregations.* These were formed, or constituted, by disciples of Christ assembling themselves together at some designated point, according to previous understanding and notices, and there covenanting and agreeing to meet together as a congregation of Christ, at some particular place or house, to worship God and keep the ordinances of His house; and manifesting this their covenanting and agreeing together, by giving each other the right hand, or in some other significant and appropriate way.

Thus *constituted,* these congregations were then *organized,* by the *appointment* and *ordination* of certain officers. These consisted of three classes only: 1. *Bishops,* or elders; 2. *Deacons* and *deaconesses;* 3. *Evangelists.* These three classes are all that are recognized in the New Testament; and each class had its appropriate duties to attend to—peculiar to itself, and not confounded or combined with those of the others; and the duties of all, in their respective spheres, are essential to the existence, increase and extension of the church of Christ—to the continuance and perpetuation of the discipleship of its members—their growth in favor, knowledge, holiness and happiness—and their perseverance in the divine life and character.

1. The *business* of the *Evangelists,* was, *to immerse penitent believers,* on a *confession* of their *faith* in Jesus Christ as the Son of God; to then form, or constitute them into congregations; and then to *organize* these, by "setting all things in order"—the appointment and ordination of the scriptural and proper officers, according to the qualifications required in the New Testament, and in the manner there authorized and prescribed; and then afterward to see that the congregations continue properly organized, as aforesaid, and to put them in order again, whenever necessary, when in confusion or out of order in any way; and to aid in correcting and putting down errors that may arise in faith and practice. 2. The duty of the *Bishops* or Elders, was to oversee, or rule the church—to teach, or feed it with the word of God—to attend to all its spiritual concerns—to exercise a supervision over all its members—to watch over the church as a body and over them individually—in short, to be the executive officers of the church, in the application and execution of the laws of the kingdom of Christ. 3. The business of the *Deacons* and *Deaconesses* was to attend to the temporal affairs of the church, and everything connected with and pertaining to them—to be its treasurers or almoners, to collect and take care of its contributions and dispense them, see to the relief of the poor and needy, &c,: Each class acting in the department peculiar and appropriate to it, and not invading the prerogatives and duties of the others—the Deaconesses attending to the *female* department of that office in particular. Of these last two classes of officers, (Bishops and Deacons,) there was always a *plurality* in every church or congregation, where necessary; and they had no jurisdiction or authority in any other congregation than the one to which they belonged.— The New Testament is an utter stranger to Romish sees and diocesan episcopacy—to Roman and Episcopalian Bishops and Arch-bishops, Priests, Rectors, Deans, &c.,—and to Methodist Bishops, Presiding Elders, Deacons, &c.— They are all of *human,* not divine origin; and have not a particle of authority—or even the shadow of it—in that divine volume.

These different congregations of the church of Christ, were entirely INDEPENDENT of each other, as regards ecclesiastical polity or church government, management of their religious affairs, &c. There was no higher body than the congregation; and to that was always the ultimate appeal, whether acting as a body, or through her appropriate officers. Sometimes they *co-operated* with each other, but always for definite purposes, and without sacrificing their independence as individual congregations. And the New Testament is also an utter stranger to all such bodies and things as "General" and "Annual Conferences,"—"General Assemblies"—"Synods"—sectarian "Presbyteries"—"Episcopalian Conventions"—Baptist "Associations," &c.

The church now which has the *organization* here described, and the *independence* referred to, is the true Church of Christ, everything else being equal; and no church can be the true church, which is deficient in these important requisites, or lacking any of them.

VII. WORSHIP AND GOVERNMENT.

The congregations thus organized met together every Lord's day, to break the loaf, or partake of the Lord's supper, and to attend to the *public* worship of God connected with that institution; and to engage in and attend upon the public religious exercises, teaching, instructing, and training of the congregation, belonging to that day; with prayer, praise, and thanksgiving; and to attend to such spiritual and temporal matters as were connected with their meeting together on that day—considered in reference to all the scriptural purposes for which they came together. (See Acts ii 42: xx. 7; 1st Cor. xi 17—34; Heb. x 25; 1 Tim. ii 1—4; Col. iv 16; 1 Cor. xvi:2; and other passages on these subjects.)

The GOVERNMENT of these congregations, was strictly that of the New Testament form, as this contained all the rules and laws which they needed and had. By that volume they were governed in all respects and in every particular; by it were all cases of discipline tried; and to it was all the appeal, and to no other documentary authority. The Bishops or Elders constituted the Presbytery or Eldership of the church, and were the governing and executive officers of the church, to see that its constitution was not violated, and to apply and execute the laws of the kingdom; while the Deacons and the Deaconesses constituted the Diaconate of the church, to attend to all its temporal arrangements, and, where necessary, to carry out such action of the Eldership as fell within their sphere.

The church now having this *worship* and this *government,* is, all things else being equal, or having all the other marks, the true church of Christ.

CONCLUSION.

We have now given the *marks*—or the most important marks—by which the *true* church of Christ may be identified and recognized.— Wherever they will all apply, that is most certainly the true church—the only organization of the kind on earth, that has the authority and approbation of God—that will prevail and triumph, and stand when all others shall fall — and the only one that the Lord Jesus Christ will own, and receive as his Bride, when He shall come again, "without a sin-offering unto salvation."

It may be said to us as it was once said to the Saviour: "This is a hard saying, who can bear it?" And it may also be said to us; "You have unchristianized every church in the land but one—but your own—and consigned them all alike to the disapprobation of God, disownment by the Lord Jesus Christ, and utter extinction and annihilation!" If so—if thus consigned—it is not *we* who have done it, but it has been done by the New Testament—by the WORD of God. If they are recognized by that, it is beyond our power to unchurch or unchristianize them—nor do we wish to do so. If they are not the *true* church—or *true* churches—of Christ, they can easily become such. Any church can become the true church by acquiring all these marks of identification, by parting with everything inconsistent with them, and by conforming to everything taught in the New Testament, as regards its constitution, organization, laws and regulations.

The church which has all these marks—to the exclusion of what, is inconsistent with them and the Bible—and claims to be the true, catholic, apostolic church—has taken high and vantage ground in religion—the highest position on earth. She has taken ground that must be sustained at every point—which she must never abandon; and which she must occupy worthily and improve perseveringly—in a manner that shall result in her own welfare and happiness, the glory of God, and her eternal redemption and salvation.

If she is no better than the sects around her—or perhaps not as good—in piety, temper, good works, the practice of Christian duty and keeping of the ordinances of the Lord's house—what will be the inducement to unite with, or enter into her?—or what advantages will she possess, by a mere *external* conformity to the Bible, in all these marks of identification? The inquiry with her should always be—"Wherein do we *excel?*" Her members should indeed be "a peculiar people, zealous of good works," and in obeying the commandments of the Lord Jesus Christ. They should endeavor to have "a good report of those without," or of the world—should avoid everything inconsistent with their high and holy profession, and be found in the daily discharge of every duty—should be "living epistles, known and read of all men," and "walking in all the commandments and ordinances of the Lord blamelessly." Then will the church be "clear as the sun, fair as the moon, and as terrible as an army with banners"—"*the pillar* and *ground* of truth."

Such must be the church, in order to be prepared for entering on the glorious period of the Millennium. She must have all these marks, and be in possession of this character. Before entering upon that she will have to pass through an *ordeal* that will try her as with fire—purge her from all that is impure and corrupting—give her members the spirit of martyrs—and make her the Bride, the Lamb's wife—the Church Triumphant.

-----o-----

Our Position as a Religious Community.
No. VIIL

Apology 5.—Having in previous articles considered four popular apologies for human creeds, we shall now proceed to consider a fifth, and the last one we shall trouble the reader with at present. It is generally couched in the following brief sentence: "Our creed will do us no harm, if it does no good." This is very soothing, quieting and relieving to the conscience. Many honest and well-meaning persons, after being awakened and brought to reflect on this subject seriously; after having their attention called to the Bible, the infallible law of the Lord, as a rule of faith—have dropped the subject, and quieted their consciences, by drawing a long breath, and saying: "Well, I know the Bible is infallible, the only sure guide to heaven—' the only infallible rule of our faith and practice'—but our creed will do me no harm; I never read it, do not know what is in it, nor care anything about it." This makes the matter assume the appearance of being of but very little consequence. But the matter cannot be disposed of in such an easy way as all that. There are certain great principles—most important and leading principles of Christianity—that all human creeds are in eternal hostility to, and the issue between those principles and all human creeds must exist, until one or the other is overcome. The Lord prayed for the believers—those who should believe on him in all time to come, through the words of the Apostles, *"that they may be one, that the world may believe."* All Christians will admit, that the belief of the world is essential to its conversion. The world can never be converted without believing. No man can fail to see, that our Lord in this prayer, (John xvii. 20, 21,) makes the belief of the world depend upon the oneness, or the union of the believers. He says: "I pray for them, that they may be one, that the world may believe that thou hast sent me." The reason He assigns for desiring the unity of believers, is *"that the world may believe,"* or that the world may be converted.

Now, that believers never can be one till we get rid of human creeds, is just as clear as that Jews and Christians never can be one, with the law of Moses in full force over one party, and the law of Christ in full force over the other; or that the Methodists and Presbyterians never can be one, while the Confession and Discipline are both in full force; or that Mohammedans and Mormons never can be one, till the Koran or the Book of Mormon is set aside. There never was, and never can be, such a thing as two religious parties becoming one, with two creeds remaining in full force. Two parties cannot, in the very nature of things, become one, without disposing of one of the organizations. This cannot be done without disposing of the constitution and laws of the organization dispensed with. We have now an immense number of organizations, mostly formed upon human creeds. These creeds, and the organizations under them, must be thrown aside, before the union of believers ever takes place; for no man of reason ever thinks of all ever uniting upon anyone human creed; nor is anyone party thinking of all ever uniting with them. It cannot, with any reason, be expected, that all the good, pious, devoted, and truly Christian, ever will unite upon any human platform; for no one can ever show any superior claims to all others. Before a union of all the believers, the truly pious, devoted and Christian, can be intelligently prayed for, expected, and confidently urged upon all the followers of Christ, a basis superior to all others, characterized by infinite wisdom, and clothed with the authority of the Almighty, must be urged. This, no human creed claims, or can claim. No man claims that he has one particle of divine authority for his creed. No one thinks of such a thing as claiming that God required or authorized his creed. No party thinks that any man is bound to believe his creed; for all parties admit that persons can be, and are Christians, who neither believe nor submit to their creed. This is admitted in regard to every creed. Then, a man can be a Christian, and neither believe nor submit to any human creed. It is not the belief nor submission to a human creed, then, that constitutes a Christian. These human creeds, then, in the place of having *superior* claims, have no claims at all. That which God has never required, never authorized, which makes no man a Christian, but which men can be Christians without believing, has no claims upon Christians, to say nothing of *superior* claims.

But the Bible has superior claims. The "law of the Lord is perfect, converting the soul:" it is the "perfect law of liberty." Men cannot be Christians without believing it. As it converts the soul, men cannot be converted without it; and as it is the perfect law of liberty, men cannot object to it as the rule of their faith and practice. No good man can coolly and carelessly see it set aside, and a human creed substituted in its place, and let it all pass, with the careless and thoughtless expression: "Our creed will do us no harm." It does harm, even if you never saw it, for it prevents you from union with those whom you admit to be Christians, who believe the Bible, the gospel, Christianity, and love the Saviour as ardently as yourself. Why not, then, in the name of all that is sacred, unite upon the Bible, the gospel, Christianity, the Saviour of the world, to whom you are indebted for every pious impulse, for every spiritual impression, for every joyful feeling, for your conversion from sin and your hope of heaven, and forget your creeds, to which you are indebted for nothing, except your lamentable divisions, and leave them forever? Do you say that Unitarians dishonor our Lord, in making him a mere prophet, merely a distinguished reformer, one highly gifted and favored of God, &c.?—In this, no doubt, you are perfectly right, but how much more do you dishonor him, in substituting a human law for his? You pray to him, and argue his essential deity and equality with the Father, but how much confidence do you show the world, Unitarians, unbelievers and all, you have in Jesus Christ, as a lawgiver, governor, ruler and king? Is his law your law—your *only law,* as he is your *only lawgiver, saviour and king*? As you exalt him in your prayers, in your arguments on his divinity and co-equality with the Father, do you honor his word, his gospel, his religion, his holy law, above all words, religions and laws? How can you call him your only king, your guide and ruler, unless you call his law your *only law* and your *only ride* of faith? How can you believe he will hear your prayers, however highly you may speak of his divinity, while you adopt a human creed in the place of his divine and infallible rule of faith and practice? He rules, like all rulers, by his law, and the man who sets aside his law and submits to a human law, sets him aside, as his ruler, and gives a human ruler the preference! or, to express it in scripture style, declares that he will not have him to rule over us. Is not this offering a dreadful insult to his dignity, as the great law-giver, governor, ruler, and king of kings, and lord of lords? To think that he is our wisdom, our righteousness; the way, the truth and the life—that no man cometh to the Father but by him—that he was lifted up to draw all men to him—that he, as the supreme ruler, has issued a law; declared it a "perfect law;" nay, more, *"the perfect law of liberty"*—commanded it to be published to every creature, with the assurance that he who would believe it and submit to it should be saved, but that those who should reject it should be lost, and that man should ever have attempted to made a law, a rule of faith, or creed to bind upon those who have received the great Ruler and his law, is perfectly overwhelming! Such an insult to his majesty, offered by his professed friends, under the idea of aiding and honoring him, is ridiculous in the extreme. There is not any earthly king or potentate in this world, that would not call a set of men to account for such an attempt in his government and punish them sorely.— He would look upon them as wicked and dangerous persons, who impeached his government, and consequently him as a governor, as insufficient and not capable of ruling them; and he would look upon them as arrogant, in claiming the ability to make a law that would supply the deficiency in his law, and as usurpers, trying to wrest the government out of his hands that they might rule themselves, and would punish them accordingly.

With what ineffable contempt, then, must the ruler of the universe—the only potentate; the king of kings and lord of lords, the Almighty, look down upon a council of poor, short-sighted, finite and erring creatures, that ought to be upon their knees praying God that they might understand *his law;* who have assumed that the law of God—the *perfect law*—is not sufficient to govern his people, and assumed the responsibility of making a law, better adapted to the work, more convenient, more easily understood and that can accomplish what the law of God cannot do. If it should be said, this law is not intended as a substitute for the law of God, but merely to aid it, the idea would be as ridiculous as he who would light up candles and lamps to aid the sun in its beams at noonday in giving light. It still dishonors the law of God, and also the law-giver, as incapable of answering the purpose, as being insufficient and needing aid. The whole procedure of creed-making, and the reasons for it, grow out of a dissatisfaction with what the Lord has done, what he is now doing, and a desire to improve upon it. There must be a dissatisfaction with the law of God, and our adorable Lord and Saviour Jesus Christ as law-giver and ruler; faults must be found with his law; complaints must be made against it; a desire must exist to get out from under it, or to have something else to aid it, before the idea of another law can enter the mind. Can one who has all confidence in him; one who wishes to commend him to an unbelieving world, as his only King and Saviour; who would honor him above all law-givers, and as worthy not only of the homage, the reverence and faith of all men, but as having a right to demand the implicit submission and obedience of the human race-let such thoughts ever enter his heart, to say nothing of expressing them? Let believers show implicit confidence in him and his law and the world will believe. B. F.

-----o-----

Noblesville Matter Again.

BRO. FRANKLIN—The following is the last latter of Bro. Cole to you:

NOBLESVILLE, Indiana, March 30.

BRO. FRANKLIN, Dear Sir—Your letter of the 21st, was received on the 24th inst., and on to-day, was laid before our congregation, I am instructed to reply as follows:

We understand ourselves in our note of the 17th inst., as fully and unequivocally accepting the suggestions and advice of yourself and others in your communication of the 15th of October last.

Our understanding of said document, as set forth in our note of the 17th inst., was for the purpose of avoiding any equivocation on the part of our opposing Brethren before the committee contemplated.

For it is well known here both in public and private, that they have, or profess to have at least, a very different understanding of the object and design of said letter of the 15 th of October last, from that entertained by us—we understand the object of yourself and other Brethren to be an investigation of all matters of complaint and difficulty, resulting in the division now existing among us, for the purpose of bringing about a settlement of these difficulties, and a reconciliation of the divided body of disciples in Noblesville. They say the object was and is to inquire as to which is the scripturally organized body in this place, theirs or ours. We desire a full, fair, and impartial investigation for the purpose of showing to the world, who it is that has caused so much difficulty, strife and division; and let the wrong-doers make restitution, whether it be individuals or parties.

We believe this to have been the object, design and import of said letter of the 15th of October. Should we, however, have misapprehended the design and meaning of the brethren as set forth in said document, you will correct such misapprehension, and thus we shall feel called upon more fully to respond to your requisitions. But as we now view things, we can give no other answer than that already in your possession, with the foregoing reasons there for:

Yours still in hope of peace,

N. B. COLE.

This letter, and the one written to you by Bro. Cole, dated March 17, 1856, and which appears in your last, shows that the congregation, of which Bro. Cole and the undersigned are members, did unequivocally accept the proposition and suggestions of Bro. Mathews and others, of the 10th of October last—according to its obvious import and meaning—and that they who contend otherwise, are liable to the charge of evasion and of spurning some other issue than that contained in the original proposition.

G. H. Voss.

There can be no misunderstanding in regard to this matter. The reader only need look over the letters of Bro. Cole, to see that our statement is entirely correct and unprejudiced. Let these brethren commit their case, without specifications or conditions, to a committee, in precisely the same manner as the other party has done, thus putting themselves upon an equal footing with them, showing a willingness to have the matter settled, manifesting confidence in their brethren, who may be appointed a committee, and confidence in the rectitude of their conduct and position. But they have not accepted the proposition of Bros. Mathews and others, without conditions, and conditions too, that show misgivings at an important point, as any man can see who will read both letters of Bro. Cole; and this same Bro. G. H. Voss, on the same day on which he wrote the above, in reply to all my persuasions to induce them, unreservedly to agree to the reference to a committee, repeatedly declared that they *would not*. B. F.

-----o-----

Spirit Manifestations.—Sorcery.

No. I.

Among all the contributors to the torrent of infidelity now sweeping over the land like a mighty avalanche, none is to be found more variable and active than the so-called "Spirit-manifestations," or, as first styled, "Spirit-rappings." This delusion carries those caught by it—gulled into its meshes by its subtleties, with the velocity of a lightning train down into the vortex of ruin. It so effectually closes their ears, extinguishes their vision and neutralizes their sensibilities, that no expostulations of friends, warnings of scripture, or threatenings of the Almighty, can deter them. The leap, though wholly in the dark, they will make; the risk, though it be the loss of everything, without the probability of gaining anything, they will run. Still, as some distinguished reformer said of the pope—"that the prophecies of scripture would not be fulfilled without him"—so we say of these modern Spiritualists; wicked and sinful as they are, hurling men into infidelity, the prophecies of scripture would not be fulfilled without them. One of the clearest evidences that omniscience dictated the New Testament, is found in the fact that it contains clear predictions of things most accurately fulfilled before our eyes. Let us attend to an expression or two of the New Testament. *"Now* the Spirit speaketh expressly, that in latter times some shall depart from the faith, giving heed to seducing spirits and doctrines of devils; speaking lies in hypocrisy, having their conscience seared with a hot iron." 1 Tim. 4: 1, *2.* The import of the expression, "seducing spirits," is the same as that other expression, "unclean spirits," and "doctrines of devils," the same as doctrines concerning demons. The many who are now giving heed to seducing spirits, teaching doctrines concerning demons and departing from the faith, at the peril of their eternal all, are fulfilling most accurately clear and explicit predictions of the New Testament.

The Lord said, "There shall arise false christs and false prophets, and shall show great signs and wonders; insomuch that, if it were possible, they shall deceive the very elect."— Matt. 24:24. Let no one, therefore, be alarmed nor deceived by any of these signs or wonders, for, in doing them, they are simply fulfilling the Lord's word—doing precisely what he said they would do. Notice too, that he does not say, that "they shall *pretend* to show great signs and wonders," but *"shall show great signs and wonders,"* and this deception shall be such, that, "if it were possible, they shall deceive the very elect." They are not to operate with some trifling and significant delusion; but it is to be a great one, showing "great signs and wonders"—upon a magnificent scale, malignantly trifling and sporting with the credulous and gullible portions of our unfortunate race, and sundering them from all that is near and dear to them. We must remember the Lord's admonition, in regard to this delusion. His holy and solemn admonition is, *"Believe it not."*

But we must enter the merits of the case. What is a *necromancer?* Webster says:—"Properly, one who pretends to foretell future events by holding converse with departed spirits. One who uses enchantment or practices sorcery. The latter is now the more usual sense. Syn. conjuror; enchanter; wizard; sorcerer or magician." The same high authority defines *necromancy* as follows: "Properly the art of revealing future events by means of a pretended communication with the dead.—Enchanter; conjuration. This is now the more usual sense." The word necromancy, is a compound of two Greek words. The Greek word *nekros,* means *dead;* and the Greek word, *manteia,* means *divination.* The pretence of netting communications from spirits, is *necromancy,* and he who does it, is a *necromancer,* sorcerer, wizard, or consulter of familiar spirits." Malcom, in his Bible Dictionary, says: *"Witch* is a woman, and *wizard* is a man, who has, or is supposed to have dealings with Satan." The same good authority defines "Sorcerers as conjurors, or those who undertake to disclose secrets, or foretell events, by magical or diabolical power. Acts 13: 8. They claimed the power of calling up departed spirits. 1 Sam. 28; of inflicting plagues, Ex. 8: 18, &c. The damnation of such as addict themselves to the practice of sorcery, is often declared. Isa. 47: 7, Prov. 21: 8, and 22: 15. Let us now open the Bible, and see what we can turn up. Deut. 18: 10, 11, 12, we find the following: "There shall not be found among you any that maketh his son or his daughter to pass through the fire, or that useth divination, or an observer of times, or an enchanter, or a witch, or a charmer, or a consulter with familiar spirits, or a wizard, or a necromancer. For all that do these things are an abomination unto the Lord; and because of these abominations the Lord thy God doth drive them out from before thee." Now, what is a modern Spiritualist, but a "consulter with familiar spirits"? or one "that useth divination"? Consulting familiar spirits and obtaining divinations from them is the ostensible and avowed work of modern spiritualism. How shocking it is that men will tamper with such unworthy influences, in the face of the clear declaration of the Almighty, that "all who *do these things are an abomination to him,"* and that on account of these abominations the Canaanites were driven out of their land.

Let us hear the Lord again: "Regard not them that have familiar spirits, neither seek after wizards, to be defiled by them: I am the Lord your God." Lev. 18: 31. What is a "spirit medium," admitting what is professed, but one having a familiar or unclean spirit? and what language could be more explicit than the above, forbidding us to regard or consult such characters. But if the reader is inclined to consult those who deal with familiar spirits, we invite him to consult the following sketch of the character of one. If his match, for idolatry and atrocity can be found in all paganism we know not where. His name was Manasseh. The faithful and inspired historian says: "Also he built altars in the house of the Lord, whereof the Lord had said, In Jerusalem shall my name be forever. And he built altars for all the hosts of heaven in the two courts of the house of the Lord. And he caused his children to pass through the fire in the valley of the son of Hinnom; also he observed times, and used enchantments, and used witchcraft,, and dealt with familiar spirits, and with wizards; he wrought much evil in the sight of the Lord, to provoke him to anger." 2 Chron. 33: 4, 5, 6. On account of these abominations, the Lord sent upon him the Assyrians who carried him away to Babylon, where he was humbled and made to confess his sin against God. It was then as it is now; when anyone turned away from the clear revelations of heaven, to consulting familiar spirits, witches wizards, etc., there was no stopping place short of the very sink of heathenish idolatries. Let us hear the word of the Lord again on the subject. "And the soul that turneth after such as have familiar spirits, and after wizards, to go a whoring after them, I will even set my face against that soul, and cut him off from among his people." Lev. 20: 6. Be it observed here, that God declares that he will set his face against the man who goes after those who have familiar spirits.— The threatenings of the Almighty are not only against those who have, or profess to have, intercourse with familiar spirits, but those also who go *after them*. Let us hear the prophet of the Lord once more: "And when they shall say unto you, seek unto them that have familiar spirits, and unto wizards that peep, and that mutter; should not a people seek unto their God? for the living to the dead? To the law and to the testimony: if they speak not according to this word, it is because there is no light in them." Isa. viii: 19, 20. How utterly inconsistent the consulting of familiar spirits, witches and wizards, compared with the clear and wonderful revelations of heaven.

If parents would see what will befall them, if they run into these sorceries and enchantments, look at the following: "But these two things shall come to thee in a moment in one day, the loss of children and widowhood; they shall come upon thee in their perfection, for the multitude of thy sorceries, and for the great abundance of thine enchantments." Isa. xlvii: 9. The Lord said, Ex. xxii: "Thou shalt not suffer a witch to live." If the reader would see further the fate of such characters, under Moses, see the following: "A man also or a woman that hath a familiar spirit, or that is a wizard, shall surely be put to death; they shall stone them with stones: their blood shall be upon them." Lev. xx: 27. Such was the penalty under Moses. In the New Testament, witchcraft excludes from the kingdom of God. Paul, Gal. v: 20, classes witchcraft with the works of the flesh, and at the bottom of his classification of a catalogue of sins, containing the lowest corruptions on earth, concludes by saying, "that they who do such things shall not inherit the kingdom of God." John, Rev. xxi: 8, gives us a list of those who "shall have their part in the lake which burns with fire and brimstone; which is the second death;" and in the midst of that list we find the *sorcerers*. Rev. xx: 15, in enumerating those without the kingdom of God, John the apostle, puts the *sorcerer* in the midst. The Almighty classes the necromancer, wizard, witch or sorcerer, with murderers, liars and the vilest characters, punished them with death under Moses, and, under Jesus, declares that they shall not inherit the kingdom of God, but shall be punished with the second death. No Christian man can have anything to do with it, only to resist it with every power of his soul. It is a work of the flesh, will destroy the faith, corrupt the morals, ruin the families and sink the souls of those who practice it in perdition.

B. F.

-----o-----

Review of Dr. H. M. Shaffer on Infant Baptism. No. 1.

My worthy old friend and quondam opponent, Dr. Shaffer, commences his work in defense of infant baptism, by introducing and replying to objections against it. The first objection he comes in contact with, is that there is no express or positive command for it. This, too, is a pretty formidable objection; but formidable though it be, the Dr. summons his courage and walks up to the work to meet it. In looking over his effort, we could but think of a case mentioned to us a few months ago. A lady, a member of the Presbyterian church, desired to have her first-born, an infant, baptized. But her husband, not a member of any church, did not believe in it and opposed it. The lady, being distressed about it, stated the case to her minister. He advised her to invite her husband to hear him preach on the subject and he would convince him. She accordingly obtained her husband's promise to hear the sermon, and informed the preacher. The announcement was made when the discourse would be delivered. At the time the gentleman and lady were present. The preacher commenced by saying, "Our Baptist friends are not fair in demanding express Scripture authority for infant baptism. We admit that there is no express

Scripture for it." When he said this, the gentleman walked out, and passing to a window, where he caught his lady's eye, beckoned to her to come out. She accordingly met him at the door. "Come," said he, "let us go home; the preacher says there is no Scripture for infant baptism, which I told you before was the case, and it is no use to hear him any further." They immediately left, and the lady concluded that if the Lord had required her, or anyone else, to have infants baptized, he would have said so, but till she could see it in the Bible, she would have nothing to do with it. If parents would say to the preachers, when you show us infant baptism in the Bible, we will have our infants baptized, and not before, and stand to it, not another infant would ever be baptized. Or if they deemed this an unreasonable demand, if the parents would say, show us one mention of infant baptism, in any shape or form, and we will have our infants baptized, but not before, and stand to it, not another infant would ever be baptized. Not a preacher in the world can show one word about it, in any shape, in the whole revelation from God to man. Not one passage, ever quoted in all the arguments upon the subject from the Bible, contains one word about it. Not one ray of light on the whole subject, nor a single mention of it is found in all the writings in the Bible, or out of it, in a single document written in the first two centuries of the Christian era, that has escaped the ravages of time: We might as well search the ancient records for Romish penance, counting beads, worshiping relics and images. There is not one syllable about it in any way.

We know what Dr. Shaffer can say on this point; we shall never forget the confusion manifested by him and several of his preaching brethren, when we pressed it upon him in our oral discussion, in the presence of several hundred people. But he is not to be intimidated by finding that there is not one word about it in the Bible. He insisted then, as he does in his book, that he could prove it, though he did not find one word about it in the Bible. But the reader is anxious to know how he answered the objection, that there is no express Scripture for it. That was a light matter with him. He says, there is no express Scripture for female communion, and Baptists practice it; upon the same principle, he practices infant baptism. But this little sophistry, or artifice, is too stupid, though it has emanated from the pens of some great men. Baptists who understand themselves have no such an institution as *"female* communion," or *"male* communion." They have no such an institution as *"male* baptism," or *"female* baptism." They have a communion for the Church of God, and baptism for believers. The communion is not for *male* or *female, young* or *old.,* but for disciples of Christ—children of God—saints—the Church of God. To be a child of God, in the church, entitles one to the communion. It is not *male* or *female, adult* or *infant* communion, but "the communion of saints." The same is true of baptism; it is not *adult,* baptism nor *infant* baptism, but believers' baptism. The communion was not delivered to *males* nor *females,* but to the church. To whom did Paul address his first letter to the Corinthians? He says, 1 Cor. 1: 2, "Unto the church of God which is at Corinth, to them that are sanctified in Christ Jesus, called saints, with all that in every place call upon the name of Jesus Christ our Lord, both theirs and ours." Now, Dr., look over these words right carefully, and see who is included. You see "the church of God at Corinth," "them that are sanctified," the "saints," and "all that in every place call upon the name of Jesus Christ," are the persons addressed. Now, sir, were there any *females* among these? Come, my old friend, we must have no inference here, but "express Scripture." Were there any females in the "church of God at Corinth?" Put on your spectacles and look at 1 Cor. xi: 3, 5, 6, 7, 8, 9, 10, 11, 12, and 15, and you will find *express* mention of "woman." Well now, sir, what does Paul say in this same letter, addressing himself to all these?1 Cor. xi: 2, he says, "Now I praise *you." "You,"* who? Why, *you*—the church of God at Corinth—the sanctified in Christ Jesus, the saints, with "all that in every place call upon the name of Jesus Christ," with *women* expressly mentioned. What does Paul say to all these—*women* and all?" Now," says he, " I praise you, brethren, that ye remember me in all things, and keep the ordinances as I delivered them to you." The ordinances were delivered to all these, the *females* as much as the *males*.

But, Dr., as you are slow of hearing, run your eye down the same chapter, to verse 23, where the holy apostle is addressing all those mentioned above, and on the communion, which he had received of the Lord, and delivered to the church. He says, "I received of the Lord that which I also delivered unto you, that the Lord Jesus, the same night in which he was betrayed, took bread," etc. To whom does he here say he delivered the communion? To " the church at Corinth," the " sanctified in Christ Jesus," " all that in every place call upon the name of Jesus Christ," the whole of them, *women*. and all. This, Dr., is "express authority" for an institution—the communion—by positive, divine authority delivered to the church—the whole church. Notice, Dr., as you are slow to learn, that it was not delivered to *males* nor *females*, but to "the church of God at Corinth," with "all that in every place call upon the name of Jesus Christ." You will observe, sir, that it is no *inference*, that there were *women* in the number here described, to whom the communion was delivered, as much as to men; for they are expressly mentioned many times over in the same chapter. Now, sir, show express authority for infant baptism, or one mention of it in the whole revelation of God to man, and we will be silenced. But this, you know, you cannot do; this, you know, you failed to do in our oral debate, in the presence of hundreds, among whom were many of your warmest friends, who desired you to do it, thought you could do it, but were sadly disappointed when they saw you fail, and close *without quoting one word about it from all the Bible*.

But after writing some twenty pages to show us that we ought to receive infant baptism upon inference, the Dr. says, page 23, "But we think there is express command for infant baptism in Mat. xxviii: 19, 'Go ye, therefore, and teach (*matheteusate*, disciple), *all nations*, baptizing them," etc. Now, Dr., as you are in search for "express command," we must sharpen our perceptive powers, and make an effort to perceive it. To begin, then, we enter no demur against the position, that *matheteusate*, here translated " teach," in the common version means *disciple*. The command, then, is, "Go ye, therefore, and disciple all nations, baptizing them," etc. Your position is, that "all nations" includes infants, and that the command is as much to disciple them as anybody else. Well, sir, *matheteusate*, or disciple, in this commission means the same to all to whom the commission extends. Discipling is the same in all cases. Whatever process is contained in discipling in one case, is in every case. If you please, do not now begin to invent a system of discipling for infants, and another for adults. There is but one commission, and but one system, or process, of proselyting. Keep this in mind. On page 24, the Dr. quotes the words, "Go ye into all the world and preach the gospel to every creature," and remarks: "Now as far as the command to disciple extends, the command to baptize reaches, and both are as extensive as human population." This statement we deny, and if we cannot show it to be incorrect, we will give up the whole controversy. There can be no doubt but "all nations," Mat. xxviii: 19, and "all the world," Mark xvi: 15, are the same in extent, showing to whom the gospel is to be preached, but not describing who are to be baptized. This the Lord's own words show, as would have appeared in the Dr.'s quotation, if he had not cut the commission in two precisely in the middle, as if to disallow the Lord, in his own words, in the Dr.'s book, to tell for whom baptism was intended. He quotes the words, "Go into all the world and preach the gospel to every creature," leaving out the very next words, "He that believeth and is baptized shall be saved, and he that believeth not shall be damned." Why did he leave this out? He would not allow the Lord, in his book, to say, in the very commission which he was quoting, who is entitled to baptism. He was trying to prove infant baptism, and to do this, he used an argument that would entitle any infidel in the world to baptism. He maintains that the commission is to every creature—to the whole race, and that the command to baptize reaches the same number; but this is not so, for while the command to preach is to "every creature," the baptizing is limited to those who believe. But after the Dr.'s flourish to make the commission extend to the race, that it may include infants, on the very next page, commenting upon Mark's record of it, he says, "This text has exclusive reference to adults." This is certainly true, and as this is the same commission that Matthew is talking about, it has exclusive reference to adults all the time, no matter which one of the sacred writers mentions it But my worthy old friend, Dr. Shaffer, can make the same commission include infants, when commenting upon Matthew's account of it, and then exclude them when commenting upon Mark's account of it! But here we must leave him for another month, when we will carefully attend to this commission.   B. F.

-----o-----

Politics and Religion.

IN every great political excitement, the cause of religion suffers in this country, more or less, in every church that has any spirituality in it. The Romish church, having nothing spiritual in it, and being itself as much a secret political organization as the organizations of Know-Nothings or Sag-Nichts, suffers nothing from political excitement except when defeated; or, in other words, suffers nothing only as all political parties suffer, when defeated by some other party. But when a church, its ministry, creed or influence is allowed to be made a tool, an engine, a political instrumentality, an auxiliary to some political party or policy, we care not what, nor whether good or bad in itself, it is perverted from the entire object of its divine founder, and becomes a mere carnal and worldly establishment. One of the most sublime evidences that Christianity is from God, is found in the fact of its non-interfering spirit with any of the secular institutions, civil governments and administrations of any country in the world, whether good or bad. It never tries to get the sword into its hand, but once commanded a worldly-minded preacher—one who yet thought the kingdom of God was to be a political institution—whose eye had not yet reached a spiritual institution—to put up the sword, assuring him that they who take the sword shall perish by the sword. This lesson many of the carnal-minded preachers of this land have not even yet learned; nor have we any reason to believe, from their present course, that so heavenly and divine a lesson will soon find a place in their hearts. They are not only worldly-minded, carnal, fleshly and riveted to human ambition, but appear determined to make the whole kingdom of God a mere instrumentality for the accomplishment of the objects of their worldly schemes and human ambition.

We are aware that we are using some pretty strong terms, terms that we have hesitated for months to use, but which it is no use to withhold longer. The time has come when every man must show where he stands, be tried and separated off into his appropriate place. We have identified our all with Christ and the apostles—with pure Christianity. But the time has come, when we are to be tested, brow-beat, misrepresented, slandered, abused and a clandestine effort made to injure our influence and cut off our support, because we will not consecrate our *Christian Review,* our *Christian* efforts in the pulpit, with the *church of God,* so far as possible, to the service of politicians. But our mind is decisively established on this point. We are not to be swerved to the right hand nor to the left. We shall not use the Lord's name as a pretext, nor religion as a cloak; but shall maintain religion for its own sake, for the sake of its Author, and for the sake of the only hope of fallen man. There was more sound reason than some men have, in the Quaker, when about to fight. He laid off the Quaker hat and coat, saying, "Lay there, Quaker, till I chastise this man." In the same way, all those religious editors, preachers and churches now converted into political engines, who only use the Lords name as a cloak, his religion as sugar-coating to sweeten some political pill, should lay off the religious garb, the name of the Lord, the name of the church, and the name of the preacher, and stand out where they belong, fight under their proper motto, and stand upon a level with their fellow-citizens of the world.

If a man has a leading object in view, no matter whether religious or worldly, let him come out in his proper color, declare his object, and drive directly at it. If a man has a favorite political scheme, let him declare it, publish a paper advocating it, or maintain it in public addresses; but not under the name of *Christian;* not in the name of the Lord, nor under a pretence of preaching Christ; for this would be a manifest imposition, no matter how good the political doctrine. But every attempt to make the religion of Christ auxiliary to political ends is a perversion, and in direct opposition to the whole spirit and entire bearing of the Lord's own reply, when charged with being a political aspirant. When arraigned before Pilate, and charged with claiming to be a king, he explained the matter, and obviated the charge, or set it aside, by saying, "My kingdom is not of this world; if my kingdom were of this world, then would my servants fight, that I should not be delivered to the Jews; but now is my kingdom not from hence." John xviii: 36. While he frankly admitted that he was a king, and that he came into the world to bear witness to the truth, he set aside all ground of suspicion against him as an aspirant to the throne, or any other part in the civil government, or one who would in any way meddle in the civil institutions of his country, by declaring that his kingdom is not of this world. This declaration was no evasion, but a clear, important and divine truth, and must be shown in the lives of the disciples of Christ, by following his example, or the cause will suffer immeasurably.

Our Lord was so careful to keep his kingdom and his mission distinct from civil affairs, that when he was appealed to, to arbitrate a dispute touching an inheritance, he inquired, who made him an arbiter in such matters, or where there was any authority for him to step aside from his mission, or rather, pervert his mission and his office from their high, spiritual and divine object, to a worldly, temporal and business object. He was so careful to keep his mission distinct from the world and worldly relations, that when engaged in the work of his mission, he refused to recognize a fleshly relation.—his own mother, brother and sister. In his kingdom, he recognized no fleshly relation, as a basis for any application to him, or a reason for his institution conferring any benefit on any human being, not excepting his own mother according to the flesh. Those who *do the will of God,* regardless of all fleshly ties, political conditions, or worldly circumstances, whether male or female, bond or free, are mother, sister or brother to the Redeemer and Saviour of man. So perfectly distinct did our Lord and the apostles keep their mission from politics, that there is not the remotest hint that they ever participated in civil affairs in a single instance, in the whole of the sacred record. They either never participated in politics in any way, or else looked upon the whole matter as so distinct from their mission and work, as not to be once mentioned in the whole Christian revelation. So distinct is the New Testament from political institutions, that it contains not one word of instruction to civil officers in regard to their duties, not one hint what kind of men we should vote for, or what form of government we should favor. It simply enjoins that Christians "obey every ordinance of man for the Lord's sake;" "submit to the powers that be; for the powers that be are ordained of God," and declares that "rulers are not a terror to good works, but to the evil;" that "the ruler is the minister of God, and bears not the sword in vain."

The Christian law enjoins that we "follow *peace* with all men and holiness, without which no man shall see the Lord." It is not enjoined that we follow peace with a political party, but "peace with *all men,*" and holiness. The Lord said, "Blessed are the *peace-makers,* for they shall be called the children of God." The angels of God shouted when Jesus was born, "Glory to God in the highest, and on earth *peace* and good will toward man." Shall that religion, enjoining its adherents to "follow *peace* with all men," promising a blessing upon the peace-makers, whose divine Author was introduced into the world with an angelic shout of *"peace* on earth," be made an instrument in the hands of a misguided and worldly priesthood, in the political strifes of the world? If it shall, wo betide him who does it. It will kill every preacher and every church that ever had the spirit of God in them, to do it. Indeed, all of this description are now dead. Not a man nor a church among them, throughout the length and breadth of the country is doing anything for the cause of God. Not a sinter is converted by them, nor a saint comforted. Many of them, old men, that formerly had the spirit of the Lord, preached Christ with great power, with their souls full of the love of God, converted sinners, edified and comforted the children of God, now sit in the company of worldlings, read and discuss politics on the Lord's day, while the house of God is forsaken.

Some of this description are not contented even with this, but are anxious to impair the influence of others, because they will not run into the same wild career. They can see the church of God shut up, the place where the Lord's name was recorded, desecrated, their children living in their sins, and not attend to an ordinance of the New Testament; and are not satisfied with this, but are determined as far as possible to limit the influence of the only men that are maintaining the cause, and still not seem to be conscious that they are wrong. One, in a private correspondence on some matters of this kind, says, "Your writings are *pro-slavery,"* as an apology for the state of things in his church. But this charge, all know who have read what we have written, *is not true.* We never wrote or spoke a proslavery word, or had a pro-slavery feeling in our life; nor have we any commission from Jesus Christ, as a religious teacher, or a preacher of the gospel, to discuss the merits or demerits of any system of slavery or antislavery in the world. Our mission is to preach Christ, Christianity, and to disentangle it from all connection with these side-artifices devised to draw men away from the Lord. We have only alluded to slavery and the excitement about it, so far as to discover the proper course for a Christian, but not to discuss its merits as a system at all. In doing this, we have simply applied to it the rule that we do to all questions of the kind, viz.: To inquire for the *course pursued by the Lord, the apostles, and the first Christians, and follow it as infallibly safe and right.* In doing this, we have certainly shown that those warring upon us in this matter have no commission from heaven, from Christ, or his apostles, or in anything in all their lives and practice. We shall, therefore, as far as God shall enable us, preach the pure gospel of the grace of God, both north and south, east and west, to all, both great and small, high and low, rich and poor, bond and free; and thus labor to bring them into the kingdom that is not of this world—a kingdom that cannot be moved —where the pure in heart can enjoy God, his Holy Spirit, and his people, though the wicked rule and the civil governments are corrupt, with the blessed assurance that they shall one day be delivered from all the perplexities of an imperfect and sinful state. Here we must all turn our attention at last. Civil governments can never be perfected. They will always be working wrongs and cruelties some place. The wisdom and power of man cannot avoid this. The wickedness and selfishness of men also are in the way, so that the civil institutions of the country can never be perfected; and he has studied Christianity to but little purpose, who thinks its aim to be the perfection of the human contrivances of the world. It looks above this, to the purification and perfection of *individuals,* in their regeneration and personal sanctification, and preparation for a better state. It does not, like some fleshly systems, look upon this world as *man's all;* but as momentary, a pilgrim state, not our home, not our continuing city, but merely the preparatory state to a better world. How soon this world will all be nothing to all these political wranglers, who have suffered themselves to be made tools for political parties, to the neglect of the church of God, without one soul ever being able to see that all their noise ever did any good in any way. How silly it is, as well as unchristian, for old friends, neighbors and *brethren* to disagree and fall out about the intricate and deceptive schemes of political wire-workers. Such men are doing no good for their church or country. The very circumstance of their falling out with their best friends, shows that they are insane upon the very subject upon which they propose to enlighten the world, and of all men in the world the most unsafe to guide either church or state.

B. F.

-----o-----

Independency and Co-operation.

These are subjects of incalculable value to the well-being and universal triumph of *the Christian* religion. They have oft-times enlisted the best talents, sanctified by the most enlarged attainments in sacred literature, and the deepest-toned piety, in their investigation, elucidation and development. In the conflict of mind with mind, ill-feelings have been engendered in consequence of the indulgence in personalities, and the impeachment of motives. Many of the *choice* spirits of this reformation are deeply grieved for the past; and the man who would now enter the *arena* encounters a most fearful array of suspicion, jealousy and rivalry. Deeply impressed with the importance of the subject, and the responsibility of assuming any position, the undersigned would modestly submit a few suggestions for the serious consideration of all concerned.

1. The Christian religion is designed to bless the world, to impart wisdom, purity and happiness in this life, as a preparation for eternal life.

2. To accomplish an object so desirable, the congregation of Christ was originated and organized; and the obligation cannot be evaded.

3. It seems to be universally admitted that independency and co-operation must exist to a certain extent, in order to the grand end to be attained. What that extent is, according to the divine standard, is the delicate question.

4. Each congregation acts necessarily in its own vicinity in the conversion of sinners, and in the perfection of its members for the everlasting kingdom. Its discipline is necessarily confined to its own body, with the liberty of calling for light, advice or assistance from the entire brotherhood, as occasion may demand. It must have the elements of existence within itself, so far as its membership is concerned. Its officers must be of its own approval and selection, and subject to its control.

5. Co-operation to some extent is just as fundamental as the other. The world's conversion is demanded by the Saviour, and this can never be accomplished without a concentration and co-operation of all the talents, learning, piety, liberality, zeal, courage and influence of the entire brotherhood. Love to God and love to man is the fulfillment of the law and the prophets, and this love must develop itself at home and abroad, for sinner as well as saint.

6. As to the *how* this co-operation is to be brought about; whether the district shall embrace a county, a dozen congregations, more or less, etc., etc., much depends upon expediency. In all such matters, as well as in the selection, employment and compensation of evangelists, a spirit of compromise and forbearance is indispensable.

7. The evangelists already ordained by the congregations, constitute the body from which the co-operation must select speakers to accomplish their objects; and the entire co-operation must have an equal choice in the selection, as well as equal power to discontinue the evangelist. Otherwise it would be a perfect anarchy. The continuance or discontinuance of an evangelist, in cases involving no delinquency in morals or doctrine, ought not to involve unpleasant feelings.

In cases of delinquency in morals or in the faith, the co-operation must necessarily possess the power to act and to decide, so far as their responsibilities are concerned. It must have power to examine the case, to suspend the evangelist, if the case demands it, and to report the delinquent to the congregation of which he is a member. A congregation may act indiscreetly, and withdraw from the co-operation—the responsibility is theirs. A co-operation may withdraw their fellowship from a congregation, for supposed or real corruption in morals or the faith—the responsibility is theirs. The mode of conducting business, and the manner of ascertaining the mind of the congregations, *in all cases*, is a matter of judgment. If possible, doubt and uncertainty must be avoided.

8. It seems to be universally conceded that the co-operation possesses power to appoint a Board, or Committee, to act in vacation, and to execute the wishes and desires of the body. The power confided to this committee embraces the selection of evangelists qualified for the work, their fields of labor, their compensation, etc., etc.

9. Each congregation possesses the inherent power to contribute according to its own judgment, subject to the Judge at the great day. Where the proper spirit prevails, a difficulty would rarely occur. The congregations should adopt the most prudent means to ascertain the available wealth of each, and as far as possible, the contributions ought to be equalized.

10. This body possesses no ecclesiastical power to make or ordain elders, deacons or evangelists. It possesses no power to try an officer or member from a congregation. Nor has it the power, as a body ecclesiastic, to pass judgment on a congregation of Christ. Each congregation, as a congregation of Christ, possesses the power to act for itself, upon its own responsibility. There are powers conferred, and responsibilities devolved upon the congregations, that cannot be transferred, shifted or evaded—the power to receive and expel members, the power to appoint and dispense with officers. But there are certain powers that may be confided, by the congregation to the co-operation, without which it could not exist, and without which, nothing of importance could be accomplished.

11. The co-operation must necessarily have power to engage evangelists; to appoint the fields of labor; to superintend the entire work; to agree upon the compensation to be made to the laborers; to take charge of the means, and to see to its faithful disbursement.

Besides, it has power to suspend an evangelist, either for inefficiency, delinquency in morals, or a departure from the faith. In these latter cases, there is an obligation to report the delinquents to their congregations, for the action of the congregation according to the law of Christ. Here the matter ends with the co-operation. But suppose a congregation should act basely, or depart from the faith, what power does the co-operation possess in reference to it? It possesses none; for it is a body constituted by the congregations for a different object. Yet there are certain obligations and responsibilities devolving on this body in reference to such a case, that can no more be evaded than a single member of a congregation can be relieved from his obligations. It would most certainly be the duty of the co-operation to report such a case to their respective congregations, and thus have the matter investigated and settled by each congregation. The entire wisdom, advice, influence, piety and counsel of the body might be brought to bear in the investigation and decision. The action and decision of the congregations could be reported to the co-operation, and through their co-operation, an announcement could be made to the world, so as to relieve themselves from the odium and responsibility that would otherwise be incurred.

It would be a strange affair if the congregations could not in some way, without infringing upon their rights, or surrendering their powers, embody their influence in disclaiming fellowship with a congregation that had departed from the faith. When we come to understand each other, there may not be as much difference as is imagined. Let us all keep cool, abstain from personal reflections, and endeavor in all sincerity to ascertain the truth. Let us love one another with pure hearts fervently; acknowledge and ask pardon where we have done injustice, and make a united effort to give a fresh impulse to the best cause on earth.

Most affectionately,

J. T. JOHNSON.

-----o-----

A DISCUSSION of three days' continuance has just closed at Florence, Ky., between Eld. Willson Thompson, of Ind., and the editor of this paper. The topics had respect to the office of the ministry, conditionally of salvation, and final perseverance of the saints. The crowd was large, and very attentive. The disputants conducted themselves with Christian propriety. May the debate result in good.

M. B. HOPKINS.

Queries Answered.

I. Is it right for any Christian congregation to grant any member the privilege of withdrawing membership, without desiring to unite with another congregation, but simply wishing withdrawal from the church? Should such request be granted? or should such a one be excluded for making such a request?

Yours truly, WM. JARRETT.

We are of the opinion that after due time for reflection is given, with proper reasonings and expostulations, that a letter of dismission should be given to every person that demands one; but let these letters always be genuine exponents of the case. A Christian church cannot, in good faith, give a letter recommending a person as in *good standing and full fellowship,* when it is known that the letter is demanded on account of disaffection. These letters should be of different grades, some recommending persons in full fellowship and good standing; some recommending the moral character, but on account of dislike to the church, or some of its members, or some of its obligations; the lukewarmness of the person demanding the letter, his lack of interest in the cause, love to the brethren; his inattention to prayer and reading the Bible—he had been dismissed, at his own request, from the church. Or a letter might be given in a case where a member cannot be reclaimed from sinful practices, setting forth the objections to him, with his dismissal, and the desire that he would return again to his duty; and in all these cases, let the causes of separation be clearly stated in the letter, and upon the church record, and we shall soon be excused from applications for letters, where the ground of the application is disaffection. In all cases of disaffection or immoral conduct, it would amount virtually to an exclusion, and so set it forth in the letter, and upon the church record.

There cannot be anything more preposterous, than for a person who has objections to a church, does not love it, fellowship it, nor desire to remain in it, to request that church to grant him a letter, recommending him as a member in good standing and full fellowship. If a person has no fellowship for the church, is not of the same spirit as the church, and is alienated from it, let this be stated in his letter, as the cause of his dismission, and upon the church record; or if he wishes to leave the country, or whatever the cause may be, let it be stated in the letter. If a man is in good standing and full fellowship, has good feelings to the whole church, has done nothing wrong, desires to do his duty, and intends to remain where he is, there can be no reason for a letter, and no one would demand one.

If you think proper, please give us an exposition of Gal. iii: 27, in connection with Rom. xiii: 14. The subject is "Putting on the Lord Jesus Christ." 1. Are there two methods of putting on Christ? 2. If so, what are they?

R. B. HENRY.

The passage, Gal. iii: 27, is: "For as many of you as have been baptized into Christ have put on Christ." The passage, Rom. xiii: 14, is: "But put ye on the Lord Jesus Christ, and make not provision for the flesh, to fulfill the lusts thereof." The former of these passages alludes to adoption, or the putting on of Christ in adoption. In our induction, we took the authority of Christ upon us, or the Christian obligation. This was in baptism. But the passage, Rom. xiii: 14, cannot refer to the same, because it is a requirement of those in Christ—already baptized. They had, however, been partially drawn away by divers fleshly inducements, and to some extent thrown off the authority of Christ. The Apostle's admonition is simply to return to their former Christian obligations, and maintain their position under Christ.

Please give us your views of Luke xvi: 16.

Does our Saviour mean to say, that His kingdom or church was established when He uttered these words? Also, your views of Luke xvii: 20-21. E. ALEXANDER.

The passage, Luke xvi: 16, is: "The law and the prophets were until John: since that time the kingdom of God is preached, and every man passeth into it." The Lord did not *mean to* say, and certainly *did not say,* in this passage or any other, that His kingdom was established when he uttered these words. If the translators had been as free with their supplements here as in other places, we should read: "The law and the prophets *were preached* until John: since that time the kingdom of God is preached," etc. The law and the prophets were in full force, when these words were uttered, and never died till the Lord expired on the cross—the "hand-writing of ordinances" was never taken away, till this wonderful event. But we cannot elaborate the subject now.

The other passage, Luke xvii: 20-21, is: "And when he was demanded of the Pharisees, when the kingdom of God should come, he answered them and said: The kingdom of God cometh not with observation: neither shall they say, Lo, here or Lo, there! for, behold, the kingdom of God is within you." The kingdom of God was within or *among* them, not established, fully developed and progressing in full glory, but in its inefficient or embryo state, embodied in the Lord, and its approach announced by John the Baptist, the Lord, the Twelve and the Seventy, in all its fullness and glory.

IV. Brother C. V. Bristow, of Ill., says:

"There is a question on which the brethren, both preachers and private members, are divided, and the little brotherhood here is divided on it. The question alluded to is the ordinance of washing the saints' feet. Some think it a command, and necessary to be attended to. Others say it has had its day and ceased. Those who believe and practice this ordinance, disagree, some putting it in the church, and some in the household."

We have neither the time nor the space to elaborate this subject. There is no such *ordinance* in the New Testament as *washing the saint's feet*. The Lord, in the family capacity, after a common supper, gave the apostles a practical lesson of humility, to counteract that kind of spirit which led to dispute who should be the greatest. He commenced washing their feet. Peter objected through shame. The Lord commanded him to yield, or he should have no part with him. The Apostle then cheerfully yielded. The Lord then proceeded to make the practical deduction: "If I, your Lord and Master, wash your feet, you ought to wash one another's feet." If He, though greater than all, humbled himself to the most lowly service, we should humble ourselves to any service for the most humble and lowly of the human family.

Such a thing as a ceremony called "the ordinance of feet-washing," practiced in the congregation met to worship, among the primitive Disciples, is unknown to all history. Owing to their wearing sandals, and their sandy country, it was an important item to bathe the feet before retiring, both to cleanse them and prevent soreness. It was consequently an important item in hospitality, to furnish water and bathe the feet of a friend in entertaining him. In this sense Paul looks at it, in the only mention of it in the apostolic writings. It is mentioned in a catalogue of good works, such as lodging or entertaining strangers, bringing up children, guiding the house, etc.

We cannot discuss the subject now; we have, on some previous occasion, examined every mention of it in the Bible, in some former volume.

-----o----

[From the Louisville Courier.]

Bible Union—Father Maclay's Pamphlet.

The New York Times has recently published a notice of a pamphlet purporting to be written by Dr. Maclay, late President of the Bible Union. The Times announces that the Bible Union is in an uncomfortable position before the public at this time, but we beg leave to assure all who think thus, that the discomfort arises entirely from the fact that Dr. Maclay has been put to services in his present condition of mind, that are at war with all the services of the days of his intellectual vigor. The old gentleman has been induced lately to lend himself to purposes at direct variance with his labors and proclamations of the past few years, and he has been carried so far into the regions of wrong-doing, that his managers have required that the pamphlet against the Bible Union, of which he is the putative author, shall be sedulously kept from the *friends* of that body, and placed in the hands only of the most violent and virulent *enemies of the cause,* with injunctions not to permit any friend of revision to see it. Does truth or honesty or honor ever require such services as these? The most earnest efforts have been made by the friends of the Bible Union for two weeks, in the city of New York to obtain a copy of this pamphlet, this secret emissary, but even those who admitted that they had a copy of the work, declared that they were enjoined not to show it. But an enemy of revision, the Philadelphia Chronicle, has published the precious document in that paper.

We have been well acquainted, for weeks, with the matters of which Dr. Maclay complains. We shall not burthen this communication with their enumeration, but content ourselves with saying, that all of these complaints, that have any truth in them, were as palpable to him, as open to view, as common to all the members of the Bible Union, when Dr. Maclay was an agent of the society, boldly proclaiming the superlative claims of the Bible Union to the confidence and support of all true men, as they now are to the defected ex-President. He is made ridiculously to assert that he has just discovered these wondrous secrets, and while every employee of the Bible Union was perfectly posted in them, he claims that he was a dupe for years! And if he was thus duped for years, may not some such work still be in progress?

At the instance of Father Maclay, a committee was organized by the Bible Union to investigate every complaint made by him. That committee labored long and sedulously and patiently, in hearing the querulous carpings of the old gentleman. It gave the matter so much time that some complaint was made about the delay of the report. The pamphlet says that the committee has not reported, but we have the report before us, and we quote enough of it to refute all the criminations of Father Maclay. It is as follows:

"Your committee, appointed to inquire into the present condition and practical working of the enterprise, respectfully report, that after a careful examination into its affairs, they are satisfied that its executive officers have laboriously and honestly discharged their duty to the Union, and they see no reason to recommend any change in the practical working of the enterprise.

"W. COLGATE, EZRA SMITH, W.H. WYCKOFF, SAM'L BAKER, S. E. SHEPARD, T. B. STILLMAN, J. W. SARLES."

In addition to this, the Bible Revision Association instituted an independent investigation of all these troubled dreams and fancies of Father Maclay, and after a thorough inquiry into them, unanimously resolved that the Bible Union is acting in strict accordance with fidelity, and is abundantly worthy the esteem and confidence of every honest and truthful mind. The attempt by a few ambitious spirits to make the Bible Union subservient to *their uses,* has been promptly met and put down, and the Bible Union is honestly, faithfully and nobly performing all its duties to God and man, which it assumed in undertaking a faithful revision of the Holy Oracles. There is not even the shadow of a foundation, in the management of the Bible Union, for the charges, the conduct, or the dereliction of Father Maclay—the infirmities of age are rapidly pressing him down, and while we grieve over the fact that such a man has become a castaway from the noblest cause of the age, we rejoice to know that neither his example nor his criminations have in the slightest degree effected the Bible Union, or checked its onward progress. The great scholars of the Bible Union, Conant, Lillie, Schaff, and numbers who approach them in scholarly attainments, all of whom know the revisers of the Bible Union, look with contempt upon the silly ravings that falsely say the tribunal of revisers are incompetent It is absurd to suppose that the Baptist and Presbyterian scholars we have named, would be associated as co-laborers with such scholars as Father Maclay is made to say some of the revisers are.

These facts explain what is called the "uncomfortable condition" of the Bible Union, and will answer in advance, whatever may be said by a partisan religious anti-revision press, which unblushingly announces, that it will publish only one side of these matters, "because a different course [that of letting both sides be heard] would be unfair to its readers." If any words of admonition on our part would be of any use to the enemies of revision, we would caution them to handle these affairs carefully, for we assure them that we have fullness enough of information in all the premises, to enable us to say that the Bible Union is anxious to court the largest inquiry into its conduct, and that it will triumphantly come through the ordeal, to the joy of its friends, and the discomfiture of its enemies.

JAMES EDMUNDS,
T. S. BELL.

BIBLE REVISION ROOMS,
July 22nd, 1856.

P. S.—May we not ask such of the secular press as may publish an account of Dr. Maclay's pamphlet, to republish this response to it?

[Since writing the note touching the above matters, found upon another page, we have received the foregoing, and insert it at our earliest convenience.—ED.]

FINCASTLE, Putnam Co., Ia., 24th June, 1856.

BRO. FRANKLIN: *Dear Sir*—Often do I think of and pray for you, that the Father of our spirits may greatly strengthen and confirm you unto the end; that you may live long and he greatly blessed in sowing the seed of Christ's kingdom in good and honest hearts, and in building up believers in the faith once delivered to the saints.

But the main object of this is to give a short notice of a Universalian meeting held in our house last Lord's day, and a synopsis of the discourse preached at the time, and their attempt to organize, etc. At the time appointed, the speaker arose and read the 57th Psalm, took for his text the 16th verse of the chapter read. Here it is: "For I will not contend forever, neither will I be always wroth; for the spirit should fail before me, and the souls which I have made."

He began by defining some of the words of his text. Said "contend" meant "to be opposed to." Forever, he said, must be understood to mean a limited time, when applied to things in their nature *temporal,* and endless, when relating to things necessarily *endless.* Pretty good, thinks I, hope we will have some good logic to-day, for I did not hope to escape the everlasting song at trying to prove there is *not* any *future* punishment. And here, while I think of it, permit me to affirm. Just take this *"not,"* this *"is not* any future punishment," from under the Universalian structure, and it falls a baseless fabric, with not one wreck behind. But the speaker made quite a show of fairness; said all he was after was the *truth,* and really appeared to be *honest.* But he here gave us a maxim or two about this thing called *honesty,* that was good. He said that a man's being ever so honest, did not prove him to be *right.* Thinks I, your own rule applied would ruin you, sir. But all at a bound, he dashed right into the subject; made the old prophet say that God would not *contend* or oppose the wicked forever, endlessly. But here he was compelled to admit, that God would endlessly contend with or oppose the wicked or sin. *"But,"* making a grand summerset backward, said he, "the reason God will not endlessly oppose the wicked in the future is, there will be no wicked, no sin to oppose in the future." But he took good care not to offer the shadow of proof to sustain this miserable *ad captandum* of Universalists. It is an awful blunder upon which thousands are *leaning* for the future, viz.: that because there is *no future* punishment, therefore I will be saved!! Candid reader, open your Bible at the 57th Isa., seriously ponder it over, and with myself you will say, the prophet has alone in his eye the idolatries of the Jews. Verse 5 says, "Inflaming yourselves with idols under every green tree," etc., to 11th verse. "And of whom hast thou been afraid or feared, that thou hast lied, and hast *not remembered* me." Now for all this idolatry. God says, ver. 13, "When thou criest, let thy companies deliver thee," etc., "but he that putteth his trust in me shall possess the land, and shall inherit my holy mountain." All this can only apply to the idolatrous Jews and the land of *Canaan.* Now to these ungrateful idol-loving sons of Abraham, God, by the mouth of the prophet, adds ver. 16, the text of the speaker; for were God to continue for a *limited time,* much less endless, the sore calamities he often sent upon this people for their idol worship, they would indeed have "failed before him," the race would have been utterly destroyed, an event God has always prevented.

All that followed was only repetition of the assertion, that if God did or would not contend *endlessly* with the wicked, it was because there was a time coming when there would be no sin, nor wickedness to oppose or be wroth with; for God's nature would endlessly be wroth with and opposed to all sin and sinners. Another reason he said endless punishment could not be true was, 'twould *annihilate* the spirits and souls God had made!!

Why, sir, it is *only annihilation* that can enable the Universalists to span the *great gulf* that lies right between all who die in their sins, and the Paradise of God; for all know they do not pretend to deny that *many "die in their sins,"* nor do they pretend to account for, when or how the sinner gets rid of his sins after death. You will remember, when you pressed this matter on

Mr. Curry last winter, he frankly said, "I don't know," a fatal admission for men *do die in their sins;* for many men, with *murder* in their hearts, and the steel in their hands, have in a moment been cut down by the arm of justice. But remember, reader, God has said, "The abominable, and murderers, and whoremongers, and sorcerers, and idolaters, and all liars shall have their part in the lake which burneth with fire and brimstone, which is the second death." But *annihilation* will not light up that dark abyss in which Universalism endlessly leaves its votaries, for then the "abominable" would never get into Abraham's bosom, being *annihilated,* and this will not do, for, say they, "*all men,*" including the abominable, of necessity, "will be made holy and happy."

In my next I shall notice the organization, etc.
ONESIMUS.

-----o-----

CADIZ, Henry co., Ind., May 15, 1856.

BROTHER: You will please send the *Review* to Rev. John Smith, Abington, Wayne county, Ind. He desires to receive it from Jan. No. 1. He is a minister of the United Brethren church, and travels this circuit. He is the most distinguished debater of that denomination; he entirely demolished the great Spiritualist, who declared the Bible had done more harm than all wars, etc. He (Smith), says that "the whole Christian world will have to come to the Bible alone and immersion alone, and they are now rapidly coming to it; weighing down instead of enlarging their discipline."

Bro. Enos Adamson held a several-days' meeting for us, and did much good; his efforts were well received by all classes and sects, and our brethren felt strengthened; we thanked God and took courage. Tell all the saints to pray that the Word of God may have free course.

Bro. Ebenezer Thompson is laboring with great success at Middletown. Many have already bowed to Messiah, and been buried with their Lord in Baptism. Four of Mr. Cooper's girls are among those added to the saved.

We are not very able to pay largely, but we are very willing to give of our sustenance so that our ministers shall not have fears about their temporal wants. We need preachers to proclaim the Word in our midst.

Bro. S. S. Bennett, of Ogden, is now debating with a Spirit-Rapper infidel at Greensboro, and is doing good service in the cause of truth.

JOHN C. BECK.

A Word to the Brethren.

We have recently read some articles from the pens of some of our gifted scribes, upon the "cause of our downward tendency," but we can- not agree with some of them, that it is owing to our want of a sufficient organization. I am tardy to believe that all the luke-warmness and difficulties of the churches are attributable to an inefficient organization; for I believe that we have that organization taught and recognized by the New Testament, viz: congregations of brethren, with their elders, deacons and evangelists. I am still more tardy to believe that the New Testament is not explicit enough upon all things necessary to our faith and practice; for I believe with Paul, that all Scripture given by inspiration of God, is profitable for doctrine, for reproof, for correction and instruction in righteousness; that the man of God may be perfect, thoroughly furnished unto all good works. But my object is not to engage in a controversy, already too protracted, personal and sarcastic, to be productive of much edification or usefulness. I merely beg leave to suggest a few thoughts to my more gifted brethren. I am willing to admit that we have in some of our churches luke-warmness, coldness and difficulties. I am willing to admit that there is not near as much zeal and devotion among us as there ought to be. I am willing to admit that there is too little of the love of Christ, and too much of the love of the world and its pleasures, in the congregations. I am willing, in a word, to admit that we do not pray enough, do not preach the gospel as we ought, do not study the Bible as we ought. I repeat it, I admit all these, and to *these* I attribute the "cause of our downward tendency." Now, brethren, in all kindness permit me to suggest that we cease writing our long and too often acrimonious articles upon the above subject, and betake ourselves to praying more fervently, studying the Bible more faithfully, preaching more zealously, and living more Godly. That we consecrate our whole body, soul and spirit, together with our substance, to the advancement of the Redeemer's kingdom, and we shall no more hear the cry of inefficient organizations, no more be called upon to lament the downward tendency of the Redeemer's cause; but our hearts will be filled with joy at the triumphs of the "gospel of the grace of God." This is the way the primitive Christians did, and this is what we MUST DO if we would fulfill our mission, and secure the everlasting smiles of our Heavenly Father. That we may live in peace and love, one with another, and finally be all united in heaven, is the sincere prayer of your brother in the kingdom and patience of Jesus Christ.

R. C. MORTON.

OBITUARY.

Bro. JOHN WILLIAMS WILSON fell asleep in the arms of our blessed Saviour, on the evening of the 22d inst., aged 28 years and 21 days.

Bro. Wilson was a straight-forward, plain man, and a true Christian; he had long been a member of the Christian church. Although he suffered much, he bore it with Christian fortitude and patience, and calmly breathed his last like a child falling asleep. He left a wife and two small children, an aged mother, besides many relations and brethren, to mourn his departure. We repeatedly heard such expressions as these fall from his lips: *"I have a home in Heaven,"* "Blessed Saviour!" "Vain world, adieu!" "Obey the Lord." Some two days before he died, he called all his friends around him, and told them he was going home to his Father's house, and prayed for the time to come when he would leave this world of sorrow and affliction. He desired his sister to sing a favorite hymn of his, commencing,

"When for eternal worlds we steer,

And seas are calm, and skies are clear,"

after which he exhorted all to continue in *the Faith*, and meet him in heaven, the Christian's home. He then seemed contented, and slept for some time; then woke up, and seemed astonished that he was still in the body, and told me he was sorry he was here; he thought he had left us. "Oh!" said he, "I will have to die again; but the Lord's will be done." After that he became deranged at times, until just before his death, when he came to his senses. He again desired the same hymn to be sung until he died, and in a few minutes breathed his last, praising the Lord.

W. M. HELLINGS.

West Middlebury, Ohio.

"Leaves have their times to fall.

And flowers to wither at the north winds breath.

And the stars to set—but all,

Thou hast all seasons for thine own, O Death."

Died, at his father's residence, in Carlisle, Kentucky, the 24th day of March, 1856, in the 26th year of his age, John W. Rogers, son of Elenora and Elder John Rogers. The deceased had been afflicted for several years previous to his death, with a hemorrhage of the lungs. Thus admonished of his approaching end, he contemplated the period of his departure from this world of sorrow and suffering, with great calmness. He frequently remarked to his friends during the past winter, that the cold, bleak storms of March would take him away. But he was prepared to meet his death. He was a Christian. He was an obedient subject of the blessed Son of God, and delighted to commune with his brothers and sisters in the sanctuary of the Most High. When deprived of the privilege of going to the house of God, he took great pleasure in reading the Sacred Scriptures, conversing with his friends and relations, and in hearing sung the songs of Zion. He admonished the unconverted to think of their condition, and prepare for the solemnities of death and eternity. He urged his friends and relations to persevere in well-doing, that they might finally attain everlasting life. He desired to meet them in the "better land."

By faith he viewed the mansions of rest, and contemplated the bliss of the happy inhabitants. By faith he saw the triumph of the Christian, saw the crown of life, incorruptible and star-gemmed, given to the conqueror; saw his entering into the glorious city of our God—the new Jerusalem; in which tears are never shed and night is unknown; in which there is no suffering, no death, no separation; and thus resigned in the prospect of a blessed immortality he fell asleep in Jesus, who is the "resurrection and the life." He has passed the portals of the grave, and is now where "the wicked cease from troubling and the weary are at rest." We sorrow not as those who are without hope; assured that our loss is his gain. "Death is the crown of life; were death denied, poor man would live in vain. Death wounds to cure. We fall, we rise, we reign." We will see him no more, until the bright morning of the resurrection. "Blessed are the dead which die in the Lord, from henceforth, yea saith the Spirit, that they may rest from their labors, and their works de follow them."

W. C. R.

Editor's Table.

Office of the *American Christian Review,* West Fourth street, No. 60, on third floor, open stair way from outside. Signs will be seen at the entrance.

Dr. Barclay—Jerusalem Mission. On Wednesday night, July 23d, we had the gratification to hear our distinguished brother, our missionary to the ancient city, Jerusalem, Dr. Barclay. We saw him once before, but did not have a clear recollection of his personal appearance. He is a man of goodly stature, well formed, and fine appearance. He is extremely modest and unassuming; yet appears much at ease in the pulpit, or in front of it, for he was wise enough not to be propped up in the ungained pulpit, corner of Eighth and Walnut streets. He spoke with ease and distinctness. He glanced at the territorial condition of Jerusalem and the environs, then the political state of things, then the moral condition, and closed with a brief argument in favor of the position that the Jews will be converted. The speech was full of interest throughout, but, as we took no notes, we attempt nothing like an outline here.

We were much pleased with Dr. Barclay, as well **as** with his speech. He had every appearance of the candid, unassuming Christian man. We were truly happy to know that he and his family were in our midst, after a perilous adventure of some four years about six thousand miles from us, and after he had been the object of so many prayers and anxieties on the part of the children of God.

But where is the missionary spirit among us now? O! where? Jerusalem may cry for help! England may cry for help, and thousands of disciples reveling in luxury, and not even evangelizing our own country! God will soon call us to account for all these things.

THE regular yearly meeting of the Sixth District of Indiana will commence on Wednesday, August 27th, at nine o'clock, A. M., at Bentonville, Fayette Co. Addresses expected on special subjects by Brethren B. F. Reeve, Benj. Franklin, David Franklin, Henry Pritchard, S. S. Benette, Jas. P. Orr and S. K. Hoshour.

Churches in the district will please report by delegates without further notice.

As these meetings are for the special benefit of the brethren at large, they are earnestly requested to attend. By order of President

B. F. REEVE.
JAS. P. ORE, Sec'y.
July 21th, 1856.

Campbell and Rice Debate.—We were surprised, on calling at the Presbyterian Book Store for a copy of the Debate held in Lexington, Ky., between Pres. A. Campbell and Rev. N. L. Rice, Dec. 1843, to find but two miserably old shelf-worn and damaged copies, and no account of a new edition ! Nor could we learn of any place where the work is kept for sale, or whether it is in print! What does this mean ? Is it the policy to let it die and go out of print? Is this the interest Presbyterians take in this work ? Did they secure the copy right merely to put the light under a bushel ? Is this grand effort thrown aside, and resort now to a little tract of forty pages? Here is a Presbyterian comment upon the effort of Dr.no; we mistake; he was not *doctor then,* but was made such since, to give effect to a work which they are ashamed to circulate! Can we not secure the plates and circulate this book? The copy right will soon be out.

Bible Union.—We regret to learn that Drs. Maclay and Judd have become disaffected, and issued a pamphlet injurious and highly prejudicial to the great work of the Union. This alienation, or disaffection, in this great and, as we have constantly thought, harmonious work, is a most lamentable and mortifying thing. It will be a sweet morsel under all the tongues and pens of the enemies of this great and good work. We have advices of different kinds, but nothing that we shall stand upon to give an opinion, as to where the blame lies; and we do hope that all the friends of this great enterprise will suspend any opinion till a fair and impartial investigation into all the merits of the case, by an impartial and disinterested committee, which we trust will be called, shall report in the premises.

It is useless for any friend of Revision to become disheartened at this. All great moves have their difficulties, and all men have human nature and human weaknesses, not excepting Bible Union men. We cannot have Gabriel, Michael, or any other angel, or committee of angels from heaven to do this great work. It must be done by men, and imperfect men, for we have no other kind. Hence no reasonable man need expect that such a great and important work will be completed without human weakness and imperfection being found. The very men that have disagreed in this case, are about as great and good men as the world contains; and we trust a gracious overruling Providence will save us, in this most important instance, from shame and disgrace; and that this great work will be completed. Cannot this breach be healed? A mighty responsibility will rest upon him who is the cause of this offense.

ELD. M. B. HOPKINS has been unwell for some days, so much so that he has been unable to fill his appointments. He is better, and we hope will be in the field soon

Success of the Gospel.

Bro. Wm. Wm. Jarrett, Williamstown, Ky., July 17th, reports three additions at Fork Lick Creek, and two at Elizabeth, Ky.

Bro. Finley Oakes, Mt. Morris, Va., July 4th, reports seven received into the church; three by baptism.

Bro. S. W. Irvin, Poplar Plains, July 7th, says: "Yesterday we had three accessions to the church here; one by letter, two by confession and baptism. Old Father Smith, one of the most honorable and venerable men in this community, surrounded by a large circle of children and grand-children, vowed allegiance to the great King, and' added greatly to the interest of the occasion. An amiable and interesting daughter-in-law went with him, and they were together buried with the Lord, and rose to walk in newness of life. May God's grace attend them."

Bro. A. Adams, New Liberty, Ky., July 20th, says: "We have had a protracted meeting at White's Run, embracing the first Lord's day in June, at which we had four valuable additions, and the brethren and sisters seemed much stirred up Bro. Lockwood, of Madisonville, labored for us du ring the meeting."

Bro. E. Thompson, July 16th, says: "I have just closed two meetings of four days continuance each; one at Quincy, Ill., and the other at Independence. At the former we had eleven additions, at the latter sixteen, making twenty-seven at the two points, embracing the first and second Lord's days in July. Also, some thirty have been added to the churches during the Spring and Summer, (up to this time), in the bounds of my labor. To the Lord be all the praise.

-----o-----

Several Presbyterians have referred to the Confession of Faith, and not finding our quotations upon the pages referred to, disputed their authority, they had a like difficulty once before, from the fact that we quoted from an old edition, the pages of which did not correspond with late editions. We immediately secured the correct edition; but as this has been several years, this mutable concern has been again changed, so that the pages do not correspond. All our quotations are genuine, and to be found in the late edition, but not upon the pages referred to.

-----o-----

We had an encouraging account of matters pertaining to Bacon College, from Bro. J. A. Dearborn, which came a little too late for No. 7, which we regret to say has, by some means, been mislaid. We are truly sorry that this important document could not have gone out in the present number, for the encouragement of the friends of that institution.

The Daughters' College.—Our esteemed brother, John Aug. Williams, having resigned the Presidency of Christian College, Columbia, Mo., and purchased the elegant property of Bro. Mullins, near Harrodsburg, Ky., designs commencing his labors in the Daughters' College in September next.

-----o-----

Revision—*First and Second Thessalonians.*— The revised copy of Paul's first and second letters to the Thessalonians, printed upon pages of three columns, the left hand column containing the common version, the middle column containing the original Greek, and the right hand column containing the revised version; also a complete copy of the revised version in paragraphs, by itself, with critical notes, giving the authority for alterations, in a neat bound volume of 75 pages. We have read it through with both pleasure and profit. It is now committed to the world for criticism. Every man who is studying the Bible should have it, whether he is pleased with it or not, as it contains the original and two translations, with many valuable notes and authorities. Price 60 cents, bound in cloth; 40 cents in paper. We will order it to any person who desires it, or keep it for sale if the demand will justify it.

-----o-----

Religious Telescope.—Such is the title of a weekly sheet, of respectable dimensions and interesting matter. The editor is an interesting and rather an independent man, in the denomination wearing the singular misnomer, "United Brethren in Christ."

-----o-----

To Correspondents.—Many queries have been on hand for months. Some are prepared for insertion and crowded out; some we have not had time to consider and answer, and some are so purely speculative that we cannot turn them to any practical account, and are compelled respectfully to pass them by. Many brethren have requested private letters upon matters that would require hours to look up and respond to; some making inquiries into business matters in this city, that would require much time and walking to look up. Now we have a great desire to accommodate everybody; but in this respect, anyone who will reflect a minute must see the thing *is impossible.*

-----o-----

Bro. Ayers has had a lengthy document to hand for some time, kindly written, headed, "Central (Ky.) Christian Union," which we should certainly have no objections to publishing, only that the question discussed has not only "waxed old and is ready to vanish away," but has actually gone by. The esteemed Bro. Anderson, some months since, published an excellent article in the *Age,* in the true Christian spirit, assuring his brethren that he should give them no trouble, but that he should co-operate with them. The beloved B. F. Hall has also expressed himself in similar style and spirit. If Bro. Ayers pleases, then, we will let the matter rest for the present, read the Bible, pray that we may understand it, and all be of the same mind and of the same judgment.

THE AMERICAN CHRISTIAN REVIEW.

Vol. 1.]   CINCINNATI, SEPTEMBER, 1856.   [No. 9.

THE MORAL CHARACTER OF CHRIST.
BY B. F. HALL

"We preach Christ!" What theme so sublime, so thrilling, so appropriate! The Apostles preached him; prophets preached him; angels preached him. Jesus was the sum of every message from God; the spirit of every promise; the substance of every ceremony; the burden of every song; the subject of every Divine prediction. Jesus was the key-note in every anthem sung by the Levite choirs; the theme of all the Jewish prophets; the subject-matter of apostolic preaching.— Angels sung at his birth; they waited on him during his eventful life; they ministered to him in his agonizing death; they hailed him when he rose, in conquering majesty, from the grave, and escorted him back to Heaven.

"They brought his chariot from above, To bear him to his throne;

And with a shout exulting cried, The glorious work is done!"

The Holy Spirit preached Jesus. The Apostles heard it, and echoed the theme the world around. They preached Jesus to the traditionalized Jew, the superstitious pagan, the philosophic Greek, and the war-worn Roman. They preached him in Jerusalem, in Corinth, in Athens. They preached him among all nations, and to all classes of men.

VOL. 1., NO. IX.—15.

In the Seven-Hilled City, and to Caesar's household; they preached him as the King of kings, and Lord of all. "I am not ashamed of the Gospel of Christ," exclaimed a Heaven-sent Apostle of Jesus—a model-man, one of the noblest spirits that ever inhabited a human body, or that angels ever bore on golden pinions to glory and to God.

We are not surprised that the Apostles preached Jesus. They knew him, and loved him; nor that martyrs bled and burnt for him. There is a charm in his name, a power in his religion, that made them glory in his cross, and rejoice that they were counted worthy to suffer for his religion. Jesus is the spirit, and life, and light of both Testaments. He is the source of all Divine influence, the center of all moral attraction. *Jesus* is the theme of our present discourse. In him we behold what most concerns us to understand—what is most necessary for us to know in Christianity—*the character of God, the import of the Divine law, and the standard of moral excellence.*

The character which the Evangelists have given of Jesus Christ is unique, consistent, uniform, natural, perfect. It stands alone in the history of the world—alone without an archetype, without a parallel. Other persons have been remarkable for individual excellencies; but in Jesus there is a beautiful and attractive harmony of all the virtues; and from their perfect combination results the spotless luster of his character, as the purest white is the effect of the union of all the primitive colors.

Jewish history contains a succession of patriarchs and prophets and saints distinguished for particular virtues—as Job for patience, Moses for meekness, Elijah for zeal. The heathen world boasts of a Socrates, a Pythagoras, and a Zoroaster. But Jesus travels across this galaxy of illustrious men, like the full moon in all the brightness of her course, with a luster totally unborrowed from them, and casting their feeble and collected light into distant obscurity, by the mild yet overwhelming power of his rays. All the lights of the earth pale in the resplendent rays of the Son of Righteousness.

In Jesus we see conjoined in profoundest harmony, not only those remarkable qualities which have been exhibited by different individuals, but we discover also new forms of virtue, and new manifestations of greatness. In his mysterious person were united eternity and time, Divinity and humanity, heaven and earth; majesty never before displayed was blended with meekness unexampled. In Jesus we see dignity clothed with condescension; temperance and self-denial softened by gentleness and suavity; indignant sensibility to sin by weeping compassion for the sinner. In him were united the splendor of the Divine nature with the humility of a little child; a determined perseverance in the path of duty, which no array of dangers could deter, with a heart so attuned to compassion, that the faintest appeal of misery arrested his progress as with the power of Omnipotence. Embracing the mightiest plans, he yet stooped, without trifling, to the smallest circumstance. Like his Almighty Father, sustaining vast, stupendous, and unnumbered worlds, revolving through illimitable space, yet stooping to succor the falling sparrow, and to admire the humble lily. He one moment conversed with angels, and the next listened with delight to the lispings of infant praise, or bore with meekness the obtuseness of his disciples. His character, though original, is natural. It is a harmonious whole, a self-consistent character. Whatever is majestic in greatness, touching in mercy, and condescending in goodness, collected into one assemblage, formed his character. As shade softens into shade, and color melts into color in the rainbow, so attributes of character before considered antipodal and contradictory, are seen to mix and mingle in the peasant of Galilee; and altogether form a character so splendid with virtues, as to render poverty venerable and humility august—a character on which envy never fixed a stain, nor malignance cast a shade; a character so pure as to baffle the scrutiny of malice, and to force from the Roman Procurator, who had often sported with the rights of innocence; the reluctant confession—"I find no fault in this man;" a character so great, and so perfect, as to excite the admiration of ages, and the wonder of the world. It was a character supremely good and perfect—so perfect that the most captious have not been able to detect in it a single instance of error, imprudence, sinister intention, or evil passion; a single instance of impotence, or ignorance; a single fault. All is perfect uprightness, innocence, wisdom, goodness, truth. The picture has been hung on high for the inspection, the scrutiny of the world. It has challenged the most rigid criticisms of eighteen centuries; and no blemish has yet been detected. Its grandeur compels our homage; its benevolence and purity touch our hearts. What a dazzling constellation of the most sublime, and difficult, and useful virtues does the picture exhibit. What a perfect test of the truth, what a glorious display of the efficacy and fruits of the religion which he taught! Such virtues define the furthest limits of excellence; they bear the impression of the Divinity. Surely this is the Son of God!

Power, calculated to impress the beholders with the most reverential awe, in him was united with a familiarity which admitted on easy terms of communication all grades and classes of society. He united zeal with candor, the utmost activity with a prudence which never deserted him, and irresistible power with unassuming gentleness. Sensible of his high character, he was yet meek and unresisting. Though he abated not from the rigor of his Father's law, he was the preacher of a religion which offers pardon to the guilty penitent, relief to the burdened, and succor to the helpless. Such was the life of Jesus, that in all the busy murmurs of history about the character of men, not a whisper can be distinguished which calumniates the founder of our faith.

The doctrine and precepts of Jesus are in strict accordance with all we know of the character of God, and are strictly adapted to the capacities of mankind; and yet they are delivered with a simplicity and majesty wholly divine. He spake as never man spake. He spoke with authority, and yet he addressed himself to the understanding and reason of men; and he spoke with wisdom which men could neither gainsay nor resist.

In his private life Christ exhibited a character, not merely of strict justice, but of overwhelming benignity. He was temperate without austerity, humble without sanctimoniousness; patient and yet energetic. Every virtue was regulated by the most perfect prudence. Such was his demeanor as to win the love of his friends, and invite the wonder and admiration of his enemies. He is like a tower seen afar off, under a clear sky, that rises in grandeur and sublimity with every step of approach. Familiarity with him excites devotion. In vain should we search for such a character in the pages of profane history, or of human philosophy. It stands confessedly unrivaled and alone, a masterpiece of Divine wisdom and power, stamped with the wisdom of the Most High God.

History furnishes us with many characters illustrious for some remarkable attribute; characters in which many great defects are concealed amid the dazzling splendor of a single virtue. But on the disk of the character of the Nazarene no dark spots are perceptible. His biographers had no defects to conceal, no faults to excuse, no crime to palliate, no weakness to deplore. There is not one dark passage in his wonderful life. In the character of the best of men there are always some rough points which jut out to mar their beauty; some essential virtue lacking, or some vice, like Satan clothed in robes of light, placed in strange companionship, among the virtues. How different is the character of Jesus. Like the finished production of an artist, the details of the picture are as perfect and as beautiful as the general outline is grand and imposing. Even his sternness of principle, and the wonder-exciting displays of Omnipotent power, were set off and relieved by his gentleness, his humility, and benevolence, as the brilliancy of the diamond is enhanced by the gems of softer ray by which it is encircled. There are spots in the material sun, but there are none in the Sun of Righteousness. His alone is a full, unoriginated, inexhaustible, and unchanging light.

It is not, however, the sublime contemplation of God, the philanthropic admiration of the character of Jesus, nor the sentimental love of virtue, that constitute Christianity. The soul cannot live on such religion. It is like feeding on dew. Religion is more than airy, sentimental, beautiful. It consists in the *imitation of Jesus.* Christ assumed human nature that we might become partakers of the Divine nature. He was given us for an example, that we should follow in his steps. His example is, in every moral respect, strictly practicable. It is an example to men in every condition. It is accommodated to the imitation of all men.

"The word was made flesh." This is the grand central truth in Christianity. *"God in Christ."* It is not God, the infinite Spirit, merely, pervading heaven and earth, whom no man hath seen, nor can see; it is God in Christ, wearing human nature, like a soft cloud on the brightness of the Godhead, and putting before his awful majesty, the sympathies and feelings of a man, to attract our feeble and sinful spirits. Christ comes to us as a friend and a brother, of whom we are not afraid; and yet when we commit our souls to him, we feel that the fullness of the Godhead dwelleth bodily in him; so that God comes to us, not as an abstraction, but as the man Christ Jesus. We rest upon this idea, in faith, and hope, and love. It is a sentiment that gives joy to the heart; it meets the wants of our entire nature by addressing us, not as mere intellectual, spiritual substances, but as *men*, with feelings and passions which cannot be satisfied, as God has constituted them, without an incarnation of religion; something brought near to our senses, which we can, as it were, look upon with our eyes, and our hands can handle. *God in Christ* does not speak to us, as he spake to Moses on Mount Sinai, amid rolling thunders, and lurid lightning, and a terrible earthquake, which shook the mountain to its base, and smote the camps of Israel with terror and alarm, and caused even Moses to fear and tremble.

The Jewish law, with its sacrifices, ablutions, ceremonies, penalties, vocabulary, types, and figures, together with its paraphernalia of ritual service—all, all were intended to teach the import, the divine signification of a few words and symbols. These constituted the elements of the Divine oracles, the first principles of Christian doctrine, the rudiments of truth to be more fully revealed at a future period. They were the alphabet of Christianity; but they required the arrangement of the great Teacher, Jesus, to make visible the illuminating and transforming truths of Heaven. To do this was one design of our Lord's incarnation. None but he could do this, for no one knew the Father, save the Son. His life was a commentary upon the Divine perfections. The character of God was seen and read in his life. He was the focus where all the rays of Divine glory met and were radiated. As the moon reflects the glory of the sun, so does Jesus reflect the glory of the Divine Father.. "He is the image of the invisible God"—"the effulgence of his glory"—"the exact representation of his character." Philip said to Jesus: "Show us the Father." "Have I been so long with you, and do you not yet know me?" said the Saviour. "He that hath seen me hath seen the Father; why do you say then, show us the Father?" The words of light and love which flowed from the lips of the adorable Jesus, emanated from the Father. The mighty and benevolent works which he wrought were the works of God, the Father; and all exhibited the gracious and benevolent character of God; for Jesus and his Father are one. The attributes of Christ's character which have excited the admiration of the world, and won the hearts of so many thousands, are the attributes of God. It is only through the medium of Christ Jesus, that the Divine character is fully and truly seen. Here is Deity dwelling among men— ineffable glory, issuing in softened radiance from the cloud of humanity in which it was invested.

"In Christ we see Christianity alive, active, moving amid human sympathies, tested by trial, triumphant in death." " Take the life and character of Jesus out of the Scriptures, and leave only his teachings, and what would remain but propositions as cold and vague as those of philosophy! The light of Divine truth would be extinguished. It would be like blotting the sun from the material universe. Something might be seen by the cold light of the stars; but nature would lie dead— the green hills, the cultivated vale, the shining river, would be colorless, indistinct, with uncertain outline and deceptive shadows."

In the face of Jesus we see "as in a glass the glory of the Lord, and are changed into the same image from glory to glory, as by the spirit of the Lord." This life explained the attributes of love, justice, holiness, goodness, truth. As the rays of light, falling upon the smooth waters, reflect a perfect image of the sun in the firmament, so the perfections of God are mirrored in the life of Jesus. It reveals the glory of the invisible God, and presents him before his creatures robed in all. the beauty of holiness, and invested with all the charms of love, mercy and grace. In the person of Jesus, the father is brought near to us without being lowered; he is here seen clothed with condescension without being degraded; and he is enthroned in majesty without being surrounded with terror.

We invite attention to the moral character of Christ as the outshining of the Divine perfections, and as the great model of excellence. In his life we see what God is, and what he would have us to be—what we *must* be, to become partakers of the inheritance with the saints in light.

Our limits will allow us to note only a few of the traits in the character of Jesus. Yet in this sketch, we shall aim to exhibit the principal outlines of the Saviour's character, so as to form, if not a picture, at least a slight sketch of those features of his grace and glory which so endear him to the hearts of his saints. My spirit fails at the thought of the wonderful task which I have essayed. Spirit of grace, aid us in our undertaking!

1. *Mark his* CANDOR. On one occasion, Jesus passed along the highway, attended by an immense concourse of people. The multitude heaved with anxiety. Every countenance was lit up with intense expectation, and reached forward to catch a glimpse of the person upon whom public attention was beginning to be fixed as the king and deliverer of the nation. The hearts of the crowd beat quickly with hope, waiting only for a signal from him to muster round his banner. But look! the peasant of Nazareth turns, and is about to speak. Every eye is fixed. Every ear is attentive. Every voice is still. "If any man will come after me," says Jesus, "let him deny himself, and take up his cross and follow me." Are these the words of an impostor? Such a sentiment at such a time—a moment of such high-wrought expectation—how convincingly does it show that he did not aim to bribe or flatter the populace. They must have been shocked beyond measure. These conditions of discipleship, expressed thus early in the ministry, show the candor of Jesus. He wished no one to commit himself in his favor until he knew the terms of entering his service. His very terms of discipleship challenge investigation of his claims. This is not the policy of an impostor; he shuns close inquiry, and scrutinizing investigation of his credentials; he resorts to arts; he folds around him the mantle of secrecy; he deals in inuendoes, in ambiguous terms, in vague expressions; he attracts by the charm of mystery; he never exposes himself to searching gaze and public scrutiny. The frankness and open candor of Jesus show his consciousness of being the Messiah, and of being able to furnish adequate proofs of the Divine origin of his religion, and to supply corresponding motives to influence the honest hearted to become his disciples.

On another occasion, one came expressing willingness to follow him whithersoever he might go. Jesus said to him—"The foxes have holes, and the birds of the air have nests, but the son of man hath not where to lay his head." The Proprietor of the Universe, he who spread out the heavens as a tent to dwell in, and fashioned our world into form and beauty, when he came to rescue fallen man, had not where to lay his head! worse accommodated in his own world than the birds of the air or the beasts of the forests! He evidently saw that this ready professor expected temporal advantage, and he undeceived him in the outset. He checked his ardor by letting him know he had nothing to give him. We see here no over anxiety to make proselytes; no excessive desire to gain adherents; no feverish solicitude about followers. Is this the language of a deceiver? It is on the contrary, another instance of the candor of Jesus.

At another time, a young man who seemed to think himself the personification of goodness, came to Jesus, and kneeling before him. asked—"Good Master! what good thing must I do to inherit eternal life?" How exceedingly prepossessing must have been the appearance of this young man, and how strong and evident the impression made upon the mind of Jesus as to cause it to be remarked, that "Jesus loved him!" But neither the winning openness of the young man's countenance, nor his posture of reverence, nor his respectful address, could dim the bright spiritual vision of Jesus, or sway for one moment his unerring heart. What was his answer? Does he instantly bid the young man to come and enroll himself among his followers? No; Jesus knew the young man's heart, and accordingly propounded to him, as the ordeal of his professed piety, the startling injunction—"Go thy way, sell whatsoever thou hast, and give to the poor, and come, take up thy cross and follow me, and thou shalt have treasure in Heaven." A test so true, yet so repugnant to unsanctified human nature, an adventurer seeking to gain proselytes to an imposture, would never have ventured to prescribe. But Jesus wanted the right kind of men; he wanted their hearts, not their wealth. The prospect of gaining a rich and youthful adherent to his cause made no impression on him, neither did it prompt him to abate one jot of his demands. Had he been an impostor or an enthusiast, he would have been anxious and impatient. He would have been disposed to gain all the proselytes he possibly could on any terms, especially such as this young man would have been.

"No man can become my disciple," said the son of Mary, the carpenter of Nazareth, "unless he hate father, and mother, and brother, and sister, his wife and children, and even his own life."What powerful evidence does this passage furnish of the candor of Jesus! He states in the strongest and most impressive manner, that no one is worthy to be his disciple who is unable to rise above the strongest tics of natural affection. He, who could not surrender father and mother, and all earthly friends, for truth's sake, is unfit to be a servant of Jesus. Thus does he depict in the strongest terms, and set forth in the clearest light, the perilous nature of his service, and the trials that awaited his disciples. He manifests no anxiety to collect a party and build up a sect. The heavy draft he makes upon the faith of his hearers, shows his candor, the confidence he felt in his cause, and the goodness of his doctrine. He decoyed no one into his service by flattering assurances never to be realized, but stated explicitly the terms of discipleship; and how high they are, and what a draft do they make on our faith and devotion!

As disciples of Jesus, it becomes us at all times to imitate his candor. We should never mistake a fact; never keep back any part of the truth, where it is proper to speak at all; never give a false coloring to any matter. The heart should be transparent, and should be mirrored in the actions, the words, the very countenance of a Christian. We should never in any way deceive a fellow mortal. This would be to imitate the arch-fiend, the first and greatest deceiver, the father of lies. All who imitate him will inevitably share in his awful doom. On the contrary, let us imitate Jesus, whose candor and honesty we cannot but admire.

2. *Behold the* COMPASSION *of Jesus.*—He had compassion on the multitude who had followed him into the wilderness, to receive his sublime but simple, heart-stirring instructions. They were so intent on hearing Jesus, they had forgotten to bring food. The day had begun to decline, and the people felt the pressings of hunger. By means of a miracle he fed the concourse, and having invoked upon them the divine blessing, dismissed them to their respective homes.

The compassion of Jesus was manifested in his deep solicitude for the welfare of his nation.

The Jews, in the Saviour's time, were a priest-ridden, formal, and hypocritical people. Their habits were such as to reduce all minds to a level of superstitious imbecility. They were also proverbially wicked. They had corrupted their religion, by adding to it numerous and gross traditions; and, losing sight of its original design, they were guilty of the most flagrant violations of its precepts. As might have been expected in the circumstances, they contemptuously rejected the claims of Jesus to the Messiahship, having lost both the spirit and knowledge of their prophets. They misapprehended the aims of Jesus, perverted his teachings, and misinterpreted his actions. They accused him of many heinous offenses; they heaped opprobrious epithets upon his head, and cherished toward him feelings of the bitterest hate. They were constantly plotting his death. All this Jesus knew. He knew, moreover, they had spies constantly on the look out to apprehend him, and that the most rigid system of espionage was observed toward him. Still Jesus loved his nation. He saw the impending vengeance that awaited them. From the summit of Mount Olivet he surveyed the metropolis of Judea, so soon to be bathed in blood. It lay spread out before him in all its extent, its beauty and pride; its white towers and palaces glittering in the sun; the city of God's former habitation, with its peerless temple majestically towering above all other buildings. But in all its beauty, and majesty, and glory, it was a city steeped in crime, and red with the blood of martyrs. The prophetic eye of Jesus read its fearful doom; for to his Omnipotent vision the future rose crowded with scenes of guilt and wo. He saw that in a few brief years that gorgeous temple would be in ashes, the city a pile of undistinguished ruins, and the people either slaughtered or wandering as outcasts among the nations. The clouds of wrath were brooding that should wrap their city in a pall of darkness; the storm was gathering which should scatter them abroad. At the thought of Jerusalem's desolation Jesus wept—wept, not over friends, but enemies; enemies who had reviled, rejected, persecuted him; enemies who had pursued him with a fiend-like desire to wreak their vengeance on his person, and to quench their malice in his blood. Yet he loved them, and wept over them. Hear his pathetic, his heart-touching lament, his piteous moans over the city of his executioners. "O! Jerusalem! Jerusalem! thou that killest the prophets, and stonest them that are sent unto thee! how often would I have gathered thy children together, as a hen gathereth her brood under her wings, but you would not. And now your house is left unto you desolate." Jerusalem was doomed from that moment; her fate was sealed; her destiny certain. God ceased to importune; angels took their flight from it, and the long-suffering Saviour gave it up to its fearful desolation. His agony of soul at that melancholy prospect, could find no relief but in a flood of tears, accompanied by the above most tender and impassioned apostrophe.

Such are the feelings which the followers of Jesus should cherish toward their enemies, implacable enemies. Instead of meditating revenge, and indulging in feelings of hatred toward them, like Jesus you should pity, and weep over them.

3. BENEVOLENCE *was another trait in the character of Jesus.*—Beneficence, active goodness, was his prominent characteristic. "He went about doing good." This brief sentence summarily expresses the object of his mission. "The labors of his life were love."

Bethany was a calm retreat, where many an hour of Christ's weary pilgrimage on earth was passed, free from the taunts and jeers, the buffetings and scorn of the heartless crowd. In this little city lived a family consisting of three persons, Lazarus and his sisters, Martha and Mary. They were all pious believers in Jesus. The Lord loved them. Lazarus died when Jesus was in a distant part of the country. This Jesus knew and communicated to his disciples, and at the same time informed them that he would go and raise him from the dead. Lazarus had been dead four days when he reached Bethany. As he approached the house of mourning, Martha saw him coming, and ran out to meet him; and prostrating herself before him, cried, "Lord, hadst thou been here, my brother had not died." Jesus told her he would raise him from the dead. But this announcement she did not exactly comprehend. She returned to the house weeping, and informed her sister Mary that the Master had come, and called for her. She ran out to meet him, and throwing herself at his feet, said, "Lord, if thou hadst been here, my brother had not died." Mary wept. She sobbed aloud. Her grief found vent only in a flood of tears. And Jesus wept. He did not look on bereavement and agony with indifference; nor contemplate death with a cold philosophy. The cords of his sympathy were exerted to the greatest tension, and quickly vibrated to the touch of sorrow. *"Jesus wept."* He wept because he was both human and Divine. It is an honor to our nature to weep. It is God-like to weep, for Jesus wept. There is a sacredness in tears. They are the messengers of overflowing grief; they are holy tokens of affection. I love to see the heart of man melted with sympathy, and to see that sympathy manifested in flowing tears. There is a pleasure in tears, a painful pleasure.

"Where have you laid him?" said Jesus. The bereaved orphans conducted him to the homely grave, attended by their sympathizing friends, who joined in the general wail. Jesus approached the grave of Lazarus, and as he gazed upon the noble, manly form, prostrate in death, he wept!

But his was a sympathy of action as well as of emotion. He lifted up his mandatory voice, so bland, yet so potent. Death reluctantly obeyed his sovereign mandate, and released its grasp. "Lazarus come forth!" and the grave yielded up it's tenant; decay bloomed into health.

Lazarus arose, and was folded in the arms of sisterly affection.

As Jesus on one occasion was entering the city of Nain, he met a funeral procession. A crowd followed the bier; and in that large procession was one lone mourner. It was an aged female, a widow. She had no kinsman.

> "Her slow steps
> Faltered with weakness, and a broken moan,
> Fell from her lips."

Deep marks of grief were thick upon her countenance, and her cheeks were wet with tears.

She had lived a widow many, many years, with her son, her only son. He was her all—the only tie that bound her to the world. It was he they were carrying to the grave. There he lay, cold and pale, in the dress of death. No smile beamed from the countenance of the pale sleeper; no flash of heaven's light streamed from his eyes, now glazed and sunken. The pall-bearers drew near the grave laid open to receive the dead. Jesus approached the bier. The aged mourner drew nearer to the clay-cold form of her son, and fixed her sad gaze upon him.

> "Jesus looked upon her, and his heart was moved.
> 'Weep not!' said he.
> With troubled wonder the mute crowd drew near,
> And gazed on his calm looks. A moment's space
> He stood and prayed! Then taking the cold hand,
> He said, 'Arise!' and instantly the breast
> Heaved in its cerements, and a sudden flush
> Ran through the lines of the divided lips,
> And with a murmur of his mother's name,
> He trembled and sat upright in his shroud."

Passing on, as his custom was, in search of the distressed, opening the eyes of the blind, curing the paralytic by a touch, and healing all manner of diseases, wiping away the tears of sorrow, and raining down blessings upon the heads of all who asked for them, the compassionate Saviour was met by a ruler of a synagogue, who, throwing himself at his feet, informed him that his daughter was at the point of death, and entreated him to go and heal her. Moved with sympathy, Jesus hasted to the chamber of disease; but ere he reached the place, he was met with the sad intelligence of the damsel's death. Still he hurried on to the house of mourning. As he neared the place, bursts of grief and plaintive moans fell upon his ear. He entered the apartment, and there lay a form lovely in death, and beautiful in the attire of the tomb. Pale disease had smitten the delicate flower just blushing into loveliness, and it withered in its natal bowers; there had withered the frail blossom of an untimely doom. The lips were white as the unstained napkin about her head. The sweet voice that had mingled so often with Judah's daughters in the anthems of praise, had murmured its last sigh; the heart was hushed to peace, and the swelling bosom had heaved for the last time. The; flattering changes which had swept over the faded cheek, marked the fond parents' hopes no longer. Jesus approached and took her cold hand. The frozen blood mounted to the lip and coursed through the veins. Light and life gleamed in the eyes just now so dark and motionless; and the damsel rose from the icy couch, glowing with returning life, and was pillowed on the warm bosom of a fond, joyful and delighted mother.

The son of Mary heard the touching cry of blind Bartimeus by the wayside. The stern multitude rebuked the beggar for what they considered his obtrusive importunity. But the compassionate Jesus halted in his journey and commanded him to be brought, and graciously opened his eyes. The blind man, restored to the light of heaven, joyfully followed in Messiah's train.

Never did a whisper of a sincere prayer escape the ear of this personification of benevolence and mercy. As he sat, an invited guest in the house of a Pharisee, a penitent female bowed at his feet weeping, and began to wash his feet with tears, and to wipe them with the hairs of her head, and anointed them with ointment. The Pharisee caviled in his heart that Jesus, claiming to be a prophet, should permit himself to be contaminated by the touch of pollution. But he had come to redeem the lost; and instead of reminding the guilt-stained and spirit-broken penitent of her past offenses, he dismissed her by kindly saying, "Thy faith hath saved thee. Go in peace!" How touching this heaven-drawn portraiture of pardoning love!

The efforts of Howard, the philanthropist, to meliorate the condition of suffering humanity excites universal admiration. He heard the cry of the prisoner, and the clanking chains forged by 'the inhumanity of man to man,' and his generous heart, touched by the tale of sorrow, moved him to go down into gloomy dungeons to wipe away the tears of anguish, to speak comfort to the child of affliction, and to smooth down the straw on which he reclined. He heard the groanings of the victims of the pestilence, and his benevolence moved him to stay the ravages of the angel of death. He fell at length on a foreign shore, a victim of the disease whose step he had gone to arrest. We love him for his benevolence, and admire his noble and generous conduct. Our hearts are moved at the mention of his name. But what was the benevolence of Howard in comparison to that of Jesus? He came from heaven to earth on an errand of benevolence, on a mission of good will to men. He went about doing good. He searched out objects of want and distress that he might relieve them. Wherever he went tears of affliction ceased to flow; the groans of anguish were hushed, and joy and smiles sat upon the countenance once beclouded with sorrow. The lame man leaped as an hart, the tongue of the dumb sang, and the blind received their sight.

Was there an outcast of society, frowned at, scoffed and trampled on? Jesus raised the wretch, and braved the opprobrium, and blessed the tears of penitence, and cherished returning goodness, and smiled on the offering of gratitude, and restored the image of God which crime had marred, and told of the joy in heaven over a recovered sinner.

By a single trait Jesus is painted in the Scriptures; and how majestic, though simple, is this trait! He went about doing good! Yes, wherever he went he bore blessings with him; he relieved indigence, consoled affliction, restored joy to the countenance of a desolate father, to the heart of a tender mother, to the bosom of a family plunged in woe. He rejected none who applied to him. Behold your model, Christians! Like your divine Master, pity the afflicted, relieve the indigent, weep with them that weep, and let unfeigned benevolence swell your soul, or else renounce the name of the Redeemer.

The Son of Man was equally distinguished for his INTEGRITY and MORAL FIRMNESS. There are times and events to try men's souls, to test their principles, to place their integrity on the rack, to put their firmness to the trial. Often did such times occur in the life of Jesus. When he stood a submissive criminal at Pilate's bar, he was asked authoritatively, "Art thou a king?" He well knew that upon his answer to this question his destiny hung. And what is his answer? Does he hesitate? Does he falter? Does he equivocate? Or does he by prevarication attempt to evade the truth? With the firmness and candor and integrity which always marked his illustrious life, he answers promptly and with an emphasis peculiar to himself, "Thou hast said it. It is as you say." The cross, the nails, the crown of thorns, the spear, and the agonizing death he was soon to suffer, all come thronging around him, yet he never swerved from the path of rectitude, but meekly confessed the truth and submitted to his fate.

Speaking of the trial and conduct of Jesus, an apostle says, He witnessed a good confession before Pontius Pilate! He made this confession as an example to us. He requires us to make confession of his name. But in what different circumstances are we called on to do so! No heartless mob surrounds us, whose noisy clamor demands our life at the hands of an obsequious judge. We are threatened with no cross and crown of thorns in the event we confess this holy name. On the contrary, anxious, weeping friends surround us; angels unseen surround us. All would rejoice to hear us confess with our lips, believing in our hearts, that Jesus is the Christ, the Son of God. Instead of a crown of thorns and an ignominious death, a crown of glory and the boon of life eternal will be the reward of such as confess before men the name of Jesus. He will confess them before his Father and his holy angels. He will confess them his in the presence of an assembled universe. But those who are ashamed of Jesus before men, he will be ashamed to acknowledge in the day of eternity, when the world shall be on fire, and the doom of the universe shall hang upon his word.

THE MAGNANIMITY OF JESUS CLAIMS OUR ATTENTION. We shall be able to note but a few of the many instances in which this trait was manifested.

Observe his conduct toward *Judas*. Jesus and his disciples were partaking of the last supper, when Judas came to the determination to sell his Lord, and left the table with the design of executing his foul purpose; and Jesus left soon after to prepare for the conflict with death. He was in the garden of agony, and while he was struggling in prayer, and covered with bloody sweat, Judas approached and interrupted the privacy of sweet devotion by hailing Jesus, and pointed him out to the infuriate mob by kissing him. For the accomplishment of his fiendish purpose he feigned sincerity. He betrayed his Lord with a kiss of hypocrisy so vile as almost to desecrate forever this pure, sweet token of friendship and holy affection. *Judas!* detested name I It has ever since represented the lowest grade of guilt, and the foulest, meanest form of human nature. Judas! Children loathe him, and stammer out execrations on his hated name. His crime places him next to Lucifer himself. The bare mention of him excites disgust, hatred, contempt. He seems almost to have "tempted the devil," and has been consigned over to him for his sin. As the wretched suicide, by his own act rid the world of a fiend so foul, demons with a shuddering yell of joy seized him as their prey, and dragged him down to his own place. In hell

"The common damned shun his society,
And look upon themselves as fiends less foul."

Our indignation rises instinctively within us at the conduct of the perfidious wretch; and we feel a burning contempt for his heartless conduct. But we must hold, Jesus did not so speak, nor so feel toward him, and his conduct in this instance is for our imitation. How did Jesus act on this occasion? How did he treat the traitor? His conduct was mild and gentle. Not a word of reproach or censure escaped his holy lips. He merely said, "What thou doest, do quickly!" He left the. remorseful culprit to the scorpion stings his own conscience, and the retributions of eternity.

What was the influence of this course on Judas? The lamb-like meekness of the Savior so affected him, that stung with remorse for what he had done, he rushed in to the chief priests with blood-shot eye, and the money chinking in his trembling hand, and said, " I have sinned in that I have betrayed innocent blood! Had he known only one thing of Jesus, anything which he could have wrested into an excuse for betraying his Lord, would he not have told it? Most undoubtedly he would have seized such an occasion with avidity. But nothing of the kind is pleaded in justification of his course, or in extenuation of his crime. On the contrary, the conscience-smitten culprit, under the weight of remorse threw down the money, rushed out of the house, fled to a field, and there amid the gloom of night hanged himself. And so,

Being tired of time, with his own hand
He ope'd the portals of eternity,
And sooner than demons hoped, arrived
In hell."

How unexceptionable then must have been the conduct of our Lord, as to defy the scrutinizing and interested search of one who had known him long and intimately, and who would have rejoiced to find a single objection to urge against him. "The catastrophe of his unfaithfulness presents an anomaly in the history of treason. Traitors have existed in every age; but none save the betrayer of Jesus was ever driven by compunction to lay suicidal hands upon himself. Treason had often caused the death of innocency and yet slept in callous indifference. Iscariot was urged to his fate by the maddening thought that he had betrayed the Messiah. In the character of Jesus he could not have been mistaken. He had spent years in his society. He had been the ear-witness of his doctrine and precepts, and the eye-witness of his wonderful works. His dying declaration, unsolicited and voluntary, was a sublime and awful demonstration of the intrinsic power of truth, bursting forth by its own volcanic force from the despairing heart."

In our Lord's conduct toward Judas, we are taught, my brethren, how we should act toward one who may have betrayed our confidence, and meanly deserted us in the hour of peril. Instead of heaping opprobrious epithets upon his guilty head, and dealing in words of bitter censure, and expressing contempt for his traitorous conduct, and pursuing him with vindictive and revengeful feelings, we should imitate the great exemplar of righteousness in his conduct towards Judas.

Witness our lord's demeanor toward *Peter*, who denied him in circumstances calculated to enhance his guilt. He had been forewarned that he would do it, thus being put on his guard against the temptation; and moreover, his lapse followed close after the most vehement asservations of enduring constancy. He denied him thrice. Once in answer to the interrogatory of a young woman. He denied him with imprecations. He basely denied all knowledge of his Lord, at a time too, when his friendship was most needed, and would have been most appreciated. Jesus was in the custody of his enemies. His disciples had forsaken him and fled. No one stood by him in this trying hour. Numerous charges had been preferred against him; charges, malicious as envy; false as perdition. His enemies were intent on his death.

In this time of extremity, Peter was found associated with the enemies of Jesus, around the fire. His first denial was a willful departure from the truth; the second was a repetition of the falsehood, confirmed by an oath; and in the third denial he reiterates the same falsehood and perjury, with startling imprecations. It was then the cock crew the second time. Peter looked up involuntarily toward Jesus, "and the Lord looked upon Peter." Oh, what a look that was! How full of meaning! What a blending of injured affection with tender sympathy; and gentle reproof with divine forgiveness! The tears of Peter attested its overpowering effect. How simple and graphic and soul-touching the words, "And the Lord turned and looked upon Peter." Those eyes, through which beamed the gentlest spirit that ever dwelt in a human bosom, were turned full, in all their awful clearness and searching scrutiny, upon the erring disciple; and it was a look of such mingled pity, reproof, and sorrow, that no wonder it flashed conviction to Peter's conscience, and dissolved his heart in tears of agonizing repentance. Peter then remembered all, and hurried out to some secret place, "and wept bitterly."

"What a strong and cheering light does the character of Jesus, as revealed in his treatment of Peter, cast upon the character of God! If we would know how God regards the sinful, we must turn to Jesus." He was one with the Father, and His conduct was the conduct of the Father. Here is nothing stern or repulsive. If any conduct justifies indignation, it is such as Peter's. But see how Jesus treated him! "He turned and looked upon him"—looked upon him with undiminished affection, and with a countenance beaming with pity. "In that look which was turned upon Peter, there is a beam that illuminates the upturned features of the penitent, and directs the contrite heart to God, as to a Father ever ready to forgive."

In this magnanimous conduct of our Lord, we are taught how we should treat an erring brother, who in a moment of weakness is overtaken in a fault. The Christian, like the adorable Jesus, should be elevated and refined from the dross of all sordid and ignoble passions.

6. The conduct of Jesus toward His *enemies* while he was on the cross, claims our marked attention. Hear the prayer which burst from His lips, in soft, sweet and gentle accents, amid the agonies of the crucifixion, "Father, forgive them, they know not what they do!" How great the generosity of feeling which dictated this petition! It came welling up from the deep fountain of His heart.

The prayer seems to have been uttered at the moment when the Roman soldiers were nailing Him to the cross, and while He was suffering the extreme torture which this cruel operation produced. What a sublime ejaculation was this which burst from the inmost soul of Jesus, under the intense agony which He was suffering! Oh, what a heart was that, who fixed Him to the instrument of His torture! The agonies of the crucifixion did not chill the warm fountain of His compassion. Not in corroding bitterness, but in cleansing, healing streams of mercy, did the sensibility of His heart flow out over the very hands of His murderers; and with His dying breath He invoked forgiveness upon those who had nailed Him to the cross. Yes; He prayed for His enemies— enemies who had rejected Him— enemies who had hunted Him down like a wild, ravenous beast; who had pursued Him from Bethlehem to Calvary, and who at that moment were gnashing upon Him with their teeth, and marking, and deriding Him; enemies who were torturing their ingenuity to increase His pains. When I behold Him, amid the agonies of dissolving nature, while ligament after ligament of His heart was being sundered, raising His dying eyes to Heaven, and forgetful of Himself, interceding with His Father, almost with His last breath, and from His very cross, in behalf of those wretches whose insatiable malice had fixed Him there—then it is, that the evidence of His divinity rises to demonstration, and I feel the influence of His dying example.

"And shall a worm, covered with crimes, and living on sufferance in that same world where the agonizing Saviour uttered His dying supplication, and left His dying example for imitation—shall such a worm, tumid with resentment, lift his proud crest to his fellow-worm, and, incapable of mercy, talk of retribution? No, blessed Jesus! Thy death is an antidote to vengeance. At the foot of Thy cross, I meet my enemies; I forget their injuries; I bury my revenge; and I learn to forgive those who have done me wrong, as I hope to be forgiven of Thee!"

"In Jesus, the real greatness of our nature—the glory of a pacific, all-enduring temper—is revealed. Let Him be lifted up before all eyes, and all hearts will be touched, and the sword and the spear and the banner bathed in blood will be buried at the foot of his cross, and it will be felt that all other courage is fear, and all other glory shame, in comparison with that spirit which subdues by mercy and reigns by suffering."

Behold the FILIAL AFFECTION *of the Son of Mary.* The infant Jesus nestled in love on the bosom of his mother in the cold manger. He lived with his mother till he was about thirty years old; was subject to her will, and toiled under a carpenter's shed in Nazareth for her support. He wrought his first miracle in honor of his mother, and for her gratification. He often makes affectionate allusion to his venerated mother during his brief but illustrious ministry. But the crowning proof of his filial affection was given in the sad hour of his affecting death. Amid the multitude that surrounded his cross, he recognized his homeless and distressed mother, standing near his favorite friend and disciple, the amiable and humble John. "When Jesus saw his mother, and the disciple standing by whom he loved, he said to his mother, woman I behold! thy son! and to the disciple, behold! thy mother!" This generous affection reveals the depth of his sensibilities; sensibilities, affection which the heart-rending pangs of a most distressing death could not quench; nay, the pangs of Calvary were absorbed in his solicitude for his agonized mother; for though tortured on the cross, parched with thirst, and amid the pains of death, he did not lose sight of her who bore him. He gazed upon her as she stood with her streaming eyes fixed upon her suffering son! Oh, what a sight for a mother to behold! His hands and feet nailed to the cross, blood trickling down over his quivering flesh; his heart throbbing with intense emotion; and the sins of a world pressing upon his holy soul; suffering agonies which sent a convulsive throe to the heart of nature; agonies, the sight of which drove back the chariot of the sun, and shrouded the earth in a pall of darkness.

As his eye rested in affection on his unprotected mother, his holy heart was moved with compassion toward her. She was soon to be left without a friend and protector. The strong, sweet tendrils of his pure soul entwined around her. She was all the world to him, for she was his *mother*. He could not die without making provision for her future comfort. To whom did he commit his precious charge, his beloved mother? Not to

The sons of thunder among his followers. He had a disciple, an humble, modest, unassuming man, but noble hearted, tried and true; the only one who had not deserted him in that trying hour. To him Jesus bequeathed his dear mother, his only, but rich legacy. How proud must the holy, and beloved disciple have been of so precious a charge! And what a compliment did Jesus pay to goodness! How much superior in his estimation, it is to greatness ! Behold! thy mother! This was enough. His wish was understood; and from that hour John took charge of the heaven-favored Mary.

No word possesses such charms, and thrilling interest as that of *mother!* It is endeared to us by a thousand fond, and tender, and stirring recollections. Young man! don't forget your mother, your dear mother! You owe her more than all the world besides. Think with what tender solicitude she watched over you in helpless infancy. With a sleepless vigilance she guarded your feet in wayward youth, and hung about your path like a guardian angel; and perhaps, this moment if alive, is sending up her prayers to. Heaven in your behalf. No labor has been too severe; no self-denials too painful; no sacrifices too great, which would contribute to your happiness. And for all this toil, and solicitude, and kindness, the only reward she asks is, that you will act worthy of yourself, and honor her by imitating the example of Jesus. And shall this requital be denied her? Will you by your follies embitter her cup of earthly consolation ; disturb her tranquility of age, and rob declining life of its few remaining pleasures, and bring down her grey hairs with sorrow to the grave?

Oh, what rapture would thrill the heart and swell the bosom of your mother, young man! to see you turn to God! It would mitigate the pain of sickness; it would soften the gloom of adversity; it would soothe the inquietudes of age; and extract more than half the anguish of the pang of death. None but a mother can tell the anxieties of a mother, and her ardent desire for the well-being of her offspring, present and future. Young man! it was for this purpose, with this desire burning in her bosom, your mother sustained you with so much affection, solicitude, and kindness. But methinks I hear one say—"My mother, alas! is no more on earth; she has gone to swell Immanuel's retinue in Heaven, and to wear his image there! O, that I were able to call her back from sepulchral ashes! Could I do this, I would pour my tears into her bosom, if thus I might wash away my crimes which disturbed her life, and embittered even her cup of death!" Ah, sir! it is not at the sepulcher your crimes are to be washed away, but in the blood of Jesus, by obeying his holy word. Your return to God would swell your sainted mother's soul with joy ecstatic.

-----o-----

The Tendencies of the Times,

A DIALOGUE—No. 1.

Present, an Episcopalian, a Presbyterian, a Lutheran, a Methodist, a Bible Union Baptist, an anti-Bible Union Baptist, a Disciple, a Quaker, a Universalist, and a Skeptic; all, except the Skeptic, *preachers,* when precisely the following conversation was heard and taken down accurately by our reporter:

PRESBYTERIAN, Gentlemen, I am truly happy to meet you all this evening, as I think it will afford us an opportunity of engaging in a most benevolent and righteous work. I am an agent of the *American Christian Union,* and wish to enlist your sympathies for this great and good work. As you are all clergymen, and it is well known that ministers receive but a scanty support, I do not, as a matter of course, expect you to contribute *money,* but I should be happy to have each of you present the matter to his church.

UNIVERSALIST. I should be happy to hear the reverend gentleman state the object of the A. C. Union. We Universalists do not accord with many things called "good works" by our orthodox neighbors.

P. The object of the A. C. Union is to convert Roman Catholics; not to operate *politically,* but simply to convert them. The Union is doing a great and good work; we have many converts in the principal cities.

U. What do you convert them to? We Universalists do not give our influence or money to convert men to orthodoxy. To what do you convert them?

P. We must not allow our peculiarities to stand in the way of our co-operation in a great and good work.

U. True; but then we must know that it is *a good work*, before we can go into it. To what do you propose to convert Romanists?

P. To what do we propose to convert them? Why, we propose to convert—we propose to convert—we must not introduce any of our peculiarities, but simply convert them from Romanism.

DEIST. That is my mind precisely. That is precisely what we *Turners* are doing; we convert them from Romanism, but not to any of your peculiarities, or to any other doctrine. I do not see why, Bro. Universalist—

U. Do not call me *brother,* if you please. Bro. Quinby and all our ministering brethren, deny the uncharitable charge, that we fellowship *infidels,* and repel it. I repel the insinuation.

D. This surprises me, sir; that you should be so indignant at me, when I call you brother. When Mr. Quinby, editor of the *Star,* asked me to subscribe for his paper, he called me *brother,* and so did you, when I subscribed fifty dollars to build your meeting house. Not only so, but you preached for an hour last Sabbath, to prove that *we are all the children of God,* and would therefore all be saved. I thought therefore, that if we are all children of God, are all to go to heaven together, and your preachers called me *brother,* when they want my *money,* that I might familiarize myself with that style of address, that it may be the more convenient when we all get to heaven.

U. It is true, as I preached on last Sabbath, that we are all the children of God, and will all be saved—but the fact is—the truth is—here lies the rub: all will be saved, because all will be saved; but you cut yourself off from Christian fellowship in *this life,* by your infidelity.

D. Then, if you please, do not call me *brother* again, when you want me to subscribe to build a meeting house, pay a preacher or for a paper, and then disown me before orthodox preachers, showing that you are ashamed of me in their presence. But why can you not agree with us, that it is right to convert Roman Catholics from *Romanism,* without converting them to anything?

P. I did not say, that we should simply convert them from Romanism, and not convert them to anything.

D. What then, sir, will you convert them to?—to Presbyterianism?

P. No, sir; did I not distinctly say, that we do not convert them to any of our peculiarities. If we should convert them to Presbyterianism, Methodists, Baptists and others would have nothing to do with it.

D. To what, then, do you convert them?

P. We convert them—we convert them to Protestantism.

D. What is Protestantism?

P. It is *protesting* against Romanism.

D. We Turners are Protestants then, for we *protest* against Romanism.

P. You are not Protestants—you are infidels; you deny the essential doctrines of the gospel.

D. I know we are infidels, and do not believe what you call the "essential doctrines of the gospel; but we believe in what you call Protestantism—protesting against Romanists. Is this all you are trying to convert Romanists to?—to protest against Romanism?

P. No, sir, this is not all; we are converting them simply to Christianity—to the Bible.

D. I understand you to say, that you do not convert them to *Presbyterianism.*

P. I did say so; we do not convert them to Presbyterianism, Episcopalianism, Methodism, etc., etc., but merely to Christianity—to the Bible—to God.

QUAKER. Thee holds then, that converting men to thy doctrine—to Presbyterianism—is not converting them to God—to Christianity! Thee will find that Friends agree with thee in thy conclusion. What church does thee unite them with, when thee converts them, as thee says, to Christianity?

P. We do not unite them to any orthodox sect, but form them into churches by themselves.

Q. What does thee call them—Presbyterians?

P. No, sir; we simply call them by Bible names—Christians, Disciples of Christ, etc.

Q. What creed does thee put them under— the Presbyterian confession?

P. No, sir; we do not put them under any creed. We have organized them into a church upon the Bible. If you will give me a few minutes, I can explain that matter so as to satisfy all present, that the American Christian Union is upon the only plan upon which we all could harmoniously co-operate in the great work of converting Romanists. It is preposterous to think of converting them to anyone of our peculiar parties; for then, we not only fail to obtain the assistance of the other parties, but must incur their opposition. But upon our present plan we avoid this. We labor to convert them simply to Christianity—to the Bible—to Christ, which we all agree in. Then, in the place of uniting the converts with any party, which all the other parties would oppose, we unite them in a band by themselves, as a church of the Disciples of Christ, which we all admit to be right. We simply call them Christians, too, against which there can be no prejudice, among any good people. We all admit that the great matter is, to be a *Christian.* Therefore, you can see, gentlemen, that the American Christian Union is established upon great Catholic principles, containing nothing but common-ground principles, admitted by us all to be right.

BIBLE UNION BAPTIST. That is my mind, precisely; and therefore, I have been favorable to this great work, and frequently raised contributions for it, during the last ten years. It is a great Protestant movement, occupying great common-ground principles believed by all Protestants. It is, in this respect, precisely like the Bible Union. It is not sectarian; does not contain sectarian peculiarities, nor anything but common-ground principles, believed by all Protestants.

P. I deny that the American Christian Union bears any similitude to the Bible Union. The Bible Union is sectarian, and I can have nothing to do with it. It originated with the *Baptists.*

B. U. B. The American Christian Union originated with some one party; but that party, as you have justly shown, did not infuse any of it's peculiarities into it; but established it upon principles admitted by us all to be true. The same is true of the Bible Union. Though Baptists were the movers in starting it, they have not infused a single Baptist peculiarity into it. Every principle in it is professedly believed by all Protestants.

P. I deny that statement, sir. The Bible Union proposes to translate *baptizo,* immerse. This you know is not a Protestant principle, but a *Baptist peculiarity.*

B. U. B. You are mistaken, sir; the Bible Union proposes nothing about *baptizo,* nor any other word, only the great Protestant principle, that the whole Bible—"the religion of Protestants," as Chillingworth called it—shall be *faithfully translated,* making no change from the King James version, except where *faithfulness to the original requires it.*

METHODIST. If I should speak, I do not know what I should say. I was in hopes that my brethren would have kept clear of this sectarian scheme of Bible-mending. But I am mortified to learn, that any Methodist minister should have been led into this unholy work. And I was more mortified and chagrined than all, to find Dr. Elliott, editor of the Western Christian Advocate, winking at this mischievous work. But I trust the castigation, so timely administered to him by Dr. McPherren, editor of the Christian Advocate, of Nashville, Tenn., will prove a savor of life to him. I pronounce the Bible Union a mischievous, sectarian scheme. Our fathers, thank God, got religion, served God, and have gone to heaven, with the old family Bible that lay on the stand. The Lord has blessed us abundantly with the common version, and is converting thousands soundly to God, every year, with it, and we will never give it up for a sectarian Bible. Thank God for the Bible!

B. U. B. I trust we all can join our brother in thanking God for the Bible; but I confess that I never thank God for the *errors* in any translation, but simply for the Bible proper— that which God gave; no more, no less.

M. I pronounce the Bible Union a sectarian and mischievous scheme, and I will have nothing to do with a sectarian version.

B. U. B. You will certainly, then, have nothing to do with the common version, for it proceeded from one sect alone, headed by an earthly king.

M. The common version is good enough for me. The great and good men of our church have been satisfied with it, lived happy under it, died in peace and have gone to heaven, and that is sufficient for me. Bless God!

B. U. B. How then, if the great men in your church were satisfied, came Mr. Wesley to publish a new translation of the New Testament?

M. Mr. Wesley?—I say, Mr. Wesley—the fact is—Mr. Wesley was a High Churchman, and did many things which we at this day do not accord with.

B. U. B. Why then, sir, does your Book Concern publish his New Testament as one of your standard works? Is this not a sectarian version, published by a single denomination? the emanation of a single individual?

M. Mr. Wesley—Mr. Wesley's Notes—the fact is—

ANTI-BIBLE UNION BAPTIST. See here, (brother M. I agree with you, that the common version that has comforted so many of our fathers, and guided them to heaven, is good enough for me. We need no new version; but if we did, I have an objection to the Bible Union, stronger than any you have brought. My objection is, the "unholy alliance with Campbellites."

Q. Thy objection then, if I understand thee, is not that it *is* sectarian, but that it is *not* sectarian. Thee would have sectarian boundaries set, and certain sects proscribed, and the work committed wholly to the hands of others. I make this remark to show thy inconsistency. Friends have no need of any of thy translations of the *outward* Word; they have the light *within* that teaches them all things.

A. B. U. B. As to your "light within," guiding you into all truth, I fear it will land you all in unbelief, before long. And as it regards your notion, that I am sectarian, it amounts to nothing with me. I shall show, if Providence permit, that there is much more of the leaven of *Bethany* in the Bible Union than Baptist doctrine.

Q. Thy trouble is then, just what I told thee; not that the Bible Union *is,* but that it *is not* sectarian; or rather, thy trouble is. that the Bible Union contains *Bethany* leaven, and not *Baptist* leaven.

No doubt thee is correct in supposing that there is more Bethany leaven in the Bible Union than Baptist leaven; because thy society opposed revision when Mr. Campbell published a new version of the New Testament. But, it appears, that the Bethany leaven has become infused among Baptists till many of thy most distinguished men are favorable to revision. Thee is, however, inconsistent, for thee believes in going by the *outward* Word, and, therefore, should be in favor of having it translated as clearly and correctly as possible.

B. U. B. Gentlemen, these evenings are short, and the time has now arrived when we must adjourn. I now propose to meet again in one month from now, when I will demonstrate, that neither the Bible Union, nor the American Christian Union, is sectarian, and—

M. And that the principles of *Bethany* lie at the bottom of both, and—

B. U. B. I ask your pardon, sir; I can express myself, without your assistance, and that with much less confusion than was shown by yourself, a while ago. I will show that both these institutions are founded upon the great principles of truth, the great principles of Protestants, and the only principles that can preserve truth among a Christian people.

REPORTER.

-----o-----

Our Position as a Religious Community. No 9.

WE do not pen these articles because we love to annoy our religious neighbors, perplex them, or war upon that which is dear to them. We are sorry that duty, solemn duty, demands of us this examination of our position, relative to human creeds, and this expose of the barrenness of the ground they stand upon, knowing, as we do, the unpleasant sensations it produces in the breasts of some persons. But our sympathy must not get the better of our judgment, and silence us upon what we know to be a great vital point. If there are any two great objects that may be regarded as the main burden of the gospel of Christ, the main mission of Christianity, and essential to carrying out the great purpose of God, they are the following:

1. The union of all the children of God; their harmonious co-operation in all the great and good works of Christianity, as well as the Scriptural worship of Almighty God.

2. The conversion of the world.

That all Christians, or all the children of God, can never unite in the worship of God and the good works of Christianity, until human creeds are abandoned, and the Lord honored as the Supreme Ruler, and his law honored as the supreme law—the only ecclesiastical law—is one of the clearest and most manifestly self-evident propositions. And that the law of God requires such union in worship and good works—that it imperiously demands it—that it continues to demand it—that this demand comes clothed in expostulations, in inspired persuasions— that it comes clothed in all the authority of a Divine command from the law of God—that it comes with all the authority of Him who controls the thunders of the universe—no man will attempt to deny, who knows anything of the letter and spirit of the word of God. What then, shall we do? what can we do? If the Almighty requires union, and all human creeds stand opposed to union, we must reject the creeds, or stand opposed to the God of our existence. We cannot stand opposed to the Almighty. We must then, reject the creeds. If there can never be harmony or union till the power and influence of human creeds are destroyed and disregarded; and if the world can never be converted; if the nations of the earth can never be induced to regard Christianity, have confidence in it, and believe in its adorable Author, as is implied in his prayer (John xvii: 20, 21), then the world can never be converted till the abolishment of all human creeds.

But why need we argue against human creeds? Who is defending them? Who has written a book in their defense? Who has undertaken to show any Divine authority for them? We have never seen a book, any article in a book or printed publication of any description, or heard a man in the pulpit try to show any Divine authority for Human creeds. Nor have we ever seen anything like an attempt to establish their utility and necessity, in any book, important document or public speech. It is true, when Mr. Campbell affirmed, in the Lexington Debate, the schismatical tendencies of all human creeds, Dr. N. L. Rice plead "not guilty" for them; insisted upon their innocence, and tried to show that they did not do the harm alleged. But that they had any authority from God, that they did any good, or could do, in governing churches, comforting saints or preventing heresy, what the Bible *could not do,* we believe he did not attempt, by any regular course of argument, to prove. We are free to admit, that in many instances, he seemed to imply this much, but did not make it a clear point and directly attempt to establish it. Why then, if no one argues the Divine authority of human creeds, undertakes to prove their usefulness, or that they can do, in governing churches, comforting saints, or shutting out heresy, what the Bible *cannot do*—contend against them, and try to put them down? Because, though men do not contend for any Divine authority for human creeds, but generally know there is none, nor undertake to prove their necessity, or that they can accomplish what the Bible cannot do, they have them, as their rule of faith and practice, submit to them, bind others to do so, govern churches by them, and substitute them in the place of the law of God.

If a man pushes on his distillery, keeps it running and rolling out barrels of the fiery intoxicating liquor, whether he ever attempts to make any defense or not, I feel bound to speak of his ruinous operations, and try to dissuade men from countenancing his work.—Or if a man keeps his liquor shop open, continues to sell and make men drink, we must continue to speak against it, and discountenance the business, though he may never offer an argument in justification of his work, or even though he confesses all the time that it is wrong. Some of the worst sins that men are addicted to, are practiced, their perpetrators admitting them wrong all the time.

So long then, as human creeds are bound upon men, going on with their ruinous work, keeping up division, the issue exists. They are in direct opposition to the interests of the Bible. The great works of uniting all the good, the pious, those who love and desire to serve God, in one holy and happy band, that they may harmoniously co-operate in all the great works of mercy and humanity, and converting the world—the main objects of Christianity—can never be accomplished till all human creeds are rejected by Christians.

Here then, we file our reason—our main reason—for our unmitigated opposition to all human creeds. Two of the main objects for which we labor are continually impeded, obstructed, and hindered by human creeds. Our first great work—the union of all the children of God, which our Lord prayed for, the holy Apostle commanded, and which is inculcated by the whole spirit of the New Testament—we cannot give up; nor can we cease to labor for it, and in laboring for it, we must rescue those whom we labor to unite from human and put them under Divine instruction; from human and put them under Divine leaders; from human and put them under Divine law; from human and put them under Divine authority; from the fallible dictation of uninspired men to the infallible dictation of the Spirit of God; from the power of poor, erring mortals, and put them under the power of the Almighty. This is necessary—*it is essential*— to our second object, *the conversion of the world.*

The object of the Lord's mission into the world, as stated by himself (John iii: 17), is—"that the world through him, might be saved." The church, being "the light of the world," and "the salt of the earth," has an object— a mission—and that object or mission must correspond with the object of our Lord in coming into the world—"that the world through him might be saved." If the mission of the church corresponds with this object — with the idea of being "the light of the world," and "salt of the earth"—it must be to enlighten and save the world. Human creeds are in continual hostility to this work. Their horizon is too limited, narrow and circumscribed for such a work as this. They are not made for the world—for mankind, or for the human race—but merely for a party. The great objects of converting and saving the world are supremely above all the conceptions of all human creeds. The idea of being "the light of the world," or "the salt of the earth," has never entered into them. They are not designed to operate upon the world; nor are they designed for the church of Christ, as a whole, but merely for a little party; and all the provisions of every human creed have respect to some faction and their peculiar interests, and all the efforts of the party are directed in some way merely to the peculiar interests of a party.

Now to be a partisan—a mere devotee to a creed—all that is necessary is to become acquainted with the peculiar objects of the party, or the objects of the creed, and labor to promote these objects. Such persons generally fix their attention upon a few peculiarities, views, and party interests, and confine the labors of their lives to these, and suppose that such a zeal and devotion will go for Christianity, and gain the approbation of the Author of the Christian faith. But this is infinitely too insignificant, little, and circumscribed for Christianity. To become a *Christian,* in the New Testament acceptation, a man must *receive the Saviour of the world,* and not some man's *views* of him; but receive *him,* as God has revealed him, as his Prophet, Priest, King, Ruler, Governor, Lawgiver, and place himself under him, give himself to him, follow him, and put his everlasting trust in him.—He must receive Christianity itself, and not some man's *views of it;* the whole of Christianity, as set forth by Christ and the Apostles in the New Testament. He must fix his attention upon it, as the great system to which he has subscribed, and look for its great purposes, designs and objects; and never allow his objects to be circumscribed to anything more limited, narrow, and little, than the great objects of Christianity itself. He must take the church of Christ into his embrace—his fellowship, with all its great interests and objects, as a whole—and not some little insignificant party that have split off, for the purpose of maintaining and promoting some partisan peculiarity or peculiarities. He must take the great work of God upon his soul, the whole of it;

fix the purpose of God before his mind, and make the purpose of God his purpose, the work of God his work, the church of God his church, the people of God his people, the law of God his law, the book of God his book, and the will of God his will. He is not then, continually trying to prove his doctrine by Scripture, for his doctrine *is Scripture itself;* nor trying to prove his creed, for his creed is the law of God itself; nor apologizing for unscriptural names and peculiarities, for he has none. He is enraptured with the glories of his Lord, and his wonderful works to the children of men. His heart is filled with the spirit of God. He is embraced in the church of God, and all his powers engrossed in the work of God. His whole trust is in God. The Almighty is pledged for his protection, and he leans upon the blessed promises. He is girded as with the everlasting hills. The everlasting arms are underneath him. He dwells with God, and walks with God. How high his objects, how grand his work, and how expanded his soul, compared with the man circumscribed to the limited interests of a party!

B. F.

-----o-----

Bible Union Troubles.

To anyone acquainted with the history of English Bible translation, it would be something new and unprecedented to find that great and good work progressing steadily, smoothly, and prosperously, without any interruption, in the midst of all the malignant, blinding, and antagonistic influences of these times. Such a work, with the effort of the Bible Union to let the clear light of heaven, unobstructed by errors and obscurities in translation, shine upon the nations, in the midst of all the errors and sins of these times, disclosing the hidden things of dishonesty, and laying bare before all men things of the first importance for all the world to know, the enemy of all light, and truth, and righteousness, unquestionably would not see progress prosperously to completion, if by any artifice he could defeat it. To see a work set on foot, prosecuted, peaceably carried on, and consummated, that would lead the whole Christian world to read the whole Bible, from cover to cover, as they had never done before; examine it, from side to side, weighing every word and every sentence, comparing first with the common version, then with this version, then with that, now with the inspired originals, then appealing to critical authorities, commentators, history, and every possible means of knowing precisely what God has revealed to the world; thus eliciting light at every step, and disseminating it at large, without a mighty struggle of the enemy to frustrate and defeat it, is not to be expected by anyone able to say, with Paul, "we are not ignorant of his devices."

This greatest of all the great moves in Protestant Christendom, in this country, throws open the door of investigation, and enables all *men* to look down to the bottom for authority, for everything. The Bible Union is perfectly *unsectarian.* It has no concern for the doctrines of the parties and creeds of the times, or of any other times since the world was made. It knows no party, nor party feeling, nor is. it responsible for anything, except the giving to all men exact transcripts of the inspired originals of the Old and New Testaments, in the other languages of the earth. This work, all the lovers of darkness throughout the world dread. It is not merely revising the English Scriptures that they dread; but they dread all revising and translating, because it leads continually to investigation; and a kind of investigation that they of all others dread. It is not investigation to prove *your* doctrine, or *our* doctrine, but an investigation to determine *what God says*. It is no other than an effort to ascertain, as near as possible, what *God says,* and publish it among all nations and peoples of the earth. This we know to be right—*infallibly right*—no matter who is for it, or who is against it. This great and good work, in the very nature of things, we know must inevitably be opposed by the malignant influences of these times. Nothing else can be expected by any man acquainted with the ways of the world.

It is truly mortifying and distressing to any man, whose heart is enlisted in the mighty work, to find that any of the supposed friends of the undertaking should have turned traitor to it. But still, one who was a bosom companion of the Lord, and of the Twelve, who had partaken of the loaves and fishes, as well as enjoyed all the other honors and privileges of the most intimate intercourse with the Redeemer, turned traitor to him, and to his cause. The Lord said of this man, that "it had been better for him not to have been born." One historian says, that he "by transgression fell," and another says, "he was lost." How much less the wickedness of him who is the cause of this dreadful offense, and this lamentable injury, and how much lighter the condemnation that must follow? The Lord grant that he may find mercy. But, as in the case of the apostasy of Judas, so, we trust, it will turn out in this case; the former disclosed nothing injurious to the Lord, or his cause, but returned with the money he had received for betraying the Saviour, and, throwing it down at the feet of those who had led him into this dreadful crime, with his heart broken, and the pitiful exclamation, "I have sinned, in that I have betrayed the innocent blood;" so it will turn out in the case of the latter; he will disclose nothing wrong on the part of the Union, but, at the same time, develop that all is sound, and make it known to the world, as it never could have been done by the opposition of any other person.

We are aware that many are deeply mortified, that this occasion should have been afforded for the enemy to exult, and we are free to grant that it is extremely mortifying, but the Lord will bring good out of it. When the Lord was brought upon trial, and disgraceful charges were made against him, it was deeply mortifying to him and all his friends. When he was nailed to the cross, crowned with thorns, mocked, and spit upon; when he expired in the midst of enemies, and the whole powers of darkness exulted, it was truly mortifying and humiliating; but He who makes the wrath of man praise him, in the midst of this procedure laid the foundation for all our preaching, all our hopes, and eternal salvation. In fifty days after all this disgrace had been brought upon the cause, and the Author of it, the dark and gloomy clouds were dispersed, hope sprang up, the Lord was justified by the Spirit, his righteous work vindicated before the world, confidence in him planted in the hearts of three thousand people. The work spreads from city to city, the opposition lurks away in shame, and the Lord turns the whole to the advancement and establishment of the Christian religion. So, we trust, it will turn in the present instance.

The greediness with which the enemies have laid hold of this excrescence is only an evidence of the awe they feel, and the terror with which they look upon the Bible Union, and furnishes but another evidence of its importance. Their rolling this as a sweet morsel under their tongues, is only opening the way for a fuller development of their spirit and temper—only an exponent of their love of mischief, and glorying in misfortune to a cause, arising from a want of integrity, an ambitious spirit and misunderstanding. But why should any enemy catch at this? Why should opposing publications herald it from one side of the country to the other? Why should they exult? or why should any friend to the Bible Union feel in the least disheartened by it? Surely there is nothing in the whole affair that should change the mind of any good man. Nothing is developed in this affair showing the principles of the Bible Union to be anything different from what we have understood from the beginning. Nothing is developed in this to lead any man to doubt for one moment that the work will progress steadily and faithfully to its ultimate object. The separation of Dr. Judd from the Bible Union, in view of the small amount of labor performed, and the amount of funds required by him; in view too, of his restless and inharmonious state of mind, can be no disadvantage to it in any sense. With the disaffection, personal feeling, and suspicious state of mind to which Dr. Maclay seems to have been wrought up, it was out of the question for him to be of any possible service to the Union. It is true, that he has rendered great service, and would, no doubt, have continued to do so, if he had not been tampered with. But in his unhappy state of mind, it was out of the question for him to do any good. O that he may find mercy for allowing his name and influence to be used for harm! But we must look at the matter in a practical sense. We inquire then, as follows:

1. Are not the same translators engaged now that were before this rupture occurred? Precisely the same, except Dr. O. B. Judd, who was doing comparatively nothing.

2. Has anything occurred to lead us to doubt the ability of the translators? Certainly not; for neither Drs. Maclay or Judd developed anything new in regard to the qualifications of translators, or anything that they did not know before. Neither of them have seen, or can now know, what the completed version will be; and if they did know what it will be, the mere circumstance of their not liking it, would be no certain evidence that it was wrong.

3. Have funds been wasted? From the best evidence we have, we are inclined to think that some funds have been wasted, especially upon Dr. O. B. Judd; but this was not intended, but happened them, as all lodges in such efforts, contrary to their design. All men who know anything of such enterprises, know that it is an impossibility to foresee how things will work, and avoid any loss. The undertaking is a new one to every man engaged in it, and no man could see what the expense would be; and no man, nor body of men, could fail to spend some means in such a way as not to see afterward that money might have been saved at certain points. But what if something has been unnecessarily expended? Would we stop a worldly enterprise on that account? Certainly not. Remedy the defect as soon as possible; stop the unnecessary expense, raise more funds and go on with the work. How frequently it has happened that a railroad company, an insurance company, or a banking company, has squandered much more than is alleged has been squandered in this case; but do they stop on this account? Surely not; but remedy the difficulty and proceed. So must good men do in this case. What is a little money in such an immense work? It is true, we do not desire men to be prodigal with means consecrated to this great work; but when we have no reason to believe they have aimed to waste anything, it is perfectly weak and childish to stop now, and begin to talk about the expenditure. It can be regarded in no other light than an appeal to the avarice of the world, to break down the greatest work of our day and generation.

We trust, that no man, whose heart is in this great and good work, will for one moment hesitate to give it his warmest support. We trust too, that, in view of this effort to ruin the greatest and best work of our time, every man who has taken a life-membership, or life-directorship, will be the more careful to meet every installment promptly, and that thousands of others will forthwith make most liberal contributions to this most benevolent and righteous work.

It will be recollected, that the management of finances has not been entrusted to men of no experience, and no established reputation. Several of these men have had much experience in the Bible Society, before they came into the Union, and shown themselves true and faithful, during many long years. These men have not changed, and become reckless. They are as true and trust-worthy as they ever were. The truth is, the matter is in the hands of men who have long since given the most satisfactory evidence that they are as honorable, high-minded, faithful, and true men, as the world contains; and if we cannot trust them, we cannot trust any men living.

But the man who is at the bottom of all this mischief, and is doing his utmost, through the influence of a venerable name, which, by some strange and unaccountable means, he has been able to use to destroy confidence in the Bible Union, is comparatively a *young* man, made giddy by a little learning, with place and honors conferred upon him, which proved his ruin. Who is he? and what is he, compared with the honorable men of the Bible Union? Who will be led to believe, from this effort, that Conant, Wyckoff, Armitage, Schaff, Lilly, Shepherd, Campbell, Buckbee, etc., etc., have all departed from principles of integrity and honor? The thing is impossible; it is devoid of all reason; the most silly tale ever told. B. F.

Evangelizing.

We have had many long essays and sermons, upon order, church organization, church officers, etc., etc., which, though many of them were very fine, have afforded no kind of relief. They do nothing toward removing the real difficulty. On the contrary, many of these fine theories have done us immense injury. They have erected such an ultra standard for measuring church officers, that not one out of ten of the writers or speakers themselves, ever come up to it. Many good men, who were in these offices, and doing the best they could to discharge their duties, saw their pieces, became discouraged, concluded that they had not the qualifications, could not obtain them, were doing wrong in occupying a place for which they were not qualified, and declined. In almost every instance where these humble, good, and faithful men were thus driven from their post, an immense injury was done to the cause. But this only by the way. Evangelizing is our theme now.

The same kind of a course has been pursued in reference to Evangelists. We have had a continuous series of writing and preaching about properly qualified Evangelists, and numerous schemes have been set on foot and advocated, for raising up and qualifying men for this great work. Still, the Evangelical field is not at all supplied. No scheme set on foot is supplying, or likely to supply, the field. Some few preachers are being manufactured, but where do they go? and what do they do? How many of them go out into the field and preach the Gospel, convert sinners, plant, and build up churches? Where is one doing anything of this kind? In many parts of the country, they have made people believe that the old preachers who have planted the churches and made the principal part of all the converts that have been made, are behind the times, and incapable of preaching, discouraged and driven many of them from the field, and the work is not progressing. We need, and *must have,* if we ever progress, Evangelists, or missionaries, who will travel throughout the length and breadth of the country, visit the churches, "see how they do," "set in order the things that are wanting," recruit their numbers, and maintain the faith once delivered to the Saints. We need, and must have, men who will visit weak churches, enter new communities, where there are no churches —bold adventurers, pioneers—to open the immense forests, and make the rude desert blossom like the rose. This work must be done, and we *must have* the men that *can* and *will* do it.

Where are we to obtain this class of men? Can we never learn anything from the history of the past, from all experience? Where did the men come from, who have done pretty much of all this kind of work that has ever been done? Is a miracle to be expected? Will men for this work, come from a source whence such men never came? No! never, while man is man, and human nature is human nature. Men brought up in school houses, fed and clothed from their father's pockets, without ever knowing what it was to earn a dollar, or a goat for their backs, without knowing anything about the hardships and buffetings of the world, no matter if they become scholars, and learn how to say a few fine things, *never will* and *never can* do the work we are speaking of. They have not the constitution, the physical energies to do it. They have not the knowledge of the world, the ways and manners of the people to do it. They know nothing of the toils, hardships, and burdens of the masses of mankind, are incompetent to sympathize with them, mingle with them, become a fellow creature with them, and preach the Gospel of Salvation to them, in an acceptable and successful manner and save them. They not only are wholly incompetent, incapable, and could not, if they would; but it is not their atmosphere, not their congenial sphere, and they *never will* do the work in the Lord's great Evangelical field. They never have done the work and never will.

We must turn our eye in another direction. We must look to men who have come up in our midst, among the people, who are of the people, in active life, habits of industry, who have known what it was to earn a living— men who have found out what a dollar is worth by earning it; learned the people by mingling with them; developed their physical man by active and industrious life; know the ways of the world by being in it. We must look to men of this description, whose hearts have been overcome by the love of Christ, whose energies have been enlisted in the churches, and who are brought forth by the churches, and should be reared up and encouraged by the churches. Here is where we must look for Evangelists. The church must open the way for her young men, set them forth, and bring out all the talent she has within; and every man that has the natural endowment, the energy, the love for man, the anxiety for man's Salvation, necessary for one who would go out into the world to save men, will make his way into the Evangelical field, and make his mark on the world. If he lacks learning, or information, and has the proper zeal, desire for his work, and natural endowment, he will acquire the learning and knowledge. We must open the way for such, in all the churches; show our young men that we are looking for them to come forth and enter upon this great work. We must give them opportunities and encourage them to speak, to read the Scriptures and pray in public, and we shall soon find that the Lord has plenty of material of the first quality, for this great work.

Here is the source whence our laboring men have come—our active effective men who are doing, and have always done the work. It is useless for us to be deluded by the vain hope that the men we need, will ever come from any other source. We must turn our attention to the Evangelical work, concentrate our energies upon it, and do all in our power to promote it Every man that can preach at all; every man that can turn a sinner to the Lord, should be engaged in the work, with all zeal and power. We must preach the word both publicly and privately, with the tongue and pen, through newspaper, pamphlet, magazine, tract' and book; in every possible way, and by all means, we must preach the word of God from the rivers to the ends of the earth, and make all men see what is the fellowship of the mystery, which, from the beginning of the world, hath been hid in God, who created all things by Jesus Christ. "Go," brethren, the Lord says "*Go* into all the world, and preach the Gospel to every creature;" "Go," says he, "therefore, and teach all nations." Let every man go, who can call a few people together, and preach the word of the Lord to them; yes, go, if you can preach at all, turn sinners to God and save them, go and preach. Go under a sense of the mighty work, remembering the language of that great preacher and apostle to the Gentiles, "Woe is me if I preach not the Gospel." God requires those who have the Gospel and the ability, to preach it now, and this same *wo* will rest upon them if they do not do it.

What a crying sin against the Lord, who gave us the Gospel, and man, to whom He commands it to be preached, for those with the ability, to refuse to preach the Gospel of the Grace of God? Who but these shall answer to God, if the people perish for the word of God? The first disciples, when dispersed from their homes, deprived of all their earthly good, "went everywhere preaching the word." B. F.

-----o-----

Another New Book.

It would be ungenerous in us, when a neighbor produces a new book, to allow it to be *still born,* and confer upon it no attention whatever. As we do not wish to be obnoxious to such a charge, we call attention to a new book, entitled—"How God Justifies the Sinner, or a Review of the Doctrine of the Reformed Church, Compared with the Bible Doctrine on the Justification of the Sinner. By J. W. Ridgell, of the Kentucky Conference." The author of this book, of 95 pages, is a Methodist Circuit Rider, and if we mistake not, has been a Presiding Elder. He is the man of war who debated with a seceding Methodist gentleman, in Florence, Ky., by the name of Corwine, who is much esteemed in his community, but who has become disgusted with Methodism, and departed from it. We gave some notice of this discussion several months ago.—During this discussion, we heard Mr. Ridgell challenge "any man between the poles," but as yet, so far as we are informed, no man in this boundary has ventured to measure swords with him. Though we were present, and the challenge was generally supposed to be intended for us, our combativeness has not been the least excited by it, nor has the challenge called any other disputant into the arena.— Determined that the magazine in store should not lie unemployed, with a fearful enemy in full view; that mighty talents should not be hid in the earth; and that his light should not be put under a bushel, Mr. Ridgell sallies forth in the above named book. The way Mr. Campbell suffers, with all those identified with him, is only equaled by the efforts of Dr. Shaffer, Gilmore, Jameson, and a dozen or two more which we have seen of the same kind.

If such men could see their insignificant nibblings, as others see them, at a man whose writings they never read, and their minds not capable of appreciating five consecutive sentences of all he has ever published—what misfortune it would save them from, and of what an amount of deep mortification would their more enlightened brethren be relieved. Their heads contain but little more than some crude notions of half learned, not half digested nor half appreciated, but miserably garbled scraps from Wesley, Clarke, Watson, and others; and yet they entertain the silly conceit that they are in a mighty struggle with Mr. Campbell, refuting his arguments, and scattering them to the four winds! If they could see themselves, we say, as others see *them*, with what ineffable contempt would they look down upon their Lilliputian attacks upon a man who has wrestled with the great master spirits in the mighty antagonistic ranks of the world! It would remind them of Aesop's toad trying to swell himself to the size of an ox, a mouse trying to make battle with an elephant, or a mole-hill trying to stretch itself to the enormous dimensions of a mountain.

But, not seeing themselves as others see them, nor conscious of their weakness, sensible of their insignificance, or the enormous conceit that propels them onward, they must nibble, bite, scratch, bark, growl, rant, foam, and sweat. They frequently work themselves up to feel, or appear to feel, that they are not only ambassadors for Christ, but that the fate of the nation hangs upon their shoulders.—These little creatures too, have their admirers, who gaze upon them, filled with astonishment, when they hear one of them talk of "theology," the "doctrines of grace," the "Triune God," the "ever blessed Trinity," the "Holy *Shekinah,*" Biblical learning, quote Greek and Hebrew, talk of nouns, pronouns, prepositions, definite articles, etc. The astonishment still rises, and like Goldsmith's pedagogue, "Still the wonder grew, that one *small* head contained all he knew." When they sit and gaze at one of this class confounding, confuting, and literally annihilating all that Mr. Campbell has said in forty years—pulverizing it and dispersing it to the four winds, as their truly great and learned men have never been able to do, they sit in profound amazement, and wonder that this dreadful heresy of Mr. Campbell has not been banished from the land, long since; and seem to look upon it as an especial Providence, that has raised up and sent one so well prepared to do this great work. It is true, some inquisitive minds will inquire, where this mighty man has been all the time, that we never heard of him, and that this doctrine should have been allowed to spread so far before one has been sent to arrest it? But still, the time has now come when the thirty, or thirty-five volumes of Mr. Campbell, scattered largely over the civilized world, the thousands of churches, the numerous preachers, their fifteen or eighteen regular publications, all their colleges and academies, with their three hundred thousand members, shall be called to a halt! Such is the feeling sometimes manifested by one of this class of men, and one of these little books.

But what becomes of these fine dreams? In three months this man of war—this theological giant—has fired his last great gun, exhausted his magazine, and he can scarcely command hearers enough for a respectable class-meeting. In six months, the fire kindled by him is out, and the only hope of his cause and relief anticipated by his brethren, is in shipping him to some new point at the end of the year. He sells his little book—if he belongs to the class who publish a refutation of Mr. Campbell—to a few of his personal friends and admirers; but others have seen such works before, and do not want them. He sinks about one-half of his moderate year's salary, in publishing a book that he cannot sell, the book dies, and is soon forgotten—Conference sends him to astonish another community with the profundity of his knowledge and vastness of his powers. Such is an outline of the history of a vast majority of this kind of men.

"But," says one, "do you intend simply commenting upon the men and work of publishing such books, without giving any direct attention to the matter contained in Mr. Ridgell's book?" Well, to be plain, it has been such a tax on our patience to read such a book *through,* in dog-days, that it will be about all that we can do to nerve our self up to make even a pass at anything so manifestly the offspring of an inconsistent, unenlightened, and conceited mind. But still, we must touch the document itself, without attempting anything like a general review. This it certainly does not need in this community. The sum of the first thirty pages—indeed, the sum of the book—is one of the lamest and weakest efforts we ever saw, to justify the following, from the ninth article of his Discipline: "Wherefore, that we are justified by faith only, is a most wholesome doctrine, and very full of comfort," and confute the position that baptism is a condition of justification. He appears utterly unconscious that his Discipline applies the words, "born of water," to baptism, and declares that—"Our Saviour Christ saith, that none can enter into the kingdom of God except he be regenerate, and born anew of water and the Holy Ghost." His own Discipline thus makes baptism a condition of entrance into the kingdom of God, which is the same as entrance into a justified state, or entrance into justification; and what is infinitely worse for him, makes baptism the condition of entrance to infants; thus making our Saviour teach, what he never did teach, viz.: That baptism is, to infants, a condition of entrance into the kingdom of God; or except they are born of water, or baptized, and of the Holy Spirit, they cannot enter into the kingdom of God. It is a pretty dream for him whose Discipline contains, not only the doctrine that baptism is a condition, but a condition to *infants,* of entrance into the kingdom of God, or a state of justification, to attempt to raise a dust about Mr. Campbell making baptism a condition of justification to a believer! Does he claim to be an ambassador of Christ, under the Lord's commission to the apostles, and is he ignorant of the fact, that in the commission, the precise words that make faith a condition, also make baptism a condition. If he has not mind enough to see that the identical same words that make faith a condition also make baptism a condition, he is neither competent to preach nor write a book, and certainly is not sent by the Lord to do either.

Let us look at this commission. "He that believeth and is baptized shall be saved." The word "saved," here means justified, or pardoned. "He that believeth and is baptized, shall be *justified or pardoned."* Here are two conditions; one is faith, the other is baptism. They are for one object; that object is Salvation from sin, or justification. Two things are to be done by the sinner for the same purpose. These two things are, to "believe and be baptized." The purpose, or object, is justification. The same words precisely that make one a condition, make the other a condition also, and there is no escape without the most manifest equivocation. "But faith is mentioned, as in the case of the jailor, as a condition, without baptism." We are aware that it is; so is baptism mentioned as a condition, without faith, Acts ii: 38. "Repent and be baptized every one of you, in the name of Jesus Christ, for the remission of sins." Not a word about faith here! Was faith left out in the justification of the converts on this occasion? or were they justified without faith? The omission of faith in the narrative, is no evidence of its absence in their conversion. Again, Ananias said to Saul, "Arise and be baptized, and wash away thy sins, calling upon the name of the Lord." No mention of faith here, or repentance either. Was Saul justified without faith and repentance, by baptism and calling on the name of the Lord *alone?* shall we conclude, from the simple circumstance that the sacred historian did not mention faith and repentance? Certainly not. Peter alludes to baptism, without mentioning faith or repentance, in the words, "the like figure even baptism doth also now save us." Is this an evidence of justification by baptism alone? Surely not. The circumstance of faith not being mentioned in these places, is no evidence that it was ever left out in the justification of one sinner. The blood of Christ is not mentioned in every place. In many places the Spirit of God, the Grace of God, the Life of Christ, etc., are not mentioned, but certainly this does not prove that either was ever left out in the justification of one sinner. If the Grace of God, the Life of Christ, His Blood, the Spirit, Faith, or Repentance, are found connected with justification in one case, they are connected with justification in every case. The same is true of baptism; if the Lord ever made it a condition in one case, in justifying a sinner, since the establishment of the Christian religion, it is a condition in every case. No condition is mentioned in every case, yet no condition was absent in any case. If they believed in one case, they believed in every case. If they repented in one case, they repented in every case. If they confessed Christ in one case, they confessed Him in every case. In the same way, if they were baptized in one case, they were baptized in every case, whether it is mentioned in the history of the case or not.

But Mr. Ridgell, in his efforts to evade the fact, that baptism is a condition of justification, denies that repentance is a condition. It matters not with him, if the Lord did "command all men everywhere to repent," nor if He did declare, that "except you repent you shall all likewise perish," nor if the holy and inspired apostle, did, when the three thousand inquired, "Men and brethren, what shall we do?" command them to "*Repent* and be baptized," nor is it any matter with him, if the same apostle did command the penitent before him in Solomon's portico, to "*Repent* and be converted," that their sins should be blotted out, or that they might be justified, thus making repentance as clearly and manifestly a condition of justification as faith; we say, it is matter for all these clear scriptures; with Mr. Ridgell, repentance must not be a condition, or that *wholesome* doctrine, so full of *comfort*, is not true, and he will be, as Paul says, of the man with all faith, without charity, or faith alone, "a sounding brass or a tinkling cymbal," or "nothing." "Faith without works," or faith alone, is *dead,* and in the place of this faith justifying anyone, the apostle says, that the man who has it, *is nothing.* Even Abraham, the father of the faithful, and the man to whom the faith was delivered, in promise, four hundred and thirty years before the law, or the deeds of the law, was justified by works, when he offered his son Isaac.

Still, Mr. Ridgell admits that a man must repent and be baptized, but these acts are not conditions. Can a man be saved without repentance? Certainly not. Baptism is a command, can a man be saved who will not obey this command of God? We do not speak of such as *cannot* obey, for with these we can do nothing; but those who *can* obey, but *will* not; can they be saved? or preachers who encourage them in disobedience; can they he saved?

B. F.

-----o-----

Insubmission to the Plain Letter of Scripture — The cause of Distraction in the Church.

MY BELOVED BROTHER FRANKLIN — Permit me to send you a few plain practical reflections on the above subject. I am indebted to Caroline Fry, for them, and feel happy in being able to acknowledge my indebtedness to so able a Priscilla. May the Lord raise up many such in His kingdom!

"The children of this world are wiser in their generation than the children of light." They have a king, a code, a legislation of their own, and are generally content to abide by their decisions. In the kingdom of Christ, insubmission to *the plain letter* of Scripture, a wish to look into the secret purposes of God, and "to be wise above what is written," has, at all times, in some measure, and at this time in particular, distracted the church, and tainted the simplicity of divine truth. So much of corrupted nature is there in us, men will ever here be thinking for themselves, and call their views deep, enlarged. These biblical free-thinkers take the word of God for their rule, but then it is in a different sense—in any sense they do not much care what, so it be but different from that in which any simple mind would understand it. I believe this disposition to be the chief source of the divisions and extravagances that now disgrace the church. That biblical criticism, as exercised by the really studious, has thrown light on passages of holy writ, obscured by change of time, and difficulty of language; that the deep experience of the really devout has done still more to explain those passages which are mysterious only till they are realized in the heart, it is not possible to doubt; and assuredly God intended we should thus impart to others the benefits of such light as He may give to each. But it does appear to me that those who talk most of deep views, and large views, and do certainly most excel in new views, are different persons from those who, by study or experience, have really sounded the depths of divine knowledge. These last have been men of close application, and laborious research, whom the world heard little of, but by the matured and long digested product of their labors. Or they have been men, who, under severe trial of their faith, in close intercourse with Deity, and devoted administration to the secret mind of others, have obtained a peculiar insight into the language of the Holy Spirit, and tried the value of their ore in many a fire, before they produced it to the world.

These were men who spent their lives in kindling some small taper, for such it was, in comparison with the light of Revelation, and left it burning on their tombs. They were not the young, the loud, the popular, who blazon the day with torches to find out something new, and discover the secrets of the Lord; finding every day a fresh pearl, for which they are willing to sell all they have before, and this too, when they can find another. They were not critics who produce fresh readings every year, commentators who find an altered sense at every re-perusal of the word; and give to the public, not the matured result of patient study, but every crude notion as it arises. Such critics have made intellect seem the enemy of truth, which God could never mean it should be. He foresaw indeed, that it would become so. He knew how powerful an instrument in Satan's hand would be the reasoning, questioning pride of man, when induced to array itself against the reception of the word. When he determined to reveal to babes what was hidden from the wise and prudent, it was not that He held in abhorrence, gifts He had bestowed; or that superior endowments made the creature an object of dislike to his Creator, that He should exclude him from his mercy. Impossible! But it pleased Him to clothe His Gospel in such a form, that none but the simple minded could receive it; and while He gave His revelation in terms so plain, the way-faring man though a fool, could not err therein, unless willfully choosing darkness rather than light, He cast such mysterious greatness about his secret purposes, that the wisest would fail to penetrate them. It pleased Him that there should be but one way to divine knowledge; the ignorant, the poor, the simple, were ready to enter it, and His Spirit had only to unclose the gate—but for the wise, the learned, the disputatious, a previous process was required: *"If* any man will be wise, let him become a fool." They must go back and enter by the same gate of child-like ignorance, receiving the dictation of the Spirit without question, and without dispute. This the All-wise foresaw they would not do. They would take his word as if it were the word of man, and examine it by the light of their own wisdom; and doing so, would either reject it wholly, receive only so much of it as they could fully explain; or admitting its divine authority as a whole, would subject each separate part to whatever construction seemed most agreeable to their natural reason. Well might God foretell that not many such would be saved, although He named a way by which they might be. That which seemed impossible with men, was possible with God. Some such are saved; not by conforming his plan of salvation to their character, and unclosing His mysteries to satisfy their wisdom, but by a quite different process. Touched by His Spirit, they consent to become fools, to read, believe, and obey. But alas! how often is this the end, when it should be the beginning; often, even of a religious course. What years of holy contentment are lost; what season of doubt and despondency endured, because men will reason when they should believe, or will have other guides for their belief, than the plain letter of the Scriptures! There cannot be an object of more painful interest to an enlightened mind than to watch the progress of those amiable and almost holy beings, who seek peace and find none, to ask and not receive, to live in search of God, and yet to live without Him. But never can God's promise be disannulled. To him that knocks, the door must be opened; to him that asks the Holy Spirit, it must be given. There is something at the bottom that we do not see; there is a reserve, an insubmission somewhere, that blinds the eye at the very moment of its anxious search. I can imagine it was exactly such a one that Jesus saw and loved; and every pious bosom loves and wonders when it sees the same—so near the kingdom, and yet cannot enter. Jesus probed the heart, and found where the canker lay beneath the seeming promise; He brought it as He did all things, to the test of Scripture—"How readest thou?" While it responded to the test: but there was one thing too much;—he went away, and Jesus let him go. I think I read in this an explanation I could never find elsewhere. Men take their Bibles; we see them study, we believe they seem humble, but it cannot be; there must be something under all we cannot reach; we have not that penetrating eye which once glanced through the covering of moral excellence to the sordid preference which lay beneath it. But the word of God could do it: it could show to those individuals what it is they stop at; what part of its testimony it is that they refuse; which of its requirements they see no necessity for; which of its doctrines their reason disputes against. Is it what the world tells them of themselves? what it tells them of Christ? what it tells them of the world? "Whatever it be, if they would have peace, let them find it out and give it up; or it will be to them, what the young man's riches were to him. They will go away and Christ will let them go. They will still ask and receive not, because they ask amiss.

When I observe how much the simplicity of divine truth has been departed from, and man has made difficult what God has made plain, lean not but think there has been in our days, too much reading and too much talking. And though I do not say, too much teaching, it is not impossible our teachers may have too much departed from the example of Christ in the manner of their teaching. I should seem a fool to many, if I were to say how simple a thing, how plain a thing to an honest mind, I think the religion of Christ to be—so much of it as concerns our personal salvation, and the effects to be produced upon us. It might seem even bold to say, I think the Bible, for the purpose for which it was intended, the plainest and the easiest book that ever has been written; and while experience proves, what the word itself declares, that no man understands it without the illumination of the Holy Spirit—I believe he requires that assistance, not to enlarge his intellect and improve his wit, but to reduce him to the ignorance and simplicity of childhood, without which, he will not be instructed. Of this I am sure; if they, who have made some progress in a religious course, find themselves harassed by uncertainties in doctrine, or confounded by the clangor of disputation, they had better leave controversy and the opinions of men, and betake themselves in simplicity and prayer to the plain letter of the written Word. They had better become deaf till they can hear its language, and dumb till they can speak it without additions and without reserve.

May God enable us all, to search the scriptures, with more diligence and more humility of mind—enable us to trust in Him and His word, and not to learn on our understanding. Affectionately yours in the Lord,

C. D. H.

Madison, Wisconsin, Aug. 2, 1856.

-----o-----

MORAL STATE OF LONDON.—Of the immense and ever augmenting population of the metropolis, there are not less than 1,400,000 souls, who are supposed never to enter a place of worship. This vast mass has been divided into the following classes, but the statements can only be approximates to the truth. Be this as it may, they are most appalling. There are 150,000 habitual drunkards; 160,000 I living in the lowest profligacy; 20,000 beggars, 10,000 gamblers, 30,000 destitute children, and 3,000 receivers of stolen goods.

From the Christian Union. Stem and Branches.

IT is a singular and startling fact, that of the thousands of Protestants who profess to be Christians, and of the hundreds of Protestant denominations, each of which is claimed to be *a* church, there is no one, or at most, very few, who feel that they can conscientiously style either one of the many so-called churches, THE Church of Christ. The orthodox canon is, that all the evangelical (!!) denominations are respectively *branches* of the church. The orthodox inquiry is, to what *branch* of the church do you *belong?*

In the eyes of the Protestant world, it is shameless assumption for a member of any denomination to say of that denomination, that it is *the Church* of Christ. And when, as has been proved by an actual experiment, any body of men has been found, having the fear of the Lord before their eyes sufficiently to take the Bible, the revealed will of God, for their Book of Faith, Discipline, and spiritual counsellor, to the absolute exclusion and rejection of all human articles and systems of faith and discipline; and are so sincere in professing to be Christians as to call themselves Christians, and to speak of the Church which rests on the Rock of Foundation alone, as THE Church of Christ; that body has been hooted, condemned, scorned, and contemned, for *presuming* to say that they are Christians, and refusing to have any name less than the name of Christ, applied to them as their distinctive epithet.

Men seem to reason thus—We profess to be Christians ourselves, but we have not the Christian boldness to cast off the names of our systems and system-makers, and be called simply Christians, and if we do not call ourselves pre-eminently Christians, you shall not do so.

When we ask the question:—Is there any organization which all Protestantdom concedes to be the Church of Christ? the reply is, no; but every evangelically orthodox denomination is a branch of the church. Now a branch is, according to our standard lexicographers, a limb, a bough shooting from the stem, a member, or part of a body; a branch therefore necessarily implies a stem; and a stem is the principal body of a tree, the firm part which supports the branches. From these definitions, it is plain that a branch is that which *grows out* of, and is supported by a stem, and as it grows out of a stem, it must be the same nature as the stem; and as it is supported by the stem, if the stem dies, the branch necessarily dies. If the stem is not, the branches of that stem cannot be. It is simply absurd to say of a branch that it is of a different nature from its stem, or that a branch exists when it has no stem to support it.

Now applying these deductions to the case under consideration, let us question these branch advocates a little. If *all* these denominations are branches, where is the stem denomination? Answer — "All the branches united constitute the church." But who has ever heard that all the limbs or branches of a tree taken together, without the stem, made up a tree? "We do not mean that," says the branch churchman, "we mean that the *good of all parties* make the church." Very well, but where do these good come from, are they not *parts* of these same branches? Your explanation amounts to this: after the decayed parts of the branches are thrown away, the *good parts* united make up the tree. I would ask again, where is the stem?

"But," says the advocate of branches, "we teach that there is a visible and an invisible Church of Christ!" I reply, our object is not to locate an invisible church, and therefore we will not now leave the proper subject of our investigations, in an *ignis fatuus* search after a something invisible; suffice it on that point, that we nowhere hear the Saviour or his apostles speaking of an *invisible* church. I therefore admit the correctness of the proposition, that there is a *visible* Church of Christ, and press the question — "Where is that Church of Christ?" The only recourse is to the branches. But it is as undeniable as it is true, that where there is no stem there can be no branches. Look at the nature of these church branches, every one differing from the other, and all differing from the stem. What kind of a tree would it be, which, springing from an acorn, has apple, peach, orange, and almond branches; and the fruits of these branches were red and yellow apples, peaches clear and clingstone, oranges sweet and sour, almonds hard shell and soft shell? Yet such is the kind of tree, which the various denominations growing on the same stem would be.

It may be argued, that the different sects are grafts into the stem. Where then, did the scions come from? It is *generally* the case, that a bud or scion is taken from one tree and grafted on another. Is there then, one larger church tree and a nursery of little ones, whose buds are grafted in the larger one? For be it remembered, we are not considering the case of a sinner coming to Christ and being *adopted* as a child of God, but we are considering the branches, as they claim to be, branches of the church. I admit that Christ said to his *disciples,* "*I* am the vine, YOU are the branches;" but he has nowhere said—I am the stem, and the various sects are the branches. He also said—"On this rock (himself, the rock of ages) I *will* build MY CHURCH but he has nowhere said—This is my Church, and these, the sects of every name and order, are the branches. It is therefore clear, that where there is no stem church, there can be no branch churches; and even if there be a stem church, the branches are not church branches, unless they have the same nature, are governed by the same laws, and bear the same kind of fruit which the stem has, is governed by, and bears. the query, what branch of the church do you belong to? is in good keeping with the assertion, that all orthodox denominations are branches of the church, when not one of them pretends to know where the stem is, or whether there be any such thing or not, i., e., when none admit that anyone is The Church of Christ. The inquiry, I say, is in good keeping with the theology, for they ought to know that no one *belongs* to a church, but that anyone may be *a member* of a church, and that the members make the churches. Says Paul— "Ye are *bought with a price." "Ye are Christ's."

To conclude this article, I will introduce a brief definition of the expression, the churches. The word church is derived from two Greek words, *kurios* and *oikos,* and in the original *kuriake,* or church, which signifies house of the Lord, as Paul expresses it, "a temple for the habitation of God through the Holy Spirit." The word church was unknown during the Mosaic dispensation, and was never used in the Sacred Oracles, till it is used in the 16th chapter and 17th verse of the testimony of Matthew. It was not previously used, because previously there was not in the proper sense, a house of the Lord. "THE CHURCH, then, is the house of the Lord;" and Paul, in Hebrews, 5th chapter 2d and 3d verses, tells us what that house is—"Who was faithful to him that appointed him, as also Moses was faithful in all his house." "And Moses verily was faithful in all his house as a servant — but Christ as a son over his own house, *whose house are we,* if we hold fast the confidence and rejoicing of the hope firm unto the end."

*1st Cor., 6th and 20th vs.; 3d and 23d vs.

-----o-----

Deism and Christianity.

1. I have never met a man, woman, or child, who had been made better by embracing deistical sentiments.

I have met hundreds of persons who had been benefited by having embraced the principles of Christianity.

2. I have seen those who, after having abandoned the faith of their fathers, through the sophistry of the infidel, have delivered themselves up to the most fatal deviations from the path of rectitude; and I judge of Deism by its fruits.

I have seen Deists who, after having abandoned their maxims of infidelity, through the preaching of the Word, have applied themselves to the practice of the most distinguished virtues; and *I* judge Christianity by its fruits.

3. I do not remember to have met with a Deist who could assure me that his belief rendered him peaceful and happy.

I remember to have seen a great number of Christians, who have assured me that they owed to their religious sentiments a peace and happiness that passed all understanding.

4. I have nowhere found a Deist whose actions were really directed by a belief in rewards and punishments beyond the grave. The Deist says he believes in a life to come, yet acts as though he did not.

I have nowhere found a true Christian whose actions were not governed by a belief in rewards and punishments hereafter. The Christian not only says, but also evinces by his actions, that he believes in the life of the world to come.

5. I have seen many Deists, at the hour of death, with a horrible despair accusing themselves of having completely forgotten the commandments of God. Hell besieged their dying couch with all its horrors.

I have seen many Christians rejoicing at the hour of death with ineffable joy, and blessing that Lord who had brought them to the knowledge of his mercies and commandments. Heaven brightened their dying bed with all its glory.

And I said, Deism is an incomplete religion —an error of men; Christianity is a perfect religion—a revelation from God.—*Seumer*

-----o-----

THOUGHT OUR DIGNITY.—Man is a reed, and the weakest reed in nature; but then, he is a thinking reed. There is no occasion that the whole universe should arm itself for his destruction. Vapor, a drop of rain, is sufficient to kill him; and yet, should the universe crush him, man would still be more noble than that by which he fell, because he would know his fate, while the universe would be insensible of its victory.

Thus, all our dignity consists in thought. It is hence we are to raise ourselves, and not by the aid of space and duration. Let us study the art of thinking well— this is the foundation of ethics.

Editor's Table.

Correspondents. —Many documents are on hand for publication—some articles, obituaries, items of news, success of the gospel, etc.—but mostly demanding attention in some way, that we could not give, engaged, as we are, every day and every night almost, evangelizing.

☛ We invite special attention to the Sermon, for this number. Read it attentively through; and if it does not bring tears, pray the Lord that your heart may be tendered.

Literary Notices.

The Christian Banner, is a monthly of 32 pages, printed covers, neatly executed; edited by our esteemed brother, D. Oliphant, assisted by J. Butchard, jr.; and published at Coburg and Brighton, Canada West, by Oliphant & White. We have owed this valuable pamphlet, and several others, a notice some time; but our constant absence from home in the evangelical field, and pressure of engagements, have prevented us till now. Brother Oliphant is soundly educated in the Master's School, and loves the pure faith, speaks the pure language, and keeps Christianity distinct from the fooleries of these times. His *Banner* is the only publication the Brethren have in Canada, and we hope he may be well sustained. Many more Brethren in the United States would do both themselves and the cause service to take it, and aid a safe and good man.

The Christian Union. — Such is the name of a monthly pamphlet of 32 pages, printed covers, neatly executed; edited by our beloved brethren, J. S. Lamar, of Augusta, Ga., and A. G. Thomas, of Griffin, Ga. This is a healthy publication, "sound in the faith," uttering pure speech, and showing manly strength. This pamphlet is an advocate of *Christianity itself,* and not some men's *notions* of Christianity. May God preserve such men, and fill their hearts with the overwhelming matters of Christianity itself, and enable them to devote themselves to the honors of their Master; and may the Brethren give them the patronage they so justly merit.

Church. News.
July 30th, 1856.

BROTHER FRANKLIN—We have just closed a protracted meeting, held three days, commencing on Saturday and Lord's-Day; broke up on Monday evening. We had thirteen additions—seven by confession, and six by immersion—and organized a church near Vermont, Howard county, Ind. We had Bros. A. Conrod and Hull, from Russiaville, to preach for us.

May the Lord help us, in this good work.
BENJAMIN JACKSON.

Canton, Stark county, Ohio, August 5, 1856. BROTHER FRANKLIN :

Dear Sir—I have just returned from Canal Fulton, in this county. Bros. J. C. Stark, and John Sinclair commenced a meeting at that place, on Wednesday, July 23d; and on the 31st, I went to assist them, and continued until Monday last, (the 4th of August). The result was, 13 additions by confession and immersion, and the resuscitation of the congregation. There had formerly been a congregation there, but from death and removal of the leading members, the Brethren ceased to meet.— There is now a congregation of some forty members. The cause is onward in this county. To the Lord be all the praise.

I enclose $3 to you, for the American Christian Review, vols. 1 and 2—for Miss Calista Elson, Canal Fulton, Stark county, O. Mrs. Mary A. Smith, " " " " "

Yours, in the blessed hope,
P. K. DIBBLE.

Noblesville, Ind., August 13th, 1856.

DEAR BRO. FRANKLIN—We closed a meeting last night, at Miami, Ind., with 15 accessions; we baptized 11. A short time since, Brother Van Buskirk baptized one here. We received three. A few weeks since, we received three at Huntsville, Ind., baptizing two. In a little less than three months, we have reported some 50 accessions to the different churches with whom we have labored.

Yours in the Lord,
H. St. JOHN VAN DAKE.

Woodsonville, August 14th, 1856.

DEAR BROTHER FRANKLIN—I am just closing a tour of about four months, through the Green River section. New theaters, where the cause has been feeble and languishing, have been mostly occupied.— Although there have not been many additions, yet it is believed and hoped that great good has been accomplished in disabusing the public mind in reference to the bitter misrepresentations of wicked and bigoted opponents. I visited Owensboro, McKays, Madisonville, Henderson, Morganfield, Uniontown, Cypress Valley, Mumford's Coal Mines, Trenton, Elkton, Philippi, Gordonsville, Bowling Green, Pleasant Hill, Glasgow, and this place.

Brethren Lawrence and Mulkey—talented and estimable Evangelists, assisted by your humble servant— commenced here on the first day of the month; and resolved to try the power of the ancient Gospel on the minds and hearts of the people, in the midst of a contested election. Brother Mulkey remained seven days, when we had 22 additions. We close to-day, with 57 additions. It has been a glorious meeting! I have never seen more substantial persons added to the Brotherhood, in my life; and what is peculiarly gratifying, the church yesterday, withdrew her fellowship from a member who was engaged in retailing ardent spirits, and thus saved him from ruin; for he at once repented, abandoned the business, and was restored. It was a triumph. It was hailed with delight by the church and the world. There have been about 100 additions since I left home.

We enjoyed the hospitality of my beloved old friend and brother, Isaac Chaplin, late of Mercer county. He will take charge of the young Disciples, and lead them in the worship.

Thank the Lord for all his kindness to his aged servant.

Yours, affectionately, J. T. JOHNSON.

The Noblesville Matter, again.

WE have received a document from Bro. G. H. Voss, of Noblesville, Ind., commencing as follows:—

"In the last number of the Review, we appear at direct issue: You affirm that our church has *not* accepted the proposition of Bro. Mathes and others, of the 10th of October last; and I say they *have*.— Our disagreement is found in this only: You contend that the document authorizes an inquiry into our Scriptural existence as a church of Christ; and I say that document has no such meaning. Let the Brotherhood know that our acceptance amounts simply to this: That we take the document *unreservedly as it is,* and say that nothing else shall be *lugged* into the controversy but what was originally intended."

To this I reply—that the disagreement is not, that "I contend that the document authorizes an inquiry into the Scriptural existence of the church," with which this brother is identified, or that it does not. I contend nothing about what it requires; but tried to induce him and those with him, both publicly and privately, as kindly as possible, unreservedly according to the suggestion of Bro. Mathes and others, to refer the whole matter to a committee. This I could not do, without restrictions that might embarrass a committee, and prevent them from reaching the worst evil in the whole matter.

I tried to induce Bro. Voss to agree to the reference without the restrictions, the very day on which he wrote the piece that appeared in the *Review,* and he declared that they *would not do it.* He now says—"That our acceptance amounts simply to this: That we take the document *unreservedly as it is,* and simply say, that nothing shall be *lugged* into the controversy but what was originally intended."— This is all well enough, unless one of the parties is to decide "what was originally intended." Leave the committee to decide "what was originally intended," and we are ready to proceed. But it is certain that it is not my duty to say what was, or was not originally intended, nor can it be the prerogative of either of the parties. Those who signed the document, or the committee to whom the reference is made, must decide what was originally intended. This the committee can decide, from the document itself. Do you then, Bro. Voss, and the brethren with you, refer the matter *unreservedly* to a committee, to proceed as "originally intended,' leaving the committee to determine and decide what was originally intended? or do you, and those with you, hold that you have a right to determine what was originally intended? If you unreservedly refer the matter to a committee, leaving the committee free to determine what was originally intended, say so, without equivocation, and we are ready to proceed. But while you are determined to forestall the committee, and I try to leave the committee free, let it so appear to all. You can set yourselves upon a proper footing in one sentence. Either do so, or admit that you *will not*. B. F.

Franklin College.

WE feel in duty bound to say to our brethren and others who have sons to educate, that Franklin College, without doubt, offers advantages inferior to no institution in the country. The retired and beautiful location cannot easily be surpassed, and the order of the pupils and constant vigilance of the Faculty give unmistakable evidence that the influences are most favorable for moral and intellectual improvement. During the twelve years' existence of the College, the patronage has been encouraging, and we have no reason to doubt the interest will be increased.

We erected the buildings mainly at our own cost, and while we make no sympathetic appeals for patronage, we feel thankful that so far we have been able to sustain the high character of the College.— We look for success through our pupils, and while we have failed in some instances, we believe our success has been good with an unusually large number. Will the friends of the College think of these things?

Gospel Advocate.

OBITUARY.

Little York, Washington co., Ind., August 12,1856.

DEAR BROTHER FRANKLIN—It is with sorrow that I record the death of my beloved brother, JEPTHA R. HARROD. He died on the first day of August, after an attack of typhoid fever of eighteen days' duration; and although his sufferings were great, he bore them with fortitude becoming a Christian.

He had been a member of the Christian Church about twelve years, and died with a well-grounded hope of immortality and eternal life beyond the grave.

As ever, your brother,

SANDFORD H. HARROD.

THE AMERICAN CHRISTIAN REVIEW.

SERMON OCCASIONED BY THE DEATH OF SEFTON LANE.
BY BENJAMIN FRANKLIN.

TEXT.—"Lord, what is man that thou art mindful of him, or the son of man that thou visitest him —Heb. 2:6.

MY RESPECTED BRETHREN AND FRIENDS, The circumstance which has called this large congregation together is one of that solemn class that we must frequently witness in passing through this world of sorrow, sickness and death. None are so dear to us, so much beloved, or so useful as to be exempt from death. Hence it is rational for us to be always ready to meet death, either in our own persons, or in the persons of those who are near and dear to us. I am unable to express the emotions caused in my breast, by hearing of the death of our beloved and highly esteemed friend, Mr. SEFTON LANE; and in my meditations on my way from the city here this morning, as I passed in review the condition of this community, the church, and many brethren with whom I have spent some of my happiest days, and with whom I have so frequently been at the Lord's Table, while we commemorated our Lord's great sufferings for us. All is changing here, and ephemeral. Transmutation is written upon everything around us. Lord, teach us to number our days and apply our hearts to wisdom!

Since it was known to me that I was to address the friends on this occasion, but especially on my way here, I have been reflecting upon some suitable theme, that the living might be benefited by the occasion. I could think of no more fitting theme than is suggested by the words of David, found in the eighth Psalm, and quoted by Paul in the words just read: "Lord, what is man, that thou art mindful of him, or the son of man, that thou visitest him?" There are many important questions agitated and discussed among men, but none of greater moment, now that the tendency is so inevitably and rapidly to carnalism and sensuality, than the one now proposed. We therefore propose, as fitting the occasion, to consider the following points:

1. Man in the present state.
2. The boundary line of repentance.
3. The state of man between death and the resurrection.
4. The state beyond the resurrection.

What is man in the present state. That there is something more in man than the lower animals, we all are as conscious, as that we exist at all. When a man's life is in danger, the impression is different from that produced by the endangering of the life of a mere animal. When a man is lost to the community, to his family and friends, the impression is different from that produced by the loss of any property. When a man lies before us in death, and we reflect that we shall hear his voice no more, see his face, and witness his actions no more, what an impression it makes upon our sensibilities! What does all this arise from, but the estimate we put upon a man? Some speak of what a man *worth,* meaning simply his property. But the question we inquire into is what *the man himself* is worth. The scripture fact, that *God loved man,* attaches an importance to man, that this world never could have realized without the wonderful manifestations of the love of God to man. The wonderful fact, that *Christ died for man,* is another means by which we make a feeble effort to appreciate the value of a man. O, that the Lord would this day aid us in our feeble effort to grasp the idea of the worth of a human being.

We have already hinted at the fret, that the tendency of the times is to carnality, sensuality, and mere materiality. The theory that man is merely an animated, moving and thinking lump of clay, or matter, though tending to Atheism, is gaining footing and working itself through society in all the length and breadth of the land. The low and degrading notion, that after a man dies, he no more exists than he did a thousand years before his birth, is now boldly advocated and preached as the true gospel of the grace of God, to encourage the living, comfort the dying, and console the bereft. But all such idle theories have their foundation in the cold-hearted unbelief lurking in breasts from which the love of Christ and Spirit of God have departed. The fact that man cannot be satisfied with mere animal gratifications, shows that there is in him more than a mere animal man. Mere animal gratifications are all found in this life; but after man has all earthly gratifications, there is still remaining in him an ungratified nature, there still remains in his nature a demand, a craving, unsupplied. For this demand there is no supply, for this desire there is no gratification in all mere animal and material nature. This wonderful demand, craving and desire, not supplied and gratified in mere worldly and material gratifications, is spiritual. It is nothing more nor less than the demand, cravings, and desires of an immortal nature. An immaterial nature cannot be gratified with material things, or a spiritual nature cannot be gratified with sensual things. The reason religion—a spiritual system—effects man, is that it reaches the demand of a spiritual nature. Religion produces no effect upon the mere animal creation, nor would it produce any effect upon man, were it not that he has a spiritual, or an immortal nature.

This doctrine, of the spirituality, immortality and eternity of the "inner man," or "the hidden man of the heart," is abundantly set forth in the inspired revelation of heaven. This, Paul puts his pen upon as follows: "Though our outward man perish, yet the inward man is renewed day by day." 2 Cor. iv: 16. The outward man is the material man, which suffered by persecutions and perished, or died, but the inner man, or the spiritual, or immortal man, being imperishable, is *renewed* day by day, even at the same time that the outer, or material man, is perishing. He then, proceeds: "For our light affliction, which is but for a moment, worketh for us a far more exceeding and eternal weight of glory; while we look not at the things which are seen, but at the things that are not seen; for the things which are seen are temporal; but the things which are not seen are eternal." Now, here we have an outer and an inner man, the one perishable and the other imperishable, the one seen and the other unseen, one temporal the other eternal. This imperishable man, who is invisible, looks forward to the time when the external man, the material man, the house of the inner man, shall perish, to a house not made with hands eternal in the heavens. This inward and imperishable man, is called "the soul," in the following: "Fear not them who kill the body, but are not able to kill the soul." Man can kill the material, or the animal man, but the immaterial or spiritual man cannot be killed by man. The same indestructible man is referred to in the following: "Whose adorning, let it not be that outward adorning of plaiting the hair, and of wearing of gold, or of putting on of apparel; but let it be the hidden man of the heart, in that which is not corruptible, even the ornament of a meek and quiet spirit, which is in the sight of God of great price." Now what is affirmed of the "hidden man of the heart?" Why that "it is *not corruptible.*" The Greek *aphthartos,* here translated, "Not corruptible," is also translated immortal, and is used to express the immortality of the Deity. This hidden man of the heart, which is affirmed to be immortal, eternal, and which man cannot kill, it is also affirmed, "is in the sight of God of great price." This man, when dead to us, is alive to God.

2. The boundary line of repentance. Life is the boundary line of repentance. What the scriptures call "time," contains the whole period during which man can turn to God. "To-day, if you will hear his voice, harden not your hearts, as in the bitter provocation, in the day of temptation in the wilderness." If we are ever molded into the image of Christ, made conformable to his death, and prepared for the society of the blessed, it must be while we are in time. To show that we are inside of the clear revelations of God, we shall make two or three references to the New Testament. One man, more curious to know the fate of the masses, than his own duty to God and man, in our Lord's life-time, asked him: "Lord are there few that be saved?" To this, the Lord responded: "Strive to enter in at the straight gate; for many, I say unto you, will seek to enter in, and shall not be able." LUKE xiii: 23, 24. He then proceeds to the time when this shall be, as follows: "When once the Master of the house is risen up, and hath shut to the door, and ye begin to stand without, and to knock at the door, saying, Lord, Lord, open unto us; and He shall answer and say unto you, I know you not whence you are." In reply, they make an appeal to the fact that the Lord had been accustomed to eat and drink in their streets. He replies, "I know you not whence you are; depart from me all ye workers of iniquity." This must be after death, for He refers to the future, "When ye shall see Abraham, and Isaac, and Jacob, and all the prophets in the kingdom of God, and you yourselves trust out," or thrust away. It is after death, because the Master of the house has never risen up and shut to the door of the kingdom, in this life.

As we sing sometimes, "The doors of gospel grace stand open night and day." None, in this life, stand and knock at the door, crying, Lord, Lord, open to us, whom the Master refuses to receive. His language now is, "Whoever will, let him come and take of the water of life freely." "He who cometh to me, I will in no wise cast out." "He who seeks shall find; to him who knocks, it shall be opened," and "whoever calls upon the Lord shall be saved." But the time will come, when the Lord shall have arisen and shut the door, and men shall stand without, knocking and crying, Lord, open to us; but He refuses them admittance and thrusts them away, declaring that He never approved them.— Nothing like this can be found in this life. It refers to the time when the fear of the wicked cometh as a whirlwind; when distress and anguish shall overtake them; then shall they call upon the Lord, but He will not answer them. See PROV. i: 26, 27.

Another passage to which we refer, to show that death is the boundary line of repentance, is the case of the rich man and Lazarus, LUKE xvi: 19,31. This rich man died, "and in hell he lifted up his eyes, being in torments." Here we find a man in torments after death. Lazarus has also died, and been carried by angels to Abraham's bosom. Dives, once the *rich, man,* but now a beggar, looks up and seeth Abraham afar off, and Lazarus in his bosom, and cries to him, "Father Abraham, have mercy on me, and send Lazarus, that he may dip the tip of his finger in water, and cool my tongue, for I am tormented in this flame." Now the question of repentance, of obtaining relief from punishment after death, is fairly before us. In a case stated by our Lord himself, an application is made for the mitigation of torment after death. But what is the response of Abraham, who speaks in the place of the Almighty, here? It is, "Son, remember that thou in thy life-time received thy good things, and likewise Lazarus evil things; but now he is comforted, and thou art tormented." Here are two men after death, one *comforted* and the other *tormented.* Can any change be made in their condition? Let us hear Abraham. He proceeds: "Besides all this, between us and you there is a great gulf fixed; so that they who would pass from hence to you cannot; neither can they pass to us that would come from thence." This is an end of all change of condition. In that world there is no turning to God nor falling from grace. The rich man, then despairing of any mitigation of his torments, or change of his condition, makes one more appeal to Abraham. "I pray thee, therefore," said he, "that thou wouldst send him to my father's house; for I have five brethren; that he may testify unto them, lest they also come into this place of torment." Having fallen into torments, on account of his unbelief, and having five brethren also unbelievers, he desired testimony presented to them from the dead, lest they also come to this place of torment. But Abraham answers, "They have Moses and the prophets, let them hear them." The rich man persists; "If one went unto them from the dead, they will repent." This is the only New Testament account of a request for a departed spirit to be sent to our world to lead sinners to repentance; but this request, coming from one already in the torments of a wicked man after death, was refused in the following words: "If they hear not Moses and the prophets, neither will they be persuaded though one rose from the dead." This shows that God will allow no means employed to save sinners only those of His own appointment, and writes the seal of condemnation upon all visitations of the spirits of dead people to save sinners.

The next and only passage more to which we shall refer, to show the boundary line of repentance, is Rev. xxii: 11, "He that is unjust, let him be unjust still; he who is filthy, let be filthy still; and he who is righteous, let him be righteous still; and he that is holy, let him be holy still." This is an end of all repentance, of all turning to God, and also an end to all departing from Him. The holy shall remain holy and the wicked remain wicked, from this time forward. Jesus made his personal efforts to save man in this world. When He left the world, He committed to the apostles the ministry and word of reconciliation, and they made their efforts in this world.

All the means ever employed to save man, have been employed in this life. All the cases of acceptable repentance that we have ever known anything about were in this life. If, therefore, men ever turn to God, it must be in time.

3. We proceed in the third place, to consider the state of man between death and resurrection. There were, in the days of our Lord's pilgrimage, a class of materialists, who not only denied the resurrection of the dead, but that there was an angel or spirit. Many were the debates which they had with the Pharisees who differed with them upon these three points. Knowing that our Lord had sanctioned the doctrine of the Pharisees, that there were angels and spirits, and would be a resurrection of the dead, the Sadducees approached the Lord with the puzzle, touching the resurrection of the woman and seven husbands. As if they had said, "Now, Master,' you agree with the Pharisees, and teach that there will be a resurrection of the dead; but this doctrine involves a difficulty; for a certain woman, in the course of her life, had seven husbands, and we should be pleased to know which one shall have her in the resurrection?" Our Lord soon explains this matter. He says, "In the resurrection they neither marry nor are given in marriage, but are as the angels of God." He proceeds, "Now that the dead are raised, even Moses showed at the bush, when he calleth the Lord the God of Abraham, and the God of Isaac, and the God of Jacob. For He is not a God of the dead, but of the living, for all live unto Him." While those departed from this life, are dead to us, they are alive to God—*for all live unto Him.*" "The inner man," as Paul calls him, or "the hidden man of the heart," as Peter styles him, which is eternal, "not corruptible," but immortal, which Jesus says, man is not able to kill, though separated from us, or dead to us, is *alive to God,* "for all live unto Him." See LUKE XX: 27—38

The Transfiguration of Christ presents us the three states, the fleshly, the intermediate, and the resurrection, or eternal state, all at once. The Lord is changed into the glorified state, is seated upon the throne, as we would see Him to-day, if we were before Him in Heaven. Hence Peter says, "We were eye-witnesses of His majesty, for he received from God the Father, honor and glory, when there came such a voice from the excellent glory, This is my Son, in whom I am well pleased." On this august occasion, Peter, James, and John represented the fleshly state. They were present in the flesh. Moses was here, not in the flesh, for he had died some fifteen centuries before this. He was not in the resurrection state, for Christ was the first-born from the dead of every creature, that in all things He might have the pre-eminence. But he was in the intermediate state, or the man Moses was there separate from the body) alive, conscious, and held a conversation with the Lord, in regard to his great sufferings to be accomplished at Jerusalem. Though Moses had been dead to the world fifteen hundred years, and his body mingled and lost in the dust, he was alive to God all this time, and so are all the dead. He had not lost his identity, nor his name, but is known and mentioned as the *man Moses,* in a conscious state, seeing, hearing and talking. Our friend, so much loved, lamented, but now dead to us, is alive to God, and as conscious, and maintaining his identity, as much, as when here in the body. Another dignitary present at the transfiguration, was Elijah, who was taken to Heaven without seeing death. He was in the glorified state, in the body, glorified, spiritual, as all the bodies of the blessed are. Probably the Lord took him to Heaven without seeing death, in view of this very occasion. What a grand scene is now before us. The Lord of the universe is before us upon the throne; the old prophet Elijah, stands before him who was the great prophet of all the prophets, recognizing his authority, before the witnesses of Christ. Here stands Moses, the Law-giver of ancient Israel, and recognizes the Lord Jesus Christ, and surrenders up all authority to him. Just at this wonderful and interesting moment, the Almighty from the upper world, called out, "This is my Son, the beloved in whom I am well pleased: *hear him."*

Let us hear Paul once, on this subject. "Therefore we are always confident, knowing that, whilst we are at home in the body, we are absent from the Lord." In a few words, he says, "Wherefore we labor, that, whether present or absent, we may be "accepted of Him." 2 COR. v: 9. How could we be "present with the Lord," and "accepted of Him," when absent from the body, if there be not an inner spiritual man, who will exist separate, or absent from the body? No man living can ever reconcile this passage with the preposterous theory, that when a man dies, he has no conscious existence. To this we add only one more scripture. When John, in the Island of Patmos, was in awful and sublime vision, and saw the whole panorama of the future ages passing in review, he says, "I saw under the altar, the souls of them who were beheaded for the word of God and for the testimony of Jesus Christ, and they cried and said, how long, O Lord God Almighty, holy just and true, dost thou not avenge us of our blood on them who dwell on the earth." Here were souls, alive, looking back to what had been done on earth, and looking forward to what would be done in future. They had not lost their identity nor memory, forgotten the past nor distrusted the future, but were alive. The intermediate state is, therefore, a conscious state, the righteous are comforted and at rest, with the Lord, in Abraham's bosom, or Paradise; the wicked are in *Tartarus,* in prison, tormented, reserved unto the judgment of the great day, with the angels that sinned.

4. In the fourth, and last place, let us take one look forward to the eternal, or resurrection state. Looking to the close of the intermediate state, John says, "I saw a great white throne, and him that sat on it, from whose face the earth and the heaven fled away, and there was found no more place for them. And I saw the dead, small and great, stand before God; and the books were opened; and another book was opened which is the book of life; and the dead were judged out of those things which were written in the books, according to their works." REV. 20: 10 —12. After thus presenting the dead in judgment, he proceeds to tell us where they came from, as follows: "And the sea gave up the dead that were in it; and death and hell delivered up

the dead which were in them; and they were judged every man according to their works." The Greek *hades*, here translated hell, simply means the invisible, or unseen state. In this invisible state, the book of God reveals two distinct, or separate apartments. One is *Paradise* the other is *Tartarus*. In this same book of Revelations, John, speaking in the person of Christ, says, "I am he who *was dead* and *am alive forevermore;* I have the keys of hell and of death; I can open and no man can shut, and shut and no man can open." The amount of this is, that I have the keys, or power, to open the grave, and raise the bodies both from land and sea, and I have power to open the invisible state, both *Paradise* and *Tartarus,* and bring forth the spirits of the dead, both righteous and wicked, re-uniting soul and body, to stand in judgment. When the last righteous sentence is passed upon man, in the last judgment, the final separation follows. Whoever was not found written in the book of life was cast into the lake of fire. This is the second death. Here is the last account of the wicked, the incorrigible, and we must leave them where God leaves them, without any attempt to dwell upon their deplorable and irremediable condition.

Let us now turn our attention to the righteous—the good and virtuous of all ages—those who feared God and worked righteousness in every nation. John says, "I saw them coming from every nation, kindred, tongue, tribe and people, who had washed their robes and made them white in the blood of the Lamb, and they shouted, blessing and glory, and honor, and might, and dominion unto him who sits upon the throne, and to the Lamb, forever and ever!" Again they shouted, Hallelujah to the Lamb! The Lord God Omnipotent reigns! John looks again, and says, "I, John, saw the holy city, new Jerusalem, coming down from God out of Heaven, prepared as a bride adorned for her husband. And I heard a great voice out of heaven, saying, Behold, the tabernacle of God is with men, and He will dwell with them, and they shall be His people, and God himself shall be with them and be their God. And God shall wipe all tears from their eyes; and there shall be no more death, neither sorrow, nor crying, for the former things are passed away." Shall we who are bathed in tears, here to-day, reach the holy city, where we shall be called to pass through the deep waters of affliction no more; where we shall hear the groans of the sick and dying no more; where there will be no visiting of the sick, nor funeral occasions; where we shall no more be called to give up fathers and mothers in death, husbands or wives, or precious children; but where the wounded heart shall be made whole, the weary spirit shall be at rest, and the mourner comforted. How ineffable the bliss! How unutterable the joys! of a state where we shall not only be free from all the afflictions that encompass us here, but see the Lord and dwell with Him forevermore! How invaluable the rich boon proposed to man, through the Lord Jesus Christ! What everlasting obligations we are under to love God and serve Him! Let us put our everlasting trust in the Lord, our strength and our Redeemer.

Before I take my seat, I must try to utter some word of comfort to our dear sister, in view of her bereavement of her nearest and dearest earthly friend. I am perfectly aware that no words that I can utter can heal her bleeding heart. Indeed, here is where the Lord teaches us all, what poor, feeble and helpless creatures we are. We may sympathize with her, and try to enter with her into this heavy affliction and bereavement, but, though this may afford her some satisfaction, still it can give no permanent relief. We must go with her to our Father and our God, and implore Him for the comforts and consolations which she needs, and He alone can give. He says to her, and to us all, when in affliction and distress, "I will never leave you nor forsake you; but will give you grace and glory, and no good thing will I withhold from you." If "The everlasting arms are underneath," we shall be holden up. When Job was in the midst of bereavement and losses of property, in resignation, he exclaimed, "The Lord giveth, and the Lord taketh away; blessed be the name of the Lord." When our Lord, with the sins of the world upon Him, entered the garden of

Gethsemane, he fell upon his face and prayed, "O, my Father, if it be possible let this cup pass; nevertheless, not *my will* but *thine* be done." In the same spirit of resignation, let us all bow to this mysterious dispensation of God's providence. Not *our will* but *thine* be done!

Respecting our departed friend, Mr. SEFTON LANE, I presume, I speak but the mind of all who hear me, when I say that he was highly esteemed, a man of honor, integrity and morality. When I speak for myself, I must say, that I had much attachment to him, that I felt deep solicitude for him, and, some years ago, made several efforts and gave invitations with him upon my heart, to induce him to come to the Lord Jesus. I can but think that he was almost persuaded on more than one occasion. I am informed that during his last illness, he conversed upon his state, had the Bible read and friends to pray with him, and that he was willing to bow to the will of the Divine Being. But he has gone from among us; we shall see his face, hear his voice, and enjoy his society no more in this world. Our effort to speak to this dense audience on this occasion is not for him, but for the living. Shall all these warnings, in the midst of this people, fail to bring them to recognize the hand of the Lord? The aged are falling in our midst. Fathers and mothers are dying. Husbands and wives are sinking into the grave. Children are bidding adieu to parents. Many of them warn their friends in their last hours, to prepare to meet God. Shall all these solemn warnings go unheeded, and shall all the prayers and tears of all the good, fail to bring this people to Christ? Shall the love of God fail? Shall the sufferings of Christ fail? Shall all the tender mercies of our God fail? Shall the goodness and benevolence of God fail to bring this people to the kingdom of God?

May God bless and have mercy upon us all, and may He especially grant to our dear sister, grace and strength to support her in this severe trial!

In reference to time, hours and days are of great importance: in respect to eternity, years and ages are nothing.

Our Position as a Religious Community.
No. 10.

"IN having no creed but the Bible, requiring no experience, no explanation of the convert's views, his feelings and faith, except the simple confession, that he 'believes with all his heart that Jesus Christ is the Son of God,' you make the church liable to imposition, in receiving many who have no change of heart, and who will not hold out faithful to the end." In appearance, this is a very specious objection, and has no doubt, had much weight with many persons. It assumes such an air of piety, that an unsuspecting person would scarcely think of any sophistry in it. It puts on such a deep and cautious concern in regard to a thorough work in converting men, and the protection of the church from imposition, that not one out of a thousand would ever suspect it of being a most wicked and daring assumption. Still, when it is carefully looked at, it is most unquestionably such. It commences with an admitted dissatisfaction with the Work of conversion under the immediate administration of the infallibly inspired apostles of the Lamb. It impeaches the procedure of the holy apostle to whom were committed the keys of the Kingdom of God, alleging that he opened the way for imposition. It challenges the Holy Spirit of God, who led the apostles into all truth, with being too loose in the reception of the first converts to the faith of Christ, of demanding too little of them, and not using proper precautions against imposition. In one word, it impeaches the wisdom of God, in assuming that he has not safely guarded the door of admission into the Kingdom of Christ and consequently, that his system is defective, permitting persons to enter without proper feelings, views, impressions, and unprepared for admission.

Having assumed, reasoned, and decided, that the apostles, under the guidance of the unerring spirit of all truth, in receiving persons into the Christian institution, were faulty, to be complained of, and not a suitable example for preachers in our day, it proceeds to the second assumption, viz.: "That uninspired men, in their wisdom and discretion, should supply the defect in the procedure of the holy and inspired apostles of Jesus! In order to this important object, they should *add to* the simple confession, that the penitent "believes with all the heart, that Jesus Christ is the Son of God;" *or* rather, *substitute for this,* something like the following: "Do you feel a desire to flee the wrath to come? Do you feel that you are a great sinner?—that you are the chief of sinners? Do you feel that you are entirely unworthy of the Divine favor? Do you feel that if you had received your just desert, you would have been sent to perdition before now? Do you realize the heinous, awful, and damning character of sin? Do you loath and hate sin, and feel a full determination to abandon it? Do you love God with all your heart? Do you desire nothing but God? Do you hunger and thirst after righteousness? Do you feel your continued need of God? Do you feel determined, by the help of God, to seek the Lord, find him. obey and serve him all your life? Do you feel that your heart is changed, and that the love of God has reached your soul? Can you tell us what the Lord has done for you?" These questions are all found in two or three places in books I have read, and have been put to applicants for church reception, in one form or other, thousands of times. We are free to grant, that a true penitent might answer the most of these affirmatively, very conscientiously. But what would be gained by it? The most consummate hypocrite could, and would respond to them affirmatively as readily as the most sincere. So *can,* and so *do* such, tell the most thrilling experiences, and frequently call forth the greatest applause, and the most hearty approbation of the inquisitors, make their way through them all, and gain admission into churches, more readily than they pass the great confession of faith in the Redeemer, and the first solemn test of submission to him.

To a man, however, who admits the wisdom and works of God, and who has become acquainted with the great and incomparable wisdom and superiority of the arrangements of the all-wise God, above all human contrivances, it is an instructive lesson to notice some of the silly and puny efforts of man to improve upon his works; and in no instance that we know of, is it more so than in the very matter we are considering. When the Almighty revealed his Son, at his baptism, it was in the short, but comprehensive oracle, "This is my son, the beloved, in whom I am well pleased," and in the holy mountain of transfiguration, in the presence of the eye-witnesses of his majesty, when he repeated this great oracle, he added the simple, very brief, though most comprehensive and world-wide command, "HEAR HIM." In this oracle, we have the Father's own revelation of his Son, Jesus Christ our Lord, to the world; and in this command we have the authority of the ineffable Jehovah to adhere to him. In this short oracle is concentrated the whole revelation from God to man. It is the base, the rock, the immovable pillar or foundation upon which the whole rests. He who receives it, if consistent, receives the whole, and is bound to the whole. God puts the whole—concentrates the whole in it, when presented to the children of men in the confession, as the great test of faith. He who makes the great confession, acknowledges his confidence in the great Teacher; which confidence he cannot have without confiding in all he sanctions. He sanctions the whole revelation of God, and whoever believes in him with all the heart, believes in, and receives all he sanctions. In this short oracle then, or confession, is contained more than is found in all the catechisms in the world. God is in it. The Lord Jesus Christ is in it. The Holy Spirit is in it. The whole Bible is in it. The power of God is in it. The only salvation for man is in it. The only hope of the world is in it. All Christianity is in it. The whole Christian institution is in it.

"But we want something binding." Look then, at the command accompanying this oracle, or confession, or immediately following it, if you desire something binding, or authoritative. We allude to the authoritative utterance, "Hear Him." God who made the worlds— God who rules among the armies of heaven— who hurled angels down to hell for disobedience —whose voice shook the earth; God who holds the destinies of all the nations in His hand, who "weighs the hills in a balance, and handles the isles as a very little thing," in connection with the revelation of His Son, to all the nations of the earth, with

OUR POSITION AS A RELIGIOUS COMMUNITY.

all the majesty of his authority, says, "HEAR HIM;" give Him audience; regard Him; bow to Him; follow Him; be guided by Him, honor and obey Him forever. How utterly futile and insignificant the attempt of puny and erring mortals to add anything to the great oracle, or confession, in which is concentrated the Whole Christian institution, and with which is connected the authoritative words of the ineffable Jehovah, *"Hear Him."* If a man receives the revelation God makes of his son, or rather, if he receives his son, from the revelation he has made of Him, and bows in submission to Him in accordance with the command to "Hear Him," confesses with the mouth before men what he believes in the heart, that "Jesus Christ is the Son of God," and submits to the Divine test of loyalty, in the requirement to be buried with his Lord in Baptism, while that great formula is uttered over him, "I Baptize you into the name of the Father, and of the Son, and of the Holy Spirit"— he gives the highest assurance in his power to give, that he is changed in heart, that he loves God and will serve Him, and is bound by the Strongest pledge, the highest and most solemn obligation that ever did or ever can bind a human being, to love and serve God. To add a thousand human ceremonies to this, would give no higher assurance of the preparation of the heart, the designs and resolutions being genuine, and bind the individual no more solemnly to be faithful to the end. The confession that God requires is the greatest confession that man can make, and the making of it is the best evidence a man can give that his heart is right. The first test of loyalty God has required of the penitent confessor, is the strongest, highest, and most solemn to which man can submit, and the submission to it, is the strongest evidence of loyalty the person can give. The authority that requires this submission is the highest and most binding that can rest upon a human being, and if it does not govern, control, and restrain the person, no authority can.

If such a confession as this—one that takes in God and man, Heaven and earth, the Saviour and His words—the whole revelation from God—the sublime confession that Jesus Christ is the Son of God, made in a proper manner, will not show that the heart is right; you need not add any such catechisms or experiences as are common in these times. They are all perfect nothingness compared with this great confession, which, like the spider's web, may catch flies and gnats, while the dangerous wasp and hornet will pass through with ease. The safe ground, and the only safe ground, is to follow the simple and infallible leadings of the Spirit of God. Appeal to the sacred record, and examine His Divine and unerring procedure the day He came down from heaven and guided the Apostles into all truth. What did he require of men on that day before receiving them into the church? Follow Him as He guided the Apostles in all the cases of conversion mentioned in the sacred record. What did He require in all these cases? The same must be required now, and no more. We must be led by the Spirit of God in converting sinners, and not by human creeds; we must be guided by the wisdom of God and not by the wisdom of man; we must have confidence in the ways of God and show no hankering after the ways of man. God will depart from all who turn away from the simplicity of the apostolic practice, under the immediate guidance of the Holy Spirit. No man is led by, or has the spirit, who has not full confidence in requiring precisely the same of all who enter the church required by the Apostles, as by the Holy Spirit, who guided them. He simply required the *confession with the mouth, of the faith of the heart.* B. F.

-----o-----

The tools of labor are a scepter of higher empire than monarch ever swayed that of dominion over the earth and elements; they are the weapons wherewith man achieves the purest and most benignant of all conquests, the subjugation of the powers of material nature to the service of humanity; and they are instruments also of the best of all worship, that which a fertilized earth sends up toward a gracious Heaven.

A Review of the Design of Baptism, by S.W. Lynd, D. D.
BY W. C. ROGERS.

The design of Baptism is a subject of no ordinary importance. It has occupied the attention of some of the best minds of the past, and is certainly not altogether ignored in the present day, by those who desire a scriptural and rational view of the great scheme of redemption.

Dr. S. W. Lynd, of Georgetown, Kentucky, has lately written a work on the design of Baptism, which, for various considerations, is worthy of notice. I shall analyze the positions assumed by the Dr. in the light of the word of God. If substantiated by that infallible and all-sufficient standard of truth, they must stand, if not, they must fall. It is affirmed by the Dr., that "In the New Testament salvation is contemplated in different connections. First, in connection with *faith alone.* "He that believeth on the Son hath everlasting life." Secondly, with faith and baptism — "He that believeth and is baptized shall be saved." Thirdly, with *regeneration,* "Saved by the receiving of the Holy Ghost." Fourthly, with persevering obedience, "He that endures to the end shall be saved." (p. 4 and 5.)

The above statements constitute the foundation of the Dr.'s argument concerning the design of Baptism. These statements furnish him the data for all the conclusions in his essay. I will endeavor to give them a close, and impartial examination. "Has not the infinite mind, (says the Dr.), established all these connections." The above question is one of great moment. In the decision of this question the Son of God must be heard, and his teaching must be regarded as authoritative and final. God the Father has bestowed upon him all power and all authority. If salvation is contemplated in the connections spoken of by the Dr., and if these connections have been established by the Divine mind, they have been established through the great Teacher, because he came to do his father's will. But the Son of God commanded twelve persons to go into all the world and preach the Gospel. They acted in accordance with His instructions. Therefore, such connections of salvation as are found established in the commission of Christ to His Apostles will be satisfactory. "Go, therefore, and teach all nations, baptizing them in the name of the Father and of the Son and of the Holy Spirit." Matthew xxviii: 19. "Go ye into all the world, and preach the gospel to every creature. He that believeth and is baptized shall be saved; he that believeth not, shall be damned." Mark, xvi: 15, 16.

"And He said unto them, Thus it is written, and thus it behooved Christ to suffer, and to rise from the dead the third day. And that repentance and remission of sins should be preached in His name among all nations, beginning at Jerusalem." Luke, xxiv: 46,47. Any view, antagonistic to the instructions of Jesus Christ to the Apostles, could not have been proclaimed by the Apostles for the salvation of a dying world. Truth is ever consistent. The Apostles could proclaim nothing more and nothing less, than was lodged in the commission by the Son of God. Alexander Carson has made some very judicious remarks relative to the extent of the commission, which I insert, not only for the benefit of Dr. Lynd, but for the benefit of others. "It is impossible that a command to baptize believers, can be extended to include any but believers. We need not say that this cannot be done by inference; I say it cannot be done by the most express command or explanation. No command, no explanation, can bring unbelievers into the commission, that enjoins the baptism of believers. Even if I found another command, enjoining the baptism of the infants of believers, I should not move an inch from my position. I should still say this is not included in the apostolic commission. This is another commission, and cannot interfere with the former.   *   *   *   * I would gainsay an angel from heaven, who should say that this commission may extend to the baptism of any but believers. His assertion would imply a contradiction. It would imply that the same persons may be, at the same time, both believers and unbelievers. Here then I stand entrenched, and I defy the ingenuity of earth and hell to drive me from my position."

A REVIEW OF THE DESIGN OF BAPTISM.

The above remarks are pungent and very forcible. They bear directly upon the question before us. The extent of the commission was the extent of the instructions received by the Apostles. Whatever therefore they taught, they received from the Messiah. On the Pentecostal day, when the convicted multitudes cried "Men and brethren, what shall we do?" and Peter remarked, "Repent and be baptized every one of you, in the name of Jesus Christ, for the remission of sins, and ye shall receive the gift of the Holy Spirit," such as gladly received the word were baptized, and so far as we are informed, only such. But what is the meaning of the expression "Gladly receiving the word?" "He came to his own and his own received him not; but as many as received him, to them gave he power to become the Sons of God, even to them that believe on His name." Hence it is perceived, that receiving the word of Peter is equivalent to believing on the name of Jesus. But when did the three thousand believe? before or after repenting? Before. Because it is impossible from the constitution of the human mind, to suppose that a person could be sorry because of past transgression, or change his course of conduct, unless he believed he was guilty of having violated the commands of the Most High. Moreover, "Without faith it is impossible to please God." "Whatsoever is not of faith is sin." Therefore, had the three thousand believed before repenting, their service would not have been acceptable to the living God, not being mingled with faith. Hence, faith is the mainspring of all service approved by God, in becoming and after having become a member of the church of Jesus Christ. By faith the views of the sinner are changed. Previous to believing, he had looked downward for happiness—had no object of an ennobling character before the mind; nothing by which the emotions or purposes of the heart were refined. Believing the grand object of thought, admiration and love, is Jesus Christ the Son of God, the noblest personage ever beheld, the wisest teacher ever clothed in mortality, the only potent Redeemer, the only Being in whom a fallen may confide for present and eternal salvation, assured that He will never leave nor forsake. By repentance or reformation, the conduct of the sinner is changed. He is grieved on account of his sins, and is determined henceforth and forever to live a life of holiness in the sight of God. He is determined to cease to do evil, by learning to do well. By baptism, the state of the sinner is changed. "For ye are all children of God by faith in Christ Jesus. For as many of you as have been baptized into Christ, have put on Christ." GAL. iii: 26, 7.

From the above remarks, it is manifest that the penitent believer, submitting to the ordinance of Christian baptism, is baptized into Christ. Old things have passed away, all things have become new. Faith, repentance, or baptism alone, is not sufficient to introduce the sinner into the kingdom of Messiah. Because faith, and repentance, and baptism, are all found in the great commission, and therefore must be preached. Faith and repentance, and baptism were all proclaimed by the Apostle Peter, in order to the same purpose. He commanded the multitudes on the day of Pentecost, to repent and be baptized, in order to the remission of sins, and when in the presence of Cornelius and his household, said, "To Him (Jesus Christ), gave all the prophets witness, that through his name, whosoever believeth in him shall receive remission of sins." Acts, x: 43. If Peter was consistent, he proclaimed the same things everywhere. Doubtless the multitudes on the Pentecostal day, gladly received the word of the Apostle, because it is so stated, and submitted to immersion for, or in order to the remission of their sins. God is a God of order, and not of confusion. Therefore I conclude that all the Apostles preached the same things, everywhere in order to the accomplishment of the same end—the remission of sins. The consequences of remission of sins, an induction into the Son of God—the gift of the Holy Spirit—the appropriation of all those great and precious promises vouchsafed in God's word.

The proper subject submitting to Christian baptism is saved—in other words, enjoys the forgiveness of sins—is pardoned. "Buried with Him in baptism, wherein also ye are risen with Him, through the faith of the operation of

God, who hath raised him from the dead. And you being dead in your sins, and the uncircumcision of your flesh, hath He quickened together with Him, having forgiven you all trespasses." Col. ii: 12,13.

Such a person is justified. "Therefore, being justified by faith, we have peace with God, through Our Lord Jesus Christ." Rom. v: 1. "Ye see then how that by works man is justified, and not by faith only." James, ii: 24. Not by faith only nor by works only, nor by faith and works only, but by the authority of Jesus Christ, through His blood and through the favor of God. Such a one is sanctified, reconciled, and adopted into the family of God. "To them that are sanctified by God the Father." Jude. "And all things are of God, who had reconciled us to Himself by Jesus Christ, and hath given unto us the word of reconciliation." 2 Cor. ii: 18.

"Beloved, now are we the Sons of God, and it doth not yet appear, what we shall be; but we know that when he shall appear, we shall be like him, for we shall see him as he is." 1 John, iii: 2. These things being true, the position assumed by Dr. Lynd is manifestly incorrect—namely, that salvation is contemplated in the word of God with faith alone. The justification of the sinner by faith alone is the chief corner-stone in his essay. I have proved that his foundation is wanting—is too narrow—is not the foundation given in the sacred scriptures. He can find no authority from the great commission, warranting any such conviction of salvation. He can find no authority for such conclusion from prophet, apostle, or evangelist. By what authority then has he assumed such a position? Surely not from the teachings of any inspired personage.

But hear the Doctor a little further on the subject of justification. "Before we proceed to the consideration of this question, it will be proper to offer some remarks upon justification. This is a point so clearly and fully established by the New Testament, that it serves as a focus to collect all the rays of truth scattered over the sacred pages. If we are right here, we shall not be likely to go astray from any part of the truth., * * * * *Personal meritorious* justification can be applicable only to persons really innocent of the charges brought against them. Men cannot be declared righteous before God, in this sense, because they are *really guilty.* Hence, the ungodly are said to be justified, not because they are personally meritorious, but because God regards the righteousness of Christ in their behalf as if it were their own, and thus places them in such a relation to himself as they would have been in if they were personally and perfectly righteous."

"This is the justification of a sinner, or his reception for the first time into the favor of God; in which, in reference to the law and its penalty, he is viewed as if he were righteous. There is also the justification of the believer, which does not embrace the idea of restoration to the favor of God. It is simply a justification of the believer by his obedience to the teachings of Jesus Christ. The former—that is, the justification of the ungodly—is the point so frequently argued by the apostle Paul in his letters to the Romans and Galatians. The latter—that is, the justification of the righteous—is the theme of the apostle James. Both illustrated by the example of Abraham, but at different periods of his history. Abraham believed God, and it was accounted unto him for righteousness at least forty years before he was justified by works—when he proceeded at the command of God, to offer up his son Isaac. The justification of the sinner is by faith alone, without any work of law." Pp. 9, 10, 11, 12.

From the foregoing language of the Doctor, the point before the mind of Paul in his letters to the Romans and Galatians, is the justification of the ungodly, and the point before the mind of James is the justification of the righteous. Having carefully examined the teachings of Paul and James, the inevitable conclusion arrived at, is that Paul is speaking of the justification of the sinner, without the deeds of the law of Moses, and that James is speaking of the justification of the sinner by faith and works, having no allusion whatever to the Mosaic institution. In the fifth versa of the fourth chapter of Romans, Paul says, "But to him that worketh not, but believeth on him that justifieth the ungodly, his faith is counted to him for righteousness." Paul must refer to works under the law; if he does not his declaration would conflict with the argument of James. James must have reference in his remarks to the justification of sinners, because of his universal proposition, "that faith without works is dead;" and because of his affirmation that Abraham was justified when he had offered up his son upon the altar. But Paul does not say that Abraham was justified by faith alone, but that he was justified without submitting to the requirements of the law. Nor does James say that Abraham was justified by works alone, but that faith wrought with his works, and by works was faith made perfect. But let us permit Paul to define his own position. " Where is boasting then ? It is excluded. By what law ? of works ? Nay, but by the law of faith. Therefore we conclude that a man is justified by faith without the deeds of the law. Is he the God of the Jews only ? Is he not also of the Gentiles? Yes, of the Gentiles also. Seeing it is one God which shall justify the circumcision by faith, and uncircumcision through faith. Do we then make void the law through faith? God forbid. Yea, we establish the law."—Rom. iii: 27, 31. From the above passages it is evident that Paul was arguing against the idea entertained by the Jews, of being circumcised and keeping the law of Moses, in order to Justification before God. Then he alludes to the case of Abraham. " What shall we then say, that Abraham our father, as pertaining to the flesh hath found? For if Abraham were justified by works, he hath whereof to glory, but not before God. For what saith the scripture ? Abraham believed God, and it was counted unto him for righteousness." Rom. iv: 1, 2, 3. Paul does not affirm in Romans or Galatians that Abraham *was* justified by faith, or by works. If so, a word from the great apostle to that effect would be a settlement of the matter forever. Paul states that Abraham believed God, and it was *counted* to him for righteousness. Not that he was formally declared righteous, or justified, but was merely so reckoned.

James, alluding to the case of Abraham, says, "Was not Abraham our father justified by works, when he had offered Isaac, his son, upon the altar. Seest thou how faith wrought with his works, and by works was faith made perfect? And the scripture was fulfilled which saith Abraham believed God, and it was imputed unto him for righteousness: and he was called the friend of God. Ye see then how that by works a man is justified, and *not by faith only.* * * * * For the body without the spirit is dead, so faith without works is dead also." James does not say that Abraham, after having virtually offered up his son, was any longer *counted* justified, but that he *was then justified.* He was not only justified, but his faith was *then* made perfect, and that scripture was *then* fulfilled, which saith " Abraham believed God, and it was counted to him for righteousness." He who contends that faith alone justifies, must do it, bearing in mind the pointed language of James: "Even so faith if it hath not works is dead, being alone." But I will submit a brief summary of the means of justification, which I find already furnished to hand, in "Campbell on Baptism."

"It is worthy of remark, that if faith were a work of the head, or of the heart, or of both, possessing inherent and essential merit, it would be as much a work to be recorded as any other exercise of the understanding or of the heart. Love is said to be 'the fulfilling of the whole law,' and covetousness is called idolatry. Were then justification to be founded on faith, hope, or love, as works of the understanding or affections, it could be no more of grace than any other blessing received on account of anything done by us, or wrought in us."

"Hence in the evangelical dispensation of justification, it is in some sense connected with seven causes. Paul affirms that a man is justified by *faith.* Rom. v: 1. Gal. ii: 16, iii, 2-4. In the second place he states that " we are justified freely by his grace." Rom. iii: 24, Titus iii: 7. In the third place, on another occasion, he teaches that " we are justified by Christ's blood." Rom. v: 9. Again, in the fourth place, he says that " we are justified by the name of the Lord Jesus, and by the Spirit of our God." 1 Cor. vi: 11. To the Galatians, in the fifth place, he declared that "we are justified by Christ." Gal. ii: 16. In the sixth place Isaiah says, "we are justified by knowledge." Isa. liii: 11. And James says, in the seventh place, "we are justified by works." Chap, ii: 21. Thus by divine authority, faith is connected as an effect of seven causes, viz., Faith, Grace, the Blood of Christ, the Name of the Lord, Knowledge, Christ, and Works. May it not then be asked, why so many select one of these only, as essential to justification? This is one of the evidences of the violence of sectarianism, (p. 2, 7, 9.)

III. I come now to speak more particularly of the design of baptism. The Dr. alludes to the design of baptism in three points of view. I shall only notice the third or last design mentioned by the Dr. The following language is clear and conclusive. It is worthy the attention of all persons interested in their present and eternal salvation. "It is very certain that the promise of salvation is to those who believe and are baptized. "He that believeth and is baptized, shall be saved." This is God's word. Let those who do not thus put on Christ, have all the trouble of meeting and explaining away the force of our Saviour's words. Let their consciences meet it freely. Let them have the burden of reconciling their course with the declaration of the great commission. Shall we become the apologists of those whose action, if it were to become general, would obliterate from the inspired records a law of Jesus Christ?" p. 37.

The above remarks are full of fearful meaning, and I would earnestly recommend them to the serious consideration of the reader, and would ask Dr. Lynd to look them full in the face. Dr., read them seven times, and pray God, that you may appreciate their full force. But I will submit another paragraph from the Dr's, work: "There is a connection which we have not yet noticed, but which is mentioned a few times in the New Testament. It is the connection which subsists between baptism and remission of sins." * * * The Evangelist Luke, employs the same words. "The baptism of repentance for the remission of sins." On the day of Pentecost, in answer to the query, what shall we do? the Apostle Peter replied "Repent and be baptized every one of you, in the name of Jesus Christ, for the remission of sins." Acts ii: 38. Ananias is represented as saying to Saul, "Arise and be baptized, and wash away thy sins." This last passage, however, merely teaches, that in the act of baptism we figuratively wash away our own sins. It has no reference to forgiveness on the part of God. But is the beginner's own act. It is equivalent to a passage already considered, in which baptism represents the fact, or the profession, that we die to sin, and rise to a life of holiness." (p. 43-4.) Baptism is not an act on the part of the subject. The subject submits to an act. "What is the meaning of the Dr's expression, that "'Arise, and be baptized, and wash away thy sins,' has no reference to forgiveness on the part of God, but is the believer's own act." If Paul's sins were washed away before baptism, why did Ananias give the command. His views were changed, and he doubtless determined to amend his ways. But it was necessary that he should change his state, before he became a Christian. Hence he affirms, in his letter to the Romans, that he was baptized into Christ. If he was baptized into Christ before his baptism, he was out of Christ, and could not believe for one moment that his sins were pardoned, or, that he could appropriate a single promise made by the Son of God, to the Christian. But I will close the case of Paul by quoting a criticism of the Dr. "The expressions for the remission of sins, would ordinarily indicate the same as the words, *in order to* the remission of sins. Professor Hacket, of Newton, who may be regarded as good authority, has translated, in the passage, Acts ii: 38, the preposition *eis* by the words 'in order to.' In this, he will probably be sustained by the most distinguished scholars." (p. 47.)

But mark the following words of the Dr.: "It would not be wrong to grant that some diversity of views upon this point, and some latitude of interpretation, may be admitted when the convictions are right in regard to fundamental doctrines." (p. 51.) The point before the mind of the Dr., in the above paragraph, is the remission of sins. And I would ask from what portion of the sacred scriptures has the Dr. gleaned authority for such a conclusion? I am unable to determine. It does not sound well in connection with the language of the great Teacher, "Not everyone that saith unto me, Lord, Lord, shall enter into the kingdom of Heaven, but he that doeth the will of my Father which is in heaven." Nor does it agree very well with Doctor Lynd's own declaration—"Shall we become the apologists of those whose action, if it were to become general, would obliterate from the inspired records a law of Jesus Christ." Such a position is unworthy a venerable teacher in Israel. Such a position is subversive of the truth as it is in Jesus. From such tampering with God's word, dangerous, ruinous consequences have resulted.

Who has guaranteed to Dr. Lynd the privilege to grant latitude in interpreting the Living Oracles? Who has authoritatively instructed him to approve diversity of views on the subject of Christianity? He can, of right, teach nothing more and nothing less than is found in the inspired Word.

IV. I will close my review of the Doctor's extraordinary work on the design of baptism by laying before the reader a few declarations, resulting from the careful examination of his premises. But hear the Doctor once more: "It would be an extravagant view to say, that because a man is not immersed, he is in an unpardoned state, and an alien from God. He may honestly mistake his duty in regard to the ordinance, or he may believe it to be fully met, in his case, when it is not; in either view, he may be, by a living faith, really and spiritually in Christ. God suspends our justification upon faith, that kind of faith which we have described, and he knows when that faith is really exercised. We recognize our justification as suspended on faith, and thus perceive its gratuitous nature, so that we give to God all the glory of our salvation; but we have no knowledge of the reality of our faith except by its fruits. These fruits are not mere feelings of joy, arising from the conviction that our sins are forgiven. How many have had these feelings, as they supposed, who never were subjects of Christ's spiritual kingdom really and spiritually. One of the first fruits of faith is the open, formal, voluntary confession of Christ as our Lord, in the ordinance of baptism. And here we perceive, as before exhibited, its connection with salvation. Everyone can readily understand, that if baptism is in no sense necessary to salvation, life obedience to Jesus Christ is in no sense necessary to salvation." (p. 55, 56.)

In another place, the Doctor in speaking of baptism, says — "This formal subjection to Christ is an inherent element of the faith that justifies; and hence, without it, no true faith exists in the soul which does not render it— life and opportunity being granted for the purpose." (p. 21, 22.)

A person may honestly mistake his duty in regard to baptism, and be in Christ by a living faith. The language of the Doctor, then, implies, that if a person understands his duty relative to baptism, he cannot be in Christ till baptized. This is a beautiful specimen of logical and theological legerdemain. One person may be in Christ by a living faith, if he be honest; another person cannot under certain circumstances, be in Christ unless he submit to baptism. This is a rickety foundation. I have always understood that there is only one foundation—only one way. Suppose an individual honestly determines to reject the word of God? Is there any hope for such a one? Dr. Lynd's Theology would save him, perhaps, on account of his honesty. This is the legitimate offspring of his reasoning.

Honesty of purpose in religion is no criterion of the correctness of the views entertained. A man may be sincere, and yet be wrong— may conscientiously violate the commands of the Most High. Saul, when sent to destroy the Amalekites, was commanded not to save a living creature. Yet when he returned from their destruction, bringing with him Agag the king, and sheep and oxen for sacrifices, saying he had done the things commanded him, Samuel told him, that having thus acted, he rejected the word of the Lord, and that the Lord had rejected him from being king over Israel. Doubtless, Saul was honest—doubtless, he was very sincere—although he had in some degree mistaken his duty. Yet God saw proper, notwithstanding his conscientiousness, to set him aside as king. Saul of Tarsus was honest before and after becoming a Christian ambassador. But his honesty was not at any time an exponent of the relation he sustained to God. The heathen honestly bows his head, and with great ingenuousness of purpose, submits to be crushed beneath the ponderous wheels of Juggernaut. But who will contend that he is right in his views, or in his submissive action. The Dr. may affirm a thousand times, that a man honestly mistaking the ordinance of baptism, may be in Christ by a living faith; but without proof, such an affirmation is worth nothing, and may do a vast deal of harm.

"But we have no knowledge of the reality of our faith, except by its fruits." "This formal subjection to Christ (in baptism) is an inherent element of the faith that justifies."

The letters of the English alphabet are the elements of the English language. Take away one letter, and the language is imperfect.— Oxygen and nitrogen are the elements of the atmosphere. Take, away an element, and the atmosphere is imperfect.

Light is made up of seven elements. Subtract from it one element, and we have defective light. So if baptism be an element, and an inherent element of the faith that justifies, then faith without baptism is impaired, just to the extent of the design of the element, baptism. But the Dr. says—God does not require baptism of a man in the dying hour— that he is saved by faith alone. But according to the Doctor, his faith must be imperfect; and if he is justified, or saved, it must be in imperfect faith. Moreover, how the Doctor can look his own language in the face —"We have no knowledge of the reality of our faith, except by its fruits"—and make such a declaration, is enigmatical. Secret things belong to the Lord—things revealed belong to us. If it were manifest from God's mind that faith alone would save, in the dying hour, it might be easily ascertained. But it cannot be found by the strictest searching. Hence, it must be destructive to the great system of Christianity.

I regard Dr. Lynd's work on the design of baptism as one of the singular productions of the present age. At one time it is in accordance with the truth, at another in direct opposition to it. I do not say that the Doctor is not honest in his views of the system of Christianity, but I am sure he is inconsistent. His work has gone abroad. It is now accomplishing its mission. It may be claimed as orthodox by almost anybody; but it must ever be regarded by Bible students as opposed to Bible-teaching. It should be metamorphosed, and I would recommend this work to the author.

The high argument of the Doctor is a sophism, as we have proved. He has searched the sacred Word through colored glasses; hence his views are egregiously distorted. May he finally arrive at the whole truth.— And in his own closing language—"May God make us all wise to know, and to do his will, * * * * * May the time soon arrive when the watchman upon the walls of Zion shall see eye to eye, and the glory of God shall fill the earth."

-----o-----

Tendencies of the Times.—No. II.
A DIALOGUE.

Present—an Episcopalian, a Presbyterian, a Lutheran, a Methodist, a Bible Union Baptist, an Anti-Bible-Union Baptist, a Disciple, a Quaker, a Universalist, and a Skeptic.

Bible Union Baptist.— Gentlemen; I am truly happy to meet you all again, and to be so comfortably situated as we are, in this neat room, in a circle around this table, with the Bible lying upon it. I have matters of the highest importance to us all to present for our mutual consideration; and, I trust I shall be able to enlist your approbation and energies in the most important religious move in the world. We live, as I think, in the most important period in the world's history, and the work that I allude to is the most important work, in this most important period. The Bible Union——

Presbyterian.— Gentlemen, the American Christian Union, for which I have an agency, has the priority in our investigations, as I introduced it before any other subject was mentioned. Beside, this Bible Union is sectarian, and it shall never have my influence and——

Anti-Bible-Union Baptist. — That is my mind;

the Bible Union is *sectarian,* and then, the "unholy *alliance!*" *I* cannot—I will not go into such a contrivance.

Universalist.—Gentlemen, I hope you will maintain your opposition to the Bible Union. I have been opposed to this sectarian scheme from the beginning; but since I heard a speech on revision lately, I am determined to go against it with every power. It is a dangerous and mischievous piece of work. The speaker that I have alluded to, said that in the common version we have the three Greek words, *hades, gehenna* and *tartarus,* all represented by the one English word *hell.* He insisted that *hades* should never be translated *hell;* nor should *tartarus* ever be translated *hell;* but *gehenna* should always be translated *hell.*

Skeptic.—I heard the same speech; and, if you recollect, he said, the Greek word *hualos,* should not be rendered *glass,* but *mirror,* as it did not mean the material the instrument was made of, but the name of the instrument, whether of polished metal or anything else.— If this word *glass,* is to be changed to *mirror,* then my objection to the antiquity of the Bible, founded upon this word *glass,* which is of modern invention, is taken from me.

Universalist.—He also said, that the words *demon,* and *Diabolos* are translated *devil,* in the common version, whereas no word but *Diabolos* should be so translated.

Anti-Bible-Union Baptist. — In the same speech, he contended that in the place of "John the Baptist," we should have "John the *immerser."* I am a Baptist, and my father was a Baptist, but now the name Baptist must be turned out of the Bible!

Methodist.—And then, that consecrated word, *baptize,* he said, must be changed into *immersion!* A pretty Bible we shall have of it, at this rate! I pronounce it a mischievous and ruinous work, and it shall never have my influence.

Presbyterian.—A large majority of us are against the Bible Union, and cannot engage in such a sectarian work. Let us now turn our attention to the American Christian Union. It is not sectarian. We all agree that it is right to convert Romanists, and we are not converting them to any sectarian party, but merely to *Christianity.* This we all can agree in; this we all acknowledge to be right.

Quaker.—Why does thee not convert them to the doctrine of thy own church? Would thee not prefer this to converting them merely to Christianity?

P.—Because, if we should attempt to convert then to our church, Methodists, Episcopalians, Lutherans, etc., would not co-operate with us; but as the matter now stands, they can have no objection to co-operating in this great and good work. Were it not that others would not co-operate with us, I confess I would rather unite them with our own church.

Q.—Thee does not convert them to Christianity alone, then, because thee prefers it to Presbyterianism, but merely because thee can induce others to co-operate with thee! But why does thee not convert other people to Christianity alone, as thee thinks all others can co-operate in it, and thus induce all good men to co-operate in converting all men to Christianity alone? Thee is fully aware that Friends do not engage in any of thy outward schemes for enlightening the world. We look to the inward light. But I mention this to show how inconsistent thou art, in trying to convert Romanists simply to Christianity and unite them on the Bible, but yet thou wilt not unite with them. Thou art manifestly inconsistent.

Christian.—I think, Mr. P., that you make a poor show in converting Romanists to Christianity alone, uniting them upon the Bible and calling them Christians, when you have never been converted to *Christianity* alone, united upon the Bible, or called Christians yourselves. Now, sir, there is no question but you are upon the true ground in converting Romanists to Christianity alone, uniting them upon the Bible and calling them Christians. This is utterly unsectarian. There is nothing in it not professedly believed by all who have any faith in the Bible. It is common ground; or, as you say, catholic.

P.—Yes, sir, it is; we do not introduce any of our partisan peculiarities into this great movement, and consequently all can cooperate in it.

C.—True enough; and why, if we can preach to Romanists, convert them to God, unite them upon the Bible, and call them Christians, without preaching any partisan peculiarities, or sectarianism, may we not convert all others to God, unite them upon the Bible, and call them Christians in the same way?

P.— Well, but what will become of our churches in that way? How would they be built up?

C.— No matter what becomes of your churches, provided you are all united in one body upon the Bible, as Christians, or disciples of Christ, and trying to convert not only Romanists, but all others simply to Christianity.

P.—That would be carrying the matter a little too far. I did not think of such a thing as giving up our churches and uniting with the converted Romanists. All I thought of was simply converting them to the Bible and uniting them upon it.

C.—I think that it is quite as important to convert you to the Bible as Romanists. Not only so, but I have no confidence in trying to convert Romanists or anybody else to a position that I am not willing to stand upon myself. I believe the position you have presented for the Romanists—converting them simply to Christianity—is precisely right. I cannot see any reason why any good man cannot engage in striving to convert them to Christ, without infusing into their minds any of the partisan peculiarities of these times—simply turning them to God, or making them Christians. But then I can see no good reason why we should not stand united and be one with them.

P.—We cannot see alike.

C.—We can see alike in regard to Roman Catholics. All we have to do is to see the same for ourselves that we do for your converts from Romanism, and do the same you require them to do.

P.—We are all agreed that it is a great and good work to convert Romanists and unite them upon the Bible.

C.—I know we are, but it is only because the union upon the Bible is self-evidently right; and if it is right for them, it is right for us also. I therefore propose to go with you into the work, heart and hand, if you will occupy the same position yourself that you present to Romanists.

M—Mr. C., I have the same objection to the A. C. Union that I have to the Bible Union. I cannot go into an alliance with you and your brethren in either of these institutions. You are not *orthodox*.

P.—In simply co-operating in the A. C. Union, we do not endorse the doctrine of those who engage with us in this work. Therefore I can co-operate in this work with men whom I could not fellowship.

C.—But if I understand you, the converts you make from Romanists you do fellowship. I cannot, then, see why you cannot fellowship all who will stand on the same foundation, and unite with them. Why cannot you and I unite with them upon the same foundation upon which you have united them?

P.—I cannot unite—I cannot unite—the fact is—

M.—The fact is, the A. C. Union that you appear so enlisted in, contains precisely the same principles that Mr. C. has been contending for all the time. He can unite with your converts from Romanism without any sacrifice. Converting men to the Bible, and nothing but the Bible, or to Christianity, and nothing but Christianity, uniting them upon the Bible and calling them Christians, as you have been telling us you do the Romanists, is the precise thing he has been contending for all the time.

A. B. U. B.—You are right, Bro. M., and the same is true of the Bible Union. I have heard Bro. Waller, Bro. Lind, and many others making Bible Union speeches, and the language, style of argument and entire principles are precisely the same as I find infused through all the writings of Mr. Campbell.

C.—Gentlemen, I perceive that sectarianism is so in the way that no great and important work can be done without being subject to the indignation of all the little parties around us. No man among you seems to think of anything beyond the interests of his little sectarian party. One man is opposed to revising the English scriptures, because he fears that a correct translation will give us *immerse* in the place of the Greek word *baptize,* and that his darling, *sprinkling,* will be discarded. Another man is trembling for fear the darling word *baptist,* which has strangely been manufactured into a religious designation, will be changed into *immersion,* and thus that the religious designation that he and his fathers before him have venerated so long, will be turned out of the Bible. Here stands another man trembling for fear that those Greek words *hades, gehenna* and *tartarus,* in the place of being represented by the one English word *hell,* as we now have them in the common version, will be represented by three distinct terms in English. In that case, he is aware that *hades* and *tartarus* will never be translated *hell,* and his principal source of quibbling, dodging and trying to make unenlightened men believe that hell is in this world, will be cut off. Even our skeptical friend is fearful that he will lose the word *glass,* used by Paine to disprove the antiquity of the scriptures.

B. U. B.—I perceive that it is not because the Bible Union is sectarian that these gentlemen are opposed to it, but because they fear it will remove causes of sectarianism, and rid the world of bones of contention.

M—You are certain to lose your darling name, *Baptist.*

B. U. B.—If correctly translating the Bible takes from me the name Baptist, let it go. It is not the name Baptist I am aiming at; I am for the truth, the whole truth, and nothing but the truth, both for myself and all mankind.

C.—Gentlemen, we shall never do any good either with or without a new translation, till we lift our minds above these little partisan interests. There is yet something in the world that may properly be called *the cause of God.* It is wider in its range, more extended in its designs, more expanded in its benevolence, and more efficient in its operations than mere party. I am aiming to fix my mind upon this, and the minds of all others as far as possible. All other causes are nothing.

B. F.

For the American Christian Review.
Baptistries.

BRO. EDITOR.—I have proposed for some time past to call the attention of the brotherhood, through the *Review,* to the above subject. It has long occurred to me that a baptistry should be an accompaniment of every meeting house, as much so as the pulpit or table. They can be built at a cost of from twenty-five to fifty dollars, according to quality, etc., filled and emptied conveniently. Personally, when everything is favorable, such as fair weather, fine water in reasonable distance, easy of access, and plenty of time, I prefer to baptize out of doors, in a running stream or the pure clear waters of the lake; but the above favorable circumstances we are not perhaps one-half the times this ordinance is administered by us, surrounded with, but are often compelled to dash through rain, snow, mud and bitter cold to a distance of three, four, or perhaps five miles in search of a suitable place to baptize; thus subjecting ourselves to a loss of time, great inconvenience, and often suffering on the part of the attendant company. Now would it not manifestly be better for the brethren, in the construction of their houses of worship, to have an eye single to this convenience also.

But there is another reason in favor of their use that experience has suggested to me. People are always anxious to witness an immersion, hence the crowds that assemble from the cities and villages on the banks of streams where it is to be administered, but they meet you *there* only. Want of time, broiling hot sun, or excessive cold, forbid many remarks. Oh, how I have often felt my spirit stir within me to speak when I have seen the banks of the river lined with Presbyterians, Methodists, and other perverters of this ordinance of Jesus Christ, but the howling wind or falling snow forbade. Now let the baptisms be administered in the houses, and this same crowd will come there, and come at the beginning of the services, and the speaker has a fair chance to unburden his mind fully and freely to them. I am sure I have seen something gained by this.

But in addition to the above, it makes the winter season, (that part of the year which has generally been considered most unfavorable by our brethren for the success of the gospel), the most favorable. But what do you say yourself, Bro. Editor ? Speak out.

M. B. HOPKINS.

-----o-----

Letter from Elder John Longley.

BRO. FRANKLIN. — I have thought for some time, that, with your permission, I would address a few lines to the brotherhood through the *Review*. I am getting very old, and cannot preach much more; but my *experience* of over *fifty years* in the ministry, has taught me some things that would be useful to the church.

There is one subject upon which I will present a few thoughts, to wit, the adoption of a plan for the support of the Gospel "finance." I have witnessed the adoption of various plans, have seen them changed and new ones adopted in their stead. I have been among the Baptists, and have seen their plans fail. I have been among the old Christians, or New Lights, and helped them to form and adopt plans for twenty years—a new one almost every year— and have seen them all fail. I have been in the current reformation for thirty years, and attended all the state meetings, a part of the time in Kentucky, a part of the time in Ohio, and the last twenty in Indiana. Almost every year something new is brought up in reference to raising money, but as yet nothing permanent has been agreed to, so we go on forming and changing methods to raise money until preachers have to quit the field and go to some worldly employment to procure a Support for themselves and their families. It is evident that, so far, our plans have not been sufficient to meet the exigencies of the times, for many of the *sects* seem to raise means to support their preachers well, and send their missionaries abroad, besides having their old worn-out preachers provided for, while ours are not as they should be; nor do their people complain of being taxed, while ours, or many of them, do.

At the last Indiana state meeting, Bro. GEO. CAMPBELL was appointed general agent to travel the state and solicit funds for missionary purposes, and for the support of infirm and superannuated preachers, he to take fifty per cent, of the money raised, for his trouble. Suppose he collects one thousand dollars, one- half of which goes to pay the agent, which would leave five hundred, half ($250) of which would go to the missionary fund, and the other two hundred and fifty to be divided between the two named brethren, (O'Kane and myself) which would be one hundred and twenty-five dollars apiece—a very small sum to support a family upon. And this plan of collecting money must be kept up all the time, which will require much labor and expense; so it is evident to all, that this plan will not do. I will suggest a plan which I think would be superior to all others. We want a standing fund, the principal of which can never be touched, but let the proceeds of it, either at interest or stock in trade, go for missionary purposes, and the support of superannuated preachers, who are in need; and let it be called the missionary fund. This is all very good you say, but then comes the question, " How is this fund to be raised ?" I answer, it can be easily done. How many members have we in Indiana? Say 60,000 at least. Say 10,000 are not able to pay anything. Then say fifty thousand members pay 25 cents each a year to the missionary fund, which will produce $12,500 per year at 25 cents each for 50,000 members. Let the elders collect the 25 cents from each member each year, and take it to the state meeting. This would be a good run to commence with, and let it run on for five years, and the sum, with the simple interest, would amount to $66,250, and the church need never want money for any purpose, and the people would not feel it.

I have always been an unflinching advocate of the all-sufficiency of the word of God, as the only rule of faith and practice, as respects our duty to God and each other as individuals, in all our worship, in all our faith, and in all our devotions, both in the church and in our families; but it does sometimes seem to me that we are deficient in our church government, and need some kind of by-laws for local purposes of expediency. Yet it appears that there are many things in which the church as a body is left to use discretion; the *how* and *when* to do such things are not taught in the Scriptures, but are commanded, and, therefore, *positive duties,* and to be attended to. For instance, the Lord's Supper is a positive institution for every first day of the week, yet the *hour* is not given when we shall attend to it, whether in the morning before preaching, or immediately after preaching, or in the afternoon at a special meeting for that purpose, or at night. This is a question of expediency or convenience, to be decided upon by the church. It is agreed to by all lovers of God and Bible Christianity, that we should have prayer meetings, but the *when* and *where* is left to the members of the church to decide. I could mention a number of other things in the same category, in all of which the church has a right to make her own by-laws, to regulate discipline without violating the words of eternal life—the law of God.

JOHN LONGLEY.

-----o-----

MILLERSBURG, Aug. 27, '56.

DEAR BRO. B. FRANKLIN,—We are now making a last, vigorous effort to endow "The Orphan Girl's School at Midway," and, as one of its trustees and patrons, I assume the responsibility of urging every Christian brother or sister, who desires to have their name enrolled in so benevolent an enterprise, to send on their subscriptions, or contributions, as soon as possible, lest they may not share the glorious results. We hope to have many subscriptions, varying from $25 to $100, payable at a short date. In addition to this, I have another proposition to make, which would complete the Institution:—

"That we endow a Professorship of Sacred History, embracing mental and moral philosophy, and the art of teaching." To accomplish this object, it is not designed to make a general appeal to the brotherhood. I make my appeal to *the wealthy* in our ranks, and I hope some four or five will respond to it most promptly, in a noble, Christian spirit. It will be to them a monument pointing to the heavens, and worthy to be looked at. We are here laboring in the good cause, and the prospects are flattering.

P. S.—Brother J. R. Hulett is present, and says, "I endorse that."

Bro. J. J. Rogers says also, "I go for that, and I have obtained a subscription of $1,000 already on the general endowment." Two important immersions.

We have had a most delightful meeting, and we hope great good has been accomplished. The brethren have acted a most noble part. May the Lord bless them.

This moment a gentleman of the world called in, and subscribed $100 for the Orphan School. This is worthy of imitation.

The *Christian Age* and the *Harbinger* will please copy.

J. T. JOHNSON.

-----o-----

DEAR BRO. FRANKLIN:—Through the faithfulness of the Saints, some *twenty* have been added to the Christian congregations in this region since I last wrote you. The cause of our blessed Master is for the most part on the advance in this section of country, but it is a source of grief that the great political excitement now agitating this republic, is doing its destructive work in some congregations—alienating from each other the affections of brethren, producing a sad religious stupor and apathy among the members of Christ's body, blighting the fairest prospects of an abundant harvest, and rendering the momentous interests of the Kingdom of Heaven subordinate and even subservient to the civil laws and institutions of our country. Some of those who were once successful teachers in Israel, have ceased to preach "Jesus, and him crucified," and are devoting all their pulpit efforts to the investigation of political issues and untaught questions, which gender strife among the people of God. Under the labors of such teachers, sinners are hardened, saints are without the rich consolations of the gospel of Christ, and entire churches are desolated. Brethren, "these things ought not so to be." O, may all the saints be led to see and to feel their obligations to the ever blessed and only Potentate, the King of kings, and Lord of lords; and in the strength of Israel's God may they engage in the good fight of faith, lay hold on eternal life, and never yield the contest till the victory is won, and an unfading diadem of royalty secured in the blessed mansions of eternal glory.　　WM. M. ROE.

Buchanan, Sept. 6th, 1856.

Debate on Universalism.

OUR Universalian friends have been in much trouble in obtaining an opportunity for their new champion, Mr. Bosserman of Dayton, Ohio, to show his powers. According to agreement among the parties, and being selected by the Disciples, we met this gentleman on Monday, the twenty-first of September, in Lexington, Preble county, Ohio, and, we trust, satisfied his curiosity in a discussion of three days, in the presence of a large and respectable audience. If we did not satisfy that community, that Universalism has no more a pardon in it than a condemnation, no more a salvation than a destruction, no more a heaven than a hell, we missed our estimation of their decision. Mr. Bosserman, when pressed to tell what men are saved from, said, "from sin in this world." We then insisted that they had no salvation, for man, as they have it, is punished as much as he deserves for his sins in this world. He then said man is saved from the fear of punishment in this life. When pressed upon this preposterous notion, he said that "we are saved in this life, from a fabled hell." We pressed him then to know if they had no salvation after this life. He resorted to the old theory then, of salvation in the resurrection, thus leaving all the sinners who died four or five thousand years ago, unsaved all this time, but we attempt not even an outline of his meanderings in his system of unbelief.

By the request of the friends, we shall try and furnish our opening speech, of an hour's length, on endless punishment, in our next number of the Review.　　B. F.

More Darkness.

SOME person has sent us a column and a half from some newspaper, containing strictures of E. J. H. White, on a sermon delivered by a Methodist preacher. We have not time nor space now for discussing the points introduced in this letter, and simply mention it to let the friend who sent it know that it has come to hand. A man who has got the conceit into his mind that he is a minister of Christ, and does not know that the Lord has a kingdom on earth, where Messiah taught his disciple to pray that his will might be done as it is in Heaven, and does not know the difference between the terms *Bible* and *Gospel,* is very near the embodiment of the darkness of Mystery Babylon. If there is a clearly revealed thing in the Bible, it is that the gospel was first embodied in a *promise.* Hence, Paul says, "The Scripture foreseeing that God would justify the heathen through faith, preached the gospel before unto Abraham, saying, "In thee, and in thy seed shall all nations be blessed." Gal. iii: 8. The ancients received the gospel in this promise, and rejoiced in hope of good things to come. But in the fullness of time the promise was fulfilled. Christ came and died for our sins, and rose for our justification. He is presented to us in fact—the fact that he is the Christ, the Son of God. In receiving this fact, we receive the Savior, the Father who sent him, the Holy Spirit, and the whole institution of which he is the head, through which we shall be saved if we are true to him to the end.

Coming Anniversaries.

THE time of the year when the anniversaries of the Bible, Missionary, and Publication Societies, in this city, are held, is rapidly approaching. The anniversaries will commence on Tuesday, October 21st, and continue several days. It is of the highest importance that we have as extended a representation, both in person and by letter, at that time, as possible. These societies have existed long enough to show that they are not satisfactory to the brethren; and institutions, through which the brotherhood are expected to act, must meet the wishes of the brethren or be inefficient. The brethren here have from the beginning made every reasonable effort to have a full and fair representation from abroad, that everything might be done satisfactorily. Still, such a representation has never been had, and no general co-operation has ever been obtained, nor unanimity of feeling produced in reference to these societies.

The State Meeting of Ohio, passed a resolution recommending the dissolution of the Bible Society, and the transfer of whatever funds it may have to the Bible Union, if our memory is not at fault. Many brethren are now of opinion that we should have but the one society—the Missionary. Such seems to be the general feeling here, so far as we have been able to gather it. At all events it is obvious that some important move will be made, and it would truly be a happy thing if the brethren would speak for themselves. Bro. A. Campbell has proposed to be with us. Many other distinguished brethren, we understand, are making their arrangements to attend. We have no right to dictate what shall be done, and put in but the one plea, viz: the plea for as large a representation, both by messenger and letter as possible. Let us act in some way, and not let the matter go by default. Many have been dissatisfied with the Publication Society, and no doubt are still; come up then, and speak out, and let us set it aside in a formal manner, and not complain and do nothing. We are not of that class that will do nothing, unless we can have it *our* way. In all questions of expediency and propriety, we are going with the brethren, *if they will go at all*. If there be any who will go no way, the nearer they are alone, and the fewer in number, the better.

If it is the mind of the brotherhood to transfer the Bible Society to the Bible Union, let us do it; or if it is the better way to consolidate all into one society—the Missionary—thus making one effective board, to operate in foreign fields, let us go for it, go together, and go with all our strength. Or if there be any who would disband the whole, and abandon all idea of any arrangement of the kind, let them come up, or write up, declaring their mind, in reference to the course they intend to pursue. At all events, come up to this meeting, and let us have a great gathering—a great gathering of the Disciples—meet old acquaintances, see old brethren that we never have seen, greet each other, and bid all hold on their way to the end. Come brethren, the men of this world are spending money and time in their causes; have we not as much zeal and love for our cause as they have for theirs?

Come on, brethren, we will cheerfully throw open our houses, to their utmost capacities, and do our utmost to make you happy, while with us; and our hearts shall be open too, that we may greet you with a Christian reception. Come up; let us meet face to face. We are driving at the same object, and we must understand each other, or we shall never act in harmony. No one, who has never experienced it. can appreciate the strength imparted on such an occasion, the real benefit derived, and the happiness enjoyed. We have a noble band of preaching brethren, capable of meeting, deliberating, harmonizing, and pushing forward the great work to which we are called. Shall we, then, have one more great meeting? Come brethren, come, and warm our hearts and encourage us with your presence, your preaching, exhortations, prayers, singing, and Christian counsel. B. F.

-----o-----

Isaac Watts.

BELOVED BRO. FRANKLIN:—Once more I am enjoying the comforts of home—once more relieved from the arduous duties of my profession, with a mind at liberty to gratify its taste in any lawful and expedient measure. The library is a source of much enjoyment on occasions like these. O! how I love to cultivate an intercourse with old and valued monitors, and refresh my memory with their sage and beautiful reflections!

"Joy is communicative." No higher pleasure can possess the mind, than that enjoyed in communicating to other minds the materials which have been the basis of profitable reflection to itself. The biography of good men furnishes many a basis for the superstructure of that thought, which leads to reason; on which reason we build resolve, "that column of true majesty in man." Isaac Watts was a noble spirit, and Samuel Johnson a noble biographer. Scanning a volume of his biographies of the poets, these observations on the character of Watts, struck me as being worthy of being handed round among many readers. I submit them therefore to the ordeal of your judgment.

"Isaac Watts was one of the first authors that taught the dissenter to court attention by the graces of language. Whatever they had among them before, whether of learning or acuteness, was commonly obscured and blunted by coarseness and inelegance of style. He showed them, that zeal and purity might be. expressed and enforced by polished diction.

"He continued to the end of his life the teacher of a congregation, and no reader of his works can doubt his fidelity or diligence. In the pulpit, though his low stature, which very little exceeded five feet, graced him with no advantages of appearance, yet the gravity and propriety of his utterance made his discourses very efficacious. I once mentioned the reputation which Mr. Foster had gained by his proper delivery, to my friend Dr. Hawkesworth, who told me, that in the art of pronunciation he was far inferior to Dr. Watts.

"Such was his flow of thoughts, and such his promptitude of language, that in the latter part of his life he did not recompose his cursory sermons; but having adjusted the heads and sketched out some particulars, trusted for success to his extemporary powers.

"He did not endeavor to assist his eloquence by any gesticulations; for, as no corporeal actions have any correspondence with theological truth, he did not see how they could enforce it. At the conclusion of weighty sentences he gave time, by a short pause, for the proper impression.

"To stated and public instruction he added familiar visits, and personal application, and was careful to improve the opportunities which conversation offered of diffusing and increasing the influence of religion.

"By his natural temper he was quick of resentment; but, by his established and habitual practice, he was gentle, modest, and inoffensive. His tenderness appeared in his attention to children, and to the poor. To the poor, while he lived in the family of his friend, he allowed the third part of his annual revenue, though the whole was not a hundred a year; and for children he condescended to lay aside the scholar, the philosopher, and the wit, to write little poems of devotion, and systems of instruction adapted to their wants and capacities, from the dawn of reason through its gradations of advance in the morning of life. Every man, acquainted with the common principles of human action, will look with veneration on the writer who is at one time combating Locke, and at another making a catechism for children in their fourth year. A voluntary descent from the dignity of science is perhaps the hardest lesson that humility can teach.

"As his mind was capacious, his curiosity excursive, and his industry continual, his writings are very numerous, and his subjects various. With his theological works I am only enough acquainted to admire his meekness of opposition, and his mildness of censure. It was not only in his book, but in his mind that *orthodoxy* was *united* with *charity.*

"Of his philosophical pieces, his Logic has been received into the Universities, and therefore wants no private recommendation. If he owes part of it to Le Clerc, it must be considered that no man who undertakes merely to methodise or illustrate a system, pretends to be its author.

"Few books have been perused by me with greater pleasure than his *Improvement of the Mind,* of which the radical principles may indeed be in Locke's *Conduct of the Understanding,* but they are so expanded and ramified by Watts, as to confer upon him the merit of a work in the highest degree useful and pleasing. Whoever has the care of instructing others, may be charged with deficiency in his duty if this book is not recommended.

"I have mentioned his Treatises of Theology as distinct from his other productions; but the truth is, that whatever he took in hand was, by his incessant solicitude for souls, converted to Theology. As piety predominated in his mind, it is diffused over his works: — under his direction it may be truly said, Philosophy is subservient to evangelical instruction; it is difficult to read a page without learning, or at least wishing to be better. The attention is caught by indirect instruction, and he that sat down only to reason is on a sudden compelled to pray.

"He continued many years to study and to preach, and to do good by his instruction and example; till at last the infirmities of age disabled him from the more laborious part of his ministerial functions, and being no longer capable of public duty, he offered to remit the salary appendant to it; but his congregation would not accept the resignation.

"By degrees his weakness increased, and at last confined him to his chamber and his bed; where he was worn gradually away without pain, till he expired, November 25th, 1748, in the seventy-fifth year of his age.

"Few men have left behind such purity of character or such monuments of laboring piety. He has provided instruction for all ages, from those who are lisping their first lessons, to the enlightened readers of Malbranche and Locke; he has left neither corporeal nor spiritual nature unexamined; he has taught the art of reasoning, and the science of the stars.

"His character, therefore, must be formed from the multiplicity and diversity of his attainments, rather than from any single performance; for it would not be safe to claim for him the highest rank in any single denomination of literary dignity; yet perhaps there was nothing in which he would not have excelled, if he had not divided his powers to different pursuits.

"As a poet, had he been only a poet he would probably have stood high among the authors with whom he is now associated. For his judgment was exact, and he noted beauties and faults with very nice discernment; his imagination was vigorous and active, and the stores of knowledge were large by which his fancy was to be supplied. His ear was well tuned, and his diction was elegant and copious. His lines are Commonly smooth and easy, and his thoughts always religiously pure; but who is there that, to so much piety and innocence, does not wish for a greater sprightliness and vigor? He is at least one of the few poets with whom youth and ignorance may be safely placed; and happy will be that reader whose mind is disposed by his verses or his prose, to imitate him, to copy his benevolence to man, and his reverence to God."

In the hope, that these observations may have a benign influence on many minds, I abide, affectionately,

Yours in the Lord,

CHAS. D. HURLBUTT.

Hiram, Portage county, O., July 19, 1856.

-----o-----

Letter from G. W. Elley.

Lexington, August 27, 1856.

BRO. FRANKLIN—I have just returned from a series of meetings at Fisherville, in Jefferson, and Antioch and Jeptha, in Shelby counties. At the latter places, brethren W. Sharp and S. King co-operated; and brother Willis, the resident minister, at the first — all of whom did good service.

Large audiences heard the word, day after day. The churches were very faithfully taught and exhorted, sinners warned, and sectarianism fully exposed. At all those meetings, we had a large hearing from our Baptist, Methodist, and Presbyterian friends, who all seemed interested, although their peculiarities were severely though kindly handled. Thirty-nine additions were made at those points. Large additions have been made to some of the churches, recently, and the people seems at least willing to hear.

So far as I have noticed your "Review," it has been ably and faithfully conducted, and is becoming more and more acceptable to the brotherhood. The times demand men of unusual nerve and firmness, and I am glad to find that you have enough to "stand square upon the Bible." To do this, brother Franklin, requires more reverence and fear of God than can be claimed by the mere partisan. So long as you hold on to your present position, you have nothing to fear. Let us have no North or South, but Union, among God's children and every lover of civil liberty.

Wishing grace and peace, I am yours in bond,

G. W. ELLEY.

-----o-----

A year is much in human life, particularly to the very young, and very old.

Co-Operation.

BROTHER FRANKLIN: — *Dear Sir,* — "No one having drank of old wine, straightway desireth new; for he saith the old is better:" so of the *things,* and the *ancient order* of things in the church of God—the *old* is better. At the "Big Meeting," held in Connersville, in June, 1842, an effort was made, you will remember, to do something, and more than had hitherto been done, for evangelization; and it was proposed to do it by a restoration of the *things* and the *order* adopted by the apostles. A large edition of the Minutes of that meeting were published, but they were not generally circulated; and but few, comparatively, it is believed, have ever seen them. The Address, written by Elder R. T. BROWN, and annexed to said Minutes, I think is worthy of re-publication; if you think so too, the copy herewith is at your service. F. W. E.

-----o-----

ADDRESS

To the Congregations, associated on the Foundation of the Apostles and Prophets, and on Jesus Christ the Chief Corner Stone, throughout the State of Indiana:

BRETHREN: —Within the last few years, much has been done in our bounds for the glory of God and the advancement of his cause. But has all been done that might have been accomplished? Have we consecrated all the talent in our ranks to the service of the Lord, and kept it constantly employed? If we have not (and that we have not is too apparent), what is the cause of our delinquency? These are momentous questions, and deserve a serious consideration from all, in every place, who love our Lord Jesus Christ. Permit us, therefore, to express ourselves on this subject freely.

If we have not brought to bear on the conversion of our contemporaries all the powers with which Heaven has gifted us, the fault must lie, either with those possessing the talents requisite for the work, or with the brethren generally. Now that the first may be sometimes the case, we will not pretend to deny. There may, perhaps, be found a few instances, of men who wear the name of our Lord, and have the requisite qualifications to render them useful laborers in the field before us, and yet prefer the forum, the bar, or some other theater to exhibit their talents, that will promise them the fading wreath of earthly renown I We say there may be men among us thus gifted, and thus deluded; but we are constrained to believe that the occurrence of such cases is rare.

If then the church have the qualified laborers, and they are willing to devote themselves to the work, Why stand they all the day idle? The answer is, "No man hath employed us." So long as men tabernacle in the flesh, and sustain their relations to society, so long they must be governed by the laws of the one, and the circumstances of the other. The day of miraculous gifts has passed. We cannot expect that our public laborers can command the stones to be made bread; or that the ravens will feed them, like Elijah of old. If this were the case, the greater part of the brotherhood would be cut off from the glory of any active participation in the conversion of the world. But none are to be drones in the Heavenly family. It is the duty of every Christian to labor in his appropriate sphere; and if we cannot preach ourselves, we can aid in supplying the necessities of them who do, and so be joint laborers in the good cause. This is not only the rational view of this subject, but it is the statute of Heaven, signed, sealed, and delivered, by the Spirit of inspiration. When Jesus, the Lord, in the day of his sojourning with man, sent his apostles to preach the approaching reign of Heaven, he forbade them providing themselves with anything to defray the expenses of the journey: alleging as a reason, that "the laborer was worthy of his meat;" — Math, x: 10 — and Paul is even more explicit, when he says, "Even so has the Lord ordained that they who preach the gospel, shall live of the gospel."—1 Cor. ix: 14. It is therefore to be regarded, by all who respect the authority of God, as no longer a debatable question, whether those who devote themselves to the proclamation of the gospel are to be sustained. But who is to sustain them? Paul says, "If we have sown to you spiritual things, is it a great thing if we shall reap your carnal things?" — 1 Cor. ix: 11. By the decision of inspiration, then, we conclude, that they who receive spiritual blessings are under obligation to send them to others. Or in other words, on the church devolves the duty of speaking the word of life to the world. This truth in the abstract, we apprehend, will be called in question by few who venerate the authority of our King, or love his cause. But to admit the truth of anything abstractly, is a very different matter from acting on it practically. The want of energetic action on this subject may in some degree depend on a mistaken view of the matter.

The brethren have witnessed the operation of the hireling system among the sects in producing a pampered clergy, whose only business seems to be to domineer over the laity. Shocked with the scene they turn from it in disgust, and determine not to do right, because others have done wrong. But perhaps in a majority of instances, this is not the ground of delinquency. It is the direct offspring of a kind of skepticism; we call it skepticism because we have no better name for it. It is a want of confidence in God—a want of reliance on his promise! Did the brethren really believe that "the earth is the Lord's, and the fullness thereof"—did they, when they turn their eyes on their flocks and their herds, their barns and their storehouses, overflowing with the munificence of heaven—when God has poured out the horn of plenty on the land—did they REALLY believe that these were but loans from the Great Proprietor of the Universe, to test their loyalty to God, and their love of his cause—would they stand idle and unconcerned spectators of the languishing condition of that cause? Did they really believe in the promise of the Lord with as much confidence as they do in the immutability of the laws of nature, would they withhold the aid it may be in their power to give toward the triumph of the truth? God has said, "He which soweth bountifully shall also reap bountifully."—2 Cor. ix: 16. Or, "Whatsoever a man soweth that shall he reap—He that soweth to the flesh, shall of the flesh reap corruption; he that soweth to the spirit, shall of the spirit reap life everlasting."—Gal.vi: 7, 8. Brethren, if the Heavenly Father has fertilized the earth by the genial influence of his seasons, if he has blessed us in our basket and our store, in our flocks and in our herds, in our various avocations, cannot we contribute a trifle of the fruits of his superabounding goodness, to feed a starving world with the bread of life?

Men are sometimes ambitious to make such a use of their money as that their memories may live ages after they slumber in the tomb.— what a field for the laudable display of this ambition is here! Send abroad God's saving power by the hand of faithful men, and every convert that is made is a monument to your fidelity, that shall live when the very names of brass and marble are forgotten forever. Away, then, with this "covetousness which is idolatry." The condition of a priest-ridden and deluded world calls aloud upon us for action. Our duty to God, in view of the bounties of his Providence and the richness of his favor, imperiously demand prompt and energetic action in this matter.

But in what MANNER shall we raise the necessary funds to keep our laborers in the field?

This is a question that has been much agitated. Is there, or is there not, any law upon this subject in the New Testament? If there be, it becomes us to ascertain it and be governed by it. If there be not, we are at liberty to adopt any other plan or course of procedure which, as congregations of Jesus Christ, made free by the Son, we shall judge most expedient and proper. When there is no law there is no transgression, and uniformity is enjoined only, where there has been given to govern us an expression of the Divine will. The evangelist Luke says of the first Christian congregation, established at Jerusalem on the day of Pentecost, that "they continued steadfast in the apostles' doctrine, in the fellowship, in the breaking of bread, and in the prayers." Acts ii: 42. If this be a record of the established public worship of this congregation; and if, as is understood by some of our brethren, the fellowship here means a weekly contribution for religious purposes, the question, "How shall funds be raised?" is answered.

From all the data which we have before us, the present number of the Disciples associated on the foundation of the Apostles and Prophets, in the State of Indiana, is not less than fifteen thousand. Twenty-five cents only from each member, would make a fund of THREE THOUSAND SEVEN HUNDRED AND FIFTY DOLLARS!—enough to sustain the families and keep continually in the field, some eight or nine evangelists. Where, now, is the brother or sister so poor as not to be able, besides doing something for the preachers and teachers at home, to contribute this trifle annually to send the gospel to the destitute abroad? No one is so poor. We want this amount; we ask this amount; we believe that it can be raised, and that it is our duty, and should be our privilege, to raise this much this year for this purpose. It can be raised by the FELLOWSHIP; and if there be any other method of raising funds for religious purposes laid down in the New Testament, it can be raised by that other method. Let every congregation decide for itself this question. Let them decree in their hearts to raise this amount, and let them do it.

Brethren, there is an immense field of labor before us. Let us not spend our time in talking about our duty; let us act. Let us call into the field all the talent in the State, and sustain it there. We are engaged in the best of causes; let us not become weary in well doing, for we shall reap the harvest if we faint not. The signs are ominous. The powers of corruption are marshaling for one mighty effort, to stay the onward progress of truth.

Let us do battle valiantly in the cause of the Lord, and victory shall perch on the standard of truth. R. T. BROWN, Ch'n.

E. W. EMMONS, Sec'y.

-----o-----

ALFONT, IND., Aug. 7, 1856.

BRO. FRANKLIN—As we have seen nothing in the *Review* concerning the congregation here, we have concluded to let you and the brethren know that we have a congregation of Disciples numbering about seventy-five members, and are doing tolerably well at present. Emanuel Amick and Benjamin Jones are the Elders. Wm. Bannon and Joseph Wynn are the Deacons. We have a house of worship one mile southeast of Alfont, and we would be glad to have you and other preaching brethren, when passing, to call and see us. Bro. Eld. John Brown and Bro. David Franklin had a protracted meeting here; commenced Aug. 1st, and twenty-three made the good confession, and one from the Baptists. To the Lord be all the praise.

EMANUEL AMICK.

-----o-----

Just Published.

The Discussion on *Revision of the Holy Oracles,* and upon the Objects, Aims, Motives, the Constitution, Organization, Facilities, and Capacities of the American Bible Union for Revision. By two "Laymen" of the Revision Association, and five Clergymen; the latter specially appointed by a Congress of Ministers of the city of Louisville.

Price, postage paid, bound in paper, $0 25.
Do. do. in muslin, 0 50.
Do. do. extra in muslin, 0 60.
Address, JAMES EDMUNDS, Cor. Sec.,
Corner Fourth and Walnut Sts., Louisville, Ky.

We take pleasure in calling attention to the above. We hope it may have an extensive circulation, as it will throw much light on the Revision enterprise. If the five clergymen who conducted the opposition have not offered something strong here, against Revision, we know not where anything of the kind will be found. Read it and hand it round. B. F.

The New Version.
REVELATION.

I. THE Revelation of Jesus Christ, which God gave unto him, to show unto his servants things which must come to pass shortly, and sending he signified by his angel unto his servant John, who testified the word of God and the testimony of Jesus Christ, whatsoever things he saw: blessed *is* he that readeth, and they that hear, the words of the prophecy, and keep the things therein written; for the time *is* near.

John to the seven churches which are in Asia: Grace unto you, and peace, from him who is, and who was, and who cometh; and from the seven Spirits that are before his throne; and from Jesus Christ, the faithful Witness, the First-born of the dead, and the Prince of the kings of the earth. Unto him who loveth us, and washed us from our sins in his blood, and he made us a kingdom, priests unto his God and Father, unto him the glory and the power forever and ever. Amen.

Behold, he cometh with the clouds, and every eye shall see him, and they who pierced him; and all the tribes of the earth shall wail because of him. Yea, amen.

I am the Alpha and the Omega, saith the Lord God, who is, and who was, and who cometh, the Almighty.

I, John, your brother, and fellow-partaker in the tribulation, and kingdom, and patience of Jesus Christ, was in the isle that is called Patmos, for the word of God, and for the testimony of Jesus Christ. I was in the Spirit on the Lord's day; and I heard behind me a loud voice as of a trumpet, saying: What thou seest, write in a book, and send unto the seven churches; unto Ephesus, and unto Smyrna, and unto Pergamos, and unto Thyatira, and unto Sardis, and unto Philadelphia, and unto Laodicea.

And I turned to see the voice that was speaking with me; and having turned, I saw seven golden lamp-stands, and in the midst of the seven lamp-stands one like a son of man, clothed with a garment down to the feet, and girt around at the breasts with a golden girdle; but his head and hair *were* white as white wool, as snow; and his eyes as a flame of fire; and his feet like burnished brass, as if they glowed in a furnace; and his voice as the voice of many waters; and he had in his right hand seven stars; and out of his mouth proceeded a two-edged sharp sword; and his countenance *was* as the sun shineth in his strength.

And when I saw him, I fell at his feet as dead: and he laid his right hand upon me, saying: Fear not; I am the First and the Last, and the Living One; and I was dead; and, behold, I am alive for ever, ever and ever; and I have the keys of death and of hades. Write, therefore, the things which thou sawest, and the things which are, and the things which are to come to pass after these; the mystery of the seven stars which thou sawest on my right hand, and those seven golden lamp-stands. The seven stars are the angels of the seven churches; and those seven lamp-stands are seven churches.

II. Unto the angel of the church in Ephesus write:

These things saith he that holdeth the seven stars in his right hand, he that walketh in the midst of the seven golden lamp-stands: I know thy works, and thy toil, and thy patience, and that thou canst not bear evil men, and hast tried those who say that they are apostles, and they are not, and hast found them liars, and hast patience, and hast borne for my name's sake, and hast not become weary. But I have against thee, that thou hast let go thy first love. Remember, therefore, whence thou hast fallen, and repent, and do the first works; but if not, I come unto thee quickly, and will remove thy lamp-stand out of its place, unless thou repent. But this thou hast, that thou hatest the works of the Nicolaitans, which I also hate. He that hath an ear, let him hear what the Spirit saith unto the churches: To him that overcometh, to him will I give to eat of the tree of life, which is in the paradise of God.

And unto the angel of the church in Smyrna write:

These things saith the First and the Last, who was dead, and lived: I know thy works, and tribulation, and poverty (but thou art rich), and the railing on the part of those who say that they are Jews, and they are not, but the synagogue of Satan. Fear not at all the things which thou art about to suffer. Behold, the devil is about to cast *some* of you into prison, that ye may be tried; and ye shall have a tribulation of ten days. Be faithful unto death, and I will give thee the crown of life. He that hath an ear, let him hear what the Spirit saith unto the churches: He that overcometh shall not be hurt by the second death.

And unto the angel of the church in Pergamos write:

These things saith he who hath the two-edged sharp sword: I know thy works, and where thou dwellest, where *is* the throne of Satan; and thou holdest my name, and didst not deny my faith even in the days wherein *was* Antipas, that faithful witness of mine, who was killed among you, where Satan dwelleth. But I have against thee a few things; that thou hast there some that hold the doctrine of Balaam, who taught for Balak to east a stumbling-block before the children of Israel, to eat idol-sacrifices and commit fornication. So thou also hast some that hold the doctrine of the Nicolaitans in like manner. Repent, therefore; but if not, I come unto thee quickly, and will fight with them with the sword of my mouth. He that hath an ear, let him hear what the Spirit saith unto the churches: To him that overcometh, to him will I give of that hidden manna, and will give him a white stone, and upon the stone a new name written, which no one knoweth, but he that receiveth.

And unto the angel of the church in Thyatira write:

These things saith the Son of God, he that hath his eyes as a flame of fire, and his feet *are* like burnished brass: I know thy works, and love, and faith, and service, and thy patience, and thy last works *to be* more than the first. But I have against thee, that thou sufferest the woman, Jezebel, who calleth herself a prophetess; and she teacheth and deceiveth my servants to commit fornication and eat idol-sacrifices. And I gave her time that she might repent, and she will not repent of her fornication. Behold, I cast her into a bed, and those who commit adultery with her into great tribulation, unless they repent of her works; and her children I will kill with death; and all the churches shall know that I am he who searcheth reins and hearts; and I will give unto you, every one, according to your works. But unto you I say, unto the rest that are in Thyatira, as many as have not this doctrine, who have not known the depths of Satan, as they say: I cast upon you no other burden; but, what ye have, hold till I come; and he that overcometh, even he that keepeth unto the end my works, I will give him authority over the nations; and he shall tend them with an iron rod, as the vessels of the potter are shivered; as I also have received of my Father; and I will give him the morning star. He that hath an ear, let him hear what the Spirit saith unto the churches.

III. And unto the angel of the church in Sardis write:

These things saith he that hath the seven Spirits of God, and the seven stars; I know thy works, that thou hast a name that thou livest, and art dead. Be watchful, and strengthen the things remaining that were ready to die: for I have not found thy works fulfilled before my God. Remember, therefore, how thou hast received and heard, and keep and repent. If, therefore, thou dost not watch, I will come upon thee as a thief, and thou shalt not know what hour I will come' upon thee. But thou hast a few names in Sardis, which have not defiled their garments: and they shall walk with me in white: for they are worthy. He that overcometh, the same shall he clothed in white garments; and I will not blot out his name from the book of life, and I will confess his name before my Father, and before his angels. He that hath an ear, let him hear what the Spirit saith unto the churches.

And unto the angel of the church in Philadelphia write:

These things saith he that is holy, he that is true, he that hath the key of David, he that openeth and no one shutteth, and he shutteth and no one openeth: I know thy works: behold, I have given before thee an opened door, which no one can shut: for thou hast a little strength, and hast kept my word, and hast not denied my name. Behold, I give out of the synagogue of Satan, those who say that they are Jews, and they are not, but do lie; behold, I will make them to come and do homage before thy feet, and know that I have loved thee. Because thou hast kept the word of my patience, I also will keep thee from that hour of trial, which is about to come on the whole world, to try those who dwell on the earth. I come quickly: hold what thou hast, that no one take thy crown. He that overcometh, I will make him a pillar in the temple of my God, and he shall never go out more; and I will write upon him the name of my God, and the name of the city of my God, of the new Jerusalem, which descendeth out of heaven from my God, and my new name. He that hath an ear, let him hear what the Spirit saith unto the churches.

-----o-----

A Mothers's Grave.

EARTH has some sacred spots where we feel like losing the shoes from our feet, and treading with holy reverence; where common words of social converse seem rude, and the smile of pleasure unfitting: places where friendship's hands have lingered in each other's; where vows have been plighted, prayers offered, and tears of parting shed. Oh, how the thoughts hover around such places, and travel back through unmeasured space to visit them. But of all the spots on this green earth, none is so sacred as that where rest, waiting the resurrection, those we once cherished and loved—our brothers, our sisters, or our children. Hence, in all ages, the better part of mankind have chosen and loved spots for the burial of their dead; and on these spots they have loved to wander at eventide to meditate and weep. But of all places, even among the charnel-houses of the dead, none is so sacred as a mother's grave.

There sleeps the nurse of our infancy—the guide of our youth — the counselor of our riper years—our friend when others deserted us—she whose heart was a stranger to every other feeling but love, and who could always find excuses for us when we could find none for ourselves. There she sleeps, and we love the very earth for her sake. With sentiments like these, I turned aside from the gaieties of life to the narrow habitations of the dead. I wandered among those who had commenced life with me in hope. Here distinctions were forgotten; at least by the quiet slumberers around me. I saw the rich and the great, who scorned the poor, and shunned them as infected with the plague, quietly sleeping by their side.

-----o-----

Song of the Seasons.
BY CHARLES MACKAY.

I HEARD the language of the trees
    In the noons of the early summer,
As the leaves were moved with rippling seas
    By the wind—a constant comer.
It came and it went at its wanton will,
    And evermore loved to dally
With branch and flower from the copse of the hill,
    To the warm depths of the valley.
The sunlight glowed, the waters flowed,
    The birds their music chanted,
And the words of the trees on my senses fell,
    By a spirit of beauty haunted.
Said each to each in mystic speech,
    "The skies our branches nourish:
The world is good—the world is fair—
    Let us enjoy and flourish."

Again I heard the steadfast trees:
    The wintry winds were blowing;
There seemed a roar as of stormy seas,
    And of ships to the depths down-going;
And ever a moan through the woods was blown,
    As the branches snapped asunder,
And the long boughs swung like the frantic arms
    Of a crowd in affright and wonder.

EDITOR'S TABLE.

Editor's Table.

Office of the *American Christian Review*, West Fourth Street, No. 60, on third floor, open stairway from outside. Signs will be seen at the entrance.

The Circular Letter.—This document came too late to be published in the *Review* to be of any service to the Indiana State Meeting.

---o---

Western District Annual Meeting of Ohio.— This meeting will commence on Wednesday, 15th of October, two o'clock, at Bethel, Wayne Co., Ind. This is a short distance from the State line, and is appointed in Indiana on account of some brethren in Indiana who belong to the co-operation. It is important that there be a large and faithful attendance, with liberal donations for the support of the cause. Come up, brethren, strong and numerous.

---o---

Eureka College.—We have just received the Catalogue of this flourishing young institution. To call attention to this institution, we give below the Faculty, the time the session begins and ends, and the location—Ed.

Faculty.—Eld. William M. Brown, President; A. S. Fisher, Professor of Mathematics, and Principal of Preparatory Department; John Neville, Professor of Greek and Latin Languages, and Literatures; O. A. Burgess, Professor of Natural Sciences, of Moral and Mental Philosophy, and Lecturer on Sacred Literature; Miss E. F. True, Teacher of Vocal and Instrumental Music; Miss S. Caroline Neville, Governess , R. A. Conover, J. H. Rowell, Teachers in the Primary Department.

Terms.—The collegiate year, or session, begins the second Monday of September, and closes on the 4th day of July. It is divided into two terms. The first term begins with the session and continues twenty-one weeks. The second term comprises the remainder of the session.

Eureka College is located in Walnut Grove, Woodford county, nearly midway between Peoria and Bloomington, and about twenty miles from either city.

---o---

Success of the Gospel.

Eld. B. K. Smith, writing from Indianapolis, Ind., Sept. 18th, says that "on a late tour in Indiana seven were added; six at Unionville, one at Mt. Giliad."

Under date Sept. 8th, Bro. Wm, Halstead informs us of a meeting of five days, at Josiah Creek, Ind., held by Eld. E. Thompson, at which four were added. The same letter states that since the first of last March, under the labors of Eld. E. Thompson, one hundred have been added.

Bro. W. S. Brown gives an account of a church being built in his neighborhood in February last, of eleven members; since which time fourteen have been added, but does not tell where his neighborhood is, nor date his letter.

Bro. John Lanam, Sec., August 11th, reports a co-operation meeting, of Washington Co. Dist., Ohio, assembled with the Salt Run congregation. Eld. Devoir reported one hundred and fifty-two immersed by him last year. Other important items are contained in the report, but we cannot publish reports unless they are condensed to about one-fifth their usual length. The audience was addressed during the meeting by Chas. S. Devoir, Hughs, Poulten, J. J. M. Dickey.

Bro. E. Thompson, Aug. 20th, says that "Quincy, Ill.," in his of last month, should have been Quincy, Madison Co., Ind., and that it should have been eighty additions in all, instead of thirty. He now has increased the number to one hundred and five.

Two were baptized in Covington, Ky., by Bro. Hathaway, on the second Lord's day in Sept. Bro. Thos. N. Arnold preached.

Within the last two months we baptized four at Nicholasville, Ky., fourteen in Boone Co., Ky., six at Middletown, Ind., and fifteen in the Rich Woods, Ind., making in all thirty-nine. Eld. S. Rogers aided in Boone, Ky.

Bro. V. O. Pinkard, Maysville, Sept. 20th, writes that Bro. John O'Kane, of Ind., had closed a meeting at Beasly's Creek, Ky., with twenty additions.

Bro. Jas. Renner, of Albion, Ill., Sept, 10th, says, "I have recently witnessed the addition of sixty members to different congregations. The little congregation at Republican, in Edwards Co., had the greatest number — thirty-two at two meetings. Brethren Phelps, Hale and Morrel were the principal laborers.

Bro. G. W. Thompson, Oceola, Iowa, Sept. 15th, says, "Bro. P. T. Russell informed me that he has immersed over fifty in the last six weeks.

Gillespie. Aug. 27th Bro. Benjamin Franklin—We have a small flock here and no shepherd. Bro. G. E. Sweeney has been preaching here and at Litchfield. We have a house there, and about thirty-five members. These are now flourishing on the A. & T. H. R. R., and now is the time to give them the truth; it must be done before other denominations get organized. Please tell the traveling brethren to give us a call.

With the kindest regards, I am yours,

John H. Cheery.

Bro. P. R. Dibble, Canton, Ohio, July 16th, 1856, says: "Our meeting at Sparta closed with twenty-two additions, after which, Bro. Lockhart went to Magnolia, and gained nine to the Lord — four by confession. On Saturday, July 5th, I commenced a meeting in Waynesburg, in this county, assisted by Bro. J. C. Stark, of Massilon, where we continued ten days. There were fifteen immersed and two from the Baptists. We there "*organized,*" (for the use of a better term), a congregation of thirty members. To the Lord be all the praise."

BENTONVILLE, IA., Sept. 12, 1856.

BRO. FRANKLIN,—*Dear Sir*—Our meeting at this place, which you left on the 29th ult., was continued until the 2d inst. Bro. Pritchard was with us most of the time. Five persons made the "good *confession,*" and were buried with their Lord in baptism.

The attendance was good to the close; the hearts of the brethren were much encouraged, and considerable interest prevailed.

May the Lord speed the good work.

Yours in the Lord, DAN'L R. VAN BUSKIRK

. BOONE CO., MO. Aug. 17th, 1856.

ELD. BENJ. FRANKLIN, — *Dear Bro.*—Bro W. H. Hopson and I recently held a meeting at Danville, with ten additions when I left, and the meeting still in progress.

Bro. Hopson, with other teaching brethren, have recently held meetings at Louisiana, with seven additions; at Frankfort, with thirty; at Paynesville, with forty-three; and at Louisville, with thirty-one additions.

In haste, I am affectionately

And fraternally yours,
T. M. ALLEN.

Literary Notices.

The Sacred Plains.—Such is the title of a valuable volume, by J. T. HEADLY. It begins with the plains of Shinar, takes the reader over the plains of Jordan, Mamre, Moab, Jericho, Sharon, Shiloh, Moreh, Dura, Esdraelon, Damascus, and Galilee; showing him, in an able and reliable manner these sacred plains, and at the same time opening to his mind important antiquities pertaining to them. The author makes the reader almost realize that he is walking through these plains, in actual company with the ancients.

The Economic Cottage Builder. — Such is the title of a beautiful volume by CHARLES P. DWYER, dedicated "to the failing millions, whose means are small, yet whose desires are great to possess a home where industry and contentment shall be household gods, and independence be allied with happiness." Many are the books and orators trying to show how to obtain a home by means of great gain, but this book has a shorter, easier and more accessible road to all; that road is *economy*. No temporal subject needs closer study in our time.

Study for Young Men A "Sketch of Sir Thomas Fowell Buxton, by REV. THOMAS BINNY," delivered in Exeter Hall, London, upon "the improvement of the spiritual and mental condition of commercial young men," is certainly a valuable treatise.

The Signet Ring.—This little book is certainly a rich gem, impressing a divine lesson in a most graphic manner.

The Hallig.—This work, also called "The Shepherd in the waters. A tale of Humble Life on the Coast of Schleswig. Translated from the German of Bier-natzki, by Mrs. GEORGE P. MARSH," is lying before us. We have not had opportunity to peruse it with sufficient care to recommend it, but see that it is highly recommended in some prints.

Each of the above can be had at Blanchards, between Main and Walnut, south side, and also at this office.

Eld. M. B. Hopkins has had such poor health that he has been unable to attend his appointments for several weeks past, and is yet measurably confined to his room.

Eld. M. B. Hopkins expects to make Louisville, Ky., his head quarters as soon as his health will permit, where the *American Christian Review* and all our other works will be published by him. His pen will also contribute to our columns. The arrangement will be such, that all orders addressed to him . at that place will be filled, the same as if addressed to us here.

Obituary.

DIED in Sharpsburg, on the 26th Aug., 1856, at the residence of her son-in-law, Wm. Peck, Mrs. ELIZABETH STEPHENS, in the eighty-eighth year of her age.

In April, 1791, Mrs. Stephens removed with her husband from Loudon Co., Va., to Fleming Co., near the Poplar Plains. In that early period that section of country was in almost a wilderness condition, subject to the marauding incursions of hostile Indians. With her husband she withstood the privations incident to frontier life, and reared a large family of children. In 1817, she removed to Sharpsburg, and in the Summer of that year her husband died, full of years and highly respected. Four of her children reside in and near Sharpsburg, all highly respectable and good citizens.

The distinguishing features of this venerated lady's character were a sprightliness and energy of disposition, which carried through in success her designs. She ruled firmly, but in grace and mercy. Sixty four years ago she became a member of the Calvinist Baptist Church, in which she lived until twelve years ago, when she connected with the Christian Church, adorning her life by a devotion and consistency, marking her strong faith and reliance upon "Him who is mighty to save."

Numerous descendants mourn the death of the loved and venerated mother, but they mourn not without hope. Her aged form will no longer be seen. Her cheerful smile and sage counsels will no longer enliven the home circle, and the hearts of numerous friends. She is gone—exchanged this sinful world for a higher and brighter land, "where the wicked cease from troubling and the weary are at rest."

"Friend after friend departs;
  Who has not lost a friend?
There is no union here of hearts,
  That finds not here an end."

THE AMERICAN CHRISTIAN REVIEW.

Vol. 1.] CINCINNATI, NOVEMBER, 1856. [No. 11.

OPENING ADDRESS.

THE following is the opening address of the editor on Endless Punishment, delivered on the second day of the debate on the claims of Universalism, with Rev. Bosserman, of Dayton, Ohio, in Lexington Ohio, September 22, 1856. By the request of many friends who heard the speech, we lay it before our readers. It was delivered perfectly extemporaneously, as every speech of ours was, as we had not time to open a single book to make the slightest preparation after we knew the debate would certainly take place, until we were on the ground. This will account for any lack of method or arrangement in the speech. We have aimed to write it out as near in the precise words in which it was delivered, as possible, from memory, and a brief skeleton prepared during the short intermission of an hour and a half that preceded its delivery, in the midst of talking and greeting friends, who were taking some refreshments on the ground.

We will just observe, that if our Universalian friends complain of our publishing this speech, that we will publish the reply to it—the author furnishing it—if the *Star* will publish ours. If that is not satisfactory, and they wish to try the strength of the pen, we are ready to enter into a volume of some four to six hundred pages, each party having equal space, upon the same propositions discussed in this debate. If they feel any delicacy on the subject, they may consider this a *direct challenge to their entire fraternity.* We have had no hand in getting up a debate with them for years, but they have drawn us into several; we, therefore, propose to end the whole matter so far as we are concerned.

B. F.

GENTLEMEN MODERATORS, LADIES AND GENTLEMEN:—I have appeared before you only as a respondent during this discussion till now. Heretofore I have simply replied to the effort of my opponent to prove that all men will be finally reconciled, made holy and happy. Having, in my reply, not only defeated the argument of my friend, but brought negative proof ruinous to his whole system, and going far to establish my affirmative proposition, I am now to proceed to discuss Future Punishment. The proposition, as written by my friend, reads as follows: "Will any part of the human family suffer endless torment?"

Mr. Bosserman has made several strong appeals to your prejudices, only calculated, whether so intended or not, to prevent a candid hearing and deliberate decision. Similar appeals might be made to induce you not to believe in the existence of a fine, chain-gang, prison, penitentiary or gallows, in this world; but, after all, his fine rhetoric, sensible people would still believe in the existence of such places of punishment. Nor would it avail anything with them should he read to them as tenderly and affectionately as he told his experience last night, during which he shed tears, or thought he did, as I judged from his applying his handkerchief to his eyes. He might, in the most feeling manner he could invent, tell the mothers present, that if there be such places of punishment, they know not but the tender infants in their arms may be the victims, and they may be separated from the objects of their fond embrace. But not many of the mothers here could be induced, by such arguments, to deny the existence of such places of punishment, or to try to reform their children by making them believe that there are no such punishments. Good mothers believe, or rather they *know,* there are fines, jails, etc., and let their children know it, and advise them how to live so as to avoid them. In the same way, a good mother does not deny the existence of a place of punishment for the wicked after death, but labors to direct her children as the Lord commands her, to walk in the way that leads to life. The same is true of a good minister of the word of God. He does not deny, nor attempt to quibble round the punishment threatened in the Bible, but guides the people in the way to life. No good guide was ever yet found who would deny the dangers to which they are exposed, whom he professes to guide safely.

Upon this momentous question the Bible is the supreme authority. Whatever the Bible teaches is true, whether it suits our notion or not; and it is much easier for us *to bow to the Bible* than to *bend' the Bible to us.* We shall, therefore, proceed to make a condensed statement of the argument now before you, with some additional argument, to show that people who die in their sins will be judged and punished after death, and that the punishment will be endless. In so doing, I shall grasp as many of the principal passages that I rely upon as possible, that my opponent may have a fair opportunity to make the best response in his power.

1. There is punishment or torment for wicked men after death. The case of the rich man and Lazarus is recorded Luke xvi: 19—31. At verse 22, we are informed that "the rich man died and was buried, and in hell he lifted up his eyes, being in torment." Such is the testimony of the Lord. The rich man himself testified, saying, "I am tormented in this flame." Abraham testified, saying, "Thou art tormented." The only use we now make of this case is, to show clearly that a man was in torment after death. In connection with this quote from Luke xii: 4—5, "Be not afraid of those who kill the body, and after that, have no more that they can do; but I will forewarn you whom you shall fear: Fear him who, after he hath killed, hath power to cast into hell; yea, I say unto you, fear him." Here we find our Lord admonishing his disciples to fear God, because he not only can kill, but after that cast into hell. This could not be true if there were no hell beyond death. This *Valley of Hinnom* my opponent must find after death—after the body is killed— not merely a place to burn bodies, but in which both *souls* and bodies may be destroyed after the body is killed.

2. The next passage I shall quote to show that the Lord reserves the ungodly unto the day of judgment to be punished. 2 Pet. ii: 9. "The Lord knoweth how to deliver the godly out of temptations, and to *reserve* the unjust unto the day of judgment to be punished." In the same letter, iii: 7, the apostle says: "But the heavens and the earth which are now, by the same word are kept in store, *reserved* unto fire against the day of judgment and perdition of ungodly men." Both of these passages are in the same spirit, setting forth the fact that the world is *reserved* for the day of judgment; and the latter connects the coming of Christ with the day of judgment. Let us hear Paul, whom Mr. Bosserman tried to prove a Universalist on last night, giving a charge to a young preacher: "I charge thee, therefore, before God and the Lord Jesus Christ, who shall judge the quick and the dead at his appearing and kingdom."

2. Tim. iv: 1. Here we have an account of judging the *dead* at the appearing and kingdom of Christ. This connects the coming of Christ and judgment together, and shows, by "the *dead,*" as well as the quick or the *living* being judged, that it will be after death. But we must hear the Apostle Peter in his first sermon to the Gentiles, Acts x: 42. "And he commanded us to preach unto the people, and to testify that it is he who

was ordained of God to be the judge of quick and dead." Here again we nave judgment of both the *living* and *dead.* We must be explicit on this point, and afford clear light to show that the dead will be judged, as my friend is slow to learn. The Apostle Peter, speaking of a certain class of the dead, viz: The Antediluvians tells us for what the gospel was preached to them, in the days of Noah, as follows: "That they might be judged according to men in the flesh, but live according to God in the spirit."—1 Pet. iv: 5. In the verse preceding this, speaking of other vile characters: "Who shall give account to him that is ready to judge the quick and *dead,"* we find the dead included.

If the foregoing does not satisfy any candid mind that our Lord will judge the dead, look at the following: "But I say unto you, it shall be more tolerable for Tyre and Sidon at the day of judgment than for you."—Mat. xi: 22. Hear the Lord again: "For I say unto you, 'that it shall be more tolerable for the land of Sodom in the day of judgment than for thee.'" The Sodomites had been buried in ruins ages before this; the cities of Tyre and Sidon were destroyed from the face of the earth many long centuries before the Lord uttered these words; yet he declared that they should be in the judgment with the generation to whom he spoke. No man ever made even a plausible show of argument on the question here in dispute, who denies that this passage teaches a judgment after death? Let us attend to the teaching of the Lord again. He says: "The men of Nineveh shall rise in judgment with this generation, and shall condemn it, because they repented at the preaching of Jonas; and behold a greater than Jonas is here. The queen of the South shall rise up in judgment with this generation, and shall condemn it, for she came from the uttermost parts of the earth to hear the wisdom of Solomon; and, behold a greater than Solomon is here."—Mat. xii: 41—42. We have now found that the antediluvians, those of Tyre, Sidon, the land of Sodom, the Ninevites, and the Queen of Sheba, all dead and gone ages before our Lord's lifetime, are included in the judgment of which he spoke. But this is not all; there are more than these to be there.

Look at the following: "For if God spared not the angels that sinned, but cast them down to hell, and delivered them into chains of darkness to be reserved unto judgment." 2 Pet., ii: 4. Here we have the angels that sinned reserved unto judgment. Let us hear about these angels that sinned once more: "And the angels who kept not their first estate, but left their own habitation, he hath reserved in everlasting chains, under darkness, unto the judgment of the great day."—Jude 6. There has been no judgment in this world since the writing of these Scriptures, at which the citizens of Tyre, Sidon, the land of Sodom, Nineveh, the Queen of Sheba, the antediluvians, the angels who sinned, with those to whom the Lord spoke, to say nothing of all who have lived since, were present. The reason is that, "as it is appointed unto men once to die, but after this the judgment; so Christ was once offered to bear the sins of many; and unto them who look for him shall he appear the second time without sin (or sin offering) unto salvation."—Heb. ix: 27—28.

3. We shall now connect the coming of Christ, day of judgment, and resurrection of the dead together. Indeed, the passage just quoted puts judgment after death, and the coming of Christ at the same period. The gentleman has quoted Isa. xlv: 23—25, and, applied it to the resurrection state. In this he is right; for Paul quotes the same passage and applies it to the same state, to prove that we shall all stand before the judgment seat of Christ—Ro. xiv: 10—11. Let us hear him: "But why dost thou judge thy brother? or why dost thou set at naught thy brother? for we shall all stand before the judgment seat of Christ." Now, Paul, let us hear you prove this: "For," says he, "it is written, as I live, saith the Lord, every knee shall bow to me, and every tongue shall confess to God. So then, every one of us shall give account of himself to God." The identical passage then quoted by my opponent to prove that all will be saved, is quoted by Paul to prove a judgment; and, as it relates to the resurrection state, it proves a judgment at the resurrection of the dead.

But my friend, no doubt, is anxious to hear

from 1 Cor., xv: 22—23. Let us hear the Apostle then: "As in Adam all die, even so in Christ shall all be made alive. But every man in his own order; Christ the first fruits; afterward they that are Christ's at his coming." The making all alive, predicted in this passage, is the raising all from the dead. This, the passage declares, shall be "at his coming." This beyond controversy connects the coming of Christ and the resurrection of the dead. But this passage does more than this; at the coming of Christ and the resurrection of the dead, it discriminates between those "that are Christ's" and those that are not his. The expression, "they are Christ's," implies that there are some *not his,* and this is at his coming and the resurrection of the dead. These discriminations between those who are Christ's and those not his, at his coming and the resurrection of the dead, are ruinous to the whole theory of my friend. Paul makes the same discrimination speaking of the just and unjust, in his allusion to the resurrection of the dead, in reply to Tertullus. Acts xxiv: 14. "There shall be a resurrection of the dead, both of the just and unjust." The Lord himself makes the same discrimination in the words: "Thou shalt be recompensed at the resurrection of the just." An intimation of the same discrimination, in the resurrection, is found, Luke xx: 35, in the following words: "They who shall be accounted *worthy* to obtain that world, and the resurrection from the dead." See also Dan. xii: 2, "And many of them that sleep in the dust of the earth shall awake, some to everlasting life, and some to shame and everlasting contempt." He follows in the same passage: "And they that be wise shall shine as the brightness of the firmament; and they that turn many to righteousness, as the stars forever and ever." The same is inculcated, John v: 28—29. "Marvel not at this; for the hour is the coming in which all that are in the graves shall hear his voice, and shall come forth; they that have done good unto the resurrection of life, and they that have done evil unto the resurrection of damnation." Thus you perceive that in every allusion to the resurrection, the Lord discriminates in some form or other between the righteous and wicked. We will close this part of the argument with John's account of the matter. In his splendid vision, in the island of Patmos, he appears to have presented to him, and passed before him, in one grand panorama, the whole period called "Time," the delivering up of the souls in the invisible state, the collecting of the bodies from both land and sea, or the resurrection of the dead; and he says: "I saw the dead, small and great, stand before God; and the books were opened; and another book was opened, which is the book of life; and the dead were judged out of those things which were written in the books, according to their works."

Now, cast your eye back and take one solemn look at these expressions touching the resurrection, and see the discrimination between the righteous and wicked — such as "they that are *Christ's* at his coming"—"they that shall be accounted *worthy"*—"the resurrection of the just"—"a resurrection both of the *just and unjust*"—"they that be *wise"* — "they that shall *turn many to righteousness*"—"they that *have done good*"—"were judged every man according to *their works*" and then, tell what these continued and oft repeated discriminations between the righteous and wicked mean, made at the resurrection of the dead, the coming of the Lord and day of judgment! Recollect it is after death—the quick and dead are present. The antediluvians, Tyre, Sidon, those of the land of Sodom, the Queen of Sheba, Nineveh, the angels that sinned, those to whom the Lord, in his lifetime, spoke, and all that are in the graves, with all alive on the earth, are there to be judged according to their works. "Those whose names were not found written in the Book of Life were cast into the lake of fire." Here is the last state of the disobedient.

But while I am making an effort to grasp as full a summary as possible, in my opening address, that my friend may have a fair opportunity to make a response, if he has any, I proceed to another class of evidence upon the state of those who die in their sins. These passages are negative proofs, some of which have been referred to. The Lord says: "He that believeth on the Son has everlasting life, and he that believeth not the Son shall not see life; but the wrath of God abideth on him."—John iii: 36. This passage looks forward as far as unbelievers can be found, and declares that "he that believeth not the Son *shall not see life.*" Jude, 12 and 13. describes these; he says: "They are clouds without water, carried about of winds; trees whose fruit withereth, without fruit, twice dead, plucked up by the roots; raging waves of the sea, foaming out their own shame; wandering stays, to whom is reserved the blackness of darkness forever." This description certainly follows these down to their last state. Let us hear the holy apostle again: "For many walk, of whom I have told you often, and now tell you even weeping, that they are the enemies of the cross of Christ, whose end is destruction."—Phil, iii: 18—19. The end of these corrupt persons is unquestionably their last state. If their *last state is destruction,* as here affirmed, it is all the veriest nonsense to speak of their ever being saved. The same high and holy authority, comparing corrupt characters to "thorns and briars," says they are "rejected, and nigh unto cursing; whose end is to be burned."—Heb. vi: 8. Here is the last state of a man whom the Lord declares it impossible to renew again to repentance; "he is *nigh unto cursing, and his end is to be burned."* Let us hear the Lord while upon this fearful and momentous point. He says: "If ye believe not that I am he, ye shall die in your sins."—John viii: 24. Just before he had said "Ye shall seek me, and shall die in your sins; whither I go, ye cannot come." One of these expressions declares that those who believe not shall die in their sins, and the other declares that those who die in their sins shall not go where the Lord is, or shall not enjoy him. This passage never was and never can be harmonized with the theory that all will be saved.

One man, while the Saviour was upon his public mission, like many idle speculators of our time, more curious to know the precise number that will be saved, than desirous to learn his Lord's will, or do it when learned, inquired, "Lord, are there few that be saved?"

Now I can but think that if my friend had been there, that he would have responded, "Why, my dear sir, they will all be saved. At least such is the doctrine he is here to prove. But such is not the doctrine taught by our Lord. He gave that man a much more solemn lesson. Let us be attentive to his words: "Strive to enter in at the straight gate, for many, I say unto you, will seek to enter in, and shall not be able. When once the Master of the house is risen up, and hath shut to the door, and ye begin to stand without, and to knock at the door, saying Lord, Lord, open unto us; and he shall answer and say unto you, I know ye not whence ye are; than shall ye begin to say, we have eaten and drunk in thy presence, and thou hast taught in our streets. But he shall say, I know you not whence you are; depart from me all ye workers of iniquity."—Luke xiii: 23—27. This language can never apply to men in this world. The language of the Lord to men in this life is, "They who seek shall find"— "they who ask shall receive"—to "those who knock it shall be opened." "Whoever will, may come"—"he who cometh to me, I will in nowise cast out." As we sing, "The doors of gospel grace stand open night and day." But this language applies to a time when the door of grace will be shut; when the applicant for admission shall not gain an entrance, but shall be thrust away, followed with the awful language, "Depart ye workers of iniquity, I know you not." Here follows the Lord's own reason: "Because I have called, and ye refused; I have stretched out my hand and no man regarded; but ye have set at naught all my counsel, and would none of my reproof; I also will laugh at your calamity; I will mock when your fear cometh; when your fear cometh as desolation, and destruction cometh as a whirlwind; when distress and anguish cometh upon you; then shall you call upon me, but I will not answer; they shall seek me early, but they shall not find me."—Prov. i: 24—28. This reaches beyond time—beyond the day of grace—beyond this world, and beyond all gospel invitation—beyond all repentance. To this list I will add but one more passage on this point. I allude to the closing words of the New

Testament: "If any man shall take away from the words of the book of this prophecy, God shall take away his part out of the book of life, and out of the holy city, and from the things that are written in this book."—Rev. xxii: 19.

Let us glance our eye over this list and grasp as far as possible the amount of it. What then, shall we think of the man who would try to prove that those will be saved, whom the Lord declares "shall not see life"— "upon whom the wrath of God abides"— "who die in their sins"—of whom Jesus said "whither I go ye cannot come"—those whom he styles "trees twice dead and plucked up by the roots"—"to whom is reserved the blackness of darkness forever" — "whose end is destruction"—"rejected, nigh unto cursing; whose end is to be burned"—"who shall seek to enter in, but shall not be able"—but shall be thrust away with the sentence, "Depart from me, all ye workers of iniquity"—whom the Lord will "mock when their fear cometh" —"who shall have their part taken away out of the book of life, and out of the holy city, and out of the things which are written in this book!" We say, what shall we think of him who teaches, and tries to make men believe, that those to whom this language applies, shall be saved? Does he believe his Bible?

Having now followed punishment, not only to the after death state—not only to *hades,* but to the day of judgment, at the coming of the Lord and the resurrection of the dead, when those whose names are not written in the book of life are sentenced to the lake of fire— as our Lord expressed it, "cast into hell; where the worm dieth not and the fire shall never be quenched" — or *Gehenna,* we are ready to Took at its duration. My friend need not trouble himself about old *Gesohenna,* near Jerusalem, where criminals were executed, and dead bodies consumed; for its fires had gone out some four hundred years before our Lord uttered this fearful language. The Saviour was not threatening a punishment—like our Universalian friends, in finding a hell for the wicked at the destruction of Jerusalem—that he knew to have been done away four centuries when he uttered the language. But we must proceed to the duration of this punishment. We do not read of an "endless hell," my friend says. True, for the good reason that hell is a place; and an endless place would be rather a long place. We affirm nothing about the length or width of this *place* of punishment; but the duration of the punishment we affirm is endless. This is intimated, in our Lords words: "He who shall sin against the Holy Ghost hath *never* forgiveness; but is in danger of *eternal* damnation." Mark iii: 29. Here the terms used to express the perpetuity of the unpardoned, or condemned state, are as unlimited in duration as human speech can employ. How can you express the unlimited duration of a man's unpardoned state in stronger terms, than to say, "he hath never forgiveness?" The same kind of unlimited duration, or perpetuity, is given to the fire of hell. The Lord says, "It *shall never be quenched."* What is the meaning of this? and what shall we think of him who will try to prove that this punishment shall have a termination? This can only he, when that which the Lord says *"shall never be,"* shall come to pass, or when Universalists shall prove that our Lord's words are not true.

My opponent is right in applying the expression "The Lord God shall wipe off all tears," to the eternal state. John so applies this expression, Rev. xxi: 4; but John soon finishes his description of those in the holy city, New Jerusalem, and just four verses after gives an account of others not in the holy city, but of whom we have the following overwhelming language: "But the fearful, and unbelieving, and the abominable, and murderers, and whoremongers, and sorcerers, and idolaters, and all liars, shall have their part in the lake which burneth with fire and brim- stone; which is the second death." Recollect this is in the resurrection state, at the precise period when all tears shall be wiped from those in the holy city, where there shall be no more death. As my opponent desires a little light, touching the object of this "lake of fire," I am willing to contribute my might to enlighten him. Mat. xxv: 41, we are informed that it was prepared for the devil and his angels." As he has also asked so significantly, learnedly, and piously, "What or who is the devil?" I feel also under some obligations to assist him a little on that point. The Lord says, "He was a murderer from the beginning." Again he says, "When he speaketh a lie, he speaketh of his own; for he is a liar, and the father of it." John viii: 44. Such is a hint of his character. In the same connection we are informed that "he abode not in the truth." From this we learn that he was in the truth, but abode not in it. This "everlasting fire," Mat. xxv: 41; prepared for the devil and his angels, is the same that the Lord says shall never be quenched, into which vile characters shall be cast immediately after the judgment, which we have seen followed immediately the coming of the Lord and resurrection of the dead.

The angels who sinned, we are informed, Jude 6th, "he hath reserved in everlasting chains of darkness unto the judgment of the great day." "*Chains*, under darkness," here used as a figure of the power by which they are held, or bound, are called *everlasting*. "Everlasting" here, does not come from the Greek *aionion*, but from *aiodios*, which occurs in but one other place in the New Testament. In that place it expresses the perpetuity of the Godhead and his power, in the following words: "Even his eternal power and Godhead." This word means endless, or unlimited duration, and is so used in the only two occurrences it has in the New Testament. The same word then, used in the Christian Scriptures, to express the perpetuity or eternity of the power and Godhead of the Deity, expresses the perpetuity, or eternity of the powers by which the angels that sinned are bound in punishment. The chains, or powers, in which they are bound, are everlasting. See Jude 6. The fire prepared for the devil and his angels is everlasting. Matt. xxv: 41. The punishment is everlasting. Matt. xxv: 46. Angels cannot die, in any such sense as to be incapable of punishment, nor can men in the resurrection "die anymore," in any such sense as the natural death, for the Lord says of those in the resurrection, "neither can they die any more, but are as the angels." This corresponds with the Lord's own words: "Their worm dieth not." In this same sense, the Lord affirms that man "is not able to kill the soul." It cannot die as the body dies, and become incapable of punishment. But it can suffer the "second death," which means the same as "destroy in hell," or "lose his own soul," or "suffer the vengeance of an eternal fire," or "everlasting punishment."

Some deconstructionists have concluded, that if the wicked have eternal existence, they will have "eternal life." But this only shows how loosely and carelessly they have thought upon the subject. "Eternal life," in no place, that we are aware of, in the New Testament, means simply *eternal existence*. Nor does immortality ever simply mean eternal existence. These terms always mean more than mere eternal existence. Where eternal life is presented as an object to be sought, it is not mere eternal existence; but it includes all the blessedness and glories of the redeemed. It is that form of speech in which a part is used for the whole. The same is true of the word "lost." When the Lord speaks of a soul being lost, the word *lost* involves all the evils of the state of perdition. The single expression "second death," involves the same. Lost, destroyed, perished, all mean the same, and indeed, come from the same Greek word, and when applied to the wicked in the future state, involves precisely the same as punishment, tormented or misery, involving all included in the state of perdition. Any man who undertakes to explain "second death," to mean one thing, "lost" another, "perished" something else, and "destroyed" different from all the balance, will only blind himself, and all who hear him, in the labyrinths of his meanderings in the dark. No matter how many forms of speech, both figurative and literal, may be applied to the punishment of the wicked in the eternal state. The thing they refer to is one—*always the same*. Every expression that refers to that thing, *always means the same*. The same is true of the state of glory; it is no matter whether it is called "life," "eternal life," "immortality," the "joys of the Lord," or "a crown of life," it means the same.

The Lord involves the whole, on both sides, in the two expressions, " everlasting punishment," and "eternal life." All that awaits the disobedient, and will ever be visited upon them on account of their sins, is embodied in .the short, but awful expression, " everlasting punishment." All that the whole Bible means by every expression, touching the state of the wicked after the resurrection, no matter what the form of speech, nor whether figurative or literal, is concentrated and embodied in this short, but fearful expression, "everlasting punishment." In the same way, all that the Bible means by all the expressions, both figurative and literal, touching the state of glory, is embodied or concentrated in the short, but important expression, " eternal life." The latter includes heaven and all that heaven means; the former includes hell and all that hell means.

The passage that we are now commenting upon is the close of our Lord's discourse, Matt, xxv: 46. The first thing we shall observe is the ground of admission, or that which the Lord gives as the reason of the separation of the two classes. He says, a few verses previous to the one we have been commenting upon, and when drawing his discourse to a conclusion, he will say to the righteous, or those on his right hand, " Come ye blessed of my Father." His reason for this invitation is, " When I was hungry you fed me," etc. They inquire of him, "When ?" He answers, " Inasmuch as you did it to one of these the least of my servants, you did it to me." He will regard your acts of beneficence to the poor as done to him in person. But to those on the left hand he will say, "Depart, ye cursed, into everlasting fire, prepared for the devil and his angels." His reason for this Sentence is, " When I was hungry you fed me not," etc. They inquire, " When ? " He responds, " Inasmuch as you did it not to one of these the least of my servants, you did it not to me." He regards their omission of humanity to the poor as done to him in person, and makes this the basis of his procedure in the last judgment. So much for the Lord's reason for his decision.

The sentence is, " These shall go away into everlasting punishment, but the righteous into life eternal." The next thing to observe is that the judgment of both parties is *at the same time*. The sentence of both parties is on the same occasion. The entrance of both parties into the respective places assigned them is *at the same time*. The entrance of the righteous into " eternal life," is not their entrance into Christianity, for the Lord never refers to a man's previous Christian acts of beneficence as a reason for his reception into Christianity; but these had gone through their Christian life, and the Lord refers back to their Christian acts of humanity as a reason why they should enter into everlasting life. If this is not entering heaven and all the joys that heaven unfolds to man, I know not where the passage is to be found that speaks of the entrance into that state. But it is the entrance into heaven itself into " life eternal." At the same time then, that the righteous enter " life eternal," or heaven; the incorrigible enter "everlasting punishment," or hell. This shows that the states, the state of glory and the state of punishment, in point of time lie side by side. In point of time, the parties enter and start forward at the same period.

How long will these states, or that which is received in them, last? Respecting the state of glory, or the " life eternal," there is but one mind. Its perpetuity shall be co-existent with the years of God. In the same sentence then, in reference to those who enter their final destiny at the same time, the Lord used the same word to express the duration of the state of glory that he does to express the duration of the punishment of the wicked. That word is *aionion,* here translated " everlasting " in one place, and " eternal " in the other. As Dr. Clarke says, " It is as likely that the state of glory shall have an end, as that the punishment of the wicked shall terminate." The word *aionion,* here used by our Lord, can mean nothing but duration, and the same duration expressed by it, in one part of this sentence, is expressed in the other. If it mean endless life, as all admit in one places then it must mean endless punishment in the other. It cannot be used in a limited sense in one part of a sentence and unlimited in another. Let no man then, trifle with this fearful, momentous and awful passage; but remember this, that the judgment of all is at the same time; the sentence of all is passed at the same time; the entrance of all into their final state is at the same time; and the duration of the condition of all in their last state is, by our Lord, in the same short sentence of two lines, expressed by the *same word*. As certain as "life eternal" is endless, so certain is the punishment of the wicked endless.

The expression "forever and ever," occurs some twenty-three times in the New Testament, and means unlimited duration, or endless in every case. It is never used in a limited sense in one place, in the New Testament. It expresses the duration of the existence of God, of Christ, of the praises of God and the punishment of the wicked. It is used in such expressions as the following: "Him that liveth forever and ever,"—"Blessing, and honor, and glory and power, be unto him that sitteth upon the throne, and unto the Lamb, forever and ever." That these expressions mean unlimited duration — in one instance, the unlimited duration of the life of God, and in the other, the unlimited duration of the praises that shall ascend to him, no man doubts. This expression is found thirteen times in the single book of Revelation, and ten times expresses the duration of the life of God, the life of Christ, and the praises that ascend to heaven. In all these places, it expresses unlimited duration, all admit. The same expression precisely is applied to the punishment of the wicked three times, in this same book. Twice it is said, the "smoke of their torment ascended forever and ever." Once it is found, as follows: "And the devil that deceived them was cast into the lake of fire and brimstone, where the beast and the false prophet are, and shall be tormented day and night for. ever and ever." Rev: xx: 10. My opponent may make the old Universalian reply that "there is no day and night in eternity." But that is home-made Scripture. No passage in the Bible says so. One passage speaking of the holy city, New Jerusalem, says: "there shall be no night there." In the same passage, speaking of the holy city, it is said there shall be no need of the sun, nor of the moon; but the reason given for this is not that day and night have ceased; but "the glory of God and the Lamb is the light thereof." That day and night have not ceased, is evident from the statement that "the gates shall not be shut at all by *day."* Rev. xxi: 25. David, as quoted by Paul, Heb i: 12, speaking of God, says: "thy *years* shall not fail." Years are made of days, and if the *years* of God fail not, and if the gates shall not be shut by *day,* there will still be days in eternity. This is the period when all tears shall be wiped from the eyes of those in the holy city, which my friend has rightly applied to eternity. This is also the same period in which "the devil who deceived them shall be cast into the lake of fire where the beast and the false prophet are, and shall be tormented day and night forever and ever." The same expression here also that expresses the perpetuity of the state of glory, expresses the duration of the punishment of the wicked. The same expressions used to express the duration of the life of God, of Christ, of the praises of God, and the state of glory in heaven, are used to express the duration of the punishment of the wicked. What then, ever put it into the heads of men that the state of glory shall be perpetual, but the state of punishment limited? Certainly no Scripture, no argument, no reason, or anything else, only *their desire to have it so.*

I admit the conclusion is momentous, fearful, and overwhelming. But it is to be recollected that the mission of Christ is the last effort to reclaim our race. Jesus, of Nazareth, in his teachings, life, miracles, and death, is the last great exponent of the love of God to man. He is presented as the chiefest among all the ten thousands and altogether lovely, to woo our whole rational nature and bring us to God. He presents a crown of glory in heaven, with the high and holy inducements of heaven, with all that heaven means, to enlist us and bring us to God. And then, as a last resort, he unveils a judgment after death, a "lake of fire prepared for the devil and his angels," and declares to the rebellious—the incorrigible—that "their end is destruction"—"to be burned"—to "go away into everlasting punishment" — "tormented day and night forever and ever." Do you say "the thought is awful!" Then repent; flee to God and seek salvation. You can then know what salvation means. It is not an idle bubble about the salvation of a people never in any danger of being lost; but salvation of those already lost—a salvation of their souls from sin now, and both the soul and body from the danger of destruction in hell in the world to come. This does, as no other conclusion ever can, explain the labors, tears, persecutions and sufferings endured by the apostles and first Christians.

-----o-----

A Crowd of Methodist Preachers.

On Monday, Sept. 29th, we went to our wharf to find a boat for Maysville, Ky., on our way to Flemingsburg, where we were expected to spend five or six days in the proclamation of the word. But, on arriving at the steamboat landing, we found less water in our beautiful river than we ever saw, and the only boat, with steam up, was one of the least and most uncomely stern-wheels to be found. We hesitated whether to go on board; but as she was about backing out, there was no time to be lost in consultation. As she shoved out, we walked up into the cabin, which we found crowded to its utmost capacity with some seventy Methodist preachers and a few other passengers. Starting in a little confusion, owing to several friends calling on us just on the eve of starting, we left without a book to read, the like of which we have not done in a year before. Not only so, but this little crowded cabin afforded no opportunity for writing. The question immediately came up in our mind, What are we to do for a livelihood on this tedious trip? We concluded to spend the time in an effort to *read human nature,* in this body of ministers. We, therefore, commenced reading and soon arranged in our mind the following classification:

1. The Bishop.
2. Presiding Elders.
3. Circuit Riders.
4. Local Preachers.
5. Editors.

We then commenced reasoning upon these men, as follows: We will now say nothing of the strong and just objections that may be urged against the system advocated by this large and powerful body of men, but will try to estimate the men and appreciate their work and condition:

1. They are on their way to Ripley, Ohio, to the Annual Conference, and appear quite cheerful and happy. Their salutations, when they first meet, and when new accessions to their number come on board, at every port, are pleasant, brotherly and joyful.

2. They appear to be pleasant and agreeable passengers, accommodating and kind to one another, especially to their *superiors* in office.

3. Little as we think of Methodism, as a religious system, we could but notice that these men, in all that ennobles man, are vastly elevated above men who are without religion.

4. During the afternoon, we gave them credit for being rather a noble band of gentlemen, and they rather won upon our feelings.

5. Occasionally some of the younger men would attempt to find out our whereabouts. One approached us in most reverential and respectful style, and asked if we were an Elder? When we informed him that we did not belong to their ministry at all, he excused himself and sidled away. We had not proceeded far when we were pointed out as "a *Campbellite* preacher and editor," after which we were not troubled with many questions on any subject. One or two made unavailing attempts to draw us into political discussion.

6. All parties seemed to regard it as a great matter to go to Conference, and were speaking with great interest of the appointments that would be made.

7. Bishop Ames is probably fifty years of age, has a good countenance, an intelligent appearance, and is a fine and elegant looking, man. His manners are easy, pleasant, and agreeable. His whole bearing is becoming, kind and winning.

8. Those we took for Presiding Elders, are grave, respectful, and dignified men, and conducted themselves worthily.

9. Dr. Elliott, former editor of the *W. C. Advocate,* is a venerable, grave, and intelligent looking man. Indeed, he is rather a remarkable man for his age.

10. A majority of the remainder of the preachers conducted themselves worthily and becomingly; sufficiently so to render them an example worthy of imitation. But we are sorry to be compelled to say that some things occurred that we thought exceedingly unbecoming, on the part of some few. When it came time to retire for the night, an appropriate hymn was sung, after which all bowed in prayer. This was all very well; but what immediately followed was ridiculous in the extreme. Some wag, a wit, we know not who he was, lay opposite our birth on the floor; and Munchausen himself could not have competed with him in telling big stories. He would tell of the singular prayers he had heard at their various meetings, of which he mentioned the prayer of some old preacher, which will serve for a specimen. The prayer, as near as we can now recollect, ran as follows: "O Lord, bless the circuit; come down and bless them at Zanesville, Newark, Circleville, and Chillicothe; and then, Lord, come down here, (the place where the preacher was praying) to this poor, little, dirty Saltillo, and have mercy upon it also." This elicited the loudest, longest, deepest and heartiest laugh from the general body we almost ever heard. We had frequently heard others tell of their ridiculous expressions, in their prayers, and laugh over them, but we were not aware that the preachers themselves entertained one another in that way.

We must mention one more case, as a kind of exponent of what followed the solemn prayer before retiring. One man, we think an old man, told of a revival meeting he had held in a school house. He said, "a strapping great big fellow come to the mourner's bench; and while we were praying for him he got under conviction; and in his struggle, got down flat on the floor, and twisted round till he got under the stove; and then he got religion, jumped up, threw the stove down, scattered the fire all over the school house, and would have burnt it up, if it had not been for some sinners who put the fire out." We pretend not to describe the laughing that followed this. In one word, more laughing, jesting, and foolish talking we have not heard in any company in twenty years.

One old man was inquiring about the state of things at Fort Black. Some young man talked as if he were lately from there. Among other inquiries, the older one asked, "what has become of them Water Fowls up there?" The answer was that "they went ahead rapidly for a while and were dipping somebody at almost every meeting, but at present, I am in hopes the thing is dying out." He gave a hideous account of these "Water Fowls," and, I have no doubt, had his troubles with them. From his own account, we should not be surprised if he did not have to imitate the "Water Fowls," and "go down into the water," according to Scripture, and *immerse,* as the word *baptize* means. Many pious Methodist preachers, and, probably, some not very pious, have been compelled to this; in doing which they are simply doing what their Discipline requires, where the candidate desires it. What a state of things, when men, professedly preachers of the gospel, nickname and ridicule others for doing what the Lord requires, and what they will do themselves rather than lose a member.

We are informed that there were more than three hundred preachers at Conference. What an amount of good these might do, if their entire energies were devoted to Christianity, in the place of Methodism. But, at present, their thoughts extend not beyond their mere party and its aggrandizement. The kingdom of God is too wide a scope to take into the horizon as a partisan. The Church of God is entirely too expanded to have a place in the soul of a mere sectionist. The benevolence of the Bible; the grace of God; the mercy of our Lord Jesus Christ, extend too wide, for a man with his eye upon an insignificant human party, with a human name, a human creed, and, in itself, nothing but a human system.

-----o-----

SPEAK as you mean, do as you profess, and perform what you promise.

Our Position as a Religious Community.
NO. XI.

We have been satisfied that the main difficulty to be encountered in calling the people of this generation back from the doctrines and commandments of men, to the simplicity of the ancient faith and practice of Christianity, would be found among the professors of religion; that it would be found in *the churches,* and what is vastly more lamentable, among *preachers;* and, still worse, that the difficulty itself, is to induce them to love, admire and delight in the ways and works of God more than in the ways and works of man; to have more confidence in, and be more willing to be led and guided by the glorious Redeemer; or, in other words, to have more confidence in, and be more willing to be led by the Holy Spirit of the living God, than poor, weak, and erring mortals; to prefer to honor and exalt the wisdom of God above the wisdom of man. Whatever spiritual influences men may believe in and plead for, however much they may contend for an abstract influence of the Spirit, or an influence separate from and independent of the word, it is manifest that the inspired scriptures are the teachings of the Spirit of God, and that no man is a Christian who does not adhere to and follow the scriptures. "They who are of God, hear us, and they that are not of God, hear not us," says the holy and inspired Apostle of the Lamb. No preacher in his revival operations, or any other work he may engage in, has the Spirit of God, or is guided by the Spirit, or is of God, who does not hear the Apostles, both in converting men and teaching the church. The command of an Apostle is, to follow him as he followed Christ. No man who preaches to sinners, who does not preach what the Apostles did when they preached to the same class, need claim that he has the Spirit of God, or is guided by him; nor need any man, when directing penitent sinners how to come to God, who does not give the same directions the Apostles did in all the conversions under their ministry, claim that he is led by, or has the Spirit of God, for the spirit of God must agree with himself. If men could prove a thousand operations of the spirit, separate from and independent of the Bible, all these operations and influences must lead men to obey the Bible, or else the Bible must be set aside.

Some men are guided by *reason,* other by *providences,* and others by spiritual *influences,* separate from, or without the word of God. In regard to all this, it is not necessary to make much war upon them, provided *their* reason, providences, or influences, lead them to obey the Gospel, which we know was preached with the Holy Spirit sent down from Heaven. But it is a sad comment on *their* reason, providences, or spiritual influences, when it leads them to disobey the teachings of the Spirit of God in the Bible. Right reason, true providences, or real spiritual influences, could not lead any in our day to disregard what the Spirit of God taught in the establishment of Christianity. In one short sentence: "The Spirit of God would not lead men to disobey what He has clearly required in the Bible." No reason, providences, or spiritual influences, therefore, can be of the Spirit of God, to lead men to disobey what the Spirit of God taught in the Bible, or required at the beginning. The Spirit of God required precisely the same of all persons who sought the way into the Kingdom of God in the days of the Apostles, that he does of all who seek the way now. The Holy Spirit has not changed. It is then a most arrogant and unfounded pretense for any man who now attempts to set forth the way for sinners to come to God, to claim that he is led by the Holy Spirit, while he evades and refuses to set forth the plain and unequivocal requirements of the Holy Spirit as set forth in the New Testament, or attempts to improve upon them. Nothing can be taken from those requirements or added to them without incurring the curse of Heaven. The Spirit of God, if he did lead men independent of his word, could not lead them to incur this awful curse; he, therefore, manifestly, does not lead any man who will add anything to, or take anything from, what he required when he spake through the Apostles, of all whom he showed the way into the Kingdom of God. That which he required in one case, he required in all cases. If he required one man to believe, in order to become a disciple, he required all to believe. If he required one man to confess Christ, he required all to confess him. If he required one man to repent, he required all to repent. If he required one man to "be baptized in the name of Christ for the remission of sins," he required all to do the same. If he promised one man pardon and the impartation of his Holy Spirit, upon his compliance with his requirements, he promised all who complied with the same, whether all the items mentioned in one case are found in all or not. No matter if faith is not mentioned in the case of the three thousand on Pentecost; it is not left out; they all believed, for without faith it is impossible to please God. They that come to God must believe. No matter if repentance is not mentioned in Saul's conversion. Acts xxii: 16, he repented, for God requires all men everywhere to repent. The same is true of all the items.

We, therefore, are the only people now known, who proceed upon the infallibly certain method of collecting and arranging in proper order all the items required by the Holy Spirit in the conversion of sinners; we mean the inductive mode of reasoning. We have no preference for any particular part of scripture; it is all precious to us. We have no particular class of scriptures, as Calvinists. Universalists, Unitarians, etc., but we take the whole scripture; not to prove our doctrine, but as the perfect and complete system of doctrine itself. When we wish to examine any point of doctrine, we proceed upon the inductive plan, and take all the Bible contains as the mind of God upon that point. When we would ascertain what the Holy Spirit of God requires of sinners in their conversion and admission into the Kingdom of God, we proceed through all the conversions of the New Testament, collect all the items, and ascertain their order, and insist that the Holy Spirit requires the same now; nothing more; nothing less. Let us, then, take a brief look through the New Testament, at all the conversions, and ascertain precisely what is required and what is promised.

We open at the following words of the Philippian Jailor: "Sirs, what must I do to be saved?" Here is a Pagan whose attention is for the first time called to the subject. What reply does the Apostle make to him? The answer is, "Believe in the Lord Jesus Christ, and thou shalt be saved, and thy house."— Acts xvi: 30—31. Here is an important item in the form of requirement, and one, too, that cannot be dispensed with, for the Holy Spirit says: "He that cometh to God *must* believe." It is not only a requirement that he should, but a positive and unequivocal demand is that he *must* believe, and this indispensable demand of him that "cometh to God." See Heb. xi: 6. But now for the order of this item. Is it a first, second, third, or fourth item? It is the first item, for the Apostle says, in the context, "Without faith it is impossible to please God." It is in vain, then, to try to do anything else to please him so long as a man does not believe. It is the first item, because the Apostle required it first of a man who had complied with no other item in such a way as to lead him to believe on the Lord Jesus Christ the first thing he did. It is the first item, because "whatever is not of faith is sin."—Roms. xiv: 23. It must, therefore, be the first item, because everything else proceeds from it and is done by it. The first item in the commission is Faith, and he that sets aside that item will be condemned, let him think and act as he may in regard to all other items. "He that believeth and is baptized shall be saved, and he that believeth not shall be damned," says the Lord. The first requirement, then, is to "believe on the Lord Jesus Christ," and without complying with this requirement, or taking this step, no person can ever take another. There is no reaching the second step without taking the first. Unless the first step is taken, it will eternally stand between any man and the second. This indispensable step was required of, and taken by, all who came to God under the guidance of the Holy Spirit who spoke through the Apostles to the people to lead them to God. Never did one, from the days of the Apostles to the present time, get round, or by, this great requirement, and come to God. It is true, that when the Pentecostians and Saul inquired what they should do, they were not commanded to *believe;* but it was not that faith was dispensed with in their cases, or that the Lord had a different method of conversion for them, but for the good reason that they *already believed,* and their faith caused them to inquire what they should do.

Acts iii: 19, we find the following requirement laid down: "Repent ye, therefore, and be converted, that your sins may be blotted out, when the times of refreshing shall come from the presence of the Lord." This requirement was uttered to an assembly that had just witnessed one of the most manifest miracles of the apostles—one which the enemies mentioned shortly after, admitting that it was known to all who dwelt in Jerusalem and that they could not deny it, and at the close of a discourse which they had heard and which had convinced them that the work was of God. The Holy Spirit, on this occasion, demanded of them to repent, reform, or amend their lives. This demand too, is as wide as the actual sinners among men. In the times of ignorance before the gospel, God did not hold men to a strict account for their sins, "but now he commands all men everywhere to *repent,* because he hath appointed a day in which he will judge the world in righteousness." Acts xvii: 30-31. Repentance, too, is indispensable. "Except ye repent, ye shall all likewise perish." Lu. xiii: 3. What does the Lord mean by this word, "except"? John iii: 3, he says, "except a man be born again, he cannot see the kingdom of God." Two verses after this, he says, "except a man be born of water and of the Spirit, he cannot enter into the kingdom of God." Here we have the same word, "except," again. What does he mean by it? At verso seven he explains as follows: "Marvel not that I said unto thee, *Ye must be born again."* You must repent or perish then, is the meaning of the Words "except ye repent ye shall perish." Repentance is then required of "all men everywhere," and is indispensable—*must be.*

But what evidence have you that repentance is the second item? It is the second item, because we have shown that faith is the first, which shows that repentance cannot be the first; and because Peter, Acts ii: 3, and iii: 19, addressing people who believed, but had not repented or done anything else, commanded them to repent. He makes it the second item. It is the second item, because a man cannot repent till he believes in the Lord before whom he must repent, and who convinces him of sin, for "by the law is the knowledge of sin," which shows that it must follow after faith; and because there is no other item in all the records of conversions required, that he can acceptably comply with till he does repent. An impenitent person cannot pray, confess, be baptized, or do anything acceptable to God. The person, therefore, who is a believer in our Lord Jesus Christ, cannot get over repentance, or do anything else acceptable to God till he repents. His faith will do no good so long as he continues in impenitence. For his impenitence, if he persists in it, he must perish. In the order of God, it is the second step, and unless taken, will eternally stand between him and the third step. No advance can ever be made till he repents. "Except ye repent, ye shall perish." It is true that Ananias did not command Saul to repent; but it was not because it was omitted in his case, for no man ever entered the kingdom of God without repentance; but he was not commanded to repent, for the good reason that he had repented before Ananias came to him. We are not to expect any historian, in giving records of conversions, and so many instances, to mention all the items in each case. B. F.

-----o-----

Eastern Tour.

On Thursday, Oct. 9th, we left the dear ones in Cincinnati, and took cars for our first trip over the mountains. At six o'clock in the morning, the steam-horse hied us away at the rate of some 33 miles an hour, over the beautiful Little Miami railroad, through Xenia, Columbus, and Zanesville, without any interruption for some 200 miles, which brought us opposite and some 10 miles from where we were brought up. But here we called a halt. In a few minutes, impatient passengers began to grumble: "What are we stopping here for?" "Are we to remain here all day?" "We shall miss the connection at Wheeling." "I would not be detained a day for twenty dollars," etc., etc. But all this grumbling availed nothing; here we remained. Among the anxious passengers was a stump orator, due at some point ahead, to make a speech at night, "to *save his country"* which, we have learned, means, to save an office, or salary. The anxious man showed that he felt the importance of his mission, and the serious danger that the speech in store, consisting of explosive and fiery elements, like the rumbling fires of Etna or Vesuvius, would have to remain penned up and burning in his soul over night. But it was soon found that neither the urgency of his case, nor that of anyone else, availed anything in our condition. A stupid switchman had neglected to have his switch in order when a freight train ahead approached, by which means it was thrown off the rails, but stopped on and obstructing the track so that we could not pass.

Here we had to wait some two hours for the eastern train to meet us, when we were ordered to change trains. Here another hour was spent in exchanging passengers and baggage. Our new train now moved slowly and cautiously backward. In some ten miles we halted again, when we came to a switch, when more time was lost in changing the locomotive from the rear to the front of the train. We then proceeded to Cambridge, O., when our locomotive was detached from the train and seen to leave us. The intelligence was brought that it was going ahead to a turn-table to turn round. After it had been gone about an hour, and another locomotive had made a trip to it and back, we learned that it was off the track. It was now manifest that our conductor was a stupid creature who never should have been entrusted with a more important conveyance than an ox-cart. Passengers proposed to him to take one of the four or five locomotives at hand and proceed with the train. But he expatiated on the dangers of running a locomotive backward until he filled a portion of the passengers with fear, so that they were willing to remain. At length the word came that our locomotive was on the track, but not turned, when the cry of the passengers was unanimously, "Proceed."

After thus detaining not only to miss the regular connection at Wheeling, at 4 o'clock, P. M., which was unavoidable, but stupidly and entirely unnecessarily detaining so as to miss the connection with the 11 o'clock at night train, when threatened that he should be published for his stupidity and mismanagement, he proceeded, reaching Wheeling at 12 o'clock at night. Here we got a sound sleep from one o'clock till six in the morning. At seven o'clock, we took the accommodation train, on the Ohio and Baltimore road, in place of waiting till four o'clock, P. M., for the express, that we might pass the mountains in day-time.

This day presented us some of the grandest objects of admiration, both of nature and art, we ever beheld. Here we saw some of the grandest, most stupendous and wonderful achievements of human enlightenment, combined with industry, we had ever seen. At one moment we found ourselves hundreds of feet above the tall pine-trees away in the valley below, where, if we had been thrown off the track, we must have been precipitated hundreds of feet down among the craggy rocks. In another moment we passed from the skirts of tree-tops, plunging into the dark and dreary tunnel, cut through solid rock, hundreds of feet underground, where we could no more see than if we had never had eyes. Truly is this a mighty and wonderful achievement for mortals—poor, weak, and dying mortals! It is overwhelming that *men* should ever have projected, prosecuted, and completed such a conveyance as this such a vast distance through this expanded and rugged region of country!

But, vast as this achievement may appear, when we are looking at it as a *work of man,* it diminishes, dwindles and sinks into utter insignificance and nothingness, when we lift our eyes above it, to "the everlasting hills," the workmanship of Him who "weighs the hills in a balance and handles the isles as a very little thing." Also, how our hearts are filled with reverence and our spirits impressed with awe, when we lift our eyes above the hills, to the vast mountains, and think of the thousands of miles over which this mighty range extends, as well as others on our great continent, vaster and greater than this, and reflect, that, stupendous as they appear to us, they are all as nothing with that Almighty and incomprehensible Being—the Infinite One, who created and upholds that overwhelming and illimitable something which we call *the universe!* We are, at the same time, filled With awe and gratitude, that we have the blessed assurance that we are not overlooked, forgotten, and lost in the immensity of the innumerable works of the Creator! But, blessed be his glorious name, vast and innumerable as are his marvelous works, he has the time, the goodness and compassion to provide for the fowls of heaven, and the fish of the sea, as well as the beasts of the forest. Among all the variegated multitudes of the feathered tribes, not even a sparrow falls to the ground unobserved by Him; and, by the same Omniscient One, we are assured, by our adorable Redeemer, the hairs of our heads are all numbered. To the same amount, and for the same purpose, he says, "If an earthly parent knows how to give good things to children, how much more shall the Heavenly Father give his Holy Spirit to those who ask him!" How comforting to think that he has promised, saying, "I will never leave you nor forsake you, but will grant you grace and glory, and no good thing will I withhold from you!" How secure, too, we can feel, and how strengthening to reflect, when dashing through these fearful mountains, conscious that though in one moment an accident might occur by which our earthly career might be terminated, the everlasting arms are underneath; and though the earthly building may be destroyed, we have an house not made with hands eternal in the heavens. To his Almighty hand we commit our all; in Him is our everlasting trust. To him be praises forever and ever.

At 6 o'clock and 40 minutes in the evening we reached Cumberland, Md. Here the accommodation train stopped, and here we had to remain till the express arrived at 2 o'clock in the morning. Here we thought would be an opportunity to sleep from 8 o'clock till 2. But being thrown 24 hours behind time, and fearing that it would derange our operations, filled us with too much anxiety to sleep much.

We did, however, sleep some. In due time our faithful landlord had all the passengers awakened and in readiness, when the train arrived, and the cry was heard, "All aboard." Stepping upon the train, we soon found several passengers from Cincinnati, who had started one day later than we. At daylight in the morning, we were at Martinsburg, Va., our stopping place; where in a very few minutes we engaged a boy to carry us to Hagerstown, Md., 18 miles distant. On reaching Hagerstown, we learned that the beloved brother, Benj. Whitmer, had been there punctually to meet us, the day before, and made arrangements with a gentleman to carry us some six miles to Beaver Creek. After taking a little refreshment, having endured some fasting, much loss of sleep, and the fatigues of nearly three days and two nights, we reached the residence of Bro. Benj. Whitmer, where we met a hearty welcome and every comfort that could be desired. Nothing was omitted that this precious Christian family could do, to render us happy and make us feel the value of friendship and hospitality.

We soon learned that Eld. Lefever, from Cumberland county, Ta., and Eld. McComas, from Hagerstown, Md., were in the neighborhood, and had been edifying the assemblies convened to hear the word previous to our arrival, to both of whom we were introduced and with whom we formed a short but agreeable acquaintance. After lying down and sleeping some two hours, we rose and took some refreshment and repaired to the commodious meeting house, which was filled to its utmost capacity. This audience, consisting of respectable and intelligent young people mainly, gave unabated attention for an hour and a half, to a discourse on reconciling both the Jews and Gentiles in one body in Christ. On the next morning, Lord's day, we addressed a dense assembly; and again still a larger assembly at night. Thus we continued from day to day, at 10 o'clock and at night, till Wednesday night. On Thursday, an elderly gentleman, a member of the Lutheran church, Mr. JACOB FUNK, died in the neighborhood. The Disciples' meeting house is on one side of the road and the Lutherans' house on the other side. We preached at 10 o'clock, and, the announce ment was made, that a Lutheran minister from Hagerstown, would preach at the funeral, at one o'clock. At the hour, the procession arrived at the Lutheran church, with the corpse, but no preacher appeared. After waiting, hesitating, and consulting, the request was made that we should address the assembly, which we cheerfully did, and, as we learned, much to the satisfaction of all concerned. At night we addressed a full house, on the Great Commission, at two hours' length, which was heard with profound attention. One worthy sister, who had been baptized, but who had been with the Methodists several years, united with the church. Another valuable lady was immersed during the meeting.

But now the time had come to part from these precious brethren. In the midst of many tears, warm grasps of the hand, good wishes, and a very commendable liberality, we separated, exhorting each other to persevere to the end, that we may meet in a better world. On Thursday morning, we bid farewell to the beloved Witmer family, and being helped on our way by the worthy and esteemed brother, John Flaugher, we went five miles to Boonsboro, where we received a hearty welcome, in the kind and hospitable family of Bro. Jacob Keedly. Here we were in the house that the esteemed, faithful, and lamented evangelist, Eld. G. H. CALDWELL, died in. This brought to our mind the happy days we spent with him and the labors we performed together in advocacy of the cause of God. We also saw his grave, where his body rests, while we are assured that the noble being—the spirit—that dwelt in that body, is with the Lord, whom he loved and delighted to honor. We also saw the widow, his excellent lady, who, though left to struggle with the adversities and asperities of this world, while we confidently trust her husband is at rest in Abraham's bosom, enjoys the same universal esteem and confidence of the Disciples in Maryland, she did in Indiana.

The Lutheran church, the most ancient house in appearance we ever saw—a stone house—readily opened to us in Boonsboro', and on Thursday morning, we addressed the small congregation collected with a short notice, from the midst of political excitement and the attractions of a great fair at Hagerstown, at 10 o'clock. Those present, principally old people, appeared deeply interested, and to feel that it was good for us to be here. At night, we again spoke to a respectable audience, in the same house, at much length, where the profoundest interest prevailed. Two ministers were present, one an Episcopal Methodist and the other a United Brother. The former we were introduced to, and when requested to close the services, he prayed with us; but the prayer was the most precise and non-committal we ever heard. He was as careful not to allude to anything said, or to us as a people, or the occasion, as if aiming to keep the whole matter a profound secret from the Lord. The other gentleman we had no introduction to.

On Friday, 17th, helped on our way by Bro. Keedly, to Kearneysville, Va., we took cars for home, and on Saturday, 18th, at 5 o'clock in the evening, reached our city, found all well. We traveled almost 1200 miles and preached twelve discourses in 11 days.

-----o-----

LEXINGTON, Oct. 13, 1856.

DEAR BRO. FRANKLIN:—Our venerable and devoted Bro. J. T. Johnson handed me, a day or two since, the accompanying communication, with the request that, after reading it., I would send it to you for publication. Surely suggestions coming from a brother of the age, opportunities of observation and experience of the writer, should receive the attention and prayerful examination of our Brotherhood, and the adoption of the practice recommended, so far as in their judgment they are in accordance with the teaching of inspiration. His remarks on the subject of long prayers, meet my cordial assent, as well as those on the importance of promptness in assembling and engaging in worship at the appointed time; indeed, as I remarked before, all claim due consideration, and in connection with those made by Brother Johnson, I take the liberty of adding, that it frequently appears to me that in returning thanks for the bread and wine, the emblems of the broken body and shed blood of the Saviour of mankind, too much is often prayed for and thanks offered, for to suit this solemn and soul-reviving feast; but, my Brother, we may engage in all these services in the most approved and acceptable manner to the Brotherhood, and the word, if our worship be without love to God and good-will to man, and the unction of the Holy Spirit, our worship will be in vain. God knows I am no fault-finder, but I will venture a hint relative to an evil which I have noticed for years, and which, in my opinion, is the cause of bitter feeling in the bosoms of good men. I mean a certain class of men who shall be nameless, it is that of (shall I say it) Envy and Jealousy. Possibly I have said too much. May God. our Heavenly Father, enable us all to be humble and entirely devoted to his cause. Amen.

JOSEPH WASSON.

-----o-----

The Proper Method of Conducting Worship.

IT is the privilege, as well as the duty, of: the aged and experienced, to give the results and benefits of their observations and reflections to those who are to come after them. The cause of Christ has suffered greatly in the hands of good and sensible men, for the want of prudence and discretion in matters that are considered by many of little importance. Having observed the most disastrous consequences resulting from an imperfect knowledge of human nature; of the genius and spirit of Christianity, as adapted to all ages, sexes, and conditions; and ignorance in respect to the tastes and capacities of others to receive, digest, and hear, I have concluded to venture a few pages for the benefit of all concerned. In the first place, I will speak of the management of congregations, inasmuch as great defects exist; and much complaint has been made as regards the delinquencies of the members in attending their weekly meetings. The fault may be owing as much to the managers of the congregation as the managed. Therefore, the following suggestions are submitted, in the hope that good may result. Most frequently the officers and congregations assemble after the time appointed for the worship. A calm, or indiscriminate, boisterous conversation ensues, for twenty or thirty minutes; a hymn book is opened, and the leaves are turned for some five or ten minutes. The throat is then cleared for about the same time, and then commences a hymn. After a while another hymn is sung; then a *long* reading is indulged in, with, perhaps, some comments; then a prayer three times too long, offensive to the Lord and the congregation. And now, when the time has arrived for closing the worship, the leader enters upon the administration of the supper, preceded and followed by tedious, common place, and a thousand times repeated, observations and comments. The time occupied in all this display, is, perhaps from half after 10 o'clock A.M., to 1 o'clock P.M. It may be asked, to whom will the above apply? Let us all take it to ourselves, and if faulty, we will be sure to profit. But the misfortune is, that we are too apt to apply to our neighbors what belongs to ourselves. Let each examine himself. Let me now suggest the Christian course. Meet precisely at the moment—engage at once in singing—read a brief, interesting, appropriate paragraph (not a chapter)—put up a brief petition to the Lord, appropriate to the occasion and circumstances — make some few comments, embracing not more than ten minutes—partake of the supper—attend to the contributions, and adjourn. Such a course as this, free from scolding, would soon interest all the pious, valuable members of the congregation, and all would be life and animation. Try it, persevere in it. Begin at the time, don't delay; dismiss at the time, don't prolong. From half after 10 to 12 o'clock is long enough, at any one time, for the worship.

A prayer meeting, Bible class, or Sunday School, ought never to be prolonged beyond an hour.

Be punctual to engagements, be punctual, be punctual. What a mighty revolution would be accomplished by it! The most successful men on earth have been punctual to their engagements, yea, to the very moment.

It must be remembered, however, that the most perfect adherence to time and order, will never supply the deficiencies of unqualified elders, or bishops, and deacons. And it is equally true, that nothing can fill up the chasm of love and devotion for the cause. We may endeavor to bind and organize, and we may complain and scold, but it will all be in vain, unless the members are bound together by love. Converted by love, we must be disciplined in love. Love must be the ruling, reigning passion.

To succeed well, the officers must be Scripturally qualified. We might as well expect an army to be successful with unqualified officers and undisciplined soldiers. And if; qualified as officers and soldiers, success never can be expected from an indolent, slovenly army, regardless of the high trust committed to it. Let us, one and all, endeavor, in the spirit of kindness, to carry out more perfectly the divine science of salvation, as inscribed in the pages of the divine volume. J. T. J.

Suggestions in conducting the worship of a congregation in cases where a speaker is present, and a sermon is to be delivered:

1. The congregation should be punctual to the time, and the speaker should commence his discourse at the moment fixed by the congregation. Everything should be arranged to this end.

2. Let each part of the worship have its allotted time—the singing, the prayer, the reading, the preaching, and the supper, etc.

3. By all means, brevity should be observed in all that is done. Avoid all attempts at a long prayer—what miserable things *expletives* are in prayer.

4. All should be attended to with life, spirit, and animation.

These may be considered little matters, but we may rest assured that mighty results for good would be the consequence. J. T. J.

-----o-----

REMARKS.

We fully accord with every word in the foregoing: it comes from one who shows his faith by his works. He has a plan of operation, easy, simple and efficient—the one under which we are made what we are as a people, and the one under which he has labored some twenty- six years, and under which he is still laboring and bringing many souls to the kingdom of God; many others are doing the same, and wherever one of this classes found, the wonk is progressing. But what are those doing who oppose him on these points? Are they advancing the cause? Those who preach and write upon "the *decline* of the Reformation," are they advancing the cause? Are they building up anything? Where they go and labor do they produce love, good-will, benevolence, and convert sinners and strengthen saints? We have a right to look to these matters. hollow Bro. John T. Johnson, and others laboring upon the same principle, and try them by the same rule.

We have listened to all this cant about "our decline," "going down," "the Reformation a failure," etc., etc., for years, and know the meaning of it. Some men, because of their impracticable and extravagant notions, or their lack of zeal, earnestness and perseverance, or their dictatorial, tyrannical or despotic course have made a most manifest failure *themselves'*; but this is no failure in the *cause;* it is *their* failure and *their* shame, and the time has come when *they* must take the responsibility, and not think to shift it off upon the cause. Let them go to work and work for God, with spirit, zeal and earnestness, and they will prosper and the cause will prosper. B. F.

-----o-----

To the Brethren in Kentucky.

OUR present aspect as a religious people, in contrast with our wonderful success a few years back, has been a fruitful theme of speculation of late. Though there is no body of professing Christians adding numerical strength in a greater ratio in the Middle and Western States, at the present time, than our own, yet this success does not fill the measure of expectation, with those brethren and friends who have never ceased to appreciate the power of truth, when brought into action under favorable circumstances. We are yet progressive—but tardily so.

The time was when the ranks of partyism thinned down and melted away, under the constant and vigorous blows of our simple-hearted but strong-minded pioneer fathers. They clad themselves in God's armorial, and went forth to conquest, with no other weapon of offense than the naked "sword of the spirit"—"The word of truth." Theirs was the courage and self-sacrifice of heroism. The Ricketts, and Mortons left the anvil—the Curtis Smiths the saddler's shops—a Johnson the halls of Congress—and how many John Smiths the plow handle, to battle for truth? As the drilled soldiery of Europe could not stand before the rustic militia-men of the revolution, so the rank and file of sectarianism, drilled as they were in the arts and cunning of polemic theology, were scattered and defeated by these militia of our Lord. In each case, the victorious fought with a deep and full conviction of the justice of their cause. If we should assume it as our province to represent the motives and means of each arrayed party, we should say, that on the one hand were the well trained place-men of sectarianism, sustaining that organization from which they secured their livings, or because they were baptized in the traditions and prejudices of their fathers, with that sophistry and artifice which too often deludes, but never enlightens; while opposed to them were simple hearted men, too unsophisticated to handle such weapons if they had been willing, yet irresistibly strong in the earnest and determined energy of confidence and conviction in the unadorned truths of the gospel—contending for that freedom for others wherein Christ had made them free. Their mighty power lay in the naked simplicity of truth. They told the simple story of the cross—but oh! how earnestly— how affectingly! Their labors were done with oneness of purpose—with singleness of heart— as Jesus of Nazareth done his. Such labors in such a cause, never were unfruitful, in the history of man.

But what were the effects upon the masses? Wherever the ears of the people could be had, the truth prevailed. Christianity was the earnest theme, not only in the pulpit, but upon the highways and in the social circle. Nothing supplanted it, because the teachers taught and talked of but little else.

When our preachers evangelized, and our elders taught, the people willingly heard and obeyed. Where the Gospel was preached—where the elders taught and prayed and labored —there the congregations grew in grace and numbers—there they attended to the ordinances of the Lord.

Though we are far from saying that this work was perfect, yet it combined the elements of success in a greater degree than any religious effort before or since, after the apostolic age. In this fact of our early history, may we not discover and profit by the plain examples of a correct philosophy?

But at this day, and for two or three years back, it has become plainly evident that we have not been enlarging the boundaries of our Lord's kingdom as steadily and rapidly as we could wish. It is right and necessary that those who feel a deep and vital interest in the progress of Christianity, should canvass these facts, and discover, if possible, the source of the evil.

We may first inquire—have we not as good material out of which to constitute teachers of the Word and servants of the Church, as when this reformation had its beginning? Have we not as sound doctrine? Have we not the same liberty to proclaim the Gospel? All these questions must be answered in the affirmative. But here, we think, the analogy between our past and present state of affairs ceases. We have, it is true, elders or bishops and deacons in the churches, after the *form* of the wisdom and polity of the Apostles— *but we are almost entirely destitute of Evangelists.* Not that we are left without material to make efficient evangelists—for we have got with us Rickets, Rice, Gano, Williams, Pinkerton, Rogers, and a host of others, who might take the field with as much hope of success as crowned the pioneer efforts of our early fathers. But where are these? They have suffered themselves to be counted among that nondescript class of co-operants in the kingdom of Messiah, *unfortunately known* as—monthly preachers—a class so universally known, too, that we shall give their character and official identity only in a single brief sentence. Authentically considered, they are one-fourth pastor, without pastoral authority; one-fourth evangelist, without evangelical efficiency; and two-fourths *nothing.* A fungous growth—unknown to scriptural precept or scriptural example, and which we pray

God, may not much longer be known to us—superinduced by evils and errors on the part of both preachers and people, as we most humbly submit.

The error, upon the part of the people, has been the withholding, as is affirmed, an adequate support from our missionary preachers. With how much justice this affirmation is made, we shall not pause to inquire. We take for granted that it is partially true—but not the whole truth. How many of those who have placed their trust in God, entered resolutely and energetically in the field, and labored successfully—forgetting self, and all things else save Christ and his kingdom— have been heard complaining that they were starved out? We know that even these encountered many difficulties, and oftentimes preached to people whose hearts were more easily moved than their pockets. But amid all such discouragement, they pushed on the work with a faithful reliance on Him whom they served. David wisely said, many centuries ago—"I have been young, and am old now, yet have I never seen the righteous forsaken, nor his children begging bread." So of the righteous servants to this day. We look in vain for any who have been forsaken to poverty, or whose children were driven to beg bread. Indeed we cannot point to an instance in our knowledge which is an exception. But let no man flatter himself that he can be excused from paying his proportion toward an adequate support of those who depend on their labors in the Gospel for their living. I would as soon appear at the bar of God with the crime of theft upon my conscience, as to be accused there of having caused a preacher of the Word to suffer from my covetousness.

There are yet many who do not, or will not, recognize their obligation to bear their portion in supporting elders and evangelists. That it is their duty to make at least this small sacrifice. is as plain as the hand-writing upon the wall; and we appeal to all such, to answer, in good conscience, whether it be their avarice or their ignorance that prompts them in sending the minister from them in want? If it be the former, they must be conscious of base motives —if the latter, let them not be deceived with the assurance that a plea of ignorance, in this day of light, will not fait But we have heard those who complained loudest, testify, of late, that a revolution had taken place to some extent—that a spirit of liberality was generally diffusing itself among the brotherhood in Kentucky, and that most of the ministers were well supported. If our brethren have thus responded to the appeals set forth, and shown their willingness to do their duty, when enlightened with regard to it, may not our preachers be encouraged to dispossess themselves of all fears and misgivings in regard to a support, quit their monthly preaching and enter the field as true evangelists? The press of public and general want of their labors in this field, is surely worth the trial. As one of the people we promise a hearty response to those who are competent evangelists, if they are ready and willing to make the sacrifice, for Christ's sake.

But we have said that the preachers were at fault too, in this practice. They have lent themselves, *too willingly,* to the abominable practice. Instead of meeting the difficulties with a firm front, and with firm voice warning and rebuking against this tendency, in some of the churches, they have tacitly yielded to popular caprice, and fallen in with the current. Let us look for a moment at the suggesting motives, the operations and consequences of this practice. There is a prevailing prejudice among the masses of Christians, that the preacher is a sort of priest standing as mediator between them and God; and if they employ a preacher all they are obliged to do is to pay him and go to hear him—and that is the end of Christian practice. There is another prejudice equally as absurd—that the worship is not worth attending—that it is a bore—unless the preacher is popular enough to draw a crowd from the world. These forget that every disciple is "a priest unto God," and that the regular service of each Lord's day is for the edification and spiritual advancement of the congregation, and not for the conquest of the world. The former may always be secondary matter with the evangelist—the latter a secondary consideration with the bishop or pastor. The primary duty of the evangelist is to convert sinners—that of the pastor to edify and advance the congregation. To gratify this eccentric desire, a preacher, with all the prestige of official dignity, must be had. He is rarely employed, in his weekly ministrations, at a single point—sometimes he serves a congregation twice a month, but generally not more than once. The congregation, saints and sinners, listen—go home, exchange opinions as to the merits of the sermon, and forget it. Their "itching ears" are tickled for the time, and they imagine they have been devotional. If this service is once a month, or twice a month, the Lord's day service of the remaining days of worship is voted a bore by a large proportion of the members. We can testify, that as far as our experience goes, the churches do not often grow even under the weekly ministrations of our anomalous preacher of the present day. Generally shifting himself from place to place every year, he often preaches to congregations one-half of whose members he is unacquainted with, or but partially so, when he is called, at the expiration of a twelve-month, to preach his valedictory. These are not the bishops of the New Testament, as we shall see before we conclude.

The congregation, therefore, must have a preacher, and if they feel themselves unable to employ him to preach every Lord's day, they will strike a bargain for one or two Sundays in the month. With the preacher the position is one of easy indulgence, and certain and profitable remuneration, compared to the responsibilities of the true Christian evangelist. On the one hand, are the trials of the Christian servant, on the other, the temptations of— we must not say it! Did our preaching brethren ever think of monthly preaching in this light? No! for then they would never have engaged in it. They may even now refuse to see it from our stand point. But we ask them to be candid.

Thus, from mutual blindness, or mutual misconception of their responsibilities, preachers and laymen have suffered—or rather encouraged the practice among us, until it has become a consuming monster, exhausting our strength and leaving us helpless to the evils of stagnation. What are the facts apparent to every-one who observes?—*about one-half of the wealthier churches have retained the services of those who ought to be evangelizing, while the other half, with the world, are famishing for the bread of life thus unjustly taken from their mouth!*

Preachers and people! We ask you, in our Master's name—in behalf of our Master's cause—think of this! How many young and partially helpless congregations have we seen struggle against opposition and difficulties for years, and efficient men, in hearing distance of their cry for help, tramp, tramp their monotonous round of monthly preaching, refusing to stretch forth the helping hand, even to the exhausted and dying! Oh! there is a cruel selfishness in the hearts of preachers and people, in these things, that strikes upon the car too much like the story of poor Lazarus at the rich man's gate.

Yet there are some among us, in the face of our condition and necessities, would persuade the congregations to employ these brethren who ought to constitute our evangelical strength, as regular preachers or pastors of single churches. What would be the result? As there are not more than one preacher to every five churches in the State, four-fifths of our congregations would be cut off from all prospect of support from competent evangelists, and left to struggle on hopelessly to an end, over which we gladly drop the curtain of the future. It is idle to talk of supplying all the congregations with efficient pastors, with a competent corps of evangelists left, while society is rent into fragments by the curse of sectarianism. In almost every community, where there is only enough material for one good congregation, and enough talent for its pastoral and evangelical wants, we find about four churches, with these elements of strength divided among them. So they struggle on in weakness, blindness and folly. Who of our preachers are ready to cut themselves loose from this unscriptural and ruinous practice of periodical preaching? To some, we fear, we appeal in vain; they are too much joined to their idol. They love their ease too much to bear the cross of Christ. They tremble and hesitate to let go these indulgent livings, and cast themselves upon the mercy of God. Their faith is not strong enough to trust him. How fearful, in the present day, to start upon the mission of the Gospel, without gold or silver in their purses, scrip for their journey, or a change of garments! O brethren! have you not confidence to trust the assurances of God? Try it—once! Throw away your theories—your new organizations! We want work! self-sacrificing work! New organizations—new theories can do us no good. They may divide us into factions and discordant parties, but they are neither scriptural food nor strength nor growth for us. We are not wanting in the theory of organization, but in labor and resources to develop and perfect our strength.

[TO BE CONTINUED.]

-----o-----

Letter from J. T. Johnson.

LEXINGTON, Oct., 1856.

DEAR BRO. FRANKLIN:—To convert and save a ruined world was the grand, the sublime, the glorious design of the mission of the Son of God. He formed a nucleus, around which the world might rally, arming his followers with motives as lofty as the heavens, as deep as perdition, and as lasting as eternity. He gifted them with his own spirit to enable them to make every sacrifice, to endure the severest tortures, and to triumph over every obstacle. This trust, of priceless value, was committed to his followers before he left the world, and it will remain a charge upon them until he comes to give them a triumphal entry into the city above.

This is the theme of themes; the object of objects; and it is only astonishing that it does not engage all our powers, day and night, during life, to accomplish an object so far surpassing all that the mind of man can grasp or conceive.

With all our efforts we are dissatisfied; and so little is accomplished that we become despondent and melancholy; surmising that something is wrong; that the machinery is out of order; that the system is defective; we begin to find ways and means to remedy the defects.

The greatest success that ever attended the labors of the disciples was in the age of the Apostles, and that immediately succeeding, when fire and faggot stared them in the face; and before any grand ecclesiastical organization was affected, Christians felt as one, and acted as one. They loved one another as the Son of God loved them. They were animated by the same hope. They were inspirited to accomplish the same object. The congregations had their own officers. They attended to, and managed their; own discipline. They felt the deepest interest for their own purity, and did not rely on others to set them right, or keep them pure.—They elected their own officers, keeping in view their own edification, purity, and happiness, and the conversion of the world. Notwithstanding all this, they acted as with one mouth, one heart, one spirit. There was a love and benevolence that knew no bounds.

With all our civilization and learning, our efforts at co-operation by district and state meetings, are as a Lilliputian to a giant. Truly something is the matter."What is it? It is not the want of organization. Neither is it the want of a state or district meeting *so organized,* as to be empowered to select and ordain, and to try evangelists and churches for heresy, or misconduct of any sort. It seems to me a very poor business, if the congregations are incapable of selecting and trying their own officers, whether bishops, evangelists, or deacons; and of disciplining their own members. There may be cases where helps may be needed. Let them be asked for, and they will be granted. If not, the consequences must be met. If we must have a fire, let it be confined to one house, instead of a city.

But where is the fault? There are many true hearted, loyal Christians, even in Kentucky. They are prepared for any sacrifice, if they see their way clearly. They have shown it, when appealed to properly. They have shown it lately, in appeals for the orphan girl school, the evangelical educational fund, and Bacon College.

If we desire permanent action; constant action; dispensing with these ephemeral appeals, some system must be adopted, more scriptural perhaps, and more in accordance with the philosophy of man, and of Christianity, than any we have yet practiced, as a body. The congregations must get right, and start right. If one congregation can accomplish a given object, do not divide the responsibility between two. For example, if a congregation is wealthy enough to supply her own wants, and sustain an evangelist in the general field, a co-operation of other congregations ought not to relieve her, or lessen the obligation. The Lord may require it at the hands of both parties.

Whenever we begin to divide responsibilities, it is natural for each party to compare their capacities, and to act in that ratio. In thus acting, injury is the invariable result to the parties, and the cause.

It seems to me, then, that co-operations should be confined to very small districts. It would succeed better in every respect. The meetings could be much more' frequent— the brethren would form a more intricate acquaintance—the cause would be brought home to every one—the interest would be a thousand fold more. The means would be multiplied five hundred fold, and the good resulting would be correspondent.

Take, for instance, the four counties of Fayette, Scott, Woodford and Jessamine. Let them have two district meetings in the year— in April and October. Let these meetings be faithfully attended by every preacher and evangelist; and let the brotherhood meet in a mass, so far as practicable. Let them continue together a week at least, and longer if good can be done. I will venture the assertion, that these four counties would raise at least two thousand dollars for evangelical purposes. By these means, three evangelists might be sustained— one within the district, and two without. This would be worthy of them and the cause. I do not like to take ground against any benevolent enterprise in which the brotherhood may be engaged, but I have for sometime felt that our state enterprise is a very little affair; unworthy of us, as a state and people. And I feel prepared to abandon it. and adopt the district system, that brings the matter home to the congregation and members. What is one for an entire state? Even after such an effort, the districts require or request, that their contributions may be spent within their respective bounds. It would be a thousand times more creditable and charitable to spend the whole amount in a mission to England or Europe; and I would give my vote for it now.

If my mind remains the same at the next state meeting, I will most cheerfully vote for a dissolution, in order to make an experiment upon the plan suggested. Whether we adopt a plan or not, the Lord will hold us accountable, both as individuals, and as a community, for all the means we possess, whether pecuniary, or intellectual, or moral.

Let each one take the cause home to his own bosom, and decide whether he is doing what he should for the cause, at home, and abroad; and conclude whether he can stand the test. By the time we have swept our own house clean, we shall have very little time to find fault with, and scold others.

May we all so act, as to be prepared to hear the plaudit, "Well done," in the great day, is the prayer of one who wishes all well.

J. T. JOHNSON.

P. S. Last year, just ending, I acted as evangelist for the State Board, to the entire satisfaction of both parties. This year I calculate on acting as an evangelist on my own responsibility, with the sanction of the organization of which I am a member.

I prefer this course, because I shall feel free to visit my friends in any part of the United States. This course lies nearest my heart, and I desire, before age bows me down, to travel, and build it up, in places far distant, that I have never seen, and where I have long had a strange desire to labor. I anticipate with great pleasure, the meetings I may have with old friends, and the converts I have been the means of bringing to the fold of Christ. May we all meet in heaven.

J. T. J.

-----o-----

ANCIENT superstition introduced the fine arts into her train, called the powers of genius to her aid, and employed the painter and the poet to hold out her charms to the world.

Anniversaries of our Societies in Cincinnati.

As announced in sundry publications, the anniversaries of the societies in this city commenced on Tuesday, October 21st—spending the first day with the Bible Society, the second with the Missionary, and closing on the third day with the Publication Society. The attendance was not large, but yet of such men, and the work done of such a nature, that we think much good will result from the occasion. The unanimity in regard to the course that should be pursued, of mind and feeling in general, was encouraging. It appeared as if all had come up, not only with the determination to agree, but in actual agreement in almost everything. It was resolved that the Bible Society ought to dissolve, and appropriate its proceeds to the Missionary Society, and arrangements were made to bring this about as soon as possible. It was also resolved that the Publication Society should dissolve and cease to exist, and arrangements were made to wind up its affairs in order to that. end. The constitution of the Missionary Society was amended, as was thought, so as to give it more efficiency, and better adapt it to its work; and the way is now opened for the brotherhood to concentrate and combine their hearts, minds, energies and means in one grand enterprise, which we trust will meet the good-will and hearty co-operation of the general body.

There may be, and we doubt not is, some discrepancy in regard to missionary fields, among the brethren; but certainly there is but one mind in regard to the propriety and legitimacy of the missionary work. Every member of the church is, in the very nature of things, a missionary; every congregation of disciples, no matter whether large or small, is constitutionally and in the very nature of the case, a missionary society, with a command from Heaven, to "Disciple, convert or proselyte all nations." We may not always precisely agree in that which is left to human prudence and discretion, but as to the importance of the work of "preaching the unsearchable riches of Christ," of "making all men see what is the fellowship of the mystery, which from the beginning of the world hath been hid in God, who treated all things by Jesus Christ; that now unto the principalities and powers in heavenly places might be known, *by the church,* the manifold wisdom of God," there is no disagreement. The goodness, benevolence and mercy that moved the Infinite One to send the remedial system to the human race, and moved the Word, who was with God, who was God, by whom and for whom all things were made, to leave his abode in heaven, become incarnate, clothed in humanity, the seed of Abraham, a little lower than the angels, that he might "save that which was lost," "that the world through him might be saved we say, that the same goodness, benevolence and mercy, if it has made its proper and divine impression upon our hearts, must draw us out in the deepest anxiety, most ardent solicitude and awful concern for the conversion and salvation of man. If the mission of Jesus, the mission of the apostles, the lives of the first Christians, the testimony of all the holy martyrs, with all that God has said and done, impress anything upon the soul that has been enlightened and felt the powers of the world to come, as well as known the love of God—it is, that man is lost, sinful and wandering from God, and must sink in everlasting ruin if not rescued and turned to God. The world still is measurably lying in sin, under the wicked one, and the highest and best effort in the power of the church should be made, not only for its perpetuity and well-being, but for the rescue of poor, fallen humanity from the manacles of sin and death. In this transcendent matter all are agreed.

As to the best fields of labor, the finger of divine providence should be our guide, aided by enlightened, enlarged and ennobled reason and sound understanding. The apostles themselves looked for an open door and an open heart; nor are we aware that they ever continued and persevered where the people would not hear them, but turned to others who would hear. Wherever God, in his divinely ordered providence, opens a door, or a heart, for the word, in any nation, any land, or among any people, and where they can be converted, the missionary should go. But many nations and peoples now on earth are given over to believe a lie—to strong delusion. These have so long in the presence of an immense concourse, we heard perverted their reason, their understandings and hearts, that no means short of a summons from the Almighty, to appear before him, will burst the spell and mists of delusion from their minds, and awaken them from their slumbers. But there are immense numbers in the world— especially in our own country, who are unsophisticated, uncorrupted, and comparatively in a state of innocency, especially among the young, who will receive the word into good and honest hearts, and may be saved. Wherever these may be found, there is the place for the missionary. No *one place. nation* or *time,* since the establishment of Christianity, is anything more than another, save the openings for the word of God. But on all this we can say no more now.

Our very distinguished and venerable brother, Alexander Campbell, was with us from the beginning. Many had the privilege, for the first time, of seeing him. This was a matter of great gratification. Many had seen him and stood by him when he wrestled with Robert Owen, and again with Bishop (now Archbishop) Purcell, of this city, as no man on this continent has done for the HOLY BIBLE ; and many of these were won to God by his early labors, and yet love him, and regard him, in religion, as they do no man, or no being this side of Him who sits upon the throne. Mr. Campbell showed us the Redeemer, the way to him, how to love him and serve him, in his early efforts, and from that day to this as no other man has done. He has made such a defense of Christianity against the assaults of Infidels, Romanists—such an effort to separate it from everything else, and preserve it in its purity, as no other man on earth has made in the last thousand years. To him, under the Lord Jesus Christ, we, as a great religious body, are largely indebted for our clear appreciation of the Word of Life, our tangible and unassailable position, our entrance upon the sure foundation-stone—the Rock that God has laid in Zion, which will stand when all his enemies and our enemies shall be defeated. It is, therefore, natural and rational that we should have a great regard for him, and feel a deep interest in him.

On Friday night, in the Mechanics Institute, in the presence of an immense concourse, we heard him deliver an educational address that certainly was the crowning piece. For about one hour and a half, he chained that immense assembly in the most breathless silence and intense interest. Never before did the grandeur of the very being, work and destiny of man, in connection with the Author of his existence, God's revelation to the human race, the proper place for religion and the education of man, appear more clear in a public address. With him the universe is a magnificent system. Our world is a part of it, and man belongs to our world. Man, too, is a complete being, with attributes and capacities, and his education must take into the account that he is not all intellect; spirit, soul, or body. The whole man must be educated, his body soul and spirit. But we attempt no description of his address, only to say, that for an intellectual, literary and educational effort, he showed clearly that, though time is wearing upon his physical energies, his intellect is as clear, vigorous and giant-like as ever Never before has this city been saluted with a speech containing more good to man, more sound reason, good educational philosophy and manly strength.

But mighty in all the elements of human greatness as our venerable brother is, vast as his labors have been, and much as he has done for man, no matter how great our attachment to him, time must carry him from us. His and our Lord has gone before us ; the holy apostles, prophets and martyrs have gone, with all, both good and bad, great and small, down to the mansions of the dead. We all must go, one after another, from this state, but blessed God, we shall meet again.

Brother Walter Scott, venerable and well known, was also with us, buoyant and full of faith and hope, aiding us with his counsels and prayers. Other distinguished brethren, as Johnson, Raines, Henshall, Pendleton, Davenport, etc., etc. How precious these meetings, these men and these associations ! But we had to separate, and are now distributed to our various fields of labor, with the full assurance that the Lord will be with us, whether together or separated, provided we are one with the Lord, and of the same mind and judgment. B. F.

Dr. Barclay and the Jerusalem Mission.

So far as expressed at the annual meeting of the Missionary Society, there was but one voice in regard to the re-establishment of the Jerusalem Mission. The subject was carefully considered, and much time was spent in hearing a full expression on the subject, producing great feeling and solicitude; and the resolution recommending the Board to take the matter into immediate consideration, passed without a dissenting voice. The board has also taken action upon the subject, and unanimously resolved to make an effort to send the beloved Barclay family to the holy city again.

Our Missionary, during his first residence there, immersed thirty-one persons into the one Lord, as the apostles did at the beginning. This was great success, when everything is taken into consideration. If the mission meets the minds of the brethren as it did those in the meeting, and the Board, our brother with his family, will be off in from four to six months. The manner in which the minds of the brethren will be expressed, will be in contributing freely to the support of the mission, if favorable to it, or witholding contributions if not favorable. By the way, however, if there should be brethren favorable to missions, but not the Jerusalem mission, they can designate what object their contributions are intended for.

By the way, we consider it our duty to meet a wicked and unfounded report that has been in circulation, detrimental both to the mission and Missionary. We inquired of Bro. Barclay in person, and before a witness, not because we believed he had done anything inhuman, or wicked, but that we might make a reliable statement, to save some good brethren from being misguided, in regard to his disposition of his slaves. He says that he had several slaves that had descended to him by inheritance, and one that he had bought, at the servant's own request, to be placed with a companion, the only one he ever bought. They were all Christians. When he had decided to go to Jerusalem, after prayer one evening, they being present as usual, he told them what he was about to do, and that they were all free. He told them that they could go to Ohio, Canada or Liberia, and that he would find money to take them to the place of their choice. With the exception of one, they soon decided that they would not go. One accepted his freedom at first, but after some six weeks, came back, and they all requested him to turn them over to a brother, whom they and he knew; which he did at a mere nominal price. Since our interview, we have been informed, from another source, that even this nominal price, he never received.

So far as we heard an expression from all who attended our anniversaries, the Barclay family are looked upon as a precious gift of Heaven for a great work; and we know that the Doctor left here with the best wishes, good will, and highest Christian regard, and that he will be followed by many prayers, and be most freely and liberally supported. He is an economist, humble disciple, making no worldly show, but constantly aiming for the accomplishment of the highest possible good, with the least possible expense. Brethren will you aid him? Will you pray for him? If you will, send your communications and means to Bro. C. L. Loos, Corresponding Secretary, Cincinnati, Ohio.

-----o-----

Bible Revision.

The following article was. as the reader may perceive, written for the *Nashville Christian Advocate,* the editor of which declined publishing it. It was sent to the Bible Revision Association, and placed at our disposal, and we cheerfully place it before the readers of this discussion.

JAMES EDMUNDS.
T. S. BELL.

-----o-----

TO THE NASHVILLE CHRISTIAN ADVOCATE.
"Audi alteram partem."

MR. EDITOR:—As you have published so much in opposition to the "Revision" of the Scriptures by the "American Bible Union," I feel sure, from the knowledge I have of your candor and courtesy, that you will also admit into your paper something in its favor, and that, too. by one who claims to be a "Methodist minister," but by no means a "distinguished" one. If you send forth into the world the criticisms of those who judge of that performance from what has been "told" them, you certainly will not refuse a place to a few remarks from one who has read, with the utmost care, nearly every verse issued by that society hitherto, comparing it with King James's translation and the original, and weighing well every reason assigned, in the notes, for the alterations that have been made. You are aware that, besides nearly all the book of Job, six books of the New Testament were published some time ago, with this notice prefixed: "This revision is not final. It is circulated in the expectation that it will be subjected to a thorough criticism, in order that its imperfections, whatever they are, may be disclosed and corrected." I have been in the habit, for more than twenty years, of using different versions, both of the Old and New Testament, collating them with the originals and King James's translation, with a sincere desire to ascertain the exact sense of the Spirit of God in every passage, divesting myself as much as possible of all prepossessions and prejudice, and I am constrained to declare that the version hitherto issued by the Bible Union, so far as it goes, is most decidedly and conspicuously superior to them all. This my judgment and conscience would compel me to acknowledge, even if it had proceeded from the Shakers or Mormons.

The Bible Union may have set out with a wrong motive and an unjustifiable intention. The desire to make it appear that "immersion" is the only legitimate mode of introducing persons into Christ's church, may have given rise to it; but whatever may have been its design in the beginning, I am well convinced that if it publish the remainder of the Sacred Books with the same fidelity and scrupulous adherence to the original observed hitherto, it will confer an incalculable benefit on the many millions who use the English language throughout the world. I speak not of the other versions published by this society, in French. Italian, etc., for the simple reason that I have not examined them; having read somewhere that "He who answereth a matter before he heareth it, it is folly and shame unto him." Persons who have not read a single chapter of the "revision"—nay, some who have not seen it, have raised, and are daily raising, a senseless hue and cry against it. This is unwise, unjust, and, moreover, uncharitable and unchristian. They are impeaching the motives of those engaged in the work, taxing them with ignorance, bigotry malice, etc., without any knowledge whatever of the individuals. Surely it is "folly and shame" unto those who do so. Now, after having, as already stated, perused most scrutinizing all that has yet been printed, nearly seven books, I am utterly unable to determine to what denomination of Christians the translators belong. One writer stigmatizes them as "New Version Tinkers." Tinkers, indeed! I think I can judge by a man's writings whether he is a scholar or not; and if the gentlemen who have given us these seven books in English dress are not scholars, and accurate, thorough, profound scholars, I know not in what country we are to find such. "The works that they do bear witness for them:" and, according to the highest authority, this testimony ought to satisfy all. But ignorance and bigotry are both very unreasonable things, and it is useless for any man or society of men to aim at quieting their clamor.

These translators, too, have evidently availed themselves of every aid, consulting not only all the English versions from Tyndal's down to the present day, but those made in many other languages also, as Syriac, Ethiopic, Slavonic, Dutch, German, Spanish, Italian, French, etc., besides all the lexicographers and grammarians of any note. They frequently refer to Clarke and Wesley, as authorities for some of the changes made. Who that reads the Bible in the original language, does not know that a revision is imperatively, absolutely demanded? I venture the assertion that there is hardly a paragraph in our common English Bible, from the first chapter of Genesis to the last of Revelation that is not capable of amendment. The version was good for the age in which it was executed, but it is very far from being so now. Who can for a moment believe that no progress has been made in biblical criticism in the space of nearly two hundred and fifty years? Dr. Adam Clarke tells us that this science was. in King James's time, "in its infancy, if indeed it had begun to exist." Whoever has read his commentary with care has found thousands of corrections of the common version, and no very civil epithets applied to many of the passages so corrected—such as "nonsensical," "absurd," and "no translation at all." And instead of King James's version of Isaiah —one of the most sublime and evangelical, but, unfortunately, one of the worst translated books in the Bible—he informs us he came very near inserting Bishop Lowth's admirable version. It would be very easy to show, from a multitude of theologians and commentators, that King James's version abounds in errors— some of them, too, of a very grave character. If permitted, 1 shall advert to a few of these hereafter. I have read in the Advocate, from time to time, some most ridiculous strictures on the "Revision." One gives us a long diatribe on the use of the perfect tense in Greek, referring very learnedly to

Winer, Butman and other masterly grammarians. He thinks, too, he has discovered "a stroke of Arminianism" in one passage wherein the perfect is very rightly employed in the new rendering, For myself, I must confess I am rather dull of vision, but I believe I would rather labor under this disadvantage than possess the over-excited optics of this vigilant brother. Another thinks it "furnishes infidels with the most deadly weapon they have ever used against the Christianity of the Bible." Should any persons be so extremely weak as to discredit Christianity because of a new *translation* of the Bible, let them run their own course. They certainly have not *common sense* enough to be Christians. They must be the very quintessence of *ninny- ism.* Have we not had hundreds upon hundreds of translations of the Bible; and who has ever known of one infidel being made or confirmed thereby? On the contrary, I am fully persuaded that this translation, truly faithful and beautiful as it is, will induce many to read the Sacred Scriptures who hitherto have neglected to do so, and thousands to peruse them with more care and diligence than ever before. What can be more fair than the manner of publishing this Revision? You have presented to your view, on each page, the common version, the original and the revision; and underneath you have authorities for all the amendments made. Every man who is capable, can form for himself an instant judgment as to the merits of the performance. It is forced upon no one. No one need substitute it for the old, defective translation, if he is so wedded to error. But for my part, if the rest at all equals what has been already accomplished, 1 will, if spared to see it completed, most assuredly adopt it, at least in my own family and for private use. I value it above gold, yes, much fine gold. And I will confess that my design, in writing the present article, is mainly to call the attention of my brethren in the ministry to this work. With the utmost deference I would advise every minister of the Gospel to subscribe for the "Bible Union Reporter," and to *study* it, laying aside all prejudice and passion—and I am satisfied, if he do, he will thank me heartily for the counsel. What an opportunity is hereby offered to all young ministers, of acquiring an accurate knowledge of the sacred languages'. The notes subjoined afford considerable help to the attainment of this end. They are, I venture to say, the soundest and most reliable critical and philological notes ever published. They are indeed the very cream of all that has preceded them in that kind. The Greek text is magnificent. Methinks it should tempt every preacher of the Gospel who sees it, and who has neglected the study of that language, to commence it forthwith. The whole is beautifully got up, and, besides, it is remarkably cheap—12 numbers, postage paid, for one dollar. If we, ministers of the Gospel, had but the industry and love of learning that characterized the great Adam Clarke, theological institutions would hardly be needed among us. He could preach *daily,* and yet find time to study the Scriptures in the languages of the inspired writers.

What if the authors of this revision do translate the word *"babtizo" immerse,* will that destroy the value of the whole work, or make immersionists of all who may prize and use it? By no means. I doubt whether it will make a single proselyte to immersionism. People will continue to think for themselves, on that subject as hitherto. Thousands who practice sprinkling, or pouring, believe that immersion was the primitive and apostolic mode of administering that sacrament, but, not attaching any importance to the mere mode, they still employ the more convenient and feasible methods. For instance, the late Bp. Capers believed that *"babtizo"* meant to "immerse," and that anciently that was the custom. I heard him say so myself, at Ash Spring camp ground, Logan county, Ky., only a few years before his death. Yet I believe the good Bishop died as he lived, in the bosom of Methodism. So did Dr. A. Clarke, who had the same persuasion. So have thousands of others. I wish there were less controversy among us, especially in matters of little importance, and more of that heavenly temper of mind described and recommended in the 13th chapter of 1st Corinthians. We would then no longer "bite and devour one another," as is too much the case at present. But this article being already sufficiently long, I shall close it with stating that I have marked more than fifty passages in the six books of the New Testament already published by the "Bible Union," wherein the translation is altered greatly for the better, and it would not be difficult to add fifty more to the number. The portion of Job issued is a *perfect gem*—more intelligible, without any commentary at all, than the Old Version with twenty of the best commentaries that have been written, casting their light upon it. Come, brethren, "in understanding be ye men," and do not suffer yourselves to be carried away by the popular current, but stand, consider, review, and judge for yourselves. Despise popularity, and be well assured, that so far from the "vox populi" being always "vox Dei," it is much oftener *vox Diaboli.* But more anon.

Wash'n Co., Miss. W. McCALLEN.

Christian Benevolence.

THE Christian religion, being a development of the Divine character, is essentially a religion of benevolence—that is its great and prominent feature, shining alike in its precepts and examples. " Thou shalt love thy neighbor as thyself," was the great maxim inculcated first, midst, and last, by its Divine Author. But this, in Christianity, is not a barren abstraction, a mere sentiment of the mind, unproductive of corresponding fruits. As such it is of no value. It is a living principle, to be exhibited by the Christian in works of practical goodness, in positive' acts of benevolence to the unfortunate and afflicted. The mere sentimentalist may weep over the fictitious sorrows of a romance, while he views unmoved, the sufferings of those around him— that is a spurious sympathy, utterly foreign to the practical benevolence of the Gospel. In the Author of Christianity, benevolence was not a mere sentiment, enunciated with oracular pomp. It was a living, every-day principle of action—a practical sympathy with the woes of others, evinced in substantial and timely acts of kindness: it did not mock the afflicted with professions of sympathy, while it left them without relief. He looked around 'him, and seized every opportunity to accomplish his God-like purpose of doing good. It is a great and fatal mistake, and one too prevalent in the minds of professed Christians, that the benevolent precepts of the gospel can be satisfied by a mere dreamy, sentimental feeling of sympathy for the woes of others, unaccompanied by practical and honest efforts to do them good. Christianity, the Christianity of the New Testament, the Christianity taught and practiced by the Son of God, demands something more substantial and practical than this. It calls upon its disciples to be up and doing, to look around them, to search after the victims of misfortune and woe, and " whatever their hands find to do, (for the great work of practical benevolence) to do it with all their might."—*Gospel Advocate.*

-----o-----

Christian Life.

MOST persons who spend unhappy lives are themselves chargeable with their own misery. It is no difficult matter to render ourselves wretched when we set out with a determination to do so. We can always find cause for dissatisfaction and complaint when we search diligently for it. No state of society is perfect— no man or woman is entirely free from weakness and fault. No neighbor, probably, is *exactly* what we would desire. No hour that passes over us is wholly free from pain or care. Labor anxiety and suffering continually beset us, but the glory of the Christian religion is, that it enables us to bear them all patiently and cheerfully. It teaches us that these are light afflictions, and are but for a moment, and bear no comparison to that eternal weight of glory promised in the Gospel. We gain but little from Christianity if it does not teach us to govern our passions, bridle our tongues, subdue our anger, lay aside our enmities, and cultivate in our hearts only sentiments of Love. My brethren and sisters, how many of you are wearing out your days—robbing yourselves of all peace and good feeling, and blasting forever your hope of heaven, by petty jealousies, bickerings, evil-speaking, giving heed to tales of idle and mischievous tongues ? How many families are rendered utterly unfit for anything like Christian culture, and how many neighborhoods are torn and distracted and embittered by the merest trifles? These things ought not so to be. All our wisdom, and knowledge, and talent cannot secure us the bliss of Immortality, while there is no love, no spirit of Christ in us. Let us take heed to these things.   W. L.

-----o-----

Good News from Arkansas.

OUACHITA, ARK., Aug. 21st, 1856.

DEAR BRETHREN—Under the direction and patronage of a few earnest Christians, about three years ago I commenced evangelizing in this part of the country. Pursuant to their direction and my desire, it has been my aim. not so much to gain additions, as to add strength to the Church of Christ. The result of my labors has been the formation of four congregations, numbering, in all, about one hundred and twenty disciples.

From past experience, as well as from information received from others, I am fully persuaded that many of our teaching brethren, preachers and editors, have been too superficial in presenting the apostle's doctrine. I would not say that they have said and written too much about first principles, but they have not said and written enough about *a holy life.* But the time has come when the necessity for a change in this respect is seen and felt. It is plainly apparent that many of the brethren have not the spirit of Christ—that they " *walk* as the enemies of the Gospel of Christ— *who mind earthly things''* We need more religion among us—heart-felt religion, *"pure and undefiled"* religion. I am glad to see that you are giving some attention to this matter in the *Gospel Advocate.* Give it more; we need it. I will write again ere long.

DAVID F. SALLEY.

Editor's Table

Agents for the A. C. Review.—We desire all our present agents to act for us the coining year, upon the same terms as they have the present year, except that large class who have done so much for us gratuitously. To those, we are truly thankful, and would willingly allow them the usual percentage. To those who take a deep interest and procure an extended list, we give a larger per cent. We desire as many agents as we can possibly obtain. Indeed, any person can act as agent for themselves or others, Without corresponding with us. But persons wishing to know What, percentage we will give, will please address us. A liberal percentage will be allowed.

-----o-----

To those whom it may concern.—Any subscribers having failed to get any numbers, or having received imperfect copies, by informing us shall be supplied.

-----o-----

Sincerity Seeking the Way to-Heaven.—A new and large edition of this widely circulating little book is now ready, and all orders for it will be filled soon after they come to hand. The sales of it now are three times as huge as they were one year ago. Many encouraging accounts of its good effects are now in our possession. Price.—Bound, twenty cents^ stitched and trimmed, ten cents. It will b; sent by mail at this price, and a liberal deduction made by the quantity. The *Union Movement* is also selling rapidly at tire same price. The *Contrast,* or Review of Dr. N. L. Rice, is going at a rapid rate, And doing a noble work.

-----o-----

Delay.—When we are at home, we answer to everything immediately; but we have been much from home lately, which occasions some delay ; but everything will be attended to, and answered in the most faithful manner.

-----o-----

A Fair Notice.—One more number completes our present volume. Many have doubted whether a religious publication could be sustained where the term3 are invariably cash-in-advance. The trouble anticipated is, that through inattention or neglect, many will not renew their subscription. But our notion is, that this will be the case with none who really want the publication. All such will certainly look to it, and have their subscriptions renewed. In this way, the Review will be continued to none who do not want it. In our estimation, an editor should be elected every year. The Review has now been before the people eleven months, and we have been known to be a candidate for re-election. In electing an editor, nobody votes directly against him. Those who do not vote for him are merely neutral—do not vote at all. If good is done in electing him, those who vote for him deserve the credit; if evil, they, are responsible for it. The manner of the election is very simple, and equally decisive. Those who vote for him, enclose the subscription in a letter and send it to him, with their names and place of address plainly written. When enough of that description can be found to support an editor, he is elected, and has a right to proceed to the duties of his office. In this manner we were elected for the present term, and we are now before the people for .re-election. Many votes have already been given. Indeed we consider ourselves re-elected ; but it is very desirable that the vote should be as large as possible. Those, therefore,' who do not vote for us, we shall conclude, do not desire us re-elected, and do not want the *Review,* and. as a matter of course, it will not be sent to them:' It amounts to nothing with us, that a man is a good man. Our subscribers are all good; but we must know that they want the *Review,* in the most certain way of knowing—*their sending the money for it.*

-----o-----

Anniversaries of our Societies.—According to appointment, the anniversaries commenced Oct. 21st. The attendance was larger than we have had on any similar occasion, for several years ; yet no adequate representation for an occasion of this kind. Still the meeting was one of much importance to the cause, and one that we trust will long be remembered. Arrangements were made to dissolve both the Bible, and Publication Societies, that the minds and energies of the brotherhood may be concentrated upon the Missionary Society, and the great missionary work.

-----o-----

We have no list of brethren in attendance, but from memory, mention the following: A. Campbell, W. Scott, A. Raines, W. K. Pendleton, Pettigrew, J. I. Rogers, S. Ayres, Wm. Begg.

Misunderstanding.—The announcement that Elder M. B. Hopkins would make his headquarters in Louisville, Ky., keep an office there, and publish our works there, has been misunderstood by many. This is owing to the fact, that they do not think of the distinction between *publishing* and *printing.* The works will all be *printed here* as before, and will differ in nothing from what they have been, except that Eld. Hopkins will write more frequently for the paper. He will simply keep the works there, that orders addressed to him may be filled. Everything will go on here, the same as before, and all communications for us should be sent here, the same as before.

Success of the Gospel.

Eld. E. Thompson, writing from Nameless, Ind., Oct. 15th, says, "We had four additions here; two by confession, one by relation, and one from the Baptists."

Eld. T. M. Barnau, New Paris, Ohio, Oct. 9th, says, "I have just got home from Flat Rook, Henry Co., Ind. We had truly a fine meeting, commencing last Saturday, and continuing five days, with thirteen additions by baptism. Bro. S. Bennet, and Bro. Edmondson assisted me much in the meeting. It was truly a time of rejoicing, and we thank God and take courage."

Bro. R. Rayal, Canetown, Ind., Oct. 19th, says, "I have just closed a meeting of eleven days, with the Union church, Gipson county, at which twenty confessed the Lord, and were buried with him in baptism. I was assisted by Bro. James Cum, of Graysville, Ill."

Eld. George Campbell, Oxford, Ind., Oct. 8th, informs us, that as State Missionary in Indiana, he reported at the State meeting, in Indianapolis, 118 additions, though he has been much annoyed with "chills" during the year.

-----O-----

COLLIERSVILLE, Tenn., Sept. 26th, 1856.

BRO. FRANKLIN:—I have just returned from a Meeting in Mississippi. During the meeting nineteen heard, believed, and were baptized. The laborers were Brethren Matthews, Barber and Dupuy. We have also had two additions to the church meeting in Colliorsville.

GEO. PLATTENBURO.

-----O-----

HARFORD CO., Md., 26 miles E. of Baltimore,
October 18th, 1856.

BRO. FRANKLIN On the 7th inst., I left home for an annual meeting to be held at this place, and commenced operations on Lord's day past with the aid of the Baltimore brethren and sisters, with a congregation of some seven or eight hundred persons, gathered from the surrounding country.

Brothers Austin and Dickerson from Baltimore; together with Sisters McComas, Benson, and others, rendering important aid.

I have never met with a more devoted people. In prayer, the whole congregation bow down with becoming reverence, and all the members seem to feel a direct interest in the work. And the great mass of the brethren will make prayer when called upon. They really seem to be living for God. So far, we have had four days of service, and nine confessions, three of whom were Methodists. The Weather becoming stormy, our labors have been interrupted, but we shall commence again when the weather will allow.

In all Maryland there are but five congregations known to the brethren here, and not one evangelist devoted to the work. What a picture, this! Is not this truly a proper field for missionary effort? I really feel oppressed at the thought. The church in Baltimore though without a settled minister, as we say; yet is full of preachers, and some of them able ministers of the word. Maryland, so far as cultivated, is indebted to them for the labor.

From here I shall probably go to the city for a meeting, and after a suitable effort, if the election excitement allow of a meeting, shall return home.

The third Lord's day in September I closed a meeting of some days at Blandville, in Ballard Co., in Southern Kentucky, with 21 additions.

I hope yet to do something more for the cause in this State before leaving it. Yours truly,

G. W. ELLEY

-----O-----

MOUNT STERLING, KY., Sept. 29th, 1856.

EVER DEAR BRO:—Agreeably to promise, I write you and all well. Have 110 pupils and more coming. Am laboring very hard. Think we have a very fine place for the doing of good. Have tried very hard for the Review, but *politics! politics!* What are our brethren coming to?

Have just returned from the church at Corinth (modern Corinth). Bro. Lee has held a meeting of several days, and had about forty additions. I spoke there to-day, and three came forward to the praise of the Lord. To his dear name be all the glory, now and forever. Our Christian regards to yourself and family. Write us when you have time. I would say that a meeting at Bethlehem has just been concluded by Brethren Waller and Harding, at which over seventy additions were made to the church. The harvest seems to be ripe for the sickle. Shall we not pray the Lord for laborers? Let us praise his holy name.

Fraternally in the bonds of love, J. B. CRANE.

-----O-----

Obituary.

DIED, at his residence, Meridian, Pendleton Co., Ky., on the 6th September, 1836., at the age of forty-seven years, eight months and ten days, HEBER SHOEMAKER, son of Lakey Shoemaker. The deceased was born at Flour Creek, in Pendleton Co., Ky. He became a member of the Christian church at Flour Creek Ky., Oct., 1830, and remained a member of the same until his death. He retained his senses until the last, and was sensible of his approaching dissolution, and told his companion that he was going to a better world. During his illness, he was frequently engaged in solemn prayer to God; and bidding his friends farewell, he left the world with a hope of a blessed immortality beyond the grave. He leaves a large family circle of friends who mourn his departure. In his death we lost a good citizen; his companion, a tender and affection ate husband; his children, a kind father. May God bless, guide, guard and protect his bereaved companion, little sons and daughters, is my prayer.

FERDINAND TAYLOR.

Sept. 27, 1856

THE AMERICAN CHRISTIAN REVIEW.

CAN WE INFALLIBLY KNOW THE GOSPEL WHEN WE HEAR IT?

By P. S. Fall, A. M.

"Charge some that they teach no other doctrine."
1 Tim. 1: 3.

WHEN Paul went into Macedonia, he requested Timothy to remain at Ephesus. In expressing this desire, he had in view a most important object; and for its accomplishment, instituted means as simple as they were efficient. He gave his substitute in the apostolic office there, a special charge, and succinctly stated the end he proposed thereby: "the end of the commandment is love."

For ages had the world been left to its own efforts to discover "the chief good." Question after question had been introduced and discussed. Topics in all forms and relating to all subjects, mental and material, had been offered and examined, and mankind, instead of fraternizing, as in beings of a common origin, and tending to a common destiny might have been expected, were no nearer the settlement of their differences than if no investigation had been made.

There was nothing in their debates that could promote love. The endless genealogies of the Jews, and the mythological superstitions of the Gentiles, "ministered questions, rather than godly edifying." They had missed their way, were groping in the dark, "feeling after God, if haply they might find him, though he were not far from every one of them," and were lost in the inextricable mazes of bewildering ignorance. They had before them no example by which to learn what love is; and it is not wonderful that they were "hateful and hating one another." Sadly out of sorts, the world, mental and moral, needed regulating, and could not regulate itself, as it had discovered after 4000 years of effort. This great result was to be brought about by divine means; and the publication of the gospel was that means. "After that in the wise arrangements of God, it proved that the world by its wisdom knew not God, it pleased God, by the foolishness of preaching, to save the believers." Hence the commandment to Timothy, "Charge some that they teach NO OTHER DOCTRINE."

In his memorable address to the elders at Ephesus, Paul says: "I know this, that after my departure, grievous wolves shall enter in among you, not sparing the flock. Also of your own selves shall men arise speaking perverse things, to draw away disciples after them." Acts xx: 29, etc. He knew that the success of the truth depended upon the affection of the disciples, and that there could be none of this where contention, and strife, and envying, and evil works abounded. He knew too, that if causes of dissension were introduced, either by such as would not spare the flock, or by any who from among themselves should arise, creating parties upon the basis of their perverse disputings, there could be none of that building up of themselves, so essential to the conversion of others, and therefore he warned them of their danger, and prescribed the only preventive, "Charge some THAT THEY TEACH *no other doctrine.*"

The bishops of the congregation at Ephesus were the persons upon whom Timothy was to lay this command. They were to feed the flock "over which the Holy Spirit had made them overseers," not upon the husks, that only made them fight, but upon that "unadulterated milk of the word by which they might grow and in order to make the disciples love each other, they were not only to avoid such questions as ministered strife, but were to teach only ONE doctrine.

This latter command they could not obey without observing the former; for had they given heed either to Jewish, Gentile, or old wives' fables, or to endless genealogies, there would have been no taste among their hearers for that one doctrine that should make them love each other. And how means could be better adapted to an end, it is difficult to conceive; since, instead of a multitude of views or of opinions, but *one great theme* wa8 to be kept before them, and about this there could be no debate. An example of love, so striking, so dear, was herein exhibited, moreover, that they could be at no loss for arguments teaching them to love God, each other, and mankind.

It is worthy of remark, that Christianity is everywhere represented *as a system of the utmost simplicity,* and thus its divinity is proved. For, while all that God does is characterized by this attribute, the very opposite distinguishes the efforts of man. How often do we reason falsely from these premises! We infer the greatness and the power of human beings from the complexity of their productions; as, for example, when studying an instrument that represents the motions and phenomena of the earth, the causes of the seasons, and of the different lengths of day and of night at the same place, we infer hence the mental strength of him who could conceive it. But how does the Divine Being effect the reality which it requires so great an outlay of time, of skill, and of materials to imitate? He simply bends a little on one side the axis of the earth, and ordains that it shall be always parallel to itself. A great mind never brings out even great results by complicated means. On the contrary, he that can effect great purposes by simple instruments, possesses the main attribute of greatness. He does great things quietly, and thinks that any other man could have done as much. A machine, noisy in working, is defective, a screw is loose; but the perfection of the most stupendous engine is seen in the noiseless contrivance of its resistless motions.

That is most simple, in every point of view, that is a unit; and such is Christianity. It is one in form and in essence; not Protean in character or in effect. It presents us, too, with a system of unities; one God the Father, one Lord Jesus Christ, one Holy Spirit, one Lord, one faith, one baptism, one mediation, one high priest, one sacrifice, one head, one body for one spirit, one hope, one vocation, one doctrine, one means to one end. It is adapted to one human being; and if to one, to every such one, and to him the whole of it is necessary.

Men speak of "doctrines," and contend for "essential" doctrines. No wonder, then, that they differ, even to schism. The Ephesian bishops were to teach "*no other*" doctrine" than that one which, of course, they had learned of Paul, "Thou hast fully known my doctrine." But what is a doctrine?

A *fact,* as the term imports, *is something done.* A *truth* is the *statement of a fact.* For instance, Jesus, the Messiah, was delivered by Pontius Pilate into the hands of wicked men, who crucified him. This statement is based upon what was done. The statement is not a fact, but the fact is the basis of the statement. This was made by one who *knew* the fact. It was, then, *matter of knowledge,* and hence the statement is true. The truth is not matter of knowledge, *but of belief;* and thus, while facts may be addressed to all our other senses, truths can be addressed to but one; "Faith cometh by hearing." True, as confidence results from both knowledge and belief, these words are sometimes synonymously employed; but, strictly speaking, the distinction indicated obtains; nor is it without significance.

But a doctrine, what is that? It is the *meaning* of a fact, or a truth, or of a collection of either. The above truth, founded on a fact, is of deep import, and while faith seizes upon the truth, the understanding feeds upon its meaning. It cannot be said, properly, that we *believe a doctrine.* We know a fact; we believe a truth; we understand a doctrine; and thus, while Christianity is in itself so simple, it is adapted in the simplest manner to the being it proposes to benefit. It gives him matter to investigate, to believe, and to understand, and thus captivates his heart and his intellect, and subjects his whole mental and moral being to its influence.

But why should the elders at Ephesus have been charged to teach no other than this one doctrine? Not only because any other *prevents* the end of the commandment, but because this is the only one that God has selected to *promote* it, as being adapted to man as he is. Hence Paul says, "Though we, or an angel from heaven preach *any other* gospel unto you, than *that 'which we have preached* unto you, let him be accursed." "If any man preach any other gospel unto you than that *you have received,* let him he accursed." Gal. i: 8, 9.

A very serious thing, is it not? to undertake to preach the gospel. And who would, lightly, expose himself to this terrific curse? Yet if man or angel preach anything but THE gospel which Paul preached, or which the Galatians had received, to this anathema he is certainly obnoxious. Is it not, then, possible —must it not be easy—to ascertain what that gospel is? How, otherwise, can anyone feel that he is not anathematized? A very distinguished preacher once said: "I have been trying to preach the gospel for twenty years, but am not certain whether I know how to do it yet." How terrible must be that uncertainty to a conscientious man! And how deplorable the darkness that pervades such minds as are under a system allowing of this uncertainty, and which even considers it virtuous to boast of it.

That the gospel is exactly adapted to the condition of man, many considerations will show; but of these, two will suffice for the present: and first,

1st. Man is a sinner.

Now, any system that does not need this consideration, is, certainly of no use to *him.* He must be *convinced* of sin, must be taught how to get rid of it, and must be delivered from its power. All this the gospel effects. Hence it is "glad tidings of great joy unto all people."

2d. Man is a dying sinner.

To be adapted to him, then, the gospel must teach him how to *live,* and must remove the fear of death. The same process which takes away his sins, and thus teaches him being "made whole, to sin no more," extracts also the sting of death; and thus abolishes its fear. Death is terrible to those only whose sins are not blotted out, but who expect to live in another state. The brute does not fear death: he expects not to live again. He is always ready to die. *We* sometimes speak *of preparing to die.* We ought rather to think of preparing *to live;* and this Christianity enables us to do, by training us here in the life of the future.

But this is true of Christianity *as it came from the hands of its author* ONLY. Any change of essence or of form, destroys its fitness for man. We might argue this *a priori,* from the circumstances that its author has giver to its definite essence a definite form. Any other form of the same essence, or of any other essence, would have done as well, had God chosen it; but that He has selected any form, proves *that* to be the best, and that to be alone, suited to its end. Suppose, for illustration, that a malignant disease has baffled the skill of all who undertook its cure; and that a physician, who understands it perfectly, prescribes a remedy. He gives written directions to an apothecary; and requires that five grains of one ingredient, shall be first combined with three grains of a second; after these are well mixed, two grains of a third are to be added.

The patient is to take the whole medicine, at a given hour, when in a given condition.

Now it is admitted that the physician not only comprehends the case perfectly, but that he can certainly cure the patient. His directions, however, must be literally and implicitly obeyed.

If the *apothecary,* on reading the prescription, shall say: "Why should I combine *five* grains of No. 1, with *three* grains of No. 2? Why not reverse the proportions, or use equal quantities? Or why mix No. 1 and No. 2 first, and *then* add No. 3? Will it not answer to combine No. 2 and No. 3, and then No. 1 with these?"

That he would not obey the given directions, is a sufficient answer. By substituting his own prescription, moreover, he intimates a want of confidence in the physician: and it may be added, that he may kill the patient, instead of relieving him. Or if the *patient* set up for himself and change the prescription in any way, or do not take it at the proper time, or when in the required condition, does not *he* also demonstrate his want of faith in the physician to whom, professedly, he submits? Is that physician responsible, should the remedy, thus mutilated or abused, prove a "savor of death, ending in death?" He who knows what is in man, and needs not that any should testify to him of man, knows what is best for man, and prescribes accordingly. Who then, has a right to alter the remedial agent that He, in his wisdom and benevolence, has originated? If it may be changed in form, it may, also, in essence; and who shall, in either case, be warranted in his reliance upon its salutary effects?

But, it may be asked, "Do not all Protestants, at least, preach the same gospel? In all essential matters, do they not agree?" Why, then, their divisions? Is not *the gospel* the basis of Christian union—the great center of the religious system? Why, then, do they forbid such union over the Lord's body? Why not rally, as one army, on this one foundation? It may be replied: "They are not divided about the gospel, but about minor matters— such as church government, etc., etc." The answer is: So much the worse. They have no right to create dissensions, ending in schisms, about minor matters.

Existing divisions, however, are based upon feelings much stronger than may originate about unimportant points. They are accompanied by proscription, by excisions, and by expulsion from seats at the Lord's table. All this is either deeply criminal, or the grounds of difference must be essential. And are they not essential?

A clergyman professes to be "called, qualified, commissioned, and sent forth to preach the gospel of the grace of God," and what does he preach? He affirms,

1. The total hereditary depravity of man.
2. The doctrine of personal election, if not of reprobation.
3. The doctrine of limited atonement.
4. The special influences of the Holy Spirit, applying the atonement to the elect.
5. The final perseverance of the saints—that is, of the elect.

These *five points,* established by the Synod of Dort, are regarded by their advocates as "the essential doctrines of the gospel." Now, I do not undertake to deny them. They may be true; but most certainly, they are opposed, point for point, by the doctrines of Arminius, condemned by the same synod. Now these, also, their defenders affirm to be "the essential doctrines of the gospel." Here, then, is an *essential* difference—a difference in which each affirms what the other denies to be "essential doctrines of the gospel."

As already remarked, I do not here decide upon the merits of either system. This, however, is clear: that supposing one to contain the essence of the gospel, the other does not. Two things that differ in the least, cannot be identical; much less, if one denies wholly what the other affirms. One *may be* true, but the other *must,* in that case, be false; while neither may be the gospel. Both may be false, moreover, but both cannot be true, at the same time. It may be well, then, to ascertain if we can, whether the advocates of either thesis consider it to be the gospel.

Suppose either to affirm: The system which we advocate is Christianity. It follows, of course, that the other is not; since there is but one system bearing that name. But, if it be asked: Are there any Christians among those who hold the

the opposite system? The answer is: Certainly. There are Christians in all denominations. If it be inquired, further: Do these Christians believe in your system? it is at once replied: No, they oppose it, and consider it most dangerous and unscriptural. But, it is affirmed that the system thus rejected is Christianity. Hence, there may be persons admitted to be Christians, *who do not believe in Christianity!* Now, either this absurdity must be admitted, or it cannot be contended that either system is Christianity, in essence or in form.

The arrangement of the items of the gospel is as much divine as its constitution; and will no more allow of interference. The same elements may enter into the constitutions of two systems; but if these elements be differently combined, the systems must differ. The substances constituting our atmosphere form also, when the proportions are reversed, a most deadly poison—nitrous acid. Both exist by divine appointments—that is, God has created both; but they can neither be identical, nor be substitutes.

Suppose, then, that one great school of practical or personal divinity, arranges the elementary effects of the gospel it preaches, in showing the "rise and progress of religion in the soul," as follows:

1. Regeneration, by the *immediate* agency of the Holy Spirit.
2. Conviction of sin.
3. Repentance for sin.
4. Faith in Jesus Christ, as the Saviour of sinners.
5. Hope—resulting in, or identified with conversion.
6. Baptism.

If this be the divine combination of the effects produced by the remedial system—and it is not here denied—then no other than this can be; and the nearer any system approaches this, not to be it, the more dangerous—because the more delusive it is. There can be but one divine arrangement; and therefore, if the sixth item of the above system be made the first of another, the divinity of this last, is to be at once denied. Or, if the *mediate* agency of the Holy Spirit—that is, the employment of means in regeneration—be affirmed, the difference between the two systems, made by the omission or insertion of a prefix, renders them antipodal. Any change, indeed, either in the position or the nature of the elements, or in the order of their effects, has the same result. We may combine them in many different ways; but we have a divine warrant for one only. What is THAT ONE? Can we tell?

How important it is that we should be possessed of means to decide this momentous question! Certainly, our Heavenly Father would not allow us to be without such a criterion! If, however, this *be* our condition, it is, of course, a matter of indifference to what religious party we may attach ourselves; and as well to none, as to any. Where there is no standard, there can be no error. All things are equally right and equally wrong. I have as much right to form a new sect, or to preach a new gospel, as any other man has to preach or to belong to an old one. It was idle in Paul to anathematize those who should have independence enough to think for themselves, and to preach not as he did; and all distinctions of parties, and all denominational shibboleths are mere playthings, like political issues, to be made and destroyed at will. I cannot believe that God would countenance latitudinarianism, in a matter where the eternal well-being of his creatures is so vitally involved. They are under the terrible influence of a specific disorder; and must be subjected to the action of a specific remedy. What that is, He has himself dictated; and He forbids us, upon pain of his eternal displeasure, to employ another. He cannot, then, but have enabled us to identify it.

It would be idle to spend time in examining the claims of the many systems that have originated since the days of the Apostles, but by way of testing the pretensions of all, we may study one.

Romanism either is the gospel, or it is not. If it be, then—

1. Nothing else is.
2. Every Romanist believes the gospel; and
3. None but Romanists do.

Now, although these conclusions are necessary, yet no Romanist will affirm the last; for while he may contend that the Church beginning at Rome—rather than that "beginning at Jerusalem" — the "Jerusalem which is from above, and which is free"—is "the mother of us all;" yet he dare not deny saving faith to *all* Protestants. And if there be but one, not a Romanist, who believes savingly—and he must in that case believe the gospel—then either Romanism, which he does not believe, is not the gospel; or one man may have saving faith without believing the gospel; and if this be true of one, it is of all men. To affirm, then, that anything which a man may reject without eternally perishing, is the gospel—is to deny that there is any gospel, or any Christian religion. This remark leads us to our criterion.

In Mark xvi: 15, 16, we have these words: "Go ye into all the world, and preach THE GOSPEL to every creature. He that believeth"—I dare not omit the words—"and is baptized, shall be saved. He that believeth not, shall be condemned."

Upon these remarkable words some thoughts may be offered, before our essential doctrines are tried by this standard. And first:

Let it be observed, that *no description of the gospel is here given.* We are not told what it is; but whatever it may have been, the Apostles were to preach it; and whosoever believed it and submitted to it, was promised salvation; while he who did not believe it was threatened with condemnation. How wonderful is this silence! Might not the Apostles lawfully have expected that, upon such an occasion, all possible light would have been thrown on their commission? But Jesus had not yet been glorified. He had indeed been with them forty days; and now upon the eve of his ascension, he gave them a commission upon which the fate of millions hung, but told them not *what* they were to announce. They knew that He had been crucified as a blasphemer; and that he had directed them to delay the execution of their trust; so that until the gospel was announced from Heaven, there was not upon earth, and there could not be until he was "justified by the Spirit," a single tongue authorized to speak to man in the name of God.

Next, Baptism is mentioned in connexion with a belief of the gospel, whatever it may have been; and both are represented as means to the end therein proposed. Not faith alone, then, nor baptism alone results in *salvation;* but they are conjoined in the commission. What then, is the position occupied by baptism in water, in the Christian economy? It is to be regarded, I presume to say, as the *first act of the whole person,* indicative of faith; and also as perfecting faith. It *expresses* our faith—that is, our belief in the gospel—by a significant action; and he that understands that action, considers it as the submission of the person baptized to the government of the Lord's anointed, in whom, he thus says to the world, that he believes with all his heart; whom he then confesses with his lips; and *whose name* he THEN receives.

For the sake of such only as have not been accustomed to define accurately the terms of the New Testament, it may also be stated, that the *salvation* resulting from faith and the "obedience of faith," is *not* deliverance from eternal torment. That depends upon other considerations. But it is described in the following language: "Thou shall call him Jesus, for he shall *save* HIS PEOPLE *from their sins."* "I write unto you, little children," says John, "because *your sins are forgiven you for his name's sake."* That is: "You have taken upon you that name which is above every name; and because you wear this, I will blot out your past offences." "If any man serve me, him will my Father honor." The whole passage, then, may be considered as teaching: "He that believes the glad tidings with all his heart, AND ACTS ACCORDINGLY, shall be cleansed—that is, delivered—from all his past offences."

Our criterion does not render it necessary, that in order to "try the spirits whether they be of God," or to "tell the spirit of truth from the spirit of error;" *or* even to distinguish the truth from falsehood, we should know positively what the gospel is. This is as wonderful as the "expressive silence" of the Messias. Hence, if ANYTHING be the gospel, it is not possible for a sinner heartily to believe it, and to submit to it, without enjoying the salvation it contemplates. And, on the other hand, it is as impossible for anyone to reject it without being condemned. If either can occur, God forfeits his word. We have only, then, when we hear what is brought to us, *as the gospel,* to ask a very simple question, to determine our duty, and to justify us in following the path it opens: namely, "Has God promised me that if I believe THIS, and obey it—that is, put it in practice—I shall be saved? If he have, this is the gospel. If not, I may lawfully and without danger reject it."

Suppose, then, that in a discourse professing to exhibit the essential doctrines of the gospel, the first of the five points be *demonstrated,* namely; the total hereditary depravity of man. The question is, is this the gospel? If God has promised those who hear it, that if they believe it, *and put it in practice,* they shall receive the remission of their sins, then it certainly is the gospel. Or, if this doctrine cannot be rejected without condemnation, it is again proved to be the gospel. But if, on the contrary, it admits of question, if it may be rejected by a sinner, without danger of damnation, then it is not the gospel. It may be true, *but it is not the gospel.*

The same reasoning will apply, in detail, to the other four points, and also to the five opposing tenets. These may all be true, and either system may be true as a whole, but unless belief of them, and obedience to them, be connected with salvation, and the rejection of them with condemnation, the criterion disallows them.

Nothing can be regarded as glad tidings to a sinner that does not result in the certain removal of his sins. In order to this, the means must be definite and ascertainable. They must, moreover, be indisputable; they cannot allow of debate. But all these essential doctrines do allow of debate. A truly good man may reject any one of them, and be considered a good man by the advocates of what he rejects. How true soever they may be, and I question none of them now, certainly they cannot constitute, in whole or in part, a remedy that shall inspire confidence in its results. It must not be forgotten that if anyone can believe the gospel and be baptized without being saved, God forfeits his word And likewise this is true, if he be not condemned on rejecting it.

We may also try by this test, sentiments not constituting an essential part of either of the great divisions of theological opinion; as, for example, the question, if man, as he is, can or cannot believe the gospel. If God has promised a sinner that if he believes *that he can believe,* or *that he cannot* believe, and act accordingly, he shall be saved, this is the gospel. And if he declare that anyone who does not believe one of these propositions shall be damned, this again is the gospel, and not otherwise. But neither of these propositions is matter of saving faith, or therefore forms any part of the gospel. The same may be said of almost all the doctrinal discussions that fill the pulpit and divide the religious world into endless schismatic fragments. By matters that are of no saving efficacy, even though they could be decided, has the gospel of the grace of God been lamentably supplanted.

It becomes proper now, to present in a manner as brief as possible, the gospel by which man is saved. And it may be affirmed, without fear of contradiction, that it will bear the test instituted by divine authority. Its characteristics need not be discussed, the thing itself is what we desire to hear. But it may be remarked that nothing can be the gospel that has not the following traits: 1st, It must be "*glad tidings* 2d. glad tidings "*of great joy j'* 3d glad tidings of great joy "*to all people.*" We may examine all that professes to be the gospel in this light, with the confident expectation of determining its pretensions, but as it has been proposed to consider it under another standard, this is not pursued.

That we may not err in this great matter, we must confine ourselves to *the statements* of the Divine record. No inferences are allowable here. In the words of its author we must find it, or nowhere. The criterion by which it may be known does not tell what it is. Where, then, shall we go? To many passages of the New Testament we may apply, but to none with more certainty of being fully satisfied than to the following:

"Moreover, brethren, I declare unto you the gospel which I preached unto you, which also you have received, and wherein you stand. By which also you are saved, if you keep in memory what I preached unto you, unless you have believed in vain. For I delivered unto you first of all, that which I also received, how that Christ died for our sins according to the scriptures, and that he was buried, and that he rose again the third day according to the scriptures." 1 Cor. xv: 1-4.

It is hardly possible to overlook the agreement of this passage with Mark xvi: 15-16. Paul, although acting under a different commission from that of the eleven, preached the gospel just as they did; for he says, "which *I* also received," and "whether it were I or they, so we preached, and so you believed." "I certify you, brethren, that the gospel which was preached of me was not after man, for I neither received it from man, neither was I taught it, but by the revelation of Jesus Christ." Gal. i: 11, 12.

When, seventeen years after his conversion, he went to Jerusalem, in obedience to a divine impulse, he communicated privately with those of reputation, lest he had run in vain; that is, he did not preach publicly until he had ascertained, by conversation with the apostles, that the gospel which he preached was the same as theirs. And he tells us he knew as much as any of them; "In conference they added nothing to me." Gal. ii: 6. Although therefore an apostle, created not at the same time with the others, he preached the same gospel as fully, and as much with divine approbation. Let us then see how his statement of what occurred at Corinth agrees with the demands of the commission given to the eleven.

In Acts xviii, the introduction of Christianity into Corinth is narrated. He alludes to his *success* there, in the passage above quoted from the first epistle to the church then formed, when he says: "Which also you have received, and wherein you stand." To "have *received"* the gospel, is the same thing, in other words, as to have *believed* it. "To as many as received him," "even to those who believe on his name," etc. John i: 12. The Corinthians then had heard the gospel and had believed it. They had also obeyed it; that is they had been immersed for the statement declares, "wherein you stand." To this agrees the history of the case in Acts xviii: 8. "Many of the Corinthians hearing, believed, and were immersed." To complete the case, Paul adds, "By which also you *are* saved," and thus we have all the conditions of Mark xvi: 15, 16: "He that believeth and is immersed, shall be saved."

So far we have traced the *results* of the apostle's preaching. But what did he preach? His object in this passage was to repeat what he delivered to them *"first of all,"* and of course, as he notifies them of that object, he did not neglect it. What then does he say? "I delivered unto you that which I also received, how *that Christ died for our sins,* according to the scriptures; and *that he was buried,* and that *he rose again the third day,* according to the scriptures." Here, then, we have the gospel. And certainly these are "glad tidings of great joy to all people," to sinners and to dying sinners.

It is impossible, within my prescribed limits, even were it now necessary, fully to develop these truths. Let it be remarked, however, that this inspired enunciation of the gospel, represents it as consisting of three truths, based upon three facts, and importing what eternity alone will disclose.

No one questions the truth that "Jesus died." Some, indeed, do deny that it was *"for"* or on account of "our sins." This is to invalidate the gospel, since it renders it in-, applicable to. sinners. Whether, therefore, the words of the apostle be so used as to deny the expiatory nature of Messiah's death, or as Universalists employ them, the statement is annulled. Indeed, we may even admit the statement in its apostolic sense, and yet so preach it as to produce *any* effect rather than that reconciliation to God contemplated by the death of his Son. We may place no stress upon the fact, nor upon the meaning of that fact; but may debate about "the extent of the atonement," as controlled by the "design" thereof. We may discuss questions that have long agitated the church, namely, "whether

---

* There is now no debate among the truly learned as to the meaning of the original word.

the atonement is special in its nature, its design, and its application," or if it be infinite and universal in these three respects? Whatever combination of these propositions be adopted, such investigations invalidate the death of Christ, since they divert the minds of the hearers of them from the *fact,* and from the doctrine of the fact; namely, that love wherewith God has regarded *man;* inasmuch as that "when we were yet sinners, Christ died for us."

In preaching the first great gospel truth, then, or any other, we must do it "as the oracles of God require—that is, we must state it in the terms in which He has announced it, and for the purpose he designed by it, supporting it by the testimony He has vouchsafed to give. Were we to do this, it would prove itself to be the power of God unto the salvation of him who believes; and the reasons of so little effect, *religiously,* from what is called preaching, are, that "doctrines" have been substituted for the gospel, as the matter of that preaching; and still worse, that the most absurd and disgusting anecdotes and appliances have entered the pulpit, and have been used by way of "carrying home" what is said to be truth—as if truth had not weight enough to make its own way to the mind without a bribe to the passions! It is necessary to *force* a cork under the water, but gold will sink spontaneously. Either of the above plans may convert—that is, turn human beings, the first into doctrinal disputants, the second into— anything but Christians. But as "whatsover a man soweth, that also shall he reap," it is as absurd to expect that by such means men will be converted to Jesus Christ, the great subject of the gospel, as it is to look for grapes on brambles, figs on thistles, or for barley from tares.

If a man sow Presbyterian seed, he does not intend nor expect to reap Methodists; Episcopalianism will not bring forth Baptists; nor Methodism Catholics; nor will the seed of either system produce *Christians.* The "one Lord, one faith, one baptism," "the incorruptible seed of the kingdom," the "glad tidings of great joy to all people"—*this alone* can bring forth fruit, thirty, sixty, a hundred fold to God, and this will never fail of its results.

Nor is the next great gospel truth less important than the first, namely: "*And that he was buried."* This is a speaking truth; but who has ever heard a sermon preached from these words? Yet they constitute a part of the gospel as much as "Jesus died for our sins." This point, then, should be as prominent in our exhibitions as the other. And who can contemplate the fact it portrays without emotion? The grave has gained over man a greater victory than that achieved by any other conqueror. The dead are, everywhere and by all people, with few exceptions, buried, or put out of sight in some way. The grave is terrible to those who study it not in the light of Christianity. Our flesh recoils at the idea of returning to the dust—of being disintegrated—of becoming a loathsome and disgusting mass of putridity. Hence the various but futile means to avoid this necessity. What do the recently discovered sarcophagi of the Assyrian monarchs contain, but the dust of their occupants? And what is an Egyptian mummy but a mass of atoms held together by cohesive attraction, or by the bandages that envelop it? Is it less dead or less repulsive because of its bone-like solidity?

Attempts to preserve the human body from decay, indicate an utter ignorance of that wonderful truth—"If Christ be in you,"—that is, even though Christ be in you, the body is dead, or mortal, because of sin; but "the spirit is life because of righteousness."—Rom. viii. 10. The human body has lost its original grandeur. It was made in the image of God —that is, after that model of perfection the body of the glorified Immanuel. It was as brilliant as the sun, clothed with light as with a garment. By sin it lost this glory and became what it now is. It must needs be covered to hide its sin and its shame, and the grave must receive it for the same reason. This building must be destroyed, this temple thrown down—not one stone left upon another. It is dust; and God's decree is, "unto dust shalt thou return." How vain, how utterly at variance with God's will, and with the objects of the remedial system, is the attempt to render immutable the sin-deformed body of a dead human being!

Far better is it that all vestiges of sin shall be obliterated—that the victory gained over it by Satan shall be itself conquered. Jesus came "to destroy the works of the devil;" and he will destroy that fiendish triumph in which the adversary rejoiced when he effected the mutilation of a frame constructed in the divine likeness. But death must be conquered by death, and out of a vile body shall spring one glorious and immortal!

"Jesus was buried." He entered the tomb, that those who believe in him may not fear to trust themselves there. *He* did no sin, neither was guile found in *His* lips. Hence *His* flesh did not see corruption. It was mortal, indeed, because of sin; and yet he was not a sinner. How then could he be mortal—how die? No man can account for this, except by means of the Scriptural statement, that his birth and life, his death and burial all occurred *for others*—for those who were sinners—for man and in his stead. Man then is the sinner, *his* flesh *must* see corruption in the grave where he is hidden from the view of man. But God sees him; his dust is precious; his body is a "purchased possession." It has been redeemed from under the dominion of "him who had the power of death," and that body will be reanimated. "God shall quicken your mortal bodies by his spirit that dwelleth in you." Jesus slept but three days—his disciples must rest until their bodies have been thoroughly decomposed; and when the summons of the archangel shall awaken their dust, the dead in Christ shall arise, before those who, because perhaps of their eminent piety, are alive and remain until his coming, shall be changed in a moment, in the twinkling of an eye, into his glorious image—into the original form of the first man's body. Thus, "the manifestation of the sons of God will take place,"—thus "the adoption, to wit, the redemption of the body."

What glad tidings of great joy, then, do we hear when told that "Jesus was buried?" He descended into the dark domains of the monarch enthroned over man. He took out of his hands the keys of death and of Hades, and placed them, as a victorious trophy, in his own girdle. He retains them: he opens, and no man shuts; and has declared that the gates of Hades shall not prevail against his church. Like Sampson, he stooped to conquer, and he *did* conquer.

We have heard many discourses upon the third item of the gospel, namely: "*He rose again* the third day, according to the Scriptures." Not often, however, have these differed from logical demonstrations of a physical truth. They may have exhibited the ability, the learning, the research of their authors, but they do not involve the necessity that those authors were pious men, or that they preached the gospel. Any candid man, of sufficient discernment, may take the evangelical history, and may demonstrate the resurrection of the Messiah, since he can account for some events upon no other hypothesis. But it is one thing to prove an event, and another, altogether, to announce that event as part and parcel of the gospel.

The death of Christ has formed a theme for thousands of discourses, during hundreds of years; his burial has often been alluded to, his resurrection is a standing yearly topic before many congregations, But this is one thing, and it is wholly another to put these three truths together; to declare that these constitute "the gospel;" to assure our hearers that if they heartily believe these, and submit to their power, they shall certainly be saved here, and be glorified hereafter; and that if they do not believe them, they will as certainly be condemned.

We may establish these as separate facts, beyond the possibility of appeal; and yet our hearers may hate the truths we teach, but they can-not be received as instances of God's love to man; as proofs of the triumphs of life over death; as the abolishing of death, and the bringing of life and immortality to light, without that shout of joyful gratitude: "O death! where is now thy sting? O grave! where is now thy victory?"

In *preaching* the gospel, it cannot but be seen, I think, that we must be confined to the declaration of these three truths. They constitute the whole gospel; and nothing but these, in some divinely authorized form, can be matter of saving faith. When, upon the testimony that "God has given of His Son," these are heartily believed; when confession of them is made with the lips; and when upon this confession, a sinner, taking upon him the name of Christ, is immersed unto death, and unto *his* death; he, rising to walk in a new life, and becoming thus a Son of God, needs the *development* of these truths; the *teaching* of one doctrine and no other, in order to such a life as shall end in his redemption from the grave, and the enjoyment of an inheritance among the sanctified.

Let me ask, then, Can any man, believe with all his heart, upon the testimony of *such a witness,* that "Christ died for our sins; that he was buried, and that he arose from the dead for our justification; while at the same time, he is, not in one act only, but in his whole life, controlled by this belief?" Can any such one fail to receive the pardon of his sins here, with all the blessings of the new Covenant, and in the end, life everlasting? CAN HE? If so, then, the gospel is valueless; and such an anomaly, such a disjunction of cause and effect, never entered into the list of those topics upon which the mind of man has been called to dwell. No man can be fitted for the society of heaven without taking his place in that society. What other position can he occupy? He is not fit for the society of the condemned, since he has not been educated for that. It is not possible, then, for God's promises to fail; nor for the object of the Divine Mission to be frustrated. Jesus will certainly present himself before his father, and say: "Behold I, and the children whom thou hast given me," are here.

On the other hand, can anyone deny that Jesus died, and died for our sins—that he was buried, or that he rose again, and receive the remission of his sins, or escape destruction from the presence of God, and the glory of His power? If so, then again, the gospel is valueless, since a believer in it is no better off than an infidel, and religion of any sort may be justly repudiated.

Let us not be deceived, nor lay to our souls the hope that in impugning the Divine veracity we can escape; for while he that believeth on the Son of God, hath in Him; that is, in God, a witness. "He that believeth not God, hath made God a liar, because he has not believed the record He has given of His son."—1 Jno: v. 10. If the greatest offense we can commit against our fellow beings is to doubt *their* words, what is the character of those thoughts of that language, and of a life that deny the statements of Him who has condescended to bear testimony to man, that "Jesus of Nazareth is the Messiah, the Son of the living God?"

-----o-----

A Dialogue of Devils.—No. 1.

Present, *Diabolos, Apollyon, Daimonion* and *Lucifer.*

Subject.——The most effectual method of subverting, neutralizing and defeating the word of God, and the mission of Christ.

Diabolos.—It is truly fortunate that we have thus met in this deep, dark, and secret cavern, that we may have an opportunity to discuss, plan and arrange our mode of operations, in our efforts to paralyze and defeat the word of God, and the mission of Christ. No time should be lost, now that we have met, and I am ready to hear any suggestions.

Lucifer.— I heartily agree with you, sir, that no time should be lost, and that immediate and most effectual action should be had. I therefore propose that we, without delay, fall upon some stratagem by which we can take the Bible, and keep it from the masses of the people. As long as they have the Bible, we can never have complete success in effecting their destruction.

Daimonion.—I am, sir, favorable to that suggestion. We can never succeed with the Bible in the hands of the people at large. I therefore suggest that we set on foot some scheme, by which to engage men, and raise liberal salaries, sufficient to induce them to do this work for us. The men are to be found; we *can,* and we *must* obtain them. The money will bring them.

Apollyon.—How are these men to get the Bible from the people? That statement of Chillingworth: "The Bible, and the Bible alone, is the religion of Protestants," has now become stereotyped in the minds of the people pretty much throughout the civilized world, and I see no way of counteracting it.

Luc.—The men we employ to do this work, must teach the people that they are their spiritual guides and expounders of the word of God; that they care for their souls, as those who must give account, and the people will soon and readily yield most tamely to them the right to read the Bible for them, and decide in spiritual things for them. Many now would rather give some spiritual guide a large salary for reading the Bible, thinking, and worshiping for them, than to do it themselves, as the first simple-hearted followers of Christ did. The thing, sir, can be accomplished easily.

Diab.—You must be a great set of simpletons! Have you no memories? or were you all soundly asleep for the space of a thousand years, during the dark ages? or have you read no history? or are your heads so thick that you can never learn anything? Have I not tried that scheme to perfection, during the space of more than a thousand years? I had the Bible once taken from the "common people," as I taught "the clergy" to call them, and I thought at one time the plan would prove successful; but I was defeated.

Apol.—How could you have been defeated in so admirable a plan? You know that, as prince of the bottomless pit, I was not present; but I cannot see how such an admirable plan could have proved a failure!

Diab.—Well, sir, I never could make it work precisely to my notion. When I would think I had the work almost accomplished, the first thing I would know, in some corner or other of the earth, some man would be found with a copy of the Bible, or portions of it, proclaiming to the masses of the people, at the top of his voice, "Without *holiness* no man shall see the Lord." This would create uneasiness and anxiety to hear what the Scriptures say. To counteract this state of things, I had my faithful and dutiful son at Rome, the Pope, whom I had appointed general superintendent of my affairs on earth, to authorize all the agents he had appointed to assist him in accomplishing my work—to give them power, or rather to make the *people believe* that they had power, by virtue of the keys of the kingdom, to forgive sins. This succeeded admirably for a time.

Daim.—I cannot see why it should not have succeeded to perfection. In the first place, I should have supposed, that it would exactly have suited those who had no personal holiness; and in the second place, it was a source of much gain to the priests, which would certainly have secured their hearty aid.

Diab.—Well, here was a difficulty; many would die without pardon, and the people were anxious to look into the Bible, to know what had become of these, and a continual inquisitiveness was some place or other springing up to find out what was in the Bible. To meet this difficulty, and give all my agents an opportunity to lay their hands on a sufficient amount of gold and silver to secure their devotion to my work, I ordered them to make the people believe, that if any should die without pardon, and fall into purgatory—as all most certainly would, who die in that condition—for a sufficient sum of money, by virtue of the aforesaid keys, purgatory could be unlocked, and their souls released. This satisfied many, and aided me very materially.

Apol.—I think, sir, you managed with great skill; but I cannot see how any possible failure could have attended a scheme so wisely arranged and well executed!

Diab.—It may appear strange to you that the success of my plans was not complete; but such was the case. I even extended my plans beyond what I have mentioned; for the sake of securing the aid of a large and influential class, I arranged, advocated and established the doctrine of indulgences, and carried the matter to such perfection, that I had many of my most devoted servants selling indulgences at public auction, which you all know means pardon for sins which the purchaser intends committing. I carried this matter to such an extent, that I had one of my most devoted servants to declare publicly, that he had saved more souls by the sale of indulgences, than St. Peter had by the keys of the kingdom.

Daim.—Most noble *Diabolos,* you have acted most admirably in this matter, and wisely; all that I am led to wonder at, is that your success should not have been most complete! Perhaps you should have appointed some severe punishments for all who should be found with a copy of the Scriptures, except the priests.

Diab.—I am astonished at your ignorance! Are you now to be informed of the inquisition, the gibbet, the scourge, chains, prisons, fagots, stakes, banishments, confiscations of goods, &c., &c., that I employed for more than a thousand years, to deter men from reading the Bible? If you are, you are unfit for a seat in this council.

Daim.—I ask pardon. I was not ignorant of your having employed these instrumentalities; but with all due deference to your superior wisdom and position, I think you do not give full credit to the efficiency of these means.

Diab.—Were you asleep in the time of Luther, Melancthon, and other co-workers with them? Where were you in the time of Tyndale, young Frith, Coverdale, Calvin, Huss, Servetus, &c., &c., who, though they did not agree among themselves, were all vociferating aloud, "The Bible, and the Bible alone, is the religion of Protestants," and no more regarded their lives and property, or the thunders of the Vatican, than the mild breezes of a summer's day? Are your eyes closed to the result of the operations of these men? If they are, as I said before, you are incapable of being of any advantage in this council. It is useless to speak of schemes of this description now. I have tried them to perfection; and, though they answered my purpose well in their day, their time has gone by. They may serve for a time yet for stereotyped people and antiquated countries, but other expedients must now be resorted to. Look at their free governments, free speech, and free presses; missionaries, Bible societies, and Sunday schools, spreading the Scriptures everywhere! These operations must be counteracted.

Luc.—I am convinced, most wise *Diabolos*, that you are in the right, that you have made full and fair experiments, in the effort to take the Bible out of the hands of the "common people," and that that plan will not work now. We must resort to something different, if we effect anything in these times. I think the time has come for a bold push, and I suggest that we now, as such vast numbers have the Bible, and are scattering it all over the world, come square out and deny its divinity, and the divinity of Christ. Thousands of men will fall in with this at once, and can be enlisted in our work.

Apol.—I am pleased with that idea. I should like something bold and daring, and therefore am in for striking one mighty blow, and think we can thus finish the work at once.

Daim.—Gentlemen, I like your suggestion. I think the time has come for us to sweep everything before us. All that is now wanting is to strike the blow in a bold and decided manner, and success will follow.

Diab.—I am astonished at your ignorance! You talk with as little judgment as inexperienced children. You never stop to reflect upon what has been, or you are wholly ignorant of all the past I Are you all ignorant that I made one push of that kind once, when there was an opportunity, and when I employed some of as bold and daring men as I can ever expect to find again, and that the whole thing proved a failure? I once had the great Gibbon, Voltaire, Hume, Bolingbroke, and Paine employed in an effort just such as you suggest, both with the tongue and pen.

Daim.—Wherein did the plan prove a failure? I cannot see how it could have proved a failure.

Diab.—It proved a failure in this way: It immediately called out such men as Paley, Watson, Geo. Campbell, etc., and set the whole ministry to investigating, and almost the whole civilized world to thinking on the subject, which resulted in reaction. The matter lies here: we all know that Christianity is true, and that Jesus of Nazareth is a divine person, and any move that we make to induce men to look directly at the question of the truth of Christianity, and the divine mission of Christ, must ultimately react upon us. It did react in this way when I made just such a push as you now suggest; and in the place of putting the Bible down, Bibles have been multiplied upon us thicker since than ever before.

There is no policy, nor good sense, in our coming out boldly and denying the Bible. We shall only defeat ourselves, if we try that method.

Luc.—Well, I am at a loss what course to pursue! You appear to condemn all our suggestions, and I see no general plan of operation that we can hit upon!

Diab.—If you will all come here and sit down at my feet, and confess your ignorance, I will instruct you. It is useless to speak of any "general plan." Truth is an *unit*—it is *one*. Anything else is error. There is but *one right way* to anything. Everything else is wrong. Now, that we be successful, we must not be scrupulous what we advocate, provided it is not the truth, and does not aid the truth. It is not material what the people hold, provided it is not the truth. It is no matter what way the people go, provided it is not the right way: it will answer our purpose.

Apol.—Thank you, most noble *Diabolos.* your suggestion is full of wisdom, and opens a wide field for operation. I see now how we can make immense improvements in our work of ruin.

Diab.—Improvements in our work, most certainly! What is the use of experience, if we learn nothing? We must not even deny all truth. In accomplishing our fiendish designs, it is frequently more wise to admit certain truths than to deny them. When Jesus cast out *demons*, it would only have subjected us to ridicule and derision to have denied it. I therefore admitted that he cast them out, but explained that he did it through Beelzebub the prince of *demons.* So far as this, my explanation of the matter, was received, it accomplished my malignant designs as effectually as if I could have succeeded in making men believe that he did not cast out *demons* at all.

Luc.—Most wise and worthy *Diabolos,* you have now opened a world-wide field for us. I can see now wherein we may take great advantage. It is not necessary that we should oppose all truths, and thus show all men that our cause is manifestly wrong, but merely subvert the truth so as to ruin its force.

Diab.—Certainly; you now speak like one who begins to understand his business. You all well know the truth that has given us more trouble than all the balance—the truth that Jesus Christ is the Son of God and the Saviour of the world. This truth we must evade somehow, or our cause is gone. But you must recollect that we are not to deny this right out. I have not for the last century thought it expedient directly to deny this. The only manner in which I have thought of success has been in tacitly admitting the divinity of Christ, and seeking to call off the public mind from that fact, by engrossing it upon other subjects.

Luc.—I am truly delighted with that thought. In that manner we can put forth many of our plans under the name of *orthodoxy,* by inducing speculative questions, side-issues, and delusive reasonings; infusing feuds, strife, and hatred among the followers of Christ. In this way, we can induce them to love their views, their partisan peculiarities, and organizations; preach them, try to prove and defend them, and they will soon set their whole affections upon them, and become a church founded upon these peculiarities, and not upon Christ at all. In this way, Christ will be forgotten by them, and his religion will be as effectually defeated as if they had denied him.

Diab. — Most excellent Lucifer, you now begin to talk sense. I hope you will mature these things, till we have an opportunity to meet next month, when I propose to set out my plans more fully, and show you the immense agencies I have now in lively operation, and if my success is not complete, it will certainly be very great. It is useless here, where we are not seen *by men,* and as we know God will not hear us, to adjourn by prayer; we therefore adjourn without any prayer, to this night one month. REPORTER.

-----O-----

Our Position as a Religious Body.

No. 12.

IN NO. 11, under the above caption, we commenced an induction of all the items contained in a conversion to Christianity. In that article, it was ascertained that faith must be the first item, and that everything else must proceed from faith; for "without faith it is impossible to please God," and "he that cometh to God must believe." It was also ascertained that repentance was the second item. Repentance cannot he the first item, for it is "repentance toward God," or in view of God's requirement, and which God grants unto life, which cannot exist without faith. It cannot be the third or fourth item, for the believer cannot do anything acceptable to God without penitence. The impenitent believer cannot confess, call upon the Lord, be baptized, or do anything else acceptable to the Lord. If faith does not lead to penitence, it never can lead to anything good. This is indisputably the second step. We now proceed to find the third step. This is the great confession. This is not only an item, but, like those we have considered, an indispensable. "Whoever, therefore, shall confess me before men, him will I confess before my Father who is in heaven." Matt. x: 32. Even the enemies of Jesus saw that there was something important in confessing Christ. Hence they did not form the issue upon believing in him, repenting, or being baptized, but upon *confessing him.* Hence the statement, that "the Jews agreed already, that if any man did confess that he was Christ, he should be put out of the synagogue." Jno. ix: 22. The same is seen in the following: "Nevertheless, among the chief rulers, also, many believed on him; but because of the Pharisees, they did not confess him, lest they should be put out of the synagogue." This shows that the issue was made upon the confession. The Lord required it, and the enemies opposed it. See Jno. xii: 42. Let us have a little more light on the confession. "Every spirit that confesseth that Jesus Christ is come in the flesh is of God. And every spirit that confesseth not that Jesus Christ is come in the flesh, is not of God." 1 Jno. iv: 2, 3. From this it is clear, that the Lord makes the confession the *test,* that tries the spirits whether they are of God.

We will hear the scripture again: "And many that believed came, and confessed, and showed their deeds." Acts xix:18. But we must determine what it is that is confessed. We have already seen that John defines it to be that "Jesus Christ is come in the flesh."

But Paul refers us to the period when the Lord made the confession. He says to Timothy, "I give thee charge in the sight of God, who quickeneth all things, and before Jesus Christ, who before Pontius Pilate, witnessed a good confession." What was that good confession? It was that he was the King of the Jews, though his kingdom was not of this world; but the King promised in the Jewish scripture. In a different form, though virtually the same, he made the confession under oath before the Sanhedrim. He made the confession, that he was their King—that he was the Son of God, and confirmed it by an oath. This shows what the confession was. But we will hear Paul. He says: "The word is nigh thee, even in thy mouth, and in thy heart; that is the word of faith, which we preach; that if thou shalt confess with thy mouth the Lord Jesus, and shalt believe in thy heart that God hath raised him from the dead, thou shalt be saved." Rom. x: 9, 10. Here we have precisely what is to be believed in the heart, confessed with the mouth, and the object of it. We must confess with the mouth the *Lord Jesus,* believe in the heart that God *raised him from the dead,* and the object is *salvation.*

But now for the order of this item. Is it the first, second, third, or fourth? It cannot be the first item, for we have determined that faith is the first, and there must be faith in the heart before confession can be made with the mouth. It cannot be the second item, for a confession in impenitence is an absurdity. Not only so, but we have found that repentance was required as the second item. It cannot be put off till after baptism, because, Acts viii: 37, it is made a prerequisite to baptism. The eunuch said to Philip, "See here is water, what doth hinder me to be baptized? And Philip said, If thou believest with all thy heart, thou mayest." He believed in his heart and was penitent, and answered, "I believe that Jesus Christ is the Son of God." Here in this confession, is where the soul of man yields, bows or submits to the Lord Jesus, and is pledged to him. Here the will assents, yields, and comes under him, as the infallible guide and ruler, and is pledged to do his will. After this step is taken, all is easy. His yoke is easy, and his burden is light.

The next item in the divine arrangement is *baptism*. The heart is changed, purified, or the person is converted in heart, by faith. The person is purified, changed, or converted in character by repentance, reformation, or amendment of life. The confession is the public, open, verbal recognition and reception of Christ. Although the man is changed in heart, changed in character, and has acknowledged his Redeemer, the Lord has not acknowledged him. Nor did the Almighty openly and audibly acknowledge Jesus till he was baptized. But the moment he ascended from the waters of baptism, the heavens were parted above him, and the voice came from his Father, "This is my Son, the beloved, in whom I am well pleased." The Holy Spirit did not bear witness to him till this interesting moment. But here he descended and abode upon him and John says, "He who sent me to baptize, said, On whomsoever you see the Holy Spirit descending and remaining, he is the Son of God." If, then, God did not audibly acknowledge his Son, and if the Holy Spirit did not bear witness of him till his baptism, we certainly need not look for him to acknowledge us as sons and daughters before baptism. Whether we look for it or not, he surely does not acknowledge us till we yield to him in this institution. If the Lord could say, "Thus it becometh us to fulfill all righteousness," when he bowed himself to this institution, surely we may say, *it becomes us.* "But I cannot think that baptism is essential." Well, have you the mind that was in Christ? If you have, it becomes you to submit to the Lord in baptism. Not only so, but the Lord said to persons who refused to submit to John's baptism, "You rejected the counsel of God against yourselves, not being baptized by John." How could persons reject the counsel of God against themselves, not being baptized by John, unless his baptism was essential?

Let us hear the Lord: "Except a man be born of water and of the Spirit, he cannot enter into the kingdom of God." This language he explains to be, you *must* be born of water and of the Spirit, for, at verse 7, referring back to this, he says, "Marvel not that I said unto you, Ye *must be* born again." The Lord, then, defines being born again, being "born of *water* and of the Spirit," and says, it *must be.* In the last commission, he makes baptism co-extensive with faith. "He that believeth and is baptized, shall be saved, and he that believeth not shall be damned." Here are conditions and a promise, and certainly no man can reasonably extend the promise any further than the conditions are complied with. But let any man follow the apostles under this commission, and see if they ever brought any man to salvation who did not comply with these conditions. Where did they ever receive any person without baptism? Nowhere.

Let us hear the Lord's own word in a very important case. When he appeared to young Saul, he said, "Lord, what wilt thou have me to do? And the Lord said unto him, Arise, and go into the city, and it shall be told thee what thou *must do.*" Acts ix: 6. He went to the city, and waited to be told what he must do. To fulfill this promise, in telling him what he must do, the Lord sent Ananias to him, for the express purpose of telling him *what he must do.* He did not tell him to believe, for he was brought to believe, when he heard the word of the Lord, "I am Jesus whom thou persecutest," and that faith led him to inquire what he must do. He did not tell him to repent, for he had already repented—ceased to do evil—to persecute the saints, and was trying to learn do well. What then was it, that he was to tell him that he *must do?* It was precisely what Ananias did tell him, viz.: "Arise, and *be baptized,* and wash away thy sins, calling on the name of the Lord." Acts xxii: 16.

Why not make baptism a first, second, third, or fifth step in the Divine process? We cannot make it first, for it is a command, and no command can be recognized without faith. Faith must, therefore, precede all commands. It cannot be second, for we have found that repentance is the second item, and repentance was required before baptism. It cannot be the third item, for the eunuch, when he inquired what hindered him to be baptized, was required to confess Christ. It was the fourth term, for the eunuch, immediately after the confession—the next step he took, was baptized. This is the manner in which they called upon the name of the Lord. They came by faith, with most solemn reformation, confession, and baptism, to the Lord. Here his word declares them pardoned, justified, adopted, and saved, and here he acknowledges them children. The next word after baptism, in the commission, is salvation. The next thing on the day of Pentecost, after baptism is remission of sins, which is the same as salvation in the commission. The heart is prepared for God by faith, the character by repentance, the state by baptism, the former guilt is destroyed and the power of sin taken away by pardon, and the soul of the new convert is comforted by the Holy Spirit and the hope of heaven. Thus it is that we find by a careful induction, the items in the Divine arrangement are as follows: Faith, Repentance, Confession, Baptism, Pardon, the Holy Spirit, the Hope of Eternal Life.

That some of the denominations in this country lack some of these items, pervert others, and derange them all, we not only admit, but can abundantly show beyond all contradiction. But that any denomination, or any teacher of religion, can show that they have any item of the Divine arrangement for converting sinners that we have not, or that any other order of the items is of God, we do not and never expect to believe. We are free to admit that they have items that we have not, and some that we have they have in a different order; but those which we have not are not of the Divine arrangement—not in the New Testament, and those in a different order are arranged without any regard to apostolic order or reason. To speak of an unbeliever praying for faith, or repenting, is only equaled by the absurdity of baptizing an unconscious infant, which is certainly darkness confounded. It is of a piece with men believing who never heard the gospel, of being born again to enable them to believe, and receiving the Holy Spirit to regenerate them. If we could become sufficiently stupefied and bewildered thus to derange and confuse the order of heaven, and call the items, in this confused and distorted form, "the doctrines of the gospel," "the doctrines of grace," etc., we could be orthodox and not regarded as a dangerous people. But weft betide the man, who must have all the items of the Divine arrangement, as laid down in the holy records; no more, no less; and who must have them in the precise order as arranged by the Holy Spirit of God at the beginning! We maintain, however, that the Holy Spirit gave us all the items which he requires, in the history of the first converts, and the order in which the items stand to each other, as God had joined them, and let not man put them asunder. B. F.

-----o-----

The Christian Profession, as compared with that of the Patriarch and Jew.

BROTHER FRANKLIN I held a very pleasant interview a few days since with one of my companions in travel, in which the Christian profession, as compared with that of the Patriarch and Jew, was under consideration. I received the following very interesting reflections on the subject, and inasmuch as they were freely received, I wish freely to impart them, for general benefit. I herewith, therefore, transmit them to you, with very little change in the phraseology:

"Our profession," said he, "as compared with that of the Patriarch and Jew, will be this: We profess, with them, to repent, and renounce the world and its lusts; to die to sin, and live again unto righteousness. But we do this with such a death and life being made especially imperative upon us, being also actually proposed and represented to us in the death and resurrection of the author of our forgiveness. We also profess our entire faith: in the truth of His promises. But the greater part of what were promises to them, are gifts to us; and such gifts as still remain in expectance, and not in possession, are rendered distinct, appreciable, and certain from the accomplishment of the others. They have even been exemplified to us—the life after death in the resurrection of the lord, the bounteous gifts of His spirit, in the graces and powers of His saints, from the day of Pentecost until now. Thus our profession is distinctly marked out to us. There is for doubt, no excuse for vacillation. It is not shadowy. so as to elude the grasp, it is not indefinite in any point, so as at times to escape from it; it is so substantial, so comprehensible. that if we hold it not fast, the fault lies with our own weakness and wavering. What had Adam, what had Abraham, what had the Prophets for the grounds of their profession, compared with this? Verily, the least in the kingdom of Heaven is greater than them all.

The most practical part of our profession lies in the renunciation of the world, whose ways having been far more openly detected, and awfully condemned by the Gospel, than by any previous dispensation, we are more peculiarly called upon to reprobate and abandon. What fellow-feeling can a true child of God in Christ have with it? It is bent on the joys and pleasures of this life; therefore the cross of Christ, with its crucifying afflictions, is a stumbling-block to it. It is wise in its own conceit, and therefore that cross is foolishness to it. It worships rank and power, and therefore that cross is contemptible to it. It loves its own will and ways, and therefore that cross is hateful to it. As the convert in baptism takes a new name, to show that he is a new creature, so must he take up new names for the things of the world, in which he moves as a new creature; its joy will be his sorrow, its good his evil—in all things a new vocabulary will he adopted.

The Jew bore in his body the mark of his calling in Abraham; however, and wherever he lived, his flesh bore testimony to his being a member of that covenant which gave his nation the inheritance to the land of Canaan. But our mark must be in the spirit, as heirs of a spiritual kingdom, never to be obliterated there. That mark must be a peculiarity of thought, originating a peculiarity of action, by which we may be distinguished from those without. Word, and thought, and deed, must all have upon them the stamp of the cross of Christ. Everywhere we are obliged, from our common nature, to feel and do as other men. yet here we shall discover the mark of our calling. This feeling and doing will go but a short way with the world; if developed into any continued train of reflection, or expanded into any deliberate act. the eye will immediately discover its peculiar form, and acknowledge in it our profession. How should it be otherwise? We see how deeply the characters and conversation of men are imbued with the spirit of their worldly professions. The soldier, the scholar, the merchant, carry each the peculiar stamp of their occupation into their most free and disengaged moments. Their thoughts cannot, without some effort, be broken up from those clusters into which the due performance of their several duties has a tendency to combine them. And the more strictly they perform those duties, and the more signal their success, the deeper also is the tinge of this mark. Should it, therefore, be otherwise with the Christian, the exercise of whose profession is not. like this, limited to certain places and certain seasons; who is not now in full occupation, and then in utter leisure, but is ever engaged, and has before his eyes for his reward. not the honors or wealth of this fleeting world, but the bliss of the world everlasting? Shall not his mouth speak from the fullness of his heart? And if the soldier's heart be in the camp, the merchant's in his freighted vessels, so that the language of the one would sound absurd from the mouth of the other, shall there be no such distinction between the man of this world and the man of the next? Their hearts cannot have the same object, and can, therefore, the language of the one proceed from the mouth of the other, without and immediate and glaring contradiction to his profession? Shall a clean vessel pour forth what is unclean? Shall a heart overflowing with love, joy, and thankfulness for the mercies of God shown in our redemption—shall a mind exalted in the spirit far beyond the pitch to which the natural man could attain, supported daily by the daily soaring contemplation of the unraveled mysteries of God—shall these send forth no language of their own? shall they speak but as worldlings speak? It cannot be. "The heavens declare the glory of God, and the firmament telleth his handiwork," and shall the great work of God's hands, a living spirit, twice created, regenerated man—shall not his voice be heard among them? Shall not the glory of God be manifested from him, the chief of God's works, and cast in his own image? This is the Christian's profession; thus he must be a shining light amid darkness telling from his firmament, by an inextinguishable brightness of character, and by duly regulated motions of conduct, the glory, and the power, and the dominion, and the majesty of the almighty Author of his salvation.

It is true, that in no case should we think too highly of ourselves. But in the case of our station and corresponding profession as Christians, we can never think highly enough; and our constant endeavor must be to proceed from a higher to a higher pitch, so that the note and song of our profession may, like the trumpet of God, wax louder and louder. Look at the proud ones of this world, at them who do indeed think of themselves more highly than they ought, what a constant, jealous vigilance is there to maintain their dignity; what a cautious mingling with the general world; what a barrier do they try to throw around their communications, in order to keep off all intrusion of vulgar taint. Shall not, then, the Christian, whose honor is real and not conventional; inward and essential, not outward and accidental; derived from a heavenly incorruptible fountain, not from an earthly and corruptible; from eternity, not from yesterday; immortal, and not perishing; shall he not guard this with equal vigilance and scrupulosity, and keep it pure and unspotted from the world? Still more, if earthly rank, which lives on the breath of the world, and which is averse but to its conventional and not real impurities, can draw a line of separation, shall not the follower of the cross of Christ, which is at enmity with the world, and loathes all its impurities, shall he not trace around him a clear, decided mark of distinction?"

In great thankfulness to Him to whom I am indebted for these reflections, and in the hope that they may improve all who read them, as profitably as they have him who thus transcribes them, I abide, affectionately, yours in the Lord.

CHAS. D. HURLBUTT.

HIRAM, Portage Co., O., Nov. 3, 1856.

"Sweet are the Uses of Adversity."

"SWEET are the uses of adversity." Happy is he who, experienced in these uses, comes to authority among his fellow men; whose temper, tuned to the humility of suffering, brings a heart warm with that memory, brings a mind skilled by old sympathies, springing from the knowledge of human wrongs, to some station of control wherein he may somewhat direct and shape the lot of his fellow-men. Blessed is such a man in his generation if, wisely and humbly, with due weighing of his own trials, with due reverence for that holy light these trials have thrown upon the pathway of justice and mercy along which he is commissioned to walk, he remembers, heeds, and practices the duty of guidance and instruction to his subordinates.

When I go forth to seek a leader of men in whatever enterprise, let me find him of a generous nature, of a manly, brave spirit, of clear insight of what he is and what he has to do, of study, intelligence, improved by all good studies, of honest soul, and then to all th.se rare perfections, let me add that richest grace which comes from a successful encounter with adversity—not broken by it. but taught; not hardened in heart, but mellowed and filled with pity. Such a man would be one, above all men, to follow, cherish, forever remember.

Of such are heroes made; by them is our race adorned, exalted, made worthy of history. Truly, I believe no here ever became veritable but through this high road of suffering. Mock heroes we have enough; the world is full of them who strut before the foot-lights in all manner of tinsel, who flaunt on many signposts. who fill the throats of a whole senseless generation with huzzas. Such mock heroes, with their "mad jumble of hypocrisies," we have in all times to a surfeit. But no true hero, who has not stood in many a dark day, erect and manful, trusting to his manhood, and confident to carve his way either to proud distinction or to the prosperous light. This world's vicissitudes, which men somewhat impiously call fortune, are the tests by which God has signified the true man from the false;

which checkering the progress of mortals with more or less of pain and privation, in greater or smaller degree, render them heroic; prepare Hercules for his twelve labors; prepare Jason for his long circumnavigation; prepare Columbus for his abyss of waters, and for his miraculous epic of a new world; prepare Washington to render that new world forever unchainable, forever disdainful of tyranny.

J. P. K.

-----o-----

Industry in the Ministry.—Its Support.

No subject has been more frequently thought upon, discussed, and schemed at, on the part of the ministry, than that of its own support. This has been a subject of much deep and earnest solicitude. Nor is there anything strange in this. No man, with a right mind and heart, can rest satisfied at the head and responsible before God and man for the support of his family, without a visible income adequate to that end. Not only so, but the Christian ministry cannot exist, in such form as to promise success to the cause, without an adequate support; and, consequently, to withhold support is to crush the ministry. The result that must follow will be to destroy the church, which, it is manifest, cannot exist without the ministry. Many considerations like these have moved good men to think, argue, and feel deeply concerned upon the subject. No doubt nine-tenths of all the efforts to establish and sustain certain kinds of ecclesiastical organizations for many centuries past, have been with an eye largely to ministerial support. In all great convocations of ministers, such as conferences, synods, presbyteries, assemblies, councils, etc., etc., this absorbing and engrossing question has consumed a large share of the time and labor. Still, no general and permanent relief has been found.

In some religious organizations, the ministry have managed to get the matter pretty much into their own hands, and have it about their own way, to apportion and appropriate as they please, and the people submit with some internal and secret grumbling. Others have what they call a "lay delegation," who have, or *think* they have, a voice in the matter. Another class, becoming disgusted with this theorizing, maneuvering and scheming in mere pecuniary matters, and being impressed with its incompatibility with the whole spirit of the Christian religion, have concluded that preaching must be done without any pecuniary reward, and stand opposed to the whole business of *paying* preachers. Which of these has done the more harm, it were useless to try to determine. We need something practical, and that all can understand.

1. Such a professional class as preachers of the gospel, consisting of men who give themselves wholly to the work, is scriptural and indispensable.

2. It is impossible for men to devote their entire time and energies to the work unless they are supported.

3. Where any party have repudiated the support of the ministry, a class of men are soon found occupying the place of the ministry, wholly incompetent. A few men may be found competent, who are able to support themselves, but these are not willing to spend their whole time for the good of mankind wholly at their own expense, and they know, too, that a people thinking to sustain a religious system of operations of that kind, could not succeed.

4. The other classes, who appear constantly discussing questions of ministerial support, legislating in reference to it, appear to make money the all in all. Nothing like this can be found in the Scriptures. We there simply find allusions to the subject sufficient to show, that the ministry anciently was supported by the liberality of the disciples; but not one word about any plan, for the simple, good, and valid reason that they had no plan for any such object, and needed none. In that simple age of the church, they knew how to contribute to the temporal support of a deserving and worthy man, without any plan, and so they do now, when *they desire to do it.* Where they do not desire to give, they talk about *plans.*

5. Editors, other writers, and speakers have much to say on the subject, which makes an unfavorable impression, persons looking upon it as making merchandise of the gospel.

INDUSTRY IN THE MINISTRY—ITS SUPPORT.

6. Preachers are called to fill certain stations, visit points, and perform labor. Immediately. the question arises, is discussed, and the amount must be agreed upon, as if we were engaging a man to construct a piece of railroad. All this has a most unhappy effect both upon the church and the world.

Now, that there is something decidedly wrong here, is as manifest as day; something, too, directly in the way of the support of the ministry and the prosperity of the cause. All this bargaining, chaffering, bartering, and setting prices—so much preaching for so much money—is manifestly and decidedly wrong. The same is true of this discussing, legislating, and scheming among preachers upon the subject; it is wrong, and directly in the way of the very object they wish to accomplish. We know the Christian ministry must be supported. and we have been our self supported exclusively by the liberality of the Disciples for some fifteen years. How, then, shall the difficulty be avoided? Suppose a class of physicians should meet, debate, and scheme plans for their own support; or publish documents setting forth the duty of the people in supporting doctors, what would it avail? The people would think them simpletons and laugh at them. But let one of their number, without saying anything about support, open his office, seek employment in his profession, and industriously engage himself in *curing the sick;* it is circulated throughout the community, that he is ready to go promptly and faithfully at every call, and that he is actually *curing people,* and he will find plenty to do and a good support.

In the same manner, let preachers cease inquiring for *salaries,* for support, and about money, and inquire for *work* and when they fear of any, be off faithfully and promptly, and see to it that the work is well, thoroughly, and faithfully done. Inquire for more work, and in like manner be off to that and do it, and thus keep on, without making any ado about support, faithfully and zealously doing the work of evangelists. Keep on; inquire for more to do; study how to do it; pray the Lord to enable them to do it, honestly and faithfully; let the great matter be how to do that which the Lord has committed to their hands, and thus let the report go abroad, as it will without any concern on their part, that they are doing the Lord's work—converting sinners—turning men to God, encouraging the Disciples and building up churches, and the Lord will put it into the hearts of his people to supply their wants as certain as the Bible is from heaven.

There is not a preacher of this description any place, with acceptable preaching talents, free from those untoward manners and habits which render some good men repulsive to the people, who has the least trouble to find a place or support. Men do not get a support, or do much good, in any calling, without work, and there is no calling on earth where the distinction is wider, between the industrious and indolent, than in the Christian ministry. We cannot be supported in the ministry without work, and it is not right that we should be. The Lord puts us upon the same footing as other men. We must rise early, be at our books, off to our appointments, through winds, rains, and snows, cold and heat, with zeal and earnestness; preach with spirit and power, whether the audience is great or small, rich or poor, both early and late. We must come to. the people with something cheering, strengthening, inspiring, awakening, stirring, and thrilling the hearts of men with the theme of Calvary. There must be no murmuring, complaining, and repining about the amount we have to do; we must do it cheerfully, and show that we delight in our Lord's work. It is a most sacred honor to us—a mercy from God—that we are permitted to work for him, in his most glorious cause at all; and the work must be performed cheerfully, freely, and with all the heart, or it will not be acceptable to him, whether we are supported or not.

The Lord has said that "the laborer is worthy of his hire," and if the preacher of Christ imparts spiritual things, he is to receive in return, temporal things; but a "laborer" is a *working* man, and the Divine rule is, "if we sow sparingly, we shall reap sparingly." The man who preaches the gospel, is, by all reasonable men, expected to do as much labor as his strength will permit. It is reasonable that he should be expected to apply his energies as men of other pursuits. The field is wide open before him. and he should be a zealous, enterprising, and persevering man, making full work in his calling. A man who does not work any save a little on one or two days in a week, does not receive much reward in any business, unless some fraud obtains. The physician who makes a good support, works early and late, both good weather and bad. The lawyer who makes a good support, is one of industry and energy. The farmer who prospers, rises early, toils hard, and perseveres late. In all departments, industry, perseverance and energy characterize men who prosper. This is as true of the ministry as any class of men on earth; they can never prosper without the most untiring industry and perseverance. It is utterly useless for a man of idle habits, addicted to loafing, wasting his precious time in useless gossip to speak of his wants, his lack of support, or to try to induce persons of industrious habits to feel that he is in need. They will throw the whole matter off by saying. "Let him make an effort and apply his energies, as I have to do. and he will have plenty." But let a preacher apply himself to his calling; persevere in it, making every effort in his power; thus showing to all who know him, that his labors are actually arduous and incessant, and he will receive full credit from, not only his brethren, but the community generally, for his industry and faithfulness, and his temporal wants will as certainly receive attention, as that *his work is of God.*

The Lord has men yet in this world, good and true, who will reward labors of the faithful and persevering preacher of the gospel and support him. Indeed, there is a kind of fixed principle among men, as well as in the Divine administration, that industry shall be *rewarded* and indolence *punished,* and it is not more certainly a settled principle in reference to any class of men than preachers. We cannot expect to be wrapped in cloths, silks, and satins, with fine salaries, for preaching one or two short discourses on Lord's day, and then lying in the shade all the week; much less can we expect Christianity to prosper, or the approbation of heaven to rest upon us, in such an order of things. We must penetrate the whole land in every nook and corner, and preach the word of the Living God to every creature.

We have not written this for any preacher older than our self, but for the sake of young men. whom we desire to see useful, influential, and well sustained ministers of the word of God. All such, we entreat, to study and labor to do the Lord's work, and he will supply their wants out of his inexhaustible store-house.

B. F.

-----o-----

The Political Campaign.—The Cause.

WE are thankful to heaven that another political campaign has gone into the past. Its withering effects upon religion are like a great dearth upon vegetation. It has spread desolation in religion, in many communities, that will not be overcome in many years to come. It has left many hearts cold, consciences rankling in guilt, and Christian characters ruined. Many men. now that the intoxicating influence of partisan strife has passed off, are left to reflect upon the many angry and useless disputes, the miserable waste of time, of money, as well as loss of religious influence, and evil feeling among friends, all occasioned by the unhallowed campaign of worldly strife we have passed through. How many churches now can look back to a year spent in wrestling with the potsherds of the earth, while nothing but decline and dearth has attended them! How many preachers are now abashed, that they have allowed themselves to be drawn aside from their holy calling, to grapple in the vain strifes of the world; thus robbing the cause, and the Author of the cause, of their precious services, at the very time, above all others, when their labors were most needed, to preserve the flock from ruin! Let all such look back upon their fruitless career, learn a solemn lesson from it, and resolve never again to be drawn aside from the work to which the Lord has called them. For all these things we shall give an account to the Lord. We are not our own, and our time is not our own. We belong to the Lord, and to Him we must account.

Many men in the day of judgment will look

back to the present year, to find the cause of their apostasy—the commencement of their downward course, and the date of their decline. This year will he marked in their minds as the most unfortunate of all the years of their career. They will wish that this year could be struck from the years of God. and from the records of eternity. But the work is now done. The works of the year, both good and bad, are all registered upon God's great book of eternity. No hand but the hand of Omnipotence can efface them, nor will His hand touch them without most solemn repentance.

We rejoice to know, however, that many men of God have maintained their integrity, persevered in their vocation, and in every case of this kind, the blessing of God has attended, and the work has prospered. Indeed. this year has been rather an opening for true ministers of Christ; for many of their former opposers have been so much engaged in worldly strife, that they have been drawn off from their former work of opposing the gospel The success that has attended the proclamation of the gospel among the Disciples this year, wherever living, spiritual-minded men have made an effort, has been very remarkable; and, upon the whole, we are satisfied that the success of the cause this year has been equal to that of any previous year for the last ten years. We are truly thankful to God to find the cause and the brotherhood generally standing such a deadly influence. as this year has opposed to the cause, so well, and even succeeding in defiance of it. We find here another evidence of the invulnerable position which we occupy, with our faith in God. in our Redeemer, and the word of His grace. While the storms may carry off some but loosely connected with the body, and rid it of some excrescences, the main body will remain unharmed. The rains may descend, the winds may blow, and floods may rise, but the man upon the rock of ages, true to Him that liveth forever and ever, will not only remain unmoved but immovable.

But where are the strong bulwarks—the ramparts and defenses of sectarianism? What are sectarians doing, with their "creeds to keep them together," their disciplines for a rule of faith; with all their human bonds of confederation, and ecclesiastical combinations, or systems of government? What have they been doing this year? Have they not been splitting asunder, and spreading desolation and confusion in every direction? Where has their success amounted to anything? Scarcely any place in the whole land. The great worldly strife about the presidency has engrossed their attention, not only as citizens, or individuals, but as churches; nor has this been confined to the private members, but it has extended to the preachers; not merely in their relation to society as citizens, or individuals, but as preachers; not merely using their influence, but the influence of the pulpit, or the sermon, under the name of religion. In this career, they have forgotten the struggle to separate Church and State—the importance of separating and keeping separate Church and State. But the desolations they have spread, we think, will teach them a lesson on that subject. In thousands of instances, feedings have been wounded, divisions occasioned, and organizations bursted up, that cannot be mended in ten years to come. In all this, the Lord has shown the feebleness of human bonds of confederation, the nothingness of human platforms, and the rickety and unstable character of all that goes under the name of *orthodoxy.* It is ready to be tattered by every storm that assails it—scattered and dispersed to the winds.

How different those who stand upon the simple and immutable faith of Christ, holding on to pure and simple Christianity, as God gave it; elevating it above everything, and looking upon everything around as secondary to it. The man who stands here, knows that his religion is right, whether he understands it or not, for he knows the Author of it to be right, and that He could not give a system that is not right. He may be conscious of many imperfections in *himself;* but they are not in *his religion,* for it is infallible. If anything in this world is reliable, immovable and immutable, it is the Bible. If the Bible can fail, then anything can fail. If Christianity can fail, then man has nothing to rely upon— all may fail—all may be lost, and the hopes of all nations may be thrown into confusion and uncertainty. The Bible has stood the assaults of all its most formidable assailants for many long centuries, and is now more popular and widely circulated than at any former period. Let the friends of pure and unadulterated Christianity and the Bible take courage. They and their cause will stand when the present heavens, and earth shall pass away. B. F.

-----o-----

Letter from J. T. Johnson,

COLUMBIA, MO., NOV. 6, 1856.

BRO. FRANKLIN:—With regret I felt bound to start on my tour to this State on Thursday afternoon, before the American Christian Missionary Society closed its important labors. I hope the objects and designs we had in view, were accomplished—that the Bible and Publication Societies were dispensed with as inexpedient and unnecessary, and that the Missionary Society should command all of Our energies and resources. Almost everything depends upon its President, its Corresponding Secretary, and its Board. I am, therefore, most anxious to see what was done. Be so good as to let me have the result of your labors at Fayette, or St. Joseph's, or Lexington, or Leavenworth, or Weston, or Independence, at which places I expect to be before I return to Kentucky. The liberality of our brethren does not depend upon light trooping, but upon the proper appeal upon right objects. I hope, then, that the President of the Society, Bro. Campbell, the Corresponding Secretary, and all of our preachers, will make suitable appeals to the brotherhood; and that something worthy of us be done in a general missionary enterprise, embracing this Continent and the Continents of the old world. Men of talents and influence ought to be selected to range the world in order to its conversion.

From Thursday 3 o'clock, P. M. at Cincinnati, I reached this vicinity by 3 or 4 o'clock, P. M. Saturday. I was stopped by Bro. Bradford, an old county-man of mine, and rested in his hospitable mansion, with his amiable family, till Saturday morning. Our estimable and talented Bro. T. M. Allen, whose praise is all over the land, and whose energy and untiring industry have resulted so gloriously, whose residence is near Bro. Bradford's, was absent on a tour to Fulton. On Saturday I was taken to Columbia by Bro. B., having sent notice the evening preceding, and I had the pleasure of seeing many of my old Kentucky friends, and of addressing a large and interesting congregation on the truth of the gospel. It was thought expedient, and so we concluded to make a protracted effort.

Here I met President Bro. Shannon, and found a home in his amiable, lovely, and hospitable family. I found him the same bold, fearless, ardent advocate of the truth—one of the honestest men that ever graced the earth.

Brethren Wilkes and Rogers have charge of the Christian Female College; both of them are ripe scholars, preachers of the gospel, competent to the task imposed upon them, and they bid fair to be of incalculable value to the good cause.

All the public institutions here are in a prosperous condition. The gentlemen who have charge of them are fully equal to all that is required of them, and they want all the patronage that can be bestowed on them. This moment the president, Hudson, comes in and is introduced to me. He is a man after my own heart. He is the man to succeed Bro. Shannon as president of the Missouri University at this place.

We have had a most delightful and successful meeting. Bro. Allen returned, and was with me from Monday night. Bro. Hulett, of Kentucky, came on opportunely on Friday night, and has assisted us in our labors. We have had twenty-three additions by confession and immersion, and four by letter.

I concluded, of my own accord, to make a little effort on behalf of the A. C. Missionary Society. On a visit to Bro. Allen's family, I mentioned the .subject to him, and his amiable, Christian, but afflicted daughter. She unhesitatingly became a life member, and he followed her example. I enclose a list of the subscribers for publication, that others may emulate their Christian example. Let the preachers and brethren be active in this matter. Let them cease scolding and go to work. Let us act a part worthy of us and the cause. I am no agent, nor do I intend to be one; but I intend to aid in the cause as opportunity offers.

If there is anyone object that can secure and call forth all the resources and energies of the brethren, it is this. This will effectually try all of us. We have rallied around the Bible Union. We will see who will rally around this. The results will all be glorious.

To-morrow I hold a meeting at Bro. Allen's, for the benefit of his lovely daughter. May the Lord bless her, and inspire her with fortitude, and patience, and resignation to bear bodily suffering as a Christian. I pray that she may be restored to health and society—that she may aid more effectually the good cause of the Redeemer.

Most affectionately,

J. T. JOHNSON.

-----O-----

Sunday-School Address.

The following brief extract from an address on the Moral Culture of the Mind, delivered before the teachers and Sunday-School, at Ben Davis' Creek, Rush Co., Ind., Oct. 8th, 1856, by Wm. Ging, is all we could find time to prepare for the press and space to insert. We have slightly changed the verbiage of what we have published; but the matter remains near the same as before it came to our hand. B. F.

-----o-----

PARENTS, TEACHERS, AND SCHOLARS:—I have been called upon this morning, though unprepared, to deliver an address. Not having been accustomed to speaking extemporaneously, knowing also my inability, and that there are others present more able than myself to address you, I can but feel some embarrassed, and would have preferred hearing someone else. But we can-not expect our fathers and mothers to be with us upon earth forever. They must pass down to the cold and dreary chambers of the dead, and the cares and responsibilities now resting upon them, will soon fall upon those who shall follow them. In this solemn fact we find a reason why the youths present should be cultivated both in mind and heart. Upon their intelligence and excellence, to a great extent, depends the happiness of many in years to come.

Therefore, we say the youth of the land cannot too early launch forth upon the stage of action—the field of usefulness—as the time so rapidly hastens when we, too, shall fall in death. This truth is an important one, and furnishes an important reason why we should lay aside all selfishness, buckle on the armor and fight valiantly for the good of poor suffering humanity. The subject, therefore, I am about to introduce is full of importance to the youth whom I address. Among all the questions to which I could call your attention, on this occasion, nothing that I could think of, appeared more fitting, applicable, and admirably adapted to the occasion, than the Moral Culture of the Mind.

When we ascend or descend through the records of history, we find that in old ages, when the moral culture of the mind has been faithfully attended to, man has been ennobled, happiness and prosperity have followed. But on the other hand, where this has been neglected, man has been degraded, fallen; and sufferings follow. In all ages, the moral culture of the mind has been followed by the richest rewards, in happiness, greatness, and honor. Among pagans, men of great minds have been looked to as demigods. The multitudes look to them with awe-stricken wonder, crown them with the richest and enduring honors. The pathway of cultivated mind has been strewn with flowers; its brow has worn the loftiest plume; it has set upon the loftiest throne, and held the mightiest scepter of power. This general and almost universal homage to cultivated mind, is at once a proof both of its worth and power. The universe itself proclaims both the worth and power of that which has the power of thinking.

Let us, for a moment, consider the complicated machinery of nature, so wisely, harmoniously, and beautifully ordered by the infinite mind of the Creator. All his works proclaim not only the presence of mind, in their arrangements and movements, but of the highest order of mind. Mind of the highest order is displayed in man's creation, both in his physical and intellectual structure. In all the arts and sciences mind is displayed; but in religion, the intellect is not only cultivated, but the cultivation is moral. Hence the lessons in the Sunday-School are frequently of a higher order than in those halls where science is taught. Added to the cultivation of the intellect, respect is also had to the heart, to the affections and moral feelings, and an impression is made, not only to brighten and shine with luster for a few days in time, but that will last co-extensive with the years of God.

-----o-----

Capon Bridge, Va., Nov. 1st. 1856.

BROTHER FRANKLIN:

Dear Sir—When on a western tour, from which I have recently returned, I came in contact with a gentleman, in the vicinity of Wheeling, Va,, who professed to believe in what is called "*spiritualism,*" or "*spirit-rapping,*" and as he was the first of that deluded class that it had been my fortune to encounter, and withal a man of some intelligence. I felt an anxiety to learn something concerning this new mode of being enlightened. I accordingly entered into a friendly conversation, the substance of which I here present in the form of a dialogue.

Traveler.—I understand you to believe that you can hold communication with the spirits of the departed dead, and that you may, through that medium, receive information upon any subject upon which you may desire to be enlightened.

Spiritualist.—I do not only *believe* it but I *know* it to be the case. I have no more doubt on that subject than I have of my existence.

T.—I could not possibly admit the correctmess of your statement from your mere assertion, without some additional evidence. But admitting, for the sake of argument. that you are correct, can you have converse with the wicked as well as the spirits of the righteous?

S.—Yes, we can call up any spirit we wish to converse with. Some of them are no doubt wicked spirits.

T.—Have you any rule by which you can distinguish between the spirits of the righteous and the spirits of the wicked, or between good and bad spirits?

S.—They will show themselves whether they are good or bad spirits. We can in that way determine the disposition that they manifest.

T.—Suppose, for instance, you should call up an evil, wicked spirit; would it not be likely to tell you lies? You know that in present world there are some lying, wicked characters, and if one dies in this state his spirit would be a lying wicked spirit, and consequently could not be depended on. Now, as you may be deceived by such men while in the flesh, may you not also be deceived by their spirits? Then, unless you have some infallible standard by which you may distinguish between the good and bad spirits, you must always be liable to be deceived.

S.—We must try the spirits to see whether they are good or bad.

T.—By what rule do you try them to determine this fact?

S—They will show what they are.

T.—But *how* will they show what they are? If they show what they are it must be by their conduct, and that conduct must be brought to some infallible standard to determine whether it is good or bad. right or wrong. To what standard, then, do you bring your spirits to determine whether they are good or bad, or whether they speak truth or falsehood? If I were to determine this matter for you, I would say that any spirit that teaches anything contrary to the Word of the Lord, is a lying, wicked spirit, and is not worthy of the least confidence; and on the other hand, if your spirits teach precisely what is contained in the scriptures, their teaching is of no earthly account, for the Bible reveals all necessary truth concerning both God and man. It has been revealed by the Holy Spirit of the Living God, and is well authenticated; so that it needs not the aid of the spirits of men to make it more authentic, or to add a single ray of light to its divine luster. You might as well light a candle to aid the light of the sun at noonday, as to consult the spirits of men to add a fresh luster to the volume of inspiration.

S.—As to that, a man may be a Spiritualist and not believe one-half of the Bible.

T.—Indeed! Then a man may be a Spiritualist and an Infidel at the same time. But "he that believeth not shall be damned," most assuredly, and all the spirits of the departed dead combined cannot save him. But of what account is this Spiritualism. if it will not save us from infidelity? I confess I cannot see what possible benefit can be derived from your spirit communications. If a man can be a Spiritualist and not believe one-half of the Bible, his Spiritualism must be a base deception.

S.—I would not give what I know of spirit communication for all the wealth of a continent.

T.—But of what benefit is all this knowledge? You allow a man may be a Spiritualist and not believe one-half of the Bible. Where, then, is the benefit? Can the spirits of the departed dead show you a more excellent way than that revealed in the Bible? Can you believe the spirits of men in preference to the Spirit of the Living God? Really, my dear sir. you must be laboring under a great delusion. But time admonishes me to pursue my journey—Farewell.

S.—Farewell, sir; I hope you may yet become a Spiritualist.

After parting from my spiritual (?) friend, my mind was led to the following reflections:

This, then, thought I, is a living specimen of Spiritualism. And he can be a Spiritualist and not believe one-half of the Bible. From such *spiritualism* may the Lord deliver us. Surely this is a strange delusion. But where did it originate? Certainly not from the Bible. There are, it is true, a few cases on record in the scriptures, where persons held communications with the departed dead; but none of them have any similarity to these spirit rappers. In the case of the witch of Endor, she said "An old man cometh up, and he is covered with a mantle. And Saul perceived that it was Samuel." In this case the witch saw Samuel, and Saul knew him; and Samuel spoke to Saul and foretold his final ruin. But there was no rapping; no invisible spirit called up and manifested by rapping, and explained by an ignorant *medium*. We read also of Moses and Elias appearing with the Saviour on the Mount of Transfiguration. But it was their *persons,* and not merely their spirits that was there. And indeed I do not know that we have any account of persons conversing with the spirits of men after they were dead. To be sure, we read of persons being possessed by *evil spirits*; but those evil spirits always spoke through the persons possessed by them. I cannot, therefore, regard this spirit-rapping but as a delusion of the devil. But if it were even so. what could we expect to be benefited, by these spirit communications? They could tell us nothing concerning God, Paul asks the question, "What man knoweth the things of a man save the spirit of man that is in him? even so, the things of God knoweth no man but the spirit of God." If then it were possible to hold communication with the spirits of the departed dead, they could tell us nothing of God and of Christ. They could tell us only of man. All the information therefore that is received through this medium is of but little account. The Saviour says, "It is life eternal to know the only true God, and Jesus Christ," etc. But as this knowledge can only be obtained through a revelation of God's spirit, this spirit-rapping, if true, could not impart life to a single individual.

But their opposition to the Bible is proof sufficient that their whole system is a base delusion—whose mother is sin and whose daddy is the devil. It is an unmistakable truth that every system which undervalues the "living oracles," has its origin with the father of lies. But the spirit-rappers are not alone in their indifference to Bible teaching. This is the case with every system of abstract spiritualism. So far as any man believes in an abstract spiritual influence, so far does he lose his esteem for the teaching of the inspired volume.

The Mormons believe in the immediate inspiration of the Spirit; but what regard do they pay to the Bible? Both the religion and morality of the Bible is outraged by them, and at the same time they profess to be influenced by the Spirit of God.

The Shakers believe in the abstract influence of the Holy Spirit; and to what extravagance has it led them! Their religion consists principally in setting aside one of the ordinances of the Lord, which is plainly revealed in the Bible—and in singing and dancing to mortify the flesh. Thus, the flesh. Thus, through the supposed influence of the Spirit of God, they counteract the authority of heaven, and engage in the wildest fanaticism. It is a little strange, however, that the Spirit of God should influence the Shaker to have *no* wife, and the Mormon to have a *dozen!*

The Friends also believe in the inspiration of the Spirit of God, which they style "the light within." But in what light do they view the Scriptures of truth? Let their conduct answer. They set aside the commandments and ordinances of the Lord, as of no consequence, and speak contemptuously of the scriptures as. the "outward word," "a dead letter," etc., forgetting the words of the blessed Jesus, "The words that I speak unto you they are spirit and they are life and Paul's declaration, "The word of God is quick (living) and powerful," etc.

Finally, all who believe in the immediate abstract operation of the Spirit of God, in the conversion and salvation of men, lose their esteem for the teaching of the scriptures. And this course appears to me to be consistent; for if the Spirit does everything for the sinner, there remains nothing for the word to accomplish; and hence it might as well be laid aside as an old almanac. But oh! there is a judgment approaching, and we must all account for our stewardship. And our final destiny will be fixed, not according to our *impressions* nor our *feelings,* nor *mw views*—but the Saviour says, "the *words* that I speak to you *they* shall judge you."

- But as I have protracted my remarks beyond what I intended when I commenced, I will conclude with my best wishes for your health, happiness, and prosperity.

Your brother in the faith,

CHRISTY SINE.

ELD. B. FRANKLIN, *Cin., O.*

-----o-----

Conclusion of the Volume.

THIS number closes our present volume; and this year, also, closes our thirteenth year since we took the position of a religious editor, and almost twenty-one years since we entered upon the Christian ministry. The older we become, the more confidently we lean upon the Christian religion, and the more fully we realize its value to the human race. The more we labor for its spread, and see its effects upon men, the more we delight to labor for its dissemination. This year we have performed more labor than we have in any previous year of our life—had better success, everything considered, both in the pulpit and with the pen. It has also been our happiest year; it has gone truly well with us. We have issued four thousand copies of the *Review*; put about three thousand copies into circulation, and the balance are going every day. We have put many thousands of tracts also into circulation—more, so far as we know, than has ever been put in circulation among the brethren in one year before, and have preached more than a sermon for each day in the year.

We have been well supported in our efforts in every way. We are greatly indebted to many liberal and noble-hearted brethren, for the means they have afforded us to bear our expenses on the cars and other public conveyances, over the immense districts of country through which we have passed, and supply our numerous wants. Nor are we less indebted to many who have taken an interest in circulating the *Review,* and tracts, frequently at much expense. Truly are we grateful to all who have aided us, and thankful. Many of them we shall never be able to requite for their kind assistance to do what was impossible to us without their liberal aid. They have endeared themselves to us, and are engraven upon our heart. We pray that God, who is rich in mercy, may make all grace abound to them, and bless them, with all, in every place, who call upon the name of the Lord from a pure heart. Many of those who have aided us we have never seen, but we trust that they, and those we have seen, including the precious ones we have been enabled to gather to the kingdom of God, the present year, shall meet us when all our sacrifices and labors are over.

It is true, in one sense, that in the twenty-one years now closing, we have performed a considerable amount of labor—especially when we reflect that we can appeal to the brethren where we have been, to sustain us in the statement, that we have never relaxed our energies for a single week, except in deep afflictions. But still, looking at the eternal benefits Christianity has conferred upon us, and the rich inheritance it proposes to confer in the world to come, the little a poor mortal can do in a short lifetime sinks into nothingness, and deserves not to be mentioned. When we think of him who became poor, that we through his poverty might be rich—that he became a little lower than the angels, that he, by the grace of God, should taste of death for every man—that he had not where to lay his head—that he died for us—think of the holy apostles and martyrs of Jesus, with all their labors and sufferings— all we do, .or can do, dwindles into perfect insignificance. To God, over all. blessed forever and ever, through Jesus Christ, we owe eternal gratitude, praises and thanksgiving, that he has ever received us and permitted us to labor in his gracious cause at all. To his name be honor and power everlasting.

-----o-----

Alexander Campbell.

The name at the head of this article needs no title to give it emphasis. It has been long associated with one of the multifarious religious movements of our country, of which it is made by opposers the patronymic and the shibboleth.

It is more than twenty years since we last met with Mr. C., till we saw him, the other day, at the Bible Union Anniversary; and we confess, he seems to us in body and soul ripening for that land from which there is no return. His whitened locks, furrowed features, and other marks of age—or rather, perhaps, of the severity of life's labor, have imparted to his tall and commanding person a truly patriarchal appearance. Few minds dwell in a body more expressive of their powers and proclivities than Mr. C.'s. The large Roman nose, the fiery eye, the jutting brow and lofty forehead, yea, the well turned lips and finely chiseled chin, indicative of firmness and determination, all bespeak one born to command. Age has evidently produced a mellowness of feeling and a fervor of devotion, for which we were not prepared to look in one who has his reputation as a caustic controversialist and an eager debater.

It is well known that we have never sympathized with Mr. C., in his reformation, as a general thing, though, we confess, that a few words to which he gave utterance the other day, in a short conversation we had with him, had much in them which is true and important. He said he claimed to be orthodox in the ordinary sense of the word, and that his leaning was toward Calvinism as a system, having in it more of real Christianity than any other. His object in life had been to restore to Christians a Bible TERMINOLOGY, in place of modes and habits of speaking which have been derived from ages of religious philosophizing. His idea, seemed to be that all the creeds are vitiated, and perverted from the true ways of the Lord, through corrupt intermixtures and modes of thought which began, at an early period, to be introduced, and that there is no such thing as restoring "the ancient Gospel," without adopting Bible modes of speaking.

This cardinal idea has given Mr. Campbell's literary labors the appearance of dealing more in the *letter* than in the *spirit*. It is somewhat as if Whitfield, for instance, had become strongly impressed with the departure of the English Church, in its doctrines, forms, ceremonies and ecclesiastical constitution, from those laid down in the New Testament, and had set about showing this departure by dualistic debates, periodical literature, caustic controversy and cutting satire, for the purpose of exploding them and restoring the ancient forms of Christianity. Anyone can see how different such a Whitfield would have been from the Whitfield of field-preaching, burning appeal and powerful eloquence, to persuade poor colliers, merry-andrews, thieves, pickpockets, and all the dregs of society, as well as the cultivated worldly and profane, to come to Christ and accept of instant salvation by his cross.

But that a reform in the *terminology,* as well as the *temper* of Christianity is needed, we do not at all doubt, though the one is far less important than the other.

It is indeed true that "the form of sound words" is not to be despised, and that a true biblical terminology is necessary to the purity of Christian doctrine. Those subjects which are purely matters of revelation, cannot be correctly expressed except "in the words which the Holy Spirit teacheth." This is true of the doctrine of Father, Son, and Holy Spirit, of regeneration, of spiritual influence, and of many other subjects. To invent a form of words, aside from the revelation, to express all on those subjects contained in the revelation itself, we take to be impossible. The most that can be said of a creed is, therefore, that it is simply an index to what one class of Christians educe from the words of Scripture, as distinguished from what another class educe; and hence it is, as Mr. C. holds, a symbol of division rather than union.

But whether the explosion of the creed would avail, so long as the spirit of division remains, and the differences of which it is a sign still exist among Christians, is a question. Our predilections go rather toward securing more Christian vitality, more of "the unction of the Holy One." and more of that peculiar power which "effectually worketh in them that believe," being fully convinced that "the ancient Gospel" must be in the heart before it can find expression on the lips. Whitfield's plan of striking at the conscience first, and regulating the symbol and ceremonial afterward, far better accords to our habits of thinking.

Still we do now. as we ever have done, accord to Mr. Campbell and those associated with him. the sincerest convictions, and have often looked with surprise upon the extent of the movement with which they are identified.

Bethany, a small inland town in western Virginia where Mr. C. first located on coming to America, is rendered famous by his labors— the seat of a great university over which he presides, and, in some sense, the Jerusalem or Antioch of the Disciples. Much is said of the heresy of the sect, but as someone remarked of the Catholic church, that it is impossible but that there should be some good men among a people who make so much of Christ; so we say of the Disciples; it is impossible but that a people should have some truth who make so much of the Bible.—*N. Y. Chron.*

---o---

FAYETTE, Nov. 14, '56.

DEAR BRO. FRANKLIN:

I left Columbia on the 6th inst., and preached in Rocheport, that night, to a very crowded house. Next morning I went, conveyed by my worthy and benevolent brother, T. M. Allen, through rain and sleet, to Ashland. No one there except one aged veteran, Bro. Robinson, whose hospitality we shared that evening, in company with some relatives who resided in the neighborhood. Next morning we reached this place in time for our appointment; and here I have labored until this time. The congregations have been large at night, and apparently greatly interested. We have had three valuable accessions, and prospects are good for more. Here I have seen brethren Boon, who resides in the vicinity, Proctor, Robinson, and Gains, all of them men after my own heart. If they live they are destined to be of great value to the reformation. Their hearts are in the cause. May the Lord help them.

FAYETTE, MO., NOV. 19, '56.

DEAR BRO. BEN. FRANKLIN:

The meeting at this place closed with five valuable additions. In the mean time I held forth at Ashland and Rocheport, and I had the assistance of brethren Allen and Gains; and Bro. Boone, a noble man, is the resident preacher at this place. Night before last I was at Rocheport with Bro. T. M. Allen, and had five valuable additions. Bro. Boone is now preparing to take me there to-night.

We got four life memberships for the A. C. M. Society located at Cincinnati, and I enclose you $20, the first installments of the subscribers. Be pleased to hand the enclosed to the proper officer for me, with the copy of the subscription list.

From Rocheport I shall go up the country. In great affection,

J. T. JOHNSON.

BENTONVILLE, IA., NOV. 4, 1856.

DEAR BRO. FRANKLIN:

We commenced a meeting at Clarksburg, Johnson county, on Friday night the 24th ult, and closed on Thursday night the 30th, which resulted in 33 additions to the church—20 by confession and baptism (of whom one was from the Methodists), ten by letter, one from the Baptists, and two restored. Yours,

DANL. R. VAN BUSKIRK.

Bro. Proctor has agreed to locate in St. Louis, and will be there in a few weeks He is the very man for the place.

Bro. Allen was compelled to leave me for home, a few days past, but I hope to see him at Ashland to-morrow and next day. where I have an appointment, before I start up the river. Missouri is a great State; filled and filling up with a great people, destined to exert a mighty influence in this mighty west. I hope Bro. Allen will accompany me in my trip. Yours truly,

J. T. JOHNSON.

N. B.—At night.—One more confessed the Saviour. Large and attentive crowd. Obtained three life memberships of the A. C. M. Society, and more will be done before I leave the neighborhood. Yours,

J. T. JOHNSON.

EDITOR'S PAGE.

Editor's Table.

Review Bound.—We have the *A. C. Review,* vol. I, with title page and index, neatly bound in cloth, and will send it, post paid, to any address, for one dollar. We will send the complete set of numbers, without binding or paying postage, for fifty cents. Orders are still coming for this volume every day. All who desire the present volume in a neatly bound book, postage pre-paid by us, and volume second as issued, will please enclose two dollars, and they will be faithfully sent to order.

Agents Again.—All persons who have acted as agents for us, and aided us in extending our circulation are entitled to our most sincere thanks, and are requested to aid us again. AH agents who have acted for us are entitled to the same percentage we have been giving. We desire as many others as we can obtain. All who will act for us, and receive a percentage, by writing us shall be answered, and receive term s. Any person may act for one or many, without corresponding with us at all. The only thing important in the matter is to enclose the subscription price, and write the person's name, post office, county and state, plainly.

A Perplexity.—brother, from home, writes us a letter with sundry items, requiring an answer, but does not tell us his place of address. It should be recollected that we cannot remember every man's address to whom we send the *Review*; and it is rather a tedious business to hunt through several thousand names to find one. Many brethren make short work of it when they send a name, by saying "Send to the same office with my own.".

Persons who have received the Review gratis.—We have sent the *Review* to a few of the older preachers, gratis. We have also sent it gratis to a few poor sisters. We have sent about a hundred copies in this way very willingly and freely, and will do the same the coming year, where we can hear from them and learn that they desire it; but we must *know that it is desired before we send it.*

Many pieces that we should have been glad to have published, Lave been unavoidably crowded out. We have n.tt been able to publish near one half of what has come to hand for publication. We have selected what we thought most profitable, to fill all the room we had.

Our Position at a Religious Community.—The series of articles under the foregoing head, running through the present volume, was written during the forty days confinement, while the small pox was in our family, in June and July of 1855. Nine of the articles were written before we were taken down, and the other three after we had commenced to recover. The period during which these pieces were written was the most solemn and afflicting we have ever been called upon to pass through. The dangers that hung over us were sufficient to induce us to the utmost care how we wrote every sentence. But from that gloomy period, the Lord in mercy delivered us, and has now spared us till they are all published, as we intended when we wrote them They have met with a hearty reception and may yet appear in a tract.

To the Readers of the Review.—Our subscribers visited us first, confided in us, and gave us the subscription price, and thus invited the *Review* to visit them monthly. Receiving such a cordial invitation, the *Review* has made them a visit every month during the year, with the best information we could produce. The present number completes the engagement with almost three thousand persons. This visit is his farewell with those who do not invite him to return. He is too polite to obtrude his visits where he is not invited. He wishes all well, and is anxious to extend his visits into more families, and most devoutly believes that he can do them great good; but still he does not consider it his privilege to do so, unless invited by the head of the family, or someone authorized by him or her, as the case may be. To all, then, who have not yet invited him to return, in love and Christian affection, he bids farewell, till he hears from them.

Success of the Gospel.

PALESTINE, Texas, Sept. 29th, 1856.

BRO. FRANKLIN :—We have in about two months, had fifty-four additions to the church here, and ten at Beaver, ten miles north of this. We hold meetings at nights, as business will allow—were at the water yesterday, and go again to-day. The "powers that be," in the opposing ranks are yielding, and the truth triumphing gloriously. A congregation might be reared, I think, in almost every neighborhood in the county, with moderate effort. What a chance for eternal riches I but, alas, our capital is small, and our operations must needs be circumscribed. If the Disciples would live out Christianity, the gospel would conquer the world; and the responsibility is upon us, whether we will or not. The Lord help us so to live, that we may, in the judgment, have nothing of selfishness or sloth to regret.

In the faith,

C. KENDRICK.

NEW LONDON, Pa., Nov. 5, '56.

Bro. Franklin:—Enclosed find one $2 Ky. note, for which send the *Christian Review* to F. Andrews, Downing Town, Chester county, and to Miss Mary Goodwin, Jennersville, same county and State—Pennsylvania.

I have been here ten nights with a small congregation, which is nearly destroyed by removals, etc. The weather has been stormy and unfavorable most of the time. We have had some interest and two confessions; one of whom is to be immersed this evening. This is a hard community for the Gospel; it is mainly composed of Quakers,, and old Presbyterians of the parties. We have had quite a number tint, and some very strong symptoms have been manifested.

We have preaching again to-night, and may remain longer if the indications are favorable; but having been from home much during the summer, I am anxious to see my home again. If your brethren desire a missionary field for their efforts, they need not go out of the old states to find one where all their energies can be devoted, for there are not probably, three congregations east of the Alleghenies, in this State, of Disciples. If I had the means to spare, I should like to devote one year to Pennsylvania and Maryland. Yours truly,

G.W. ELLEY.

Bro. W. D. MOORE, of Russelville, Ohio, Nov. 16th, says—"Two weeks ago to-day, we immersed three worthy females, who were added to the Liberty Congregation, Brown County. Last week, at Russelville, four were added, two by commendation, and two by baptism. In last September, at Smart's Congregation, twenty-three were added, mostly by immersion, among whom were several sprinkled Methodists. Immediately after this, at Point Pleasant, Adams County, there were seven additions. At the same place, a short time before, nine had been added."

Sister ELIZABETH A. REDMAN, Georgetown, Ill., November, says—"Our meeting-house is about one mile from Georgetown, Ill., and, comparatively speaking, we are diminutive in number. We do not have preaching every Lord's day, but there are some warm hearted Christians among us, who are determined that the cause shall not languish through lack of zeal. They are punctual in their labors as a sun-dial to the hour, and every Lord's day finds them at their post, endeavoring to train the youthful mind, and teach the young members the way of the Lord more perfectly. They desire the prayers of all the faithful. Bro. Rolla Martin has been preaching for us monthly. He is quite a speaker, well versed in the Scriptures."—This little band, if they thus continue, will prosper.

Bro. JAMES COLE, Darke County, O., Nov. 16th, says—"We have just closed a meeting which resulted in ten additions, conducted by Brethren Bernau and Bennet."

Bro. R. ROYAL, Cannelton, Ind., Nov. 13th, says—"Since I last wrote you, I have immersed two."

Bro. J. M. HENRY, Dayton, O., Nov. 12th, says—"We closed a meeting, embracing three Lord's days, on last Lord's day evening. Bro. B. K. Smith, of Indianapolis, was with us, and preached to general acceptance and much profit, I trust. The immediate results of the meeting were seven immersions, and seven more added, one of whom I immersed a week before. Blessed be the name of the Lord forever and ever."

Bro. S. S. DOYLE, writing from Portsmouth, O., Nov. 13th, says—"Since I saw you in Flemingsburg, Ky., a little more than a month, twelve have been added in the bounds of my labors in Greenup County, Ky. Also, in the same county, Bro. Moses McKay held a meeting, with twenty additions, eight from the Baptists, and twelve from the world, and organized a church with thirty-two members."

Bro. J. D. SEATON, Louisville, Ky., Nov. 24th, says—"Yesterday afternoon, eight persons took membership with the Fourth Street Congregation, and last night eight confessed,—one from the Baptists. They will be immersed to night."

Bro. B. K. SMITH, of Indianapolis, Nov. 4th, reports, as the result of his labors at several points this year, as follows: — "At Franklin, Ind., in Feb., 15 or 20 additions. A few weeks after, with Bro. Cobb, some three or four additions at Middletown, Ind. At different times, at Sulphur Springs and Cadiz, some three or four were added. At Hagerstown, Ind., three. A two weeks effort in 'Monroe County, Ind., resulted in six additions."

Bro. J. H. HEDGES, Sharpsburg, Ky., October 23rd, says—"I have been listening to Bro. Rickets proclaim the Gospel of Christ, and saw some fourteen obey."

Bro. J. B. CRANE, Mount Sterling, Oct. 25th, says "There were forty-seven additions at Corinth, in all. Bro. HON continued the meeting."

Obituary.

Death, the king of terrors, is still with remorseless hand, severing the tenderest ties of relationship, and calling tenants to the tomb. Though he is conquered, still he conquers, and gathers for himself, indiscriminately from among our friends, our fathers, mothers, brothers, sisters, and our children.

DIED, a few days ago from the effects of a burn, the infant and only son and child of our much esteemed neighbors and friends, John Brown and wife; for which they are made to mourn. W. D. M.

[*Conclusion left out for want of space.*]

www.ingramcontent.com/pod-product-compliance
Lightning Source LLC
Chambersburg PA
CBHW081438070526
44586CB00019B/2162